# Foreign Policy Reader

*Edited by*

HARRY HOWE RANSOM

*Vanderbilt University*

**Thomas Y. Crowell Company**

*New York / Established 1834*

*To Jenny, Kate, and William*

# Preface

THIS VOLUME of readings has been compiled for use by students
and instructors in courses in American foreign policy, international
relations, and world politics, or by others with an interest in public affairs.
My purposes have been (1) to assemble a varied collection of material
that concretely illustrates the issues and real choices faced by American
foreign policy makers, but without neglecting the historical context,
(2) to keep the selections within a limit that would permit this volume
to be of reasonable cost, and (3) to include selections that will sharpen
the reader's understanding of and interest in the real issues, rather than
to supply exhaustive documentation.

The noted political scientist Harold Lasswell once categorized the
major ways a nation seeks to achieve its objectives as simply these: deals,
goods, force, and ideas. My assumption is that beyond self-defense, American foreign policy objectives, often implicit, less often explicit, have
always been to prevent a monopoly of power in those areas perceived to
be of major strategic concern to the national interest. Toward this end, the
United States at varying stages in her foreign policy history has been
required to apply various degrees and types of power. The necessity to
be conscious of power and its use has become increasingly a fact of
national existence. But how does one define, think about, or analyze
this power? Ultimately, it must be defined, in my judgment, in instrumental terms, that is, in terms of the means available for applying power
in concrete situations. Translating Professor Lasswell's categories into
more standard terms, the major instruments can be categorized as military, economic, propagandistic, and diplomatic.

This collection centers on these instruments. But I have always
tried to emphasize the fact that power is a *relational* or *situational*
concept; it must be related to attainable *ends* and practical *means* in concrete situations. Emphasis in this book is on the period since World War
II, although Part II is devoted to historical background, and in each
section I have made an effort to provide the historical setting for analysis
of contemporary issues and instruments.

The problem of containing a potential monopoly of power by the
Communists in Eurasia, perceived around 1947, has had to be implemented
in a fast-moving age of technological, economic, and political revolutions.
The challenge to attempts at containment has spread from Eurasia to
many other parts of the world, particularly to Africa and Latin America.
Since 1947 new political and economic conditions have converged with
new instruments of power—products of an accelerating technology. At
the same time, nationalism and communism have come into open combat,

providing a new dynamic to international politics and to East-West, North-South relations on the globe.

In this setting, the really significant contemporary foreign policy issues for the United States involve, in the final analysis, the question of the utility of the major instruments of policy in relation to national goals. This book of readings, therefore, has been divided into the following eight parts: (I) The National Interest: Ends and Means, (II) The Historical Background, (III) The Military Instrument, (IV) The Propaganda Instrument, (V) The Economic Instrument, (VI) Secret Intervention and Unconventional Warfare, (VII) Diplomacy, and (VIII) Peace, Coexistence, or War? Appended to each section is a selected bibliography for further reading.

In sum, this volume is based on the assumption that contemporary American foreign policy is manifested, and best studied and understood, by analysis of the instruments of policy. This book is designed to encourage a realistic end-means analysis. It focuses upon national interests and objectives (ends) and upon instruments (means) as these are debated, decided upon, and coordinated in today's revolutionary world. Because events in today's world are so fast-moving, the reader must inevitably up-date, at the time of reading, the analyses in some of this book's selections.

The selections generally have been reproduced as they appeared in original publication. Any deviation from this, such as omission of footnotes or condensation, is clearly indicated in each case.

Because this compilation results from an exploration of a great mass of material, the choice has always been difficult. I am most of all indebted to the authors and publishers who have permitted the reprinting of their work, for it is they, as well as those who have published in the public domain, who have created the substance of this book.

H. H. R.

*Nashville, Tenn.*

# Contents

CONTENTS

## VII    THE DIPLOMATIC INSTRUMENT

# VIII PEACE, COEXISTENCE, OR WAR?

# I THE NATIONAL INTEREST:
## ENDS AND MEANS

## 1 / From *The Relations of Nations*

### FREDERICK H. HARTMANN

**The following selection analyzes succinctly the nature of what
we call a "foreign policy" and its limitations and complications.**

A NATION-STATE perennially faces the question: what should the
national goals be? The answer to this question we call foreign policy,
and it is at once evident that not everything that could conceivably be
desired is obtainable. The most obvious limitation on policy is power,
and therefore small powers must be more modest in their aspirations
than great powers. In the days of the Congress of Vienna in 1815 small
powers were actually referred to as "Powers with limited interests."

Yet . . . national power is limited for great states as well as small.
No matter how much a nation has, it is limited both absolutely and
relatively. It is limited absolutely, for example, in terms of the annual
production of steel, coal, and oil. It is limited relatively in that the national appetite in foreign-policy matters is always bigger than it can
afford with the power at its disposal. The list of wants is infinite, and
each must be considered against every other. Consequently, the formulation of a realistic foreign policy must always begin with an appraisal
of the power reserve upon which it must rest. A nation that overdraws
its bank account of power is courting, and often finds itself visited by,
disaster. Yet even when a state attempts to keep its policy carefully
equated with its power, it encounters at the outset several practical
difficulties in following a rational policy.

### 1. The Abstract Nature of Policy

The first difficulty is a result of the fact that foreign-policy objectives are frequently expressed in abstract terms.

Reprinted with permission of the publisher from Frederick H. Hartmann, *The Relations of Nations*, 2d ed., pp. 71–75. Copyright 1957 and 1962 by The Macmillan
Company.

Frederick H. Hartmann is professor of political science, University of Florida, and the
author of several books on international affairs.

The term *foreign policy* suggests a greater degree of rational procedure than is often observable in the way in which states actually proceed toward achieving their long-term objectives. Policy as a term denotes planning. Planning in turn suggests step-by-step procedure toward a known and defined goal. Foreign-policy goals, however, by their very nature, are frequently obviously and painfully abstract. Expressing foreign-policy goals in abstract terms inevitably divorces them one step from concrete reality, because abstractions suppress part of the truth in order to keep sight of the essential idea. Thus the term *democracy* is used with equal enthusiasm by both Washington and Moscow, and both can agree on the need for more of it so long as they refrain from going into detail.

The trouble with abstract goals is that they must constantly be interpreted in terms of immediate, practical circumstances. These immediate circumstances are stubborn and unyielding things. Unless great care is exercised by the guardians of national policy, the abstract goal is lost in the shuffle of the practical situation in which day by day it is given concreteness. As a result, policy may lose direction and, like the fictional knight, go galloping off in all directions.

Decisions must be made to deal with new crises that develop overnight. Only rarely are the nature and future implications of the crisis so clearly defined that the foreign office can make its decision in full and complete confidence that it is a direct step toward the fulfillment of an abstract goal and that it will not appear instead, in the changed perspective of a later time, as a deviation from that goal or even a step backward. The great crises, such as the bombing of Pearl Harbor and the aggression of North Korea, clearly show what must be done; great events reduce a problem to its raw essentials under the brilliant light of dramatic emotion. The lesser crises, which constitute the bulk of times when a path must be chosen, often leave unclear at the moment where one is going. Confronted with the fork in the road, however, one must make a choice, and whether or not progress is being made toward the fulfillment of the abstract goal must often be left to the verdict of history.

At this point the intellectual trap that history sets for the unwary is easily triggered. Having arrived at the goal, one is tempted to look back and divide the correct decisions from the false turns without giving sufficient weight to the fact that the path followed was hard to see at the time it was traveled. Hindsight, indeed, can posture as more perfect than foresight since the claim is in fact true.

The first difficulty in following a rational foreign policy is that the goals are frequently abstract while the choice of alternatives must always be concrete. The result may be the implementation of policy that in fact does not progress toward the desired goal. The decision may be

2

the product of ignorance of all the facts. Or the pressures of the moment may distort judgment.

## 2. One Thing Leads to Another

The second difficulty in following a rational foreign policy stems from the first, since events have a way of taking the bit in their teeth, as it were, and running away with the policy, whereas the process is supposedly just the reverse. This process is cumulative. As George Kennan remarked:

> In the fabric of human events, one thing leads to another. Every mistake is in a sense the product of all the mistakes that have gone before it, from which fact it derives a sort of a cosmic forgiveness; and at the same time every mistake is in a sense the determinant of all the mistakes of the future, from which it derives a sort of a cosmic unforgiveableness. Our action in the field of foreign policy is cumulative; it merges with a swelling stream of other human happenings; and we cannot trace its effects with any exactness once it has entered the fluid substance of history.[1]

Harold Nicolson in the course of one of his books gave trenchant expression to the way in which events may, with a will of their own, shape policy in unanticipated directions:

> Nobody who has not watched "policy" expressing itself in day-to-day action can realize how seldom is the course of events determined by deliberately planned purpose, or how often what in retrospect appears to have been a fully conscious intention was at the time governed and directed by that most potent of all factors—"the chain of circumstance." Few indeed are the occasions on which any statesman sees his objective clearly before him and marches towards it with undeviating stride; numerous indeed are the occasions when a decision or an event, which at the time seemed wholly unimportant, leads almost fortuitously to another decision which is no less incidental, until, little link by link, the chain of circumstances is forged.[2]

This kind of development may also mean that much more power is needed for successful prosecution of the policy than anyone anticipated; in the long run it may force the surrender of other foreign-policy objectives for which power is no longer available, even though such a decision would not have been made if it had been clear beforehand what was going to result.

## 3. Contradictory or Incompatible Goals

A third difficulty with following a rational policy is that foreign-

---

[1] George F. Kennan, *American Diplomacy 1900–1950*, Chicago: University of Chicago Press, 1951, p. 50. Copyright, 1951, by the University of Chicago.

[2] Harold Nicolson, *The Congress of Vienna*, pp. 19–20.

policy goals may be mutually contradictory. A nation may attempt to achieve two goals that are incompatible with each other. So long as the goals remain abstract, this contradiction may not become serious; but the minute they are given concrete embodiment and implementation, a conflict arises, which, if not resolved, may cause a sort of schizophrenia in the national character. This kind of situation is much more common with abstract than concrete goals, since it is easier to see the discrepancy in the latter case. A nation cannot seek as a foreign-policy goal both to raise and to lower its imports. It may blunder in a choice of means, but either it seeks to raise or to lower the imports. This is not so with more abstract goals such as peace and security.

It is not unusual for a nation to announce that it seeks both peace and security. The United States, for example, is on record to that effect time and time again. These goals are actually compatible . . . only as long as security can be attained through peace. Given peace, America feels secure. And given security, America feels peaceful. As long as both are obtainable, both are sought. Secretary of State Acheson remarked in March, 1950, that while the United States sought peace, it did not seek "peace at any price." Or compare the statement of Russian Ambassador Maisky in London on March 15, 1939: "The foreign policy of the Soviet Government has always been a policy of universal peace. Not a peace at any price, but a peace based on law and order in international affairs."

In other words, upon analysis, it becomes evident that security is the goal, and peace is either the means or a subordinate goal. The reader may indeed agree that this is so, but the point should be clear that America and the other powers continue to announce to the world that each of them seeks peace and security as the twin goals of her foreign policy. The intellectual confusion that results is the direct product of the failure to make the above distinctions clear.

There is a danger that decisions will be made which, while designed to preserve peace, jeopardize security. The classic illustration of modern times is to be found in the actions of British Prime Minister Chamberlain at Munich in 1938. He returned from the conference, he announced, with "Peace in our time," but as it happened he undermined British security in the process. In Winston Churchill's words:

> The subjugation of Czechoslovakia robbed the Allies of the Czech Army of twenty-one regular divisions, fifteen or sixteen second-line divisions already mobilised, and also their mountain fortress line which, in the days of Munich, had required the deployment of thirty German divisions, or the main strength of the mobile and fully trained German Army. According to Generals Halder and Jodl, there were but thirteen German divisions, of which only five were composed of first-line troops, left in the West at the time of the Munich arrangement.

Churchill goes on to point out that, in addition to this loss of some 35 Czech divisions, the Skoda Works, the second most important arsenal in Central Europe whose production between August of 1938 and September of 1939 was almost equal to British arms production during the same time, was subtracted from potential Allied strength and added to that of Germany—a double misfortune. And this was done even though "In 1935, France, unaided by her previous allies, could have invaded and reoccupied Germany almost without serious fighting. In 1936, there could still be no doubt of her overwhelmingly superior strength. We now know, from the German revelations, that this continued in 1938."[3] Ironically, Chamberlain's peace lasted little more than a year.

An unqualified seeking for peace may easily become appeasement; it does become appeasement if national security is put in jeopardy in the process. Thus the third difficulty is that, where abstract goals are involved, one goal may be incompatible with the other at a critical point, and this incompatibility may not be realized. Or it may produce an ill-fated attempt to implement the wrong goal at the expense of the right one, or it may lead to a continued clinging to both when a sharp choice is inevitable and the delaying of that choice is dangerous. The successful execution and implementation of policy is an art demanding skilled practitioners.

[3] Winston S. Churchill, *The Second World War: The Gathering Storm*, pp. 336–337.

# 2 / The Instruments of Foreign Policy

## MAX F. MILLIKAN AND OTHERS

**The United States pursues its foreign policy objectives by utilizing in various combinations and degrees the instruments of policy. Some of these instruments are listed here. The study from which this selection is taken is concerned primarily with**

From U. S. Senate Committee on Foreign Relations Study No. 12, "Economic, Social and Political Change in the Underdeveloped Countries and Its Implications for United States Policy," by Center for International Studies, Massachusetts Institute of Technology (March 1960), in *U.S. Foreign Policy: Compilation of Studies*, 87th Cong., 1st sess., S. Doc. 24 (March 15, 1961). In addition to Millikan, participants in the study included F. M. Bator, D. L. M. Blackmer, R. S. Eckhaus, E. E. Hagen, Daniel Lerner, Ithiel de Sola Pool, Lucian Pye, P. N. Rosenstein-Rodan, and W. W. Rostow.

Max F. Millikan is professor of economics and director of the Center for International Studies, Massachusetts Institute of Technology.

the role of the United States in the modernization of underdeveloped nations.

## 1. Diplomacy

The nature of the American interest in the modernization process
implies national relationships not envisaged in classical diplomacy
which was mainly concerned with external problems of power and of
alliances as between sovereign nation states at roughly similar stages
of development. American diplomacy in the modern world must embrace relationships between nations at radically different levels of
technology and power and treat with much more than external national
concerns. Broadly, such relationships must be grounded both in the
American interest in furthering a process of modernization which will
enable the transitional societies to develop their own versions of responsible government and to play a useful cooperative role in the world and
in shared efforts to those ends. Thus the American diplomat must steadily project a vision of what the domestic society to which he is assigned
may become; of what its place in an orderly world system might be;
and of what the United States is prepared to do to bring common
objectives to life.

## 2. Information Policy

It follows from the basic American relationship to the transitional
nations that the purpose of our communications with them should not
be to increase admiration for the United States or its standard of living
but to provide information helpful in the modernization process and to
project an image of authentically shared national and human objectives.

## 3. Military Policy

The men, equipment, and organizational structure of military establishments have a constructive potential now inadequately used. In
our view, it is a major and as yet unfulfilled American responsibility to
help guide the transitional countries to employ their military establishments creatively in the tradition pioneered in the United States by the
American Corps of Engineers during the first half of the 19th century.
The military establishments might, for example, participate in both
large- and small-scale construction projects and organize vocational
training and other educational programs for their recruits. The United
States should develop further educational and training programs in
this country for junior and middle-level officers from underdeveloped
countries.

## 4. Economic Policy

Economic policy is peculiarly important, not so much because the economic dimension of modernization will determine its outcome but because American economic aid is a possible and mutually accepted way of affecting the alternatives open to transitional societies and of affecting the contours of a society as a whole. Observations on four aspects of American economic foreign policy follow.

### TECHNICAL ASSISTANCE

Although technical assistance programs will not require budget allocations as large as those for capital expenditure and loan programs, their potential influence in shaping the evolution of transitional societies, especially societies in the early stages of transition, may well be decisive. The central tasks of technical assistance programs are to bring the knowledge and skills available in developed countries to bear on the problems of modernization and to develop to the fullest the human resources of the recipient country. They should offer opportunities for as many groups in the society as possible to participate in the modernization process and lead whenever possible to the building of permanent institutions performing the functions for which assistance was initially given. If properly administered and staffed, these programs can convey an image of American purposes and modes of operation which will encourage continuing future cooperation.

### ALLOCATION OF CAPITAL

If American capital assistance is to have maximum leverage in encouraging the underdeveloped countries to follow a course consistent with American interests, it must have the following characteristics:

1. The economic criteria which determine U.S. capital assistance must be clear and unambiguous; and we must be firmer than we have frequently been in the past in the application of those criteria.

2. The offer of capital on terms requiring the recipient to meet conditions for its productive use must be held out consistently over long enough periods of time to permit the incentive effects to work. Such a result cannot be expected from programs which are assured no more than 1 or 2 years of life.

3. The amounts offered must be large enough and the terms flexible enough to persuade the recipient that the game is worth the candle. This means that we must invest substantially larger resources in our economic development programs than we have done in the past. Our rough estimates suggest that a reasonable American share of an effec-

tive world development effort might involve from $1.5 to $2 billion more U.S. public investment in development annually than we have been making.

4. The kinds of capital we offer and the purposes for which we encourage it to be used must be sufficiently varied so that the lack of capital will not inhibit the growth of any important sector of the economy dependent on foreign exchange. If, for example, the use of foreign assistance is limited to social overhead or big industrial projects, there may well develop in other sectors bottlenecks which will lead first to economic stagnation and then to political and psychological frustration.

5. For political as well as economic reasons the leadership in under-developed countries should be encouraged to formulate their development goals in national terms. At an appropriate stage in the transition they should be urged to work out and discuss widely in their countries coordinated programs or plans which will underline the relationship of individual and local effort in particular sectors to national purposes and objectives.

6. In order that recipients of aid may free themselves from dependence on extraordinary external assistance as rapidly as possible, they should be encouraged to relate their own economic development to the growth of the international economy.

### ASSISTANCE TO LAND REFORM

The critical role which changes in the organization of agriculture are likely to play in the modernization of the transitional societies has implications for American policy. The United States should strongly support land reform programs. It should assist governments engaged in such programs by offering to provide capital and technical assistance and food surpluses to cushion any temporary decline in food deliveries resulting from agricultural reorganization.

### INTERNATIONAL ORGANIZATION OF AID

To coordinate the efforts of the increasing number of national and international agencies offering economic assistance is an urgent task. In our view, however, to attempt to lump the existing agencies together in a single international organization to administer aid would be neither a feasible nor a desirable solution. The resources granted to such an international pool of capital would in all likelihood not be sufficient to make a serious dent on the development problem. Each donor nation, moreover, will have a strong tendency to retain control over the administration of its assistance funds through its own national agencies.

The problem of coordination can best be solved not by creating a new aid-administering organization but by developing appropriate means of coordinating the operations of the various national and international agencies now in existence. Such coordination could be furthered by enlarging regional programs of cooperation; by creating an effective organization of lenders within the free world as well as a forum where lenders and borrowers can get together periodically; and by developing the consortium technique as a method for bringing the maximum resources of the international community to bear on the development problems of each country.

# 3 / Another "Great Debate": The National Interest of the United States

HANS J. MORGENTHAU

**The concept of the national interest defined in terms of power is set forth in the following essay, perhaps the classic writing from this point of view.**

WHAT IS THE NATIONAL INTEREST? How can we define it and give it the content which will make it a guide for action? This is one of the relevant questions to which the current debate has given rise.

It has been frequently argued against the realist conception of foreign policy that its key concept, the national interest, does not provide an acceptable standard for political action. This argument is in the main based upon two grounds: the elusiveness of the concept and its susceptibility to interpretations, such as limitless imperialism and narrow nationalism, which are not in keeping with the American tradition in foreign policy. The argument has substance as far as it goes, but it does not invalidate the usefulness of the concept.

Reprinted from the *American Political Science Review*, XLVI, 4 (December, 1952), 961–98. Copyright 1952 by the American Political Science Association. By permission.

Hans J. Morgenthau is professor of political science and director of the Center for the Study of American Foreign and Military Policy, University of Chicago. His many books include *Politics among Nations*, 3d ed. (1960) and *Politics in the Twentieth Century* (3 vols., 1962).

The concept of the national interest is similar in two respects to the "great generalities" of the Constitution, such as the general welfare and due process. It contains a residual meaning which is inherent in the concept itself, but beyond these minimum requirements its content can run the whole gamut of meanings which are logically compatible with it. That content is determined by the political traditions and the total cultural context within which a nation formulates its foreign policy. The concept of the national interest, then, contains two elements, one that is logically required and in that sense necessary, and one that is variable and determined by circumstances.

Any foreign policy which operates under the standard of the national interest must obviously have some reference to the physical, political, and cultural entity which we call a nation. In a world where a number of sovereign nations compete with and oppose each other for power, the foreign policies of all nations must necessarily refer to their survival as their minimum requirements. Thus all nations do what they cannot help but do: protect their physical, political, and cultural identity against encroachments by other nations.

It has been suggested that this reasoning erects the national state into the last word in politics and the national interest into an absolute standard for political action. This, however, is not quite the case. The idea of interest is indeed of the essence of politics and, as such, unaffected by the circumstances of time and place. Thucydides' statement, born of the experiences of ancient Greece, that "identity of interest is the surest of bonds whether between states or individuals" was taken up in the nineteenth century by Lord Salisbury's remark that "the only bond of union that endures" among nations is "the absence of all clashing interests." The perennial issue between the realist and utopian schools of thought over the nature of politics, to which we have referred before, might well be formulated in terms of concrete interests vs. abstract principles. Yet while the concern of politics with interest is perennial, the connection between interest and the national state is a product of history.

The national state itself is obviously a product of history and as such destined to yield in time to different modes of political organization. As long as the world is politically organized into nations, the national interest is indeed the last word in world politics. When the national state will have been replaced by another mode of organization, foreign policy must then protect the interest in survival of that new organization. For the benefit of those who insist upon discarding the national state and constructing supranational organizations by constitutional fiat, it must be pointed out that these new organizational forms will either come into being through conquest or else through consent based upon the mutual recognition of the national interests of the

nations concerned; for no nation will forego its freedom of action if it has no reason to expect proportionate benefits in compensation for that loss. This is true of treaties concerning commerce or fisheries as it is true of the great compacts, such as the European Coal and Steel Community, through which nations try to create supranational forms of organization. Thus, by an apparent paradox, what is historically relative in the idea of the national interest can be overcome only through the promotion in concert of the national interest of a number of nations.

The survival of a political unit, such as a nation, in its identity is the irreducible minimum, the necessary element of its interests vis-à-vis other units. Taken in isolation, the determination of its content in a concrete situation is relatively simple; for it encompasses the integrity of the nation's territory, of its political institutions, and of its culture. Thus bipartisanship in foreign policy, especially in times of war, has been most easily achieved in the promotion of these minimum requirements of the national interest. The situation is different with respect to the variable elements of the national interest. All the cross currents of personalities, public opinion, sectional interests, partisan politics, and political and moral folkways are brought to bear upon their determination. In consequence, the contribution which science can make to this field, as to all fields of policy formation, is limited. It can identify the different agencies of the government which contribute to the determination of the variable elements of the national interest and assess their relative weight. It can separate the long-range objectives of foreign policy from the short-term ones which are the means for the achievement of the former and can tentatively establish their rational relations. Finally, it can analyze the variable elements of the national interest in terms of their legitimacy and their compatibility with other national values and with the national interest of other nations. We shall address ourselves briefly to the typical problems with which this analysis must deal.

The legitimacy of the national interest must be determined in the face of possible usurpation by subnational, other-national, and supranational interests. On the subnational level we find group interests, represented particularly by ethnic and economic groups, who tend to identify themselves with the national interest. Charles A. Beard has emphasized, however one-sidedly, the extent to which the economic interests of certain groups have been presented as those of the United States. [1] Group interests exert, of course, constant pressure upon the conduct of our foreign policy, claiming their identity with the national interest. It is, however, doubtful that, with the exception of a few

---

[1] Charles A. Beard, *The Idea of National Interest: An Analytical Study in American Foreign Policy*, New York, 1934.

spectacular cases, they have been successful in determining the course of American foreign policy. It is much more likely, given the nature of American domestic politics, that American foreign policy, insofar as it is the object of pressures by sectional interests, will normally be a compromise between divergent sectional interests. The concept of the national interest, as it emerges from this contest as the actual guide for foreign policy, may well fall short of what would be rationally required by the overall interests of the United States. Yet the concept of the national interest which emerges from this contest of conflicting sectional interests is also more than any particular sectional interest or their sum total. It is, as it were, the lowest common denominator where sectional interests and the national interest meet in an uneasy compromise which may leave much to be desired in view of all the interests concerned.

The national interest can be usurped by other-national interests in two typical ways. The case of treason by individuals, either out of conviction or for pay, needs only to be mentioned here; for insofar as treason is committed on behalf of a foreign government rather than a supranational principle, it is significant for psychology, sociology, and criminology, but not for the theory of politics. The other case, however, is important not only for the theory of politics but also for its practice, especially in the United States.

National minorities in European countries, ethnic groups in the United States, ideological minorities anywhere may identify themselves, either spontaneously or under the direction of the agents of a foreign government, with the interests of that foreign government and may promote these interests under the guise of the national interest of the country whose citizens they happen to be. The activities of the German-American Bund in the United States in the 'thirties and of Communists everywhere are cases in point. Yet the issue of the national interest vs. other-national interests masquerading as the national interest has arisen constantly in the United States in a less clear-cut fashion.

A country which had been settled by consecutive waves of "foreigners" was bound to find it particularly difficult to identify its own national interest against alleged, seeming, or actual other-national interests represented by certain groups among its own citizens. Since virtually all citizens of the United States are, as it were, "more or less" foreign-born, those who were "less" so have frequently not resisted the temptation to use this distinction as a polemic weapon against latecomers who happened to differ from them in their conception of the national interest of the United States. Frequently, this rationalization has been dispensed with and a conception of foreign policy with which a writer happened to disagree has been attributed outright to foreign sympathy or influence or worse. British influence and interests have

served as standard arguments in debates on American foreign policy. Madison, in his polemic against Hamilton on the occasion of Washington's Neutrality Proclamation of 1793, identified the Federalist position with that of "the foreigners and degenerate citizens among us, who hate our republican government, and the French revolution," [2] and the accusation met with a favorable response in a majority of Congress and of public opinion. However, these traditional attempts to discredit dissenting opinion as being influenced by foreign interests should not obscure the real issue, which is the peculiar vulnerability of the national interest of the United States to usurpation by the interests of other nations.

The usurpation of the national interest by supranational interests can derive in our time from two sources: religious bodies and international organizations. The competition between church and state for determination of certain interests and policies, domestic and international, has been an intermittent issue throughout the history of the national state. Here, too, the legitimate defense of the national interest against usurpation has frequently, especially in the United States, degenerated into the demagogic stigmatization of dissenting views as being inspired by Rome and, hence, being incompatible with the national interest. Yet here, too, the misuse of the issue for demagogic purposes must be considered apart from the legitimacy of the issue itself.

The more acute problem arises at the present time from the importance which the public and government officials, at least in their public utterances, attribute to the values represented and the policies pursued by international organizations either as alternatives or supplements to the values and policies for which the national government stands. It is frequently asserted that the foreign policy of the United States pursues no objectives apart from those of the United Nations, that, in other words, the foreign policy of the United States is actually identical with the policy of the United Nations. This assertion cannot refer to anything real in actual politics to support it. For the constitutional structure of international organizations, such as the United Nations, and their procedural practices make it impossible for them to pursue interests apart from those of the member-states which dominate their policy-forming bodies. The identity between the interests of the United Nations and the United States can only refer to the successful policies of the United States within the United Nations through which the support of the United Nations is being secured for

---

[2] "Helvidius, in Answer to Pacificus, on President Washington's Proclamation of Neutrality," in *Letters and other Writings of James Madison,* Philadelphia, 1867, Vol. 1, p. 611.

the policies of the United States. [3] The assertion, then, is mere polemic, different from the one discussed previously in that the identification of a certain policy with a supranational interest does not seek to reflect discredit upon the former, but to bestow upon it a dignity which the national interest pure and simple is supposed to lack.

The real issue in view of the problem that concerns us here is not whether the so-called interests of the United Nations, which do not exist apart from the interests of its most influential members, have superseded the national interest of the United States, but for what kind of interests the United States has secured United Nations support. While these interests cannot be United Nations interests, they do not need to be national interests either. Here we are in the presence of that modern phenomenon which has been variously described as "utopianism," "sentimentalism," "moralism," the "legalistic-moralistic approach." The common denominator of all these tendencies in modern political thought is the substitution for the national interest of a supranational standard of action which is generally identified with an international organization, such as the United Nations. The national interest is here not being usurped by sub- or supranational interests which, however inferior in worth to the national interest, are nevertheless real and worthy of consideration within their proper sphere. What challenges the national interest here is a mere figment of the imagination, a product of wishful thinking, which is postulated as a valid norm for international conduct, without being valid either there or anywhere else. At this point we touch the core of the present controversy between utopianism and realism in international affairs; we shall return to it later in this paper.

The national interest as such must be defended against usurpation by non-national interests. Yet once that task is accomplished, a rational order must be established among the values which make up the national interest and among the resources to be committed to them. While the interests which a nation may pursue in its relation with other nations are of infinite variety and magnitude, the resources which are available for the pursuit of such interests are necessarily limited in quantity and kind. No nation has the resources to promote all desirable objectives with equal vigor; all nations must therefore allocate their scarce resources as rationally as possible. The indispensable precondition of such rational allocation is a clear understanding of the distinction between the necessary and variable elements of the national interest. Given the contentious manner in which in democracies the variable elements of

---

[3] See, on this point, Hans J. Morgenthau, "International Organizations and Foreign Policy," in *Foundations of World Organization: A Political and Cultural Appraisal,* Eleventh Symposium of the Conference on Science, Philosophy and Religion, edited by Lyman Bryson, Louis Finkelstein, Harold D. Lasswell, R. M. MacIver, New York, 1952, pp. 377-383.

the national interest are generally determined, the advocates of an extensive conception of the national interest will inevitably present certain variable elements of the national interest as though their attainment were necessary for the nation's survival. In other words, the necessary elements of the national interest have a tendency to swallow up the variable elements so that in the end all kinds of objectives, actual or potential, are justified in terms of national survival. Such arguments have been advanced, for instance, in support of the rearmament of Western Germany and of the defense of Formosa. They must be subjected to rational scrutiny which will determine, however tentatively, their approximate place in the scale of national values.

The same problem presents itself in its extreme form when a nation pursues, or is asked to pursue, objectives which are not only unnecessary for its survival but tend to jeopardize it. Second-rate nations which dream of playing the role of great powers, such as Italy and Poland in the inter-war period, illustrate this point. So do great powers which dream of remaking the world in their own image and embark upon world-wide crusades, thus straining their resources to exhaustion. Here scientific analysis has the urgent task of pruning down national objectives to the measure of available resources in order to make their pursuit compatible with national survival.

Finally, the national interest of a nation which is conscious not only of its own interests but also of that of other nations must be defined in terms compatible with the latter. In a multinational world this is a requirement of political morality; in an age of total war it is also one of the conditions for survival.

In connection with this problem two mutually exclusive arguments have been advanced. On the one hand, it has been argued against the theory of international politics here presented that the concept of the national interest revives the eighteenth-century concept of enlightened self-interest, presuming that the uniformly enlightened pursuit of their self-interest by all individuals, as by all nations, will of itself be conducive to a peaceful and harmonious society. On the other hand, the point has been made that the pursuit of their national interest by all nations makes war the permanent arbiter of conflicts among them. Neither argument is well taken.

The concept of the national interest presupposes neither a naturally harmonious, peaceful world nor the inevitability of war as a consequence of the pursuit by all nations of their national interest. Quite to the contrary, it assumes continuous conflict and threat of war, to be minimized through the continuous adjustment of conflicting interests by diplomatic action. No such assumption would be warranted if all nations at all times conceived of their national interest only in terms of their survival and, in turn, defined their interest in survival in restrictive and

rational terms. As it is, their conception of the national interest is subject to all the hazards of misinterpretation, usurpation, and misjudgment to which reference has been made above. To minimize these hazards is the first task of a foreign policy which seeks the defense of the national interest by peaceful means. Its second task is the defense of the national interest, restrictively and rationally defined, against the national interests of other nations which may or may not be thus defined. If they are not, it becomes the task of armed diplomacy to convince the nations concerned that their legitimate interests have nothing to fear from a restrictive and rational foreign policy and that their illegitimate interests have nothing to gain in the face of armed might rationally employed.

# 4 / From *Contemporary Theory in International Relations*

## STANLEY HOFFMANN

**Professor Hoffmann finds many inadequacies in Hans J. Morgenthau's "realist" concept of the national interest defined largely in terms of power. In the following selection he gives his reasons for the inadequacy of this as well as other theories of international politics.**

IN RECENT YEARS, there have not been many *general* theoretical efforts at explaining world politics. Partial explanatory theories, such as theories of imperialism, have been more frequent. If we concentrate on the former, we can distinguish two rather different types, which have in common the desire to provide us with master keys: the "realist" theory of power politics, and modern philosophies of history.

### 1. The "Realist" Theory of International Politics

The theory which has occupied the center of the scene in this country during the last ten years is Professor Morgenthau's "realist"

Reprinted from Stanley Hoffmann, ed., *Contemporary Theory in International Relations*, pp. 30–39. Copyright © 1960, by permission of Prentice-Hall, Inc., Englewood Cliffs, N.J.

Stanley Hoffmann is professor of government, Harvard University, and one of the leading scholars in the field of international politics, law, and organization.

theory of power politics. It is an attempt at providing us with a reliable "map" of the landscape of world affairs; an effort at catching the essence of world politics. The master key is the concept of interest defined in terms of power. To what extent does the theory accomplish its mission? It succeeds in focusing attention on the units which remain the principal actors in world affairs: the States. The theory also stresses the factors that account for the large degree of autonomy of International Relations: the differences between domestic and world politics which thwart the operation in the latter of ideas and institutions that flourish in the former, the drastic imperatives of survival, self-preservation and self-help which are both the causes and the products of such differences.

However, as a general theory, the "realist" analysis fails because it sees the world as a static field in which power relations reproduce themselves in timeless monotony. The map is inadequate for two main reasons. First, the "realist" analysis of power is a very debatable one. The cornerstone of the realist theory is the statement that the political sphere is just as autonomous as the respective spheres of the economist, or the lawyer, or the moralist. This we can certainly accept. But what kind of an autonomy are we talking about? There are two possible versions: a sphere can be autonomous either because it is concerned with a specialized and limited set of variables, or because it is concerned with *all* the variables with which the various specialized spheres deal—it then differs from these spheres by its own generality and by the way in which all these different variables are combined here. When Mr. Morgenthau discusses the need for theory and for a hierarchical integration of the various disciplines which contribute to the study of international relations, he rightly says that politics must play the role of the common, integrating core and thus adopts the second version.[1] But in the bulk of his writings, and particularly in his statement of the realist theory . . . , he interprets autonomy in the first sense: the political realist "thinks in terms of interest defined as power, as the economist thinks in terms of utility; the lawyer, of conformity of action with legal rules; the moralist, of conformity of action with moral principles."

Now, the decision to equate politics and power would be acceptable only if power were analyzed, not as a limited and specific set of variables, but as a complex and diffuse balance between all the variables with which the social sciences are concerned.[2] Political man should properly be seen as the "integrator" of moral man, economic man, religious man, and so on—not as a creature reduced to one special facet of human nature. Unfortunately such an Aristotelian position is not

---

[1] Hans J. Morgenthau, *Dilemmas of Politics*, Chicago, 1958, pp. 98-100.
[2] See Talcott Parsons, *The Social System*, Glencoe, 1951, pp. 551 ff.

adopted here: the decision to equate politics and the effects of man's "lust for power" is combined with a tendency to equate power and evil or violence—a combination which mutilates reality. A "power monism" does not account for all politics, when power is so somberly defined; even in world affairs, the drive for participation and community plays a part, and the image of political man interested exclusively in the control of the actions of others for the sake of control, is simply not acceptable as a basis for theory.

Furthermore, the extent to which power as a carrier of evil and violence expresses a basic human instinct is questionable. Much of the international (or domestic) evil of power is rooted not in the sinfulness of man but in a context, a constellation, a situation, in which even good men are forced to act selfishly or immorally. Discrimination between the inherent or instinctive aspects of the "power drive," and the situational or accidental ones, is an important task. However, reactions to shifting situations are scarcely considered by the theory.

Also, it is dangerous to put in a key position a concept which is merely instrumental. Power is a means toward any of a large number of ends (including power itself). The quality and quantity of power used by men are determined by men's purposes. It would have been more logical to begin with a theory of ends rather than with the notion of power, which is here both ambiguous and abstracted from its ends. The "realist" theory neglects all the factors that influence or define purposes. Why statesmen choose at times to use national power in a certain way (say a policy of "imperialism") rather than in another is not made clear. The domestic considerations that affect national power— the nature of the regime, the structure of power, beliefs and values which account in great measure for the nation's goals and for the statesmen's motivations—are either left out or brushed aside. For instance, it is not enough to say that "the political cohesion of a federal system is the result of superior power located in some part of it," [3] for what remains to be explained is how such superior power got to be located there, what convergence of interests or what community of values led to its establishment and underlies its authority. Similarly, internationally shared beliefs and purposes are left out. Reality comes out oversimplified, for we get a somewhat mechanistic view of international affairs in which the statesmen's role consists of adjusting national power to an almost immutable set of external "givens." Professor Morgenthau's metaphor about theory which, like a portrait, and unlike a photograph, should try to show "one thing that the naked eye cannot

---

[3] Hans J. Morgenthau, "Another 'Great Debate': The National Interest of the United States," *American Political Science Review*, Vol. XLVI, No. 4 (December 1952), p. 968.

see: the human essence of the person portrayed" is most revealing. It is quite possible that there is a human essence of the person; but even if we had been able to discover it, we would still have to account for all the twists and vagaries of the person's existence and we cannot assume that they would be easily deducible from the "human essence" discovered. The same is true in world politics. Unfortunately, the "realist" world is a frozen universe of separate essences.

Even if the role of power were as determining as the theory postulates, the question arises whether any scheme can put so much methodological weight upon one concept, even a crucial one; for it seems to me that the concept of power collapses under the burden. It is impossible to subsume under one word variables as different as: power as a condition of policy and power as a criterion of policy; power as a potential and power in use; power as a sum of resources and power as a set of processes. Power is a most complex product of other variables, which should be allowed to see the light of the theory instead of remaining hidden in the shadow of power. Otherwise the theory is bound either to mean different things at different steps of the analysis (or when dealing with different periods), or else to end by selecting for emphasis only one aspect of power: either military force or economic strength.[4] Thus, instead of a map which simplifies the landscape so that we can understand it, we are left with a distortion.

There is a second reason for the inadequacy of the map. The rigidity that comes from the timeless concept of power is compounded by the confusing use of other concepts that are dated in more ways than one, and which the theory applies to situations in which they do not fit. The model of the "realists" is a highly embellished ideal-type of eighteenth and nineteenth century international relations. This vision of the golden age is taken as a norm, both for empirical analysis and for evaluation. A number of oddities of the theory are explained thereby. First, the lack of an adequate discussion of ends; for when all the actors have almost the same credo, as they did during most of that period, it becomes easy to forget the effects of the common credo on the actors' behavior, and to omit from among the main variables of the theory a factor whose role seems constant. It is nevertheless an optical illusion to mistake a particular historical pattern for the norm of a scientific system. When we deal with a period such as twentieth century world politics, whose main characteristic may well be the division of an international society which had previously been rather coherent into rival groups devoted to mutually exclusive purposes and values, the neglect of ends is a fatal mistake.

---

[4] On this point, see for instance Mr. A. F. K. Organski's economic power monism in his *World Politics* (New York, 1958).

Second, the analysis of power apart from the processes and pressures of domestic politics follows from the same optical illusion. It is easy to understand why public philosophers should bemoan the days when no visible and organized groups challenged the primacy of foreign affairs, the continuity of diplomatic action, unsentimental equilibrium calculations, and privacy. But these principles are not eternal; the Greek city-states did not observe them—at their own peril, of course, but then the world restored in 1815 balanced its power and played its cards into the abyss of 1914; and no one has yet found a way of reversing the trend and of insulating the experts on Olympus from the germs carried by the common men in the swamps below.

Third, the conception of an objective and easily recognizable national interest, the reliable guide and criterion of rational policy, is one which makes sense only in a stable period in which the participants play for limited ends, with limited means, and without domestic kibitzers to disrupt the players' moves. In such a period, the survival of the main units is rarely at stake in the game, and a hierarchy can rather easily be established among the other more stable and far less vital interests that are at stake. In such a period, the influence on foreign policies of factors such as geography, natural resources, industrial capacity, and inherited traditions of national principles is particularly strong and relatively constant. Today, however, survival is almost always at stake, and technological leaps have upset the hierarchy of "stable" factors. The most divergent courses of action can be recommended as valid choices for survival. Ordinarily less compelling objectives, such as prestige, or an increment of power in a limited area, or the protection of private citizens abroad, all become tied up with the issue of survival, and the most frequent argument against even attempting to redefine a hierarchy of national objectives so as to separate at least some of them from survival, is the familiar fear of a "chain of events" or a "row of dominoes falling." In such circumstances of mutual fear and technological turmoil, interpretations of the national interest become almost totally subjective and the relative weight of "objective" factors which affect the states' capabilities and thereby influence state policies is almost impossible to evaluate. Consequently, a scholar attempting to use the theory as a key to the understanding of, or successful influence upon, contemporary realities risks being in the unhappy position of a Tiresias who recognizes interests which the parties concerned refuse to see, who diagnoses permanence where the parties find confusing change and whose ex post facto omniscience is both irritating and irrelevant.

Fourth, the idea that the national interest carries its own morality is also one which makes sense almost only in a stable period. For it is a period in which an international consensus assures at least the possibility of accommodation of national objectives; the conflicts of interests

which are involved are not struggles between competing international moralities. The philosophical pluralism implicit in the "realist" theory (which purports to be both normative and empirical) is not sufficiently thought through. For in periods of stability and moderation, which bloom only because of a basic agreement on values, the national interest can be said to be moral and legitimate only because it expresses aspirations of a community which do not rule out those of another group. What is moral is not the national interest as such but its reasonableness, which insures its compatibility with the interests of other states and with the common values of international society; and what is legitimate is the possibility for each group to have such temperate aspirations recognized. This is, at best, the kind of pluralism which is implied by *one* particular set of values—those of liberalism. As for periods of "nationalistic universalism," of secular religions and incompatible ideologies—here the tolerance characteristic of liberal pluralism makes no sense whatsoever. It is one thing to say that ideological differences do not justify crusades which would push the world into the chaos of total war; it is quite another to suggest that *all* national interests (as they are defined by statesmen) are to be given free play and recognition, in a period when one state's interest all too often resides in eliminating another state. A difference must be made between the pluralism of harmony, and the pluralism of the jungle.

Fifth, the emphasis on the "rationality" of foreign policy and the desire to brush aside the irrational elements as irrelevant intrusions or pathological deviations are understandable only in terms of cabinet diplomacy, where such deviations appear (especially with the benefit of hindsight) to have been rare. There, rationality seemed like the simple adjustment of means to stable and generally recognized ends. These concepts are far less applicable to a period in which the political struggles involve primarily the determination of ends. [5] In such a period, a conception of rationality adequate only for the selection of means cannot help us evaluate and classify the ends of states (the narrowness of the theory's conception of rationality makes it even more easy to understand why ends are insufficiently examined). Also, revolutionary periods are often characterized by the selection of means which are perfectly irrational from any point of view, *including* that of the adequacy of those means to the previously selected ends. Forgetting these two facts can entail serious mistakes. Thus, on the one hand, to apply a rationality of means to the selection of ends can have disastrous consequences in areas such as contemporary strategic doctrines. For instance, it can lead us to advocate limited nuclear war as the most

---

[5] These arguments are developed by Henry A. Kissinger, *A World Restored*, Boston, 1957.

rational way of employing the military resources of the West in the case of a conflict, without however having faced the previous question: whether such a strategy fits entirely the purposes the West has set for its relations both with the Communist camp and with the uncommitted nations, or, to put it somewhat differently, whether the purpose of this strategy—economy of force—is the highest end the West pursues. On the other hand, to forget that a nation might at some point select totally irrational means and be pushed by the dark logic of mutual fears into the very abyss of war that it wanted to avoid, is to assume too lightly that cool calculations of interest necessarily guide a nation's policy, or that mistaken calculations do not occur. Now, as the reader will see, debates among sociologists about the nature of war are not conclusive enough to allow us to assume that nations make war only because, and when, their leaders see in war a rational instrument of policy. In other words, a theory of world politics should certainly be rational but there is no need to suppose that reality is generally rational too.

Finally, the exclusion from the pale of world politics of those activities which were not undertaken by the states as such (i.e., by their governments), or which do not represent an obvious attempt to gain control over other nations (such as the signing of extradition treaties, or exchanges of goods and services, to use Mr. Morgenthau's own examples), is also understandable in certain periods only. It makes sense when a considerable range of activities which do, if only indirectly, affect the political power of the state, is left to private citizens (as was the case in the century of the liberal states). It makes sense when these activities are carried out unobtrusively within the common framework in which "power politics" operate, instead of serving as counters in the struggle for the establishment of a new framework. Nevertheless, even in the study of stable periods, the total exclusion of these acts is a mistake, because their temporary removal from the range of issues that involve directly the states' power is precisely the underpinning and one of the defining features of international relations in these periods— the submerged part of the iceberg. Behind the claim to realism, we thus find a reactionary utopia.

The consequence of this inadequacy of the map is that the theory's usefulness as a general theory for the discipline is limited. In the first place, from the point of view of systematic empirical analysis, it is too static. The price one has to pay for identifying the "timeless features" of the political landscape is the sacrifice of understanding the processes of change in world affairs. The theory stresses the autonomy of international relations to the point of leaving outside its pale the forces which work for change and which, cutting across the states, affect the states' behavior. Consequently the study of international relations tends to be reduced to a formalized ballet, where the steps fall into the same pattern

over and over again, and which has no story to tell. To be sure, we are informed that the dancers do not have to remain the same: there might someday be other units than the nation states; but we cannot deal with the problem of knowing how the dancers will change. On the contrary, we are instructed that in the meantime "the national interest as such must be defended against usurpation by non-national interests"; in other words, new dancers might well appear but there is no intermission in which the turnover could happen and while they are on stage their duty is to stay on the job. To change the metaphor, we are presented both with a single key to the closed room of politics among nations, and with a warning that the room is in a house whose key we cannot have, or whose opening must be left to the "workmanlike manipulation of perennial forces." We are not told what they are, or how they operate. Consequently, when they disturb the model, the model's builders are reduced to imprecations against these forces, or to devil explanations.

We reach at this point one of the most fundamental ambiguities of the theory. Realism quite correctly denounces the utopian's mistake of swinging from the goal of a universal harmony to the assumption that in the world as it is the conditions for such harmony already exist. Realism commits exactly the opposite mistake. The postulate of the permanence of power politics among nations as the core of international relations, tends to become a goal. The static qualities of the theory lead to confusion between the phenomenon of power conflicts and the transitory forms and institutions in which such conflicts have been taking place in recent centuries. Why should the sound reminder that power is here to stay mean that the present system of nation states will continue, or change only through forces that are of no concern to us? Such an attitude evades both the empirical duty of accounting for change, and the normative task of assessing whether the present system should indeed continue. It is one thing to say that change will have to be sifted through the slow procedures of present world politics, and meet with the states' consent. It is quite another thing to suggest diplomacy as the only effective procedure and the only meaningful restraint. I cannot help but feel that in spite of Mr. Morgenthau's qualifying statements, there is behind his theory the old position that whatever has been, must continue.

This brings us to a second limitation. A theory which stresses necessity in policy-making rather than choice, and adjustment to the environment or to the existing element of national power, rather than value objectives and the adjustment of the "givens" to such purposes, a theory concerned with the preservation of the present units rather than with change, has disturbing normative implications. It is something of a success philosophy. The criterion of a good foreign policy is its rationality, but the touchstone of rationality is success. Unfortunately the

23

standards of success and failure are not made clear. First, how will we distinguish between the follies of straight utopianism and the fallacies of wrong realism—realism that did not work? Secondly, from what viewpoint shall we decide whether a statesman has succeeded or failed? Shall we turn to history alone? But at what stage? Metternich had succeeded by 1825, and failed by 1848, and writers disagree whether he had succeeded or failed by 1914. If we want an answer from history alone, we will be driven either to pure irrationalism ("it is a tale full of sound and fury . . ."), or to passive contemplation, or to elementary Machiavellianism: "within itself, history has no standard of value but success, and no measure of success but the attainment of power, or survival for a little longer than rival individuals or institutions have survived." [6] If, as we must, we set our standards outside and above history, then we must avoid trying to prove that history will inevitably recompense policies that meet our standards. Otherwise, we become salesmen for a philosophical stand, who travel the roads of history in search of a clientele of confirmations; we are no longer either scholars testing a hypothesis, or philosophers interested in an ideal which history cannot promise to bless at all times.

The former position we wish to avoid. It is particularly uncomfortable when one's basic postulate about human nature is such that history cannot be anything but a tale full of sound and fury, signifying nothing. For it is a postulate which stresses the inevitability and universality of evil, and which assumes that reason, "far from following its own inherent impulses, is driven toward its goal by the irrational forces the ends of which it serves." [7] Now, this view makes it almost impossible to understand how there could be a rational theory of rational human behavior. This is not the last contradiction: the "realist" theory combines a Hobbesian image of naked power politics with an attempt to show that states are nevertheless not condemned to a life that is "nasty, brutish, and short"; "realism" thus puts its faith in voluntary restraints, moderation, and the underlying assumption of possible harmony among national interests—points scarcely admitted by the original postulate, and justified only by a view of power and politics that makes some place for, let us say, a reasonable view of reason. The key to this riddle is to be found in another contradiction which our previous discussion should have suggested: the sharp contrast between the original postulate, whose logic is a permanent clash of forces of evil, and the norm of eighteenth and nineteenth century international relations—the period in which the world's state of nature

[6] Alfred Cobban, "The Decline of Political Theory," *Political Science Quarterly*, Vol. LXVIII, No. 3 (September 1953), p. 333.

[7] Hans J. Morgenthau, *Scientific Man vs. Power Politics*, Chicago, 1946, p. 154.

was most Lockian or Humean, and Mr. Morgenthau's view of human nature most unjustified.

With such flaws and contradictions, the policy guidance the realist theory is able to afford is limited. "Realism" allows us to eliminate those policies that would foolishly forget the prerequisite of power; but it does not go much further. Too often, it is possible to build alternative and conflicting cases of "realist" policies, or to justify in "realist" terms a policy that can also be defended on "utopian" grounds. Too many factors are left out for "realist" policy advice to avoid the dilemma of homilies and admonishments, or suggestions inappropriate for revolutionary periods, such as the advocacy of "peace through accommodation," diplomacy and compromise—a policy which runs against some of the facts of present international life, in particular against the unwillingness of the Soviet side to accept such rules and to seek such deals. The light that illuminated the landscape in the quiet obscurity of nineteenth century politics, is blown out by today's tempest.

## 2. Philosophies of History

There are other attempts at providing us with a master key, and at explaining as large an amount of data as possible. I refer to philosophies of history, to which specialists in international relations have sometimes turned and are likely to turn. Like Hegel and Marx, Spengler and (especially) Toynbee are in the process of being adopted by political scientists after having been repudiated by historians. They avoid many of the shortcomings of "realism." Whereas the latter is too much concerned with timeless propositions and permanent necessities, the former are rightly dealing with problems of time and change, and with the effects of changes within the units of the world on the relations between these units. Whereas "realism" puts the State at the center of its analysis, philosophies of history remind us that world politics is more than the intersection of various foreign policies, and that these policies often depend on whether the states address themselves to other members of the same civilization or culture, or to complete outsiders. If it is true that "only a universalist perspective permits a scientific understanding of international reality,"[8] these philosophies are indispensable. They are useful also because of their method: the comparison of cultures or civilizations as if they were contemporary carries a lesson for international relations. Finally, philosophers of history have a disarming way of making explicit, and even central, assumptions about man, society, and history which are often repressed but nevertheless operating in all social

---

[8] Antonio Truyol, "La teoria de las relaciones internacionales como sociologia," (here trans. by S. H.), *Revista de Estudios Politicos*, Vol. 96, (November-December 1957), p. 335.

scientists' schemes. Such candor is to be commended.

However, we are once more in the presence of a short cut. Here, a teleological interpretation which discourages further research and twists the facts into a predetermined pattern is substituted for careful and systematic explanation. It is "a set of advance-judgments,"[9] a flaw we found already in "realism." Hence many similarities. First, the net is too wide to catch all the main factors in world affairs and to account for the main forces at work in a given period. Thus, it has been remarked that Toynbee's formula of challenge and response as the explanation of the genesis of civilizations amounts in practice to the arbitrary selection of one cause only: "in every given historical situation it refers to only one element, one out of many, one which, when we are concerned with historical presentation, cannot be abstracted from the others."[10]

Second, history is again ransacked for confirmation of a postulate, and facts that do not fit are left out or thrown together under headings that are sometimes more tautological than explanatory, such as the notion of withdrawal-and-return, used to describe the action of creative individuals and minorities—an umbrella under which such different actors as Buddha, Dante, Kant, and England in modern history are supposed to find shelter. As for the postulate which history is begged to demonstrate, the difference with "realism" lies mainly in its nature: organic metaphors or spiritual revelations replace the power drive. The value of such sweeping hypotheses as explanations of reality is dubious; references to a permanent lust for power in human nature, or to a necessary cycle of birth, growth, maturity and decline, or to successive civilizations as steps in religious progress, represent an escape from the task of causal explanation rather than the victorious accomplishment of this task. Indeed Spengler denied altogether the possibility of causal analysis and systematic understanding in history, when he stated that causes operate only in the natural sciences and destiny in history.

Third, it is not surprising that the criteria of fitness of civilizations or nations should once again be success or survival, for philosophies of history of the kind we are discussing try at the same time to assert the purposiveness of the universe, and the possibility of deducing historical laws from empirical reality; now any attempt to find purposiveness in history itself rather than in man's moral nature crashes into the impasse and inconsistency of setting up "a normative pattern for the evaluation of laws derived empirically"[11]—and the usual result consists of seeing

---

[9] Ernest Barker in M. F. Ashley Montagu (ed.), *Toynbee and History*, Boston, 1956, pp. 94-95.

[10] Peter Geyl in Geyl, Toynbee, and Sorokin, *The Pattern of the Past*, Boston, 1949, p. 23.

[11] Henry A. Kissinger, *The Meeting of History*, unpublished dissertation, Harvard University, 1950, p. 143.

in the success or the decline of cultures and peoples the sanction of their conformity to the great design which reveals itself in history.

Since philosophers of history see in history the unfolding of a design rather than the mere repetition of a basic pattern, the world is treated no longer as a field, but as a plan in which certain forces work toward an end wanted by God, nature, or history itself. Consequently, the main units of analysis are entities less likely to resist such a scheme than the ordinary units of historians or social scientists. The units of analysis used by the philosophers are huge aggregates such as classes, peoples, civilizations, cultures. Sometimes these units are useful to us; nevertheless they cannot be our only analytical tools, since we must deal primarily with those more modest but less hypothetical basic communities into which the world has been divided: the states, the empires. Sometimes the philosophers' units are altogether artificial congeries whose construction, number, existence, homogeneity and use are open to challenge, such as Spengler's Magian culture, whose reality remains in doubt. Thus we can pick out of these schemes useful insights, and think about suggestive hypotheses. But this road ends in the sky, not in a theory for international relations.


# 5 / From *System and Process in International Politics*

MORTON A. KAPLAN

Is the national interest objective or subjective? Is it the same for democracies and dictatorships? Professor Kaplan explores these and related questions with reference to attempts to define or conceptualize the national interest. The influential book from which this selection is drawn demonstrates the potentialities of systems analysis for the study of interacting foreign policies.

A DEBATE HAS RAGED concerning whether the national interest is

Reprinted, with permission, from Morton A. Kaplan, *System and Process in International Politics* (New York: John Wiley & Sons, Inc., 1957), pp. 151–61.

Morton A. Kaplan has taught at the University of Chicago and has been affiliated with the Hudson Institute. He is a leading explorer of the new frontiers of theory in the fields of foreign policy and international politics.

27

objective. Those who regard the national interest as objective usually regard national interests as permanent, unchanging, and related to power. Those who regard the national interests as subjective usually affirm that it includes values other than power. They also cite disagreement between individuals and groups of individuals concerning the national interest as proof that it is subjective. Objectivists reply by making a distinction between interests and passions or between interests and opinions.

The interest of a system is to obtain the valuable. The interest of a nation is to satisfy national needs. Thus national interests are objective, and there are as many national interests as national needs.

However, what lies behind the distinction between "passion" and "interest" which historically has been commonplace in discussions of statecraft? Does a sharp distinction between analytic levels of action permit a more precise analysis of the problem of the national interest?

### Passions and Interests

National interests have been identified as objective although related to the national level of action and to the structure of the system of action at the national level. However, this does not account for the historic distinction between "interest" and "passion." Does this distinction reflect simply a dispute concerning the national interest? Or is some more basic issue involved?

Many times policies have been opposed as based on passion or sentiment rather than on interest. Somehow this use of "passion" and "interest" implies that some objectives are more ephemeral or less real than other objectives. Although the distinction between "passion" and "interest" rarely is precisely explained, it appears to rest upon the belief that national actors are concrete physical entities. Somehow this physical substratum appears to be the most important element in national life. Therefore national power is the supreme goal of national action. National power is both the means and the objective of statecraft. The more power a nation has, the more secure its life. Other objectives are regarded as ephemeral, or even as dangerous to the life of the nation.

This position has been argued as if it constituted an eternal law of nature rather than a prescription for action within a particular international system of action. The "interest" formulation constitutes both a description of what has occurred and a prescription for national policy.

The "interest" doctrine is a reasonably adequate description of the "balance of power" international system, although, at times, sentiment or "passion" did seem to outweigh "interest," for example, Palmerston's support for Greece and British neutrality in the American Civil War after Lincoln's Emancipation Proclamation.

As a prescription for action, the "interest" doctrine accords reasonably well with the essential rules of the "balance of power" international system, although it does not take proper account of the possible dangers arising from deviant national actors. As interest is understood in this volume, Palmerston may have been wise in running some risks to encourage non-directive national actors. Such action may have had long-term value for stabilizing the "balance of power" system by inhibiting deviancy.

The "interest" doctrine also neglects the consideration that external policy has the function of maintaining a given social structure within the national system as well as the function of preserving the security of the national system against potential enemies. If there really were a sharp segregation between domestic and foreign policy, conditions in the international system would be inconsequential for the internal life of the national system—provided only that the system were secure against enemies.

However, efforts to protect national systems externally affect the internal life of the national system. Things like the draft, industrial mobilization, and problems of security affect the national system. In an age when small professional armies waged war, when conscription affected only the poor and the rootless, these consequences may have been obscure.

The policy best adapted to maintaining external security may not be the best policy from the standpoint of maintaining internal values. Likewise, an external policy that would be best if supported internally may be poor if it arouses opposition within the nation or if it creates economic hardships which lead to apathy and indifference.

If the "interest" doctrine, based upon the concept of national power, is correct, it should be confirmed by the permanency of national policy regardless of changes in government within national actors. Proponents of the "interest" doctrine long have used the striking continuity of foreign policy and the abandonment by incoming governments of positions on foreign affairs taken while out of office as confirmation that the national interest rests on solid realities rather than on "ideas," "opinions," or "passions."

In part, the proof is an artifact. In non-directive systems governments usually rest upon center-based majorities. The majority is usually provided by the great "middle mass" of citizens. A radical break with past policy most often would condemn a party to the status of a permanent minority. Therefore, from a political point of view alone, great changes in foreign policy cannot often be expected simply because one party rather than another comes to office.

However, it must be admitted, some parties out of power, particularly socialist parties, have miscalculated the extent to which foreign policy

can be independent of the instrumental means of implementation. At times, popular policies are espoused out of office only to be forsaken when office is attained.

National actors in a "balance of power" or bipolar system require for their defense and also for the effectiveness of policy allies, bases, access to raw materials, and so forth. These needs, although they may be implemented in different ways, cannot well be eliminated by changing office holders.

Moreover, a number of factors may reinforce the specific objectives or means of implementation chosen by preceding governments. In the first place, enunciated objectives tend to become imbedded in the information states of the decision makers who choose them and also in the information states of those decision makers who come to office later. In the second place, once an objective or means of implementation is pursued, the investment in that objective is lost if a change is made. Other actors have already pledged their cooperation. Claims have publicly been made. Reversals would cloud the entire issue and make policies appear arbitrary. Besides, time, money, and personnel have already been expended. Moreover, the organization is structured to scan for information which seems consonant with the given objective and to ignore information which appears to conflict. This is particularly true at non-political levels in the administration. Furthermore, these levels in the administration brief political appointees and play a large role in directing their attention toward given courses of action and away from other equally plausible courses of action.

Alliances and blocs in particular represent large investments of effort and resources. New administrations may intend to make changes, but it is difficult to make changes at a single point without touching off a ramified series of consequences. It is much easier to maintain existing agreements than to negotiate new sets of agreements.

The Republican administration in 1953—even had it wanted to—was in a poor position to renegotiate the role of national forces in NATO or to take a position quite different from the position of the Truman administration with respect to German rearmament. The Republican administration was free to suggest minor modifications, but it would have raised the wrath of its treaty partners had it claimed that it was not bound or committed by the agreements of the government that was its predecessor. Indeed, such a position would have set a most undesirable precedent. Would even a more conservative Republican group have been willing to pay the cost of reassessment each time the French, Italian, or Belgian cabinet changed?

Generally, only when internal changes within a national system lead to radical changes in the political system of that nation may a change of alignment become a matter of necessity rather than convenience. Obvi-

ously, if Italy were to acquire a Communist government, both the United States and Italy would desire to examine the role of Italy in NATO.

Logistic considerations also predispose nations to some objectives rather than others which—apart from logistic considerations—may be equally desirable. Thus air fields in Patagonia may serve as well to service bombing missions as those in Libya except that they are farther from potential targets. Raw materials may be as cheap to acquire in one place as another, except that the transportation route may be safer, and so on.

For these reasons, and perhaps for some others also, it is rare that the foreign policy objectives of a national system change radically. If the Communists, for instance, were to take over Italy, the foreign objectives of Italy would change radically. But most governmental changes are not that sweeping. Particularly in non-directive national systems, the changes rest upon a framework of national consensus.

The replacement of a Labour government in Great Britain by a Conservative government may change national values somewhat. But the place to look for the consequences of the change is not in a vast and sweeping replacement of previous national policies. Rather changes in the priorities accorded alternative objectives or the speed or willingness with which given policies are carried out may characterize the change in governmental policy. The Labour government probably gave India and Burma their freedom faster than a Conservative government would have. But a Conservative government almost surely would have granted independence eventually.

Nevertheless, these differences in priority are not lacking in importance. Indeed, India might not have remained within the Commonwealth had not the grant been made when it was. France finally accorded independence to Viet Nam. But it might have been much better for France if Mendes-France had come to office a year earlier.

### Distinctions between the Interests of Different System Levels

The distinction between the interests of different system levels rests upon the consideration that systems of action are analytic rather than concrete entities. This does not signify that they are unreal but only that classes of actions with relatively permanent characteristics are segregated and treated as independent systems. Indeed, a system may be dominant over the actors within it.

National systems of action, like other systems, are organized to satisfy system needs. Their essential rules represent their adjustment to their environments in terms of the relations of the actors within the system rather than in terms of specific instrumental goal objects.

For instance, curbs were placed on the movement of labor and capital in wartime England. When, however, the external environment be-

came favorable, that is, when the war was won, it became possible to implement the values and thus to satisfy the needs of the national system better by removing some of the wartime curbs.

A national system cannot continue to regulate itself well unless it can satisfy at least some of the needs of at least some of its subsystems. Therefore, the national interest will include the satisfaction of at least some of these subsystem needs. However, even when the national system is not regulating pathologically, there may be conflicts between the interests of the national actor and interests of subsystems of the national actor system.

For instance, it may be in the interest of the political system to send an espionage agent on a dangerous mission or to nationalize an industry. Except for some peculiar conditions, these decisions will not be in the interests of the espionage agent or the industry or the owners of the industry. Although the industry may resist nationalization in the name of the national interest—and although in some cases it may be correct in this claim—the claim, theoretically at least, can be determined independently.

Analytically, the interests of individuals, subnational systems, national systems, supranational systems, and the international system stand on an equal footing. There is no natural order of priority such that one system level ought to defer to another.

There may be occasions when various system interests coincide. Although taxes in general are burdensome, taxpayers may, in keeping with their interests and those of the national actor, vote additional tax monies for defense purposes. Military appropriations may be directly valuable to the national actor and indirectly valuable to citizens whose interests are defended by the national actor.

On other occasions, the national actor may make a decision contrary to the interests of some individual, but it may nevertheless be in the interest of the individual to comply with the decision. Nationalization of industry may be a case in point. The decision may be contrary to the interests of the stockholders but—once taken—the penalty for attempted non-compliance may be sufficiently great to contra-indicate that course of action.

On still other occasions, the decisions of the national actor may be so contrary to the interests of individuals that resistance is indicated regardless of the chances of success. Jews being herded into Hitler's gas chambers had no good reason to comply with the decisions of the national government.

There may be still other occasions on which the interests of the government are so opposed to those of the body of citizens that the government will collapse and be replaced by another form of government. The French and Russian revolutions illustrate this point. Reform was no longer possible within the old institutions. The attempt to defend these institu-

tions was doomed to failure. Yet there was no reason from the point of view of the governmental subsystem why the attempt should not have been made.

National systems may be so in conflict with the interests of individual citizens and groupings of citizens that they may be merged within supranational or international political entities. Efforts to forge a United States of Europe rest upon the claim that existing organizational entities are outmoded. Yet the interests of the national actors may lie in resisting such efforts though the interests of subsystems of the national system possibly may sanction attempts to alter or to destroy national institutions. Only if such an integrative merger is the only way left to preserve some of the values of the national system, will the interests of the national actor and of its subsystems prove parallel. Even here, however, there may be conflicts with respect to speed and degree of integration.

There is in nature no inherent priority for the national actor system over any subsystem of that system or over supranational or international systems. As far as individual citizens are concerned, the interests of the national actor within which they hold citizenship have no natural priority over the interests of other national actor systems.

Should the anti-Nazi German have aided loyally in the defense of the Hitlerite regime, or should he have cooperated with the enemies of the regime? It was, in fact, to the interest of the anti-Nazi to cooperate with the Western powers and to the interest of the Nazi regime to discourage and to punish such treasonable and subversive activities.

Should decision makers within a small democracy sacrifice that democracy to give larger and more powerful democracies time to prepare against a totalitarian national actor? Individuals, after all, have no biological ties to the nation. They need not be destroyed with it nor need their values perish with the values of the national actor. Indeed, the destruction of the national actor may facilitate the preservation of individual values. In the first place, citizens may be able to flee and thus to escape the fate of the national actor. In the second place, if the national actor is sacrificed, other democratic or non-directive actors may be given time to destroy the directive national actor.

If the sacrifice is made, the nation may later be reorganized, or it may be absorbed within a supranational non-directive system. If, however, an accommodation is reached with the directive national actor, the national system may survive in a form contrary to the interests of the individual citizens.

Obviously, it is difficult to generalize in the absence of a concrete case. Nevertheless, the distinction between the interests of different system levels is compelling. Interests are objective, but what the national actor ought to do may differ from or conflict with what an individual or subsystem of the national system ought to do.

Some disagreements concerning the national interest may only represent errors in judgment. However, some disagreements may represent clashes between different subsystems concerning their interests but may be phrased as if those interests were the national interest.

Moreover, some disagreements may represent attempts to change the national interest, that is, to change the form and structure of the national system, to change its essential rules and its needs, and to change the relations of dominance within the system. In this sense, disagreement would concern not what the national interest *is* but what the national interest *ought to be* from the standpoint of or according to the interests of the subsystem making the claim.

### Decision Makers and the National Interest

The sharp distinction between the interests of different system levels raises a specter. What if decision makers make decisions which implement their interests rather than those of the national actor system?

To some extent, fear that this may happen lies behind the democratic distrust of foreign policy officials. Within any system the agency dealing with a given sphere of activity will have some degree of subsystem dominance over that particular range of activity. Those who make the decisions scan for information which accords with their expectations. They are attentive to the problems which seem important within the communicative frameworks which structure their activities. They are responsive to their individual interests and to the interests of the subsystems to which they belong, whether by birth or by selection.

In general, no objection can be made to this state of affairs except in terms of different subsystem interests. Any substitution among the decision-making personnel would only change the values and subsystem interests to which attention was given. In terms of national essential rules, a different segment of the nation would become dominant over foreign policy.

There may, however, be cases in which foreign policy decision makers act contrary to the national interest because their subsystem interests conflict with the national interest. Decision makers, like other individuals, respond to their multiple roles. Their role in some other subsystem of the national system may conflict with and dominate their role in the foreign policy subsystem. There are a number of systems in which foreign-policy makers may hold roles which conflict with their foreign-policy-making role.

Political parties with international organizational ties may have interests opposed to the national interest, that is, opposed to the preservation of the nation as an entity with distinctive territorial bounds, or possibly, opposed to the preservation of the national political system except insofar

as it adheres to essential rules consonant with the interests of the international party.

Religious, economic, and fraternal groups may have interests which are either consonant with those of some supranational system or independent of national interests insofar as their pursuit is not dependent upon the existence or nonexistence of the national actor system.

To some extent, however, differences concerning the national interest may reflect differences concerning the external environment or concerning the consequences of given actions. Quisling activity represented to some extent interests at variance with the national interest. However, probably some who joined these movements believed that only in this way could they accommodate to Nazi victory and conserve any of the values of the national system.

The situation of decision makers at lower ranks who believe that the national interest is being violated by those in superior positions either through ignorance or contrary interests, is poignant. Should such decision makers carry out policies they believe wrong or even disastrous? Or should they oppose such policies and brave the consequences?

The statement of this problem may stir the fear that anarchy will result if each decision maker, regardless of level in the administrative apparatus, implements the policies he thinks correct and fails to implement policies determined at higher national levels. If proper distinctions are made, such fears lack foundation. It would of course be anarchic if different policies were substituted at each hierarchic level in the administrative apparatus by decision makers who rejected the decisions of those above them in the hierarchy. However, common sense demonstrates that those lower in the hierarchy—regardless of their disagreements with those higher in the administrative hierarchy—are not likely to sabotage policy in this manner.

Many policies which *would* be better if adopted at higher administrative levels are worse if substituted at lower levels. Those lower in the administrative hierarchy—apart from lacking the information upon which the decision was based at the highest levels—are faced with different problems.

Lower ranking officials no longer have the problem of deciding high national policy; they have the problem of implementing that policy and of adjusting it to local conditions. Their very freedom not to apply that policy if it fails to satisfy local conditions maintains the flexibility of the administrative apparatus.

If the interest of lower ranking officials is consonant with the national interest, administrative flexibility in the implementation of decisions will raise no difficult problems. If officials are incompetent, they may overlook their paucity of information or the consequences for the national interest if they substitute their private judgment for that of their superiors.

But this becomes a matter of choosing competent officials. It would be equally bad to have officials who blindly applied policies regardless of local conditions or who were unable to make local adjustment without referring everything back to their superiors. During the war, for instance, one official without proper authority ordered a captain of a ship in port to unload a cargo of rotten potatoes which was causing the boat to sink. This was in violation of a directive to carry the potatoes to England. But common sense prevailed over red tape.

Suppose a higher ranking official is pathological. Suppose an American officer in charge of occupying a Japanese village had ordered his troops to burn it to the ground although the natives were cooperating with the occupying authorities. It is at least plausible that the national interest would be better served if the troops arrested their officer, ignored the order, and appealed to still higher authority to intercede. It is possible that the order might have been based upon secret information and that the troops therefore might have acted unwisely. But no rules for action are likely to apply to every possible contingency.

On the other hand, the interests of a decision maker may conflict with the interests of the nation. Although the previous examples illustrate cases in which national needs are best satisfied if orders from above are disobeyed, there may be cases when, rather than exercising discretion in implementing policy, a decision maker may be acting contrary to the national interest. Consider a German officer who refused to carry out Hitler's order to devastate a French village and to kill its inhabitants. Refusal to use terror might possibly injure the German war effort. Yet some officers might prefer to injure the war effort—or even to lose the war—rather than to engage in inhumane activity.

National actors have an interest in preventing decision makers from acting contrary to the national interest and in punishing those who do. National actors even have an interest in exaggerating the bad consequences of such actions or of convincing decision makers that such actions are morally wrong. But there is no good reason—except *perhaps* fear of personal consequences—why an administrator who views national values with abhorrence should not sabotage the implementation of those values. Indeed, the myth that administrators have no responsibility except to carry out legally prescribed national policy has been responsible for some of the most sordid violations of individual values in the history of mankind.

From the point of view of the political system, human beings are instrumental for maintaining the existence and interests of the political system. However, from the point of view of individual human beings, the political system has value only as an instrument for implementing human values. There is no reason in logic or theory why individual needs should be subordinated by human agents to the good of the political system.

# 6 / The National Interest and Current World Problems

## CHARLES BURTON MARSHALL

In the following essay, Mr. Marshall both praises and questions the term "national interest" with reference to its analytical
or operational utility. Here is an argument that the national
interest is essentially a subjective matter to be dealt with in
political terms, that is, the "art of the possible."

MY ASSIGNMENT calls for me to relate the national interest to the
problems of the United States in the present world situation. Let me
comment first on that phrase, "the national interest."

Only a few years ago the economic interpretation of virtually everything was in vogue. Writers of considerable repute were fobbing off the
significance of the national interest as a factor in foreign policy, interpreting it as merely a facade to conceal special interests and to deceive the
public. The return of the phrase to respectable parlance, indicating the
recognition of a valid national interest paramount over particular interests,
is a gain for straight thinking.

Often a decision in foreign policy is inseparable from the question
of the domestic consequences of the decision. It is necessary in such an
instance to recognize that our national destiny in a world of many nations
is more important than the domestic group interests affected by the decision. In settling questions of conflict between the necessities of national
security and group interests, the idea of national interest is valid and
essential. The phrase, moreover, indicates a step away from the utopianism beclouding too much the discussion of international affairs in the
sequel to both World War I and World War II.

Nations do have interests. In some instances their interests coincide
with the interests of other nations. Sometimes interests of different nations
harmonize without coinciding. Sometimes they differ, but not incompat-
ibly. Sometimes they are mutually exclusive. Out of these variations comes

Reprinted from U.S. Department of State, *Department of State Bulletin*, XXVI
(May 5, 1952); derived from an address made before the American Academy of Political and Social Science April 18, 1952.

Charles Burton Marshall is a former member of the Policy Planning Staff of the
Department of State. A leading essayist and critic in the field of American foreign
policy and diplomacy, he wrote *The Limits of Foreign Policy* (1954).

the real nature of international life. It is useless to try to ignore this by talk about global harmony and the universal state. Such talk, while edifying to those who like it, only hinders—it does not help—the handling of world problems.

So it is good to hear people talk about international problems again in terms of national interests rather than in the abstractions of world government and world law. Indeed, it would be a blessed thing if all differences among nations could be translated into differences of interest alone and not differences of basic purpose and principle. It is unselfish to compromise on interests. It is unseemly to compromise on one's principles.

Here I myself stray off into utopianism of another sort. The world is nowhere near that stage of adjustment where all national differences can be dealt with as solely differences of interest, and the coming of that day is too remote for prediction.

I have said enough in praise of the idea of national interest. Now let me say some things in criticism. The usefulness and significance of the phrase are limited. It begs more questions than it answers. In appraising the significance of the national interest, I must distinguish between instances in which the decision turns on weighing our world position as a Nation against the claims of particular domestic interests and instances in which the issue lies simply between lines of action in the foreign field.

I know of no case of the latter character in which the settlement of an issue of our national policy in the line of responsibility would have been facilitated by injecting the question: Shall we or shall we not try to serve the national interest?

The question in the arena of responsibility in handling an issue involving foreign policy alone is not whether, but how, to serve the national interest. That involves the question of what is the national interest in a particular situation. The question of serving the national interest is always a subtle and complex one in real situations.

I am sure all of the following things are clearly in our national interest: to avoid war; to preserve our institutions; to have strong allies; to avoid inflation; to have a prosperous civilian economy; to find common grounds on which to stand with the various nations which have newly come to responsibility; to preserve our access to strategic waterways and vital raw materials; and to protect the property and safety of our nationals abroad. I could extend this list by dozens of items.

Now any matter of foreign policy pertaining only to the realization of one of those items would not present an issue at all. No one would have to work his brains overtime on it. No series of exhaustive meetings would have to be held. No protracted debate about the nuances and contradictions would be necessary. In such an instance the policy decision would crystallize spontaneously.

In any practical question presenting a real issue the national interest

has several aspects. Indeed, there are many national interests, not just one. The difficulties arise in the conflict of one interest with another; for example, in the clash of the interest in peace with the interest in preserving national institutions, in the clash of the interest in having a strong defense with the interest in having a strong civilian economy, or in the clash of the interest in preserving access to a waterway with the interest in eliciting the adherence of another country to one's cause.

I trust I have made my point in the inconclusiveness of the national interest as a guide in any particular policy problem. Beyond that, I believe the concept of national interest is inadequate and misleading even as a broad concept on which to found a policy.

It seems to me that a more appropriate guiding principle is the idea of responsibility. This is a very different sort of idea. I want to take the rest of my time in talking about the contrast between national interest and responsibility and examining the idea of responsibility as it enlightens our present problems.

First I want to discuss our special role in the world today.

The great political issues of our time revolve around rival approaches to the handling of the problems growing out of such circumstances peculiar to modern times as the massing of peoples—their expanded numbers and their increased concentration; the sharpening of the clash between cultures due largely to awakened consciousness of the disparities in well-being between peoples in relation to the advance or lag of production techniques, and the destructiveness of modern war due both to the concentration of industry and population and to the greater inherent efficacy of modern weapons—their huge lethal power and the capability for distance and stealth in attack.

One approach would exploit these circumstances for the purpose of widening the scope and strengthening the foundations of a monopoly of political power. The other approach seeks to compose clashes of interest and to work out patterns of accommodation.

The legitimate question of politics is not how to eliminate conflict of interest—a utopian concept—but how to organize society so that conflicts can be adjusted rather than fought out. This difference in approach is brought to bear both within and among nations. The lines of difference are intertwined and subtle, for the lines along which great issues form are never as sharp as a razor. Insofar as the issue has crystallized among nations, however, the Soviet Union stands clearly as the champion of the first approach.

Internal political circumstances cast the Soviet Union in that role. It is ruled by tyrants, who reached the seat of power through conspiracy and, having achieved power, have not dared risk their hold on it by resort to a valid procedure of consent. They have remained conspirators after becoming governors, combining the usages of conspiracy with the prerog-

atives of the state. Both at home and in the world at large, the conspiracy that walks like a state requires tension and conflict to maintain its grip. In the service of this purpose it employs a doctrine emphasizing the patterns of conflict—class war, subversion, and the like.

This rule is established over a great range, commanding great resources in people and materials. Huge military forces at its disposal are deployed in positions bearing on northern and central Europe, the eastern Mediterranean, the Middle East, Southeast Asia, the Republic of Korea, and Japan. The Soviet Union has auxiliaries in the form of embryonic governments under the guise of domestic political groups in territories beyond its imperium. The Soviet power is such that no combination of nations adequate to cope with it is conceivable without the support and participation of the United States.

The United States thus finds itself in the position of leadership among peoples which prefer to work out a method of handling the problems of our times alternative to the pattern offered by the Soviet and which are impeded in this effort by the fact of Soviet opposition.

A failure to exercise this leadership would almost certainly result in a world power situation endangering the survival of our constitutional values. These are the values expressed in the Preamble of our Constitution. I do not doubt that you know them all, but let me enumerate them anyway.

The first is the perfection of our Union, the concept of a nation with steadily growing public values.

Second comes the idea of justice—of power subjected to standards superior to the mere attainment of the ends of power.

Third in the enumeration is domestic tranquility, conveying the idea of a nation at peace with itself, a nation where issues can be decided by reason, by discussion, and by compromise.

Then we come to the common defense—the protection of the nation from penetration from the outside.

The idea of the general welfare is another of the values set forth. It embodies the idea of a government which serves and is not master, which is accountable to all of its people as contrasted to a government which serves the exclusive interest of a dominant group.

Finally, we have the blessings of liberty—the situation in which each person can make choices for himself, regarding his life, the life of his children, his religion, and his thoughts.

The fundamental and enduring purpose of our foreign policy is to maintain in the world circumstances favorable to the continued vitality of these values in the United States.

I want to stress the novelty in the American consciousness of the responsibilities which the present world situation imposes. Our power, whence come our responsibilities, has three main foundations: position,

political strength, and economic resourcefulness. The circumstances surrounding the development of each of these were such as to conceal their eventual implications. The diffusion of power among several nations of great magnitude provided the relatively stable and protective situation which enabled the Americans to move onward from an Atlantic beachhead to become a continental Nation, singular among the great powers in that it lies in both the Northern and Western Hemispheres, faces on both the Atlantic and the Pacific, and stretches from the tropics to the Arctic. The same circumstances enabled the Americans to preserve and mature a Government based upon stipulated principles of accountability and freedom. Their purpose in doing this was purely domestic. The strength of the Government thus established is one of the great political facts of our time, important for all the globe. The Americans developed a fecund agriculture and productive industry, without equal, through the expansion of an internal market. That circumstance concealed from them the eventual world importance that American economic strength would have.

Some 60 years ago Lord Bryce described the United States as living "in a world of peace" and as "safe from attack, safe even from menace." Such was the national situation in the historic past, when the United States was a remote and intermittent factor in the ratios of world power and when Americans were concerned almost exclusively with the problems of their own national development. Lord Bryce added: "For the present at least—it may not always be so—America sails upon a summer sea."

Within a lifetime the summer sea vanished. The world frontiers closed. Two world wars were fought. Germany and Japan were eclipsed in defeat. Other great powers suffered relative declines. Patterns of empire were sundered. Many erstwhile dependencies attained sovereignty. Revolutionary communism established a power base. Two nations emerged into positions of primary magnitude—the United States as one and the Soviet adversary, the other.

So great an accession of responsibility in so brief a span has placed great moral tests on this Nation. One difficulty rises from the sense, as expressed recently by former Chancellor Robert M. Hutchins of the University of Chicago, that "this country has been thrust against its will into a position of world leadership." True, no referendum on the issue whether or not to be a nation of such wide responsibilities was ever held. The choice was made unconsciously in many decisions of our past. We were thrust ahead not against but by our wills. The choice is nonetheless binding for having been made in unawareness of the consequences.

Here we have a paradox—an accession to great power accompanied by a sense of deprivation of freedom. We feel that paradox in another way. In our historic past we viewed our role as that of standing normally

aloof from the power balance whose benefits we enjoyed. At most we would entertain the idea of throwing in our weight only momentarily to re-establish the balance whenever it might break down in general war.

We regarded our role as like that of a pedestrian who might choose to vary his solitary walks by intermittently riding with others, without foreclosing himself from choosing to walk alone again. Now that is changed. Our power makes our interposition essential to the preserving of the causes with which our interests lie. We must go along with others if we are to keep others with whom to go along. Our power is the basis of our essentiality, and our essentiality compels us to replace our historic sense of freedom by a new consciousness of responsibility. While losing a sense of freedom, we lose also a sense of effectiveness.

In the era when we stood normally aloof from the balance of power, our decision to become a world factor for a season had drastic and immediate results in redressing the balance. Now, by having become permanently involved in preserving the balance, we are no longer vouchsafed the opportunity to alter the situation dramatically and radically by sudden action.

This involvement leaves for us the exacting course of seeking a solution in the long pull through persistent effort to make the best of the situation stage by stage in the knowledge that such is the only way of making the situation better.

Let us look for a moment at the foreign policy which this situation imposes. It gives us no promise of arrival at some calculable moment at which we can say that all our troubles are behind us, that everything henceforth will be tidy and easy, and that we have crossed the one last river.

I said this to a group of Texans with whom I was discussing our national policy recently. One of them asked me whether I actually thought coexistence with the Soviet Union was possible.

This is a curious question. It makes a matter of speculation out of something known to be true. Coexistence with the Sovet Union is not simply possible; it is a fact. Coexistence with a great power that tries to lead a double life as state and as conspirator is vexatious for sure, but it is preferable to the tragedy of general war and its sequel, whichever side might win. Our policy seeks to avoid the tragedy of war, to abate the difficulties of coexistence by correcting the circumstances affording special advantage to the adversary, and to work with other nations as best we can to guide international life toward the patterns of conduct preferable to us.

This policy, often called the policy of containment, is sometimes criticized as if it aimed for a protracted, static confrontation—a sort of perpetually frozen *status quo*. Such perpetual equilibrium is foreign to the processes of history. The policy is based upon no assumption of arresting

change. It rests rather upon the assumption that the factors of position, population, talents, resources, and moral values redound to the ultimate advantage of the side of our interests, and that, in the long pull, it will be the adversary who must adjust his purposes.

This is not a foregone conclusion. What we and our friends do will be an essential factor in determining the outcome. This is no cause for disquiet. History presents no foregone conclusions. I know of no way to formulate a policy that will absolve us from the subsequent necessity of exercising resolution and restraint and paying the costs, whatever they may be.

The policy works along three general lines. The first is to make coexistence more tolerable. This calls for improving our armed strength and that of the nations standing with us and combining them more effectively through a system of alliances; for helping the depleted and dislocated economies of our friends to regain a healthy level of activity; for helping the economically lagging countries to improve their production methods; and for widening the area of peace by bringing the former enemy countries, Japan and Western Germany, back into collaboration with other countries.

The second line is to prevent serious deterioration in the conditions of coexistence by avoiding losses in areas of sharp political conflict.

The third general line relates to the development of international usages and institutions of responsibility as instruments of free collaboration among nations instead of the collaboration by intimidation offered by the adversary.

To succeed in these endeavors will require the collaboration of others. They will not work along with us on the basis solely of our national interest. The collaboration must be founded on an identity among their interests and ours. The primary responsibility for discovering and developing that identity of interests is ours, because we are in the position of greatest strength. This is not a simple responsibility. It is irksome and expensive and contains no easy formula for complete success in a stipulated interval.

The policy of responsibility lacks the simplicity—here I use the word "simplicity" in the sense of Proverbs 1:22—of the counsel of unlimited violence, a counsel based on the fallacy of trying to reduce all problems of power to the limits of the problems of force. The policy lacks the utopian tidiness of the dream of solution by world government. It lacks the traditional ring of the counsel of solution by default, by which I mean the idea of confining our security to this hemisphere—a counsel put forth by some claiming the mantle of statesmanship even though the formula on which it rests contains a fallacy recognizable to any school boy familiar with solid geometry. The fallacy inheres in this: Two points on the same sphere can never be farther than a hemisphere apart; hence the whole

world lies in the same hemisphere with us.

The policy based on the principle of responsibility lacks the crisp appeal of a phrase like "the national interest." It involves this paradox—that we can serve our national interest in these times only by a policy which transcends our national interest. This is the meaning of responsibility.

No nation could ask more of history than the privilege of coming to great responsibility. To satisfy our American professions of the values of competition, we have at hand one of the most exacting contests in ideas ever experienced. To test our faith in freedom, we have abundant opportunity to make choices of action that will profoundly affect the course of human affairs. To test our devotion to values, we have the opportunity not simply to proclaim them but actually to support them by gifts and deeds and perseverance.

This juncture in our experience is not comforting for those who take the utopian approach to international problems—those who remind one of Kipling's lines:

> Thinking of beautiful things we know;
> Dreaming of deeds that we mean to do,
> All complete, in a minute or two—
> Something noble, and grand and good,
> Won by merely wishing we could.

I recall the words opening one of Christina Rossetti's poems:

> Does the road lead uphill all the way?
> Yes, to the very end.

That is the road which a great and responsible nation must tread. It is an uphill road all the way. For Americans who do not mind walking that kind of a road, this is not a time for misgiving but a great time in which to live.

# 7 / National Security as an Ambiguous Symbol

ARNOLD WOLFERS

Quite commonly, national security is considered to be a prime
national interest which if not protected would make it unlikely
that other national interests could be pursued. But, as Professor Wolfers demonstrates, the term "security" is often
ambiguous, covering a wide range of goals and an equally
wide range of policies and "instruments" for their attainment.

STATESMEN, PUBLICISTS AND SCHOLARS who wish to be considered
realists, as many do today, are inclined to insist that the foreign policy
they advocate is dictated by the national interest, more specifically by
the national security interest. It is not surprising that this should be
so. Today any reference to the pursuit of security is likely to ring a
sympathetic chord.

However, when political formulas such as "national interest" or
"national security" gain popularity, they need to be scrutinized with
particular care. They may not mean the same thing to different people.
They may not have any precise meaning at all. Thus, while appearing
to offer guidance and a basis for broad consensus they may be permitting
everyone to label whatever policy he favors with an attractive and
possibly deceptive name.

In a very vague and general way "national interest" does suggest a
direction of policy which can be distinguished from several others which
may present themselves as alternatives. It indicates that the policy is
designed to promote demands which are ascribed to the nation rather
than to individuals, subnational groups or mankind as a whole. It
emphasizes that the policy subordinates other interests to those of the
nation. But beyond this, it has very little meaning.

When Charles Beard's study of *The Idea of National Interest* was
published in the early years of the New Deal and under the impact of
the Great Depression, the lines were drawn differently than they are

Reprinted from the *Political Science Quarterly*, LXVII (December, 1952), 481–502.
By permission.

Arnold Wolfers is professor emeritus of international relations, Yale University, and
since 1957 has been director of the Washington Center of Foreign Policy Research,
The Johns Hopkins University. He is the author of *Britain and France Between Two
Wars* (1940) and the editor of *Alliance Policy in the Cold War* (1959) as well as
numerous other works.

today. The question at that time was whether American foreign policy, then largely economic in scope and motivation, was aimed not at promoting the welfare interests of the nation as a whole but instead at satisfying the material interests of powerful sub-national interest or pressure groups. While it was found hard to define what was in the interest of national welfare or to discover standards by which to measure it, there could be no doubt as to what people had in mind: they desired to see national policy makers rise above the narrow and special economic interests of parts of the nation to focus their attention on the more inclusive interests of the whole.

Today, the alternative to a policy of the national interest to which people refer is of a different character. They fear policy makers may be unduly concerned with the "interests of all of mankind." They see them sacrificing the less inclusive national community to the wider but in their opinion chimeric world community. The issue, then, is not one of transcending narrow group selfishness, as it was at the time of Beard's discussion, but rather one of according more exclusive devotion to the narrower cause of the national self.

There is another difference between the current and the earlier debate. While it would be wrong to say that the economic interest has ceased to attract attention, it is overshadowed today by the national security interest. Even in the recent debates on the St. Lawrence Seaway, clearly in the first instance an economic enterprise, the defenders of the project, when seeking to impress their listeners with the "national interest" involved, spoke mainly of the value of the Seaway for military defense in wartime while some opponents stressed its vulnerability to attack.

The change from a welfare to a security interpretation of the symbol "national interest" is understandable. Today we are living under the impact of cold war and threats of external aggression rather than of depression and social reform. As a result, the formula of the national interest has come to be practically synonymous with the formula of national security. Unless explicitly denied, spokesmen for a policy which would take the national interest as its guide can be assumed to mean that priority shall be given to measures of security, a term to be analyzed.[1] The question is raised, therefore, whether this seemingly

---

[1] Hans Morgenthau's *In Defense of the National Interest* (New York: Alfred Knopf, 1951), is the most explicit and impassioned recent plea for an American foreign policy which shall follow "but one guiding star—the National Interest." While Morgenthau is not equally explicit in regard to the meaning he attaches to the symbol "national interest," it becomes clear in the few pages devoted to an exposition of this "perennial" interest that the author is thinking in terms of the national security interest, and specifically of security based on power. The United States, he says, is interested in three things: a unique position as a predominant Power without rival in the Western Hemisphere and the maintenance of the balance of power in Europe as well as in Asia, demands which make sense only in the context of a quest for security through power.

more precise formula of national security offers statesmen a meaningful guide for action. Can they be expected to know what it means? Can policies be distinguished and judged on the ground that they do or do not serve this interest?

The term national security, like national interest, is well enough established in the political discourse of international relations to designate an objective of policy distinguishable from others. We know roughly what people have in mind if they complain that their government is neglecting national security or demanding excessive sacrifices for the sake of enhancing it. Usually those who raise the cry for a policy oriented exclusively toward this interest are afraid their country underestimates the external dangers facing it or is being diverted into idealistic channels unmindful of these dangers. Moreover, the symbol suggests protection through power and therefore figures more frequently in the speech of those who believe in reliance on national power than of those who place their confidence in model behavior, international coöperation, or the United Nations to carry their country safely through the tempests of international conflict. For these reasons it would be an exaggeration to claim that the symbol of national security is nothing but a stimulus to semantic confusion, though closer analysis will show that if used without specifications it leaves room for more confusion than sound political counsel or scientific usage can afford.

. . . . .

. . . Attention should be drawn to an assertion of fact which is implicit if not explicit in most appeals for a policy guided by national security. Such appeals usually assume that nations in fact have made security their goal except when idealism or utopianism of their leaders has led them to stray from the traditional path. If such conformity of behavior actually existed, it would be proper to infer that a country deviating from the established pattern of conduct would risk being penalized. This would greatly strengthen the normative arguments. The trouble with the contention of fact, however, is that the term "security" covers a range of goals so wide that highly divergent policies can be interpreted as policies of security.

Security points to some degree of protection of values previously acquired. In Walter Lippmann's words, a nation is secure to the extent to which it is not in danger of having to sacrifice core values, if it wishes to avoid war, and is able, if challenged, to maintain them by victory in such a war.[2] What this definition implies is that security rises and falls with the ability of a nation to deter an attack, or to defeat it. This is in accord with common usage of the term.

Security is a value, then, of which a nation can have more or less and

---

[2] Walter Lippmann, *U. S. Foreign Policy* (Boston, 1943), p. 51.

which it can aspire to have in greater or lesser measure.[3] It has much in common, in this respect, with power or wealth, two other values of great importance in international affairs. But while wealth measures the amount of a nation's material possessions, and power its ability to control the actions of others, security, in an objective sense, measures the absence of threats to acquired values, in a subjective sense, the absence of fear that such values will be attacked. In both respects a nation's security can run a wide gamut from almost complete insecurity or sense of insecurity at one pole, to almost complete security or absence of fear at the other.[4]

The possible discrepancy between the objective and subjective connotation of the term is significant in international relations despite the fact that the chance of future attack never can be measured "objectively"; it must always remain a matter of subjective evaluation and speculation. However, when the French after World War I insisted that they were entitled to additional guarantees of security because of the exceptionally dangerous situation which France was said to be facing, other Powers in the League expressed the view that rather than to submit to what might be French hysterical apprehension, the relative security of France should be objectively evaluated. It is a well-known fact that nations, and groups within nations, differ widely in their reaction to one and the same external situation. Some tend to exaggerate the danger while others underestimate it. With hindsight it is sometimes possible to tell exactly how far they deviated from a rational reaction to the actual or objective state of danger existing at the time. Even if for no other reasons, this difference in the reaction to similar threats suffices to make it probable that nations will differ in their efforts to obtain more security. Some may

---

[3] This explains why some nations which would seem to fall into the category of *status quo* Powers *par excellence* may nevertheless be dissatisfied and act very much like "imperialist" Powers, as Morgenthau calls nations with acquisitive goals. They are dissatisfied with the degree of security which they enjoy under the *status quo* and are out to enhance it. France's occupation of the Ruhr in 1923 illustrates this type of behavior. Because the demand for more security may induce a *status quo* Power even to resort to the use of violence as a means of attaining more security, there is reason to beware of the easy and often self-righteous assumption that nations which desire to preserve the *status quo* are necessarily "peace-loving."

[4] Security and power would be synonymous terms if security could be attained only through the accumulation of power, which will be shown not to be the case. The fear of attack—security in the subjective sense—is also not proportionate to the relative power position of a nation. Why, otherwise, would some weak and exposed nations consider themselves more secure today than does the United States?

Harold D. Lasswell and Abraham Kaplan, *Power and Society* (New Haven: Yale University Press, 1950), defining security as "high value expectancy" stress the subjective and speculative character of security by using the term "expectancy"; the use of the term "high," while indicating no definite level, would seem to imply that the security-seeker aims at a position in which the events he expects—here the continued unmolested enjoyment of his possessions—have considerably more than an even chance of materializing.

find the danger to which they are exposed entirely normal and in line with their modest security expectations while others consider it unbearable to live with these same dangers. Although this is not the place to set up hypotheses on the factors which account for one or the other attitude, investigation might confirm the hunch that those nations tend to be most sensitive to threats which have either experienced attacks in the recent past or, having passed through a prolonged period of an exceptionally high degree of security, suddenly find themselves thrust into a situation of danger. Probably national efforts to achieve greater security would also prove, in part at least, to be a function of the power and opportunity which nations possess of reducing danger by their own efforts.

Another and even stronger reason why nations must be expected not to act uniformly is that they are not all or constantly faced with the same degree of danger. For purposes of a working hypothesis, theorists may find it useful at times to postulate conditions wherein all states are enemies—provided they are not allied against others—and wherein all, therefore, are equally in danger of attack.[5] But, while it may be true in the living world, too, that no sovereign nation can be absolutely safe from future attack, nobody can reasonably contend that Canada, for example, is threatened today to the same extent as countries like Iran or Yugoslavia, or that the British had as much reason to be concerned about the French air force in the twenties as about Hitler's *Luftwaffe* in the thirties.

This point, however, should not be overstressed. There can be no quarrel with the generalization that most nations, most of the time— the great Powers particularly—have shown, and had reason to show, an active concern about some lack of security and have been prepared to make sacrifices for its enhancement. Danger and the awareness of it have been, and continue to be, sufficiently widespread to guarantee some uniformity in this respect. But a generalization which leaves room both for the frantic kind of struggle for more security which characterized French policy at times and for the neglect of security apparent in American foreign policy after the close of both World Wars throws little light on the behavior of nations. The demand for conformity would have meaning only if it could be said—as it could under the conditions postulated in the working hypothesis of pure power politics—that nations normally subordinate all other values to the maximization of their security, which, however, is obviously not the case.

There have been many instances of struggles for more security taking the form of an unrestrained race for armaments, alliances, strategic

---

[5] For a discussion of this working hypothesis—as part of the "pure power" hypothesis—see my article on "The Pole of Power and the Pole of Indifference" in *World Politics,* Vol. IV, No. 1, October 1951.

boundaries and the like; but one need only recall the many heated parliamentary debates on arms appropriations to realize how uncertain has been the extent to which people will consent to sacrifice for additional increments of security. Even when there has been no question that armaments would mean more security, the cost in taxes, the reduction in social benefits or the sheer discomfort involved has militated effectively against further effort. It may be worth noting in this connection that there seems to be no case in history in which a country started a preventive war on the grounds of security—unless Hitler's wanton attack on his neighbors be allowed to qualify as such—although there must have been circumstances where additional security could have been obtained by war and although so many wars have been launched for the enhancement of other values. Of course, where security serves only as a cloak for other more enticing demands, nations or ambitious leaders may consider no price for it too high. This is one of the reasons why very high security aspirations tend to make a nation suspect of hiding more aggressive aims.

Instead of expecting a uniform drive for enhanced or maximum security, a different hypothesis may offer a more promising lead. Efforts for security are bound to be experienced as a burden; security after all is nothing but the absence of the evil of insecurity, a negative value so to speak. As a consequence, nations will be inclined to minimize these efforts, keeping them at the lowest level which will provide them with what they consider adequate protection. This level will often be lower than what statesmen, military leaders or other particularly security-minded participants in the decision-making process believe it should be. In any case, together with the extent of the external threats, numerous domestic factors such as national character, tradition, preferences and prejudices will influence the level of security which a nation chooses to make its target.

It might be objected that in the long run nations are not so free to choose the amount of effort they will put into security. Are they not under a kind of compulsion to spare no effort provided they wish to survive? This objection again would make sense only if the hypothesis of pure power politics were a realistic image of actual world affairs. In fact, however, a glance at history will suffice to show that survival has only exceptionally been at stake, particularly for the major Powers. If nations were not concerned with the protection of values other than their survival as independent states, most of them, most of the time, would not have had to be seriously worried about their security, despite what manipulators of public opinion engaged in mustering greater security efforts may have said to the contrary. What "compulsion" there is, then, is a function not merely of the will of others, real or imagined, to destroy the nation's independence but of national desires and ambitions to retain

a wealth of other values such as rank, respect, material possessions and special privileges. It would seem to be a fair guess that the efforts for security by a particular nation will tend to vary, other things being equal, with the range of values for which protection is being sought.

In respect to this range there may seem to exist a considerable degree of uniformity. All over the world today peoples are making sacrifices to protect and preserve what to them appear as the minimum national core values, national independence and territorial integrity. But there is deviation in two directions. Some nations seek protection for more marginal values as well. There was a time when United States policy could afford to be concerned mainly with the protection of the foreign investments or markets of its nationals, its "core values" being out of danger, or when Britain was extending its national self to include large and only vaguely circumscribed "regions of special interest." It is a well-known and portentous phenomenon that bases, security zones and the like may be demanded and acquired for the purpose of protecting values acquired earlier; and they then become new national values requiring protection themselves. Pushed to its logical conclusion, such spatial extension of the range of values does not stop short of world domination.

A deviation in the opposite direction of a compression of the range of core values is hardly exceptional in our days either. There is little indication that Britain is bolstering the security of Hong Kong although colonies were once considered part of the national territory. The Czechs lifted no finger to protect their independence against the Soviet Union and many West Europeans are arguing today that rearmament has become too destructive of values they cherish to be justified even when national independence is obviously at stake.

The lack of uniformity does not end here. A policy is not characterized by its goal, in this case security, alone. In order to become imitable, the means by which the goal is pursued must be taken into account as well. Thus, if two nations were both endeavoring to maximize their security but one were placing all its reliance on armaments and alliances, the other on meticulous neutrality, a policy maker seeking to emulate their behavior would be at a loss where to turn. Those who call for a policy guided by national security are not likely to be unaware of this fact, but they take for granted that they will be understood to mean a security policy based on power, and on military power at that. Were it not so, they would be hard put to prove that their government was not already doing its best for security, though it was seeking to enhance it by such means as international coöperation or by the negotiation of compromise agreements—means which in one instance may be totally ineffective or utopian but which in others may have considerable protective value.

It is understandable why it should so readily be assumed that a quest for security must necessarily translate itself into a quest for coercive power. In view of the fact that security is being sought against external violence—coupled perhaps with internal subversive violence— it seems plausible at first sight that the response should consist in an accumulation of the same kind of force for the purpose of resisting an attack or of deterring a would-be attacker. The most casual reading of history and of contemporary experience, moreover, suffices to confirm the view that such resort to "power of resistance" has been the rule with nations grappling with serious threats to their security, however much the specific form of this power and its extent may differ. Why otherwise would so many nations which have no acquisitive designs maintain costly armaments? Why did Denmark with her state of complete disarmament remain an exception even among the small Powers?

But again, the generalization that nations seeking security usually place great reliance on coercive power does not carry one far. The issue is not whether there is regularly some such reliance but whether there are no significant differences between nations concerning their over-all choice of the means upon which they place their trust. The controversies concerning the best road to future security that are so typical of coalition partners at the close of victorious wars throw light on this question. France in 1919 and all the Allies in 1945 believed that protection against another German attack could be gained only by means of continued military superiority based on German military impotence. President Wilson in 1919 and many observers in 1945 were equally convinced, however, that more hope for security lay in a conciliatory and fair treatment of the defeated enemy, which would rob him of future incentives to renew his attack. While this is not the place to decide which side was right, one cannot help drawing the conclusion that, in the matter of means, the roads which are open may lead in diametrically opposed directions. The choice in every instance will depend on a multitude of variables, including ideological and moral convictions, expectations concerning the psychological and political developments in the camp of the opponent, and inclinations of individual policy makers.

After all that has been said little is left of the sweeping generalization that in actual practice nations, guided by their national security interest, tend to pursue a uniform and therefore imitable policy of security. Instead, there are numerous reasons why they should differ widely in this respect, with some standing close to the pole of complete indifference to security or complete reliance on nonmilitary means, others close to the pole of insistence on absolute security or of complete reliance on coercive power. It should be added that there exists still another category of nations which cannot be placed within the continuum

connecting these poles because they regard security of any degree as an insufficient goal; instead they seek to acquire new values even at the price of greater insecurity. In this category must be placed not only the "mad Caesars," who are out for conquest and glory at any price, but also idealistic statesmen who would plunge their country into war for the sake of spreading the benefits of their ideology, for example, of liberating enslaved peoples.

# 8 / The Tasks Before Us: Basic Aims and Policies

## JOHN C. CAMPBELL AND OTHERS

In the period after the first Russian Sputniks of 1957, there was much concern with and discussion of "goals for Americans"—particularly in the realm of foreign policy. The statement of foreign policy aims reprinted below was the product of an ad hoc study group of the Council on Foreign Relations, constituted as a consequence of a request from the U. S. Senate Committee on Foreign Relations for a statement on basic foreign policy aims to be included in the Senate's series of studies *United States Foreign Policy.*

BECAUSE THIS GROUP was asked to consider on a broad basis aims and policies for the future, its report should not and cannot run the whole gamut of problems all over the world, go into the details of individual questions, or make specific recommendations on the pressing

From U. S. Senate Committee on Foreign Relations Study No. 7, "Basic Aims of United States Foreign Policy," by Council on Foreign Relations (November, 1959), in *U.S. Foreign Policy: Compilation of Studies,* 87th Cong., 1st sess., S. Doc. 24 (March 15, 1961), pp. 649–58. This report should not be construed as representing the view of the Council on Foreign Relations as an institution. Members of the group whose discussions led to this report included Frank Altschul, Hamilton Fish Armstrong, Elliott V. Bell, Adolph A. Berle, Jr., Robert Blum, R. R. Bowie, Harlan Cleveland, John Cowles, Arthur H. Dean, J. S. Dickey, T. K. Finletter, W. C. Foster, Averell Harriman, Philip Jessup, Joseph E. Johnson, G. A. Lincoln, Henry Luce, James A. Perkins, I. I. Rabi, Herman B. Wells, and Dr. Henry M. Wriston, chairman. Council staff members included William Diebold, Jr., George S. Franklin, Jr., Walter H. Mallory, Philip E. Moseley, and Mr. Campbell, director of studies.

John C. Campbell is director of political studies, Council on Foreign Relations.

issues of the day. Its purpose is rather to show the nature and diversity of the problems and opportunities ahead and the magnitude of the efforts required to meet them in facing the future with hope and confidence. We are aware that aims and principles are empty of content unless sustained by performance, and that the real tests come in the field of specific policies and concrete action. But the general direction must be set if the policies are to have meaning.

## A. Building an International Order

First and foremost, the United States must have a broad, basic aim which responds to the deep aspirations of the world's peoples as well as meets the challenge from the Communist bloc. Such an aim is the building, jointly with other free nations, of a new international order.

A new world is in the making. We know that the Communist powers will do everything they can to shape it to their will. Whether they can be prevented from doing so depends in large part upon the United States. We know also that the United States will have opportunities to exert a more positive influence. For most peoples of the world this is an age of change, of liberation, of promise and of hope. If America has no aims that go beyond maintaining the status quo, it will fall short of fulfilling its full promise. Only creative policies, acts which catch the imagination of people everywhere, will lead to a world in which nations can live free of alien domination and in which the security and growth of our own society and that of others can be assured.

It is obvious that the policies to support such aims cannot be conceived and carried out purely as national policies of the United States or as a crusade for the American way of life. The search for national fulfillment in freedom and its continuing enrichment becomes a search for an international order in which the freedom of nations is recognized as interdependent, and for which policies must be jointly undertaken by various nations of the free world. Those policies should be such as to make of the free world a going concern in the success of which all peoples have a stake.

The free world, of course, is made up of many different nations with wide variations in their institutions, their aims, and their attitudes. But broad common interests, most of which are stated in the United Nations Charter, do exist and can be built upon, without requiring a rigid, uniform approach to all. There is room in such a cooperative international community for states with differing political, economic, and social systems, including states which profess or wish to be Socialist. Indeed, the close cooperation of states whose economic systems bear different labels can help to discredit the false thesis that the cold war is a struggle between socialism and capitalism instead of between

Communist imperialism and the right to freedom. Success in such common endeavors may also be the most promising means by which the free world can increase pressures within the Communist bloc for less dangerous and more accommodating policies on the part of the Communist regimes.

Central to any consideration of the future is the question of security and the preservation of peace. By force of circumstance the United States and other nations associated with it have not been able to rely solely or principally on the United Nations; for they have seen that the world organization, whose power only reflects the will and ability of member states to make use of it and to adapt their national policies to the purposes and principles of the charter, cannot reach decisions or order action that will either prevent or defeat an aggression launched against them. They have had to safeguard their security through bilateral agreements and regional arrangements, with their own military power serving as the deterrent to aggression against them. This alliance system, perhaps not in the precise forms in which it has grown up but certainly in its main elements, remains essential to the free world's security. It must be held together on a basis of mutual interest. The potentialities of the United Nations, however, are also of the greatest importance.

While the United Nations has not been the cornerstone of American foreign policy as was first hoped, it does embody the ideal of collective security which the American people have so strongly held since its founding in 1945. It surely must be our purpose to maintain it, to strengthen it, and to help it gradually to acquire more authority. This is a test of our capacity for leadership. There may be many matters on which the United Nations will provide the obvious or only seat of authority to oversee or to enforce agreements which may be reached. Agreed limitation and control of armaments, for example, will have to be policed by a body acting under international agreement. Where the United States can get Soviet cooperation to use and strengthen the U.N. machinery for this and other purposes, so much the better. Where it cannot, it should still use all opportunities to work with free world countries to the same end.

More effective use of the judicial organ of the United Nations—the International Court of Justice—is an obvious and necessary means of building a better international order. The ideal of a world under law, a goal which reflects America's own experience and its long-standing convictions, can best be approached through strengthening the prestige and the authority of the one judicial body of worldwide membership. Clearly the first step, for those nations, including the United States, which originally accepted the jurisdiction of the court only with reservations concerning matters they deem to be domestic, is to withdraw those

limitations on their participation in the processes of judicial settlement.

The United Nations has performed, and should continue to perform, many useful functions: as a forum to sound out or rally world opinion, as a channel for negotiations with friends or adversaries, and as an instrument for resolving the disputes of nations willing to respect the charter. As the countries of the free world seek closer ties among themselves, they should find that the United Nations, time and again, affords means to settle differences, to coordinate policies, and to undertake joint schemes of mutual aid, cooperation, and development. Because the specialized agencies of the United Nations may be especially suited to such efforts, the United States should seek every opportunity to use them and to support their activities, while working to overcome the existing proliferation and overlapping of their functions and to make them more effective channels of international action.

## B. The Atlantic Community

A theme which runs through the American outlook on the world since far back in our history has been the common heritage of Western civilization. Two world wars and especially our experience since the second have left no doubt that the future of America is tied to that of the Atlantic community, which includes Western Europe and the entire Western Hemisphere. However we view the future, it is hard to imagine America's place in the world other than in close association with its partners in Europe, in Canada, and in Latin America.

Many of the decisions to be taken in determining the Atlantic community's own destiny will revolve around questions of organization. At present the principal organs, of prime importance for security, are the North Atlantic Treaty Organization and the Organization of American States. There is every reason to strengthen them in every possible way. But it is essential to retain a flexibility of approach. For purposes other than security, such as the growth of economic cooperation, other organizations may prove more effective. The boldness of some of the steps taken thus far should not inhibit even bolder thinking on such questions as how fast and how far Western Europe should move toward integration, in what ways the United States should be associated with that process, and what closer ties should link Europe, the British Commonwealth, the United States, and Latin America.

It is the substance rather than the form of solidarity that is crucial. While the national framework may often provide the best means of rallying support for common interests, the United States must exert its influence against the destructive effects of national parochialism, including its own. It must strive to prevent the crystallization of rival or conflicting blocs within the Atlantic Community with vested interests in division rather than in unity.

The solidarity of the Atlantic nations, however, is not exclusive. It should not represent, or appear to represent, a common front against non-Western nations of the free world. It is rather a means by which nations which value freedom can serve the general cause of freedom.

### C. The Less Developed Areas

Vital decisions lie ahead also in the relationships between the industrialized countries of the free world (principally North America, Western Europe, and Japan) and those countries of Asia, Africa, and Latin America which are less developed. For a long time to come the latter will experience revolutionary conditions, problems of an economic growth which lags behind popular expectations, and in some cases an ominous population explosion. The economic and technical assistance programs carried on by the United States over the past decade represent a recognition of those problems and a start on attacking them. For the most part, however, they have been a mixture of emergency measures, palliatives, and efforts to strengthen allies for primarily military reasons. Most of those measures have been necessary and useful. In meeting current emergencies the economic instruments of policy are frequently the most available and the most effective. But the need for a more ambitious, longer term, and more pointedly direct approach, on a basis that is broader than U.S. programs alone, can clearly be seen.

There must be movement of capital goods from the industrial to the less developed countries going well beyond the present volume; a massive effort to build up technical and administrative competence; action to correct or minimize the effects of drastic swings in the prices of certain basic commodities, a matter of special importance to Latin America; and urgent planning on how to tackle the population problem in the areas of rapid growth before it reaches the proportions of disaster. It is in the interest of the entire free world to have some of the less developed countries, soon, reach the point of breakthrough to self-sustained development. Western Europe and Japan can and should share in these efforts to a much greater extent than hitherto. But their contribution is not a substitute but a supplement to our own, which must also be greater than in the past.

The necessary decisions for large-scale assistance to the less developed countries should not be made contingent on an agreement to reduce armaments that would free funds for that purpose. If the assistance is necessary and desirable—and it is—the advanced countries should provide it without regard to the progress achieved in limiting armaments by international agreement.

The political problems will be as formidable as the economic. Many of the new and less developed countries have no early prospect of

57

stability either internally or among themselves. Some have hardly jelled as nations. Their leadership often resorts to the emotional appeals of nationalism as a substitute for statesmanship. Serious barriers still stand in the way of cooperation with the West, some of them the result of policies in areas such as the Middle East and south Asia which Western nations considered necessary for security but which unfortunately injected them into local political conflicts and alienated those who sought a neutral position in relation to the cold war. Such policies deserve searching reappraisal.

Where the colonial issue still remains, as it does in some parts of Africa, and even in areas where relations of dependence have been liquidated, it presents special difficulties for the United States because of our ties with the colonial powers in Europe and the risks of a lasting alienation from the new nations. The essence of successful diplomacy on such issues will be the avoidance of absolute choice between Europe and Africa and the promotion of a peaceful transformation of relationships which prevents such choices from arising. Because the peoples of Africa are determined to achieve self-government, it is dangerous for the United States to be associated in their minds with policies which seem to have the effect of denying it to them. Fortunately, practically all the European powers concerned have now shown a spirit of far-sighted accommodation and statesmanship, a fact which should offer greater opportunities for America to participate in the urgent task of helping Africa's progress in freedom.

The less developed and the advanced industrial countries need each other. There is a sound basis of partnership. The task is to find and strengthen political relationships based on mutual respect, as the underpinning of common economic, educational and other endeavors. The Western nations and Japan have to keep a basic unity in policies toward the less developed countries, if only to coordinate assistance to them, but they must avoid any hint of neo-colonialism. The goal should be to offer a partnership which appeals to those peoples and to their leadership as a positive and preferable alternative to "partnership" with the Communist bloc.

The advance of human welfare and standards of living on a broad front throughout the free world, commensurate with the advances in science and technology, can hardly proceed without new forms of cooperation. As in the case of the requirements for security, many problems will be too big to be dealt with on the old basis of negotiation among a great number of sovereign national states. Others will be less and less suited to the type of bilateral arrangement on which U.S. aid programs have been based. Long-range development is a broad world problem. Handling public aid primarily as a national proposition on the part of both donor and recipient tends on both sides to inject national policies

and sentiments into the picture and thus to increase the political difficulties and jeopardize the hoped-for economic results. We know from
experience that the granting or lending country becomes the natural
target of criticism, no matter how large the programs may be.

Now that the other Western countries are in a position to join in
the providing of aid, a multinational structure including both lending
and borrowing states to carry out the necessary programs offers a means
of increasing the total effort while avoiding the difficulties inherent in the
bilateral method. It could be most helpful also in blunting the damaging
political effects of the bilateral programs of the Communist powers. It
makes it easier to tackle the economic problems on their merits without
raising fears or wounding sensibilities on such issues as political strings,
national sovereignty, and nonintervention. What advantages the United
States might lose in giving up direct control of the expenditure of funds
it should more than regain in sounder political relationships.

The multinational approach need not deprive the major providers
of a voice, a very influential voice, such as they have in the International
Bank and presumably will have in the International Development Association. Bilateral programs will continue to be useful in certain instances.
But this group is convinced that the emphasis in the future should be
on the multilateral approach.

The United States will have to look at the further possibilities of
dealing with broad economic questions on the basis of regional authority
(a process already begun in Europe) and on that of the expansion of
the scope and powers of functional across-the-board institutions such
as the specialized agencies of the United Nations, provided that they
can be organized rationally and made to work efficiently. In such a
basic question, for example, as the world's food supply and its distribution, America's great agricultural productivity is bound to be a major
factor. American surpluses have been used to good effect as a means of
helping people in critical need of food, and of transferring resources to
less developed countries. Yet policies deriving largely from domestic
considerations and carried out on a year-by-year basis are not sufficient.
If our phenomenal farm production is to play its due part in the building
up of the whole free world, the United States should be in the position
of willingness to put it on the table as a matter of international discussion
with other producing and consuming countries, and of seeking to work
out with them the necessary long-range programs. This group feels that
on such issues the United States must provide bold leadership, that it
cannot shirk taking the broader view.

### D. Meeting the Communist Challenge: The Military Needs

Thus far, this report has emphasized the need for constructive decisions and policies adequate to the demands of the next decade as we

can best foresee them. Foreign policy also has its demands of the present and the near future. Seen in the longer perspective, meeting the present and continuing challenge of the Communist regimes is only a part of the totality of the complex task ahead. But it is obviously a vital part. It is a means of buying time to achieve a higher level of sanity and order in world affairs. It lays on us certain minimum requirements of policy and action which must be met if this Nation is to survive and grow in freedom. We still have to hold the line against the expansion of the Communist empire. Further Communist territorial gains, with their inevitably wide and deep psychological effects, could mean a decisive shift in the world balance.

Some of those requirements are military. What the magnitude of the military effort should be cannot be stated with precision. This report is not primarily concerned with military estimates and planning but with the need for military power as the necessary condition for an effective foreign policy. The magnitude of the effort should be determined by military needs, determined as objectively as possible, and taking into account the needs and contributions of other nations associated with us. Obviously the allotment of national resources to military purposes cannot be made without regard to other demands on those resources or to the state of the national economy. Certain military requirements, however, are important enough to demand a margin of safety without which the Nation will be in grave danger; for example, the building up, maintenance, and protection of retaliatory power sufficient to make unacceptable to the Soviet and Chinese Communist leadership the cost of launching a major attack on the free world; the possession of mobile forces capable of selective use with those of other nations in a variety of situations, as a means of deterring aggression that is less than a major attack and of coping with it if it occurs; a research and development program which will insure all possible progress in science and technology that can contribute usefully to the military tasks of the future; and a long-range military aid program to strengthen the global defense posture of the United States and its allies, thus reinforcing strategic deterrence, the capacity for limited military operations, and the opportunities for effective political action.

It is the present policy of the United States, as this group understands it, to meet these vital military requirements, although we have serious doubts whether they are in fact being met. They are mentioned here in order to stress the absolute necessity of vigilance to see that they are met, firmly and with whatever sacrifice is necessary, in changing conditions over the years as the costs go up and the burdens grow heavier.

Military measures, however, will not provide security in any absolute sense, nor will they guarantee the attainment of national objectives or

some kind of victory in the cold war. They are no substitute for foreign policy. Indeed, undue emphasis on the military aspects can be an obstacle to cooperation with nations important to us, and to the success of our military strategy. But a basic military posture must be maintained. It is the underpinning without which the other instruments of policy cannot be effective.

### E. Limitation and Control of Armaments

Progress toward disarmament through the limitation and control of armaments is made urgent by the growing destructiveness of modern weapons, the projection of military power into outer space, and the prospective spread of nuclear weapons among an increasing number of states. The nature of nuclear warfare has made the arms race, with its dangers of total catastrophe, a matter of commanding concern to the man in the street as to the expert and the statesman. Inevitably the idea of disarmament carries a strong appeal to the world's peoples living under those dangers. The whole process of working steadily toward a better world order has a certain unreality in men's minds when they live under the threat of seeing all civilization engulfed by a nuclear war.

These considerations make it imperative for the United States to conduct serious negotiations for international agreement on limitation, reduction, and control of armaments. Despite the negative results of 15 years of negotiation and the unhopeful prospect ahead, a negative or perfunctory approach to the subject on the part of the United States cannot be permitted. It would compromise American influence abroad, jeopardize the aims of our foreign policy, and produce repercussions which might well impair the confidence of the American people in themselves and in their leadership.

Even though it may be illusory and put forward for propaganda purposes, the Soviet proposal for complete disarmament has to be taken seriously and fully explored. The United States should give further and deeper study to concrete ways of attacking the problem: such aspects as the means of control, the successive stages of disarmament, and especially the possibilities of agreements involving mutual but not necessarily uniform or similar concessions on weapons, troop strengths, bases and positions; for it is in such practical trading, taking account of the dissimilarities in Soviet and Western strengths and positions, that the best chances for progress may lie.

These points will probably have to be dealt with in direct and secret negotiations with the Soviet Government, without neglecting adequate consultation with our major allies; but simultaneous discussions should be carried on with broader participation in the U.N. framework in recognition of the interest of all nations in this matter.

There are really no sound alternatives to negotiation. We cannot be content with indefinite continuance of the present situation. We cannot look forward with equanimity to an all-out arms race extending even into the unlimited realms of space. The American people have rejected, as they must, any solution through a so-called preventive attack. Likewise, they must not fall into the trap of accepting Soviet proposals lacking the indispensable provisions for inspection and control. The United States should, therefore, take the initiative and put forward new proposals of its own, seeking continuously and in every possible way to get agreement on limited aspects of the issue and on the stages of a general plan.

This group does not presume to propose any specific plan. We know of no plan which meets all the problems and would guarantee success if adopted. We wish here only to emphasize three general points which place the question in the context of the basic aims of American policy and should guide planning and negotiation on this subject: (1) The question of limitation and control of armaments is directly related to the new international order which the United States and other free nations must seek to build; such an order cannot be one dominated by an uncontrolled arms race and the threat of unlimited destruction. (2) Significant progress in the control of arms demands a sincere commitment to the concept of collective security and to the development, gradual as it may be, of a stronger international political structure, which is indispensable to any durable arrangement for inspection and control. (3) The inevitable risks involved in any proposals for the limitation and control of armaments should be weighed against the risks of failure to make any progress at all. The present state of affairs provides no such absolute security that the United States can afford to take refuge in an excess of caution in judging proposals, whatever their source, that offer a real possibility of progress.

Let us recognize, however, that the chances for agreement and tangible progress depend on the attitudes and policies of the Communist powers. The Soviet leadership may have reasons of its own for wanting agreement on some aspects of the problem, and this possibility we should not neglect. But the ideology and past conduct of the Soviet regime give little reason to hope for an enforceable general agreement. The United States cannot risk its own and the free world's security on unsecured paper promises or inadequate provisions of control to prevent violations. Moreover, even an effective agreement to stabilize armaments at certain levels would not remove the necessity for maintaining the military power necessary under the new conditions for the purposes already mentioned in this report. Reduction of armaments should not be regarded as the only or the principal avenue to peace. Armaments tend to reflect political conflicts. Settlement or attenuation of the conflicts should automatically

reduce the dangers and burdens of the arms race; failure to settle them makes agreement on armaments terribly difficult if not impossible. Yet this country must not take the position that nothing can or should be done about this latter question until the political conflicts are resolved. It should proceed simultaneously on both fronts.

### F. Meeting the Communist Challenge: The Longer Range

Even should agreement on limitation of armaments prove possible, even if what Mr. Khrushchev says about disarmament, relaxing tension, and ending the cold war is taken at face value, this leaves no room for relaxation of effort on the part of the United States and other free nations. There is no present or prospective change in basic Soviet aims. The Soviet leaders believe history to be on their side. We cannot risk our future on the easy assumption that they are wrong. The peaceful competition which is offered demands all possible effort and sacrifice to meet it on the levels of diplomacy, economic policy, and political action. Whatever surcease the Soviets might gain from the arms race will mean increased challenges in these other fields. The rapid growth of the Soviet economy enables them to use trade and aid much more effectively than in the past as instruments to extend Soviet influence in parts of the free world.

Momentary relaxation of tensions holds out no promise of an end to the cold war. The Soviet leaders have shown that they can turn tensions on and off as it suits their own strategy. Their proposal to end the cold war is to end it on their terms, to consolidate their past gains, which the United States cannot formally recognize without betrayal of basic principles and serious loss of prestige and position, and to make the free world vulnerable to new thrusts in the future.

Acceptance of the challenge of the cold war as a long-term proposition compels the United States and the nations associated with it to maintain and to strengthen those policies already developed which are best suited to the competition, and to seek new policies which can gain maximum support in the free world to this end. The positive long-range policies already mentioned hold the promise not only of finding common ground within the free world for tackling its basic problems, but also of effective defense and the reduction of the proportions of the Communist threat. It is not possible at present to see the end of the struggle or to fashion a national strategy which will guarantee victory in the sense of the end of communism. What the United States can rationally seek is an eventual modification of the nature of the competition, a gradual change in Soviet policies so that they no longer suppress or threaten the liberty of other nations. Such an outcome—now merely a hope—will depend primarily on developments within the Communist bloc itself, but

the process will be influenced, perhaps considerably, by what happens outside, and especially by what America does or does not do.

Negotiation, too, must play its part in the American response to the Communist challenge, both as an arm of strategy and as a means of seeking mutually acceptable arrangements, if only limited and partial ones. The importance of acceptable agreements on such questions as disarmament and Germany is such that a continuing reappraisal of the possibilities and probing of the adversary's positions is necessary. This report cannot go into the detail of possible proposals on specific questions such as Germany. We wish to stress, however, the need for seeking ways to break out of the present impasse. On certain issues the United States has no choice but to stand firm. But there is no status quo which it cannot expect to see, and should not wish to see, changed. The question is how it will be changed. There is nothing sacred about a status quo which denies unity to nations longing for it or subjects peoples to foreign domination. The play of political and other forces keeps the world in a state of flux, especially in those areas where no stable settlements were reached after the Second World War; our problem in negotiation, as in other aspects of carrying out our foreign policy, is not to be left with untenable positions and bankrupt policies as and when the situation changes.

All opportunities for settlement should be exploited, without sacrificing vital interests or concluding agreements in which those interests become dependent solely on the Communists' good faith. Most of these efforts will be fruitless. We do not, however, know how the Soviet and Chinese societies will eventually evolve. The evidence available now does not justify a prediction of basic change, but it is at least possible that time will bring to the fore new elements less dedicated to expansion and more willing to settle outstanding issues with the West; the continuing process of negotiation may even encourage such trends. We should be aware that international alignments are not timeless and unchanging; China's role in another generation, for example, should occupy our attention now, as it must also occupy the attention of the Soviet leadership. Such factors suggest the need to avoid stereotyped images of the Soviet threat and the Moscow-Peiping axis, and to be alert to changing conditions and new opportunities.

Accordingly, it is desirable that channels exist for communication with the Communist regimes. Regardless of what is done or not done on the specific question of recognition, the United States will have to have lines of communication open to the Government of Communist China because it wields power and controls territory which cannot be left out of account. If such a matter as the general control of armaments nears the point of international agreement, Communist China will have to be brought in as a party. In general, the most promising channels for

communication with the Soviet Union and Communist China will be regular or ad hoc contacts maintaining the necessary conditions of true negotiation, which may at times be at the highest level, but not public performances of ministers or heads of government.

The strength of the position of the United States and other nations of the free world—their military, political, and economic strength— should contribute to successful negotiation, just as it is necessary for holding vital positions in the competition of "coexistence."

# 9 / From *The United States in the World Arena*

WALT W. ROSTOW

There are many ways to define the national interest. Indeed, one of the precepts of the democratic idea is that each man is free, within some limits, to define it for himself. The following statement represents one man's view of the national interest—in the judgment of the editor, a sophisticated view. It is one of the most explicit statements available on the subject, allowing the reader to see the author's presuppositions and to subject them to critical analysis.

## A Definition

It is the American interest to maintain a world environment for the United States within which American society can continue to develop in conformity with the humanistic principles which are its foundation. This definition, in terms of the progressive development of the quality of American society, would, of course, include the physical protection of the country; but the protection of American territory is viewed essentially as a means to a larger end—the protection of a still-developing way of life.

Reprinted from Walt W. Rostow, *The United States in the World Arena*, pp. 543–50. Copyright © 1960 by the Massachusetts Institute of Technology. Reprinted with the permission of Harper & Row, Publishers, Incorporated.

Walt. W. Rostow has been a special assistant to President Kennedy; counselor and chairman of the Policy Planning Council, Department of State, under both Presidents Kennedy and Johnson; and professor of economic history, Center for International Studies, Massachusetts Institute of Technology. His writings include *The Stages of Economic Growth* (1960) and *View from the Seventh Floor* (1964).

The operative meaning of this definition derives from the geographic position of the United States. For no substantial period in the nation's history has the American interest been automatically assured by geographic isolation. Contrary to a mythology which still strongly affects American attitudes and the nation's performance, the American interest has been chronically in danger from the late eighteenth century forward. This danger arose and continues to arise from the simple geographic fact that the combined resources of Eurasia, including its military potential, have been and remain superior to those of the United States—Eurasia being here defined to include Asia, the Middle East, and Africa as well as Europe.

The United States must be viewed essentially as a continued island off the greater land mass of Eurasia. Various combinations of power in Eurasia have been and remain a potential threat to the national interest. American independence was achieved in the eighteenth century only because Americans could exploit a conflict between Britain and France. A united Britain and France could have stifled the American Revolution. During the nineteenth century the nation expanded and consolidated American power on the North American continent and in the Western Hemisphere by exploiting the power conflicts of Eurasia; and in the twentieth century the United States has been thrice placed in jeopardy, and instinctively sensed that jeopardy, when a single power or combination of powers threatened to dominate Western Eurasia, Eastern Eurasia, or both.

There is, then, much in the whole sweep of American history which denies the notion of an America safely isolated by act of God and geography; and there is nothing fundamentally new in taking the American relationship to the power balance in Eurasia as central to the nation's security problem.

### The Dual American Interest in Eurasia

If the problem of the national interest is viewed as a question of protecting not only the nation's territory but also its basic values as a society, it follows that the United States has two distinct but connected interests in Eurasia. Since the combined resources of Eurasia could pose a serious threat of military defeat to the United States, it is the American interest that no single power or group of powers hostile or potentially hostile to the United States dominate that area or a sufficient portion of it to threaten the United States and any coalition the United States can build and sustain. But under modern conditions of communication, there is a second threat to the nation's interest. Whatever the military situation might be, a Eurasia coalesced under totalitarian dictatorships would threaten the survival of democracy both elsewhere and in the United States. It is, there-

fore, equally the American interest that the societies of Eurasia develop along lines broadly consistent with the nation's own ideology; for under modern conditions it is difficult to envisage the survival of a democratic American society as an island in a totalitarian sea.

### Three Clarifications of the American Ideological Interest

This proposition must be immediately clarified in three respects.

First, the United States need not seek societies abroad in its own image. The United States does have a profound interest that societies abroad develop and strengthen those elements in their respective cultures that elevate and protect the dignity of the individual as against the claims of the state. Such elements of harmony with the Western democratic tradition exist in different forms everywhere; and they have been strengthened by the attractiveness of the Western democratic example at its best, notably by the example of British parliamentary government, the American Revolution, and the values on which American society was erected. But the forms of legitimately democratic societies can vary widely.

Second, the democratic process must be viewed as a matter of aspiration, trend, and degree, not as an absolute. The value judgments which underlie the political, social, and economic techniques of Western societies might be summarized as follows:

1. Individual human beings represent a unique balancing of motivations and aspirations which, despite the conscious and unconscious external means that help shape them, are to be accorded a moral and even religious respect. The underlying aim of society is to permit these individual complexes of motivations and aspirations to have their maximum expression compatible with the well-being of other individuals and the security of society.

2. Governments thus exist to assist individuals to achieve their own fulfillment, to protect individual human beings from the harm they might do one another, and to protect organized societies against the aggression of other societies.

3. Governments can take their shape legitimately only from some effective expression of the combined will and judgments of individuals on the basis of one man, one vote.

4. Some men aspire to power over their fellow men and derive satisfaction from the exercise of power aside from the purposes to which power is put. This fundamental human quality in itself makes dangerous to the well-being of society the concentration of political power in the hands of individuals and groups even where such groups may constitute a majority. *Habeas corpus* is the symbol and, perhaps, the foundation of the most substantial restraint—in the form of due process of law—men have created to cope with this danger.

From Plato on, political scientists have recognized that men may not understand their own best interest, and, in particular, that they may be shortsighted and swayed by urgent emotions in their definition of that interest. As between the individual's limitation in defining wisely his own long-run interest and his inability wisely to exercise power over others without check, democratic societies have broadly chosen to risk the former rather than the latter danger in the organization of society, and to diminish the former danger by popular education, by the inculcation of habits of individual responsibility, and by devices of government which temper the less thoughtful political reactions of men.

From this definition the democratic element within a society emerges as a matter of degree and of aspiration. The pure democratic concept is compromised to some extent in all organized societies by the need to protect individuals from each other, by the need to protect the society as a whole from others, and by the checks required to protect the workings of the society from man's frequent inability wisely to define his own long-run interest. Even when societies strive for the democratic compromise, the balance between liberty and order which any society can achieve and still operate effectively, and the particular form that balance will take, are certain to vary. They will vary not only from society to society but also within each society in response to the state of education of its citizens and the nature of the specific problems it confronts as a community at different stages in its history.

It is evident that some present societies have not had and do not now have the capability of combining effective communal action with a high degree of what is here called the democratic element. Both history and the contemporary scene offer instances of governments in which the balance of power is heavily in the hands of the state rather than in the hands of the individual citizens who comprise it.

The legitimate American ideological interest is not that all societies become immediately democratic in the degree achieved in the United States or Western Europe, but that they accept as a goal a version of the democratic value judgments consonant with their culture and their history and that they move toward their realization with the passage of time.

Now a third clarification of the American ideological interest. Since the American interest does not require that all societies at all times accept democratic values and move toward their achievement, the nation is concerned not with total ideological victory, somehow defined, but with the balance and trend of ideological forces in Eurasia. Therefore, the application of the limited, but real, margin of American influence on the course of other societies can and should be selective. Given the nation's geographic circumstance, its history, and the quality of its society, the American interest demands, in a sense, that Americans be crusaders; but the American ideological crusade must be tolerant, long term, and directed

toward areas of importance where the nation's margin of influence may be effective. The United States is concerned not with absolutes but with the direction of political trend in Eurasia.

### Current Threats from Eurasia

In more specific geographic terms, it is a persistent interest of the United States that no single power or power grouping militarily dominate either Western or Eastern Eurasia.

In Western Eurasia the threat of such an outcome is posed by the possible absorption within the Soviet empire of East Germany and Eastern Europe. The threat would become a reality should West Germany be drawn into the Soviet power orbit; and the threat would be made acute by the ideological defection of Italy, France, or both. In the East the threat of such an outcome is posed by the close alliance of the Soviet Union and Communist China. In Asia there are two major centers of power, Japan on the one hand and India on the other, the latter being key to the complex stretching from Indochina around to Pakistan. In Asia the threat to the American interest would become virtually a reality should either Japan or India be lost to the Free World.

At the present time the intentions and capabilities of the Communist Bloc pose two threats to the United States—a military threat and an ideological threat. These threats are clearly related; the ideological loss of India, for instance, would raise important military problems; the military loss of northern Indochina has raised important problems of ideological orientation throughout Southeast Asia. But the two American interests are not and should not be considered identical. The time necessary and the kind of effort required to cope with the military threat are likely to differ from those required by the ideological threat. The military threat to South Korea was dealt with in a few years; defeating the ideological threat to South Korea may prove a creative Free World task for a generation.

### The Interweaving of Power and Ideological Interests

If this view of the American interest is correct, the debate which has been proceeding in the United States over recent years as to whether the nation's interests should be defined in power terms or in terms of the ideological principles to which American society is attached is a somewhat misguided debate. This is so in two respects.

First, if the essential American interest is to preserve a world environment within which its chosen form of democratic society can persist and develop, then the nation's stake in the ideological and political balance in Eurasia is as legitimate as its interest in the military balance of power in Eurasia. Two national efforts, one military and the other political, inter-

acting intimately, must go forward together as part of a total effort to protect the interests of American society.

There is a second sense in which the debate appears misguided. It appears to be a characteristic of American history that this nation cannot be effective in its military and foreign policy unless it believes that both its security interests and its commitments to certain moral principles require the nation to act. From the Spanish-American War to the present, the nation has acted effectively only when both strands in its interest were believed to be involved—in the Spanish-American War itself, in the First and Second World Wars, in the effort to reconstruct and defend Western Europe in 1947–1950, in the early phases of the Korean War.

When idealism alone seemed to be the basis for the positions taken, the nation did not back its play, as, for example, in Wilson's ideological formulation of the American interest at Versailles. Equally, the nation has not been effective when confronted with situations where its power interests might be involved but where a persuasive moral basis for American action was not present. The notion of American imperialism, popular in certain American circles at the turn of the century, died quickly when it confronted the abiding American instinct in support of political independence in the case of the Philippines and elsewhere. Similarly, a major reason why the United States was ineffective in the Indochina crisis of 1954 was that it was then extremely difficult simultaneously to deal with the Communist menace and to disengage from French imperialism in that area; and in the summer of 1956 the United States was gravely inhibited in dealing with Nasser because, among other reasons, his claim to national sovereignty over the Suez Canal had a certain resonance in the American image of its historic meaning on the world scene as the friend of those struggling for independence.

The wisdom of American policy in Indochina and at Suez is, of course, debatable. Moreover, a nation's belief that its ideals are or are not involved is by no means an unambiguous criterion for performance. Nevertheless, it is unrealistic to expect American society—given its history and values—to perform in terms of pure power criteria.

The components in the American ideological interest can, then, be distinguished and summarized in the following three propositions:

1. The ideological loss of key areas in Eurasia would have major military consequence for the United States.

2. Apart from its military consequences, the ideological loss of the balance of power in Eurasia would, under modern conditions, have major adverse consequences for the quality of American society and for the viability of the humanistic principles which underlie it.

3. Among the qualities of American society threatened by the loss of the ideological balance of power in Eurasia would be the historic sense of American democratic mission on the world scene, present since the

nation's founding, which has given to American life much of its moral worth, its distinction, and its forward momentum.

The art of American statesmanship is to formulate and to sustain courses of action which harmonize in specific settings abiding American interests and abiding American ideals, steadily preserving the dual power balance in Eurasia, preventing by forehanded effort the emergence of such crises as those which hitherto have been required to evoke a major American effort at self-preservation.

The requirements of protecting the military balance of power and developing the ideological balance of power will not always converge. Foreign policy is full of painful choices. There may be times when in order to maintain military positions action must be taken which will conflict with the norms of the American ideological interest; and there may be occasions when it will be proper to take military risks to permit movement toward ideological objectives. But in the world of 1958 and beyond there are many more points of convergence than are now being exploited. If the dual character of the national interest—as a democratic island off a potentially threatening Eurasian mainland—is accepted, and if the interrelations of the two objectives are perceived, courses of action still appear open to the United States which will protect and sustain the quality as well as the existence of the nation's life in the face of current and foreseeable challenges.

### The United States and the Decline of Nationhood

Among those challenges is the problem of using American power and influence to tame military force by effective international accord; for the nature of modern weapons in a context other than American monopoly is a danger to the national interest sufficiently grave to justify acceptance of important constraints on the nation's sovereignty. Put another way, it is a legitimate American national objective to see removed from all nations—including the United States—the right to use substantial military force to pursue their own interests. Since this residual right is the root of national sovereignty and the basis for the existence of an international arena of power, it is, therefore, an American interest to see an end to nationhood as it has been historically defined.

The pace at which means of communication are now under development argues, further, that the present nations of the globe will move into relations of increasing intimacy and interaction.

Between them, the urgent imperative to tame military force and the need to deal with peoples everywhere on the basis of an accelerating proximity argue strongly for movement in the direction of federalized world organization under effective international law. And, should effective international control of military power be achieved, it might prove con-

venient and rational to pass other functions upward from unilateral determination to an organized arena of international politics.

It is not easy or particularly useful to peer far beyond the time when this great human watershed is attained. Nevertheless, it can be said that the American regional interest would still continue to embrace elements from the long sweep of the past. Convergent and conflicting relationships of geography, of cultural connection, of economic interest would in substantial measure be simply transferred from a setting where military force enters the equation of negotiation to one of global domestic politics. When the great conference has ended and the freely moving inspectors take up their initial posts from one end of the world to the other and the nightmare passes, the agenda of international politics will look not unfamiliar. Much in the historic relation of the United States to the balance of affairs in Eurasia will remain. There will be, however, a special dimension to global politics with special meaning for Americans—the problem of so conducting the world's affairs as to avoid a dissolution of the federal machinery and civil war.

# For Further Reading

ACHESON, DEAN. *Power and Diplomacy* (Cambridge, Mass.: Harvard University Press, 1958).

BEARD, CHARLES A. *The Idea of National Interest* (New York: Macmillan, 1934).

COOK, THOMAS I., and MALCOLM MOOS. *Power Through Purpose* (Baltimore: The Johns Hopkins Press, 1954).

HALLE, LOUIS J. *Dream and Reality* (New York: Harper, 1959).

LERCHE, CHARLES O. *Foreign Policy of the American People* (Englewood Cliffs, N.J.: Prentice-Hall, 1961).

MARSHALL, CHARLES BURTON. *The Limits of Foreign Policy* (New York: Henry Holt, 1954).

MORGENTHAU, HANS J. *Politics Among Nations*. 3d rev. ed. (New York: Knopf, 1960).

MORISON, ELTING, ed. *The American Style* (New York: Harper, 1958).

OSGOOD, ROBERT E. *Ideals and Self Interest in American Foreign Policy* (Chicago: University of Chicago Press, 1953).

PADELFORD, NORMAN, and GEORGE A. LINCOLN. *The Dynamics of International Politics* (New York: Macmillan, 1962).

ROSENAU, JAMES, ed. *International Politics and Foreign Policy* (New York: The Free Press of Glencoe, Inc., 1961).

SNYDER, RICHARD C., and EDGAR FURNISS, JR. *American Foreign Policy* (New York; Rinehart, 1954).

SPROUT, HAROLD, and MARGARET SPROUT. *Foundations of International Politics* (Princeton: Van Nostrand, 1962).

TANNENBAUM, FRANK. *The American Tradition in Foreign Policy* (Norman, Okla.: University of Oklahoma Press, 1955).

THOMPSON, KENNETH W. *Political Realism and the Crisis of World Politics* (Princeton: Princeton University Press, 1960).

U.S. Congress. Senate. Committee on Foreign Relations. *United States Foreign Policy: Compilation of Studies*. 87th Cong., 1st sess., S. Doc. 24. Washington: 1961).

WESTERFIELD, H. BRADFORD. *The Instruments of America's Foreign Policy* (New York: Thomas Y. Crowell Co., 1963).

# II HISTORICAL BACKGROUND OF AMERICAN FOREIGN POLICY

## 10 / Historic Aims of American Foreign Policy

### JOHN C. CAMPBELL AND OTHERS

In the preparation of this overview of the history of American foreign policy, the author was aided by an ad hoc discussion group of members of the Council on Foreign Relations. In the selections following this one, some of the major issues and events in the background of American foreign policy will be treated in greater detail.

DURING THE NINETEENTH CENTURY the basic aims of the American Nation, which are best expressed in the preamble of the Constitution, were shaped by its geographical position on what had been a virtually empty continent, by its urge for rapid growth, by the nature of its free institutions, and by a sense of destiny and of difference from the old world. Its foreign policy was directed largely to ensuring the Nation's ability to grow in freedom and to carry through its expansion to the Pacific. Two historic policies supported that basic purpose: the policy, embodied in the Monroe Doctrine, of preventing non-American powers from establishing themselves in the Western Hemisphere, and the concomitant avoidance of involvement in the alliances and conflicts of the great powers of Europe.

Although insulated by geography and by these policies from the politics and wars of the major powers, the United States was no hermit state. It was a part of the Western World, of the international community of that time. It stood for freedom of the seas, the free exchange of ideas, and

From U. S. Senate Committee on Foreign Relations Study No. 7, "Basic Aims of United States Foreign Policy," by Council on Foreign Relations (November, 1959), in *U.S. Foreign Policy: Compilation of Studies,* 87th Cong., 1st sess., S. Doc. 24 (March 15, 1961), pp. 641–42. This report should not be construed as representing the view of the Council on Foreign Relations as an institution.

A brief biographical sketch of the author accompanies selection 8.

freedom for its citizens to trade and to do business abroad without discrimination. It stood for respect for international obligations and the promotion of peace through techniques of negotiation, arbitration, and judicial settlement. It stood also—and this made the United States a revolutionary influence in the world of that time—for the right of all peoples to national and individual freedom, a principle which has remained ever since a salient element of America's attitude toward the world.

Foreign policy in practice, of course, rarely corresponds fully to broad statements of aim and principle, for it must be based also on calculations of national interest in the specific circumstances in which decisions are made and actions taken. American concern for the cause of freedom abroad was an aspiration which colored national attitudes rather than a concrete objective engaging the Nation on behalf of popular revolutions all over the world. Nevertheless, the example of America as a working democracy served as a symbol of freedom, and the boldness of its declared position unquestionably exerted a significant moral and even political influence beyond its borders. Thus, when the United States came onto the world stage in the First World War and the peace settlement which followed, it was a great moral force as well as a principal member of the victorious Allied coalition.

That war was a turning point in American history. The prospect of a German victory had threatened to demolish the protective hedge behind which we had been able to concentrate on cultivating our own garden. By its intervention in 1917 the United States showed that its weight could be thrown onto the scales to prevent an aggressive power from gaining dominance in Europe—a consideration which again came into play when Nazi Germany and later the Soviet Union presented a similar threat. By the time of the First World War, moreover, the United States had become so large, productive, and potentially strong that it was bound to be a major factor in the world balance.

The two main elements in President Wilson's program—a just peace settlement based as far as possible on self-determination, and a world organization for collective security—were basically consistent with historic American attitudes, even though the American people were not ready after the war to accept the responsibilities of full participation in world affairs. After the twenty-year interval between the two wars had demonstrated the futility of isolation, they again turned to those two goals. America's peace aims in the Second World War, expressed in a series of congressional resolutions, official statements and international agreements, envisaged a just and stable peace settlement, a world organization to keep the peace through collective security and to protect human rights, and a set of international economic arrangements and institutions that would insure maximum trade, set up safeguards against crisis, and encourage economic growth.

75

The American people accepted the fact that the United States must play a leading role in the postwar world. They have continued to accept it. But the conditions under which those responsibilities have to be carried out have brought new and unprecedented challenges. Some became apparent as early as 1945; others later. The magnitude of the responsibilities, both of American leadership and of the Nation as a whole, is driven home to us every day.

# 11 / From *The Farewell Address*

## GEORGE WASHINGTON

**In the formative period of the republic, few documents in American history have had greater influence in shaping American attitudes toward foreign policy than the first President's farewell address "to the people of the United States" on September 19, 1796. The fact of great geographical isolation of the United States led Washington to state his "great rule of conduct" regarding this nation's relationships with foreign nations. The reader may want to speculate as to what Washington's advice would be under the influence of contemporary technology.**

OBSERVE GOOD FAITH and justice towards all nations; cultivate peace and harmony with all. Religion and morality enjoin this conduct, and can it be that good policy does not equally enjoin it? It will be worthy of a free, enlightened, and, at no distant period, a great nation, to give to mankind the magnanimous and too novel example of a people always guided by an exalted justice and benevolence. Who can doubt but, in the course of time and things, the fruits of such a plan would richly repay any temporary advantages which might be lost by a steady adherence to it; can it be that Providence has not connected the permanent felicity of a nation with its virtue? The experiment, at least, is recommended by every sentiment which ennobles human nature. Alas! is it rendered impossible by its vices?

In the execution of such a plan, nothing is more essential than that

Reprinted from 86th Cong., 1st sess., H. Doc. 96 (Washington, D.C., 1959), pp. 27–35.

permanent, inveterate antipathies against particular nations and passionate attachments for others, should be excluded; and that, in place of them, just and amicable feelings towards all should be cultivated. The nation which indulges towards another an habitual hatred, or an habitual fondness, is in some degree a slave. It is a slave to its animosity or to its affection, either of which is sufficient to lead it astray from its duty and its interest. Antipathy in one nation against another disposes each more readily to offer insult and injury, to lay hold of slight causes of umbrage, and to be haughty and intractable when accidental or trifling occasions of dispute occur. Hence, frequent collisions, obstinate, envenomed, and bloody contests. The nation, prompted by ill will and resentment, sometimes impels to war the government, contrary to the best calculations of policy. The government sometimes participates in the national propensity, and adopts through passion what reason would reject; at other times, it makes the animosity of the nation subservient to projects of hostility, instigated by pride, ambition, and other sinister and pernicious motives. The peace often, sometimes perhaps the liberty of nations, has been the victim.

So likewise, a passionate attachment of one nation for another produces a variety of evils. Sympathy for the favorite nation, facilitating the illusion of an imaginary common interest, in cases where no real common interest exists, and infusing into one the enmities of the other, betrays the former into a participation in the quarrels and wars of the latter, without adequate inducements or justifications. It leads also to concessions, to the favorite nation, of privileges denied to others, which is apt doubly to injure the nation making the concessions, by unnecessarily parting with what ought to have been retained, and by exciting jealousy, ill will, and a disposition to retaliate in the parties from whom equal privileges are withheld; and it gives to ambitious, corrupted or deluded citizens who devote themselves to the favorite nation, facility to betray or sacrifice the interests of their own country, without odium, sometimes even with popularity; gilding with the appearances of a virtuous sense of obligation, a commendable deference for public opinion, or a laudable zeal for public good, the base or foolish compliances of ambition, corruption, or infatuation.

As avenues to foreign influence in innumerable ways, such attachments are particularly alarming to the truly enlightened and independent patriot. How many opportunities do they afford to tamper with domestic factions, to practice the arts of seduction, to mislead public opinion, to influence or awe the public councils!—Such an attachment of a small or weak, towards a great and powerful nation, dooms the former to be the satellite of the latter.

Against the insidious wiles of foreign influence, (I conjure you to believe me fellow citizens,) the jealousy of a free people ought to be

*constantly* awake; since history and experience prove, that foreign influence is one of the most baneful foes of republican government. But that jealousy, to be useful, must be impartial, else it becomes the instrument of the very influence to be avoided, instead of a defense against it. Excessive partiality for one foreign nation and excessive dislike for another, cause those whom they actuate to see danger only on one side, and serve to veil and even second the arts of influence on the other. Real patriots, who may resist the intrigues of the favorite, are liable to become suspected and odious; while its tools and dupes usurp the applause and confidence of the people, to surrender their interests.

The great rule of conduct for us, in regard to foreign nations, is, in extending our commercial relations, to have with them as little *political* connection as possible. So far as we have already formed engagements, let them be fulfilled with perfect good faith:—Here let us stop.

Europe has a set of primary interests, which to us have none, or a very remote relation. Hence, she must be engaged in frequent controversies, the causes of which are essentially foreign to our concerns. Hence, therefore, it must be unwise in us to implicate ourselves, by artificial ties, in the ordinary vicissitudes of her politics, or the ordinary combinations and collisions of her friendships or enmities.

Our detached and distant situation invites and enables us to pursue a different course. If we remain one people, under an efficient government, the period is not far off when we may defy material injury from external annoyance; when we may take such an attitude as will cause the neutrality we may at any time resolve upon, to be scrupulously respected; when belligerent nations, under the impossibility of making acquisitions upon us, will not lightly hazard the giving us provocation, when we may choose peace or war, as our interest, guided by justice, shall counsel.

Why forego the advantages of so peculiar a situation? Why quit our own to stand upon foreign ground? Why, by interweaving our destiny with that of any part of Europe, entangle our peace and prosperity in the toils of European ambition, rivalship, interest, humor, or caprice?

It is our true policy to steer clear of permanent alliance with any portion of the foreign world; so far, I mean, as we are now at liberty to do it; for let me not be understood as capable of patronizing infidelity to existing engagements. I hold the maxim no less applicable to public than private affairs, that honesty is always the best policy. I repeat it, therefore, let those engagements be observed in their genuine sense. But in my opinion, it is unnecessary, and would be unwise to extend them.

Taking care always to keep ourselves by suitable establishments, on a respectable defensive posture, we may safely trust to temporary alliances for extraordinary emergencies.

Harmony, and a liberal intercourse with all nations, are recommended by policy, humanity, and interest. But even our commercial policy should

hold an equal and impartial hand; neither seeking nor granting exclusive favors or preferences; consulting the natural course of things; diffusing and diversifying by gentle means the streams of commerce, but forcing nothing; establishing with powers so disposed, in order to give trade a stable course, to define the rights of our merchants, and to enable the government to support them, conventional rules of intercourse, the best that present circumstances and mutual opinion will permit, but temporary, and liable to be from time to time abandoned or varied as experience and circumstances shall dictate; constantly keeping in view, that it is folly in one nation to look for disinterested favors from another; that it must pay with a portion of its independence for whatever it may accept under that character; that by such acceptance, it may place itself in the condition of having given equivalents for nominal favors, and yet of being reproached with ingratitude for not giving more. There can be no greater error than to expect, or calculate upon real favors from nation to nation. It is an illusion which experience must cure, which a just pride ought to discard.

# 12 / *The Monroe Doctrine—Cornerstone of American Policy*

### DEXTER PERKINS

**James Monroe was in public service for a half-century as a United States Senator, governor of Virginia, minister to France, Great Britain, and Spain, Secretary of State, Secretary of War, and fifth President of the United States. As President, he presided over an "era of good feelings." His most lasting impression on American diplomacy, the "doctrine" bearing his name, was pronounced in December, 1823. It is analyzed below by one of the foremost authorities on the subject and on American diplomatic history in general.**

THE FAMOUS DECLARATION of December 2, 1823, that has come to be known as the Monroe Doctrine, had a double purpose and a double

Reprinted from E. S. Miers, ed., *The American Story* (New York: Channel Press, 1956), pp. 131–36. Copyright © 1956 by Broadcast Music, Inc. By permission.

Dexter Perkins is professor of American civilization, Cornell University, and the author of numerous works, including *The American Approach to Foreign Policy*, rev. ed. (1962).

origin. On the one hand, it originated in a dispute between Russia and the United States, with regard to trading rights on the northwest coast of America, in the region known as Alaska, then under Russian sovereignty. Referring to this dispute, President Monroe laid down the principle in his message to Congress "that the American continents, by the free and independent condition which they have assumed and maintain, are henceforth not to be considered as subjects for future colonization by any European powers." On the other hand, the declaration was provoked by the fear existing in Washington in the fall of 1823 that the Continental European powers would intervene by force of arms to restore to Spain her lost colonial dominion in America. "With the governments [that is, of the Spanish American republics] who have declared their independence and maintained it," wrote the President, "and whose independence we have, on great consideration and just principles, acknowledged, we could not view any interposition for the purpose of oppressing them, or controlling in any other manner their destiny, by any European power in any other light than as the manifestation of an unfriendly disposition towards the United States."

While it is the second of these two pronouncements that raises the most interesting and important questions, some attention must be paid to the first. The so-called "Doctrine" relating to the Russian matter is almost entirely the work of John Quincy Adams, Monroe's Secretary of State. It was Adams who, from the very first, conducted with Russia the negotiations arising out of the Russian government's decree of September 16, 1821, which excluded American trading vessels from the shores of the Northwest down to the line of 51 degrees. Adams saw "an abuse of government" in measures of colonial exclusion of this kind, and as early as November, 1819, was disposed to challenge completely Russian claims in the Northwest. By the summer of 1823 there had taken form in his mind the idea which was later to be incorporated in the message of the President. It formed a part, at that time, of his instructions to Richard Rush, our minister in London, and it was explicitly stated to Baron Tuyll, the Russian diplomatic representative at Washington. "I told him specially," wrote Adams in his diary about the interview on July 17, 1823, "that we should contest the right of Russia to *any* territorial establishment on this continent, and that we should assume distinctly the principle that the American continents are no longer subjects for *any* new European colonial establishments." Though Adams did not instruct the American minister at St. Petersburg to press the point, he reiterated the view expressed to Tuyll in a draft presented to the President for the preparation of the annual message. Monroe took it over virtually in the form in which his Secretary of State drafted it.

The noncolonization principle springs in part from Adams's interest in trade. It was directed against limitations on this trade, but it rests upon a

shaky legal basis. Adams's own defense of it was on the ground that the American continents in 1823 "consisted of several sovereign and independent nations, whose territories covered their whole surface." Such a statement appears hardly true, in the light of the conditions that then existed. There were certainly unsettled areas in both South and North America in 1823, to which title had not been definitely determined. Adams also sought to rest his case on the claim that the United States had derived a valid claim to all the Northwest by virtue of the treaty of February 22, 1819, with Spain. In that treaty, Spain renounced all territorial claims north of 42 degrees. But the weakness of the original Spanish title to this region makes this argument as unconvincing as the previous one.

The noncolonization principle played no great part in the actual settlement of the dispute over the Northwest. The Russians preferred to ignore it, "to waive all discussion upon abstract principles of right," as Nesselrode [1] put it. An agreement was reached which restricted Russian claims to the line of 54 degrees and which granted to American citizens rights of trade for a ten-year period. The only effect of the pronouncement was to cool the interest of Great Britain (who also had claims in this area) for joint negotiation with the United States against Russia.

With regard to the other part of the message, the most important facts are these. In the summer of 1823, the administration in Washington received word from Richard Rush of talks that Rush had had with Canning, the British prime minister. These conversations suggested that the Continental European powers, having set about the suppression of revolution on the European continent, and having, through France as their agent, stamped out a revolutionary movement in Spain, might turn their attention to Latin America. A little later, two communications from the Russian government accentuated the apprehensions of Monroe and his advisers. In October, 1823, momentous discussions in the Cabinet took place. Canning had suggested joint action in behalf of the Latin Americas. The President, who had consulted Madison and Jefferson, was disposed to accede to this suggestion. But Adams stoutly maintained that "it would be more candid as well as more dignified, to avow our principles explicitly to Russia and France, than to come in as a cock-boat in the wake of the British man-of-war," and his view of the matter prevailed. It was not Adams, however, who had the idea of broaching the warning in the forthcoming Presidential message. This idea was Monroe's own. The famous pronouncement was read with dismay by those who had hoped for the suppression of revolution in Spain and Greece, as well as in Latin

---

[1] Count Carl Robert von Nesselrode (1780–1862), Russian statesman who, as the chief contriver of the "Holy Alliance," made Russia virtually supreme in Europe. Nesselrode's power lessened under Emperor Nicholas; he retired after the accession of Alexander II.

America. He wished to "make an American cause, and adhere inflexibly to that." Here again he got his way.

Canning, who had in October been reassured by the French government with regard to intervention in Latin America, was by no means delighted with Monroe's declaration. The United States had stolen a march on Great Britain in competition for the favor of the Latin Americans. It was Canning's object, following 1823, to redress the balance; and in 1825 Britain, first of all European governments, recognized the independence of the new states.

Monroe's declaration was variously received in Latin America. The plain truth of the matter is that the material power of the United States was not such as to furnish a very impressive guarantee of the independence of the new states, without British support. When, moreover, in 1824, various of the Latin American republics approached the government at Washington with a view to translating Monroe's generalizations into binding pledges, they found no disposition on the part of the administration to commit itself. The debates in the American Congress in 1826 underlined the determination of most Americans to refrain from pledges of any kind. The significance of the message, so far as Latin America was concerned, remained, therefore, largely moral.

The warning to Europe, like the noncolonization principle, is open to substantial criticism on grounds of logic. Monroe sought to place his admonition on the principle that European intervention would be dangerous to our peace and safety. Yet it is difficult to believe that in the conditions of 1823 the re-establishment of a colonial regime in some remote part of Latin America would have been a source of peril to the United States. Indeed, so true is this, that for many years to come, the practical application of the doctrine was restricted to the region of the Caribbean. The sweeping language of the President outran the facts of his own time.

Nonetheless, the Monroe Doctrine is of the highest historic significance. In the first place, it is an interesting, if not a decisive, episode in the clash of two points of view—the principle of intervention on the one hand and the principle of nonintervention on the other. In the history of the self-determination of peoples, it will long have a place as a resounding expression of a theory that has had wide influence in the past, and that has wide influence today.

In the second place, the technique of the message gives it substantial importance. The United States was, from an early period, a practitioner of that open diplomacy that has played an increasing role in our own time. There are few more striking examples of that diplomacy than the message of 1823. Rarely, too, has the weapon of open diplomacy been more effectively used. Granted the premises on which Monroe and Adams acted, what could have been more skillful than this public assertion of principle? How much more gratifying to the national pride, how much

more productive of prestige in Latin America, how much more disconcerting to Europe than an unostentatious diplomatic protest!

Thirdly, it hardly needs to be stated that almost no other document in American diplomatic history has had a more pronounced effect in the long run. Enunciated with a view to a special situation, it was to grow into a guiding principle of action, powerful in its appeal and far-reaching in its influence.

Finally, it symbolized the thought of an era. It was a declaration of the separation of the New World from the Old. The idea has become outmoded. But it exercised a powerful influence on policy for many generations, and did much to shape the diplomatic action of the United States.

# 13 / *McKinley and Manifest Destiny*

### JULIUS W. PRATT

**Few historic landmarks are more important in their effects upon American foreign policy than the war with Spain. That war has much to teach us about how foreign policy is influenced by the political context in which it is made and how a policy, once made, can in turn influence the future political setting. The administration of William McKinley, twenty-fifth President of the United States, provided a major turning point in American foreign policy.**

MEN WERE DYING in Cuba with Cuban insurgents and Spanish soldiers shooting each other in guerilla fighting. Women, children, and old men were dying too, huddled in concentration camps where were harbored the supposed friends of the government, not its enemies. Cubans who refused to come into the camps were held to be hostile and shot on sight. Those who came in were promised safety, but food, shelter, sanitation, medicine, and medical care were all lacking. According to some accounts, starvation and disease carried off 200,000 of these people in two years.

Reprinted from E. S. Miers, ed., *The American Story* (New York: Channel Press, 1956), pp. 260–65. Copyright © 1956 by Broadcast Music, Inc. By permission.

Julius Pratt, professor of history at the University of Buffalo, is the author of *Expansionists of 1898* (1936), *A History of United States Foreign Policy* (1955), and other works.

What was it all about? Spanish government in Cuba was harsh and undemocratic. Taxation was heavy, and 90 per cent of the taxes collected went to pay Spanish officials, Spanish troops, and a debt resulting from earlier insurrections. Little was left for roads, schools, hospitals, or other public services. Discontent was chronic, but to add to the island's woes, in 1893 came a worldwide depression. The demand and the price for sugar, Cuba's chief product, fell off so sharply that workers in the cane fields and the sugar mills lost their jobs or were put on starvation wages. In February of 1895, thousands of them joined with leaders who raised the cry of Cuban independence. They formed an insurgent government and army. They burned cane fields and sugar mills to make the island valueless to Spain.

Spain countered by sending more troops and a new Captain General, Valeriano Weyler ("Butcher" Weyler he was nicknamed in the United States). Weyler tried to end the rebellion by herding loyal Cubans into the concentration camps and shooting those who stayed out. For three years the war dragged on. Agriculture and industry were at a standstill. A shocking number of Cubans had died; many more were incapacitated by famine or disease. Yet there was no sign of victory for either side.

Cuba lay at the very door of the United States. The struggle of the Cubans for independence, and the suffering of innocent civilians in the concentration camps, made a strong appeal to the sympathy of the American people. Terrible as they were, these sufferings were made to appear even worse by sensational American newspapers, the so-called "yellow press." The American Red Cross sent food and medicines; its head, the venerable Clara Barton, went in person to Cuba to supervise the work in a great effort to relieve the sufferings of the Cuban civilians.

But relief of suffering was not enough. There was a growing demand in the United States that this government should intervene, by force if necessary, to secure independence for Cuba. Newspapers, Senators and Congressmen, clergymen of all the large Protestant churches, were soon crying out in the name of humanity and Christianity that it was the duty of the United States to put an end to this abuse on its doorstep. On the other hand, many conservative people, many businessmen, some politicians like President McKinley's friend and confidant, Mark Hanna, opposed intervention. They doubted the ability of the Cubans to govern themselves, and they feared the effect of a war with Spain on American business.

Grover Cleveland, President till March 4, 1897, held out against intervention. So did his successor, William McKinley, during his first year in office. Then the pressure on him became irresistible. In December, 1897, there were riots in Havana, and as a safeguard for American lives and property, McKinley sent the battleship *Maine* to Havana harbor. There, on the night of February 15, 1898, a terrific explosion sank her at her

anchorage. Two hundred and sixty American bluejackets died in the explosion or were drowned in their quarters.

Who or what caused the destruction of the *Maine* has never been certainly revealed. Two boards of American naval officers concluded that she had been sunk by a mine or torpedo exploded under her hull. There is, on the other hand, a possibility that the only explosion was an internal one. Spain made a reasonable offer to submit the whole question to arbitration. But the American public, led by the yellow press, assumed that the *Maine* had been deliberately sunk by an agent of Spain. "Remember the *Maine!*" became the popular watchword.

President McKinley yielded to the pressure, and late in March in 1898 sent Spain an ultimatum. She must agree to an armistice and revoke her concentration camp policy. Spain grudgingly yielded on both points, but too late to satisfy the American President or Congress. On April 20, Congress formally demanded that Spain give up Cuba, and five days later formally declared war.

A strange war it was, and a one-sided war. Both contestants were unprepared, but Spain's lack of preparation was much worse than ours. Supposedly the purpose of the war was to make Cuba free—Cuba libre, as the Cubans said. Yet the first serious blow was struck half-way around the world from Cuba at Manila Bay in the Philippines. There, on May first, Commodore George Dewey led his ships through the mine fields at the entrance to the harbor. In a few hours the antiquated naval vessels of Spain's Asiatic squadron had been destroyed—all without loss of an American life.

Why did the war for Cuba libre begin in the Philippines, thousands of miles from Cuba? First, because the Spanish ships there, if not destroyed, might attack and damage American commerce. But there was a deeper reason. To some Americans, Spain's empire in the Philippines, rich in sugar, hemp, and coconut products, with a wonderful harbor at Manila, looked like a rich prize. To some Americans it seemed that the United States had kept too long within its continental boundaries. The time had come, they thought, when it should reach out for distant naval bases and colonial possessions in competition with other great powers.

Several lines of thought led to this conclusion. American devotees of Charles Darwin's theory of evolution pointed out that upward progress came through a "struggle for existence," in which "the fittest" survived and passed on their victory-giving qualities to posterity. Let the United States, they said, join the international struggle. Surely the American people have what it takes to survive and conquer. That way lies progress.

A second line of thought, a racialist line, acclaimed the political genius of the "Nordic" races, especially the Germans and Anglo-Saxons. These Nordics were adept at government. Let them, therefore, bring good government to the ill-governed regions of the world.

A third line of reasoning, spearheaded by the scholarly naval officer, Captain Alfred Thayer Mahan, emphasized the important role of sea power in making a nation great and strong. And sea power included not only a navy and merchant marine, but colonies and naval bases in distant quarters of the globe.

All of these ideas were brought to a focus and given practical application by the coming of the war with Spain. Here was the opportunity, all at once, to join in the international struggle for power, to extend the blessings of American government to colonies long misgoverned by Spain, to acquire a rich colony in the Philippines, and naval bases from among Spain's other possessions in the Caribbean and the Pacific. An old phrase of the Mexican War period was revived. "Manifest Destiny" pointed to American expansion in the Caribbean and the Pacific.

And so the war to free Cuba became a war of expansion, of "Manifest Destiny," though William McKinley was hardly aware of the transformation till it was all over. Among the men who shaped the new policy of expansion were Theodore Roosevelt, Assistant Secretary of the Navy before the war began and later lieutenant colonel of the "Rough Riders" in the war in Cuba; his friend, Henry Cabot Lodge, Senator from Massachusetts; and Captain Mahan. It was Roosevelt who had planned the attack on Manila Bay and had picked Commodore Dewey to lead it.

Two months after Dewey's victory at Manila, the main Spanish fleet was destroyed in a running fight near Santiago, Cuba. The city of Santiago was under attack from the landward side. On July first "Teddy" Roosevelt led the footsore "Rough Riders" (their horses had been left in Florida!) in a charge up San Juan Hill, or more accurately its neighbor, Kettle Hill. Other outer defenses were taken on the same day, and on July 17 the city was surrendered. Spain now asked for peace. An armistice was signed on August 12, and in October, American and Spanish commissioners met in Paris to write a treaty.

President McKinley, slowly feeling his way, at last adopted the program of the "Manifest Destiny" boys, who insisted that we must follow up Dewey's victory by keeping the Philippines. He was under several kinds of pressure to do so. Businessmen, who had been reluctant to go to war with Spain, now saw in the Philippines a guarantee that the United States should have its full share of trade with China. The Protestant churches sensed a divine call to mission work among the Filipinos even though most of them were Catholic Christians. It was argued too that if we did not keep the islands, the alternative was their misgovernment by Spain or their seizure by some rival power, like Germany or Japan.

So McKinley decided. The commissioners in Paris were told we must have the Philippines—for which we paid Spain $20,000,000; also the little island of Guam in the Pacific and Puerto Rico in the Caribbean. Hawaii, an independent republic, had joined us voluntarily during the war. Cuba

would become free, but held for a while with leading strings by the United States.

So, in the treaty signed on December 10, 1898, and ratified a few weeks later, the United States took its place as a great power on the world stage. It accepted the imperial mission to which, as people like Theodore Roosevelt believed, "Manifest Destiny" called it. That mission, as we now know, was to be one not of perpetual empire, but of preparing colonial peoples for self-government or independence. Its chief fruits are seen today in the self-governing commonwealth of Puerto Rico, remaining of its own choice under the Stars and Stripes, and the independent Philippines, the most dependable outpost of the free world in the Far East.

# 14 / *America's Emergence as a World Power: The Myth and the Verity*

## THOMAS A. BAILEY

**How long has the United States been a world power? A great power? Some of the prevailing assumptions with regard to these questions are examined here.**

EVERY AMERICAN SCHOOLBOY KNOWS—or would know if he bothered to read his textbook—that the United States did not become a world power until 1898. Commodore Dewey, according to the traditional tale, staged our memorable coming-out party at Manila Bay on May Day of that year. At the risk of arousing the United Spanish War Veterans, I venture to take issue with this melodramatic interpretation and to suggest that the United States became a world power 122 years earlier, on the day of its official birth, July 2—not July 4—1776.

I have collected the titles or subtitles of more than a dozen books that associate America's so-called spectacular eruption with the era of

This essay was Professor Bailey's presidential address to the Pacific Coast Branch, American Historical Association, in 1960. It is reprinted from the *Pacific Historical Review*, XXX (1961), 1–16, by permission.

Thomas A. Bailey is professor of history, Stanford University, and the author of *America Faces Russia* (1950), *A Diplomatic History of the American People*, 6th ed. (1958), and numerous other works.

the Spanish-American War. This formidable phalanx of error does not include the scores of chapter titles or subtitles or magazine articles that reaffirm the May Day myth. I shall not name names, lest I redden the faces of certain scholars present, while magnifying my own sin. The embarrassing truth is that for eighteen years I further misled the youth of this land with a chapter title which I have since then unobtrusively corrected.

I cannot exculpate myself completely by pleading that at a tender age I was misled by my elders and betters, or that I later erred in distinguished company. By the time I became a graduate student I should have realized that cataclysmic changes, especially in the power position of a nation, seldom or never occur overnight. I should also have known that the very first obligation of the scholar is to examine critically all basic assumptions—the more basic the more critically. The majority is often wrong, and repetition does not make things so.

The pitfalls of periodization have no doubt contributed richly to our misunderstanding. Watershed dates like 1898 are useful as pedagogical landmarks, and although the careful historian has mental reservations while using them, the rote-minded student is likely to accept them as gospel.

More misleading is the singular indifference of many scholars to precision in terminology. Unabridged lexicons exist for standardizing the language, and we historians would do well to thumb them occasionally. The least unsatisfactory definition of a "world power" that I have uncovered is given by Webster as follows: "A state or organization powerful enough to affect world politics by its influence or actions." This concept is obviously too broad, and I therefore propose to narrow it to exclude "nuisance value" power, such as that exerted by Serbia in 1914. My rewriting reads: "A nation with sufficient power in being, or capable of being mobilized, to affect world politics positively and over a period of time."[1] The term "great power," as distinguished from the less exalted "world power," will be considered later.

Did the United States in 1776 measure up to the world-power formula that I have just propounded? The answer, in my judgment, is an emphatic affirmative.

First of all, what are the components of national power? I have made up a detailed list of about one hundred items, major and minor, tangible and intangible, but I shall not inflict them all on you. Let us examine a

---

[1] The *New Standard Dictionary of the English Language* (Funk and Wagnalls) defines a world power as "A state whose policy and action are of world-wide influence or concern." Professor A. C. Coolidge defined the world powers in 1908 as "powers which are directly interested in all parts of the world and whose voices must be listened to everywhere." *The United States as a World Power* (New York, 1908), 7. A literal application of this definition would have disqualified all nations.

few of the more noteworthy with reference to the United States during the era of the American Revolution.

In territory, we exceeded all the European states, except Russia. In population, we outranked many of the European nations, and possibly excelled them all in birth rate. In quality of population, we could boast what was perhaps the most literate people in the world, and certainly one of the more ingenious. In moral force we were from the outset probably the most influential power of all—the lodestar of liberals and the mecca of the masses. In statecraft and diplomacy we could point pridefully to Franklin, Washington, Adams, Jay, and Jefferson, to name only a corporal's guard of the Founding Fathers. In military strength we could muster adequate militia for defense, though shunning large professional armies. In the capacity to attract allies we could offer economic concessions and diversionary or additive military strength. In richness of soil, salubrity of climate, abundance of natural resources, and general self-sufficiency we were almost certainly the most blessed of all peoples.

Finally, in merchant shipping we were from the beginning a leader, ranking in the same top bracket with Britain, France, Spain, and Holland. In the days of the windjammer and smoothbore cannon an amphibious nation could so easily improvise a navy that a great maritime power could hardly escape being a world power.[2] Privateers played a devastating role in our two wars with Britain, and although we lost about as many ships as we captured, we bloodied our enemy's nose while getting our own bloodied. The menace of more privateers gave Downing Street nightmares during every Anglo-American crisis of the nineteenth century.

The power position of the United States, already formidable, was immensely strengthened by six fortunate circumstances. First, we had between us and Europe the watery vastness of the Atlantic Ocean—America's greatest liquid asset. Second, we had defense in depth, as the footsore British redcoats learned to their dismay in two frustrating wars. Third, we had the precarious European balance of power, which caused our potential adversaries to fear the dagger thrust of an envious neighbor. Fourth, we had an imbalance of power in the Americas, with the United States enjoying the top-dog position from the outset, and with our weak neighbors dreading us rather than our people dreading them. Fifth, we had Canada under the muzzles of our muskets, as a hostage unwittingly given to us by the British for their good behavior.

---

[2] President John Adams told Congress in 1797, on the eve of the crisis with France: "However we may consider ourselves, the maritime and commercial powers of the world will consider the United States of America as forming a weight in that balance of power in Europe which never can be forgotten or neglected." J. D. Richardson, comp., *Messages and Papers of the Presidents* (Washington, 1896), I, 238.

Finally, we had mountainous surpluses of foodstuffs, cotton, and other raw materials, upon which our most redoubtable diplomatic rivals, notably Britain, developed a dangerous dependence. Every time the British faced up to the prospect of again fighting the Yankees, they had to reckon with the sobering consequences of cutting their own economic throats. All this adds up to the conclusion that from its birth the United States has been incomparably the luckiest of all the great nations—so far.

I have said that the United Colonies became a world power in July, 1776, when the Continental Congress solemnly severed the umbilical cord. I might start even earlier and assert that in a broad sense we had become a power before we became a nation.[3] Charles and Mary Beard dated America's birth as a "world power" from Edmund Burke's masterly speech of 1775 on conciliation—an appeal in which the orator revealed that the resources of the colonies were so boundless as to render them unconquerable.[4] I do not accept this particular date, primarily because Burke's views did not prevail with Parliament, and because his speech neither added to nor subtracted from our power potential.

But America's strength was already considerable by 1775. Her trade, as Burke revealed, was nearly equal to that of England's with the entire world in 1700. Her manufacturing, despite the frowns of the Mother Country, was prospering; in fact, her iron foundries, though smaller, were more numerous than those of England. Her economic coercive power was such as to force Parliament to repeal the detested Stamp Act in 1766. Her nautical biceps were bulging. Benjamin Franklin noted that the total tonnage, gunnage, and manpower of the colonial privateering fleets in the war with France ending in 1748 equaled the entire English navy which had defeated the Spanish Armada in 1588.

In manpower and military strength—the conventional criteria of world power—the homespun colonials were far from contemptible. Thomas Paine, referring in *Common Sense* (1776) to the veterans of the recent French and Indian War, numbering about 25,000, could state with some exaggeration that we had "the largest body of armed and disciplined men of any power under Heaven." After Lexington, Washington commanded an army of some 20,000 men that trapped the British in Boston and finally ejected them. In the winter of 1775–1776, some seven months before independence, the brash Americans, not content with purely defensive operations against the world's greatest power,

---

[3] Colonial military and naval contributions in the Seven Years' War indirectly affected the fall of both India and the Philippines to the British.

[4] Charles A. and Mary R. Beard, *History of the United States* (New York, 1921), 477. The Beards asserted that the United States (even during the Critical Period) was continuously a world power from March, 1775, "to the settlement at Versailles in 1919." The curious implication is that the United States ceased to be a world power after 1919.

launched a two-pronged invasion of Canada which narrowly missed capturing the Fourteenth Colony.

In my view the most satisfying date for emergence is July, 1776, when the United States proclaimed a clean break with Britain. The Founding Fathers themselves believed that they were launching a new world power on the turbulent sea of international politics. The proud preamble of the Declaration of Independence proclaimed an intention "to assume among the Powers of the earth the separate and *equal* station to which the Laws of Nature and of Nature's God entitle them." John Adams, who quarreled in Paris with Foreign Minister Vergennes, informed him in 1780, "The United States of America are a great and powerful people, whatever European statesmen may think of them." [5]

But actions speak louder than verbs. The strength of the upstart colonials was so apparent that France, seeking to redress the world balance of power, undertook to wean them away from their imperial apron strings and embrace them as allies. This move, the French reasoned, would have a double-barreled impact. It would not only add to the strength of France but it would subtract correspondingly from that of Britain. The French consequently provided secret aid for about three years, and in 1778 finally came out into the open with twin treaties of alliance and commerce. One of the most striking features of these pacts was that in tone and terminology they implied an agreement between two equal and long-established powers.

The British, unwilling to lose their most prized overseas possessions, had countered belatedly with an offer of home rule. The two most powerful nations of the world were thus openly bidding for the favor of the robust young republic. The anxiety of both rivals indicates that America's strength was regarded as sufficient to tip the balance.

But the embattled British, outbid in 1778, turned the tables in 1782. Fighting desperately against a fearsome coalition, they in effect seduced America from the French alliance—a counter-seduction if you will—by offering incredibly generous terms of peace. These concessions were both the measure of Britain's desperation and of America's substantial weight in the world balance of power.

Yet many historians, awed by the magnitude of open French aid, are apt to downgrade the basic strength of the Americans. The truth is that the ex-colonials carried the burden of battle alone for three years—and against two nations. So tough was the colonial nut that the British were forced to seek assistance abroad, and in hiring some 30,000 so-called

---

[5] The passage continues: "If we take into our estimate the numbers and the character of her people, the extent, variety, and fertility of her soil, her commerce, and her skill and materials for ship-building, and her seamen, excepting France, Spain, England, Germany [?] and Russia, there is not a state in Europe so powerful." C. F. Adams, ed., *The Works of John Adams* (Boston, 1852), VII, 226–227 (July 13, 1780).

Hessians made what amounted to a military alliance with a second power. American privateers, whitening the seas, established a partial blockade of the British Isles during the three years before France threw off the mask of neutrality. After Lexington, the raw colonials pinned down tens of thousands of British troops, and in 1777, at Saratoga, compelled the surrender of the largest force that Britain had yet yielded to a foreign foe.

I would be the last to discount the French role during the American Revolution, especially secret aid and the naval contribution at Yorktown. But the United States could conceivably have won its independence without open assistance from France. After the signing of the alliance of 1778, a kind of let-François-do-it attitude began to prevail, and American enlistments declined in a ratio roughly corresponding to the size of the French expeditionary forces. If we gained from the alliance, so did the French. If they had not calculated that we would be of about as much value to them as they would be to us, they almost certainly would not have struck the perilous bargain.

More than a century later, when the Philippines fell as a gift from Heaven—or was it Heaven?—American imperialists insisted that we had to keep the islands to prove that we were a world power. To this argument the anti-imperialist Carl Schurz replied early in 1899: "Well, we *are* a world power now, and have been for many years." [6] William Jennings Bryan, in his acceptance speech of 1900, was more specific: "The forcible annexation of the Philippine Islands is not necessary to make the United States a world power. For over ten decades our Nation has been a world power." [7] But both Schurz and Bryan, the one a professional calamity howler and the other a hardy quadrennial, were voices crying in the cornfields.

Of different stature was Professor A. B. Hart of Harvard, who published a challenging article in *Harper's Magazine* in February, 1899.[8] He cogently argued that the United States had been a world power from 1776 on, and he may have conveyed this notion dimly to Bryan. But the idea apparently wilted in the feverish imperialistic atmosphere of the era, and Professor Hart himself evidently weakened in the faith. In 1907, eight years later, he edited as one of the volumes of the *American Nation Series* a contribution by Professor John H. Latané, entitled, *America as a World Power, 1897–1907*. Professor Latané himself declared cautiously (p. 318) that "the United States has always been a world power *in a sense*." He then went on to discuss our influence in

---

[6] Carl Schurz, *American Imperialism* (n.p., 1899), 28.

[7] W. J. Bryan, ed., *Speeches of William Jennings Bryan* (New York, 1909), II, 14.

[8] Later published in expanded form as chap. 1 of A. B. Hart, *The Foundations of American Foreign Policy* (New York, 1901).

shaping civil liberties and international law the world over.[9] But Professor Hart is the only spokesman whom I have found, historian or layman, who unreservedly dates our birth as a world power from the declaring of independence.

Try as I may, I cannot escape the unflattering conclusion that we historians are largely responsible for the perpetuation of the Manila Bay hallucination. Certainly the Fourth of July orator never doubted for one moment that we were not only the greatest power of all time from the very beginning, but had twice whipped the next greatest power.[10] How did the trained scholar—the professional custodian of our traditions—get so far off the track?

First of all, we historians have been unduly swayed by the smallness of our army and navy.[11] We tend to judge national power by the size of armed forces *in being*. Until the present century the United States relied heavily on land militia and sea militia, and although amateurs rarely do as well as professionals, we somehow managed to muddle through with a minimum of disaster. Huge military establishments, contrary to popular fancy, are a source of weakness rather than of strength. They reduce productive employment, burden the taxpayer, and unless assembled for blatantly aggressive purposes, are an almost infallible symptom of insecurity and fear.

The United States was the only first-rate nation that until recent times could afford the luxury of a third-rate army. In 1812 Madison invaded Canada with some 6,000 men; simultaneously Napoleon invaded Russia with some 600,000 men. The erroneous assumption is that France was one hundred times stronger than the United States. The fact is that we may not have had much of an army but what we had we had here, and Napoleon was powerless to come to grips with us. He was

---

[9] Italics inserted. Seth Low, former president of Columbia University, wrote two years earlier with similar qualifications: "From the beginning of its history the United States has been a world power, *in the sense* that it has profoundly affected the movements of thought and of action outside of itself." He refers to our influence on the French Revolution, our stand for neutral rights and arbitration, our example of fair dealing with neighbors, our reception of immigrants, and our contributions to education. *Annals of the American Academy of Political and Social Science,* XXVI (1905), 6. Italics inserted.

[10] Col. A. L. Snowden, in an Independence Day address delivered in 1895 before Independence Hall, attributed American superiority largely to a superior national character. "The Foremost Nation of the World," *American Historical Register,* III (1895), 65–70.

[11] Even so acute an observer as James Bryce, writing in 1901, could refer to the United States in 1834 as follows: "Already a great nation, it could become a great power as soon as it cared to spend money on fleets and armies." James Bryce, *Studies in History and Jurisprudence* (Oxford, 1901), I, 395. An unwillingness to recognize the power position of the United States did not negate that power, as Mexico learned to her sorrow in the war of 1846–1848.

more than one hundred times stronger than we were in Europe, but we were stronger than he was in America.[12]

A two-way provincialism thus continues to curse American historiography. If American historians are too America-centered, many European historians are too Europe-centered. A true perspective lies between these extremes.

Certain historians have also misinterpreted our early isolationism. We did not want to become one of the great powers of Europe, not so much because we were weak as because we thought it prudent to take full advantage of our unique geographical location and our phenomenal fecundity. Lord Castlereagh was quoted as saying that the fortunate Americans won their victories not on the battle field but in the bedchamber. Certainly to play for time, to avoid unnecessary entanglements, to fatten as feeders while the Europeans famished as fighters—all this was statesmanship rather than timidity.[13]

The Monroe Doctrine has further muddied the waters. Some writers have hailed it as a virtual alliance with England, which it emphatically was not—quite the reverse.[14] In 1823 the British and the Americans, both intent on keeping inviolate the newly opened trade of Latin America, were pursuing a parallel policy. This meant that the mighty British navy, yardarm-to-yardarm with the modest American navy, was prepared to thwart possible intervention by the so-called Holy Alliance. The legend has therefore taken root that the Monroe Doctrine was upheld by the British navy throughout the nineteenth century and beyond. We thus have a mental image of the Yankee cringing behind the oaken petticoats of the Mother Country—a posture that hardly suggests world power.

The disillusioning truth is that the British navy upheld the Monroe Doctrine only when the policies of Downing Street and Washington ran parallel, as they definitely did not during much of the nineteenth century. The sacred dictum of Monroe was flouted—or allegedly flouted—a score or so of times before 1904; and the British were involved in

---

[12] Such a concept inspired this piece of extravagance in a speech by young Abraham Lincoln in 1838: "Shall we expect some transatlantic military giant to step the Ocean and crush us at a blow? Never! All the armies of Europe, Asia and Africa combined, with all the treasure of the earth (our own excepted) in their military chest; with a Buonaparte for a commander, could not by force, take a drink from the Ohio, or make a track on the Blue Ridge, in a trial of a thousand years." R. P. Basler, ed., *The Collected Works of Abraham Lincoln* (New Brunswick, 1953), I, 109.

[13] Washington's Farewell Address, in urging the desirability of staying out of European embroilments, tended to overemphasize the weakness of the United States.

[14] See Walter Lippmann, U. S. Foreign Policy: Shield of the Republic (Boston, 1943), 16–22, for a full statement of the legend. Secretary Adams' famous remark about a "cockboat" coming in "in the wake of the British man-of-war" was obviously designed to stress not so much our weakness as the desirability of pursuing an independent course. C. F. Adams, ed., *Memoirs of John Quincy Adams* (Philadelphia, 1875), VI, 179.

many of these infractions, either actively or passively. Beyond a doubt, the Royal Navy could have hamstrung or halted all such encroachments, had it been the protector-in-chief of the Monroe Doctrine. And as far as defending the United States was concerned, during the dozen or so Anglo-American crises between 1823 and 1898, we rightly regarded the British navy as our most formidable single adversary.[15]

Still another source of misunderstanding was the alleged absence of a far-flung American colonial empire until 1898. An authentic world power seemingly had to be burdened with overseas liabilities, as well as huge armies, navies, and national debts. The point is often missed that during the nineteenth century the United States practiced internal colonialism and imperialism on a continental scale. When the Western European nations expanded, they had to go overseas; when we expanded, we had to go west.[16] We self-righteously preened ourselves on not becoming an imperialistic power until 1898, when we acquired Spanish real estate in the Philippines, Guam, and Puerto Rico. Yet hundreds of Spanish place names pepper the land from California to Texas, all of which, curiously enough, somehow managed to come under our nonimperialistic flag a half century earlier. As for the claim that the Philippines added to our national strength, the troublesome islands proved to be a perennial liability—militarily, economically, politically, and morally.

Another misleading cliché of the nineteenth century was that the United States, though still a lusty adolescent, loomed as *the* great power of the future. British editors condescendingly conceded that in the fullness of time—and thanks largely to our British blood and breeding —we would arrive.[17] Long after we had indubitably "arrived," the mis-

---

[15] On this point see Theodore Roosevelt's remarkable letter of November 30, 1918, in E. E. Morrison, ed., *The Letters of Theodore Roosevelt* (Cambridge, 1954), VIII, 1407–1409. A writer in the Manchester *Guardian Weekly* recently stated that "American security was, in fact, a by-product of the strength of the British fleet." LXXXII, 10 (June 30, 1960). It is true that Britain helped preserve the balance of power in Europe, to our incidental advantage, but if there had been no British navy, the balance would presumably have been redressed by other navies, or by a stronger American navy. Similarly, if there had been no United States navy to back the Monroe Doctrine, the Latin American republics would have had to maintain larger navies.

[16] Tariffs to protect our domestic market were in some degree the equivalent of European imperialism for establishing overseas markets. Both American tariffs and European imperialism affected foreign peoples adversely.

[17] For examples of British opinion see *Scots Magazine*, LXXVII (1815), 63; Edinburgh *Review*, XXIV (1814), 292; *ibid.*, LXXXVI (1847), 395–396. Whig, rather than Tory, journals were disposed to play up the actual or potential power of the United States. See Richard S. Cramer, "British Magazines and the United States, 1815–1848" (unpublished doctorial dissertation, Stanford University). In 1765, eleven years before independence, the London *Gazette* remarked: "Little doubt can be entertained that America will in time be the greatest and most prosperous empire that perhaps the world has even seen." Quoted in Hart, *Foundations of American Foreign Policy*, 12.

leading habit persisted of referring cheerfully to America as the nation of the future.

Additional confusion came from British travelers and others who harped on the youthfulness of America. We started as the youngest of modern republics, and we revealed a boyishness of spirit as we proceeded to crystallize our dreams into realities. But as the nineteenth century lengthened, as dozens of new nations sprang into existence, and as we developed a continental spread, critics continued to comment on our youth. Oscar Wilde, writing in 1893, had one of his characters quip, "The youth of America is their oldest tradition. It has been going on now for three hundred years." The juvenile behavior of some Americans, especially when abroad, still gives support to this illusion.

A false estimate of our power position has also contributed lushly to the legend of 1898. I have already said that the United States, from the very day of its legal birth, was the strongest nation in the Western Hemisphere—a basic fact often overlooked.[18] In the pubescent period of the republic, France, Britain, Russia, Prussia, Austria, Spain—to name no others—could all marshal larger armed forces *in Europe,* but not effectively against us. As for the other sister republics of the Americas, the epithet "Colossus of the North" carries its own melancholy implications.

The United States from the outset was a European power—on those infrequent occasions when it chose to exert its power in Europe.[19] The panic-inspiring raids of John Paul Jones on the British coasts, to say nothing of the ravages of American privateers in British waters during two Anglo-American wars, are twice-told tales. Less familiar was the damaging effect of the American Embargo Act and the Non-intercourse Act, which together forced the British to suspend their infuriating orders in council before we declared war on them in 1812. The simple fact is that in the years before the Civil War the coercive power of King Cotton on British textile manufacturers was so potent that in an economic sense alone America was a world power.

The United States was also an African power in the nineteenth century, when it chose to be one. Most Americans have forgotten, if they ever knew (that William Eaton, the incredible Connecticut Yankee, led a motley army of some 500 men across the desert from Egypt to

---

[18] In 1856 a writer in *Blackwood's Edinburgh Magazine* thus described the United States: "The dominant power of the New World, and with three thousand miles of sea separating it from the great military states of Europe, the Union has found on its own continent no power which unaided can check its aggressions, and as yet no European state but Great Britain has had either an interest or the power to enter the lists against it." LXXX (1856), 116–117.

[19] The Czar of Russia thought well enough of the United States to invite it to join the Holy Alliance in 1819.

Tripoli and captured Derne in 1805. Most Americans have forgotten, if they ever knew, that the United States was the nation that chastised the cutthroats of Morocco, Algiers, Tunis, and Tripoli in naval campaigns extending from 1801 to 1815. Most Americans have forgotten, if they ever knew, that the United States launched Liberia in the 1820's, and in 1884, following the spectacular explorations of the American journalist Henry M. Stanley, joined the other great powers by invitation at the Berlin Conference on the Congo.

The United States was a Far Eastern power in the nineteenth century—fifty years or so before our ill-informed expansionists clamored for the Philippines so as to make America an active force in the Eastern Hemisphere. It was Commodore Perry who, with seven warships and the velvet glove, forced open the bamboo portals of Japan in 1854. It was "Blood-is-thicker-than-water" Tattnall who went to the rescue of the British off the Chinese forts in 1859. It was an American warship, in the midst of our own Civil War, that helped punish the Japanese feudal lord at Shimonoseki in 1864. It was a fleet of five American warships that demolished five Korean forts and killed some two hundred Koreans in 1871. And it was Commodore Shufeldt who initiated our diplomatic relations with Korea in 1882.[20] On the other side of Asia, it was an American man-of-war in Turkish waters that forced an Austrian warship to release the Hungarian refugee Martin Koszta in 1853. Nor does this catalogue take into account the moral influence of America through educational and missionary establishments, ranging all the way from the missions of China and Japan to Robert College at Constantinople.

In short, critics have often failed to recognize our three-ply policies in the nineteenth century: voluntary abstentionism, as a rule, in Europe; unilateral intervention in the Americas and Africa; and unilateral or joint-power intervention in the Far East. One reason for associating our advent as a world power with 1898 is the popular but erroneous assumption that the acquisition of the Philippines marked a complete break with the past. We are told that hitherto we had shunned colonizing (which is untrue), that we had formerly been isolated (which is untrue), and that thereafter we were internationalist (which is also untrue).

The May Day misconception can further be traced to the testimony of contemporary Americans and Britons—our esteemed primary sources. In 1898 a number of editors, further proving that propinquity often dulls perception, hailed America's sudden and sensational advent as a

---

[20] As far as the nineteenth century as a whole was concerned, Britain, and possibly Russia and France, were the only powers that exerted more influence than the United States in the Far East. Germany, Italy, and Austria-Hungary, the other three great powers of Europe, certainly exerted less.

world power.[21] Americans are notoriously afflicted with "hurryupitis," and the concept of emerging in a hurry chimed in with the national psychology. President McKinley himself remarked in 1899 that "in a few short months we have become a world power."[22] But let us bear in mind that McKinley, to put it charitably, was slightly confused. Ex-President Benjamin Harrison, writing in 1901, and thinking of our unchallenged primacy in the Americas, declared that before 1898 we had been half a world power—as though world power could be divided and compartmented.[23]

If my reasoning is sound, the United States became a world power in 1776 and has never fallen below that exalted status, except for the six-year hiatus of the so-called Critical Period following the Revolution. A nation that was militarily impotent, diplomatically despised, financially bankrupt, and politically fragmented ceased to be a power, much less a world power. We almost ceased to be a nation, for British and Spanish forces held or controlled about one half of our territory. The Constitution of 1787 was in part designed—and successfully so—to restore and strengthen American prestige.[24]

The next question is: When did we step up a rung and become a great power? Webster, apparently the only lexicographer to spell out this distinction, defines the great powers as "The most powerful nations of the world, especially in political influence, resources, and military and naval strength." The "Great Powers of Europe," as the pat phrase went, formed a kind of exclusive club, and by the 1890's included Britain, France, Russia, Germany, Italy, and Austria-Hungary. When did the United States deserve the status of a great power in its own right, rather than as an influential counterweight in the world balance?

A possible date is 1803, when we dramatically doubled our original birthright by the windfall of Louisiana. "From this day," exulted Minister Livingston in Paris, "the United States take their place among the powers of the *first* rank.[25] But this self-congratulatory assessment seems unduly optimistic.

I likewise reject the miserable little War of 1812, from which we were

---

[21] See *Public Opinion* XXIV, 580 (May 12, 1898); *ibid.*, 615 (May 19, 1898); *Westminster Review,* CL (1898), 168; *Nineteenth Century,* XLIV (1898), 194. A British comment ran: "Unless all signs deceive, the American Republic breaks from her old moorings, and sails out to be a 'world power'." *Blackwood's Edinburgh Magazine,* CLXIII (1898), 703.

[22] Cortelyou's Diary, Aug. 17, 1899, quoted in Margaret Leech, *In the Days of McKinley,* (New York, 1959), 464.

[23] *North American Review,* CLXXII (1901), 177–190.

[24] Modern scholarship has undertaken to show that domestic conditions under the Articles of Confederation were not so bad as traditionally pictured, but the nation's posture in foreign affairs was still weak.

[25] François Barbé-Marbois, *The History of Louisiana* (Philadelphia, 1830), 310–311. Italics inserted.

lucky to escape with a relatively whole skin. Yet forty-seven years ago the historian Charles Francis Adams, Jr., published an article strangely entitled: "Wednesday, August 19, 1812, 6:30 P.M.: The Birth of a World Power." [26] He referred, of course, to the first frigate duel of the War of 1812, in which "Old Ironsides" partially restored American self-esteem by smashing the aged and overmatched *Guerrière*. But the tiny United States Navy, despite heroic individual efforts on the high seas, was ultimately wiped out. The Americans did manage to win a grudging degree of diplomatic and naval respect, particularly for their postwar chastisement of the Barbary states, yet on balance the War of 1812 added little, if anything, to our over-all strength.

I also reject the enunciation of the Monroe Doctrine, which likewise added nothing substantial to our national power. Much as it tickled our own fancy in 1823, it annoyed rather than alarmed Europeans. In their eyes, we seemed to be shaking our fists behind the stout wooden walls of the British navy.

A good case can be made out for the Mexican War as marking the emergence of the United States as a great power—and an imperialistic power at that. We impressed European skeptics, but we impressed ourselves even more. Henry David Thoreau ceased communion with the woodchucks long enough to mention in *Walden* the current discussion of America's being "a first rate power." [27] In an imperialistic coup worthy of the Romans, we sheared away one-half of Mexico, assumed sway over thousands of Spanish-speaking peoples, added one-third again to our continental domain, won a panoramic Pacific frontage, and further validated our claims to being both a Pacific and a Far Eastern power. While still one month deep in the war with Mexico, we stared the British down over the issue of the Oregon boundary, and forced them to yield the disputed triangle north of the Columbia River. This in itself was no mean feat, especially when one considers the booming broadsides of the British navy. But again the European balance of power and the might of the rival French fleet strengthened our hand. [28]

[26] *American Historical Review*, XVIII (1913), 513–521. Adams, oddly enough, refers to the United States in 1812 as "a power of the third class," ranking below Portugal and "more nearly on the level of Algiers" (p. 514).

[27] Henry David Thoreau, *Walden* (Mt. Vernon, N. Y., [1956]), 317. The British scientist Alexander Mackay wrote in 1850 of the United States as being in "the first rank amongst the powers of the earth." *The Western World, or, Travels in the United States in 1846–1847* (London, 1849), II, 284. A British consul in Japan in the late 1850's informed the Japanese that "there were five great nations, viz. France, the Germanic Confederation, Great Britain, Russia, and the United States." C. P. Hodgson, *A Residence at Nagasaki and Hakodate in 1859–1860* (London, 1861), 308.

[28] British statesmen feared that hostilities with America might prompt the French, whose new steam navy was about as strong as Britain's, to invade England with a powerful steamer-borne army. John S. Galbraith, "France as a Factor in the Oregon Negotiations," *Pacific Northwest Quarterly*, XLIV (1953), 69–73.

The end of the Civil War, in my judgment, marks the arrival of the United States as a great power. We were now the third most populous white nation, ranking behind only Russia and France. We had achieved peaceful coexistence among the sections by the greatest constitutional decision of them all: that handed down by Grant at Appomattox Court House. We had washed away the moral incubus of slavery in a bath of blood. We had attained a staggering agricultural productivity, while our smokestacks ranked second only to Britain's. We had an immense navy of about 500 ships, with numerous ironclads, and we boasted the largest standing army in the world—a battle-singed army at that. When Secretary of State Seward demanded that the French clear out of Mexico, he spoke with the voice of one million bayonets—and Napoleon III, for reasons both foreign and domestic, took French leave of his ill-starred puppet Maximilian.

The Civil War had presented both Britain and France with the opportunity of the century. They had long distrusted our explosive power in this hemisphere, they had since 1783 pursued a policy of containment, and they had prayed for the day when they could engage in the hoary game of divide and dominate. But such was the strength of the United States—even a disunited United States locked in the throes of fratricidal conflict—that the two greatest powers of Europe, individually and collectively, shrank from the bloody consequences of armed intervention.[29]

After the Civil War America turned inward. The navy fell prey to worms and decay. Not until the end of the century did we have a modern steel fleet that had forged into about sixth place.[30] The standing army had dwindled to some 28,000 men by 1890, and ranked about thirteenth, below the armies of Belgium, Bulgaria, and Sweden. The usual over-reliance of Europe-centered scholars on military force recently prompted a gifted young diplomatic historian to write for the Voice

---

[29] A writer in the London *Spectator* (March 16, 1861) conceded that the North alone would have enough strength left to "be entitled to rank as a first-class power." XXXIV, 273. Richard Cobden wrote to Charles Sumner in March, 1865, that it was "nothing but your great *power* that has kept the hands of Europe off you." *American Historical Review*, II (1897), 318. The *Spectator* declared in February, 1866, "Nobody doubts any more that the Union is a power of the first class, a nation which it is very dangerous to offend and almost impossible to attack." XXXIX, 177. The same journal conceded in February, 1869, that America was "the greatest power in the whole world." *Ibid.*, XLII, 250. Ignorance of such facts prompted the German General Friedrich von Bernhardi to condemn Britain's "unpardonable blunder" in not supporting the South. *Germany and the Next War* (trans. by A. H. Powles, London, 1914), 94.

[30] Such estimates can be only approximations, owing to differences in types of ships, guns, armor, crews, bases, and other factors. Many European warships were built for short-range operations, and consequently lacked the bunker capacity to cross the Atlantic and engage the American navy.

of America, "Before 1890 the United States was at most a second-rate power."[31]

Let us take a hard look at this "second-rate power" in the eight or so years before the Spanish-American War. By 1890 we were the number two white nation in population, still trying to catch up with the Russians. We had bounded into first place in total manufacturing, including top rank in iron and steel—the standard indices of military potential. In addition, we held either first or second place in railroads, telegraphs, telephones, merchant marine, and in the production of cattle, coal, gold, copper, lead, petroleum, cotton, corn, wheat, and rye. The armies and navies were not there, but we had the means of creating them when we needed them—and did.

The diplomatic box score is most revealing. In a series of breath-taking crises, we forced our adversaries—three of them "great powers"— to come to terms or knuckle under: Germany over the Samoa scramble in 1889; Italy over the New Orleans lynching bee of 1891; Chile over the *Baltimore* brawl in 1891; Britain over the Venezuela boundary imbroglio in 1896.[32] Spain capitulated diplomatically over Cuba in 1898, but we picked a fight with her anyhow and forced her to capitulate militarily.

The flash of Dewey's guns merely spotlighted a maturation that had long since taken place. The irony is that we finally won belated acceptance into the great power "club" by thrashing a second-rate power in two naval engagements that cost us only one life.[33]

I fear that some critics will regard my remarks . . . as academic hairsplitting. Power, world power, great power, superpower—what difference does it all make?

First of all, a failure to read and heed our history contributed to our costly overseas aberration in 1898. If enough of our historians—and

---

[31] Program of October 15, 1959. Ex-Secretary of State Richard Olney, writing in the *Atlantic Monthly* of May, 1898 (and presumably shortly before Dewey's victory), declared "The United States is certainly now entitled to rank among the great Powers of the world." LXXXI, 578.

[32] As early as 1879 the London *Saturday Review* had referred to the United States as "A Power of the first rank." XLVIII (1879), 226. Five years later it bracketed America with "all other great Powers." *Ibid.*, LVII (1884), 333. See also the *Nineteenth Century*, XXI (1887), 799; *Spectator*, LXVII (1889), 532; *Westminster Review*, CXXXI (1889), 508; *Public Opinion*, VII, 229 (June 22, 1889). For an unfavorable view of America's power position, see *Nineteenth Century*, XXXIX (1896), 906–913.

[33] In 1909 Professor F. A. Ogg discerned three schools of thought: (1) we had always been a world power, (2) we became a world power with the Spanish-American War, (3) we had never become a world power. *Dial*, XLVI (1909), 44. Some scholars, mostly European or Europe-centered, would not accord the United States great-power status until 1917–1918, if then. They have been misled by the reluctance of American isolationist elements to face up to the responsibilities of world leadership.

their former students—had been able to say at the time that we had been a world power since 1776, that we had always been a colonizing nation, and that we did not have to wallow in the cesspool of overseas imperialism to prove our stature, we might have spared ourselves the tribulations of keeping up with the imperialistic Joneses.

A misreading of our history likewise accelerated the deadly isolationist drift of the 1920's and 1930's. With uncharacteristic modesty, we Americans confessed that we were greenhorns at the poker table of world politics. We were content to let the white-spatted British and French, old hands at the diplomatic game, breathe life into the stillborn League of Nations. If we had only realized how long, and in what varied areas, we had in fact been a great power, we probably would have been more willing to play a role commensurate with our monstrous strength.

A further misreading of our history has caused us to forget that national power is moral as well as physical. In the formative years of the republic, the three most feared "isms" in the world were probably American republicanism, constitutionalism, and liberalism. They no longer are. Unless we can rekindle some of the dynamic faith in our democracy that we displayed in the nineteenth century, our adversaries will bury us.

Finally, many Americans—including some in high places—evidently have not examined our past with sufficient care to appreciate the extent to which national power is relative. In 1789 we were absolutely weak but relatively strong. Today we are absolutely strong but relatively vulnerable. We can blow up more people than ever before, yet we were never in such mortal danger of annihilation. If we are a supercolossal power under these terrifying conditions, one can hardly avoid a degree of nostalgic respect for the United States of 1776. We were then only a newcomer in the family of nations, but we were, I submit, a world power, and within less than a century we were destined to become a great power.

# 15 / Will We Stay Out of the Next War?

WALTER MILLIS

**Historians have never ceased to debate the causes of World War I, and American historians in particular still speculate**

Reprinted from *The New Republic*, July 31, 1935, pp. 323–27. By permission of the author.

Walter Millis is one of the leading authorities on military history and questions of war and peace. His books include *The Martial Spirit* (1931), *Arms and Men* (1956), and, with others, *Arms and the State* (1958).

about the ultimate causes of America's entry into that war. America's abandonment of neutrality for intervention as a policy instrument was, indeed, a major event in the history of American foreign policy. The way in which we became involved had a great effect on the disillusionment that followed and, over a longer range, on the coming of World War II. So it is useful to examine how the United States became involved in the "Kaiser's war." Although written in 1935, the following analysis remains among the most perceptive.

THE CURRENT DEBATE upon the question of how the United States is to avoid entanglement in the next war should naturally begin with the problem of how, in fact, we got into the last one. In confronting the future, the first guide is the experience of the past. As such, the experience of 1914-17 has the defects of most historical experience. It is confused and baffling in the extreme. The deceptive simplicity of the facts conceals a matted jungle of motives, of conflicting economic and psychological influences, of unstated assumptions as to the proper bases of national action or the nature of the social process. Even to traverse this jungle to any purpose it is necessary first to agree upon certain fixed-datum points, concerning which there is today no agreement; to establish the "cause" of the American declaration of war in April, 1917, one must solve an equation in innumerable variables, although there is as yet no consensus as to the values that should properly be attached to any of them.

It is not difficult to describe what happened. When the European complex exploded in August, 1914, the shock to the American economy was almost as violent as that to the American emotions. The situation was in both respects something with which American opinion and American statesmanship were utterly unprepared to deal. The government issued its formal proclamation of neutrality and consigned the problems of our practical relationship with the warring powers to the uncertain and contradictory principles of international law. The more influential and more vocal elements of public opinion took refuge in an attitude of hostility towards the Central Powers—as reactionary, autocratic governments that had willed the war in the hope of achieving world hegemony—and of sympathy for the Entente as the defenders of ideals and political institutions similar to our own against a brutal and unwarranted aggression. If the government, however, was willing to leave the future to international law, this majority opinion was no less willing to leave it to the Allies. There were very few, in or out of

the government, who either grasped the possibility that the United States might be involuntarily entangled or saw any reasons of national interest that might compel us to become a participant. The United States proposed to take up the role of interested spectator.

Immediately, however, as one writer has recently put it, "the truism that the world is economically interdependent became grimly apparent." It did not appear, it is important to note, in the form of a question as to whether the United States should retreat into a prudent isolation until the storm had passed. We found ourselves isolated, with a devastating abruptness. European selling forced the New York Stock Exchange to close on July 31, 1914, and it dared not reopen until December. Practically the whole of our trans-Atlantic commerce came to a standstill; and if the two belligerents had been equally able to interfere with each other's trade, we might have found ourselves cut off for an indefinite time from all our more important foreign markets. Germany's geographical disadvantage and the overwhelming superiority of the British navy combined to prevent this; the seas were soon reopened, but not to commerce with the Central Powers. Cotton, one of our two great export crops, of which Germany was a heavy taker, could not be sold, and the South was brought to the verge of ruin. At the same time, the normal trade with the Entente countries was, of course, seriously dislocated; and the late summer and fall of 1914 saw our already somewhat depressed economy sinking towards prostration.

The first economic problem presented by the War, consequently, was not one of eschewing the excess profits of death; it was one of regaining some of the ordinary profits of peace. The unemployed, who were filling the streets in the latter part of 1914, had to be provided for no less than the stockholders. Two methods presented themselves. The State Department devoted itself to reopening, so far as possible, the normal channels of trade with the civil population of the Central Powers. The business men, and subsequently the bankers, turned with a greater realism to develop from the war needs of the Entente a substitute for the markets of which they had been deprived in Germany and Austria.

The State Department's attempt to obtain the adoption of the Declaration of London was essentially an attempt to confine the savage violence of the European War within the gentlemanly limits which the Great Powers had in the past been able to impose upon such private quarrels as that between Russia and Japan in 1904. While the armies fought, the normal business of the world would be conducted as usual. The attempt promptly failed, partly because our diplomatists had no conception of the pressures they would have had to apply if it was to succeed; but the Department continued to work to the same end by insisting upon strict construction of the elaborate precedents concerning

blockade and contraband, which are supposed to establish the rights of neutrals in time of war. It was continuously baffled, both by the elusive and frequently inapplicable nature of the precedents and by the practical fact that the British navy possessed the physical power to enforce its own interpretation of them.

Upon this solid basis of sea power, the Allies had, by the beginning of 1915, erected an intricate structure of controls over American foreign commerce. It amounted to a practically complete blockade of our direct trade to and from the Central Powers and a hardly less complete interdiction upon trade by way of the European neutrals. Many of these controls were indirect, maintained by threats and promises rather than by official action, and policed by the "voluntary" undertakings of American business men themselves. It is difficult to say that any of the main features of this system were flatly "illegal," although the British were hard put to it to defend a number of the important details from the bitter protests launched against them by the State Department. Whether the controls were legal or illegal, however, it is possible that the United States could have compelled their relaxation had it applied economic pressure or the threat of war; it is certain that, given the preponderant naval power of the Entente, it could have kept the seas more or less open in no other way.

Such pressures, however, were never seriously applied. Here was the first important consequence of the fact that the majority sentiment of the country had not actually been neutral from the outbreak of the War. The President, his more influential advisers, all the important people in the foreign service (except Secretary Bryan), shared the hostility towards Germany and the sympathy for the Entente that filled every leading newspaper and the after-dinner speeches of most public figures. These sentiments were now being powerfully reinforced by the Entente propaganda; they were likewise being reinforced in another way. American business had turned to solve the problems of war depression by seeking war markets in the Entente. By the end of 1914 it was beginning to find them. The United States started out to supply the Entente because the Entente markets alone were open and because the United States badly needed business. But as the war demand rapidly developed (after the end of the 1914 campaign had revealed to the belligerents the colossal material requirements of the new warfare), it began to be realized that the United States had stumbled upon a gold mine. The Allies' power to offer or withhold these stupendous contracts became one of their most useful instruments in organizing American enterprise to enforce the boycott of Germany while serving the needs of the Entente. The contracts themselves, needless to say, intensified the emotional fervor of all the leading elements of the community for the Entente cause, just as the original sympathy for the

Entente had facilitated the development of the war-supply business.

For the State Department to exert any serious pressure upon the Allies in order to keep open some trade with Germany early became a political, a psychological and an economic impossibility; while the unexpected, seemingly miraculous, appearance of the huge war-supply business removed the original economic motive for such an attempt. Many different and intricately interrelated factors (not all of which need by any means operate in the same way in the event of another foreign war) had combined to produce this result, almost accidentally. Not because of any conscious policy—rather indeed because of the lack of any sufficiently conscious policy—the United States had become a chief source of supply for one side in a life-and-death struggle, at the same time acquiescing in the complete exclusion of the other side from her markets.

The other side inevitably sought for some means of reacting against this situation; and in the spring of 1915 a means was discovered. Here again there is an accidental element in the sequence of events. Had the Germans earlier developed the submarine as a commerce destroyer, it is possible that our economic alliance with the Entente would not have become established as it did; if, on the other hand, they had waited to perfect the weapon before resorting to it, American policy might more clearly have recognized its importance and adjusted itself to the new factor. From the American point of view, the German declaration of the submarine war zone, in February, 1915, came at just the wrong time. It was too late then to revert to the original policy of forcing open the seas for commerce with the civil populations of the belligerents; it was too early to realize the immense strategic value of the new weapon. President Wilson summarily ordered the Germans not to use their submarines as they proposed to do against the American traffic with the Allies. Only later was he to perceive the difficulty of enforcing such an order.

This refusal to accept, or at the least to discuss, the German theory of a maritime war zone must be ascribed in part to the personal temperament of Mr. Wilson, a strong moralist who was at bottom emotionally enlisted on the side of the Allies; in part to the similar temper of the public; in part to the resultant political considerations that made it difficult for any official to seem to favor Germany; in part to Allied propaganda, which discounted the submarines as strategically ridiculous. Though the Germans had a legal case for this use of the submarine, it was, at any rate on the surface, a much weaker one than the Allies' case for their blockade measures; it challenged the conventional ideas of national right in a much more dramatic way, while the whole issue was of course profoundly obscured in the fogs of passion that had accumulated.

Had the proposed war zone ever been seriously discussed, economic considerations must likewise have come into play, for it would have been obvious that the United States could not appear to sanction a free war upon a trade that promised the one means of escape from a serious depression. Actually, few seem to have supposed that the submarines could materially affect our exports, and the issue was met upon a more emotional plane. The President did not attempt to defend the great bulk of the war-supply business that was carried under foreign flags. He did commit himself irrevocably to the demand that the Germans desist from the destruction either of American flag ships or the lives of American citizens on the high seas.

A war situation had thus been prepared, for ultimately there was no peaceful issue from this demand except acquiescence by Germany or its withdrawal by the United States. A war situation does not, of course, inevitably produce a war; accident, however, was again to play a part in intensifying the crisis. The submarine campaign might have developed gradually, in a slow crescendo of incidents, permitting both statesmanship and opinion to work out some peaceful adjustment to the problem. Instead, from February until May the campaign proceeded almost unnoticed, confirming the view that the whole matter was of small consequence, only to explode on May 7, with the torpedoing of the "Lusitania," in an incident so shocking and so unexpected as to render any dispassionate treatment of the broad question very nearly impossible. The "Lusitania" did not bring the United States into the War; it did not even convince any decisive majority of the American people that war was desirable. It did have the important psychological effect of surrounding the President's position on the submarine campaign with an intense emotional field which added to the natural difficulties of retreat and constantly impeded any attempt to remove the war danger that had been created.

The war propaganda continued to operate to bring the public mind to a point at which it would support, if not clamor for, participation in the conflict. The preparedness agitation—in which patriotism seems so inextricably interwoven with less attractive motives that it is now useless even to try to disentangle them—undoubtedly contributed to the same end. The original sympathy with the Entente had been refined and deepened, through the operation of many factors, into an influential belief that permanent world peace might be erected upon an Entente victory; and this supplied a high and impressive reason for bringing the United States into the struggle to assure the victory and participate in the peace system. The growing dependence of our domestic prosperity upon the Entente war orders exerted its far-reaching, if perhaps somewhat subtle, influence. The more closely we became a partner of the Entente, the more genuine a menace, both politically and economically,

did the prospect of German victory become. If at any time the Entente had actually seemed to be on the verge of defeat, the economic factor might have appeared more plainly as a positive force driving us into the war; as it was, its influence was rather the negative one of hindering any attempt to restore the country to a position of more genuine neutrality. The actual declaration was precipitated in another way; and in spite of all these forces working in the direction of our entanglement, it is still not inconceivable that the United States might have remained technically at peace.

It is fair to say that in one sense the United States had entered the European War by the middle of 1915. We were an intimate part of the war complex. Our economic power was wholly enlisted upon one side, and we were no longer neutral either in sentiment or in policy. Even so, a military participation, though likely, was hardly inevitable. In considering a future war there is the question of whether the development of this kind of one-sided relationship to the struggle can be avoided; but there is also the narrower question of whether, once it was established, an astute statesmanship might not still manage to retain a legal neutrality.

What actually effected the transition from legal neutrality to practical belligerence in 1917 was the war situation, prepared by Mr. Wilson with his first stand on the submarine and set, as it were, by the emotional shock of the "Lusitania." The President was able to postpone the crisis for some two years by forcing upon the Germans a long series of compromises and partial surrenders. Although the submarines managed to torpedo many vessels and kill a considerable number of American citizens in the course of this correspondence, the Germans never forced the President to abandon his fundamental position. From the "Lusitania" crisis until the declaration of unrestricted submarine warfare on February 1, 1917, Mr. Wilson emerged substantially successful from each incident that arose. It was in this way that he avoided war. But each success only made a subsequent retreat more difficult for him; as time went on he became more and more the prisoner of his own victories.

The final victory came in May, 1916, when to surmount the "Sussex" crisis he compelled the Germans to agree formally to use their submarines only in accordance with the rules of visit and search. In doing so, however, he posed an issue of American rights upon the high seas in such a form that there was no possible future escape from it. This would have been a satisfactory method of keeping us out of war had Mr. Wilson possessed any threat powerful enough to compel the Germans to live up to the engagement. Unfortunately, he did not; for it requires a very powerful threat indeed to compel a power fighting for its life to leave untouched a weapon it believes to be the key to victory. In January, 1917, the Germans took it up again. They had done what

the President had declared would be a *casus belli,* and what every shade of influential opinion, including his political opponents as well as many of his supporters, had agreed with him would be a *casus belli.* President Wilson found himself almost automatically at war.

This, in brief, is more or less what actually happened. Yet to recount it leaves one with a sense of dissatisfaction. Even at the time, the specific issue of the right of certain American citizens to travel through a war zone seemed inadequate to explain why the people of the United States should be going down into the most frightful and most exhausting war in history. Many of those who urged us on at the time (including the President) were careful to explain that it was not really because of the ship question that we should take up the sword—but in the interests of peace and civilization, or the Monroe Doctrine or international law. Since then, many quite different reasons have been advanced to resolve the conundrum that unquestionably remains. Why did not the United States modify its position on the submarine when the issue was presented with the Gore-McLemore resolutions in February, 1916? We might have warned Americans not to travel in the war zone, left the question of ship sinkings to post-war adjudication (as we left the questions of Entente interference with our cargoes) and allowed the belligerents to decide the issue of the sea war themselves. Why did Mr. Wilson in February, 1917, at once break off diplomatic relations instead of accepting the German action and making the best of it? Why did Congress pass the war resolution, when there was no passionate demand for war in the country and when many of the members themselves probably preferred not to?

For the answer it is necessary to seek among the factors that have already been mentioned—the propaganda, the economic relationships, the personalities of statesmen, the exigencies of domestic politics, the fears and hatreds (whether well founded or not) of German imperialism, the altruistic dreams of world peace. These, however, are all elusive and insubstantial quantities, one shading into another in a baffling fashion and each presenting, when the attempt is made to isolate it as the primarily significant factor, certain difficulties. The influence of "Allied propaganda" for instance is today very generally misconceived. The effective propaganda for the Entente cause was that generated in the United States and by the Americans; undoubtedly it was powerfully reinforced by the spontaneous outpourings from all sources of Entente opinion, but the conscious use of censorship and official propaganda bureaus hardly did more than give precision and effect to forces that could never have been created in that way.

"The bankers" present a similar difficulty. J. P. Morgan and Company, and the other houses that participated in the Entente financing, appear to have been much more the channels than the generators of the forces

they are supposed to have wielded. In the early days they assisted greatly in setting up the machinery that connected the American need for markets with the Entente need for supplies, but they could never themselves have established the tremendous potential they thus helped to discharge. Their machinery at first ran almost entirely upon cash. It was not until the late summer of 1916 that it was necessary to resort to credit upon a significant scale, and by that time domestic prosperity had become so intimately dependent upon the war-supply business that credit must almost certainly have been forthcoming even had the bankers been less eager to supply the facilities. Finally, the private loans floated from that time onward were in general fully secured. The financial crisis that appeared with the beginning of 1917 arose from the fact that the Allies' security was beginning to run out. The point of Mr. Page's famous telegram of March 5, 1917, urging the President to enter the War to save the war-supply business was not that the government should bail out the bankers, but that it should replace them. Here again one must set down the role of the specifically banking interest as at most an indirect one.

One may broaden the charge to cover the whole complex of profit-making business of which the bankers were an essential part. No doubt the "profit motive," as a generalized concept, may be held responsible for almost anything in a profit-making society. More narrowly, there were quite probably many individual business men who perceived that their bread was buttered on the side of belligerency. It is difficult to detect any specific intrigue, however, in which such men selfishly applied pressure to influence the critical decisions of the President or the Congress in regard to the submarine. The profit motive may have helped to get us into a war situation and hindered our attempts to get out, but it did not directly control the transition from formal neutrality to formal belligerence.

There is a similar elusiveness about each of the many other factors that have been cited by one or another commentator as the decisive one. Those who pin the major responsibility upon the vanity and irascibility of President Wilson seldom attempt to explain how another statesman might, in fact, have met the situation as it was abruptly presented to him in February, 1917. Those who cling to the wartime view that the United States actually entered the struggle in order to preserve democratic institutions and the freedom of peoples from a German aggression must still meet many metaphysical difficulties in showing why there was so long a delay in taking up the issue, why so many in 1917 refused to accept this as the true issue and why the mass of the population was still hoping that war would be avoided at the moment it was finally declared upon a point that even at the time seemed to be of relatively minor importance.

The facts of the period from 1914 to 1917 are complex enough to

support almost any theory of historical causation that one may apply to them, at the same time that they are obstinate enough to resist almost any theory of how the ultimate entanglement could have been prevented. An examination of the facts must remain as an essential foundation of any policy designed to control a similar situation in the future. Yet it is to be suspected that before the facts can be of much use there will have first to be agreement upon many profound issues as to the ends which the control should serve, the proper philosophy of international relations, the real character and objects of the state in the international and domestic complex—issues the very existence of which seems to be scarcely realized as yet by most of those participating in the current debate. They have so far confined themselves to the problem of how the nation is to avoid entanglement in another foreign war. The far more important question of whether the nation (whatever they may conceive that to mean) will want to avoid entanglement has hardly even been raised.

# 16 / Failure after Versailles

## JOHN A. GARRATY

If America's entry into World War I was a significant land-mark in the history of United States foreign policy, so the postwar rejection of an organization to enforce the peace was of even greater significance. The Senate's rejection of Woodrow Wilson's idea of "the reign of law, based upon the consent of the governed, and sustained by the organized opinion of mankind" is a major element of America's foreign policy heritage.

AT THE APPROACH of the long-awaited moment, an electric tingle ran through the troops. Thousands of doughboys glanced anxiously at their watches, sweating out the last minutes of a long, brutal, and dirty war. Precisely at eleven o'clock, all along the front from Sedan to the Moselle, the big guns fired a thundering salute. As the echoes reverberated, the

Reprinted from E. S. Miers, ed., *The American Story* (New York: Channel Press, 1956), pp. 289–93. Copyright © 1956 by Broadcast Music, Inc. By permission.

John A. Garraty is professor of history, Columbia University, and the author of *Henry Cabot Lodge: A Biography* (1953), *Woodrow Wilson: A Great Life in Brief* (1956), and other works.

final shells whined across No Man's Land to explode in a chaos of mud, steel, splinters, and human flesh. Then silence. The war was over.

But for the grey, long-jawed, one-time professor in the White House, November 11, 1918 was not an end but a beginning. As countless helmets, grey and olive drab, rose warily from the opposing trenches in the strange stillness of the battlefields, as bold black headlines proclaimed the end of Armageddon, as hysterical civilians stormed and shouted in the streets of Paris, London, and New York, Woodrow Wilson realized that the peace was but a prelude. Ahead lay the vast task of rebuilding battered Europe and establishing a world order that would make another tragic conflict impossible.

No one could say he was not ready. Long months beforehand he had formulated his "Fourteen Points," outlining his blueprint for the better world that was to come with victory. If the plans were somewhat vague, they also vibrated with a high idealism: national self-determination for Europe's oppressed minorities; an end to diplomacy behind closed doors; freedom of the seas and a freer world trade; disarmament; a new colonial policy based on justice to native peoples; and, above all, a League of Nations to guarantee "political independence and territorial integrity to great and small states alike."

To convert this blueprint into a concrete structure, Wilson broke the tradition that no President should leave the country while in office, and ventured in person to Paris, where the world settlement was to be made. At the palace of Versailles, with its vast cobblestoned courtyard, its miles of corridors, its acres of parks and gardens, he met with Britain's Lloyd George, France's Clemenceau, and Italy's Orlando, pitting his idealism and faith against their cynicism and self-interest.

Sitting around a table with these three stocky, white-moustached Europeans, each devoted to the goals of his own nation, Wilson faced an almost impossible task. Clemenceau, "the Tiger," remembering two Germanic invasions of his homeland and determined there must never be another; Lloyd George, "as direct as a zigzag, as unwavering as a weathercock," with one eye on the European balance of power and the other on the ebb and flow of British public opinion; Orlando, silent and almost ignored during the Conference, but stubborn enough to quit it when Italy did not get what he thought was her due—these men had little confidence in Wilson's dreams. Yet by determined adherence to his principles, by pure personal force, Wilson emerged from the grueling Paris discussions with an agreement generally in line with his "Fourteen Points." National self-determination, if not completely carried out, was largely achieved. According to Winston Churchill, the treaty left only 3 per cent of the people of Europe under governments they disliked. A system of international supervision of the former German colonies was set up. And a League of Nations was organized as an integral party of the treaty.

To Wilson, this last was the key to the future hope of the world. To attain it he had sacrificed part of China to Japan, allowed Italy to swallow up some former Austrian territory, and made other concessions. "The structure of peace," he said in a speech, "will not be vital without the League of Nations." But through the League, the principles of disarmament, free trade, freedom of the seas, and open diplomacy—those parts of his fourteen-point program which he had not won in Paris—could eventually be realized.

Wilson returned to America in July, 1919. Though the back-breaking work of treaty making had brought him to the edge of physical collapse, his spirits were high, buoyed up by his bright visions of a new day. The cheering throngs that greeted him in New York and Washington, and the widespread newspaper support for his League of Nations idea, were most encouraging. But trouble loomed ahead. A treaty, as Wilson well knew, was not really a treaty until two-thirds of the Senate had approved it. And Senate approval was not to be easily won.

First of all, a narrow majority of the Senators were Republicans who would be tempted to balk at the work of any Democratic President. Wilson had made a bad mistake in failing to take some important GOP Senator to Paris, thus missing an opportunity to gain bipartisan support for his handiwork. Now success for the treaty might add to the prestige of the Democrats alone, an outcome to be avoided at all costs in Republican eyes. This political difficulty was reinforced by barriers of principle. Membership in an international organization meant abandoning America's "traditional" isolationism and surrendering some measure of the sovereign authority of the United States, so dearly won in the Revolution and enshrined in Jefferson's immortal Declaration of Independence. Some Senators (and a few Democrats were among them) were unalterably opposed to any League of Nations. Led by the shaggy-browed William E. Borah,[1] these so-called "irreconcilables" intended to fight it to the death with every weapon of logic, politics, and emotionalism at their command.

But despite these difficulties, the prospects of Wilson's treaty were not entirely hopeless. The "irreconcilables" were only a small minority. Nearly all the Democrats would back the President, and most Republicans accepted the League idea in principle, arguing only about details. Wilson's driving leadership, the basic sympathy of the people for a plan

---

[1] Borah, "The Lone Lion of Idaho," was consistently a Senator who embraced causes that pleased his own conscience, so that he would be best known (aside from helping to create the Department of Labor) for his advocacy of Woman Suffrage and Prohibition and for his opposition to the internationalism of Wilson and Franklin D. Roosevelt. Told Borah had gone horseback riding, Coolidge looked dubious. "I have always understood that a horseback rider has to go in the same direction as the horse," Coolidge said, a mild-mannered man having a bit of mild-mannered fun.

to promote world peace, and the universal desire to bring a formal end to the war by signing the treaty, all worked in its favor.

Yet there was sure to be a fight. The Republicans were led by Henry Cabot Lodge[2] of Massachusetts. Possessed of a keen intelligence and great oratorical powers, Lodge had an absolute mastery of the ins and outs of parliamentary procedure. His greatest weakness as a statesman was his extreme partisanship. Throughout his career he came perilously close to arguing that the only good Democrat was a dead one. His attitude in 1919 was further colored by his antipathy to Woodrow Wilson, the result of a long series of clashes before and during the war. He once said to Theodore Roosevelt: "I never expected to hate anyone in politics with the hatred I feel towards Wilson." Though Lodge claimed to believe in a bipartisan foreign policy, this hatred was bound to distort his views. Further, as leader of his party his chief aim was to keep it united, which involved concessions to its isolationist wing.

Lodge had little faith in the effectiveness of a world organization. But he was not opposed to the experiment if it were given a Republican stamp, and modified to protect American rights. He therefore proposed a series of reservations, spelling out the obligations of the United States to the League, and the right of Congress to decide just when these obligations should be met.

Some of these reservations were mere quibbles over wording. One, for instance, exempted the Monroe Doctrine from League control, although the treaty had already done so. Others, such as the provision that the United States would not endorse Japan's seizure of Chinese territory, were added only to embarrass Wilson by pointing up compromises he had been forced to make at Versailles. The most important reservation stated that America's obligation to guarantee the territory and independence of League members against aggression could not be invoked "unless in any particular case . . . Congress . . . should by act or joint resolution so provide."

But the President would not agree even to minor modifications. Already some of his Fourteen Points had been lost at Versailles; he had made his last concession. As sentiment for further changes developed he resorted to a desperate step. Against the advice of his doctors, who told him he must not submit his already exhausted body to further strains, he embarked on a nationwide tour to rally the people to his cause. But before he had carried his campaign far enough to test its effectiveness, the

---

[2] Lodge, Republican leader of the Senate Foreign Relations Committee, had lectured at Harvard and won recognition as an historian at the age of thirty. He was one of the group whom Wilson castigated as "a little group of willful men, representing no opinion but their own." Curiously, and with history's rare sense of humor, Lodge's grandson and namesake became the American representative to, and stanch supporter of, the League's successor organization, the United Nations.

predictions of the physicians came to pass. After making a speech in Pueblo, Colorado, Wilson collapsed, and suffered a crippling stroke. For months thereafter he was confined to his bed, inaccessible to friend and foe alike.

Thus the Democrats, already a minority, were deprived of his leadership in the battle over reservations. One by one, under the masterly hand of Lodge, the Republicans tacked their reservations to the Covenant. That accomplished, all but the "irreconcilable" die hards were ready to ratify it. Then, as the final vote approached, Wilson stirred himself. To vote for the treaty now, he warned the Democratic Senators, would not be to ratify it but to nullify it. "I trust that all true friends of the treaty will refuse to support the Lodge resolution."

On November 19, 1919, before packed galleries, in an atmosphere charged with tension, the Senators responded to the calling of the roll. When it was over, the treaty had failed—the Democrats had joined with the "irreconcilables" to defeat it.

So perished Wilson's dream of American participation in the League of Nations. An effort to revive the treaty a few months later met a similar fate. We shall never know what course history might have taken had the United States joined. But looking back from our present position of international leadership, this much is clear. Without America, the League failed. Millions of lives were sacrificed in a second catastrophe, which real international co-operation could have prevented.

Who must bear the blame? Certainly the "irreconcilables," who set their faces against the march of progress and spread prejudice and hatred among the people. Certainly also Lodge, who put his party above patriotism and cynicism above hope. But also Woodrow Wilson. When every responsible leader—Democrat and Republican alike—urged compromise, he alone stood stubbornly against Lodge's reservations. Former President Taft, who worked harder for the League than perhaps any single American, summed up the situation in a sentence: Wilson and Lodge, he said, "exalt their personal prestige and the saving of their ugly faces above the welfare of the country and the world."

# 17 / Building the Atlantic Partnership: Some Lessons from the Past

MC GEORGE BUNDY

A sharp contrast exists between the isolationist American foreign policy of the 1920's and the 1930's and America's involvement in the defense of the nations of the North Atlantic—and elsewhere—since 1949. In the following selection, Mr. Bundy considers "some lessons from the past" and some requirements of the future, with particular reference to Western Europe.

. . . THERE ARE very large negative lessons for us in the record of the years between 1925 and 1940 and very large affirmative lessons in the record of the years between 1947 and the present.

We all know the gloomy record of Atlantic diplomacy between Locarno and the fall of France, and it is not my aim here to recapitulate it. The greatest of our failures, of course, was in the failure to develop common policies and purposes of sufficient coherence to prevent—and later to deal with—the rise of Adolf Hitler. In this failure there is blame enough for all of us; I do not know of a country now in the Atlantic alliance whose people and leaders I should wish to represent today in a claim before history of total innocence. Each of us is able to write and speak with particular zest, perhaps, of the shortcomings of others—but this is hardly a profitable exercise. Let me instead suggest a series of more general comments.

## The Legacy of the Thirties

In the first place one must put the dangers of neutrality or appeasement as means of dealing with a determinedly expansionist power. This is a point which needs no laboring in this audience. But it is not always the simple points which are the least important. This one deserves continuous and straightforward repetition.

From U. S. Department of State, *Department of State Bulletin*, XLVII (October 22, 1962), 601–4.

McGeorge Bundy is a political scientist who has been dean of the Faculty of Arts and Sciences, Harvard University, and special assistant for National Security Affairs in the administrations of Presidents Kennedy and Johnson. He is co-author, with Henry L. Stimson, of *On Active Service in Peace and War* (1948) and editor of *The Pattern of Responsibility* (1952).

Second, and more subtly, we can, I think, discern in the history of the years from 1925 to 1939 an astonishing tendency to miss the real issues through a preoccupation with rivalries that became wholly pointless when the real themes of history were unfolded.

What do we care now for the contest between the franc and the pound which so engrossed able and determined men on both sides? At the onset of the thirties what we remember now is only that this contest was a part of the shortsighted and self-destructive approach to money which deepened the great depression and helped Hitler to power.

What do we now remember of the revulsion against war and its propaganda which led Americans to suppose that the Allies, not the U-boat, had been the real cause of our entry into the first war, so that our contribution to the keeping of Atlantic peace in the 1930's was a series of solemn legislative acts against commitment—acts of neutrality. What matters today is that those acts, in the early years of Hitler's weakness, served to give him assurance that America saw the enemy more in alliance than in aggression.

And we forget, behind the general failures named appeasement, how often in the 1930's it was a narrow suspicion of the wrong people that became the immediate cause, or excuse, for inaction—the Italians mistrusting the French, the French mistrusting the British, the British mistrusting the Czechs, Mussolini mistrusting everyone until in a final irony he was the last to try trusting Hitler. This detailed record of the follies of nations which tried to act alone carries a deeper lesson than simply the warning against appeasement. And that lesson is that already in the 1930's no foreign nation could serve itself well if it tried to serve itself alone. The aggressions of Hitler and Mussolini proved it for everyone else, and their failures proved it for their own still unhappier countries.

A third lesson from the 1930's is that governments without courage can be expected at critical moments to take wrong decisions which they will defend on grounds of domestic political necessity. Perhaps the sorriest of these demonstrations is to be found in the history of the war debts from start to finish, but other examples are available in such numbers that the choice is one of taste. Over and over again, when the need was urgent and the right course clear, men in authority held back their diplomatic hands lest they lose their political heads.

It is not for any officeholder to assert that this course is always wrong. Diplomats who ignore domestic political realities are deeply unprofessional. But it remains fair to remark of the 1930's that they record an immensely long list of follies committed in shortsighted subservience to supposed opinion—and a correspondingly short list of men who preferred retirement to timidity.

In this assertion I do not mean to leave public opinion itself exempt from criticism. This is no place for an excursion into the endless fascina-

tions of the relation between opinion and leadership; my argument does not require any assumption that the fault was all with statesmen. Opinion too was at fault—and in a variety of ways—and it may well be that in the widest of perspective later students may find that what was needed to permit avoidance of all the errors I have cited was precisely the terrible process of retribution and instruction which we call the Second World War. But we cannot afford additional instruction today.

Finally, in this set of gloomy flashbacks let me recall what we may call the error of the empty commitment. The greatest of failures was the League, and the earliest of blows to that institution was struck by the United States. But there is in addition a long and melancholy set of ties that did not bind and words that did not work: The Kellogg-Briand Pact was always empty and the French tie to Czechoslovakia broke only when it was needed, but there remains a family resemblance among them. Both represented efforts to exorcise by words a problem which could only be dealt with by will and by works. Promises—to oneself or to others—cannot prevent danger unless they mean to meet it.

### The Affirmative Present

I hope you will feel, as I do, that it is time to move to more cheerful themes, to the set of lessons of a very different sort which may be drawn from our common experience in the years since we set about the great business of Atlantic reconstruction and reordering, since 1947. And let me urge it upon you, sweepingly, that the record shows us to have made much progress in avoiding all four of the major failures I have just charged to an earlier time.

First, we have abandoned neutrality and appeasement in the face of the Soviet threat, which in its gravity and in long-range importance has required the structure of political and military commitment that we call NATO. This is not so remarkable a change for some of our nations as it is for others, but here in Copenhagen I may perhaps fittingly note how deep and significant the decision has been for countries as different—and as much alike too—as Denmark and the United States. Indeed for us Americans it is this single, simple fact of commitment to the Atlantic alliance that is repeatedly decisive in the whole range of our relations to Europe. We are in, and in to stay.

Second, we have all of us succeeded, over and over again, in putting the larger common interest ahead of small national rivalries. One thinks here of such notable and farsighted acts as that of France in the Saar—and indeed of the wider process of reconciliation which has marked the behavior of many countries toward Germany. One thinks also—as Mr. Stikker [Dirk Stikker, Secretary General of NATO] so generously said . . . of the Marshall Plan, and in return I may say that in America we

understand also what an important, and unprecedented, trust the old and proud people of Europe have shown in us by their acceptance of special American leadership in the military affairs of NATO. We believe that the tradition of Eisenhower, Gruenther, Ridgway, and Norstad has been a notable one—and we expect it to continue in distinguished fashion under General Lemnitzer. But we do recognize that it takes maturity to accept as well as to offer this kind of leadership.

But perhaps the most striking example of choosing the wide as against the narrow interest is to be found in the policy followed with such determination, for so long, by the German Federal Republic under Chancellor Adenauer. Not many years ago one could find in German politics many deeply different tendencies. There were some who hoped that answers might be found in some form of neutralism; others appeared to lean toward a renewed nationalism in which German and only German aspirations would govern policy. But in the event what has prevailed is a policy of determined devotion to freedom, determined and ever more intimate integration both in Europe and in the Atlantic alliance, and determined reconciliation among all the Western Europeans who shared, on either side, in the catastrophe of nazism. Never giving up the deep concern which all of us feel for all the Europeans—Germans, Poles, Czechs, and others—whose true destiny is to rejoin us in the tradition of civility and the purpose of freedom, the Chancellor has never wavered in his knowledge that progress toward these hopes can be made on no other basis than that of unity and mutual commitment as among ourselves. This has seemed to us in America, for 15 years, to be a wise, brave, and farsighted policy, and it has had our steady support.

Third, and still in contrast with the time before the Second War, we have repeatedly seen since 1947 that political courage does exist—and is not always punished—in our affairs. I have just spoken of the special leadership shown in the Federal Republic. Other notable cases are to be found in many countries, in the processes which have led to the construction of the new institutions of Europe. Now that the Common Market is a great success, we tend to forget that brave men had to press for it against wide and varied opposition. And courage of a high and tempered variety has been shown too in the extraordinary successes of transmutation under which so many colonial holdings have been wisely set free. The diplomats and political leaders who have accepted and defended their part in these events will not be badly treated by history. Indeed their wisdom is already apparent as the new and postcolonial Europe moves forward like a swimmer who has dropped a heavy weight.

Finally, in this catalog of happy changes we may set the fact that we now have treaties and commitments whose reality is attested in a thousand ways. Again this needs no proof to you, as friends of NATO; so let me simply cite as an immediate example the case of the United States.

We have not merely signed article 5; we have not merely joined in mutual defense arrangements for arms and equipment of constantly more modern types; we have not merely committed our prestige and our purpose by a series of appointments of our leading soldiers to the NATO command in Paris: We have emplaced in Europe weapons—of all sorts—in a strength which far outweighs the total explosive power employed by both sides in both wars, and we have sealed the whole by the presence in Europe— essentially in forward development and above all in Germany—of 400,000 men. Insofar as American strength can defend it, free Europe is as safe as any State in the American Union. This American strength will remain as long as it is wanted in Europe and as long as the alliance continues to grow on the basis of shared trust and shared effort. To think otherwise would be to mistake the 1960's for the 1930's.

There are other lessons, beyond these of direct contrast, to be drawn from our experiences of the last 15 years:

There is our new skill in creating international institutions—squaring the circle of traditional political theory by showing that in societies which wish it so high responsibilities can be shared without destroying the nation.

There is our success in growing a new generation of professional servants of the West, men whose loyalty to their own countries remains undoubted while at the same time they see the military—or the monetary— or the trading problems of the whole of our community as one. These new expert professionals are not always right. Political leadership is properly needful and decisive in the community as a whole, just as it is in each individual state. Still there is a special meaning to these new classes of men who work as colleagues in the professions that underpin the community; it is and should continue to be a source of strength to us. And I will not labor on other points, because your presence shows that you believe it: The new Atlantic community has been extraordinarily dependent throughout its life on the support, the understanding, and the leadership of private citizens.

I have come a long way through two contrasting chapters of the past toward my few comments on the future. Fortunately most of what I want to say I have managed to say along the way, and I can summarize it in one or two sentences.

We must avoid false hopes of isolation; we must rise above petty national rivalries; we must see to it that our commitments are real and strong; we must—people and leaders alike—have the courage of our convictions. We must go on, step by practical step, with the construction of a partnership in which the United States—and other countries too—will be closely bound to the emerging Europe in a series of constantly growing ways.

# 18 / United States Tasks on the World Scene

WALT W. ROSTOW

The following selection is a succinct history of the cold war:
It categorizes two major Communist offensives in the cold
war, that of Stalin and the later one of Khrushchev. Mr.
Rostow made this analysis while serving as counselor and
chairman of the Policy Planning Staff, Department of State.

I SHOULD LIKE to consider with you today where we stand in the
cold war. . . .

It is more than seventeen years now since, in a speech of February,
1946, Stalin made absolutely clear that the Soviet Union intended in the
postwar world not to make peace, but to struggle actively for world
power. Thus, we as a nation have been at the business of cold war for
almost a generation.

What has it been like? What shape can we perceive, looking back
from the autumn of 1963, in this tangled story of struggle which has absorbed so much of our resources, talents, and energy and is likely to do
so over the foreseeable future?

## I

Broadly speaking, what we have experienced are two major Communist offensives. The first was Stalin's. Beginning in 1946 he launched
major thrusts: first in the West, then in the East.

In the West, Stalin, although set back in Iran, increased Soviet pressure against Turkey by diplomacy and threat during the summer of 1946;
in Greece, by supporting substantial guerrilla warfare; and in Italy and
France, by vigorous Communist Party efforts to gain parliamentary power.
In 1947 he accelerated the movement toward total control in Eastern
Europe, symbolized by the creation of the Cominform in September
1947. He succeeded in Prague (in the coup of February 1948), but failed
in Belgrade where Tito's defection was announced in June 1948.

But from early 1947 the Western counterattack began with the Truman Doctrine and the Marshall Plan. The election in April 1948 saved

---

Reprinted from U. S. Department of State Press Release No. 594 (November 19,
1963), pp. 1–5; excerpt from an address by Mr. Rostow at the University of California
at Los Angeles, November 20, 1963.

A brief biographical sketch of Mr. Rostow appears with article 9.

Italy, and the Communist effort in Greece fell apart in the face of the Greek effort and Communist schisms. France found a group of center parties capable of governing, if uncertainly, and containing the domestic Communist menace.

Germany drifted, from the spring of 1946, toward a split; and the resulting deadlock in the Berlin Control Council was dramatized by the Soviet walkout of March 20, 1948, which set the stage for the full blockade on the ground three months later. The success of the airlift ended, in effect, Stalin's main thrust to the West. The process set in motion by his offensive, however, yielded not merely the Marshall Plan but the Brussels Pact (September 1948), NATO (March 1949), and the creation (May 1949) of the Federal Republic of Germany with its close ties to West Berlin.

As this duel in the West proceeded, Stalin launched an offensive in the East which can be roughly dated from the injunction of Zhdanov to the Communist parties in Asia at the founding meeting of the Cominform in September 1947 to shift from politics to insurrection. Open guerrilla warfare began in Indochina as early as November 1946; in Burma, in April 1948; in Malaya, in June; and in Indonesia and the Philippines, in the autumn. The Indian and Japanese Communist parties, with less scope for guerrilla action, nevertheless sharply increased their militancy in 1948. As the Communist victory was won in China in November 1949, Mao's political-military strategy was openly commended by the Cominform to the Communist parties in those areas where guerrilla operations were under way. The meeting of Stalin and Mao early in 1950 undoubtedly confirmed the ambitious Asian strategy and planned its climax in the form of the North Korean invasion of South Korea, which took place at the end of June 1950.

The American and United Nations response to the invasion of South Korea, the landings at Inchon, the march to the Yalu, the Chinese Communist entrance into the war, and the successful United Nations defense against massive Chinese assault in April–May 1951 at the 38th parallel brought this phase of military and quasi-military Communist effort throughout Asia to a gradual end. Neither Moscow nor Peiping was willing to undertake all-out war or even to accept the cost of a continued Korean offensive. And elsewhere the bright Communist hopes of 1946–47 had dimmed. Nowhere in Asia was Mao's success repeated. Indonesia, Burma and the Philippines largely overcame their guerrillas. At great cost to Britain, the Malayan guerrillas were contained and driven back. Only in Indochina did local conditions favor real Communist momentum; but Ho Chi Minh was finally forced to settle for half a victory (Geneva, 1954) in the wake of Stalin's death and in the shadow of possible United States intervention.

Where were we, then, when the truce negotiations on Korea began in

the summer of 1951? Stalin had consolidated Eastern Europe; Mao, China. But the global balance of power still lay—even if precariously—with the Free World. And the West, led by the United States, had answered three basic questions which underlay the hopes of Communist planners. First, it was demonstrated that the United States commitment to Europe had survived the war. We had not repeated our tragic return to isolation which followed victory in 1918. Second, it was demonstrated that Western Europe had emerged from the Second World War with the capacity to find again its economic, social and political vigor and, with American aid, to fend off the Communist thrusts against the Eastern Mediterranean, Italy, France and, climactically, against Berlin. Third, it was demonstrated in Korea that the United States and the Free World as a whole had the will and capacity to deal with an aggressive thrust with conventional forces across the truce lines of the cold war.

## II

After an interval of relative quiet in the cold war—roughly between the summer of 1951 and the launching of Sputnik in October 1957—the second great Communist offensive was launched. This was Khrushchev's bid decisively to shift the balance of world power against the West.

It is worth asking why the negotiations, looking towards peace, undertaken in the 1950's and the mood of *detente* created, for example, by the Summit Conference of 1955, were broken. In retrospect I think the answer is clear. Two major new factors had emerged on the world scene, and Soviet policy-makers evidently came to the conclusion that they could be turned to major advantage. It was on these two new factors that Khrushchev's offensive was built.

First, there was the emergence in the 1950's of thermonuclear weapons and the possibility of their delivery over long distances by rockets. For the first time the Soviet Union was put in a position of being able to threaten the destruction of Western Europe and the imposition of massive direct damage on the United States. Contemplating these instruments, Moscow evidently judged it possible, in their shadow to force the West to make limited diplomatic concessions at decisive points. The theme of nuclear blackmail first emerged in Soviet policy in 1956, most notably during the Suez crisis.

The second great new factor on the world scene, which evidently inflamed Soviet hopes, was the marked acceleration in the revolutions of nationalism and modernization in Asia, the Middle East, Africa and Latin America. There is no doubt that Moscow came to believe that it had deeply rooted advantages in seeking to expand Communist power and influence in these regions, at the expense of the West, by orchestrat-

ing flexibly the devices of subversion and guerrilla warfare; trade and aid; appeal to anti-colonialism and nationalist sentiments; and by the claim that communism was not merely the fast-closing rival of the United States, but the possessor of a method for the more efficient—even if ruthless—modernization of an underdeveloped region. The 1955 arms deal with Egypt and the agreement to build the Aswan Dam represented the first major efforts along these lines.

But it was only after the launching of Sputnik in October 1957 that the second great Communist offensive of the postwar years was fully launched. It was in 1958 that Moscow laid down its ultimatum on Berlin. It was in 1958 that the Communist Party in Hanoi announced it would undertake a guerrilla war in South Viet-Nam. Soon afterward, the Pathet Lao, with the active help of Communist North Viet-Nam, resumed their effort to take over Laos. It was in these first post-Sputnik years that the Soviets sought to exploit the potentialities for acquiring in the Congo a Communist base for operations in central Africa; it was then they invested a billion dollars in military aid in an effort to induce friction, if not war, between Indonesia and the Netherlands over West New Guinea and also to strengthen Soviet influence and the Communist position in Indonesia. It was also, perhaps fortuitously, at the end of 1958 that Castro took over in Cuba.

At two points the forward momentum of the post-Sputnik Communist thrust was slowed down by major and successful United States actions: in the Lebanon-Jordan and Quemoy-Matsu crises of 1958. But, as of January 1961, Khrushchev's offensive had considerable momentum in Southeast Asia, Africa and Latin America.

### III

The first charge on the Kennedy Administration in 1961—somewhat like the challenge faced by the Truman Administration early in 1947—was to turn back this Communist offensive by demonstrating that the two hypotheses on which it was built were not viable. Roughly speaking, between May 1961, when a precarious ceasefire in Laos was arranged, and the October 1962 missile crisis in Cuba, the task was substantially accomplished.

The answer to the first question posed by Soviet policy—our possible vulnerability to nuclear blackmail—was given by the whole course of the Berlin affair in 1961–62, including especially the President's July 1961 speech and the subsequent military build-up. After the failure of the Soviet effort in February–March 1962 to crack the unity of the Western Alliance by intruding into the Berlin air corridors, Moscow apparently judged the Berlin position of the West too difficult to undermine directly. The Cuban missile gambit was then mounted, and

its *dénouement* brought to an end, for the time being at least, the notion that vital interests of the Free World would be surrendered under the threat of nuclear war.

The answer to the second question—concerning the ability of the West to avoid Communist takeover in the underdeveloped areas—had to be given at many points by many devices: In Laos, by an evident determination to frustrate a Communist takeover; in Viet-Nam, by the mounting from December 1961 of a massively enlarged counter-insurgency program; in Indonesia, by the successful negotiation over West New Guinea by the Netherlands and Indonesian Governments; in Africa, by the whole cast of our approach to the new African nations— in particular, our support for the United Nations effort in the Congo; in Latin America, by the isolation of Communist Cuba, combined with the Alliance for Progress.

By the end of the Cuban missile crisis in the autumn of 1962, the momentum had drained out of Khrushchev's post-Sputnik offensive, despite the unresolved crises in Cuba and Southeast Asia.

In the course of this sequence, situations emerged which were bound to affect the future of Soviet policy. First, Western Europe continued to display an astonishing economic momentum, not matched since 1914; and it moved toward great-power status, with a strong likelihood of expansion, in one form or another, of its nuclear role. Moscow cannot count on Western Europe remaining indefinitely a hostage to Soviet MRBM's without actively participating in the task of deterring those MRBM's.

Second, quite aside from the efforts of the United States to deal with the major dimensions of the Communist thrust into underdeveloped areas, those nations and peoples demonstrated a capacity to defend their independence with increasing skill and determination and with an increased understanding of Communist objectives and methods. The over-all trend of recent events in Asia, the Middle East, Africa and Latin America, while still marked by dangerous instability capable of Communist exploitation, made the notion of Moscow control over those areas an increasingly unrealistic prospect, although this difficult conclusion has evidently not been fully absorbed in the policies of Moscow, let alone Peiping, Hanoi, and Havana.

Third, within the Communist bloc the assertion of nationalist impulses—notably in the Sino-Soviet split, but elsewhere as well— shattered the intellectual unity and organizational discipline of the international Communist movement. The process also yielded the possibility that the Chinese Communists might emerge with some kind of independent nuclear capability within a time span relevant to current planning.

Fourth, quite aside from the chronic inability of Communist nations to grow food efficiently, a marked industrial deceleration began to take

hold in the Soviet Union and Eastern Europe as the heavy industry sectors on which postwar momentum was built ran their inevitable course. In 1962 the countries of NATO had an average growth rate of 4.8 percent of GNP; the Communist bloc—leaving wallowing Communist China aside—of 3.6 percent. The effect of this deceleration, which has brought the over-all Soviet growth rate down in recent years from something like 7 percent to, perhaps, 4 percent or less, is to reduce the annual increment of Soviet resources available for allocation to military, foreign policy and domestic purposes, although the declining industrial growth rate is still quite high.

Finally, while Moscow's post-Sputnik offensive was being conducted with great éclat and considerable acceptance of risk, long-run trends operating in Russia and Eastern Europe tended to liberalize somewhat those societies, as well as to strengthen nationalist strands within them and the popular will for peace.

# For Further Reading

ADLER, SELIG. *The Isolationist Impulse* (New York: Abelard-Schuman, 1957).

ALMOND, GABRIEL. *The American People and Foreign Policy*, rev. ed. (New York: Praeger, 1960).

American Academy of Arts and Sciences. "American Foreign Policy—Freedoms and Restraints," *Daedalus*, Fall, 1962.

CARLETON, WILLIAM G. *The Revolution in American Foreign Policy* (New York: Random House, 1963).

Council on Foreign Relations. *The United States in World Affairs*. 15 vols. (New York: Harper, 1947–64).

CRABB, CECIL V., JR. *American Foreign Policy in the Nuclear Age* (Evanston, Ill.: Row, Peterson and Co., 1960).

EARLE, EDWARD MEAD. "A Half Century of American Foreign Policy: Our Stake in Europe, 1898–1948," *Political Science Quarterly*, June, 1949.

FEIS, HERBERT. *The China Tangle* (Princeton: Princeton University Press, 1953).

————. *The Road to Pearl Harbor* (Princeton: Princeton University Press, 1950).

FLEMING, D. F. *The Cold War and Its Origins*. 2 vols. (Garden City, New York: Doubleday, 1961).

HUNTINGTON, SAMUEL P. *The Soldier and the State* (Cambridge, Mass.: Harvard University Press, 1957).

IRISH, MARIAN D., ed. *World Pressures on American Foreign Policy* (Englewood Cliffs, N.J.: Prentice-Hall, 1964).

KENNAN, GEORGE F. *American Diplomacy 1900–1950* (Chicago: University of Chicago Press, 1951).

LIPPMANN, WALTER. *U.S. Foreign Policy* (Boston: Little, Brown, 1943).

LANGER, WILLIAM L., and EVERETT S. GLEASON. *The World Crisis and American Foreign Policy: The Challenge to Isolation, 1937–1940* (New York: Harper, 1953).

LEOPOLD, RICHARD. *The Growth of American Foreign Policy, A History* (New York: Knopf, 1962).

NEUSTADT, RICHARD E. *Presidential Power: The Politics of Leadership* (New York: John Wiley and Sons, 1960).

PERKINS, DEXTER. *The American Approach to Foreign Policy*, rev. ed. (Cambridge, Mass.: Harvard University Press, 1962).

REITZEL, WILLIAM, MORTON A. KAPLAN, and C. G. COBLENZ. *United States Foreign Policy, 1945–1955* (Washington, D.C.: The Brookings Institution, 1956).

ROBERTS, HENRY L. *Russia and America* (New York: Harper, 1956).

ROSTOW, WALT W. *The United States in the World Arena* (New York: Harper, 1960).

STEIN, HAROLD, ed. *American Civil-Military Decisions: A Book of Case Studies* (University, Ala.: University of Alabama Press, 1963).

SPANIER, JOHN W. *American Foreign Policy Since World War II*, rev. ed. (New York: Praeger, 1962).

WESTERFIELD, H. BRADFORD. *Foreign Policy and Party Politics: Pearl Harbor to Korea* (New Haven, Conn.: Yale University Press, 1955).

WILLIAMS, WILLIAM APPLEMAN. *The Tragedy of American Diplomacy* (Cleveland, Ohio: World, 1959).

# III  THE MILITARY INSTRUMENT

## 19 / The Development of Political-Military Consultation in the United States

ERNEST R. MAY

Until recently, the United States during most of her history has conceptualized peace and war, power, and diplomacy in separate compartments. Thus, military power was not regarded as a standard foreign policy instrument but rather as a last resort when policy "failed." And when war came, the idea of the primacy of political objectives was neither followed nor understood. Little attention was paid to the logical maxim of Karl von Clausewitz that "war is nothing but a continuation of political intercourse with an admixture of other means." This selection traces the history of political-military coordination which, until very recent times, has been in fact more a history of the failure to coordinate power and diplomacy.

. . . MILITARY FORCES are the rooks and bishops behind the knights and pawns of diplomacy; although the rooks and bishops move less frequently, their rôle in the game is not less decisive. Before the executors of foreign policy can decide what the nation ought to do, they must learn from political and military experts what the nation is able to do. They must lay objectives alongside capabilities, in the same way that business men compare the blueprints of design engineers with the estimates of cost accountants. In making foreign policy, in other words, ends must be measured against means.

Although this rationale won acceptance only recently, it is not new, even in the United States. Nowhere, in fact, is it more vigorously summarized than in Number 23 of the *Federalist Papers*, written by Alex-

Reprinted from the *Political Science Quarterly*, LXX (June, 1955), 161–80. By permission. Footnotes have been omitted.

Ernest R. May is professor of history, Harvard University, and the author of *The World War and American Isolation* (1959), *Imperial Democracy* (1961), and other works.

ander Hamilton. But long years of isolated safety smothered the idea of political-military collaboration. It found no new spokesman until Captain Mahan began to preach, late in the nineteenth century. Even then, the idea was not translated into action until after the conquest of the Philippines, when a few Americans, looking across six thousand miles of water at their new colony, began to believe that the United States had grafted to itself an Achilles heel. They perceived that the safety of this faraway member could not, like the safety of the homeland, be entrusted to Providence.

Realizing the need for hard, far-sighted planning, this handful of Americans also realized their lack of any planning instruments. The State Department, as Tyler Dennett characterizes it in his life of John Hay, was an "antiquated, feeble organization, enslaved by precedents and routine inherited from another century, remote from the public gaze and indifferent to it. The typewriter was viewed as a necessary evil and the telephone as an instrument of last resort." Although the Army and Navy had professionals, while the State Department had none, the armed services were still no better outfitted for strategy-planning than the State Department for policy-planning. Before the Army and Navy could produce coherent advice they had to nurture brains or general staff organizations, and such brains developed slowly. The Army's General Staff, for instance, was "only just growing to man's estate" fifteen years after its founding, according to the 1918 report of its Chief of Staff. This General Staff and the Navy General Board faced, in addition, the problem of welding Army and Navy differences, so that military advice on policy could be based on estimates of the total military power of the United States. Until a Joint Board of the Army and Navy and the State Department, too, perfected their internal workings, the coördination of strategy and policy could only be haphazard.

During the first two decades after the War with Spain, as a result, consultation among the State, War, and Navy Departments took the antique form of correspondence among the three secretaries. The Navy Secretary, advised by his General Board, would write to the Secretary of State, proposing acquisition of a certain naval base on foreign soil. After referring the proposal to such experts as he could collect, the Secretary of State would return his judgment, either killing the idea or pushing it up for final decision by the President.

Like sophomore letters home, these begging communications from the Secretary of the Navy sometimes hinted casually at subjects under study. The Navy revealed its concern with Panama, for instance, by requesting bases across all the sea approaches to the Isthmus—on the coast of Peru, off the Pacific coast of Panama, on Fonseca Bay, and in Cuba. Never, before completion of the canal, did the Navy General Board say that the Isthmus was of vital importance to the military

security of the United States. Alert eyes in the State Department might have detected this thought in the Board's selections of naval bases. And eyes even less alert might have perceived the concept in two bolder letters, reminding the State Department that no great Power should be allowed to perch on Ecuador's Galápagos Islands or on Haiti's Môle St. Nicholas. But the Navy and Army rarely let fall such clues to their strategic thinking.

Neither did the State Department share its political thinking with the services. In the archives of the McKinley, Roosevelt and Taft Administrations, I have yet to find a letter from a Secretary of State, asking for a military cost accounting before some diplomatic stroke. Although Taft's Secretary of State did occasionally ask the fleet to back up his diplomacy, he never inquired ahead of time about the fleet's location and make-up. Thus, in May 1912, when unrest was sweeping Cuba, the Secretary asked for "a considerable naval force . . . in the vicinity of Havana." Only by chance, or as a result of naval clairvoyance, did nine warships happen to be handy at Key West.

Letter writing in the State, War, and Navy Departments failed to bring about effective coördination of policies. As a rule, in fact, diplomatic and military recommendations reached the White House separately, and the relationship between political aims and military capabilities had to be gauged, if at all, by the President. Although this rule-of-thumb system could work for a strategy-minded President like Theodore Roosevelt, it displayed its failing even in his time.

In the summer of 1907, for example, the budding American high command, the Joint Board of the Army and the Navy, discussed the hostility growing between the United States and Japan. Realizing that war, if it came, would find most of the American fleet in the Atlantic, the Board proposed a precautionary shift of battleships to the Pacific, then asked the Secretaries of War and the Navy to suggest such a shift to the President. The Secretaries did so, writing to Roosevelt at Oyster Bay, and Roosevelt agreed, choosing, however, to disguise the movement as a good will cruise. Although he seems to have reached this decision without delay, Roosevelt waited from late June until mid-July before notifying his Secretary of State, who was still in Washington. For several weeks, therefore, the Secretary of State duelled with Japanese diplomats, wholly unaware, so far as the records show, of the Navy's preparations for a warlike gesture!

The first advances from haphazard coördination-by-letter to coördination-by-conference were made, paradoxically, under an administration that would never have endorsed the rationale of political-military collaboration. President Woodrow Wilson may even have denied the need for long-range military planning. At any rate, two generals swore after World War I that Wilson had given verbal orders forbidding the Army and Navy to construct hypothetical war plans. During his Administration, further-

more, a pacifist sat for two years as Secretary of State, a near-pacifist ruled the Navy Department, and a Quaker became Secretary of War.

Perhaps a prevailing attitude of the Administration was expressed on one occasion by this pacifist Secretary of State, William Jennings Bryan. Renewed tension with Japan had brought before the Cabinet another Joint Board recommendation for a fleet movement to anticipate the possibility of war. According to one member of the Cabinet, David F. Houston, this recommendation angered Bryan, who "flared up . . . got red in the face and was very emphatic. He thundered out that army and navy officers could not be trusted to say what we should or should not do, till we actually got into war; that we were discussing not how to wage war, but how not to get into war."

Yet the Wilson Administration, with Bryan as Secretary of State, saw uniformed officers and black-tied diplomats sit down together to discuss questions of foreign policy. Tension with Mexico, during the first year of the Administration, brought Bryan himself to the White House for a conference with the War and Navy Secretaries, the Army Chief of Staff, and the head of the Navy General Board. After war exploded over Europe, Bryan and his subordinates found a recurring need for special consultations with representatives of the Army and Navy. The uncertain character of neutral rights and duties brought into being a permanent Joint State and Navy Neutrality Board, an advisory body on diplomacy and international law. The amount of correspondence among assistant secretaries of the three departments increased three times over the pre-war average. And Bryan's successor, Robert Lansing, met almost daily, according to his desk diary, with officers from the Navy General Board and the Army General Staff. Thus conferences, letters and committee meetings began to knit the three departments together.

But American policy failed to benefit from this increasing teamwork, for Wilson reached his decisions with little assistance from any of the three departments. Lansing had come into office, in Colonel House's words, as a man "to do the details intelligently," and his Department's share in policy-making was never large. Meanwhile, the military planning agencies lacked not only the Administration's trust but also the ability to justify such trust if it were handed them. The Joint Board of the Army and Navy had virtually disbanded, because one of its recommendations had piqued the President. The Army General Staff had slipped into torpor, while the Navy General Board languished as a casualty of Josephus Daniels' perpetual feud with his admirals. Collaboration among these powerless agencies could result, at best, in a coördination of futilities.

The idea of political-military collaboration nevertheless survived. Since the war had revealed defects in the State Department and in the Army and Navy, the post-war years saw reforms in all three: the Rogers

Act for the State Department, reorganization of the Army General Staff, progressive change in the new Office of Naval Operations, and creation of a new and stronger Joint Board of the Army and Navy. To some men in the War and Navy Departments experience had also proved the need for regular, official consultation with the State Department. And these men put forward two successive proposals for consultative organizations.

The first and most ambitious of these proposals came from Franklin D. Roosevelt, then acting as Secretary of the Navy. On May 1, 1919, Roosevelt wrote to the Secretary of State:

> It is a fundamental principle that the foreign policy of our government is in the hands of the State Department. It is also an accepted fact that the foreign policy of a government depends for its acceptance by other nations upon the naval and military force that is behind it. . . .
>
> It is probable that certain policies are of such importance to our national interests that they must be defended at all cost.
>
> On the other hand certain policies are not, by the expense they would entail, justified if they lead to war.
>
> Hence it is submitted that in the framing of our policies, it is necessary for the State Department to know how much they will cost to maintain by force, in order to assign them their relative importance.
>
> Conversely, it is necessary for the Navy Department to know what policies it may be called upon to uphold by force, in order to formulate plans and building programs.

Enclosed with this letter was a giant sheet of blueprint paper, charting with boxes and arrows an organization for planning against all possible wars. Prepared by the Naval War College, this neat chart outlined duties for a State Department planning agency, for the Army General Staff, for a naval general staff, and for a Joint Plan Making Body, composed of officers from all three staffs. To this Joint Body was to go responsibility for estimating national resources, both American and foreign, and the key rôle of defining American objectives for each possible war and assessing the force needed for success.

Although this grandiose scheme was probably unworkable, hard-headed discussion of the Navy's proposal might have engineered some practical organization for national defense. No such discussion ever took place, and, in fact, Roosevelt's letter was not even acknowledged. The letter and its enclosure went, by mistake, to the State Department's Division of Latin American Affairs. After some misspent months in that Division's filing cabinets, the document was interred in the general records, never opened by the Secretary of State. Indeed, when I found the original of Roosevelt's letter in the State Department archives, the blueprint was stapled to it, closed, and, as far as I could tell, the staple had never been removed. Such was the fate of the first proposal for a National Security Council.

The second proposal came on December 7, 1921, this time sponsored jointly by the Secretary of the Navy and the Secretary of War. Considerably less pretentious than the original Navy blueprint, this joint proposal offered only the idea of collaboration between the State Department and the Joint Board of the Army and the Navy. But the reasoning in the service secretaries' letter closely resembled Roosevelt's.

They put forward three proposals. The State Department should designate "a responsible official" to sit in with the Joint Board when "questions involving national policy are under consideration." For similar discussions, one or more State Department people should sit in with the Joint Board's Planning Committee. Finally, the State Department should "refer to the Joint Board those national policies which may require the potential or dynamic support of the Army and Navy" and find out "whether the Army and Navy as at that time constituted and disposed are capable of supporting the policy in question. . . . All such opinions and recommendations of the Joint Board," the Secretaries added, "will be referred to the Secretaries of State, War and Navy for approval."

This letter at least reached the desk of Secretary of State Charles Evans Hughes, but Hughes brushed it into his "Out" basket, noting: "This appears to me to be in substance a suggestion that at least provisionally matters of foreign policy be submitted to the Joint Board. I question the advisability of this." Taking their lead from Hughes, the undersecretary and the assistant secretaries questioned its advisability even more seriously. Consequently, Hughes suavely replied: "The only officials of the State Department who can speak for it with authority on questions of national policy are the Secretary and Undersecretary of State, and it is impossible, in the existing circumstances, for either of them to undertake this additional duty."

Since War and Navy Department officials believed their proposal to be of great importance, they refused to accept the Secretary of State's negative reply. They countered with a new suggestion: the Joint Board should inform the State Department "whenever a subject comes before them for consideration which in their opinion is interwoven with the international policies of the United States." The Secretary of State or his representative could then attend the Joint Board's meeting. To this proposal the Secretary of State gave perfunctory agreement, thus providing the Army and Navy with a valve for starting a flow of military-political discussion. But the military leaders did not open this valve for over thirteen years.

Perhaps this long delay resulted from the series of slights administered to the military departments by the Secretary of State during the Washington Conference on Naval Limitation. Preparing for that conference, Secretary Hughes "worked closely with the Navy," his biographer says, and "was scrupulous in exploring the Navy's point of view while

insisting that civilian statesmanship rather than naval strategy should guide the conference." The General Board, anxious to push the Navy's ideas, presented Hughes with long, hard-thought essays on the questions apt to come up for negotiation. The Board advised that the United States fleet should equal the combined fleets of Britain and Japan, cautioned against any let-up in the naval building program, and portrayed the vital importance of fortifying Oahu, Guam and Manila Bay. But Hughes rejected each item of the Board's advice. In his opening speech to the conference, he not only proposed a 5:5:3 ratio among the three naval Powers but also offered to scrap thirty American capital ships. Later he proposed a general agreement not to fortify islands in the Pacific. Undoubtedly, Hughes based these stands on careful reasoning and broad advice, but the Navy's feelings were badly hurt, and a sense of resentment over the Washington Conference colored the writings of Navy and Army officers for decades.

As a result, these officers became even more circumspect than before in dealing with political questions. Furthermore, they fell altogether from public favor, as, during the twenties, newspapers and magazines drummed disillusionment, isolationism, and new forms of pacifism and anti-militarism. Whereas to Secretary Hughes a suggestion for political-military collaboration had seemed only imprudent, to either of his successors a similar suggestion would have seemed rash and startling. When Hoover's Secretary of State was preparing for the new naval conference of 1930, for instance, he rejected out of hand suggestions from the General Board and took with him to the conference only one uniformed adviser, an admiral "carefully selected . . . by the administration's civilian leaders," one who "took a different position . . . from most of his colleagues."

During these years, nevertheless, the general staffs were improving their minds by cloistered study of possible wars, and junior officers in the armed services were building friendly ties with their counterparts in the Foreign Service. They were exchanging intelligence data, a practice started soon after World War I, and they were meeting on various interdepartmental boards, like the Radio Advisory Committee and the committee on strategic raw materials. Early in the twenties, too, Foreign Service officers began to attend the Army and Navy War Colleges and to give lectures before War College classes. Thus the future heads of divisions and branches within the three departments laid a foundation for later coöperation on questions of policy.

Over this foundation a structure began to rise shortly after Franklin D. Roosevelt became President. His Secretary of State, Cordell Hull, found himself dealing with a newly barbarous Germany, an emboldened Italy, and a hostile Japan. As Hull stated to the Pearl Harbor investigators:

. . . soon after I came into the State Department, when I would be talking

with the representatives of the thugs at the head of governments abroad . . . they would look at me in the face but I soon discovered that they were looking over my shoulder at our Navy and our Army and that our diplomatic strength . . . goes up or down with their estimate of what that amounts to.

Consequently, Hull took more interest than his predecessors in military plans and opinions. Preparing for yet another naval conference, he asked the Navy to detail its wishes, and he sent to London, not just a "carefully selected" admiral, but the Chief of Naval Operations and a sizable band of naval officers. In the same year, too, he named a high State Department officer to sit in with the Joint Board's Planning Committee for a reëxamination of America's military position in the Far East. Early in his term, thus, Hull began to seat military and political thinkers at the same tables.

As Europe's war drums beat more insistently, Hull drew the State, War, and Navy Departments closer together. After suggesting special conferences on Axis infiltration of Latin America, he proposed a standing interdepartmental committee to consider, among other things, "matters of national policy affecting the three departments." He nominated Undersecretary Sumner Welles to represent the State Department. The President chose the Chief of Naval Operations and the Army Chief of Staff to be the committee's other members, and this three-man group took the name, Standing Liaison Committee. Thus was formed the first American agency for regular political-military consultation on foreign policy.

The Standing Liaison Committee lasted until 1943. Though it handled chiefly questions of hemisphere defense and Good Neighbor relations, it still gave the military chiefs an opportunity to learn the trends of policy thinking in the State Department. Later, too, it gave the State Department's second officer a chance to learn highly secret Army-Navy plans for possible war, plans formerly withheld from State Department eyes.

Rarely, however, did questions of policy come up for the Committee's discussion, perhaps because the members had little time for talk. The military chiefs were busy, fabricating fleets, armies and air forces out of raw metal and rawer men, while the undersecretary and his department were swirling through diplomatic crises that absorbed their time and powers. So the Liaison Committee failed to march with the perilous times.

In only one instance did the Liaison Committee handle an important issue of policy, and then it patched together a compromise instead of building a solution. The issue came before the Committee in the summer of 1940, when Hitler was looking acquisitively at the Vichy fleet. The Army and Navy, fearing that Germany might seize control of the Mediterranean, proposed a shift of the American battle fleet from the Pacific to the Atlantic. But the State Department disagreed. More fearful of a

Japanese attack on Southeast Asia than of German naval expansion and aware that Britain held the same fear, the State Department believed the fleet more effective, stationed at Pearl Harbor, where it might deter Japan from rash aggression. Since the undersecretary and the military members all stood fast behind their differing views, the Liaison Committee's decision solved nothing. The fleet, they agreed, "should be withdrawn from Hawaii only if the Germans actually secured control of the French fleet." If that happened, of course, the issue would still exist and would simply be more urgent.

Other than this decision, the Liaison Committee accomplished little that touched the great issues drawing the United States toward double war. After November 1940, furthermore, its functions shifted to other committee and council tables. A new Secretary of War started weekly conferences with his State and Navy counterparts. The President began to deal directly with his chiefs of staff, by-passing not only the State Department but also the civilian Secretaries of War and the Navy. By the autumn of 1941, in the tempestuous twilight before Pearl Harbor, the President was convening a War Council, made up of his State, War, and Navy Secretaries, and his chiefs of staff.

Despite the resemblance of his War Council to the present-day National Security Council, it hardly served as a palette for the mixing of military and political views. Rather, it provided the President with a platform from which to announce decisions already reached with the help of the chiefs of staff. After November 5, 1941, the War Council spent its time devising ways to carry out the strategic concept long ago devised by the Joint Board and now ratified by the President: "War between the United States and Japan should be avoided while building up the defensive forces in the Far East, until such time as Japan attacks or directly threatens territories whose security to the United States is of very great importance." Then, when war broke out, the President stopped inviting Hull to the War Council's meetings, and the Council, while it lasted, became nothing more than a board of strategy.

The idea of coördinating strategy and policy seemed, indeed, to die out with the onset of war. The President began to consult only with his chiefs of staff and with a few para-military officials like Harry Hopkins. Not only was the Secretary of State excluded from meetings of the War Council, but he was left at home when the President went abroad to meet British and Russian leaders and even left outside when Roosevelt met with Churchill in Washington and Quebec. During most of the war, as a result, the State Department became almost an auxiliary arm of the military services.

Uniformed officers meanwhile filled the chairs left vacant by diplomats. Eisenhower, Stilwell and Wedemeyer negotiated with allied governments. The service chieftains, reorganized as the Joint Chiefs of Staff, met

face to face with their allied counterparts and negotiated agreements that were, in effect, military treaties, requiring for ratification only the countersignature of the President. Although the Joint Chiefs continually disclaimed any authority in political affairs, their decisions, in fact, directed American policy. When they concluded, for example, that Russian aid was essential to victory in the Far East, they said, in effect, that American diplomacy should subordinate other aims in order to bring about a Russian declaration of war on Japan. Had professional diplomats desired to challenge this ruling, they would have been unable to do so. In 1944, as a matter of fact, when the State Department wanted the Dumbarton Oaks conferees to begin discussions of post-war boundaries, the Joint Chiefs checked any such discussions. Quarrels among the Allies might result, the chiefs asserted, and Russia might find cause for delaying her entry into the Pacific war. Thus, during World War II, the strategists took command, and the military-State Department relation was reversed. No longer were the military leaders seeking parity with diplomats; on the contrary, the diplomats were looking for space alongside the chiefs of staff.

Not until the last year of World War II did the State Department begin to regain its lost status. Then the need for military government directives and surrender terms caused the creation of the State-War-Navy Coordinating Committee, the National Security Council's immediate ancestor.

This Coordinating Committee, composed of assistant secretaries, prepared the plans for occupying Germany, Austria and Japan, and pondered, in addition, many other questions of post-war policy. Since most or all of these questions involved fleets and forces in the theaters of war, the Coordinating Committee had to clear its decisions with the Joint Chiefs of Staff, and officers representing the Joint Chiefs sat in with the Coordinating Committee's staff groups. Before the Committee's recommendations went to the Secretary of State and the President, therefore, any differences with the Joint Chiefs had already been discovered and explored.

Such a process brought forth, as an example, the Committee's recommendations on post-war aid to China. Had these recommendations been compounded by the State Department alone, Herbert Feis tells us in his recent book, *The China Tangle*, they "would have subordinated the program of military aid to the satisfaction of . . . political ideas"— democratic government and political unity for China. Recommendations drafted by the Army, Navy, and Air Forces, on the other hand, would have fixed on two different objectives—territorial unity for China and military strength for the Chinese government. Thus, while the State Department thought of aid for China as a means of exerting pressure on the Kuomintang, to force a political strengthening of the Nationalist government, the armed forces tended to think of this aid solely as a means for strengthening the battle capabilities of the Nationalist forces.

Since the choice between these points of view depended at all times upon detailed, expert information, the State Department and the military had to reconcile, or at least define, their differences before going to the White House with a program for immediate post-war aid for China. The State-War-Navy Coordinating Committee was an obvious arena where these views might be tested against each other.

The State Department drew up a statement of China policy, emphasizing the political objectives of unity and democratic government. Although this statement of policy has not been printed, an earlier model of it is visible in the MacArthur hearings, and the views of the State Department's chief Far Eastern planner, John Carter Vincent, have been published at length in the records of the McCarran committee. In the final proposals of the State-War-Navy Coordinating Committee, quoted in Feis's book, one can therefore detect phrases written in with stubby blue pencils by the War and Navy Departments and the Joint Chiefs of Staff:

> The achievement of [American] objectives in China requires a friendly, unified, independent nation with a stable government resting, *insofar as practicable*, on the freely expressed support of the Chinese people. . . . The following should be established as policies of the United States: . . . .
> (b) *To assist and advise China in the development of modern armed forces, ground, sea and air, for the* . . .
> (1) *Maintenance of internal peace and security in China including the liberated areas of Manchuria and Formosa.* . . .

One can see also the unaltered will of the State Department in such a sentence as: "The extent to which political stability is being achieved in China under a unified, fully representative government is regarded by the U.S. as a basic consideration which will at all times govern the furnishing of economic, military, or other assistance to that nation...."

Thus were political and military views brought into line, through the agency of the State-War-Navy Coordinating Committee. That line admittedly jogged and wavered. And one can argue that events in the Far East would have followed a different course had the opinions of one department or the other prevailed. It remains true, nevertheless, that the State Department and the military departments disagreed, and this disagreement was due, not to a personal difference between John Carter Vincent and some general or admiral, but to a real difference between political and military perspectives. General Marshall, while Chief of Staff, opposed the State Department's idea of using aid to promote reforms in the Chinese government. Then, when he became Secretary of State, he defended this very idea against challenges voiced by the new chiefs of staff. Such real disagreements between the State and military departments had to be reconciled in some place like the State-

War-Navy Coordinating Committee, or such a committee had to define the points at issue for the President's adjudication.

But the Committee had its limitations. It suffered, in the first place, from its inability to make policy. Although the Committee was capable of rapid staff work, as evidenced in its eight-day fabrication of a workable surrender instrument for Japan, its mill of subcommittees hummed uselessly in the spring of 1945 when Marshal Tito threatened to march against Allied forces in Trieste. The question of American action simply fell beyond the powers of the assistant secretaries who made up the Coordinating Committee; and the Trieste decision had to be made by the President and his Cabinet Secretaries with little or no preliminary staff study.

In the second place, the Committee went to work only when a question was referred to it by one of the departments. As a result, it failed to handle some questions well within its purview. The four-Power arrangements for occupation of Berlin were worked out hastily by soldiers and diplomats in the European Theater and approved by a nod from President Truman. The Coordinating Committee never had a chance to examine these arrangements and no provision was made for guaranteeing access to the city.

The nation needed the Coordinating Committee, but it also needed a policy-making agency with the power to review all questions. President Truman fully realized this need, and so did his Cabinet Secretaries, particularly Secretary of the Navy James Forrestal. Within two years after World War II, consequently, Mr. Truman, Mr. Forrestal, and a staff of experts had worked out a plan for a National Security Council. Bedded in the unification act of 1947, this plan received the approval of Congress, and the United States acquired a regular, legally established, cabinet-level agency for the coördination of political and military views on foreign policy.

Fifty years of growth and experiment lay behind this Council, and additional years of experiment lay ahead of it. The original Council showed signs, some said, of being dominated by its military members. As a result, Congress changed the membership in 1949, dropping out the Secretaries of the Army, Navy, and Air Force. And the composition of the Council has since been altered several times, by executive order or simply by invitation. Thus, . . . President Eisenhower has invited his secretary of the Treasury to sit with every session of the Council, so that dollar costs may be reckoned with political and military costs.

These alterations, of course, reflect a change in the Council's functions. Still the patching and mending is all applied in one place, on the National Security Council, and with one aim—to perfect that Council. Instead of replacing one experiment with another, in other words, we are striving now to improve a working model.

Mechanically, of course, the National Security Council is still in its scraps-of-wire and bits-of-chewing-gum stage. While its general purposes are clear, its specific functions are not. There seems real doubt, particularly, whether the Council is meant to resolve differences of opinion or simply to bring them into the open. Is it to copy the British Committee of Imperial Defense, where variant ideas are exposed to endless debate, or Japan's pre-war Liaison Conference, where decision was the goal, and difference often resulted in resignation? Which direction the National Security Council means to take is, at this writing, far from sure.

A reflection of this uncertainty has been the tendency of the Council and its predecessors to work like church councils or party platform committees, rather than action groups. Compromises have been forged, it seems, simply for an inner feeling of righteousness and an outward appearance of unanimity. In the State-War-Navy Coordinating Committee paper on China quoted earlier, for example, the State Department and the military departments did not really reconcile differences. They simply agreed on an ambiguous formula. With easier consciences, thus, each department could do what it wanted to do in the first place. Forrestal's notes on subsequent National Security Council discussions, testimony at the MacArthur hearings, and Chalmers Roberts' reports in the Washington *Post and Times Herald* on the Indo-China and Quemoy mix-ups of 1954 suggest that there have been later instances of meaningless compromise. Realization of the need for a coördinating committee has, in other words, sometimes obscured the truth that decision-making can become more realistic, but it cannot become easier. Coördination is no substitute for thought.

Neither has the problem of coördination itself been fully solved. While executive departments may treat one another with increasing frankness, the executive branch and the Congress retain the relationship of unfriendly sovereignties. Beside the monumental problem of harmonizing executive and congressional foreign policies, the relatively recent and minor problem of harmonizing executive views shades into insignificance. Even the simplest questions of executive-congressional coördination present absurd difficulty. "If you tell Congress nothing," as James Reston remarked, "they go fishing; if you promise nothing, they go fishing; if you tell them all, they go wild." And, as Hanson Baldwin states the larger question: "Are national policies ever really forged in secrecy and by a small group? Do they not require the support and substantiation of Congress and public opinion?"

These unsettled questions of function and competence, relations with Congress, and relation to public opinion ought not to cloud the progress that has been made. A committee that effects some political-military coördination has come into existence. Fifty years ago such a committee could not openly have existed in Washington. Had it existed in secret,

it would very likely have been ineffective. During World War I, when a need for coördination was recognized, actual coördination was at best haphazard, and the new crises attending World War II saw one experiment tumble after another. The National Security Council is thus the product of a long and painful history. Whatever its present inadequacies and whatever the trials that lie ahead, it is still an institution. It answers an enduring need, and it is likely to be a permanent feature of American government.

# 20 / Evolution of United States Military Strategic Thought

## CHARLES H. DONNELLY

**Military strategy for an isolationist foreign policy is one thing. A strategy for deterrence and containment of a powerful adversary is quite another. American military thought not only has had to adapt itself to America's new world role since World War II; it has had to keep up with an accelerating military technology. The evolution of United States military strategic thought is analyzed here.**

MILITARY STRATEGIC THOUGHT in the United States until the end of the Second World War was relatively uncomplicated. It followed three precepts:

1. Keep out of war if you can.
2. If war should come, keep the combat zone away from the United States.
3. Once involved in war, destroy the armed forces of the enemy as quickly as possible.

War was recognized as a means of carrying out national policy—a means not to be used except as a last resort but, once engaged in, to be

---

Reprinted from *The Military Review*, October, 1959, pp. 12–24.

Colonel Charles H. Donnelly has had a distinguished military career, serving on the staff of the U. S. Joint Chiefs of Staff, various NATO committees, and military assistance groups. Since 1956 he has been senior specialist in national defense in the Legislative Reference Service at the Library of Congress. He is the author of numerous Congressional reports on American military policy since World War II.

fought with all of the vigor and resources of which the Nation was capable. Complete and early victory was the goal.

The harnessing of nuclear energy and its use in a new weapons system uncovered some implications which have brought about sober reconsideration of strategic thought. Armed force remains an important instrument of national foreign policy but, today, the danger inherent in its use has caused the world powers to turn more frequently to other means of attaining national objectives. These means include use of political or diplomatic pressure; economic measures, such as loans, grants, favorable trade arrangements, and technical cooperation; and psychological methods which include propaganda, threats, gestures of good will, and sometimes domestic policies intended to impress other countries.

Military strategy, therefore, is a part of national strategy which considers all available means by which foreign policies may be implemented and plans the timing, sequence, combinations, and degree of effort to be expended on each. While the deadly effectiveness of modern weapons has all but ruled out deliberate warfare between the great powers, smaller countries and factions, not having access to means of mass destruction, are not so inhibited. There is also the possibility of war through miscalculation when a country is maneuvering on the "brink," or through deliberate attack if an aggressor judges a military imbalance to be enough in his favor to enable him to gain a military victory at a price he thinks he can afford to pay.

While a great power will make full use of its political, economic, and psychological means before turning to armed force to gain its ends, it still must have sufficient military strength to make the other means effective. No diplomat wants the embarrassment of negotiating at the council table with his hole card exposed, and that is what happens when his opponents know that he lacks the military strength with which to back his diplomatic moves. He may have plenty of moral strength behind him but, unfortunately, armed force still gets more respect in an international poker game. As long then as armed force remains so important, so will the military strategy by which the use of this force is planned.

The evolution of strategic thinking in the United States has been influenced during the past 13 years by a series of events falling into fairly definite periods. The discussion, therefore, will be presented in that manner.

### Demobilization Period

Americans have a quality of directness which tends to make them impatient and unsympathetic with the slow and often devious ways of

diplomacy. This same quality causes them—when they find themselves engaged in some disagreeable but inevitable situation, such as war— to try to finish it as quickly as they can so they can return to what they consider normal living. The end of World War II saw so strong a public demand for fast demobilization that the result was, as General Marshall put it, not demobilization but disintegration.

We were immensely proud of our Armed Forces while the war was still being fought, but as soon as the fighting was over the public lost interest rather quickly in the military. After all, what was the point in keeping up a big armed force? The enemy had been soundly whipped; Soviet Russia had been fighting on our side and that made us friends, did it not? The other nations were either good friends or too weak to pose any threat to our security. Besides, if any trouble did arise the United Nations could take care of it.

The possibility that there might be serious trouble with Soviet Russia did not disturb the man in the street very deeply. How could a nation which had lost between 15 and 20 million people and had suffered such severe damage to its industry and homes offer any serious threat to the United States? It would take them years to recover from their war wounds, we reasoned; besides, allies who fight and bleed together do not turn right around and square off against each other, do they?

This feeling was not unanimous; some military and diplomatic people who had dealt with the Soviets at short range during the war tried to sound a warning but it was not taken very seriously. Even if the Communists did make trouble, only the United States had an atom bomb, said the optimists—although by this time our Armed Forces had disintegrated to the point where effective use of the bomb was doubtful, if the need had arisen.

To sum up, strategic thinking during the demobilization period was almost nonexistent as far as the public was concerned. Military planners, faced with the realities of rapidly dwindling forces as well as public interest in military matters, revised the national strategic concept to include the vast capabilities of air-nuclear power. However, lethal as it is, an atom bomb by itself is not enough; a balanced military force still is necessary to cope with most situations involving combat. The American forces were becoming more unbalanced by the hour, but this seemed to worry no one except the authorities charged with carrying out occupation and demobilization responsibilities. The popular attitude was: The United Nations would keep the peace.

### 1946–48: Disillusionment

Within the first few years after the war a series of incidents convinced the American public that Soviet prewar goals for world communization

had never been abandoned; they had just been set aside during the war and now they were being pursued as vigorously as ever. Hopes of postwar friendship and cooperation with the Soviet Government began to dwindle.

One of the first evidences of Soviet intransigence was the difficulty which General Hodge had in working out any agreement for establishing an independent government for a united Korea. Then came reports from our representatives on the Allied Control Commissions in Bulgaria and Romania of insults, humiliations, and frustrations. In the United Nations the Baruch Plan for the internationalization of nuclear energy suffered a Soviet rebuff. During this period, too, there were Soviet threats against Iran and Turkey, pressures against Finland, a Communist uprising in Greece, and the overthrow of democratic government in Czechoslovakia.

In the spring of 1948 another event occurred which came to have strategic significance in the United States. With scant warning the Soviet Union cut off all land and water access to West Berlin with the evident purpose of creating a showdown in which the West would have to withdraw or fight. Our ground forces were badly outnumbered by the massive Soviet Army and the Reds did not seem to be worried about the possible use of our atom bomb. But they made the mistake of underestimating our resourcefulness. We chose neither alternative. Having determined not to be shoved out of Berlin, we came up with the idea of aerial supply of the civilian and military populations of West Berlin; the success of the airlift is a matter of history.

In other instances, threats to the United States had been indirect, as in the case of Greece and Turkey. The Berlin blockade was something else—a direct challenge to the United States. Had the Soviet maneuver succeeded the West would have had to leave Berlin. Once that had occurred, the setback to American prestige would have been so great that it would have been possible for the Soviets to follow with actions which could have meant our complete withdrawal from Germany, possibly from Europe.

The strategic significance of this period is marked by the constant probing of weak spots by the Soviets and by American efforts to salve and bandage the sores at which the Reds kept picking. The pattern of Soviet strategy was quite apparent—to keep the initiative in the cold war, stopping just short of bringing on a general war but never giving any respite. As fast as we quenched one blaze, another was lit; the initiative was with the Soviets and we were always a step behind.

Although it is dangerous to try to evaluate the significance of important events too soon after they occur, it appears that the Soviets may have overstepped themselves when they attempted the Berlin blockade. Our response was so swift, determined, dramatic, and effective that the propaganda loss to them was enormous. Even more important, this was the action which was largely responsible for reversing the trend in the

*145*

United States which had begun with rapid demobilization. We did two things: we began to reestablish our military posture and we began to build a new strategy which we had never before used in peacetime—the use of a system of collective defense.

This was an important turning point in American foreign policy. It meant forsaking the traditional policy of avoiding foreign entanglements and it also meant, in the field of foreign relations, that the United States was facing realities, hence maturing. The way for this new policy was opened when on 11 June 1948 the Senate passed the Vandenberg Resolution which informed the President that it was the sense of the Senate that the United States should associate herself "with such regional and other collective arrangements as are based on continuous and effective self-help and mutual aid, and as affect its national security."

Another important development in our strategic thinking came at this time. As part of the plan to reconstitute United States forces to meet the Soviet threat, President Truman advocated adoption of universal military training and, as a temporary measure, immediate revival of conscription. When this came before Congress for consideration, some witnesses at the hearings tried to make out a strong case for air-nuclear power as the answer to our security needs. The House rejected this and in its report preferred the concept of "balanced military forces." This excerpt from the report explains the reason for this action:

. . . no single military arm can be fully effective unless adequately supported by the other arms. . . . A powerful Air Force is today unquestionably the first line of American defense, but it is not sufficient of itself. It cannot be effectively utilized as an offensive weapon far beyond our shores, except as it is supported and supplied by strong ground and naval forces. A powerful Air Force is not a panacea for security. A 70-group Air Force is not a substitute for Selective Service. The committee considers that nothing could be more dangerous to the national security than for the American people to accept such an illusion.

### 1949–June 1950: Collective Security

By the spring of 1949 the Soviet Union had called off the Berlin blockade but not soon enough to discourage United States moves toward collective security arrangements. A collateral effect of the blockade was the stationing of two United States strategic bombardment groups in Britain. This gave us a nuclear counterattack capability and led the way to the creation of our strategic airbases in North Africa and Spain. This is the point at which our "massive retaliation" concept began to crystallize.

By the end of 1949 the North Atlantic Treaty Organization had been formed and had adopted a strategic concept which envisioned the use of ground forces (such as we could scrape together at the time), with such support as our fleet could give on the flanks, to delay any attack against

Western Europe. We would retaliate with our nuclear bombs. The Soviet Union had exploded a nuclear device in August 1949 but we calculated that it would be some time before the Soviets would have an air-nuclear capability. This event gave the NATO concept added significance and urgency, however.

As we progressed with our collective security plans in 1949, another move took place affecting our Armed Forces. The release from tension which came with the lifting of the Berlin blockade and the lack of any other Soviet irritant moves of importance at the moment was the signal for another period of retrenchment. The size of the Armed Forces was cut so that the gains which had resulted from the Berlin blockade scare were practically canceled by June 1950. The Navy and the Marines were hit a bit harder than the Army and Air Force but all were affected by the economy wave. The Navy had to scrap the keel which had been laid for the new attack carrier, the *United States.* Since the only adversary in sight was Soviet Russia, ran the argument, and since it had no fleet worthy to be called such, our Navy was gearing up to fight a nonexistent force.

It is interesting and significant that this line of reasoning overlooked the possibilities of limited or small wars; we appeared to be thinking only in terms of possible general war with the Soviet Union.

Congress had voted the funds for the *United States* and the congressional committee had answered the opposition arguments by saying that the service of primary interest was best qualified to judge what weapons it should develop and use; nevertheless, the Secretary of Defense stopped the construction.

Another retrenchment move came in this period. Secretary of State Dean Acheson, in a major policy speech in January 1950, drew a line on the map which delineated our defensive perimeter in the Far East. This line ran from the Aleutians to Japan, thence to the Ryukyus and the Philippines. Korea and Taiwan were outside this line. Secretary Acheson indicated that we would not guarantee these two countries against attack. Although we would continue to help them, their security was largely in their own hands. If attacked, we might come to their aid but we made no commitment. As part of our retrenchment policy we had already withdrawn our forces from South Korea and we had none on Taiwan.

To summarize this period: it was the beginning of the new strategy of collective security. The principal contributions of the United States would be the air-nuclear deterrent, plus arms and equipment for the ground and tactical air forces of our allies. Our own tactical forces were to be cut back in order to finance the military assistance program and, at the same time, balance the budget.

*June 1950–53: Limited War*

Apparently the Communists thought Korea would be a good place to

probe next. The danger of starting a world war did not seem too great, since the American flag was not present in the area and we had, in effect, told the world that the South Koreans were on their own.

The invasion of South Korea had the immediate effect of crystallizing our foreign policy toward the Far East. Hitherto we had handled such matters practically on a case by case basis. Again we were responding to Communist initiative and, in doing so, came face to face with a startling fact: we were badly equipped to fight a limited war. It became apparent very quickly that our plans had not seriously taken into account the prospect of our being involved in a small war; our concern had been mostly with the possibility of another world war, not with a limited action at some faraway place such as the mainland of Asia.

Nevertheless, when the North Koreans attacked, our response was immediate and wholehearted. The American policy of helping free countries to avoid inundation by communism was crystallized. People who had sometimes given hypothetical consideration to the possibility of an invasion of South Korea were usually inclined to take a dim view of any American involvement. Faced with the actual fact, however, the American people suddenly realized that here was a challenge to their future way of life and they solidly backed the President's action.

The Korean war has a special significance for American military men. This was the first time that our field commanders had to watch a war end without achieving the military victory of which they believed they were capable. Political objectives became more important than military objectives. They saw the war end without ever having been allowed to use their most effective weapon.

General Douglas A. MacArthur stated the case for military victory during the Senate hearings which followed his relief from duty:

> The general definition which for many decades has been accepted was that war was the ultimate process of politics; that when all other political means failed, you then go to force; and when you do that, the balance of control, the balance of concept, the main interest involved, the minute you reach the killing stage, is the control of the military. A theater commander, in any campaign, is not merely limited to handling of his troops; he commands that whole area politically, economically, and militarily. You have got to trust at that stage of the game when politics fails, and the military takes over, you must trust the military, or otherwise you will have the system that the Soviet once employed of the political commissar, who would run the military as well as the politics of the country.

General Omar Bradley, then Chairman of the Joint Chiefs of Staff, stated the views of the Joint Chiefs of Staff. He said he was under no illusion that the limited war strategy being used would guarantee that a world war would not result but that we could not afford to become more heavily

committed, at least until we had improved our military power. General Bradley said:

Red China is not the powerful nation seeking to dominate the world. Frankly, in the opinion of the Joint Chiefs of Staff, this strategy would involve us in the wrong war, at the wrong place, at the wrong time, and with the wrong enemy.

When the truce was finally concluded we had achieved the stated United Nations objectives of repelling armed attack and restoring international security in that area but one could hardly claim that peace had been restored.

Strategic thinking had now accepted the concept that general war between nuclear powers was too dangerous—not only to the participants but to the rest of the world. Therefore, if war continued to be used to gain foreign policy objectives, it would have to be held within bounds. To do this the objectives must be such that their attainment would not cause either opponent to expand the conflict into a general war.

In Korea the first objective which we tried to attain resulted in expanding the war. The objective was then lowered to reestablishment of the ante bellum *status quo* and this was achieved without further enlarging the conflict. We had learned how to fight a limited war, but some did not particularly like the rules under which it was fought.

### 1953–October 1957: Deterrence and Economy

We now come to a period when our strategic thinking was centered on effective deterrence of war while we put our fiscal house in order. Since a deterrent, to be effective, must be based upon a strong military force, there is a degree of conflict between the two operations. Major national security expenditures represent around 60 percent of our total national governmental expenditures; hence it is obvious why the military is always a prime target when there is budget balancing or tax cutting to be done. What we needed, the experts said, was a formula which would produce the most defense for a dollar.

#### Massive Retaliation

At this point the "New Look" planners, as they were referred to, began to give serious thought to the massive retaliation strategy which had really been in effect since the 1948–49 period. By dramatizing this policy it was thought that it might be the answer to both defense and fiscal problems.

The President brought up the massive retaliation policy in his State of the Union message, 7 January 1954, saying: ". . . we and our allies have and will maintain a massive capability to strike back." A week later this

was said again, in more detail, by Secretary of State, John Foster Dulles:

The basic decision [has been taken] to depend primarily upon a great capacity to retaliate, instantly, by means and at places of our own choosing. Now [we] can shape our Military Establishment to fit what is our policy, instead of having to try to be ready to meet the enemy's many choices. That permits of a selection of military means instead of a multiplication of means. As a result, it is now possible to get, and share, more basic security at less cost.

To be an effective deterrent, massive retaliation depends upon two factors: it must be backed by a force which can survive a crushing surprise attack and go on to deliver the same kind of an attack in reprisal; and the potential enemy must be convinced that if we were attacked, we would respond with all of the force at our command.

We had the force in our Strategic Air Command (SAC) and the air-nuclear capability of the Navy. It was about this time that the nuclear tests during Operation *Castle* confirmed that a cheaper, much lighter thermonuclear bomb was feasible than previously had been thought possible. This opened the way to carrying the bomb in lighter aircraft as well as making thermonuclear warheads practicable for long-range missiles.

Nuclear airpower is costly, however, whether it is based on the use of manned bombers or missiles. There was no question of the need to keep this deterrent strong and that meant constant measures to keep it as modern and well-protected from surprise attack as possible. To get the money to do this, one of several things had to be done. Taxes could be raised, nondefense expenditures and foreign military assistance could be cut, or we could trim our tactical forces. It was never determined whether or not the public would have stood for a tax increase, and domestic policies made it difficult to make sizable cuts in nondefense spending. The Mutual Security Program was showing good results and there were good reasons for not trimming this too much. Something had to give and it was the so-called conventional Armed Forces which took the brunt of the retrenchment.

When Secretary Dulles enunciated the massive retaliation policy in his January 1954 speech, it was quickly interpreted to mean that we were going to depend upon the devastating power of the hydrogen bomb to handle every military conflict which came our way—large or small. There was criticism, both domestic and international. It became so loud in a few months that Mr. Dulles tried to clarify his position. What he had meant, he indicated, was that we "must have the mobility and flexibility to bring collective power to bear against an enemy on a selective or massive basis as conditions may require. . . . It is not our intention to turn every local war into a general war."

The fallacy of relying on massive retaliation as a policy to meet all

degrees of aggression is, of course, that you leave yourself no flexibility. A shrewd, aggressively minded nation would calculate that we would never face the approbrium which would fall upon us if we attempted to solve every brush fire conflict with a thermonuclear bomb. Hence if that is the only weapon in our arsenal, we expose ourselves to being nibbled to death.

### Graduated Deterrence

A result of the massive retaliation policy was that some critics began to seek an alternative which would meet our needs without abandoning the deterrent effect of reprisal. One suggestion which had a strong following was "graduated deterrence." By this was meant that aggressions would be dealt with on a "let the punishment fit the crime" basis. It was suggested that mass destruction of enemy populated areas should be renounced by us unless the enemy first attacked our cities. Small conflicts should be handled with only the degree of force needed to do the job.

This policy would not work unless it included a capability of dealing with all types of situations, large and small. In other words, we would need a full limited war capability as well as an effective deterrent to general war. Since cost was a matter of importance, the debate over the size and shape of the forces needed to carry out this concept became rather sharp. The point of the argument was whether to rely on large forces armed with conventional weapons or to attempt to reduce the power of nuclear weapons to tactical dimensions—even to the squad level, some said—and rely on the power of these new weapons to make up the deficiency in conventional forces.

The answer is history; we began to substitute new weapons for men. This necessitated another policy. What limitations should be placed on the use of tactical nuclear weapons? Could they be used without bringing on a general war? Many thought they could. The official position became that we would use nuclear weapons whenever it was to our advantage to do so. This meant that, regardless of the size of the conflict in which we were involved, if there was a military advantage in using a nuclear weapon, we would use it, provided there was no overriding political or other reason why such a weapon should not be used.

In summary, the period from the closing months of the Korean war until the appearance of the *Sputniks* is characterized by the attempt to maintain our national security through a policy of massive retaliation while making a determined effort to put the national budget back into balance. When the flaws in massive retaliation as a policy were realized, a move was made to broaden the weapons base and to get away from the single-weapon concept of dealing with all conflicts, regardless of size. Economy still was the dominant factor, however, and conventional arms

and forces continued to be cut back as the way was opened for use of small-yield nuclear weapons on the battlefield.

### October 1957: Post-Sputnik Military Thinking

The appearance of the Soviet satellites brought double-barreled reactions. The American people were shocked when they realized how badly they had underestimated the capabilities of the Soviets and were filled with apprehension as to what these new scientific marvels might mean in terms of national security. Space activities had been regarded with a kind of tolerant amusement—something to amuse the children in the comic strips. Now the activities of Buck Rogers suddenly took on stature.

The immediate effect was to put aside fiscal restrictions in order to expedite our outer space and ballistic missile programs and to bolster our strategic deterrent. The SAC dispersal program was expedited and efforts were made to compress the time when the *Polaris* fleet ballistic missile would be operational. The antimissile defense program was given a national priority status, putting it on a par with the intermediate range ballistic missiles and intercontinental ballistic missiles, and strenuous efforts were made to get our own outer space program rolling. Note, however, that this burst of activity was directed largely toward improving our posture toward the threat of general nuclear war.

While we were heavily occupied in our catching-up activities, two minor conflicts, but each having ominous implications, demanded our serious attention. The situation in the Middle East deteriorated to the point where we thought it necessary to send forces into Lebanon to preserve the integrity of the Lebanese Government. Hardly had this situation cooled when the Communist Chinese threatened—with words and hardware—to take over the offshore islands of Quemoy and Matsu. Again the United States Government took a firm stand and, again, the crisis passed without our forces having had to engage in any actual fighting.

During the period since the first Soviet *Sputnik* appeared, United States military strategic thinking has been centered largely on what is needed to enable us to catch up with (or keep ahead of—depending on the individual point of view) the Soviet Union, and to maintain our ability to meet our military commitments around the world. This has been expressed in the form of debates over the adequacy of our ballistic missile program, the value of aircraft carriers in any future wars, the feasibility of a defense system against hostile ballistic missiles, the value of shelters and other passive defense measures, and the need for limited war capabilities versus general war capabilities.

On one side is the view that it is not only unfeasible but unnecessary to try to match the Soviets man for man, gun for gun, missile for missile, and submarine for submarine; that it is the total strength of our forces

against that of the Soviets which is important. This view also takes into consideration the collective strength of our NATO and other allies and holds that we can look to them to supply much of the conventional force strength which might be needed in future crises.

The other view is that, in declining to match the various elements of our military strength with those of the Soviets, we are in danger of becoming outmatched in aggregate strength; some think this has already happened. Those who take this view point to the tendency on the part of the British and some of our other allies to cut back their own conventional forces as we have done, and for the same reason—economy. They also mention the possibility that, when needed, these forces may not be available because of prior commitments (like the French preoccupation with Algeria) or because of adverse internal situations. Therefore, they hold, we must never let our own military strength deteriorate to the degree that we may have to depend upon the uncertain strength of an alliance to protect our Nation. *They believe in collective security but deplore using it as the keel of our national security.*

### What of Tomorrow?

American strategy is still firmly based upon the determination to use our massive retaliatory capability to discourage military attacks against us. This strategy has worked and it should continue to be effective just as long as the Communist bloc does not attain *either* of these advantages:

1. The capacity to mount a surprise attack on such a scale that they could wipe out the bulk of our retaliation forces with the first blow, leaving us incapable of effective retaliation.

2. A defense so effective that it could reduce the damage from any counterattack we might make sufficiently to make the cost to them worth the gains they might expect to make in the exchange of blows.

There is no effective argument against the correctness of this strategy, or the need to maintain scientific, technological, and military advantage so that the strategy can be implemented. What disturbs many, however, is that in our preoccupation with our deterrent we may be overlooking other threats which may not seem as perilous at the moment but could be just as dangerous over a long period. Termites do not destroy as quickly or sensationally as fire but, given enough time, they too can make a house uninhabitable.

The Communist leaders have been most adept in the use of all forms of warfare and the fact that they have not made direct military attacks against the United States adds to the insidious nature of the war they practice. The satisfaction which comes with the belief that a big threat has been blocked, at least for the present, tends to make smaller threats seem less ominous. But the Soviets are skilled in all kinds of warfare, hot

and cold, and they mix their attacks with the skill of a good quarterback. Under the umbrella of a big threat they have made gains since World War II which may have been small individually but which add to an impressive total.

In the last 12 months Soviet initiative has created two crises and has taken advantage of a third. While the West has been isolating trouble and starting the healing process in one area, the Communists have started jabbing in another. First, it was the Middle East; then Taiwan Strait; now it is Berlin. If Leavenworth [the Army's Command and General Staff College] had prepared a course on how to conduct modern aggressive warfare, it could hardly have chosen three better examples to illustrate the technique.

So far the United States has been fortunate in having to deal with only one crisis at a time. As a party to eight different bilateral and multilateral defense treaties and with moral obligations to several countries with whom we have no treaties, we have military commitments all over the Free World. What happens if crises arise in several areas at one time? It may have been part of the Soviet plan to avoid this to keep from the possibility of shoving the United States into a mobilization, but can we count on it in the future?

### Limited War Capabilities

In the last 500 years important armed conflicts have occurred at the rate of one every 17½ months; since World War II the rate has been about double this figure. The possibility of limited or brush fire wars is great and, in this troubled postwar period when the upsurge of Nationalist feeling is so great and Communist policy is to stir up trouble rather than alleviate it, it does not seem likely that the trend is about to be reversed.

Some believe that if we are prepared to fight a general war, we can take care of smaller conflicts. That should be true if our forces have retained a flexibility of armament and the capability of rapid deployment to any trouble area. Experience has proved, however, that our big deterrent does not stop small conflicts from starting. For example, it did not hold back the Red Chinese from attacking Quemoy even though they were aware that the United States had a mutual defense treaty with the Nationalist Chinese. Nor is a nuclear weapon carried by a B-52 or a long-range missile quite the weapon to use in dealing with these small conflicts. Conversely, the deterrent value of conventional forces, both land and sea, has been demonstrated many times.

The sobering effect of combat forces carrying the American flag has been quite evident. Except for some of our military aircraft which were close to Communist territory, there is no known instance of an overt attack against American combat forces since World War II, unless our forces

intervened in a situation as they did in Korea. Besides the psychological value of "showing the flag," the United States Army has been instrumental in helping to equip, train, and indoctrinate some 200 allied divisions. The value of having experienced and combat-wise troops teamed with these less experienced divisions was proved during the Korean war.

In a general nuclear war the ground forces might or might not be heavily engaged in the first phase. In the case of a surprise attack, it might be some time before the Army and Marines came to grips with the enemy. But if a general war were to grow out of a local war, all forces probably would be involved from the beginning. *In either event, the ground forces must be used eventually in order to decide the outcome of the conflict.* No matter how badly hurt a nation may be from a nuclear attack, the final act in its submission comes when the enemy ground forces come in and take over.

With the present trend of replacing men with increased firepower— particularly nuclear weapons—the question facing us is: How much longer will the Army be able to deploy meaningful forces in the trouble spots of the world, maintain a strategic "fire brigade" ready to rush to any place where needed, continue to aid in the building of our allied divisions, provide a cover during, and cadres for, mobilization (if we should be forced into such an unhappy situation), and carry on the multi-tude of housekeeping chores for itself, the Navy and Air Force, and the other governmental departments? There are still many tasks which must be done by people, regardless of the ingenuity of modern machines.

# 21 / *The Requirements of Deterrence:*
# *The Great Debate*

HENRY S. ROWEN

A "balance of terror" equation in which the United States and the Soviet Union are able to destroy each other several times over with the forces each has in being has engendered a great debate in the United States, as elsewhere, over the

Reprinted from U. S. Congressional Joint Economic Committee Study Paper No. 18, *National Security and the American Economy in the 1960's* (January 30, 1960), pp. 2–7.

Henry S. Rowen, formerly a RAND Corporation economist, has been, since 1961, a high-ranking defense planner in the Defense Secretariat, the Pentagon.

requirements of deterrence. The arguments have run all the way from those that say war has completely outmoded itself to those that advocate more and more sums for defense and an arms race spiraling indefinitely into the future. Various categories of thought on the requirements of military forces in the contemporary setting are analyzed in this selection.

THE MAJOR DEFENSE OBJECTIVES the United States has adopted in the postwar period can be summarized as follows: Deterring nuclear assault on the United States, limiting damage to this country if war comes, while seeking a favorable war outcome; deterring aggression against our major allies and aiding in their defense; and, finally, helping to defend other allies and the free world.

The principal objective of U.S. military policy has come to be the deterrence of nuclear attack on the United States. We *must* attain it. But attaining it means having the ability to receive a well-designed and well-executed surprise nuclear attack and to strike back effectively. The advantage a nuclear-armed aggressor possesses in a surprise attack is formidable, and we must not depreciate the great effect of the many obstacles to retaliation the aggressor can create. This task of deterring attack will remain difficult not only because of the rapid growth of Soviet nuclear strength but also because of revolutionary changes in military technology that are taking place, some of which may introduce greater uncertainty into the military balance. We will have to work hard and work continually throughout the decade of the 1960's to try to preserve a strong retaliatory power. And, should we succeed, we will not have complete assurance that war will not come, for the power to retaliate is not identical with the power to deter. General war might still come, perhaps by miscalculation, perhaps without either side really preferring war to peace.

If general war were to come, our military forces would be primarily concerned with limiting damage to the United States and its allies and with obtaining the best civil and military outcome that could be obtained. We should not expect the best outcome to be very good, however. Each delivered enemy bomb could do great damage, especially given our low level of civil defense preparation, and a large attack might destroy most of our population and economy. However, there are important possibilities for limiting damage through a combination of active and passive defense, through the use of offensive force, and, especially, through preparations which would enable us to fight a general nuclear war in a controlled manner. With an expanded program aimed at limiting nuclear damage, and with luck, much of our population and economy might survive a general war.

In our defense of Europe we have evolved a dual strategy: that of

opposing invading forces directly on the ground along with the strategic nuclear bombing of the Soviet Union. However, over time we have emphasized more and more the purely deterrent aspect of our strategic attack threat. Although the growth of Soviet nuclear power has weakened the effect of this threat, it undoubtedly retains much force in the defense of so vital an area as Europe. Even a small probability of a large nuclear war happening may serve to keep Soviet forces out of Europe. But this policy risks great damage to both the United States and Europe, and its credibility will lessen, perhaps dangerously, in the 1960's. As a result, interest is being focused on more direct methods of defense abroad. The need for such direct defense methods is still more obvious when we consider the problem of defending less vital areas abroad, areas for which we are most unlikely to want to undergo a great risk of all-out war.

These major objectives of our defense policies are widely, although not completely, agreed on. There is much less agreement on how to attain either our general war objectives or those associated with direct defense overseas. On general war, it is convenient to distinguish five distinct positions:

### The World Annihilation View

Not everyone holds that it is rational to deter war through the threat of nuclear retaliation. Many distinguished people regard a general thermonuclear war as risking all mankind. They hold that nuclear war cannot be a rational instrument of policy. This view focuses attention on the worldwide effects of radiation that would follow a general nuclear war. It appears that such a war would lead to a shortening of life, an increased incidence of genetic defects and of leukemia and bone cancer throughout the world. Serious as these effects are, these worldwide radiation effects would probably come to less than that from natural background radiation. Moreover, there is little evidence that the nuclear powers are planning to procure weapon systems that will lead to greater worldwide fallout damage in the future. The opposite may be true. Without depreciating the awful consequences of a large nuclear war, especially for the participants, it would be dangerous to assume that an aggressor would be deterred from launching a war by worldwide radiation effects. However, there are uncertainties: the fallout problem is not entirely understood, more serious effects may yet be discovered, and new and more devastating weapons may be developed and procured in the course of the 1960's. In any case, there would be worldwide damage from a general nuclear war, and governments have an urgent obligation to take this damage into account in their preparations just as they have an obligation to weigh the prospective damage to their own population, that of their immediate neighbors, their allies, and their enemies.

## The Mutual Suicide View

Much more serious would be the effect of a general nuclear war on the participants. Possible attacks, equivalent to several thousand megatons of TNT delivered on the United States, could kill over half of our population. Moreover, our entire population is at risk. This fact, along with the expectations that Soviet civil society is similarly exposed, leads to the view that a general war would inevitably mean the destruction of both sides.

Belief that nuclear war inevitably would result in mutual suicide results in an almost exclusive focus on deterrence-only policies; that is, policies intended to prevent war, not to mitigate its consequences if it were to come nonetheless. This view, often implicit, is made explicit in the doctrine of finite or minimum deterrence. ("Minimum" deterrence, in another sense, that of preventing war at minimum cost, enjoys practically universal acceptance.) The minimum deterrence doctrine holds that we should unilaterally reduce our general war capability by cutting down the active defenses of our cities, by not spending money on civil defense, and by limiting our offensive forces to a level adequate to destroy in retaliation some, perhaps only a few, enemy cities. It assumes that deterrence is *easy* and that working toward deterrence is *enough*.

The minimum deterrence doctrine recognizes two important truths: First, that it is not necessary to promise total destruction to a nation to deter it. Second, that the strategic nuclear balance is unstable and that we should try to stabilize it. However, this doctrine has important limitations. Contrary to the view that deterrence is easy, the difficulties of assuring retaliation *are* great. The effective weight of attack delivered in retaliation might be very much less than the level that would be lethal to a nation. It might, in some circumstances, permit the aggressor to recover rapidly. Most importantly, this view assumes that both sides would inevitably direct a great weight of attack against opposing civil targets. It is by no means certain that this would happen in a general war; both sides might have a great incentive to avoid cities. A nuclear war might be blind destruction, but on the other hand it might not. At best, it would offer a risky prospect. Nevertheless, although well-chosen defense policies can reduce the likelihood of war, it seems doubtful they can reduce its likelihood to zero. These considerations argue for something more than complete dependence on nuclear deterrence.

### Deterrence plus Insurance

This view gives great emphasis to the difficulty of having an assured retaliatory capability. It also holds that different possible outcomes of a general war can be distinguished and that the outcome would depend on the preparations of the contenders, their war objectives, and circum-

stances at the war's inception. This view does not place primary reliance for the defense of any very large part of the world on the threat of general nuclear war. For that objective, it emphasizes capabilities for direct defense abroad. It includes insurance as well as deterrence capabilities—insurance in the form of strong active and passive defenses in the United States and strategic forces designed to attack the enemy's military forces. And it includes insurance in the form of an ability to fight a nuclear war in a controlled manner. Finally, it is concerned about the stability of the balance of terror, the danger of a crisis exploding into a general war.

### Extended Deterrence

Much of the burden of the defense of Europe in the 1950's has rested on the threat of a U.S. attack against the Soviet Union even in the face of nonnuclear aggression. The extended deterrence doctrine recognizes that the threat of U.S. initiation of general nuclear war has been and is an important bulwark of our defense abroad and seeks to make it more credible. (It should be distinguished from the declaratory policy of making threats of general war in circumstances in which very great devastation to the United States would seem to be a *certain* result.) This increased credibility would come from an expansion of offense forces, our air defenses, and our civil defenses. However, although much could be done to strengthen our ability to wage general war, the net effectiveness of such a program in the 1960's must inevitably be uncertain. And a greatly expanded program to increase our general war capabilities might increase the chances of general war, because it would make us look more threatening. It might increase *his* likelihood of hitting us first. This is not to say that a program aimed at sustaining the force of our general war threat as a deterrence to aggression abroad would be infeasible or without effect; it is to say that such a program would be difficult, costly, uncertain, and risky.

### Massive Retaliation

This doctrine applies the threat of general nuclear war, or the threat of actions which make a big war substantially more likely, to the defense of much of the free world. However, if our threat of general war retains some validity in the defense of so vital an area as Europe, it loses much for other parts of the world. And the expected shifts in the military power balance in the 1960's will diminish the validity of this doctrine throughout. In sum, it appears that a greater concentration on direct defense of all overseas areas will be needed.

The principal views to be found for the direct defense of overseas areas are as follows:

## DEPENDENCE ON TACTICAL NUCLEAR FORCES

A policy of defending overseas areas by using small nuclear weapons on the battlefield would interpose a level of defense between the use of nonnuclear weapons and all-out nuclear war. They would give us graduated deterrence. However, the Russians have these weapons, too; a tactical nuclear war would be two-sided. One consequence is that such an exchange might result in great civilian damage in the area fought over. Another is that although any war between the United States and the Communist bloc carries the grave risk of exploding into all-out war, a nuclear war would seem substantially more likely to do so than a nonnuclear one. Even so, we cannot dispense with a tactical nuclear capability; in some circumstances we might elect to initiate this type of war. On the other hand, perhaps we are preparing our overseas forces too exclusively for this type of combat, and neglecting preparation for nonnuclear conflict.

## ESTABLISHMENT OF INDEPENDENT NUCLEAR FORCES

A second alternative for the more direct defense of overseas areas, one already chosen by Britain and France, is to build up independent nuclear forces. Or a European force might be created. However, if either a European or separate national force is to have a suitable retaliatory capability in the face of a nuclear assault, it must be designed to survive an enemy first strike. This task is difficult even in the United States. If not attained abroad, or worse, if not even attempted, additional nuclear forces could be seriously destabilizing to world peace. And for the United States to aid in the establishment of independent nuclear forces runs counter to our policy of discouraging the spread of nuclear weapons around the world. This policy has been based on the belief that the long-term security of the United States and the entire world would be prejudiced by the wider diffusion of bombs—especially if they were to get into the hands of irresponsible powers. Nevertheless, the process of diffusion is underway. Though difficult or impossible to stop it, it may be possible to slow it down. In the end, we might find ourselves forced to help build up the nuclear capabilities of some of our allies if feasible alternatives have been foreclosed. We should be ready for this contingency.

## USE OF NONNUCLEAR FORCES

The distinction between a nuclear and a nonnuclear bomb detonation is now, and will remain for some time, unmistakable. It is this distinction that gives most support to the hope that a nonnuclear limited war could be kept limited. This distinction seems worth preserving. Moreover, contrary to the widespread belief, we do *not* have a basic inferiority in nonnuclear capabilities in many areas abroad. For example, the economic re-

sources, population and technology of the NATO powers are superior to those of the Warsaw Pact countries. (The situation of the non-Communist countries of Asia is less favorable.) In Europe—where we are strong—we have not drawn sufficiently on our underlying nonnuclear strength. Actually an economically feasible goal for NATO would be nothing less than the ability to defeat Russian forces, allowing for the mobilization potentials of both sides, at the nonnuclear level. Such a policy, although not a complete one for the defense of Europe, would do much to free NATO policy from having to face the grim alternative of ineffectual action or nuclear war. However, the history of NATO throws serious doubt on the political likelihood of such a course, in the absence of a crisis.

No informed person can view the longrun prospect for peace with any equanimity. We are in an urgent arms race; in fact, we are in several. There is the race in military technology, the race in trying to preserve retaliatory capabilities, the race toward outer space, and others. Some are harmful to the cause of world peace, but not all of them. This fact makes it important to distinguish among them. Those aspects of the race that promise to reduce the likelihood of war or its excesses if it comes, deserve support; this is not true of those that act to make war more likely or excessively destructive. And there are several ominous developments of the latter kind: the possibility that the uneasy balance of deterrence may be upset, the diffusion of nuclear weapons throughout the world, and, perhaps most importantly, the longrun consequences of advancing military technology.

In addition to seeking a peaceful solution to our security problem through national defenses we can try to mitigate the worst aspects of the arms race through disarmament. Or rather through *arms control*, for attempting to control arms seems to be a more fruitful approach toward a stable peace than the attempt simply to do away with arms. In fact, some agreements aimed at eliminating arms might in fact make war more likely. Although agreements on the control of arms have proven difficult to conclude in the postwar period, there seem to be several possible areas of mutual interest between the Soviet Union and ourselves. Agreement might be reached on measures to reduce the likelihood of a deliberate surprise attack, or to reduce the possibility of a war by miscalculation, or on the diffusion of nuclear weapons, or on some form of disengagement abroad. Such partial agreements might be useful because, if our goal is a peaceful evolution of our society and that of other countries rather than the elimination of armaments per se, agreed measures would not be intended as a replacement for national defenses.

In sum, the decade of the 1960's will be a decade of great danger. We have been thrust into a situation in which nuclear threats, counter-threats, and coercion seem inevitable. In this situation we are faced with three broad choices: (1) The defense objectives we will support, (2) the

extent to which we are willing to risk all-out war in support of these objectives, and (3) our willingness to make economic sacrifices. If we try holding Communist military power behind its present boundaries, and if it presses openly against them, then we might be forced into a large defense effort—or alternately forced to abandon some of our defense objectives abroad. If, on the contrary, the Communists come to accept the status quo, some of our defense efforts could be reduced. We should be clear, however, that preserving a secure retaliatory power will be difficult in any case. Beyond that we should be prepared to meet aggression over a wide spectrum. Where possible, we and our allies should build up defenses abroad that do not force us to step up the level of violence substantially if these defenses are to be effective. This is not to say that we might not choose to increase the level of violence, for there may be circumstances in which we would not only want to threaten greater violence but to carry out our threat in defense of our interests.

Our preferred general war alternatives for the 1960's would seem to center on the deterrence-plus-insurance position. This view does not deny extended deterrence some value; rather it holds that the defense of overseas areas should depend more on direct defenses abroad. And probably the single most useful direction in which we should move abroad is to emphasize nonnuclear defenses more in our network of alliances.

It is not possible to predict with any confidence the pattern of the defense budget over the next decade. There is too much uncertainty in technology, in the future behavior of the Communist bloc nations, and in our own responses to challenges. An extrapolation of the trend of the past few years suggests that defense budgets might drift downward as a percentage of our gross national product. However, if we try to maintain a more certain ability to retaliate after attack and to limit damage to the United States, while maintaining strong forces abroad, our defense budget may have to increase at a rate comparable to the rate of growth of our GNP or faster; perhaps faster because the rapid growth of the Soviet and Chinese economies and, possibly, defense budgets may force us to—unless we limit some of our overseas objectives or succeed in shifting more of the burden of defense to our allies.

Alternatively, if we were to adopt the minimum deterrence doctrine for general war, and if Communist bloc reductions in ground forces, along with its recognition of current boundaries seemed to reduce the threat of aggression abroad, we might reduce our defense budget sharply. On this assumption, it might fall during the 1960's to, say 5 or 6 percent of our GNP from the present level of 9 percent.

Finally, we must continue to keep in mind the possibility that a great war crisis could occur sometime between now and 1970. If so, our defense budget might have to be greatly expanded, possibly to $100 billion a year or more.

# 22 / The Crisis of Strategic Nuclear Deterrence

ARNOLD WOLFERS AND OTHERS

One central question in the great debate over American military strategy and force requirements has involved two competing concepts, "counter-force" strategy vs. "minimum deterrence" or "finite deterrence" strategy.

## 1. Introduction

American military policy in the cold war is primarily concerned not with the fighting and winning of war but with the discouragement of aggression by the Sino-Soviet bloc, either upon the United States or upon its allies. Logically, therefore, the emphasis is on a strategy of deterrence. While the goal of deterrence itself is not in doubt today, serious questions have been raised about the means by which it can be pursued under present and foreseeable conditions. Specifically, the deterrent value of the U.S. strategic force, on which so much reliance is placed, is being diminished by the rising strategic power of the Soviet Union. The change in the strategic equation . . . threatens the security of our overseas allies, particularly with regard to the less provocative forms of conceivable Sino-Soviet aggression, and, for a temporary period at least, has greatly increased the risk of a Soviet attack on the continental United States.

If the American nuclear monopoly, coupled with an ample supply of nuclear warheads and delivery vehicles, had continued to exist, the reliability of the American nuclear deterrent would not now be open to question. The United States and its allies could have remained confident that the threat of massive retaliation against Soviet cities in response to any

Reprinted from U. S. Senate Committee on Foreign Relations Study No. 8, "Developments in Military Technology and Their Impact on United States Strategy and Foreign Policy," by The Washington Center of Foreign Policy Research, The Johns Hopkins University (December, 1959), in *U.S. Foreign Policy:* Compilation of Studies, 87th Cong., 1st sess., S. Doc. 24 (March 15, 1961), pp. 775–78. Footnotes in the original report have been omitted.

Arnold Wolfers is a scholar of diplomacy and strategy. Two of his associates in the preparation of this study were James E. King, Jr., a leading American civilian strategist and high-ranking official of the Institute for Defense Analysis, and Paul H. Nitze, who has served in the Department of State, the Pentagon's Defense Secretariat, and as Secretary of the Navy. All have written extensively on defense and related questions.

serious Soviet aggression would have been both credible and effective. As a nuclear monopolist, the United States would not have had to fear the self-mutilating consequences that could follow a strike on an opponent able to retaliate in kind.

With the advent of Soviet nuclear striking power, the situation radically changed. Now, neither side, if it initiates the use of strategic force, can be certain that it would avoid being struck itself by nuclear weapons, unless it can predict with assurance that its first-strike blow against its opponent's strategic forces will be almost totally effective. If one side should achieve such an overwhelming counterforce ability, it could gain or regain the position of a monopolist by employing its strategic power against the strategic forces of its adversary.

Development of the capabilities required for such a knockout blow by either the United States or the Soviet Union is not now likely, although it cannot be ruled out as a future possibility in view of the rapid pace and uncertain predictability of technological developments. . . .

However, neither the United States nor the Soviet Union can ignore the possibility that its adversary might someday settle for less than a knockout blow and, rationally or irrationally, be content with a strike at its adversary's retaliatory forces sufficiently crippling to make tolerable the damage it might suffer in return. Conceivably, for instance, one side or the other might consider even very grave damage more tolerable than the risks of allowing its adversary to strike the first blow, should such a strike appear imminent.

### 2. Deterrence of a Soviet Attack Upon the Strategic Forces of the United States or Its Allies

In order to clarify the problems of American military strategy, deterrence of an all-out Soviet attack, including an attack on the United States and its strategic forces, must be treated separately from deterrence of lesser attacks, restricted in geography or means, because it is the one contingency in which the American ability to retaliate might be gravely impaired—if not destroyed—by the effects of a Soviet first strike against the U.S. strategic force itself.

In view of the assumed disparity between American and Soviet missile capabilities, the dangers of a Soviet surprise attack against SAC must be taken very seriously in coming years. At least through the early 1960's, the American retaliatory force, composed of manned bombers and located on unhardened and unhidden bases, will remain highly vulnerable to such an attack, and this vulnerability will increase as long-range missiles of growing power and accuracy become the principal components of the Soviet strategic force. It is clear, therefore, that American security against a Soviet first strike rests not on the prehostilities strength of SAC, which

remains impressive, but rather on the degree of its security against nuclear attack.

Only an assured second-strike or retaliatory capability, sufficient to impress the Soviets of the intolerable level of its destructive potential, can provide even a relatively effective deterrent against a Soviet attack on the continental United States and its overseas allies.

It is unlikely that there will be an abrupt decline in the deterrent value of the U.S. strategic force against a Soviet nuclear attack. Even a relatively small number of surviving bombers, armed with multiple thermonuclear weapons and capable of penetrating to their targets, poses a threat of severe retaliatory destruction. Furthermore, the United States has a variety of delivery systems, including both planes and missiles. One should not exaggerate the dangers of the missile gap period.

But while one should not exaggerate the dangers of the missile gap period, they can also easily be underestimated. A deterrent can never be wholly reliable. There is no certainty that in Soviet estimates a sufficient number of SAC bombers would escape destruction, or reach their targets, or cause damage regarded as intolerable by the Soviets under the given circumstances.

Another consideration influences the effectiveness of the deterrent. It should be recalled that a second-strike or retaliatory capacity must serve two functions: first, to deter an all-out strategic attack, and secondly, if war occurred, to maximize the destruction of the enemy's forces, and to reduce, as much as possible, the destruction to the victim of the attack in subsequent strategic exchanges. These functions suggest conflicting and, in some instances, contradictory target strategies for the second-strike force.

Whereas the aggressor's force must seek to destroy the strategic forces of its adversary in a counterforce blow, the victim in its retaliatory second strike may choose ( a ) a counterforce strike against those of its opponent's strategic forces that have not yet gone into action, in addition to other targets of particular military significance ( i.e., communications centers, air defense centers, strategic air bases, gasoline refineries and storage sites, and sensitive industrial targets); ( b ) a strictly terror or city-busting strike; or ( c ) a combination of the two target strategies.

Strategy ( a ) makes the most military sense in the postattack situation —when deterrence has failed—because it seeks to minimize the destruction that the victim of the initial attack may expect to suffer from the aggressor's subsequent strikes. Yet, the deterrent effect of threatening to execute such a strategy may be minimal, particularly if the adversary's strategic forces are isolated from his key civilian and industrial installations, and its actual execution in war may be severely restricted by the opponent's active and passive defenses, by false or inadequate target intelligence, by a paucity of valuable targets (the most dangerous of enemy

weapons would have already been used), and, finally, by the diminished size of the second-strike force itself.

Strategy (*b*), the city-busting threat sometimes called that of finite or minimum deterrence, may appear to be the more efficient *deterrent* since it promises a high level of general and indiscriminate destruction to the attacking country. It lacks credibility as a deterrent threat, however, since the victim of the initial attack might be extremely reluctant to invoke the repeated strikes against his own cities that would be sure to follow if he himself struck only the aggressor's civilian targets and left residual strategic forces intact. The probable result of such a strategy would be a round of city-busting strikes in which the aggressor would hold the advantage.

Some authorities have questioned the deterrent value of the strategy of minimum deterrence on these grounds and have suggested that the Soviets might well doubt the credibility of an American threat of city-busting retaliation if they were themselves certain of their ability to pinpoint a first strike on American military targets in such a way as to minimize damage to the American civilian population. The execution of the retaliatory threat against Soviet population centers, invoking subsequent Soviet counterretaliation, would appear to be a strategy of little utility and of particularly devastating consequences for the United States in view of the increasing differential between American and Soviet levels of civil defense preparedness.

Nevertheless, it does not seem probable that the Soviets would lightly risk the possibility of a mistaken estimate of American intentions. However irrational a city-busting retaliatory strategy might appear, the United States might well respond to a first strike with all its remaining strategic forces against whatever Soviet targets could be hit, since it would have no time in which to revise its strategic plans. Readiness and a determination to strike back would have to be preserved until the very last minute if the American deterrent is to operate at all.

Finally, strategy (*c*) for the second strike, a combination of the counterforce and city-busting strategies, appears to be that which would almost inevitably be followed in practice, since in such a strike accurate discrimination between civilian and military targets would prove a very difficult task. As General White put it:

> The [second-strike] mission would be . . . to do the greatest possible damage to the Soviet Union as a whole with attention to applying that destruction in such a way as to do as much damage as possible to their residual military striking power.

Nevertheless, in order to maximize the military value of such a strike and to minimize the dangers to civilian populations, a major effort can and

should be made to direct the retaliatory attack against the enemy's strategic forces and targets as much as conditions permit.

As was suggested earlier, a "balance of terror" does now exist in the sense that neither side would rationally start a war by an intentional city-busting or terror attack which would leave its adversary's strategic forces intact. It seems more than likely, however, that attacks on cities would occur during the course of a nuclear war either as an act of retaliation or byproduct of counterforce operations or as a result of strategic blunders. This is the rationale behind the belief that civil defense measures would prove worth the costs and efforts required to put them into effect.

During what we have here referred to as the transitional phase of the nuclear-missile weapons generation, the possibility of a Soviet first strike against the continental United States cannot be denied, particularly as SAC will continue to depend heavily on manned bombers vulnerable to missile attack until the mid-1960's. The strategic equation will exhibit a high degree of instability during this period unless some form of effective arms control agreement is reached. It is impossible, of course, to predict whether the Soviets would in fact take advantage of a surprise attack capability if they believed they had attained it through their missile lead. Despite continued high risks discouraging such an attack, they might be tempted to strike if they foresaw an early end to their advantage. Or they might be inclined to exploit their lead before attaining an unmistakably effective first-strike capacity if they feared that the United States would attack first in order to forestall a further serious weakening of its strategic position.

The present high degree of instability in the strategic equation has been hopefully called "transitory" in the belief that the great dangers of the missile gap will diminish as the United States acquires a missile retaliatory force of high invulnerability, numerical strength, and great variety. Once the United States acquires such a retaliatory force, the dangers of a premeditated first strike at the strategic forces of the United States and its allies will be greatly lessened, and the American strategic deterrent will regain a considerable measure of reliability. It should be stressed, however, that new technological developments favoring the offense or a relaxation of American efforts to maintain an adequately protected and effective second-strike capability could again rob the American retaliatory force of its ability to strike back. Because technological developments will continue and, possibly, at an accelerating pace, a continuous and most costly effort will be necessary to preserve the effectiveness of the deterrent. The degree of effort required, and the form it will have to take, will be largely determined by our estimates of the size and quality of Soviet counterforce abilities in the decade ahead.

### 3. Deterrence of Attacks on America's Overseas Allies

We must now turn to the second danger posed by growing Soviet strategic capabilities—the diminishing effectiveness of American strategic nuclear power as a deterrent against a wide spectrum of aggressions against overseas free world areas or against other violations of vital American overseas interests.

Under conditions of American nuclear supremacy, SAC was able to spread a protective "nuclear umbrella" over the rimland countries of Eurasia by its threat of strategic intervention. Now, however, with the rising Soviet strategic counterdeterrent, the credibility of this American threat is being questioned, and its usefulness as a rational instrument to aid in the protection of our overseas allies has proved limited, as applied to all but the more serious and unambiguous forms of Sino-Soviet aggression.

In order to have a reliable deterrent against overseas aggression, the United States would have to possess a counterforce capability for a first strike at the Soviet Union that could be expected to reduce Soviet counterretaliation against the United States to tolerable proportions. This precondition raises two serious problems. First, the acquisition of such a counterforce capacity in the missile age may prove impractical in terms of the number of missiles required, and, secondly, the efforts required for its attainment would greatly increase the instabilities of the strategic equation and thus the risk of total nuclear war.

As indicated in an earlier chapter, the maintenance of an effective counterforce capability would require not a mere matching of Soviet missile forces, but the accumulation of American missiles in numbers substantially exceeding the numbers of Soviet launching sites. The low relative accuracy, reliability, and warhead power of at least the first generation missiles suggest that from 6 to 60 of them may be needed to "take out" a single enemy launching site under various circumstances. Although this disproportion will be reduced by refinements in nuclear warheads and missile accuracy, it is unlikely to approach a 1:1 missile-to-target ratio against hardened or mobile military targets.

An effort to attain adequate strategic counterforce capability would remain practical if the Soviets continued what appears to be their present pattern of creating only a counterdeterrent force. That this is the Soviet objective today is suggested by the limited size of the Soviet bomber fleet, as well as by Mr. Khrushchev's recent statement [May 11, 1959] that the Soviet Union already possesses the number of missiles requisite to implement its strategy. However, the United States can ill afford to rely on such a reassuring estimate of Soviet intentions, nor can it assume that Soviet force goals will not be increased in the future. If the Soviets utilized their assumed capacities for the production of

long-range missiles, they might in the course of a few years achieve a formidable retaliatory force. Thereafter, an attempt to create a force capable of "taking out" or severely crippling Soviet retaliatory power might prove not only prohibitively expensive but impossible in view of the number of American missiles and the amount and quality of target intelligence required. The goal of only a moderate amount of counterforce ability, on the other hand, would do little to increase the deterrent effect of our strategic force against Sino-Soviet aggression on our allies, although such a level of counterforce ability may prove useful for purposes that will be discussed later. The threat of an ineffective counterforce first strike at the Soviet Union that would invite devastating Soviet retaliation would be little more credible than the threat to hit Soviet cities. There is no half-way station on the road to first-strike capability, and the trends in technological development and the race for increased invulnerability of retaliatory power militate against reaching this destination. Any attempts to overcome these obstacles, moreover, must almost necessarily provoke a spiraling and extraordinarily costly arms race.

The second dilemma in the attainment of preservation of the strategic deterrent is the incompatibility between the goals of continued counterforce capabilities and of minimizing the risk of total nuclear war. In line with the strategy of deterrence pursued to date, the United States has equipped itself with forces that are obviously and, in some instances, uniquely fitted for a counterforce first strike. These include our medium-range bombers supplemented by IRBM's in advanced positions that are both highly vulnerable and therefore more suitable for a first strike than a second. With these characteristics, the present U.S. strategic force may in fact be regarded by the Soviets as evidence of American "aggressive" intentions. The mere existence of a strategic force of this character could tempt them therefore to undertake a preventive counterforce attack, once they attained an adequate counterforce capability. Similarly, a buildup of Soviet forces designed for a first strike would be regarded as provocative by the United States, and would in turn lead to a high level of instability in the strategic equation.

The emergence of the Soviet counterdeterrent does not mean that the threat of American strategic intervention has lost—or is likely to lose —all of its deterrent value against every kind of Sino-Soviet aggression in the Eurasian rimland areas, particularly in areas of vital interest to the United States. On the contrary, the threat of a retaliatory first strike against a Soviet *nuclear* assault on Allied countries will remain virtually as credible as the threat of strategic retaliation against a Soviet attack on the United States itself. The Soviet risks in such an assault would exceed all rational limits, since, in sparing the United States, the Soviets would be leaving SAC intact, and, therefore, able to retaliate with its

full prehostilities strength. Even if retaliation by SAC left the Soviets with the capacity to do serious damage to the United States in return, the probability that SAC would fulfill its retaliatory threat should be sufficiently high to deter a Soviet nuclear assault on allies of the United States.

There is little reason, therefore, for these allies, particularly those in NATO, to fear that a nuclear stalemate would turn the United States and the Soviet Union into sanctuaries of a future war, while leaving other free world countries exposed to Soviet nuclear attack. Instead, these countries too would benefit from the protection such a stalemate would offer against all strategic nuclear aggression.

Against other less extreme forms of aggression, the American nuclear deterrent will continue to decrease in credibility as Soviet counterdeterrent power increases. It will, therefore, become a less reliable and appropriate instrument for the policy of containment that seeks to protect the overseas countries against a wide range of possible forms of aggression below the strategic level of nuclear attack. Sino-Soviet threats to free world security range from such nonmilitary acts as a blockade of West Berlin, or subversion on the Czech model, to aggression with substantial conventional military forces.

It is generally conceded already that the threat of "massive retaliation" does not apply to peripheral cases of aggression, or to indirect aggression. There is little possibility that the threat of SAC's intervention will appear credible in these cases, in view of the disproportion between the relatively low American interests at stake and the losses the United States would suffer if it fulfilled its threat.

Between such peripheral threats to free world security and a Soviet nuclear attack on the United States or its allies there remains, however, a large "middle ground" of conceivable Sino-Soviet provocations, and it is in this area that the questionable reliability or wisdom of American strategic intervention has become an issue of grave concern. These uncertainties stem from the fact that no realistic alternative to the instrument of American strategic power is presently available for the protection of our overseas allies.

It would be too pessimistic to assert that the threat of American strategic intervention has lost all deterrent value with respect to this middle ground. An important role is played here by American determination to intervene, a determination forcefully expressed in both official and unofficial circles in this country. Whether or not American intervention would be a rational move, the Soviet Government can never be sure that it will not take place. Because the Soviets can never be certain of the level of aggressive actions that would provoke American retaliation, they would be risking the destruction of much of their strategic force and many of their cities in committing one of the "middle

ground" acts of aggression. It is doubtful that they could believe the gains they hoped to achieve in such attacks would outweigh the risks incurred. In this sense, the uncertainty of U.S. intentions and reactions continues to exert a valuable deterrent effect upon Sino-Soviet expansionist moves.

Nevertheless, the United States and its allies remain in a dangerous position as long as they must rely primarily on the effectiveness of such a form of deterrence. The consequences would be grave, indeed, should this deterrent fail to deter. If the Soviets regarded the threat as a bluff, if they misjudged the limits of the peripheral forms of aggression they might safely undertake, or if they attacked regardless of the threat—through irrationality or fanaticism, under strong provocation or in despair—the United States would be forced to choose between allowing its allies to be overrun by Communist bloc forces or engaging in a course of action that might well result in the nuclear devastation of large areas of the United States.

The precariousness and dangers of these situations will necessarily increase as growing Soviet strategic power diminishes the credibility of the American deterrent. Therefore, both the United States and its allies have a vital interest in establishing a more reliable deterrent to limited Sino-Soviet assaults and in creating thereby less self-destructive defenses than American strategic forces can now provide. In fact, if no military alternative is found, the underpinnings of the American collective defense system, on which American foreign policy now rests, will be gravely weakened, and the United States might be left with only the desperate alternative of retrenchment and isolation in a Fortress America.

### 4. Alternatives to the American Strategic Deterrent

#### A. INDEPENDENT ALLIED STRATEGIC POWER

One alternative to the obvious expedient of strengthened local forces should be mentioned here, since it has gained wide attention in Britain, France, and, to a lesser extent, in other European countries. It is asserted that independent Allied strategic nuclear forces would have more deterrent value than SAC because their intervention, in case of an attack on the countries in question, would not be open to doubt. The validity of this view can, however, be very seriously questioned. It is hard to see how these independent but necessarily very weak strategic forces could exert any appreciable deterrent effect that is not already being provided by the U.S. strategic force. A relatively small number of nuclear warheads and carriers, such as Britain possesses and France and other countries hope to acquire, can support, at best, a

strategy of "minimum deterrence"—the threat of a terror attack on Soviet cities, not a counterforce blow at Soviet strategic forces. But if, as was suggested earlier in this chapter, a threat of city busting even by the United States or the Soviet Union will lack credibility except in response to a nuclear attack, it is much less credible that a country attacked by *conventional* forces would initiate rounds of city busting in which it must expect the obliteration of most of its urban centers in return for its destruction of only a few Soviet cities. If, instead, a European country were attacked with nuclear weapons, it is not only doubtful whether its small strategic forces would be able to survive and to retaliate at all, but such an attack on American allies is almost inconceivable unless coupled with a counterforce attack on SAC which would provoke American retaliatory action far more devastating than anything European countries could hope to produce.

### B. NONSTRATEGIC FORCES

If maintenance of American first-strike counterforce capabilities comes to be regarded as an impossible or—if stability is given high priority—an undesirable objective, U.S. strategic nuclear power will have lost much of its effectiveness as a deterrent against limited Sino-Soviet attacks on our overseas allies. If, at the same time, American second-strike capabilities continue to operate as an effective deterrent against a Soviet first strike, a nuclear stalemate or a condition of relatively stable mutual deterrence will exist on the strategic level. Under these conditions, neither side will regard the initiation of strategic nuclear war as a rational military policy, either in response to a nonnuclear attack or for aggressive purposes, either between themselves or in defense of their allies.

Such a stalemate, it must be emphasized, is no guarantee against either war by accident or war in general. Rather than discouraging or deterring limited and local wars, the strategic stalemate puts a premium on the use of superior nonstrategic military power by aggressive nations pursuing goals they cannot expect to attain without violence. Therefore, unless a nuclear stalemate, or state of mutual deterrence, is extended to the nonstrategic level, Soviet superiority on this level will represent a serious threat to the security of our overseas allies. Moreover, this asymmetry is a possible source of wars that may get out of hand and become "total," despite initial limitation.

The present nonstrategic capabilities of the United States and its allies should not be underestimated. In some instances of "brushfire wars"—even in wars as extensive as the war in Korea—the Western forces deployed locally or in the vicinity of the conflict, reinforced by forces located elsewhere or by subsequently mobilized reserves, may be

able to cope with a nonnuclear Communist assault. In the case of Que-moy, for example, it would appear that sufficient forces were available for its defense, and that there was little need for the threat of American strategic intervention, however credible that threat might have been against a country deemed incapable of nuclear retaliation.

The ability of American and allied forces to cope with a similar Communist threat might be in question, however, if a number of rela-tively minor assaults were launched simultaneously at widely scattered points along the fringes of the Iron and Bamboo Curtains. Such a situa-tion might easily overtax the modest American ready reserve forces as well as the now minimal U.S. airlift capacity with which to supplement inadequate allied and American forces already deployed overseas.

A major dilemma facing the United States and its allies today is the problem of providing the NATO area with adequate protection against Soviet assaults that would either be so limited or so ambiguous as not to provoke American strategic intervention or that would have tragic consequences, if they did. As we have seen, the existence of the Ameri-can strategic striking force sets a ceiling on the size of such Soviet assaults on Western Europe not coupled with a concomitant strike on American strategic power.

To date, the overwhelming potential of Soviet conventional capa-bilities has tended to discourage local NATO efforts to remedy the imbalance by providing an adequate NATO "Shield." There was little incentive for such efforts as long as European confidence in the Ameri-can "Grand Deterrent" (the NATO "Sword") remained unshaken. NATO planners have not regarded as impractical the task of building up a NATO Shield of local forces that could prevent Soviet armies from overrunning Western Europe on the assumption, however, that American strategic intervention would take place and would cripple the ability of the Soviet Union to reinforce its armies in the field and to continue the war. While the early Shield force goal of 96 divisions, envisioned at the Lisbon Conference of 1952, was soon abandoned, in the face of political, psychological and economic obstacles in Western Europe, NATO turned in 1954 to tactical nuclear weapons as a hope-fully less costly substitute for the defensive power of the unattainable conventional ground divisions. At the time, it was assumed that these weapons would provide enough firepower to counter the offensive abili-ties of numerically far superior Soviet ground forces.

Grave doubts about the wisdom of the NATO decision to rely so heavily on the use of tactical atomic weapons have been raised. Tactical nuclear warfare, as has been pointed out by both United States and Soviet military authorities, may easily require more manpower rather than less because of high casualty rates that will rapidly be sustained. It is doubtful in this context whether a small defensive army, equipped

173

with tactical nuclear weapons, could hold against a larger one equally armed. The European peoples are, in any event, awakening to the fact that a tactical nuclear war on their soil could easily obliterate many of the areas that it was intended to defend.

As mentioned earlier, it is conceivable that, by tacit agreement or as part of an international arms control scheme, general support could be gained for the proposition that the unilateral defensive use of tactical nuclear weapons by a victim of invasion is permissible within its own borders and airspace, while the invader may not reciprocate in kind.

Under present circumstances, it would appear that the NATO Shield forces need tactical nuclear weapons less as a means to counter a non-nuclear Soviet attack than in order to deter Soviet employment of tactical nuclear weapons. The possession of these weapons by both sides tends to enhance the possibility that a state of mutual deterrence may be extended to the tactical nuclear level in Europe. If it is, the great numerical superiority of the Soviet conventional ground force is brought into full relief.

In Europe, as well as in the United States, it is widely held that NATO cannot afford—financially, politically, or psychologically—to support dual-purpose forces (able to fight either a nuclear or a conventional war) strong enough to deter or, if necessary, to stop the Soviet "steamroller" from overrunning Europe. It is argued that Europe either must be protected by American and European strategic deterrents, or it will be at the mercy of Soviet capabilities and intentions. It may be questioned, however, whether this proposition is not excessively defeatist, despite the ominous implications of the receding deterrent value of strategic nuclear force.

As mentioned earlier, if the Soviets did, in fact, contemplate a conventional military assault on Western Europe, the larger the attack they made, the greater the risks they would be taking of American strategic intervention. It seems unlikely, therefore, that the Soviet Union would dare launch against Western Europe the mass armies presently stationed between the Iron Curtain and the Urals, a form of attack that would almost certainly trigger SAC's intervention. The Grand Deterrent still operates to discourage all but the more limited or ambiguous military assaults on Western Europe.

The real danger is not the threat of invasion by Soviet mass armies but of a surprise attack by the Soviet forces currently deployed close to the Iron Curtain, particularly the 22 combat-ready and well-equipped Soviet divisions stationed in East Germany. Despite the odds, the Soviets might conceivably gamble that, in such an attack, they could create a fait accompli in Europe with such speed that the United States would hesitate, after the fact, to launch a first-strike retaliatory blow of possible devastating consequences to itself. Another danger is a nonmilitary Soviet

act, like a blockade of Berlin, against which the threat of massive retaliation might not seem credible. In neither of these cases nor in other similar contingencies would NATO face or have to match the massive power of the Soviet "steamroller."

In the light of these considerations, the demand of General Norstad, the Supreme Commander of NATO forces in Europe, for a Shield of at least 30 divisions is a reasonable request. Provided they are trained and equipped as dual-purpose forces, these divisions should be able to hold against an attack by the 22 Soviet divisions presently stationed in East Germany and supplemented by other Soviet divisions now deployed in nearby countries. In an operation of this kind, however, NATO should be able to count upon a far greater supply of readily available reserves than exist today.

The establishment of a Shield force of 30 divisions, backed by adequate and readily available reserves, can hardly be assumed to exceed the capacity of the present economies of the NATO countries. The major obstacle blocking General Norstad's goal is a psychological one that stems in part from the continued European hope that protection will be provided by American strategic power. In part, it arises from the belief that the development of independent European strategic deterrents will obviate the necessity of a larger Shield. And, finally, there is a general and deep-seated skepticism in Europe concerning the possibility of countering Soviet numerical superiority with anything but nuclear weapons.

The extent to which this skepticism is justified is a question of the greatest importance for American consideration, since the United States is vitally interested in the creation of adequate local defense forces in Europe as well as elsewhere around the perimeter of the Soviet bloc. If European skepticism on this score is not justified, it should be dispelled. For this purpose, further investigation should be made of the technological improvements applicable to localized and regional warfare, such as the "ground effect" troop and weapons carriers and the lightweight anti-tank missiles earlier discussed. It is possible that a concentrated effort to develop capabilities of this order could do much to offset Soviet numerical and mechanized strength.

Recently, there has been a marked tendency in military thinking and analysis, both in the United States and abroad, to become more and more absorbed in the problems raised by the advent of nuclear weapons and by the distribution of power on the strategic level. While these problems are grave and immediate and deserve serious consideration, greater efforts should be made to investigate the neglected problems of nonnuclear armaments and warfare and the methods by which the effectiveness of conventional defensive forces and tactics can be enhanced. It would be a calamity if, in the event of a nonnuclear war, military thought and military preparations of the free world were found to have

been based chiefly on weapons, tactics, and experience of past wars instead of having taken full advantage of new technological opportunities in the field of nonnuclear warfare.

These opportunities should not be neglected on the assumption that tactical nuclear weapons can compensate for military weakness in other areas. As earlier mentioned, it is far from established that tactical nuclear weapons can make up for numerical inferiority to an enemy similarly armed, or even that their employment will tend to favor the defensive in land combat.

No clear distinction exists between tactical and strategic nuclear weapons, or tactical and strategic targets, and there are real dangers that a tactical nuclear war might rapidly degenerate into that general nuclear war which it is our purpose to avoid. There are, in addition, areas of the world in which the initiation of nuclear war in any form would hold severe political and psychological penalties for the United States.

Even should tactical nuclear war appear clearly in our interest in some specific instance, such warfare—as it is now envisaged—will require a very high level of ability in military transport, communications, target reconnaissance, and other "conventional" capabilities.

### 5. Preservation of a Measure of Counterforce Ability

It has been suggested that the growing invulnerability of strategic forces and the desire to minimize instabilities in the strategic equation may lead the United States and possibly the Soviet Union to abandon their efforts to strive for effective first-strike counterforce capabilities. However, preservation of some measure of counterforce ability remains useful for other purposes and, in fact, a decision to abandon the first-strike race would not eliminate all American counterforce capabilities, since some of the weapons and delivery systems necessary for a retaliatory second-strike capacity will be sufficiently accurate and powerful to perform counterforce missions as well as terror attacks.

There are several considerations that call for a continuation of present efforts to maintain counterforce capabilities, even if the goal of an effective first-strike force itself were relinquished.

First, if war should break out, even a localized or limited war, the United States would be severely handicapped in its strategic and political choices if it had no means of hitting elements of the enemy's strategic force, while the enemy had substantial counterforce capabilities. In a war confined to the Middle East or Asia, for example, an ability to take out strategic targets within a limited geographical area would seem indispensable, even if mutual deterrence on the highest strategic level precluded an all-out counterforce strike.

Second, in the case of a total strategic nuclear war in which the United States was the victim of a first strike, the counterforce abilities of the American second-strike force would enable the United States to conduct militarily useful operations and to minimize the damage to its own population and industrial centers that might be inflicted by subsequent Soviet strategic strikes following the initial attempt at a knockout blow.

Thirdly, a strong case can be made that only by continuing its research efforts in the field of counterforce weapons can the United States attain any degree of insurance against upset of the strategic balance by as yet unforeseen Soviet weapon developments.

Finally, American maintenance of even a moderate inventory of counterforce weapons would, it is argued, force the Soviets to divert funds from efforts to achieve an effective first-strike counterforce ability into expensive efforts to protect their existing strategic forces. In the absence of this pressure, it is said, the Soviets would be able to concentrate on their counterforce drive and would have an easier task in breaking the nuclear stalemate. Against this argument, however, it can be held that the ratio of expenditures favors the defense, not the offense, since the side seeking counterforce abilities must spend a multiple of the sum spent by its opponent on the invulnerability of its strategic retaliatory forces. Therefore, if the United States exploited the advantages of this ratio by concentrating on the protection of its second-strike force rather than on first-strike counterforce abilities, it might force the Soviet Union either to abandon hopes of overcoming U.S. retaliatory abilities or to risk financial exhaustion and possible failure in such a race.

In summation, the critical situation created by the decline in the deterrent value of the American strategic force, a result of technological developments and corresponding changes in the strategic equation, demands new military efforts by the United States and its allies. If they are made—and made in time—it will not be necessary to consider revisions in the basic objectives of American foreign policy or to sacrifice the present alliance policy which is a precondition of their pursuit. On the contrary, it is not overoptimistic to expect that a relatively stable strategic-nuclear stalemate and a reasonable degree of protection against nonstrategic aggression can be established, provided the United States equips itself with a secure retaliatory missile force and, with its allies, creates strong dual-purpose defense forces backed by readily available reserves.

# 23 / Limited War: Conventional or Nuclear? A Reappraisal

HENRY A. KISSINGER

A continuing question in the nuclear age involves the impact
of nuclear weapons on military instruments and military
planning for less than all-out war. This question and the
related issues it raises are analyzed in the following essay,
which constitutes the author's "second look" at the problem
of nuclear weapons in limited war.

FEW ISSUES have aroused more controversy than the relative role
of conventional and nuclear weapons in Western strategy. Its resolution
is of vital significance for our strategy, our policy in alliances, and the
future of arms-control negotiations.

Two facts need to be understood at the outset: no war in the nuclear
age can ever be completely free of the spectre of nuclear weapons—at
least, not until arms-control measures are much further advanced and
much more reliable. In a war between nuclear powers, even if no nuclear
weapons are used, both sides would have to take account of the possibility that they *might* be. The tactics would necessarily differ from those
of World War II; deployment would have to guard against the sudden
introduction of nuclear weapons. Diplomats would have to negotiate
with the knowledge that any prolonged conventional war may turn into
a nuclear conflict, if not a final show-down. Every war henceforth will
be nuclear to a greater or lesser extent, whether or not nuclear weapons
are used.

A second fact is equally important: the choice between using conventional or nuclear weapons is no longer entirely up to us. The Soviet
nuclear arsenal is growing. Soviet military journals report tactical exercises with nuclear weapons. We cannot gear our strategy or stake our
survival on the assumption that nuclear weapons will *not* be used against
us. Even if we prefer to resist with conventional weapons, we have to

Reprinted from *Daedalus,* Journal of the American Academy of Arts and Sciences,
LXXXIX (Fall, 1960), 800–17. By permission of the American Academy of Arts and
Sciences and the author.

Henry A. Kissinger is professor of government, Harvard University. His earlier
views on the subject of the essay reprinted here are contained in his *Nuclear Weapons
and Foreign Policy* (1957). The questions discussed in the present selection, and
related issues, are dealt with more extensively in his *The Necessity for Choice* (1961).

be prepared for nuclear war as well. Only our being ready for limited (in addition to general) nuclear war will give us the option of a conventional strategy.

### Nuclear Strategy

With this background, we can summarize the arguments for both sides. The advocates of a nuclear strategy—a strategy of initiating the use of nuclear weapons in limited war—emphasize the disparity in mobilizable manpower between the Communist bloc and the free world, a disparity made even more acute by the Communist ability to concentrate their whole weight against states much smaller and much less well-equipped. Nuclear weapons, it is claimed, can serve as a substitute for manpower. At the very least, they will force an aggressor to disperse his forces and prevent break-throughs of established defensive positions and the consolidation of occupied territory.

The proponents of a nuclear strategy admit that if nuclear weapons were simply added to the tactics of World War II the result would probably be the complete devastation of the combat zone. They point out that such a course would be senseless. The cost of a nuclear strategy must be judged in terms of the tactics appropriate to nuclear weapons. Since nuclear weapons are so destructive and at the same time so easy to transport, large military formations cannot be maintained in the field. And they are unnecessary because fire power is no longer dependent on massed armies. To concentrate is to court disaster. Safety resides in mobility. Logistics must be simple. The traditional supply system is too cumbersome and too vulnerable. Accordingly, a great premium will be placed on small, self-contained units of high mobility. In such circumstances, it is argued, damage would not be excessive; indeed it might be less than that of a conventional war of the World War II variety with a flankless front line rolling over the countryside.

A nuclear strategy according to its proponents would have these advantages. (a) The dispersal of troops would separate the requirements of victory from those of controlling territory. To prevail in a nuclear war, it is necessary to have small, highly mobile units. To control territory, larger concentrations are required, particularly in the key centers of administration. For example, the Soviet army required some twenty divisions to crush the Hungarian rebellion. Crushing the rebellion, it is argued, would have been clearly impossible if the Soviets had had to face nuclear weapons. (b) Nuclear war would complicate the aggressor's calculations—if only because it is an unfamiliar mode of warfare. The Soviet Union and Communist China possess many 'experts' in conventional warfare; but with respect to nuclear war, the calculations are theoretical. There would always remain the inevitable uncertainty of

embarking on a course in which no experience is available. (c) Nuclear war would be an effective device to weaken the Communist control of Soviet dominated areas. The small detachments that are appropriate for nuclear war will be extremely vulnerable to guerilla activity and can be handicapped severely by a hostile population. Since the population on the Western side of the Iron Curtain is more loyal to its governments than are those under Communist rule, a nuclear war is thought to be the best means of exploiting Soviet political difficulties—at least, in Europe—and therefore the most effective means of deterring Soviet aggression. (d) Nuclear weapons are our 'best weapons', the result of our most advanced technology. To forego using them is to deprive ourselves of the advantages of a superior industrial potential. (e) Any other course would impose impossible force requirements. It is admittedly impossible to fight a conventional war against a nuclear enemy without having a nuclear establishment in the field—otherwise, the temptation for the aggressor to use nuclear weapons and sweep all before him might become overwhelming. This means that we would need a well-protected retaliatory force, a capable limited war force, and increasing conventional strength. Since the expense of maintaining each category even at present levels is multiplying, and since the military budget is shrinking, any attempt to build up conventional forces must result in a fundamental, perhaps fatal, weakness in each category.

## Conventional Strategy

The advocates of a conventional strategy reply that the decision to use nuclear weapons is inconsistent with the very concept of limitation. Pointing to such military exercises with nuclear weapons as 'Carte Blanche' in Europe and 'Sagebrush' in the United States, they stress that the inevitable consequences of nuclear war will be the desolation of the combat zone and the decimation of the population. No country would wish to be defended at that price. Even a 'successful' nuclear war would provide a conclusive argument for future Soviet blackmail.

Moreover, once nuclear weapons are used, so this school of thought reasons, all restraints may disappear. It will be difficult enough to establish the limits of a conventional war. Because of their very unfamiliarity, nuclear weapons would make the task nearly impossible. The very fact that there exists a continuous spectrum of destructiveness in nuclear weapons, so often invoked by advocates of a nuclear strategy in defence of their thesis, is used by their critics against them. If the distinction between the low-yield and high-yield weapons is so difficult, if so much depends on the manner of employing them, any effort to set limits based on explosive equivalent will be meaningless. The temptation to resort to even more destructive weapons will be overwhelming.

Proponents of a conventional strategy question not only the possibility of limitation but also the efficacy of the tactics thought to be appropriate for nuclear war. Small detachments, they contend, whatever their nuclear fire power, would be extremely vulnerable to harassment and defeat by conventional forces. When confronted by an opponent possessing both a nuclear and a conventional capability, they are almost certain to lose, for they would be largely defenceless against small conventional raiding parties. Nuclear weapons, it is contended, are not a substitute for manpower. On the contrary, because of its high rate of attrition, nuclear war would probably require more manpower, not less.

Finally, our industrial potential will be less significant in a nuclear war. Since nuclear weapons provide greater destructiveness per unit cost than do conventional explosives, reliance on them enables economically weaker nations to redress the strategic balance much more easily than they could with conventional forces. A point is likely to be reached for any given objective or area at which additional increments of explosive power are no longer strategically significant. When this 'saturation point' is reached, superiority in nuclear weapons may be meaningless. And nuclear weapons place a premium on surprise attack and sudden thrusts to which the defender is much more vulnerable than the attacker. To rely on a nuclear strategy, it is urged, would thus be adopting a course of conduct which rewards the qualities in which potential aggressors excel.

A conventional strategy according to its advocates would have these advantages. (1) It would provide the best chance to limit any conflict that might break out. (2) It would use our industrial potential to best advantage. Since the destructive power of individual conventional weapons is relatively low, victory can be achieved only through a substantial production effort which puts a premium on our special skills. At the same time, the relatively slow pace of military operations—at least, as compared to nuclear war—and the need to build up supplies before such a new advance give the maximum opportunity for attempting a political settlement. (3) Conventional defence provides the best means of preventing the occupation of threatened countries. The concept of a flankless line which advocates of a nuclear strategy wish to abandon is likely to be considered by threatened countries as the best guarantee of their safety. Liberation will always be a less attractive prospect than protection. (4) If, after all, nuclear weapons were used, the onus of initiating such a war would be shifted to the Communist states.

### The Debate

One of the difficulties in resolving these arguments is that the moral fervor of the debaters sometimes obscures the nature of the issues and

often causes them to claim too much: those who think that to forego nuclear weapons is an offence against progress have as their counterpart those who are passionately convinced that even to consider modalities of nuclear warfare is to insult morality. As a result, arguments that closer examination would reveal at least as imprecise and sometimes as erroneous have been elevated into dogma.

For example, it is often said that a nuclear war cannot be limited because neither side would accept defeat without resorting to even larger weapons. Now there are many good reasons for concern about the possibility of limiting nuclear war. But the argument that neither side will be prepared to accept a setback implies that it is somehow worse to be defeated in nuclear than in conventional war. In reality, it seems much more likely that the decision as to whether a war is to be expanded depends more on the value attached to the objective than to the weapons used to attain it. It is not clear why a country should be more willing to acquiesce in a conventional than in a nuclear defeat. Whatever the technical difficulties of limiting nuclear war, the political argument that it makes defeat unacceptable does not bear scrutiny.

On the other side of the debate a nuclear strategy is often justified by the spectrum of available weapons. The smallest nuclear weapons, it is said, are less destructive than the most powerful conventional devices. There is therefore no technical reason to recoil before nuclear warfare, and every reason to use our most 'advanced' technology. However, the effort to base a nuclear strategy on the discrimination of nuclear weapons surely goes too far. The chief motive for using them is, after all, their greater destructive power and their lower weight per explosive equivalent. Nuclear weapons no more destructive than conventional ones would probably not be worth the increased risk of 'escalation' inherent in an unfamiliar mode of warfare.

The frustration in the debate is all too often caused by the fact that both the proponents and the opponents of a nuclear strategy are right: their disagreements arise from the perspective from which they consider the issue. Looking at the problem from the point of view of deterrence, the advocates of a nuclear strategy argue that nuclear weapons are the most effective sanction against the outbreak of a war. Considering the actual conduct of a war, the opponents of a nuclear strategy are above all concerned with reducing the impact of military operations and increasing their predictability. The destructiveness of individual weapons and the uncertainties of an unfamiliar mode of warfare which are correctly adduced as contributing to deterrence can, with equal justification, be cited as working against effective limitation.

Much of the debate therefore turns on the question of what should be stressed: deterrence or the strategy for fighting the war. Obviously, an overemphasis on destructiveness may paralyze the will. But an over-

concern with developing a tolerable strategy for the conduct of war may also reduce the risks of aggression to such a degree that it will be encouraged. While the deterrent threat must be credible, the quest for credibility must not lower the penalties to a point at which they are no longer unacceptable. The frequency of warfare since the Middle Ages demonstrates the difficulty of achieving deterrence with conventional weapons alone. On the other hand, a course of action that increases the opponent's uncertainties about the nature of the conflict will generally discourage aggression. If war should break out, however, through accident or miscalculation, it may make limitation extremely difficult.

Some years ago this author advocated a nuclear strategy. It seemed then that the most effective deterrent to any substantial Sino-Soviet aggression was the knowledge that the United States would employ nuclear weapons from the very outset. A nuclear strategy appeared to offer the best prospect of offsetting Sino-Soviet manpower and of using our superior industrial capacity to best advantage.

The need for forces capable of fighting limited nuclear war still exists. However, several developments have caused a shift in my view about the relative emphasis to be given conventional forces as against nuclear forces. These are: (1) the disagreement within our military establishment and within the alliance about the nature of limited nuclear war; (2) the growth of the Soviet nuclear stockpile and the increased significance of long-range missiles; (3) the impact of arms-control negotiations. The first of these considerations raises doubts as to whether we would know how to limit nuclear war. The second alters the strategic significance of nuclear war. The third influences the framework in which any strategy will have to be conducted and determines the political cost.

While it is feasible to design a theoretical model for limited nuclear war, the fact remains that fifteen years after the beginning of the nuclear age no such model has ever achieved general agreement. It would be next to impossible to obtain from our military establishment a coherent description of what is understood by 'limited nuclear war'. The Air Force thinks of it as control over a defined air space. The Army considers it vital to destroy tactical targets which can affect ground operations, including centres of communications. The Navy is primarily concerned with eliminating port installations. Even within a given service, a detailed, coherent doctrine is often lacking. The Strategic Air Command and the Tactical Air Force almost surely interpret the nature of limited nuclear war differently. Since disputes about targets are usually settled by addition—by permitting each service to destroy what it considers essential to its mission—a limited nuclear war fought in this manner may well become indistinguishable from all-out war. At least, it would diminish our assurance and subtlety in an operation in which everything would depend on the ability to remain in control of events.

## Problem of Allies

The disagreements between our services are repeated in relations with our allies. Few of our allies possess nuclear weapons. Those that do have emphasized the retaliatory and not the tactical aspect of nuclear warfare. Public opinion in most allied countries has been mobilized against nuclear weapons by a variety of agents. And these attitudes are reinforced by current trends in arms-control negotiations. In these circumstances, it will become increasingly difficult to concert a strategic and tactical doctrine that is accepted by the alliance and maintained with conviction in the face of Soviet pressure. This raises doubt as to whether the West will possess either the knowledge or the daring to impose limitations. If it relies *entirely* on a nuclear strategy, its vulnerability to nuclear blackmail both before and during hostilities would be considerable.

To be sure, any limitation of war is to some extent arbitrary. There is probably some disagreement even as to the nature of limited conventional war. The problem of communicating intentions to an opponent during a conflict will be difficult regardless of the mode of warfare, but this makes it all the more important that the limitations which are attempted be reasonably familiar. Even with the best intentions on both sides, a nuclear war will be more difficult to limit than a conventional one. Since no country has had any experience with the tactical use of nuclear weapons, the possibility of miscalculation is considerable. The temptation to use the same target system as for conventional war and thereby produce vast casualties will be overwhelming. The pace of operations may outstrip the possibilities of negotiation. Both sides would be operating in the dark with no precedents to guide them and a necessarily inadequate understanding of the purposes of the opponent, if not their own. The dividing line between conventional and nuclear weapons is more familiar and therefore easier to maintain—assuming the will to do so—than any distinction within the spectrum of nuclear weapons. This uncertainty may increase deterrence. It will also magnify the risks of conflict should deterrence fail.

These considerations are reinforced by the strategic changes wrought by the advent of the age of nuclear plenty and the long-range missile. When nuclear material was relatively scarce, it was possible to believe that tactical nuclear weapons might give the West an advantage in limited war. Under conditions of nuclear scarcity, the Soviet Union would have had to make a choice: it could not simultaneously push the development of its retaliatory force and also equip its ground forces for nuclear war. Whatever alternative was chosen would produce a weakness in *some* category. Since the logical decision for the Soviets was to give priority to the retaliatory force, it was then held that tactical nuclear

weapons could be used to offset Soviet conventional preponderance.

In the meantime, the Soviet nuclear stockpile has multiplied. A nuclear strategy will now have to be conducted against an equally well-equipped opponent. In these circumstances, numbers become again important. Because of the destructiveness of nuclear weapons, the casualty rate among combat units is likely to be high. The side which has the more replacements available therefore stands to gain the upper hand. The notion that nuclear weapons can substitute for numerical inferiority has lost a great deal of its validity.

The development of missiles has accentuated the strategic problems of limited nuclear war. As long as delivery systems were composed of airplanes, air domination over the battle area on the model of our experience in the Korean war was conceivable. And tactical skill in handling the weapons *within* the combat zone might lead to victory on the nuclear battlefield. However, as missile forces grow on both sides, as even airplanes are equipped with medium-range missiles, this possibility steadily diminishes. For one thing, it seems unnecessary to introduce major nuclear forces into the combat zone, since nuclear weapons can be delivered accurately at considerable distances. More importantly, the only way of achieving what used to be considered air superiority is to destroy most of the opponent's medium- and intermediate-range missiles. Such an operation is difficult to reconcile with an attempt to limit hostilities. If, however, the areas where these missiles are located become sanctuaries, it would appear that a stalemate is almost inevitably the outcome of a limited nuclear war.

Of course, such a result must not be minimized. An aggressor, certain that his attack would be checked, would presumably be deterred. The difficulty is the devastation of the combat zone, which would be the price of a stalemate. In some situations, it may be to the Communist advantage to settle for the *status quo ante* in a war that obliterates the disputed area. If a Soviet attack on Western Germany should lead to the desolation of the Federal Republic, the Soviet Union would score a major gain even if it offered at some point to withdraw to its starting point. The devastation of Germany might be a means of convincing all other threatened areas of the futility of resistance. An 'unsuccessful' attack of this nature might ensure the success of all future Soviet blackmail.

### Strategy and Arms Control

Finally, it would be idle to discount the impact on strategy of the pattern of arms-control negotiations. At each conference, nuclear weapons have been placed in a separate category and stigmatized as weapons of mass destruction without any distinction as to type or device. The goal of eventual nuclear disarmament has been avowed by all states.

A moratorium of nuclear testing has been in existence for two years, and it is probable that a formal agreement will be signed. Future negotiations will almost inevitably reinforce this trend. The consequence will be that the inhibitions against using the weapons around which the West has built its whole military policy will multiply. Whatever the other consequences of a nuclear-test ban, it will reinforce the already strong reluctance to use nuclear weapons in limited war.

These factors will create an extremely precarious situation if the free world continues to rely primarily on a nuclear strategy. The more the pressures build up against *any* use of nuclear weapons, the greater will be the gap between our deterrent policy, our military capability and our psychological readiness—a gap which must tempt aggression. The years ahead must therefore see a substantial strengthening of the conventional forces of the free world. If strong enough to halt Soviet conventional attacks—as in many areas such as Europe they could be—conventional forces would shift the onus and risk of initiating nuclear war to the other side. Even where they cannot resist every scale of attack, they should force the aggressor into military operations which leave no doubt as to his ultimate aim. They would thereby make an ultimate recourse to nuclear weapons politically and psychologically simpler, while affording an opportunity for a settlement before this step is taken.

Many of the assumptions regarding the impossibility of conventional defence and of 'hordes' of Communist manpower are either fallacious or exaggerated. Both in total available manpower and in its industrial potential, the free world still is superior. And conventional warfare favours the defence. It has been truly remarked that but for the development of nuclear weapons, the defence would long since have achieved ascendancy over the offence. Even in World War II, the attacker generally required a superiority of three to one.

To be sure, in other areas the problem is more complicated. In the so-called 'grey areas' of the Middle East and South-east Asia, the Communist bloc can concentrate its manpower and material against countries weaker and less closely allied than are those of the North Atlantic Community. On the other hand, these are also the areas where the political penalties for aggression would be the greatest. An attack on an emergent country would antagonize all the other uncommitted nations and would lead to an increased mobilization of Western resources. Moreover, difficulties of terrain and communications place a ceiling on the number of troops an aggressor could effectively utilize even there. The inability to protect every area locally is no excuse, nor is failing to secure those areas where protection is possible.

At a minimum, the conventional capability of the free world should be of such a size that a nuclear defence becomes the *last* and not the *only* recourse. The best situation is one in which the conventional forces

of the free world can be overcome *only* by nuclear weapons. There is no technical reason why this should not be possible, in Western Europe, at least. Such forces would remove many opportunities for Soviet gains achieved merely by the use of threats. They would increase the flexibility of our diplomacy. They would enable us to negotiate the control of nuclear weapons with confidence.

### Dangerous Conclusions

While a substantial build-up of conventional forces and a greater reliance on a conventional strategy is essential, it is equally vital not to press the conclusions too far. In their attempt to prove their case, many of the proponents of a conventional strategy have thought it necessary so to deride *any* reliance on nuclear weapons, or to paint so awful a picture of atomic war that they may defeat their own object. For, against an opponent known to consider nuclear war as the worst evil, nuclear blackmail is an almost foolproof strategy. Conventional forces will be of no avail if an aggressor is convinced that he can probably force surrender by threatening to use nuclear weapons. A greater emphasis on conventional defence presupposes that the aggressor cannot promise himself an advantage either from the threat or the actuality of nuclear war. However much conventional war may be preferred to the use of nuclear weapons, limited nuclear war is preferable to all-out war.

Conventional forces should not be considered a substitute for a capability of waging a limited nuclear war, but a complement to it. It would be suicidal to rely entirely on conventional arms against an opponent equipped with nuclear weapons. Such a development would probably provide the precise incentive an aggressor needs to employ nuclear weapons and to sweep all before him. A conventional war can be kept within limits only if nuclear war seems more unattractive.

This becomes apparent when we analyze what options we have if, despite our best efforts in the conventional field, nuclear weapons are actually used against us. We would then seem to have three choices: to accept defeat; to resort to general war; or to seek to conduct limited nuclear war. If we are unwilling to accept defeat—and to do so under such circumstances would make us forever subject to nuclear blackmail —our choice resolves itself into all-out war or limited nuclear war. All-out war will become increasingly senseless as the missile age develops. Hence, conventional war can be kept conventional only if we maintain, together with our retaliatory force, an adequate capability for limited nuclear war. The aggressor must understand that we are in a position to match any increment of force, nuclear or conventional, that he may add. This realization would reduce the incentive to engage in aggression, and should deterrence fail, it will provide the best chance of limiting hostilities.

It may be argued that this line of reasoning demonstrates the absurdity of a greater reliance on conventional weapons. Nuclear weapons must favour one side or the other. If they favour us, we should use them. If they give an advantage to the Communists they will use them. But this is not necessarily the case. Unless the superiority of one side grows overwhelmingly, the increased risks of an unfamiliar mode of warfare may outweigh the purely military benefits.

The relation between conventional and nuclear capabilities is subtle and complex. If we are serious about placing a greater reliance on conventional forces, we must reassess a notion which has become almost axiomatic in our military establishment: that our military forces can be equipped and trained as dual-purpose units capable of fighting both nuclear and conventional war. This concept has merit as regards the Navy and the Air Force—or any other unit not in constant contact with the opponent and therefore subject to more or less continuous control from higher levels. But it is fallacious with respect to ground operations. To be sure, troops can be trained to use both nuclear and conventional weapons. They should at least be aware of the elementary forms of protection against nuclear attack. But once committed to combat, the units actually engaged in military operations must opt for one mode of warfare or another. For one thing, it is probably impossible to shift from conventional to nuclear war at the opponent's initiative. The side using nuclear weapons first can disperse, while the side relying on conventional weapons must remain concentrated in order to have the necessary fire power. The front-line units of the side conceding the first nuclear blow will almost certainly suffer heavily should the war turn nuclear. Their protection is not so much nuclear weapons of their own as to have *available* within striking distance *other* units capable of conducting nuclear operations.

If nuclear weapons become an integral part of the equipment of *every* unit, it will be next to impossible to keep a war conventional, regardless of the intentions of both sides. Even if the intention is to employ nuclear weapons only as a last resort, this becomes empty when the interpretation of this step becomes more and more decentralized. A regimental or even a divisional commander should not be the judge. Lacking the over-all picture, he will always be tempted to utilize all his available weapons. When he is hard-pressed, it would require superhuman discipline not to use arms which he believes may solve his difficulties. And the further down a unit is in the chain of command, the less can its experience be taken as a guide to the general situation. Regiments or divisions have been destroyed even in the midst of an over-all victory.

While a great deal of attention has been given to the diffusion of nuclear weapons to new countries, the diffusion downward of nuclear weapons *within* our military establishment is also a cause for concern. The more foci of control, the greater the possibility that these weapons

will be used—not so much by the action of the 'mad' major of the horror stories of accidental war as by the best judgment of a hard-pressed officer in the confusion of combat. An action which would bespeak our increased emphasis on conventional weapons more convincingly than any declaration would be to create nuclear and conventional commands for purposes of combat. The units could be trained interchangeably. But once committed, the conventional forces would not have nuclear weapons at their direct disposal. Deterrence as well as the conduct of nuclear war would be in the hands of separate commands whose weapons would be made available to the conventional forces only on the basis of an explicit decision at the highest level.

The need for separate commands indicates that a conventional capability cannot possibly be accommodated within present force levels. In the absence of reliable arms control, larger military budgets will almost surely be required. This is a price worth paying. But we should not imagine that the shift to a greater reliance on conventional weapons requires only the decision to do so. It will involve substantial efforts, intellectual and material, and it will be neither cheap nor easy.

### Superiority of Resources

It is sometimes argued that a conventional strategy does not necessarily require an increase in conventional forces. Our national history reminds us of many wars where we prevailed, despite initial defeats, because of the might of our industrial potential. An aggressor, so the argument goes, would be more deterred by the possibility that we would build up our strength during a conflict than by the forces-in-being available to us at the beginning. The Korean war is only the latest demonstration of our ability to build up fairly quickly, provided only that we are able to hold the initial thrust of the aggressor for some time.

This view has great merit. Conventional weapons have a relatively low order of destructiveness and yet require a fairly substantial production effort. They therefore do place a premium on the West's industrial potential. At the same time, care must be taken not to draw extreme conclusions from this fact. In both World Wars our side not only had a superior industrial potential but also a vast preponderance of manpower. Nevertheless, victory required a build-up of nearly two years and protracted campaigns whose bloodiness must not be obscured by the horror of nuclear warfare.

Whatever the significance of prolonged mobilization in the era of what is now called conventional technology, it becomes an extremely risky course in the nuclear age. When both sides possess nuclear weapons, there is always the danger that they will be used, regardless of declarations and perhaps even intentions. The risk of 'escalation' is a product

of two factors: the nature of the limitations and the duration of the conflict. A limited nuclear war lasting one day may involve a smaller danger of 'escalation' than a conventional war lasting a year. Aggression may be tempted by the prospect of dramatic victories and the possibility that the free world may not be willing to run the risks of nuclear war inherent in a prolonged mobilization. Forces-in-being are therefore more important than at any previous time in our history. This does not mean that they must be able to hold every square inch of every threatened area. It does indicate that enough of an area must be protected so that the governments concerned consider resistance not simply a quixotic gesture. And the prospect of restoring the situation must be sufficiently imminent so that the aggressor sees no prospect in creating a *fait accompli* and then 'out-enduring' his opponents. In short, greater reliance on a conventional strategy implies that we are prepared to maintain conventional forces and mobilizable reserves in a higher state of readiness than ever before. It is as dangerous to think of a conventional strategy as if somehow nuclear weapons could be eliminated from our calculations as it is to continue to consider nuclear weapons from the perspective of our now-ended invulnerability.

These considerations bear importantly on the question of how the decision to place greater reliance on conventional weapons is to be made manifest. Many thoughtful persons have proposed that we should strive in arms-control negotiations to bring about a mutual renunciation of the first use of nuclear weapons. We should, it is urged, resist Communist aggression with conventional forces and resort to nuclear weapons only against nuclear attack. Nothing less, so the argument goes, will induce us to develop the necessary conventional forces and doctrine. It would end the possibility of nuclear blackmail. It would remove the immediate danger of a nuclear holocaust.

There is no doubt that such an agreement has many tempting aspects. It would be a stunning initiative if we proposed a formal agreement to renounce the use of nuclear weapons and perhaps a serious Soviet political setback if it were rejected. It would force us to come to grips with the problems of conventional strategy more urgently than seems otherwise possible. Indeed, *if* a mutual renunciation should be thought desirable, it may well be that a unilateral Western step would be the wisest course. A formal agreement has the advantage that the Soviet Union would have to violate a solemn treaty if it resorted to nuclear weapons or to nuclear blackmail. But this inhibition would hardly be greater than one produced by a unilateral renunciation by the United States. Nuclear blackmail would put an end to our renunciation, and *a fortiori*, so would the first Soviet use of nuclear weapons. In both cases the onus for returning to a reliance on nuclear weapons would be placed on the Soviet Union— within the limits of certainty produced by what will almost surely be a

highly ambiguous situation. The slight additional advantage of a formal agreement would be more than made up for by the clarity and initiative achieved by a unilateral declaration.

### Propaganda and Strategy

However, the propagandistic gain does not outweigh the political and strategic disadvantages. A really effective renunciation would imply that either side—or at least the side renouncing nuclear weapons—would prefer to be defeated by conventional weapons rather than employ its nuclear arms. This in itself will be a hard decision to make. Would we be prepared to lose Europe to a conventional attack? If we are not—and we cannot be—a formal renunciation may be meaningless. On the other hand, if the aggressor accepts a renunciation of nuclear weapons at face value as indicating a decision to accept a defeat by conventional forces, aggression may actually be encouraged.

Assuming that it were possible to return to a *pure* conventional strategy—with either side preferring a defeat by conventional weapons to a nuclear war—what would be the consequences? It seems inevitable that deterrence would be weakened. The history of warfare in the conventional era indicates that it is not easy to convince an aggressor of the risks of embarking on war. Because of the relatively low destructiveness of individual weapons, the side which can suddenly mass its forces can usually achieve a breakthrough. The key to success is the ability to concentrate more forces *at any given point* than the opponent. In both World Wars, Germany began the war even though it was numerically inferior, relying on tactical skill and mobility. Victory was ultimately achieved only after prolonged and ruinous conflict, which indicated that the certainty of defeat required for deterrence is not easy to obtain with conventional weapons. Arms control can ameliorate this situation, but not eliminate it. Even if forces on both sides are stabilized, it will not be easy to stabilize tactical skill and mobility.

On the historical record, then, conventional weapons are not very effective for deterrence. This situation may even be magnified in the nuclear age. An aggressor may seek to achieve a victory by conventional means and then protect it by nuclear arms. We will then face the dilemma of either accepting the defeat or engaging in a kind of warfare which our renunciation of nuclear weapons was designed to avoid and which seems incapable of depriving the aggressor of his prize. If the Soviet Union should succeed in overrunning Europe or even Iran with conventional forces, it could then offer peace while threatening to resist the restoration of the *status quo ante* with nuclear weapons. It would appear extremely difficult to land on a hostile shoreline or to fight our way across the Continent, say, from Spain, against an opponent prepared to

use nuclear weapons. In short, the combination of a conventional strategy for an overwhelming initial victory, coupled with a nuclear strategy to prevent a recapture of lost territories, may be the most effective form of Communist aggression.

## Merits of Uncertainty

All these risks, however, would be run for a gesture which may be meaningless. For, regardless of what we tell the aggressor or even ourselves, we could not guarantee that if pressed too hard we would not use nuclear weapons after all. This uncertainty about whether we 'meant' our renunciation or knew our own mind would add to deterrence. It indicates, however, that at best a formal renunciation of the first use of nuclear weapons would not weaken deterrence; at worst it may open a new scope for blackmail.

In the nuclear age, therefore, actions speak louder than words. What we tell the Communist countries is less important in the first instance than what we tell ourselves. We should make immediate and energetic efforts to restore the conventional forces of the free world. We must adjust our doctrine accordingly. But it would be extremely risky to create the impression that we would acquiesce in a conventional defeat in vital areas. Once the conventional balance of forces is restored, we could then responsibly announce that we would employ nuclear weapons only as a last resort, and even then in a manner to minimize damage. To the extent that the Communists are unable to defeat the conventional forces of the free world without resorting to nuclear weapons, the practical effect will be to renounce the first use of nuclear weapons. Even where this is not the case, strengthened conventional forces would pose an increased risk for the aggressor and provide opportunities either for the mobilization of additional conventional forces or for negotiations before we make the decision to use nuclear weapons. The inability to defend every area with conventional forces should not be used as an excuse for failing to build up our strength. The free world must not become a victim of asserting that if it cannot do *everything,* it will not do *anything.*

The course we adopt with respect to the relation between conventional and nuclear strategy will determine the future direction of our strategy as well as our diplomacy. This is particularly evident with respect to arms-control negotiations. In this respect, the present state of our military establishment places us at a severe disadvantage. Given the disparity in Sino-Soviet and Western conventional forces, many measures such as a percentage reduction of forces or a troop freeze may be a means of perpetuating an inequality which will be an increasing source of danger as all-out war becomes more and more senseless. The same effect will be produced by our concentrating on nuclear disarmament without address-

ing ourselves to the gap in conventional forces. We can escape this vicious circle only if we realize that the price of flexibility is sacrifice and effort. If our military establishment continues to be built around nuclear weapons, and if we refuse to make the sacrifices involved in a greater reliance on conventional weapons, the current emphasis of arms-control negotiations must be shifted. In such circumstances, it will not be wise to lump all nuclear weapons into a separate category of special horror. Rather, we should then elaborate as many distinctions between various types of uses and explosive power as possible in order to mitigate the consequences of a nuclear war. On the other hand, if we really believe in the need for a greater emphasis on conventional weapons, we must be prepared to accept the paradox that the best road to nuclear-arms control may be conventional rearmament.

This is not to say that arms control should be reserved for the nuclear field. On the contrary, the balance in conventional forces should be based on a combination of an increase of our conventional strength and control schemes to stabilize an agreed level of forces. But we cannot rely on arms control as a *substitute* for an effort in the conventional field. For, if the disparity in local power becomes too great, the Soviet Union will lose any incentive for responsible negotiations. No scheme of arms control will then seem to enhance its security as much as its existing superiority. And the requirements of inspection become excessive when the strategic position of one or both sides is so precarious that it can be overthrown by even a minor violation.

This is the measure of the task ahead: simultaneously with building up our capability for limited war and our conventional forces, we will be embarked on arms-control negotiation of crucial import. Our leadership must convince public opinion that we have to increase our military expenditures even while making earnest efforts to negotiate on arms control. The danger of slighting one or the other effort is enormous.

Yet history will not excuse our failure because the task is complex. The divorce between diplomacy and strategy will produce paralysis. If we want limited war forces we will get them only by a major effort. If we are serious about disarmament, we must restore the balance of our military establishment. To continue to combine incompatible policies must lead to disaster.

# 24 / For New Victories of the World Communist Movement

NIKITA KHRUSHCHEV

On January 6, 1961, Soviet Premier Khrushchev delivered a
20,000-word speech entitled "For New Victories of the World
Communist Movement." The purpose of this speech was to report publicly on the November, 1960, conference of Communist leaders of eighty-one nations. The speech covered
many topics, but among the most important were the Soviet
leader's statements revealing somewhat new views on war as
an instrument of policy. Differences on this question are apparently at the heart of the present Sino-Soviet disputes.
Some observers attribute Khrushchev's subsequent removal
from power in October, 1964, in part to internal disputes over
military policy. The following is a summarization—prepared
by the Legislative Reference Service, Library of Congress—
of Khrushchev's statement on war in modern Soviet doctrine.

KHRUSHCHEV DESCRIBED the problem of preventing global thermonuclear war as the "most burning and vital problem for mankind." He
warned that wars would be totally abolished only when communism tri-
umphed globally. At that time, according to Marxist-Leninist doctrine,
the division of society into "hostile antagonistic classes" would be eliminated, and all social and national causes for war would, therefore, be
removed.

Khrushchev placed war in the following categories and defined them
accordingly:

## 1. World War

Capitalist countries caused world wars; Communist countries opposed them. The "most probable" wars, he said, would occur among the
capitalist states. Soviet strength and power deterred the capitalists from
launching a war against the Communist bloc. "Peaceful coexistence" was,
therefore, assured.

---

Reprinted from U. S. 87th Cong., 1st sess., S. Doc. 14 (February 22, 1961),
*Khrushchev's Speech of January 6, 1961: A Summary and Interpretive Analysis.*

## 2. Local Wars

Khrushchev stated that capitalist states planned for local wars (i.e., "limited" war, such as the conflict over Suez) out of fear that world war would destroy their system. Opportunities for unleashing such wars, he said, were now "becoming fewer and fewer," owing to the shift in the balance of world power. Since local wars could grow into a "world thermonuclear rocket war" the Soviets had to be prepared for both types.

## 3. Wars of National Liberation

Wars of this type (i.e., as in Vietnam and Algeria) would continue as long as imperialism and colonialism existed. The Soviets regarded them as "sacred" wars. Khrushchev, therefore, pledged aid to all peoples "striving for their independence."

Khrushchev discussed in detail the grave consequences of a world war. He reaffirmed his "resolute" opposition to such wars. He confidently asserted that the "laws of historical development" gave assurances that the victory of communism was "now near" and that for this victory wars were "not necessary."

In a general discussion of foreign policy, Khrushchev made the following points:

1. The prestige of the Communist bloc had risen to "unprecedented" heights; it holds the initiative in world politics. By contrast, the "imperialist" states "defend themselves with their backs to the wall." Their prestige and influence "have never been so low."

2. The Soviet Union was determined to build its military strength, expose the "aggressive essence" of all military and political alinements of the West (such as, NATO, SEATO, and CENTO), isolate them, and ultimately liquidate them.

3. With regard to Berlin, he stated that the Western Powers must be brought "to their senses." They must recognize their "particularly vulnerable" position, take the "actual position into account," and terminate their "occupational regime." If not, the Soviet Union would take "decisive measures."

4. Disarmament was "the most important factor for averting war." This was "not a tactical move." "We sincerely want disarmament," he said. Two forces operated within the "ruling circles" of the capitalist camp: one aimed at war; the other accepted the idea of peaceful coexistence "in some form." Communists were instructed to enlist support from those elements who sought "peace."

# 25/ From *Special Message to the Congress on the Defense Budget, March 28, 1961*

JOHN F. KENNEDY

The criticisms, commentaries, and analyses in the foregoing selections reflect the turmoil in the thinking about force as an instrument of international coercion in the nuclear age. The two horns of the nuclear dilemma were: one, that surrender of our values and objectives might be required, were we not armed with the latest weapons; and two, being armed with the latest weapons is an unending road at the end of which may lie the destruction of civilization. When John F. Kennedy became President, he was aware of the arguments over strategy and the nature of the dilemma. He staffed his administration with many of the leading critics of policies that had gone before. His was an attempt to rationalize the defense system and dismiss the dilemma. The basic principles of his defense program are set forth in the following excerpt from his defense budget message to Congress of March 28, 1961.

IN MY ROLE as Commander-in-Chief of the American Armed Forces, and with my concern over the security of this nation now and in the future, no single question of policy has concerned me more since entering upon these responsibilities than the adequacy of our present and planned military forces to accomplish our major national security objectives. . . .

1. The primary purpose of our arms is peace, not war: to make certain that they will never have to be used; to deter all wars, general or limited, nuclear or conventional, large or small; to convince all potential aggressors that any attack would be futile; to provide backing for diplomatic-settlement of disputes; to insure the adequacy of our bargaining power for an end to the arms race. The basic problems facing the world today are not susceptible to a military solution. Neither our strategy nor our psychology as a nation, and certainly not our economy, must become dependent upon the permanent maintenance of a large military establishment. Our military posture must be sufficiently flexible and under control to be consistent with our efforts to explore all possibilities and to take

every step to lessen tensions, to obtain peaceful solutions and to secure arms limitations. Diplomacy and defense are no longer distinct alternatives, one to be used where the other fails; each must complement the other.

Disarmament, so difficult and so urgent, has been much discussed since 1945, but progress has not been made. Recrimination in such matters is seldom useful, and we for our part are determined to try again. In so doing, we note that, in the public position of both sides in recent years, the determination to be strong has been coupled with announced willingness to negotiate. For our part, we know there can be dialectical truth in such a position, and we shall do all we can to prove it in action. This budget is wholly consistent with our earnest desire for serious conversation with the other side on disarmament. If genuine progress is made, then as tension is reduced, so will be our arms.

2. Our arms will never be used to strike the first blow in any attack. This is not a confession of weakness but a statement of strength. It is our national tradition. We must offset whatever advantage this may appear to hand an aggressor by so increasing the capability of our forces to respond swiftly and effectively to any aggressive move as to convince any would-be aggressor that such a movement would be too futile and costly to undertake. In the area of general war, this doctrine means that such capability must rest with that portion of our forces which would survive the initial attack. We are not creating forces for a first strike against any other nation. We shall never threaten, provoke or initiate aggression; but if aggression should come, our response will be swift and effective.

3. Our arms must be adequate to meet our commitments and insure our security, without being bound by arbitrary budget ceilings. This nation can afford to be strong; it cannot afford to be weak. We shall do what is needed to make and to keep us strong. We must, of course, take advantage of every opportunity to reduce military outlays as a result of scientific or managerial progress, new strategic concepts, a more efficient, manageable and thus more effective defense establishment, or international agreements for the control and limitation of arms. But we must not shrink from additional costs where they are necessary. The additional $650 million in expenditures for fiscal 1962 which I am recommending today, while relatively small, is too urgent to be governed by a budget largely decided before our defense review had been completed. Indeed, in the long run the net effect of all the changes I am recommending will be to provide a more economical budget. But I cannot promise that in later years we need not be prepared to spend still more for what is indispensable. Much depends on the course followed by other nations. As a proportion of Gross National Product, as a share of our total budget, and in comparison with our national effort in earlier times of war, this increase in defense expenditures is still substantially below what our

citizens have been willing and are now able to support as insurance on their security—insurance we hope is never needed, but insurance we must nevertheless purchase.

4. Our arms must be subject to ultimate civilian control and command at all times, in war as well as peace. The basic decisions on our participation in any conflict and our response to any threat, including all decisions relating to the use of nuclear weapons, or the escalation of a small war into a large one, will be made by the regularly constituted civilian authorities. This requires effective and protected organization, procedures, facilities and communication in the event of attack directed toward this objective, as well as defensive measures designed to insure thoughtful and selective decisions by the civilian authorities. This message and budget also reflect that basic principle. The Secretary of Defense and I have had the earnest counsel of our senior military advisers and many others, and in fact they support the great majority of the decisions reflected in this budget. But I have not delegated to anyone else the responsibilities for decision which are imposed upon me by the Constitution.

5. Our strategic arms and defenses must be adequate to deter any deliberate nuclear attack on the United States or our allies by making clear to any potential aggressor that sufficient retaliatory forces will be able to survive a first strike and penetrate his defenses in order to inflict unacceptable losses upon him. As I indicated in an address to the Senate some thirty-one months ago, this deterrence does not depend upon a simple comparison of missiles on hand before an attack. It has been publicly acknowledged for several years that this nation has not led the world in missile strength. Moreover, we will not strike first in any conflict. But what we have, and must continue to have, is the ability to survive a first blow and respond with devastating power. This deterrent power depends not only on the number of our missiles and bombers, but on their state of readiness, their ability to survive attack, and the flexibility and sureness with which we can control them to achieve our national purpose and strategic objectives.

6. The strength and deployment of our forces in combination with those of our allies should be sufficiently powerful and mobile to prevent the steady erosion of the free world through limited wars; and it is this role that should constitute the primary mission of our overseas forces. Nonnuclear wars, and sublimited or guerrilla warfare, have since 1945 constituted the most active and constant threat to free world security. Those units of our forces which are stationed overseas, or are designed to fight overseas, can be most usefully oriented toward deterring or confining those conflicts which do not justify and must not lead to a general nuclear attack. In the event of a major aggression that could not be repulsed by conventional forces, we must be prepared to take whatever action with whatever weapons are appropriate. But our objective now is to increase

our ability to confine our response to nonnuclear weapons, and to lessen the incentive for any limited aggression by making clear what our response will accomplish. In most areas of the world, the main burden of local defense against overt attack, subversion and guerrilla warfare must rest on local populations and forces. But given the great likelihood and seriousness of this threat, we must be prepared to make a substantial contribution in the form of strong, highly mobile forces trained in this type of warfare, some of which must be deployed in forward areas, with a substantial airlift and sealift capacity and prestocked overseas bases.

7. Our defense posture must be both flexible and determined. Any potential aggressor contemplating an attack on any part of the free world with any kind of weapons, conventional or nuclear, must know that our response will be suitable, selective, swift and effective. While he may be uncertain of its exact nature and location, there must be no uncertainty about our determination and capacity to take whatever steps are necessary to meet our obligations. We must be able to make deliberate choices in weapons and strategy, shift the tempo of our production and alter the direction of our forces to meet rapidly changing conditions or objectives at very short notice and under any circumstances. Our weapons systems must be usable in a manner permitting deliberation and discrimination as to timing, scope and targets in response to civilian authority; and our defenses must be secure against prolonged reattack as well as a surprise first strike. To purchase productive capacity and to initiate development programs that may never need to be used, as this budget proposes, adopts an insurance policy of buying alternative future options.

8. Our defense posture must be designed to reduce the danger of irrational or unpremeditated general war, the danger of an unnecessary escalation of a small war into a large one, or of miscalculation or misinterpretation of an incident or enemy intention. Our diplomatic efforts to reach agreements on the prevention of surprise attack, an end to the spread of nuclear weapons, indeed all our efforts to end the arms race, are aimed at this objective. We shall strive for improved communication among all nations, to make clear our own intentions and resolution, and to prevent any nation from underestimating the response of any other, as has too often happened in the past. In addition, our own military activities must be safeguarded against the possibility of inadvertent triggering incidents. But even more importantly, we must make certain that our retaliatory power does not rest on decisions made in ambiguous circumstances, or permit a catastrophic mistake.

It would not be appropriate at this time or in this message either to boast of our strength or to dwell upon our needs and dangers. It is sufficient to say that the budgetary recommendations which follow, together with other policy, organizational and related changes and studies now under way administratively, are designed to provide for an increased

strength, flexibility and control in our defense establishment in accordance with the above policies. . . .

> *The remainder of the President's message sketched out his detailed recommendations with respect to the defense budget. The message concluded:*

Our military position today is strong. But positive action must be taken now if we are to have the kind of forces we will need for our security in the future. Our preparation against danger is our hope of safety. The changes in the defense program which I have recommended will greatly enhance the security of this nation in the perilous years which lie ahead. It is not pleasant to request additional funds at this time for national security. Our interest, as I have emphasized, lies in peaceful solutions, in reducing tension, in settling disputes at the conference table and not on the battlefield. I am hopeful that these policies will help secure these ends. I commend them to the Congress and to the nation.


# 26 / The Future of American Deterrence Policy

ALAIN C. ENTHOVEN

**In spite of the eloquence of President Kennedy and the intellectual talent he assembled in his administration, the great debate over strategy and defense programs has continued. Where are we headed? Will deterrence work in the future? Is our policy credible to our adversaries? To our allies? Have we developed an "overkill" capacity? Have we sufficient "conventional" forces? These continuing questions and related issues are discussed in the following selection.**


MILITARY FORCE is but one instrument in the hands of the President to be used in the struggle to keep us alive and free. It takes its place

From an address given by Mr. Enthoven at the Loyola University Forum for National Affairs, Los Angeles, Calif., February 10, 1963.

Alain C. Enthoven has been an analyst with the RAND Corporation and, since 1961, a high-ranking official of the Defense Secretariat in the Pentagon, where he has served as one of Secretary of Defense McNamara's principal civilian strategic planners

alongside diplomacy, economic policy, foreign economic and military assistance, alliances, and many other activities that contribute to our national security. Its ultimate purpose, like that of these other activities, is to enable the President, in co-operation with the leaders of other free nations, to establish and maintain a peaceful world order based on a belief in the worth and dignity of the individual, and on freedom for each person to develop his own capacities in the way he chooses. The role of military force, in the pursuit of this objective, is to prevent would-be aggressors who do not believe in freedom and human dignity from forcing free men to live under a system based on tyranny and coercion. The problem of formulation of defense policy is to select those forces which will contribute most effectively to these multiple objectives.

There are three related themes underlying and uniting our defense policies today. They are, first, deterrence of aggression; second, freedom for the President to select and apply the amount and kind of force appropriate to the threat at hand; and third, the controlled use of force. In the nuclear age, military force will be too dangerous to use if our objectives are not carefully chosen and limited at each step of a conflict, and if the force cannot be used in a controlled and deliberate way to achieve precisely the objectives being sought. To fight for unlimited objectives, or to fight in an uncontrolled way, would almost surely bring on almost unlimited destruction.

In order to give the President the freedom of action required to be able to limit appropriately the use of force, current defense policy emphasizes flexibility, options, and choice. One of its main objectives is to make available to the President a range of military responses appropriate for each threat to our security, so that he can apply force adequate to accomplish the objectives at hand without causing any unnecessary damage or loss of life, and while holding to a minimum the risk of escalation to a more destructive level of conflict.

A few years ago, there was a great deal of public debate as to whether limited war was possible. The theory and practice of strategic bombing in World War II, the use of the atomic bombs, and the unconditional surrender policy left in their aftermath a widespread belief that war could only be total. This belief persisted long after the armed resistance to Communist aggression in Greece and Korea. Of course total war remains possible. But as time goes by, and the size and destructive power of nuclear arsenals increase, more and more, total war between nuclear powers will mean total destruction. It is my own opinion that with the widespread realization of this fact will come the general belief that all wars should be limited. At no time should we deliberately choose to fight an unlimited uncontrolled war. The "limited war—general war" dichotomy that has crept into our language may be harmful if it suggests that there is a kind of war that it makes sense to fight without limits, though,

of course, the limits that we adopt will have to depend on the threat and on our objectives.

What this means, in practice, is that we are working to acquire a flexible, balanced defense posture giving up capabilities for the selective use of force for all kinds of conflict, from counter-insurgency and anti-guerrilla warfare through large scale conventional (non-nuclear) warfare, through major thermonuclear war. Although the choice of the amount and kind of force to be applied in any circumstance is bound to be a difficult one, we would like to make it possible in all cases, if I may borrow a phrase from the Mikado, "to make the punishment fit the crime."

Keeping the use of force appropriately limited requires control. The range, speed, and destructiveness of modern weapons makes this problem both more urgent and more difficult than it has ever been before. More than ever before, this means that the President must have communication and control facilities to provide him with timely and accurate information on the course of events and to permit him to communicate his decisions in a similar manner. It also means that the military forces must be responsive to his direction, even in considerable detail. To use President Kennedy's words, "Our weapon systems must be usable in a manner permitting deliberation and discrimination as to timing, scope and targets in response to civilian authority."

Moreover, when force is being applied, the military action must not be allowed to control events and compel the President's decisions; rather, it should be the other way around. To borrow a term from missilery, our use of military force in the cold war must be command guided, not inertially guided.

This belief may be contrasted to the view that "peace is peace and war is war," and in war military necessity is the only valid criterion for decision. Certainly the requirements of the military commander must be considered very seriously, both because our security requires success in whatever armed conflicts are thrust upon us, and because the lives of our soldiers are involved, but still, the President must be free to weigh them against other requirements and decide what is best for the security of the United States. This principle was important before nuclear weapons; it has taken on added importance in the nuclear age.

### Lesson of Korea

This was one of the hard lessons of the Korean War. The United States had to re-learn to fight for limited objectives. There were reasons which the original military commander found very compelling for expanding the scope of the conflict. But in the President's judgment, to expand the conflict would have risked touching off another world war which would have left both the South Koreans and ourselves far worse off than the final out-

come that actually was achieved. The President must be in a position to make and enforce such judgments.

The same principle of control was applied in a thorough-going way in the recent Cuban crisis. Each military move was, in effect, a carefully formulated message from the President to Khrushchev, intended to convince him that the United States would use military force to the extent necessary to achieve removal of the offensive weapons. But each move was also intended to convince him that he could withdraw without armed conflict, if he would withdraw. Because each move was a carefully formulated message, all moves had to be carefully controlled from the White House.

All this was summarized by the President in the words:

> Our arms must be subject to ultimate civilian control and command at all times, in war as well as peace. The basic decisions on our participation in any conflict and our response to any threat—including all decisions relating to the use of nuclear weapons, or the escalation of a small war into a large one—will be made by the regularly constituted civilian authorities.

Because of the importance of such control, a great deal has been done in the Defense Department in the past two years to strengthen and make more secure the means of high level command and control of forces.

### Conventional Force Build-up

How have these themes worked themselves out in the development of our defense program? One of the most important ways has been in the recent and large build-up in our conventional or non-nuclear forces.

To understand properly the importance of the build-up of non-nuclear forces, it is necessary first to understand that there is a very great difference between nuclear weapons and non-nuclear weapons. Nuclear weapons are not simply high explosives writ large. Their destructive power makes them a completely new kind of military force which must be understood and related to our national security objectives in new ways. Hiroshima was destroyed by a twenty kiloton bomb. We now have weapons a thousand times that size. Roughly 2½ million tons of TNT were dropped on Germany in World War II. One B-52 can now deliver many times that amount of destructive power, and we have the ability to deliver the equivalent of thousands of millions of tons intercontinentally. As well as the familiar effects of blast and heat, these weapons can cover many thousands of square miles with deadly radioactive fallout. All this is familiar.

There has been in recent years the development of small nuclear weapons having yields equivalent to a few thousand tons of TNT or less. The day will come, if it has not come already, when there will be nuclear weapons of smaller yield than the largest high explosive weapons. When

that day comes, will there no longer be a distinction between nuclear and conventional weapons? Some have argued to that effect. But they are mistaken. There is and will remain an important distinction, a "fire break" if you like, between nuclear and non-nuclear war, a recognizable qualitative distinction that both combatants can recognize and agree upon, if they want to agree upon one. And in the nuclear age they will have a very powerful incentive to agree upon this distinction and limitation, because if they do not there does not appear to be another easily recognizable limitation on weapons—no other obvious "fire break"—all the way up the destructive spectrum to large scale thermonuclear war.

Adequate conventional forces are important. It is for this reason that, in the past two years, we have increased the number of active combat-ready army divisions from eleven to sixteen, and our active tactical air wings from sixteen to twenty-one. It is for this reason that we have more than doubled the annual rate of procurement of army equipment, that we have speeded up the tempo of modernization of our tactical air forces, and that we have increased our outlays on naval shipbuilding. Moreover it is for this reason that we are now urging our NATO allies to increase the size and effectiveness of their conventional forces. Why?

The reason strong conventional forces are required is that there are many situations in which the use of nuclear weapons would be inappropriate. For the same reasons that a sledge hammer does not make a good substitute for a fly swatter, nuclear weapons are not a good substitute for non-nuclear forces against a wide range of military threats. Even if they could be used to apply the minimum force required to achieve our objectives, their use would risk triggering escalation to a more and unnecessarily destructive level of conflict.

A nation or an alliance which maintains a strong nuclear posture combined with weak conventional forces thereby puts itself at a great disadvantage in the confrontation with another power that has both strong nuclear and strong conventional forces. This will be true no matter how strong and effective are its nuclear forces, provided that the other power maintains a secure second-strike nuclear retaliatory capability. Because nuclear war is so destructive, the use of nuclear weapons must be reserved only for the most desperate circumstances. But if the nuclears have to be reserved for vital issues, the side with the strong conventional forces is likely to be able to have its way on all issues less than vital. The side without adequate conventional forces will have no means for effective resistance in such confrontations. The side with conventional forces can use "salami slice" tactics, or make its aggression piecemeal in the confidence that it will be able to have its way on all but life and death matters. This is the kind of threat we have been facing in Berlin. The danger in piecemeal aggression is that erosion in the position of the free world over the years can end in world domination by the Communists.

Put alternatively, the President will be in a weak bargaining position indeed if he is confronted by the Communist bloc with a choice between suicide or surrender, holocaust or humiliation. In order to resist aggression and defend our freedom, the President must have more attractive alternatives. Without conventional forces, our choice when faced with aggression may be "red or dead"; conventional forces help to deter aggression, and if deterrence fails, they can give us the opportunity to fight to stay alive and free.

### Defective Arguments

Nevertheless, the build-up in our conventional forces has been costly and controversial. Two main lines of argument have been advanced against it. The first is that it weakens our nuclear resolve. In effect, it is a message to Khrushchev telling him that we are afraid or unwilling to use nuclear weapons, and that he can commit aggression against us with the expectation that we will not use them. Of course, pushed to an extreme, such an argument would say that we ought to abolish the United States Marine Corps. But the argument is defective. The important thing is not to convince an aggressor that we will use nuclear weapons. The important thing is to convince him that we will use whatever force that is necessary to preserve our freedom. In many cases, that will be non-nuclear force. Sole or excessive reliance on nuclear weapons may tempt him to believe that we will not fight for less than vital issues. The danger is that each issue can be made less than vital. Aggression can be made piecemeal and in small enough pieces so that succumbing always looks attractive by comparison with thermonuclear war. Isn't Berlin Khrushchev's "last territorial demand in Europe"?

In fact, reflection on the problem should convince most reasonable men that the threat of the ultimate use of nuclear weapons, if required, is much more credible to an aggressor who sees that to accomplish his objective he must first defeat a large and effective conventional force. If he succeeds in doing that, the issue at stake is likely by then to be vital for the defender.

Still some argue that we should try to convince our adversaries that we would use nuclear weapons even in situations in which it is irrational to do so. Interestingly enough, Khrushchev himself has recently attacked this principle as a policy for the Communist Bloc, and in attacking him, the Chinese Communists have nonetheless acknowledged the enormous destructiveness of nuclear war. When it is clear that the Communists know the facts of nuclear destructiveness, it would seem foolish for us to base our strategy on the pretense that we do not. The trouble with trying to exploit "the rationality of irrationality," as theorists of bargaining and conflict call this, is that it simply is not a viable policy in the long run for

a democracy, especially a democracy with allies. We must have defense policies that make sense to the American people and to our allies. Moreover, threats to blow ourselves up along with the aggressor are not likely to be credible. Rather, the most credible kind of threat is the threat that we will do what in the event will be most in our interest to do. In the case of piecemeal non-nuclear aggression, that will be to apply conventional forces.

The other main line of argument against the build-up of our conventional forces is that it will be fruitless, extremely costly, and unable to achieve the objective of adequacy because we are so badly outnumbered by the Communist hordes. These arguments, though widely believed, are not supported by the facts. Conventional military strength requires fighting men; it also requires that the men be fed, clothed, and equipped with effective weapons and other material. Equipping and supporting armies requires wealth and industrial production. The NATO allies outnumber the members of the Warsaw Pact in population, men under arms, and even foot soldiers in active army forces. In the dire straits into which mismanagement has plunged their economy, the Chinese Communists appear to be far from being able to provide modern and effective equipment for an army the size of our own. Moreover, the gross national products of the United States and our allies are more than twice the same total for the Soviet Union and its allies; in terms of industrial production, the ratio is more than two and one half to one. What all of these facts suggest is that although substantial sacrifice may be involved for us and our NATO allies in equipping ourselves with adequate conventional forces, proportionally the sacrifice is much smaller for us than it is for our adversaries. Although we do need to strengthen our conventional forces some, the extra costs are not large. We have already paid the entry fee into the "non-nuclear club." It is now largely a matter of making fully effective the force levels we have already agreed to provide.

### Usable Force

A related argument has it that limiting conflicts to non-nuclear weapons puts us at a disadvantage because of our numerical inferiority, and that we need to use nuclear weapons as an equalizer in all but the smallest of armed conflicts. Leaving aside the undesirable character of the equalization they accomplish, and the unresolved question of whether the use of nuclear weapons is to our military advantage if the other side replies in kind, let me point out that our wealth and technology confer on us some important advantages in non-nuclear combat. Indeed, the effectiveness of modern non-nuclear arms is so great that they can offset substantial numerical inferiority in isolated situations in which we might be numerically inferior. The ability to produce such armaments in large

quantities is a key determinant of the effectiveness of a nation's non-nuclear forces.

In summary, conventional military force is usable force. In Korea and in the Cuban crisis, we found that the non-nuclear forces were the cutting edge of our military power. We can use conventional force with a minimal risk of self-destruction. Therefore, it provides a more credible deterrent to non-nuclear aggression. As the destructiveness of nuclear war increases, and as nuclear weapon systems become less vulnerable to sudden attack, the effectiveness of the threatened use of nuclear weapons as a substitute for conventional forces will diminish, and we will have no sensible alternative to building up our conventional forces to the point at which they can safely resist all forms of non-nuclear aggression. Our forces will be adequate if we can never be forced because of weakness to be the first to have to resort to nuclear weapons.

### The American Posture

But if nuclear forces are not an effective substitute for adequate conventional forces, neither are conventional forces an effective substitute for adequate nuclear forces. Rather, the relationship between the two is one of complementarity. Now that the Communist Bloc is armed with nuclear weapons, we cannot successfully fight conventional wars except under the umbrella of nuclear strength. This nuclear strength is required to deter the Communists from escalating a non-nuclear conflict which is not going well for them into nuclear war, and to convince them that an act of nuclear aggression would lead to their defeat, and possibly to the destruction of their society.

This then is the most important objective of our nuclear posture: to make thermonuclear war unlikely by deterring deliberate calculated nuclear aggression. We also seek other objectives. We want to make accidental, unpremeditated, irrational nuclear war unlikely also. And if war does occur, we want to be able to bring it to a speedy termination on military terms favorable to ourselves, and we want to do what we can to limit the damage caused to ourselves and our allies. How do we go about pursuing those objectives?

First, we attempt to deter deliberate premeditated attack by maintaining secure second-strike retaliatory capabilities, that is forces that cannot be knocked out in a surprise first blow. This means relatively invulnerable weapon systems like *Minuteman, Titan,* and *Polaris,* and secure, protected, survivable command and control facilities that will enable our national leadership to survive an attack and direct the use of retaliatory forces against any aggressor.

There is a great deal of literature and there are many approaches to the subject of deterrence. Some argue that, in the event of a nuclear attack

on the alliance, we should plan to retaliate strictly against Soviet cities. Others argue that we should plan to strike back only against Soviet military forces. Still others argue for both. Some believe that we should design our posture for an irrevocable commitment to a spasm of massive retaliation. Our approach is based on options, deliberation, flexibility and control. Rather than decide ahead of time which targets must be hit by which weapons, and then commit ourselves to it, our approach is to give the President a range of choices so that he can select the plan whose targets and timing of attacks are most appropriate to the circumstances at hand. I won't speculate here as to which nuclear response might be used in which circumstances. Nothing useful would be accomplished by doing so. But let me make three observations about this policy.

First, it is a policy of strength not weakness. It takes superior nuclear forces to be able to ride out any kind of attack and then retain the option to destroy most of the enemies' remaining military forces should that be appropriate. It would be a policy of weakness to commit ourselves irrevocably to a spasm of nuclear retaliation against Soviet cities.

Second, this policy requires secure forces and secure command and control. It requires weapon systems like *Minuteman* and *Polaris* that are hard and dispersed, or mobile and concealed, and that can ride out a thermonuclear attack and be held in reserve in the environment of nuclear war. This is one of the reasons why the Defense Department's procurement of strategic weapon systems in the last two years has emphasized *Minuteman* and *Polaris*.

Third, this approach to nuclear deterrence illustrates the principle that across the spectrum of conflict, military force is to be used with deliberation and control. There is, to be sure, a danger of breakdown of control in the environment of thermonuclear war. But, short of complete destruction of Western society, there is no point at which it makes sense to choose to abandon control. Even when it comes to thermonuclear weapons, if our weapons are to be used to keep us alive and free, their use must be controlled.

This emphasis on control had led us, in the past two years, to emphasize the procurement of survivable, secure, redundant, and internetted command, control, and communications facilities. For example, we now have a SAC command post with a general officer on board constantly airborne, 24 hours a day. For the top civilian authorities, we have a National Emergency Airborne Command Post, command posts on ships at sea, and various hardened underground command posts, all tied together by protected communications. As well as making a major contribution to our ability to deter deliberate attack, this strengthened command structure has made an important contribution to reducing the likelihood of such unlikely eventualities as unauthorized, accidental, or other unpremeditated attacks blowing up into large-scale thermonuclear war. And, along with

many other safety precautions that we have taken, it is making much less likely the possibility of accidental or unauthorized use of nuclear weapons on our side.

I would like to emphasize this point because some recent literature has suggested that there is a lack of concern among the military and civilian leaders of the Department of Defense for the safety and stability of our nuclear weapons posture. This suggestion could not be farther from the truth. In fact, both our military and civilian leaders take this problem very seriously and they have been willing to accept considerable costs to assure the compatibility of military readiness with the highest possible degree of safety.

### If War Occurs

But, despite our best efforts a war may still occur. In these dangerous and unpredictable times it would be foolish to base our planning on the assumption that a thermonuclear war could never happen. Despite our best efforts, almost any kind of nuclear war would be an unprecedented disaster. But if such a war were thrust upon us, there are worthwhile things that could be done to mitigate its consequences. We are making preparations whose purpose is, in the event of war, to enable us to maintain a favorable military position, to bring the war to an end quickly, and to hold to a minimum the damage to ourselves and our allies. To limit the damage, we are making a combination of plans and preparations, including Civil Defense, active air and anti-missile defense, and an ability to destroy what we can of the enemy's offensive weapons. Let me explain each one.

The largest part of our Civil Defense program is fall-out shelters for our population. One of the most destructive effects of nuclear weapons is radioactive fall-out. In a thermonuclear attack on the United States, many millions of people would die, even though they were far from the blast and thermal effects, simply from radioactive fall-out. Although there are substantial uncertainties here, and the numbers vary widely depending upon the assumptions made, most studies suggest that whereas several tens of millions might die from the blast and thermal effects of a nuclear attack on the United States, because of fall-out the total deaths could well be over a hundred million in the United States alone. In order to prevent this, the President has directed the Department of Defense to undertake an expanded Civil Defense program, which has as its first objective the provision of fall-out shelters for all of our population.

Civil Defense is very important for many reasons. Without it, our active defenses and other preparations for survival in a thermonuclear war would be rendered meaningless. For example, if we defended our cities with impenetrable anti-missile defenses, but had no fall-out protection for

the inhabitants, an attacker could still destroy all the people in those cities simply by surface bursting thermonuclear weapons upwind and killing the people with fall-out. If we do have a Civil Defense program, then active air and anti-missile defenses can also make a very important contribution to our survival. Civil Defense is also necessary if we are to have any hope of limiting the effects of a major thermonuclear war and making possible a meaningful strategy of controlled use of nuclear weapons.

As well as these measures, we are also buying strategic retaliatory forces capable of knocking out those vulnerable elements of enemy nuclear striking power remaining after an attack has been launched against us. Of course we are up against the limitation here that after such an attack, our counterattacking forces are likely to be spent destroying many empty bases and launching sites. However, our studies to date suggest that, in such circumstances, it would still be likely that there would remain vulnerable forces that could be used against us in follow-up attacks, and that their timely destruction could help to limit the damage to the United States and our Allies.

Beyond these physical measures, we are also opening up the option of maintaining some effective deterrence after a nuclear war begins. This was described last Spring by Secretary of Defense McNamara in an address at the University of Michigan. In his words,

> The U. S. has come to the conclusion that to the extent feasible, basic military strategy in a possible general nuclear war should be approached in much the same way that more conventional military operations have been regarded in the past. That is to say, principal military objectives, in the event of a nuclear war stemming from a major attack on the Alliance, should be the destruction of the enemy's military forces, not of his civilian population.

> The very strength and nature of the Alliance forces make it possible for us to retain, even in the face of a massive surprise attack, sufficient reserve striking power to destroy an enemy society if driven to it. In other words, we are giving a possible opponent the strongest imaginable incentive to refrain from striking our own cities.

Doubtless questions will arise in your minds as to whether nuclear war can and should be limited and controlled. First can it? The answer depends on our will to make it so. With the protected weapon systems, command posts and communications we are now acquiring, there is no technical reason why the use of nuclear weapons cannot be controlled in a nuclear war. The destructive power of their uncontrolled use should give all participants a strong incentive to find ways of avoiding it. Moreover, as both sides acquire protected forces like *Minuteman* and *Polaris,* the prospects are that neither side will be able to improve its military position by a sudden attack on the forces of the other. Then, if massive thermonuclear attack ever did make sense, it will do so no longer.

The other question is, "Should we try?" The argument against trying,

one that has been used against Civil Defense, is that it weakens the "fire break" between nuclear and non-nuclear war. But any thermonuclear war would be such an unprecedented disaster that it is difficult to see how anything we could do to mitigate its consequences would effectively weaken the "fire break." And the disaster of an unlimited nuclear war would be too great to permit us not to take whatever measures we can to minimize its likelihood. Moreover, the principle of controlled and limited use of military force is indivisible. If we believe in control in some circumstances and not in others, it will become more difficult to maintain it in those circumstances in which we should. An emphasis on control and limitations in the use of force is desirable across the spectrum of conflict.

### The Moral Aspects

I am sure that you are all concerned, as I am, about the moral problems raised by our military preparations. Is it right or wrong for us to be buying hundreds of inter-continental ballistic missiles, fighter-bomber aircraft, and equipment for many army divisions? Can we justify weapon systems and war plans that would enable us, if a nuclear war were thrust upon us, to fight back even though doing so might lead to the deaths of many millions of people?

These are extremely complex and difficult problems that we can neither escape nor hope to understand fully. Their moral solution cannot come from artificial simplification. Tonight what I would like to do is offer you some questions and some reflections that may illuminate some of the issues. A proper appreciation of the moral aspects of defense policy requires an understanding of Theology as well as the alternative strategies and their implications. A dialogue is required, and I offer the following remarks in that spirit.

According to traditional Christian doctrine, the use of force to repress evil can be justifiable under certain conditions including the following: First, the use of force must have a reasonable chance of success. Second, if successful, it must offer a better situation than the one that would prevail in the absence of the use of force. Third, the force that is used must be proportional to the objectives being sought (or the evil being repressed). For this to be satisfied, peaceful means of redress must have failed. Fourth, the force must be used with the intention of sparing non-combatants and with a reasonable prospect of actually doing so.

It is interesting to observe that the potentially catastrophic character of thermonuclear war has forced practical decision-makers, reasoning in a secular context, to adopt a set of criteria very much like those of the traditional Christian doctrine and to apply them to the design of the military posture of the United States. Now, much more than in the recent past, our use of force is being carefully proportioned to the objectives

being sought, and the objectives are being carefully limited to those which at the same time are necessary for our security and which do not pose the kind of unlimited threat to our opponents in the cold war that would drive them to unleash nuclear war. In the past, before nuclear weapons, deliberate limitations in the use of force did not present much of a practical problem because of the limited destructive power of non-nuclear weapons. Nuclear weapons have now given such constraints great practical importance.

Within the broad policy of armed resistance to aggression, which is one of the alternatives open to us, and in terms of the moral criteria of the traditional Christian doctrine, I think it is fair to say that we have made considerable progress. This is not to say that we have gone as far as we can go. But it does suggest that all the moral questions are not concerned with whether or not armed resistance can be justifiable.

### Never Justified?

During the past fifteen years, a number of commentators, theologians and others, have taken the position that although in former times the traditional doctrine was valid and, under appropriate conditions the use of armed force could be justified, now, in the atomic age, there can be no justifiable war. The argument has been made that nuclear war does not and cannot offer a reasonable chance of bringing about a better situation than that which would have prevailed in the absence of the use of force; that thermonuclear force, being essentially unlimited in its destructive effects, cannot be proportioned to reasonable objectives; and that with it the non-combatants cannot be spared. Therefore, many argue that the traditional doctrine is obsolete and that a new doctrine must be found. Some argue that the only morally acceptable course is to renounce nuclear weapons; others believe that we must renounce the use of force altogether.

I would not want to suggest that this line of thought is not based on good and compelling reasons, even though I have not found it convincing myself. It may prove to be the case that the danger of escalation is so great that future limited non-nuclear wars will bring with them an intolerable risk of massive thermonuclear destruction. However, experience in the past 15 years has shown that non-nuclear wars can be kept limited and that freedom can be defended from Communist aggression without massive destruction.

A question to consider in one's critical thought on this problem is whether the view that the traditional doctrine is obsolete is based on an overemphasis on unlimited nuclear war, perhaps an identification of all armed conflict with it. An unlimited nuclear war is an extreme on a broad spectrum of possible armed conflicts. Of course, it is a very im-

portant extreme because of its disastrous consequences, but it is not the whole spectrum. In fact, it is only one among many possible kinds of thermonuclear war. It can be a mistake to apply reasoning based on this extreme to all kinds of armed resistance to aggression and injustice. I think it is important to recognize this, for if our thinking is unclear on this point, and if we identify any use of armed force with unlimited destruction, we are likely unnecessarily to disarm ourselves and leave ourselves victims of Communist aggression.

It is clear that we have elected to retain the threat of use of nuclear weapons in our own defense and that of our allies. We thereby consciously accept the risk that we will have to use them. Some people believe that we should reject the use of nuclear weapons. Before accepting such a judgment, one should consider carefully the full implications of such a decision. We do have worldwide responsibilities. Many millions of people depend for their lives and freedom on our military strength. In this respect, the United States is in a very different position from any other country in the free world.

The question I would like to leave with you this evening is whether current U.S. defense policy, which emphasizes deterrence, control, and the use of the appropriately limited amount of force, represents a good reconciliation of the traditional doctrine with the facts of life in the nuclear age? We have achieved some success with the controlled use of force. We are still alive and free today, and the missiles are out of Cuba. We are running great risks, to be sure, but would the risks be ameliorated by laying down our arms? It is tragic that nations must at times resort to armed force to resolve their differences. War is destructive and it has evil consequences. But our defense posture is being designed to make war less likely and less destructive. I am not suggesting that we can make war and violence desirable. The question is whether we have a better alternative.

. . . I have defended our policies on the grounds that they make sense. Can they also be defended on the grounds that they are moral? Viewed with perspective, the two should be the same.

# 27 / Defense Through Missile Deterrence

RALPH E. LAPP

Critics of the spiraling arms race range all the way from
pacifists and unilateral disarmers to those who advocate the
continuing development of bigger and better bombs and delivery systems. The most effective critics of the nuclear arms
race and overbuilding our nuclear capability are those who
are best informed on the technical facts and can spot the
fallacies of the armament experts. The author of the following
selection is one of these, and here he sets forth his oft-ex-
pressed belief that the nation has vastly overbuilt its capacity
for nuclear destruction.

IN THE DAYS of the muzzle-loading musket and horse-drawn artillery piece, the average citizen had some concept of fire-power and a rather
clear idea of the military worth of various weapons. Limits to the military
build-up of such simple units of destructive power were thus ultimately
subject to the final verdict of a nation's common sense. The situation
today is radically altered by the fantastic dimensions of nuclear
overkill.

The average American, and presumably his Russian counterpart, has
only a very hazy concept of the kill-power which is contained in the
nuclear arsenals. Such words as kiloton (1000 tons of TNT equivalent)
and megaton (1000 kilotons) are not easily understood by laymen. Even
members of the United States Senate in the Committee on Armed
Services find it difficult to comprehend the dimensions of nuclear firepower. For example, in a recent Senate inquiry Senator Barry Goldwater,
a Major General in the United States Air Force Reserve, put a question to
Defense Secretary McNamara: "When we talk of tactical nuclear
weapons now aren't we talking about a minimum of one megaton?" Mr.
McNamara's reply was politely off-the-record but must have indicated
that the "minimum" involved was a hundred thousand times smaller than
the Senator's value.

Reprinted from *The Virginia Quarterly Review*, XXXIX (Summer, 1963), 385–
400. By permission.

Ralph E. Lapp, a physicist and distinguished writer on atomic strategy, is the
author of *Kill and Overkill* (1962) and other works.

If the nuclear yardstick of explosive power is hard to understand, think how confused the non-experts or would-be experts become when considering analyses of missile systems. The intricacies of mathematical computations of ICBM base vulnerability, circular probable error of delivered warheads, yield to weight ratios in the warheads, and the imponderables of anti-missile systems still in the embryonic stage all tend to make the Congress and public alike put their confidence in essentially uncontested decision-making in the Pentagon. Congressional appropriations committees have traditionally been unable to cope with professionalism in the military services; they have had to accept basic strategic or policy decisions and nibble away at the edges of the defense budgets.

The natural tendency of the Congress has been to vote for larger and larger defense expenditures. It is regarded as unpatriotic to oppose defense-funding and fewer than half a dozen Congressmen ever vote against the annual appropriation. The cloak of a weapons culture has enveloped our nation and its folds are most tightly drawn around Capitol Hill where legislators vie to bring larger and larger defense contracts to their states and districts. The starts and stops and sudden swerves of our arms technology, so sensitive to impulses from the research laboratory, upset the status quo of defense industry. As the emphasis shifts, for example, from aircraft to missiles, some states find their economies riding a roller coaster. In the city of Seattle over half the labor force draws paychecks countersigned by the Defense Department. About a quarter of California's income is defense-based. Thus when the arms-juggernaut careens off in a new direction, it is no wonder that powerful forces act to maintain a status quo. As a result, the nation witnesses a great tug-of-war when technology clearly shows that the days of the manned bomber are numbered; Congress applies pressure and even approves unwanted funds to develop aircraft which would only be sitting ducks in the event of attack.

The forces trying to perpetuate the manned bomber do not all originate on Capitol Hill although they do conjugate there. Bomber enthusiasts in the Pentagon fight to keep alive their obsolescent vehicles. This fight is natural enough when we consider that it is not just the aircraft that have been indicted by modern military technology. More importantly, the military—and the military mind—of essentially pre-atomic training is obsolescent and to a large degree obsolete.

The Generals are in grave danger of technological displacement. The Defense Department has for a variety of reasons—largely the tradition and inertia of the professionals in uniform—failed to develop officers with a full grasp of modern technology and its implications for defense policy. Certain patch-on attempts were made to adapt the military to changing times but these were too few and too limited. The Air Force's attempt to

cope with the problem by fostering the Rand Corporation has had curious consequences. For instance, General Thomas D. White, former chief of Staff, Air Force, in a recent *Saturday Evening Post* article, "Strategy and Defense Intellectuals," bemoaned the presence of "amateurs" in the policy-planning levels of the Defense Department, called them "termites at work." It turns out that these "intellectual termites" are largely of a Rand species. Clearly, General White views these imported civilians as dangerous "innocents" who should not be trusted with judgments formerly rendered by military men. Since General White did not specifically identify the "defense intellectuals" except as professors, computer men, and specialists, the general public may conclude that *scientists* are causing the wrath in the General's domain. Almost coincidentally, Albert Wohlstetter a veteran Rand-thinker wrote a Foreign Affairs article, "Scientists, Seers, and Strategy," attacking atomic scientists, whom he accuses of professing a sense of prophecy. This, Wohlstetter argues, has resulted in faulty counsel for the United States. His arguments on this score are both confused and confusing since he views the postwar years with hindsight that fails to take into account the technological and political changes of this tumultuous period.

General White's denunciation of defense intellectuals does serve, despite its spleenful incoherence, to direct attention to the problem of missile strategy and deterrence. If the military men are being bypassed, we need to search for the roots of decision-making—not, as Wohlstetter attempts to do, among the utterances of scientists since 1945, but rather in the tight community of analysts who have worked at a high level in the Defense Department. Unfortunately, these specialists rarely publish in the open literature. This does not mean that the security fence denies access to their thinking. There are two avenues of approach; one is to analyze the policies emanating from the Defense Department and to trace their origin; the other is to study the few pronouncements which the analysts do make.

By all odds the richest source ground for evaluating defense policy as it pertains to missiles is the voluminous testimony of high-ranking Defense officials appearing before various committees of the Congress. Perusal of these volumes is particularly rewarding because of Robert S. McNamara's great grasp of defense data and his willingness to reply candidly to questioning. McNamara's testimony this winter [1963] before the Senate Armed Services Committee represents the farthest that any Defense Secretary has gone in spelling out missile strategy. The missile force levels which are projected through 1968 are, of course, well known, but need to be summarized anew for any discussion of missile policy: 656 Polaris IRBMs; 126 Atlas ICBMs; 108 Titan ICBMs; 800 Minuteman ICBMs (currently authorized); 300 Improved Minuteman ICBMs (estimated number). The latter is a design using an improved propellant and

carries an uprated warhead delivered with twice the accuracy of the earlier version.

Both Polaris and Minuteman carry warheads of comparable weight and yield. In the 1962 configuration, a 600 pound warhead has a yield to weight ratio of 0.1 megaton (Mt) per hundred pounds of warhead weight. This 0.6 megaton warhead is expected to be uprated to 1 Mt based upon incorporation of test improvements and propellant efficiency. It should be pointed out that the deliverable payload for a ballistic missile is a function of range and deep penetration aids. Moreover, in the case of Polaris there are three series: the A-1 (1,200 nautical mile range); the A-2 (1,500 n.m.); and the A-3 (2,500 n.m.). The A-1 Polaris has been stationed aboard the first five nuclear submarine launchers; the A-2 is being fitted to the next thirteen submarines; and the remainder will be equipped with the A-3 Polaris.

With these facts and projections in mind, we may proceed to analyze how this missile force is tied to defense strategy. On January 24, 1962, McNamara first set forth his approach to determining the level of deterrent force. If we restrict the discussion to missiles, then his procedure was a two-step process. First, the number, types, and locations of the targets to be destroyed needed to be determined. Second, given this target selection, the number and power of the attacking weapons would follow from a systems analysis. In other words, the quantity and quality of the targets in the USSR would fix the range-warhead-accuracy requirements for the United States strategic missiles. However, since the Russians might strike first and "kill our birds in their nests," United States policy focused on survivability of our missiles—hence the great emphasis on Polaris with its advantages of a launcher endowed with 3-dimensional mobility and concealment. Mobility for the continentally-based Minuteman was abandoned in favor of hardened sites, i.e., underground concrete silos and quick-response times. The writer has consistently stressed the inherent disadvantages of the Minuteman: namely, improvements in Soviet missile accuracy will convert currently hard ICBM bases into soft targets; continental siting of ICBMs involves fall-out association of these bases and United States population; rapid-responding ICBMs (especially when their survivability is threatened) may narrow decision times to precarious minutes. Arguments for the Minuteman include diversification of the deterrent, ability to perform deep penetration missions, assurance of command and control, and such motivating factors as Service interest and political accommodation in site selections.

Enemy intent and capability obviously enter any evaluation of United States missile survivability. If we project to the late 1960's and pure missile deterrence (vanishing reliance on manned bombers) it is seen that the United States missile force will number about 2000 missiles. If we assume that Soviet ICBM and submarine-launched missiles have reason-

ably high accuracy, then two to three missiles will have to be expended per ICBM site. This would mean that a total of more than 3000 Soviet missiles would have to be committed to achieve a "knock-out" of the United States land-based missile force. But before we get beguiled by such numbers, we need to realize that unless the Soviets achieved near-simultaneity and complete surprise in attack, their warheads would vent their explosive concussions on empty missile shafts. Could the Soviets salvo-fire three thousand missiles and annihilate the United States second-strike? This seems very far-fetched indeed, although it is premature to ask the question since one must really estimate what missile force the Soviets are projecting. But clearly, even a successful knockout of the United States ICBMs would leave the Polaris fleet untouched.

United States intelligence about the size of the Soviet missile force has fluctuated wildly. One recalls the vertiginous predictions of Joseph Alsop and the equally morbid pronouncements of senators like Henry Jackson and Stuart Symington in the days of the "missile gap." Then came the U-2 overflights and the vanishing of the missile gap. A deeply disturbing concomitant of this gap evaporation was the United States decision to increase its defense spending. Today the United States National Intelligence Estimates are generally interpreted to give the United States a decided superiority in its missile force vis-à-vis that of the Soviet Union. No official estimates are available, but "leaked" information reaches the press and is occasionally brought up in Congressional hearings. Such an incident occurred on February 20, 1963, in the course of Secretary McNamara's testimony before the Armed Services Committee of the United States Senate. Senator Symington read into the record a newspaper account in which Mr. McNamara was quoted as saying: "In 1967 the Russians will have at least 500 long-range missiles, more than half of them carried on submarines. . . ." An upper limit of 1000 Soviet missiles was indicated and attributed to Mr. McNamara. The latter did not specifically confirm the numbers, but he did protest "leaks from executive sessions" of Congressional committees. That such numbers do actually reflect United States estimates of Soviet capability may be deduced from other statements made by McNamara before the same Senate committee. Stating that the United States would possess 800 missiles by July 1, 1964, the Defense Secretary said: "We have no reason to believe that they (the Soviets) would have or are building toward an objective of (deleted) missiles by mid-1964, and therefore I can only conclude that at the present time their strategy is as Khrushchev has outlined it, a strategy directed primarily against our cities and our urban society."

Here is an astonishing development in our defense policy. According to official estimates, the Soviets will possess in the near future a missile force only large enough to attack United States cities; on the

other hand, our missile force is being built on the philosophy that it must be large enough to withstand a first strike by Soviet missiles—a strike which appears to be well beyond their capabilities. Does not this inconsistency mean that the United States is amassing an enormous overkill capacity?

Secretary McNamara denied that the Polaris component of the strategic missile force represents a degree of overkill. Since it is quite obvious that the Soviet attacking force is far from that which could challenge the combined Minuteman-Polaris target system, it follows that the rational basis for our 2000 missile force is not keyed to Soviet attack capability. We must conclude that, if it is rationally-based, the United States strategic striking force is patterned to effective attack upon the Soviet target system.

At this point a neutral observer comparing the missiles forces of the two major nuclear powers might easily conclude that the Soviet Union by virtue of its inferior missile force could only strike at United States cities and thus must adhere to a second-strike retaliatory philosophy. On the other hand, the large numbers of United States ballistic missiles would be a persuasive argument for assuming that the United States had a first-strike philosophy—at the very least a capability for a first-strike (the two would be synonymous to a suspicious general).

The Soviet Union contains military and civilian target systems. Purely military targets would include ICBM bases, command and control centers, vital communications, and the like; they would not include factories, or oil fields, or transportation as in World War II. Targets in the civilian category would be primarily urban complexes—people and plants and communication and transportation networks. General Curtis E. LeMay, Chief of Staff, USAF, decries city-busting and maintains: "It does no good to attack Russian cities and leave their weapons intact because they will just deliver them on us. We feel we must try to lower the level of our damage by knocking out weapons that can strike us." This is counterforce theory.

United States preparations for mounting a counterforce action have evoked profound concern among the critics of United States armament policy. The argument has been advanced that counterforce is not a valid military action following a Soviet first strike. Secretary McNamara has admitted: "Fully hard ICBM sites can be destroyed but only at great cost in terms of the numbers of offensive weapons required to dig them out. Furthermore, in a second strike situation we would be attacking, for the most part, empty sites from which the missiles had already been fired." But the disparity in the projected missile forces of the United States and the USSR raises doubts about the second-strike nature of the United States strategic force. If, as the Secretary of Defense expresses it, the real targets turn out to be empty missile shafts, will there not be a great

temptation to use ICBMs in a first strike and catch the missiles in their silos? Here the development of an impressive number of Soviet nuclear submarines and Polaris-type rockets would tend to ease worries on this score.

Clues to the Defense Secretary's exposition of missile deterrence are to be found in speeches of key Defense Department personnel and in Rand documents. Specifically, the February 10, 1963, speech of Alain C. Enthoven, Deputy Assistant Secretary of Defense (Systems Analysis)and an ex-Rand economist, is illustrative of the philosophy underlying Mr. McNamara's policy on missile forces. The following paragraph is a significant excerpt:

> Some argue that, in the event of a nuclear attack on the alliance, we should plan to retaliate strictly against Soviet cities. Others argue that we should strike back only against Soviet military forces. Still others argue for both. Some believe that we should design our posture for an irrevocable commitment to a spasm of massive retaliation. Our approach is based on options, deliberation, flexibility, and control. Rather than decide ahead of time which targets must be hit by which weapons, and then commit ourselves to it, our approach is to give the President a range of choices so that he can select the plan whose targets and timing of attack are most appropriate to the situation at hand. I won't speculate here as to which nuclear response might be used in which circumstances. Nothing useful would be accomplished by doing so.

Now, if we recall Mr. McNamara's assessment of Soviet capability and his interpretation of their intent, a nuclear attack would be directed against United States cities and urban areas. What would be the United States response? Dr. Enthoven prefers not to speculate, but Mr. McNamara was more candid; he stated that "we would have no alternative but to respond with our entire force, including those portions of it targeted against their cities." Such a response, he stated, would be made with "sufficient weapons to destroy their society."

The word "destroy" as used here has been defined by Mr. McNamara to mean in "the normal sense of the words." He explained that the Soviet Union "can be destroyed as a civilized nation of the 20th century, by destroying its industrial capacity, by destroying a high percentage of the population, and by destroying its military power." Given this definition of "destroy," Representative George H. Mahon (D. Texas) entered into the following inquiry during an appropriations hearing:

Mr. Mahon: General Taylor, do you agree that we do not have and do not plan to have an overkill capacity in the field of nuclear weapons?
General Taylor: I think we now have something which did not exist in former years, when I came here as Chief of Staff; namely, a measure of sufficiency, a rationale for developing this force. Behind these figures are endless files of computations which crank in various assumptions on missile performance. . . .
I have great confidence in the approach which has been developed. I

would say it comes up now with something which makes sense and has a justification in terms of a rational approach to the problem. (Detailed discussion off the record.)

General Taylor shied away from a direct answer to Mr. Mahon's pointed question on overkill but Mr. McNamara expanded on the theme:

The question of whether we are getting to the point of sufficiency too quickly brings this about—we have asked ourselves this question particularly as it relates to the question of the size of the budget.

The pressures on me from external sources, the public, certain of the Military Departments, Congress, is to do just the reverse, get there more quickly.

Had defense officials admitted that they now possess overkill capability, they would have been greatly embarrassed in asking for redundant capability in the future. In fact, dispassionate Congressmen might justifiably seek cut-backs in defense funding.

In all of this discussion, the issue is overridden with ambiguity because there is no sharp dividing line between kill and overkill. It is a matter of judgment which no single person (or computer) this side of the Iron Curtain can make with any precision. The ultimate judicator of overkill is Mr. Khrushchev. The weight of our deterrent forces is designed to press down upon him and impose a supreme penalty for the unleashing of nuclear war. Given the momentous risks involved—the fate of our nation—our leaders can obviously not err on the side of too little. As Mr. McNamara points out, our present culture places emphasis upon weapons, and powerful forces act upon him to erect the stoutest possible Military Establishment. Yet the very nature of nuclear weapons—their cheapness, relative availability, and far-ranging effects upon the fragile structure of modern societies—makes it clear that unlimited stockpiling of nuclear weapons and the overproduction of weapons systems no longer adds to national security as it did in the pre-atomic days. Furthermore, the amassing of such superpower may have two rather lethal consequences for the future.

One possibility is that the men in the Kremlin will interpret this fantastic weapon arsenal as the basis for imposing our will upon the Soviet Union. Their military experts can point to the character of United States nuclear might and buttress their contention that the United States aims at a first strike at the Soviet homeland. This can become the springboard for an all-out military build-up within the USSR, for an even more intransigent foreign policy, and perhaps for pre-emptive action with Soviet nuclear forces.

Another possibility—and probably the more likely—is that the nonrecognition of nuclear overkill by the Congress and political leaders, not to mention the militarists and defense industrialists, will perpetuate

an arms-oriented economy within the United States. The coils of a true weapons-culture may then tighten ever more constrictively upon our nation and resist all efforts at disengagement. The political and social repercussions of an uncontrolled arms race are not difficult to foresee.

It is therefore a matter of some importance to debate the issue of overkill. The public which has the most to lose in a nuclear war is within its democratic rights in demanding some on-the-record accounting of our nuclear striking power. There can be little question about the inadequacy of the Congress and its various committees in dealing with this matter. As one looks about the Washington scene for some means of penetration, for some hope of challenging the authority of the Defense Department in this unprecedented situation, the possibility of using an agency within Government seems a rather weak one.

Two agencies might contest the Pentagon's judgment on missiles. One is the Arms Control and Disarmament Agency in the State Department. The Agency has shown enough strength to warrant being attacked by reactionary forces on Capitol Hill and elsewhere in the nation. But it would be premature to hope that the self-authority of this relatively new group could begin to cope with the specialist-computer phalanx of the Pentagon. The other is the Office of Science and Technology headed by Dr. Jerome B. Wiesner, President Kennedy's Science Advisor. Prior to taking his Government post, Dr. Wiesner was on record as believing that a finite and rather limited ("a few hundred second-strike weapons") retaliatory force would be adequate for United States security interests. However, when Defense Secretary McNamara was asked on February 20, 1963, some two years after Dr. Wiesner took office, if he knew of Dr. Wiesner's point of view, he replied: "I never heard him say that."

However, outside of Government circles, interest in arms controls and in limiting the nuclear weapons build-up has increased rapidly during the past several years. At the very foundation of this movement is the twofold belief: first, that the arms race is running out of check; and second, that smaller forces than those currently programmed can be adequate for effective deterrence.

P. M. S. Blackett in his "Studies of War" examines missile deterrence. He urges that "the two giant powers should reduce their nuclear forces to a very low and purely retaliatory rôle—that is, each should retain only sufficient invulnerable long-range vehicles to attack the other's cities if it is itself attacked; less, for instance, than 100 ICBMs. with one-megaton warheads. This is still a terrific force able to kill 100 million people or so. A reduction to a level of, say, twenty ICBMs. or less would be preferable." Dr. Blackett has no doubts about the degree of overkill already inherent in the United States missile force. Those charged with national security arrangements will reject Dr. Blackett's proposals out of hand, arguing that rigid inspection procedures would have to be adopted

under an agreed-upon system in order to be sure that the Soviets did not illicitly construct superior missile forces and thus invalidate the United States deterrent. Further, they would argue that Dr. Blackett's 20 to 100 megaton deterrent force is too casually proposed and lacks credibility.

Given today's staggering attack capability, which the author estimates at 20,000 megatons, Blackett's proposal seems fanciful. However, the present megatonnage levels result from the very large-yield nuclear weapons which are accommodated by the B-52 (50 megatons per aircraft) and the huge bomber force. The transition to dependence upon missiles will involve a deliverable payload of several thousand megatons. Thus it is at least arithmetically obvious that today's bombers possess a high degree of overkill. With the development of effective ground-to-air missiles, such as those which shot down the U-2, the on-target capability of the B-52 is severely compromised. Nonetheless, the megatonnage deliverable to the Soviet homeland, if not to assigned targets, is immense. One can predict that pressure will be brought to bear, especially by those with a superficial knowledge of defense problems and an arms interest, to fill the "megaton gap" which may develop in the late sixties. Presumably Soviet emphasis upon the 100 megaton bomb will add to popular anxiety on this score. Senator Henry Jackson (D. Wash.), for example, has urged greater emphasis, including continued atmospheric testing, to develop higher-yield ICBM warheads. General LeMay, however, has admitted that "There is not a clear military requirement for this weapon." Nonetheless, the foremost champion of the manned bomber, having taken essentially the line laid down by Mr. McNamara, went on to state that hundred-megaton weapons would be a deterrent weapon if only for psychological reasons. Here we are confronted with an outcropping of the ancient custom of military men in "matching" weapons. Mr. McNamara has stated: "I do not personally hold to the view that the greater the yield of the weapon, the greater the terror. I think a more proper standard of evaluating the degree of terror associated with a potential threat is the magnitude of the destruction which that threat, when implemented, can bring about."

In the ultimate analysis of nuclear deterrence, the problem centers upon the man who rules the Kremlin and upon the character of the advice he receives about this nuclear threat. If we accept Mr. McNamara's view that Mr. Khrushchev is preparing a strategic force aimed at city and urban targets, it must follow that he knows in advance that the full weight of the United States nuclear strategic arsenal would be unleashed in the event of an attack. Given the massiveness of the United States counterblow, Mr. Khrushchev could have little doubt of the consequences of his act. The highly advertised "controlled thermonuclear response" doctrine of the Defense Department may conceivably have value in certain strategies that the Soviets might elect to take, but in the event of a

blow at United States cities, moderation in our second strike seems most unlikely. It would be tantamount to fighting a nuclear slugfest on the installment plan. In point of fact, the massiveness of the United States striking force is so great that even partial employment of it is a fearful act of vengeance.

As we approach the end of this decade and put our trust in the power of missile terror, in the combination of the megaton and the ICBM, we shall enter a new era of warfare. Just as the H-bomb multiplied the striking power of a single warhead by a million-fold, the ICBMs high velocity compresses time to the dimension of minutes. The minute and the megaton make a nightmare of modern warfare. Their combination can make of war a mad experiment in annihilation in which no human contestant can count a win. In such a catastrophe, as General Douglas MacArthur has concluded: "No longer is (war) a weapon of adventure— the short cut to international power. If you lose, you are annihilated. If you win, you stand only to lose. No longer does it possess even the chance of the winner of a duel. It contains now only the germs of double suicide."

It seems to me that the new apparatus of war has dispossessed the generals. The conduct of a thermonuclear war is really no longer a military operation. The preparations for thermonuclear war, the determination of the adequacy of deterrence—of the quality and quantity of the ballistic deterrers—these things cannot be left to TNT-minded military men. But by the same token they should not be the responsibility of megaton-specialists and computers. Indeed, the whole character of national security has changed so much that the matter of our nuclear forces transcends the competence of the Defense Department. An establishment charged with responsibility for national defense needs powerful restraints imposed upon it if it does not itself exercise self-control. It is all too clear that the Congress is not qualified and is not oriented to impose arms limitations. Nor does United States industry seem anxious to curb the rising tide of defense contracts.

Yet controls must be imposed upon the upward arc of armaments lest the nation be caught completely in the clutch of a weapons culture. The very sinews of our democracy will be tested as the complex issue of nuclear firepower is debated. ICBMs and submarine-launched missiles are a far cry from muskets and cannon. This poses the basic question: Can a democracy come to grips with such a complex issue? Is our nation so organized that it can apply the Town Hall tradition to such intricate problems? Or have the revolutionary forces of science and technology thrust our national-decision-making into the select company of a few? If so, how can we be sure that the decisions of the few are wise?

These are momentous questions for our society. Ever since Hiroshima, a relatively small band of atomic scientists has attempted to enlarge the

area of public understanding of atomic issues. To a certain degree the passage of time has weakened their voices and no second generation of scientists equally motivated has augmented their ranks. Only very slowly has awareness of the issues caused non-scientists within the intellectual community to come forth and speak out. But as a result a real interest in the control of armaments has sprung up. It remains to be seen how effectively this small-scale movement can oppose the arrayed forces of a growing weapons culture.


# 28 / *The Spectrum of Defense*

### ROBERT S. MC NAMARA

The purpose of this speech by the American Secretary of Defense was to proclaim to the world in November, 1963, the substantial strategic superiority—in the eyes of the Pentagon—held by the United States over any other military power, particularly the Soviet Union. In this address Mr. McNamara reminded his listeners, however, that defense problems remain for the United States. Many potential danger situations were seen to exist in which this superiority would not necessarily guarantee the attainment of national objectives. Put another way, nuclear weapons would be unusable.


. . . I SHOULD LIKE to identify and discuss some basic matters on which a considerable degree of consensus seems to me both possible and desirable, although by no means assured.

These include those overall comparative strengths and weaknesses of the opposing military alliances that form the bold relief in the strategic environment. In short, they are the considerations that seem to have relatively long-term significance compared to the annual budget cycle.

Matters of that degree of permanence tend to be stamped on our minds as being unchanging and unchangeable, the unquestioned framework of daily and yearly policy-making. Yet these factors of which I shall speak do change: more swiftly and more profoundly than our picture of them tends to change. Indeed I believe it is just the fact that over the last

From an address by Mr. McNamara to the Economic Club of New York, November 18, 1963.

decade this topography has changed—while many maps have not—that accounts for some apparently irreconcilable controversies.

Let me recall the earlier period briefly, for comparison. The strategic landscape at the outset of the 'Fifties was dominated by two outstanding features. One was the practical US monopoly of deliverable, strategic nuclear weapons. The other was the Soviet Union and Communist China's virtual monopoly of ground force on the continents of Europe and Asia.

Both of these determinants of Western military policy had changed considerably by the end of the Korean War. The Soviets had produced atomic explosions and had created a sizeable nuclear delivery capability against Europe, while NATO ground forces had expanded rapidly, and military operations in Korea had greatly tarnished the significance of Chinese Communist superiority in numbers. But the old notions of monopoly persisted as short-cut aids to thinking on policy matters. And they were not so misleading as they came later to be. Soviet armed forces approaching five million men still heavily outweighed the NATO forces in Europe; and Soviet delivery capability against the US was dwarfed by that of SAC. Moreover, tactical nuclear weapons were being heralded as a new nuclear monopoly for the West.

Even as these earlier notions of monopolies grew obsolete, ideas about the feasibility of alternative policies continued to reflect them. So did ideas about how wars might be fought. Nuclear operations, both strategic and tactical, by the US in response to Soviet aggression against our allies were considered to be virtually unilateral. Hence it was supposed the problem of credibility of the US response would scarcely arise, even in the case of relatively limited Soviet aggressions. Western reliance upon nuclear weapons, in particular strategic systems, both to deter and to oppose non-nuclear attack of any size seemed not only adequate but also unique in its adequacy.

That sort of situation is convenient for policy-makers. It makes policy easy to choose and easy to explain. Perhaps that is why throughout most of the 'Fifties, while the Soviets under various pressures decreased their ground forces and the NATO allies built theirs up, and while the Soviets acquired a massive nuclear threat against Europe and laid the ground-work for a sizeable threat against the US, the picture underlying most policy debate remained that appropriate to 1949. It was a picture of a Communist Goliath in conventional strength facing a Western David, almost naked of conventional arms but alone possessed of a nuclear sling.

Towards the end of that decade, the prospect that the Soviets would acquire intercontinental ballistic missiles at a time when our strategic forces consisted almost entirely of bombers focused our attention and our budget even more sharply than before upon our strategic forces. The

urgency of the problem of deterring the most massive of attacks was a new reason for thinking that the West could spare neither resources nor thought to deal more specifically with lesser threats. The most urgent task was to provide for deterrence of massive aggression by assuring the survival under any attack of forces at least adequate, in the calculations of a potential attacker, to destroy his society in retaliation. It was now not the assurance of continued nuclear superiority that pre-empted the attention of policy-makers but, on the contrary, the struggle to maintain it.

But it is time for the maps to change by which policy is charted and justified. The old ones, which assumed a US nuclear monopoly, both strategic and tactical, and a Communist monopoly of ground combat strength, are too far removed from reality to serve as even rough guides. Neither we nor our allies can afford the crudities of maps that tell us that old policies are still forced upon us, when a true picture would show important new avenues of necessity and choice.

What most needs changing is a picture of ourselves and of the Western Alliance as essentially at bay, outmanned and outgunned except for nuclear arms no longer exclusively ours. We should not think of ourselves as forced by limitations of resources to rely upon strategies of desperation and threats of vast mutual destruction, compelled to deal only with the most massive and immediate challenges, letting lesser ones go by default. It would be a striking historical phenomenon if that self-image should be justified. We are the largest member of an Alliance with a population of almost 450 million people, an aggregate annual product which is fast approaching a trillion dollars, and a modern and diverse technological base without parallel, facing the Soviet Union and its European satellites with their hundred million fewer people and an aggregate output no more than half that of the West.

### Outdated Picture

And quite apart from ignoring the underlying strengths of the West, the outdated picture I have described takes no account of the military capabilities in being that our investment over the last decade, and specifically in the last few years, have bought for us. If new problems put strong claims on our attention and our resources today, it is very largely because we have come a large part of the way that is feasible toward solving some old ones.

Let me summarize the current status of the balance of strategic nuclear forces, that part of the military environment that has preoccupied our attention for so long. In strictly relative numerical terms, the situation is the familiar one. The US force now contains more than 500 operational long-range ballistic missiles—*Atlas, Titan, Minuteman, Polaris*—and is

planned to increase to over 1,700 by 1966. There is no doubt in our minds and none in the minds of the Soviets that these missiles can penetrate to their targets. In addition, the US has Strategic Air Command bombers on air alert and over 500 bombers on quick reaction ground alert. By comparison, the consensus is that today the Soviets could place about half as many bombers over North America on a first strike. The Soviets are estimated to have today only a fraction as many intercontinental missiles as we do. Furthermore, their submarine-launched ballistic missiles are short range, and generally are not comparable to our *Polaris* force. The Soviets pose a very large threat against Europe, including hundreds of intermediate and medium-range ballistic missiles. This threat is today and will continue to be covered by the clear superiority of our strategic forces.

The most wishful of Soviet planners would have to calculate as a certainty that the most effective surprise attack they could launch would still leave us with the capability to destroy the attacker's society. What is equally pertinent is that the relative numbers and survivability of US strategic forces would permit us to retaliate against all the urgent Soviet military targets that are subject to attack, thus contributing to the limitation of damage to ourselves and our allies.

Deterrence of deliberate, calculated attack seems as well assured as it can be, and the damage-limiting capability of our numerically superior forces is, I believe, well worth its incremental cost. It is a capability to which the smaller forces of the Soviet Union could not realistically aspire. That is one reason, among others, why I would not trade our strategic posture for that of the Soviets at any point during the coming decade.

### Beyond Offensive Reach

But given the kind of force that the Soviets are building, including submarine-launched missiles beyond the reach of our offensive forces, the damage which the Soviets could inflict on us and our allies, no matter what we do to limit it, remains extremely high.

That has been true for our allies ever since the middle and late 'Fifties. Soviet acquisition of a sizeable delivery capability against the US, and more significantly their acquisition of relatively protected forces, submarine-launched or hardened, has been long and often prematurely heralded. Its arrival at last merely dramatizes the need to recognize that strategic nuclear war would under all foreseeable circumstances be bilateral and highly destructive to both sides.

Larger budgets for US strategic forces would not change that fact. They could have only a decreasing incremental effect in limiting somewhat the damage that the US and its allies could suffer in a general nuclear war. In short, we cannot buy the capability to make a strategic bombing campaign once again a unilateral prospect.

That must, I suggest, be accepted as one of the determinants affecting policy. Another is that the same situation confronts the Soviet leaders, in a way that is even more intensely confining. In fact, enormous increases in Soviet budgets would be required for them to achieve any significant degree of damage-limiting capability. The present Soviet leaders show no tendency to challenge the basis of the US strategic deterrent posture by such expenditures.

In the last two years alone, we have increased the number of nuclear warheads in the strategic alert forces by 100 per cent. During that period we have more than doubled the megatonnage of the strategic alert forces. The fact that further increases in strategic force size will at last encounter rapidly diminishing returns—which is largely an effect of the very large investments the US has made in this area—should be reflected in future budgets. The funding for the initial introduction of missiles into our forces is nearing completion. We can anticipate that the annual expenditure on strategic forces will drop substantially, and level off well below the present rate of spending. This is not to rule out the possibility that research now in progress on possible new technological developments, including the possibility of useful ballistic missile defenses, will require major new expenditures. In any event, there will be recurring costs of modernization.

In the field of tactical nuclear weapons, the picture is in important respects similar. The US at present has in stockpile or planned for stockpile tens of thousands of nuclear explosives for tactical use on the battlefield, in anti-submarine warfare and against aircraft. They include warheads for artillery, battlefield missiles, demolition munitions, bombs, depth charges, air-to-air missiles and surface-to-air missiles. The consensus is that the US is presently substantially superior in design, diversity and numbers in this class of weapons.

This is an indispensable superiority, as we can readily understand if we consider how our problems of strategic choice would be altered if the tables were reversed and it were the Soviet Union which held a commanding lead in this field. Nevertheless, what we have is superiority, not monopoly, and even if tactical nuclear warfare can be limited, below some ill-defined threshold of strategic exchange, the key fact is that if the West initiates such warfare in the future it must be expected to be bilateral, in any theatre which engaged the Soviet Union. Again, we cannot buy back a monopoly, or the assurance of unilateral use.

Finally, there is the area of what we call our general purpose forces. Within the last two years, we have increased the number of our combat-ready Army divisions by about 45 per cent, from 11 to 16. There has been a 30 per cent increase in the number of tactical air squadrons; a 75 per cent increase in airlift capabilities; and a 100 per cent increase in ship construction and conversion to modernize the fleet.

But it is not only force size that matters. The key to the effective utilization of these forces is combat readiness and mobility.

The most recent demonstration of our ability to reinforce our troops presently stationed in Europe occurred last month on Operation *Big Lift*, the first of a series of planned large-scale, world-wide exercises. For the first time in military history, an entire division was airlifted from one continent to another. That movement could never have been accomplished without a massive increase in our airlift capability, which is still being expanded. (It will have risen 400 per cent between 1961 and 1967.) It required the development of new techniques to pre-position combat equipment, of which we have two extra division sets now in Europe. It calls for new techniques in military training and administration to make sure that units are really ready to move out on a moment's notice. This exercise, in which some 16,000 airmen and soldiers and more than 350 planes took part, is directly relevant to the needs of Europe, where it brought a seventh division to join the six that are to remain in place. It is also relevant to the ability of the US to fulfill its policy commitments world-wide, swiftly and in effective strength.

But, it might be asked, what is the significance of all this for the realistic security problems of the United States and its allies? To what contingencies are these forces expected to contribute, and how effective might they be, measured against the strength of opposing forces? How meaningful is it to talk of 16 or 20 or 30 divisions in opposing the ground armies of the Soviet Union and Communist China?

Such questions are often meant to be merely rhetorical, in view of the supposed masses of Communist troops. The fact is that they are serious, difficult questions, to which I shall suggest some tentative answers. But it is difficult to encourage realistic discussions of specific contingencies so long as the shadow of the Communist horde hangs unchallenged over the debate. The actual contingencies that seem to be to me most likely and most significant are not those which would involve all, or even a major part, of the Soviet Bloc or Chinese Communist armed forces, nor do they all involve Europe. Hence, aggregate figures of armed strength of NATO and the Warsaw Pact nations are not immediately relevant to them. But it is useful to make these overall comparisons precisely because misleading or obsolete notions of these very aggregates often produce an attitude of hopelessness toward any attempt to prepare to meet Communist forces in ground combat, however limited in scope.

### Soviet Force Cuts

The announced total of Soviet armed forces for 1955 was indeed a formidable 5.75 million men. Today that figure has been cut to about 3.3 million; the Warsaw Pact total including the Soviets is only about 4.5 million. Against that, it is today the members of NATO whose active

armed forces number over 5 million. The ground forces of NATO nations total 3.2 million, of which 2.2 million men are in Europe, as against the Soviet ground combat forces total of about 2 million men, and a Warsaw Pact of about 3 million. Both the Soviet Union and the US forces of course include units stationed in the Far East. In Central Europe, NATO has more men, and more combat troops, on the ground than does the Bloc. It has more men on the ground in West Germany than the Bloc does in East Germany. It has more and better tactical aircraft, and these planes on the average can carry twice the payload twice as far as the Soviet counterparts.

These facts are hard to reconcile with the familiar picture of the Russian Army as incomparably massive. The usual index cited to support that picture is numbers of total active divisions, and the specific number familiar from the past is 175 divisions in the Soviet Army.

This total, if true, would indeed present a paradox. The Soviet ground forces are reliably estimated to be very close to two million men, compared to about one million for the US. How is it that the Soviets can muster ten times the number of active, combat-ready, fully-manned divisions that the United States has manned, with only twice as many men on active duty? The answer is simply that they do not. Recent intensive investigation has shown that the number of active Soviet divisions that are maintained at manning levels anywhere close to combat readiness is less than half of the 160–175 figure.

What remains is a large number, but even that is misleading. For one thing, US divisions have about twice as many men in the division unit and its immediate combat supporting units as comparable Soviet divisions. A US mechanized division has far more personnel in maneuvering units, far more in armoured cavalry, far more engineers, far more signals, far more light armoured personnel carriers, and far more aircraft available in support than Soviet divisions. In addition to longer staying power, much of the US manpower and equipment margin is muscle that would make itself felt on D-Day. If, on the other hand, we were to reorganize along Soviet lines, we could display far greater numbers of divisions comparable to those of the Soviets.

The Soviet combat-ready force remains a formidable one. Moreover, the Russians do have a power mobilization capability; in particular they have a large number of lightly manned or cadre divisions to be filled out on mobilization. Still, this reality remains strikingly different from our accustomed maps of it.

I do not wish to suggest that such aggregate comparisons are by themselves a valid index of military capabilities. But they are enough to suggest the absurdity, as a picture of the prevailing military strengths on which new efforts might build, of David and Goliath notions borrowed from 1949.

None of this is to say that NATO strength on the ground in Europe is adequate to turn back without nuclear weapons an all-out surprise non-nuclear attack.

But that is not in any case the contingency toward which the recent and future improvements in the mobility and capabilities of US general purpose forces are primarily oriented. Aggression on that scale would mean a war about the future of Europe and, as a consequence, the future of the US and the USSR. In the face of threats of that magnitude, our nuclear superiority remains highly relevant to deterrence. The Soviets know that even non-nuclear aggression at that high end of the spectrum of conflict so threatens our most vital interests that we and our allies are prepared to make whatever response may be required to defeat it, no matter how terrible the consequences for our own society.

The probability that the Soviet leaders would choose to invoke that exchange seems to me very low indeed. They know well what even the Chinese Communist leaders must recognize upon further reflection, that a nuclear war would mean destruction of everything they have built up for themselves during the last 50 years.

### Spectrum of Aggression

If we were to consider a spectrum of the possible cases of Communist aggression, then, ranging from harassment, covert aggression and indirect challenge at one end of the scale to the massive invasion of Western Europe or a full scale nuclear strike against the West at the other end, it is clear that our nuclear superiority has been and should continue to be an effective deterrent to aggression at the high end of the spectrum. It is equally clear, on the other hand, that at the very low end of the spectrum a nuclear response may not be fully credible, and that nuclear power alone cannot be an effective deterrent at this level in the future any more than it has been in the past.

The fact is that at every level of force, the Alliance in general, and the US Armed Forces in particular, have greater and more effective strength than we are in the habit of thinking we have—and with reasonable continued effort we can have whatever strength we need. I have spoken already of strategic weapons, where the great superiority of the United States is the superiority also of the Alliance. In tactical nuclear weapons a parallel superiority exists—and while many of our Allies share with us in manning the systems which would use these tactical warheads in the hour of need, it is not unfair to point out that, even more than in the strategic field, the tactical nuclear strength of the Alliance is a contribution of the United States. That strength has been increased, on the ground in Europe, by more than 60 per cent in the last two years. Today the thousands of US warheads deployed on the continent for the immediate defense of Europe

have a combined explosive strength more than 10,000 times the force of the nuclear weapons used to end the Second World War. Tactical nuclear strength the Alliance has today, and we have provided it.

But neither we nor our Allies can find the detonation of such weapons—and their inevitable bilateral exchange—an easy first choice. At the lower end of the spectrum, therefore, we also need strong and ready conventional forces. We have done our part here and we continue to believe it just—and practicable—for our partners to do theirs.

The most difficult questions arise over the means for meeting a variety of dangerous intermediate challenges in many parts of the world: those which threaten the possibility of sizeable conflict while still not raising the immediate issue of the national survival of ourselves or of any member of our alliances. Conflicts might arise out of Soviet subversion and political aggression backed up by military measures in non-NATO areas in Europe, Latin America, the Middle East and Africa. There is a range of challenges that could arise from Communist China and its satellites in the Far East and in Southeast Asia. Most dangerously, approaching the upper end of the spectrum, there is the possibility of limited Soviet pressures on NATO territory itself, along the vast front running from Norway to Greece and Turkey. Both the flanks and the centre contain potential targets. And always, of course, there are the contingencies that could arise in relation to Berlin.

It is difficult to say just how probable any of these circumstances might be, although they must be regarded as more likely than still larger aggression. What one can say is that if any of these more likely contingencies should arise, they would be highly dangerous. Inaction, or weak action, could result in a serious setback, missed opportunity or even disaster. In fact, if either a nuclear exchange or a major Soviet attack should occur, it would most likely arise from a conflict on a lesser scale, which Western capabilities had failed to deter and which an inadequate Western response had failed to curb in time.

Since World War II, the expansionist impulse of the Communist Bloc is clear, but equally clear is its desire to avoid direct confrontation with the military forces of the free world. In Greece, in Berlin, and in Cuba, Communists have probed for military and political weakness but when they have encountered resistance, they have held back. Not only Communist doctrine has counseled this caution, but respect for the danger that any sizeable, overt conflict would lead to nuclear war. It would follow that no deterrent would be more effective against these lesser and intermediate levels of challenge than the assurance that such moves would certainly meet prompt, effective military response by the West. That response could confront the Soviets with frustration of their purposes unless they chose themselves to escalate the conflict to a nuclear exchange, or to levels that made nuclear war highly probable—

a choice they are unlikely to make in the face of our destructive power. The basis for that particular assurance cannot be systems in development, or weapons in storage depots, or reserves that must be mobilized, trained and equipped, or troops without transport. We need the right combination of forward deployment and highly mobile combat-ready ground, sea and air units, capable of prompt and effective commitment to actual combat, in short, the sort of capability we are increasingly building in our forces.

### Lean and Fit

This capability requires of us—as of our Allies—a military establishment that is, in the President's words, lean and fit. We must stop and ask ourselves before deciding whether to add a new and complex weapon system to our inventory, whether it is really the most effective way to do the job under the rigorous conditions of combat. We must examine constantly the possibilities for combining functions, particularly in weapons that could be used by two or more Services. Given this tough-minded sense of reality about the requirements of combat readiness, it should be possible for the United States not only to maintain but to expand this increased strength without overall increases in our defense budget. As our national productivity and our gross national product expand, the defense budget therefore need not keep pace. Indeed, it appears likely that measured in relative—and perhaps even absolute—terms, the defense budget will level off and perhaps decline a little. At the same time, we are continuing the essential effort to reduce the impact of defense spending on our balance of payments. We have already brought this figure down for $2.7 billion in FY 1961 to $1.7 billion for FY 1963, and we shall continue to reduce it, without reducing the combat ground forces deployed in Europe, and while strengthening our overall combat effectiveness.

And it must be our policy to continue to strengthen our combat effectiveness. I do not regard the present Communist leaders as wholly reckless in action. But recent experience, in Cuba and, on a lesser scale, in Berlin, has not persuaded me that I can predict with confidence the sorts of challenges that Communist leaders will come to think prudent and profitable. If they were again to miscalculate as dangerously as they did a year ago, it would be essential to confront them, wherever that might be, with the full consequences of their action: the certainty of meeting immediate, appropriate, and fully effective military action.

All of our strengths, including our strategic and tactical nuclear forces, contributed last year, and they would contribute in similar future situations to the effectiveness of our response, by providing a basis for assurance that the Soviets would not dangerously escalate or shift the

locale of the conflict. But above all, in order to fashion that response, and to promise the Soviets local defeat in case of actual ground conflict, we had to use every element of the improvements in combat readiness and mobility that had been building over the preceding year and a half, including combat divisions, air transport, and tactical air. And the last ingredient was also there: the will to use those forces against Soviet troops and equipment.

Let us not delude ourselves with obsolete images into believing that our nuclear strength, great as it is, solves all of our problems of national security, or that we lack the strengths to meet those problems that it does not solve. In the contingencies that really threaten—the sort that have occurred and will occur again—we and our allies need no longer choose to live with the sense of the reality of inferiority to the Soviet Bloc in relevant, effective force. Let us be fully aware of the wide range of our military resources, and the freedom they can give us to pursue the peaceful objectives of the free world without fear of military aggression.

# 29 / Germ and Chemical Warfare

## J. H. ROTHSCHILD

Too little attention has been given to developments in the laboratories of chemists and biologists which have opened up a Pandora's box of potential instruments for future international coercion. The existence of man's knowledge in this field and the capabilities which governments are developing, more or less in secrecy, ought not to be ignored. What some of the possibilities are in this field is revealed in the following selection.

WHERE DOES CBR—chemical, biological and radiological warfare—fit into the present and future world picture? Why is it so prominent in recent arms control proposals? As nuclear weapons become more

Reprinted from *War/Peace Report,* January, 1962. By permission.

Brigadier General J. H. Rothschild, before his retirement, commanded the U. S. Army's Chemical Corps Research and Development Command. He was thus in charge of research on chemical-biological-radiological (CBR) instruments of warfare. He is the author of *Tomorrow's Weapons* (1964) and various articles on toxic and germ warfare.

and more powerful, why worry about CBR? These are important questions, requiring objective consideration free of emotion and prejudice.

To take the last first, radiological warfare is the use of residual radioactivity to injure man. When the fireball of a nuclear explosion comes into contact with the surface of the earth, it sucks up particles which are carried by winds as radioactive fall-out. Enough has been written about fall-out to permit me to omit this portion of the subject.

In discussing chemical and biological warfare (or, more concisely, toxic warfare), I would first like to dispose of the enduring misconception about the inhumanity of these weapons. There is nothing humane about any method of warfare. War just wasn't designed that way. Burning a man to death with a flame-thrower, blasting off a couple of legs, blinding a man or injuring his mind beyond recovery with shell fire is apparently acceptable. But is it humane?

If you wish to arrange your weapons in order of humaneness, I believe the toxic weapons will come at the top of the list. A person injured short of death in biological and chemical warfare could generally expect to recover in a matter of a few weeks if he received adequate medical treatment. Permanent disabilities should be rare. Suffering while either dying or recovering would generally be less than that endured from violent injury or burns.

Toxic warfare gives the commander the first real control over the damage he will inflict. Other weapons cause death, injury and damage indiscriminately. Men close enough to a nuclear explosion will be killed; others, depending upon their distance and specific location, will suffer various degrees of violent injury, radiation damage and burns.

Selection from a range of chemical or biological agents will permit the commander to kill a number of the enemy or merely to incapacitate temporarily those affected, with relatively few deaths. A familiar example is our use of tear gas to quell riots. This is more humane than using bullets or grenades. This flexibility is possible only with the toxic weapons.

The last time gas was used on a large scale was in World War I, and on the basis of that experience it is difficult to stigmatize gas in relation to other means of war. Our soldiers in the American Expeditionary Force suffered many unnecessary casualties because they would not wear masks (the masks of that period were evidently more unacceptable than the gas). When the Germans launched the first large scale attack, however, the Allies had nothing to counter it with but propaganda. This propaganda, branding the Germans as barbarous, was found to be such an effective weapon to stir up the people of their countries that the Allies continued to use it even after they had protective masks and were using gas themselves.

Gas caused over one-quarter of the casualties in the A.E.F, and it has been calculated that it was about five times as effective as high explosives

in causing casualties. But of the soldiers who became casualties from gas, only 2 per cent died in contrast to the 25 per cent who died from wounds of other kinds. And only about 4 per cent of the gas casualties were discharged from the service as permanently disabled versus 25 per cent of those wounded by other means.

The chemical agent that caused most of these casualties was mustard gas. While we still plan on mustard as an agent, we now have nerve gases which, on inhalation, are about 10 to 15 times as effective as mustard. Moreover, these gases are colourless, odourless or nearly so, much faster acting, and absorbable not only through the lungs and eyes but also through any exposed skin. A German chemist discovered the first nerve gas in 1939 while looking for a new insecticide. By the end of World War II the Germans had a large plant for manufacturing this gas, called Tabun. The plant was captured by the Russians and moved to the Soviet Union, where it presumably is in operation today. Another nerve gas, Sarin, which is also called GB, was discovered by the Germans later in the war. It is considered even more effective militarily.

In spite of the greater effectiveness of the nerve gases, the area which can be attacked with chemical agents is measured in only tens of square miles. Thus, though chemicals would be a very efficient battlefield weapon, they are not likely for enemy attacks on our homeland except for special purposes. One of these purposes would be to cause panic and force the diversion of valuable effort and material from more important tasks. An attack on one of our major cities would certainly accomplish this.

Incapacitating agents are another new development in chemical warfare. There are two main kinds—those which affect the mind and those which affect the body. An example of the former, called psycho-chemicals, is LSD 25. A small dose of LSD 25—only a tiny fraction of the lethal dose—causes a person to become so confused mentally that he cannot carry out his normal functions. Hours later the effects may disappear, leaving no after-effects. Other drugs, often in very small doses, can cause temporary paralysis, sleepiness, blindness, deafness, loss of balance, crying, diarrhoea, vomiting and convulsions. However, not enough money has been available to pursue the search for incapacitating agents energetically.

Biological warfare falls into an entirely different class from CW for two reasons. First, except for minor incidents, it has not been used in war, and thus remains to be proven. However, there is no doubt of the feasibility of germ warfare and we do know that disease has affected, sometimes decided, the course of many wars in the past. World War II was the first war in which the number of American casualties by enemy action exceeded the number of casualties from disease.

Biological weapons present a far more efficient method of causing

disease than that used by Mother Nature. We must start with the disease organisms we find in nature as we have not been able to make new ones, but our methods of spreading them are far more efficient. Generally, the biological agents would be disseminated in the air so that the target population would inhale them. Insects may be used to spread infectious organisms, and saboteurs may contaminate food, drugs and drinks, but the major method will be via the airborne route.

The second reason why biological weapons fall into another class is that such a very small amount is needed to infect a man. Thus, sufficient material may be disseminated to blanket tens of thousands to hundreds of thousands of square miles. While it is necessary to put enough chemical into the air so that a man inhales the entire dose required to make a casualty of him, this is not true for biological materials. In that case, it is only necessary to have the man inhale sufficient to infect him and the organism will then multiply to cause a casualty. There are enough *Coxiella Burnetii*, the causative organism of Q fever, in a single ounce to infect 28 billion people (if it could be perfectly distributed, which it cannot). Major-General Marshall Stubbs, US Army chief chemical officer, has stated that ". . . biological agents exist which can be used strategically to cause casualties in an area the width of a continent."

### Suitable Agents

While most casualties from biological weapons would be casualties resulting directly from germs put into the air, there would also be a later spread of some diseases from man to man. However, this is less predictable and dependable. In a country with a fairly modern public health system in working order, epidemic spread would be unlikely. If, however, transportation, communication and health facilities were disrupted by nuclear attack, the chances of epidemic spread would be greatly increased.

Many germs are suitable as BW agents. Generally, they must be capable of being manufactured in sufficient quantities, of withstanding the hardships of storage, dissemination and sunlight, and, of course, be highly infectious. Among those which meet these qualifications are dengue fever, Venezuelan equine encephalomyelitis, yellow fever, Q fever, anthrax, undulant fever, tularemia (rabbit fever) and San Joaquin fever.

Though the reservoir of diseases found in nature is the starting point in looking for BW agents, it is possible to increase their virulence by breeding them through animals and in other ways. It is also possible to make them resistant to antibiotics, hardier in withstanding the rigors of dissemination and atmospheric conditions, and with other desired characteristics.

Antifood biological warfare is another possibility. Both agricultural

crops and livestock are vulnerable to certain BW agents. For example, foot and mouth disease, which has been eradicated from agricultural animals in the US at great trouble and expense, might be reintroduced by biological warfare. Cattle, sheep and swine might be infected following aerosol dissemination over a large area. Some crops, too, could be devastated by BW, although this country would be fortunate in that it has several years' supply of most major crops in storage and its crops are relatively resistant to most crop diseases. This is not true of all other countries.

The means of delivery for germ and chemical weapons are relatively simple, as any vehicle that can carry a nuclear warhead can also deliver CB weapons. Thus CB warfare can be waged with missiles, planes, artillery, mines, and spray tanks carried by manned or unmanned aircraft. Biological warfare is also particularly suitable for sabotage. (This raises a difficult problem, as even a small country could engage in biological warfare, and the victimized country could not be sure which country was attacking it.) Instead of the infectious organisms themselves, disease-carrying insects could also be disseminated. Examples would include the mosquito for yellow fever, the tick for Rocky Mountain spotted fever and the flea for plague. Of course, all of these means are limited by their present state of preparedness, which is classified information.

### Protective Equipment

There is protective equipment available for use against chemical and biological weapons. All the masks, including the inexpensive civilian mask, will protect the lungs against both. Equipment for detection of chemical agents is available. The great difficulty is that we have no method of detecting biological agents in time to put on the masks. Biological clouds have no characteristics detectable by the senses; they are invisible, odourless and tasteless. This is an extremely critical lack, since it means that persons over many thousands of square miles could be infected before it was realized there had been a biological attack. Although the Chemical Corps is putting much effort into research to solve the detection problem, it has not yet been successful.

The relation of toxic warfare to nuclear war is far from simple. As in most areas, we do not know the intentions of the Soviets. From all information we can get, they have the capabilities to wage both germ and chemical war and they have made public statements to the effect that they envision that "any new war will be characterized by mass use of air-power, various types of rocket, atomic, thermonuclear, chemical and biological weapons." In addition, after an exhaustive discussion of the medical and military aspects of combined CBR weapons, Soviet military medical officials concluded in a paper published in 1957 that: "the

combined use of pathogenic micro-organisms (disease-causing microbes) and radioactive substances increases the effectiveness of both types of agents." One obvious place for the potential enemy's use of biological agents would be in an attack by saboteurs on our retaliatory bases timed so the maximum number of men would become casualties at the time of their nuclear strike.

Our use of biological agents in an all-out nuclear war needs thorough discussion. There is no doubt that our present massive deterrent policy is simply punitive. We say that we will not make a first strike, but will retaliate in overwhelming force. This retaliation will include Soviet cities and industrial complexes—as well as missile sites, air bases and other military targets. In other words we will make their initiation of the war so costly that they had better not start it. If this is our objective, perhaps we should include the use of lethal biological agents along with the nuclear to be sure that our deterrent is as strong as possible. But further than this, if the Soviets developed a weapons system to stop most of our nuclear missiles before they reached their targets it might be possible that a BW attack against all of Russia west of the Ural Mountains, for example, could be launched with so few missiles, or with other means which would be difficult to defend against, that BW could well be an additional deterrent to war.

It is very likely that Red China, with its relatively few important targets for nuclear weapons and its different standards as to the value of life, might be willing to initiate nuclear war between the United States and Russia when China has nuclear weapons of its own. This it could do by exploding primitive atomic bombs simultaneously over a half-dozen of our major coastal cities using submarines or disguised small craft carrying short range and even inaccurate rockets. Even if we were in an era of a stable second strike capability, I don't believe we would wait for much investigation, but would immediately launch a rataliatory attack on the USSR and, of course, receive all of its might in return. Certainly some weapons would be fired at China, but the Chinese might figure that the material damage and the loss of life its people would suffer would be acceptable. But how many deaths would be acceptable? If China were threatened with lethal biological agents on the entire fertile crescent along her coast line, would the loss of life still be acceptable? Here is a deterrent which might be more effective against China than the threat of nuclear attack.

In limited war, nuclear or not, biological and chemical warfare clearly would have its uses. CB weapons would be extremely valuable in equalizing the Communists' superiority in manpower on battlefields of their own choosing. If the enemy were widely dispersed to avoid the effects of tactical nuclear weapons, these weapons would be useful in seeking him out. Moreover, CB weapons could be useful against

opponents occupying a friendly country, since it would be desirable to keep killing and damage at a minimum.

Chemical and biological weapons have become important in disarmament discussions for two reasons: they are very powerful and inspection for disarmament violations is very difficult. It might be possible to find plants manufacturing chemical agents by means of inspecting plants and by tracing certain basic chemicals from their sources. But it would be impossible for any inspection system to guarantee that no biological agents were being produced and transported.

Since biologicals are grown, there are no raw materials that can be easily traced. Pharmaceutical plants, hospitals, breweries or many other places could serve as secret sites for producing biologicals. The final amount required is small and easily transportable. Thus it might be said that we have a "hidden biological problem" comparable to the "clandestine weapon problem" in the nuclear area. (The clandestine weapon problem refers to the fact that we have passed the point where any inspection system could guarantee that all nuclear weapons already made could be discovered.) These two problems, if nothing else, would seem to make it clear that if disarmament is to be achieved a world security system would need considerable power at its disposal to guard against these two potential dangers.

Public discussion of these and many other problems connected with toxic warfare is urgently needed if we are to shape our policies realistically. From a military standpoint, we must establish the fact that chemical and biological weapons are a normal, usable means of war. Our military must be prepared to use these weapons and to defend themselves against them, something which is not true now. In the total context, CB warfare and particularly the biological, in conjunction with nuclear war, adds up to the fact that war in the future is a completely unacceptable method of solving world problems, and that we must spare no effort in seeking an honourable, safeguarded peace. To sweep the problem of toxic warfare under the rug, which has been the policy of the US Government in recent years, serves neither the military defense of our country nor the cause of peace.

# 30 / International Arms Control

### ARNOLD WOLFERS AND OTHERS

A veritable five-foot shelf of books exists on the subject of
arms control and disarmament, and the list grows continually.
Modern man's greatest challenge is disarmament: to establish
disarmament and peace-keeping machinery that will fulfill
the categorical imperative of any contemporary nation's foreign policy—the prevention of all-out war in the nuclear age.
The prospects and problems of disarmament and arms control
are succinctly analyzed in the following selection.

MR. KHRUSHCHEV has proposed total disarmament down to the
level of those internal police forces required for internal security. It remains to be seen whether the inspection procedures, the measures and
forces necessary to resolve and enforce the settlement of international
disputes, and a phased approach to such an objective can be satisfactorily
negotiated. But even on the unlikely assumption that these hurdles can be
overcome, there are even more basic objections which need to be thought
about. They relate to the question of just how "stable" a completely
disarmed, multinational world would actually be.

It is patently impossible to reverse or to otherwise "undiscover" those
scientific and technological advances in weaponry that have already been
made. In a world totally disarmed, if conflicts broke out between nations
over vital political and economic issues—or even threatened to break
out—a hectic race to manufacture and deploy the most efficient and
destructive weapons made possible by technology could be expected to
follow immediately. Perhaps one adversary would be in a relatively
favorable position to win such a race. In the final analysis modern
technology and its weapons would still determine the outcome. Perhaps it
is better that the influence of such weapons be brought to bear at the end
of such a conflict rather than at the beginning, but that it can be
permanently banned from influencing vital decisions in a divided world
seems hardly possible.

Reprinted from U. S. Senate Committee on Foreign Relations Study No. 8,
"Developments in Military Technology and Their Impact on United States Strategy
and Foreign Policy," by The Washington Center of Foreign Policy Research, The
Johns Hopkins University (December, 1959), in *U.S. Foreign Policy: Compilation of
Studies,* 87th Cong., 1st sess., S. Doc. 24 (March 15, 1961), pp. 764–67. Footnotes in
the original have been omitted.
Brief biographical sketches of the authors accompany selection 22.

Furthermore, it is almost as difficult to keep the clock of scientific progress standing still as it is to turn it back. Scientists will continue to think. Laboratories and computers will continue to add to scientific knowledge. Perhaps the focus of scientific thought can be turned to other subjects than armament, but that it can be kept from having any bearing on military technology is beyond the realm of the possible.

It is also doubtful that an inspection system could be devised which could disclose with a high degree of certainty that all nuclear material produced in the past has been accounted for. Geiger counters cannot detect the presence of plutonium, even at close range, if it is concealed in a lead box or underground. It has been remarked that the principal tools international inspectors would need to locate hidden plutonium would be shovels and screwdrivers. There seems to be no way of attaining a high degree of assurance (even with the most elaborate inspection systems now conceived) that material sufficient for, say, a hundred nuclear weapons had not been secreted.

The point is that absolute stability is probably not attainable through arms control, disarmament and inspection. Even more important, it is not certain that the greatest attainable stability is achievable by maximum disarmament.

Those who work in the field of electronics speak of the "noise level" of their systems. All the random and uncontrollable forces operating on and within the system are called "noise". If the noise level is high, it will blanket out weak signals which the electronic system is attempting to handle in an ordered way. If the signals are strong, they will come through above even a considerable intensity of noise. There is thus a relation between the signal strength that must be maintained and the noise level of the system if it is to operate in a controllable way.

There may well be an analogous relationship between the level and character of armaments permitted under an international agreement and the number of concealed or clandestinely manufactured weapons that could disrupt the system. An arms limitation agreement between the United States and the Soviet Union which permitted each side to retain a number of retaliatory systems capable of surviving a first strike from the other, but which were insufficient in number, destructive power, and accuracy to execute a first strike themselves, could create a ratio of controlled to uncontrollable force favorable to nuclear stability.

Let us assume that such an arms control system permitted each side to maintain 200 or 300 strategic nuclear weapons so hardened, mobile, and dispersed that to eliminate any one of them would require a substantial number of attacking weapons of great destructive power and accuracy. Under such conditions even the surreptitious addition of several hundred weapons to the attack capabilities of one side or the other would not be sufficient to upset the stability of the system. Any temptation to

violate the system would be restrained by the knowledge that a very great effort, indeed an effort so great as to run a high risk of detection, would be required before the inherent stability of the system could be overcome.

It is highly unlikely that any foolproof arms control and inspection system can ever be devised. But there are other important considerations bearing on this issue. The first is that, unless a determined effort is made to achieve some form of nuclear stability, the prospect for the next decade is one of high instability and consequent risk of allout nuclear war. We will have to run very hard in the arms race just to keep the very dangerous position which we now occupy from becoming even more dangerous. The second consideration is that other nations, in addition to the United States, have an interest in reducing the instability of the nuclear relationship.

One of the most difficult problems to be surmounted in this regard may be that presented by the accelerating rate of progress in military technology. It is conceivable that the preamble to any arms control and regulation agreement should declare the intention of the parties to preserve conditions making continued nuclear stability possible. One of the commitments mutually undertaken in pursuit of that purpose could be openness of scientific and technological research. Such a commitment may not be enforcible in detail. Violation, however, to be effective would probably have to be on a scale lending itself to detection.

Another difficult problem would be that of sanctions. What could be done, short of war, if one side or the other believes the agreement is being violated? Inspection and investigation procedures could be available to the accused side to demonstrate that the accusations were false, if that is the case. If one side, however, willfully violated the agreement and persisted in its violation, what could be done? Various possibilities are conceivable. One would be then to declare the agreement voided and to proceed to full mobilization. The secure retaliatory capabilities preserved under the agreement should give a high measure of protection against the threat that the original violator could achieve a decisive counterforce capability before mobilization added greatly to the defender's capabilities.

A further difficulty arises in relation to countries other than the United States and the Soviet Union. How is their security to be preserved, particularly against threats or encroachments by powers of the first rank? Again various possibilities are conceivable. One would be an international police force of some considerable size and strength. This possibility involves many problems concerning the manner in which such a force would be controlled, staffed, armed, and based, and the way in which decisions would be made as to when, and against whom, it intervened. It is hard to see how either the Soviet Union or the United States could

agree to the establishment of a force sufficient in size and power to intimidate it if there were any possibility that this force could fall under the effective control of its enemies. Another possibility is that less powerful countries be permitted a small number of tactical atomic weapons to be used only in defense against otherwise superior external forces and only in and over their own territory.

A few words may also be said on the problem of inspection under an arms control agreement. Inspection is likely to be ineffective unless it is coupled with a system calling for the disclosure of pertinent facts by the nation being inspected. The inspection system could then be designed to test the accuracy of these disclosures. Overlapping sampling techniques, coupled with more detailed investigation where questions arise, can give a much higher degree of confidence that there has been no violation than can a system of inspection designed to reveal everything itself. Much further technical work needs to be done to work out the possibilities and limitations of various techniques of inspection such as aerial photography, monitoring of factory production, and recording of electric power consumption.

Two further difficulties in achieving increased nuclear stability through arms control should be mentioned. The first is the problem of the asymmetry in the information that we and the Soviet Union now have about each other. The Soviet system lends itself to secrecy and ours does not. The Soviet leaders are unlikely to feel, therefore, that a scheme for equal exchange of information involves equal sacrifices toward stability by both sides. The second is that an effective and comprehensive scheme must include all important countries. An agreement which did not include Communist China, for example, would present most serious risks for our side.

A necessary corollary of seeking nuclear stability through arms control agreements might therefore be a willingness to negotiate with the Chinese Communists on a basis reasonably likely to be acceptable to them. This might well require some radical and perhaps unwelcome changes in our policies toward that nation, including that of our resistance to its membership in the United Nations.

In summary of this chapter it may be said that much could probably be done toward increasing the stability of the strategic nuclear equation. There is, however, no easy and simple road to success. Much could be done through action by the United States alone. More could be done if our action were joined by the reciprocal action of others. Still more might be possible through the addition of agreed international control and inspection machinery. But there are serious policy issues and corollaries involved in the decisions seriously to seek stability. It would be an error not to see and deal with these issues as best we can and, if possible, in advance, if this is the road we firmly decide to follow.

# For Further Reading

BRENNAN, DONALD G., ed. *Arms Control, Disarmament, and National Security* (New York: George Braziller, 1961).

BRODIE, BERNARD. *Strategy in the Missile Age* (Princeton: Princeton University Press, 1959).

CLAUSEWITZ, KARL VON. *War, Politics and Power,* tr. and ed. Edward M. Collins (Chicago: Henry Regnery, 1962).

EARLE, EDWARD MEAD, ed. *Makers of Modern Strategy* (Princeton: Princeton University Press, 1944).

FURNISS, EDGAR S., JR., ed. *American Military Policy* (New York: Rinehart, 1957).

GALLOIS, PIERRE. *The Balance of Terror* (Boston: Houghton-Mifflin, 1961).

GAREAU, FREDERICK H., ed. *The Balance of Power and Nuclear Deterrence* (Boston: Houghton-Mifflin, 1962).

GARTHOFF, RAYMOND. *Soviet Strategy in the Nuclear Age,* 2d ed. (New York: Praeger, 1962).

GOLDWIN, ROBERT A., ed. *America Armed* (Chicago: Rand-McNally Co., 1963).

HALPERIN, MORTON H. *Limited War in the Nuclear Age* (New York: John Wiley and Sons, 1963).

HEILBRUNN, OTTO. *Partisan Warfare* (New York: Praeger, 1962).

HUNTINGTON, SAMUEL P. *The Common Defense* (New York: Columbia University Press, 1961).

KAHN, HERMAN. *Thinking About the Unthinkable* (New York: Horizon, 1961).

KAUFMANN, WILLIAM W., ed. *Military Policy and National Security* (Princeton: Princeton University Press, 1956).

KAUFMANN, WILLIAM W. *The McNamara Strategy* (New York: Harper and Row, 1964).

KISSINGER, HENRY A. *The Necessity for Choice* (New York: Harper, 1961).

KNORR, KLAUS, and THORNTON READ, eds. *Limited Strategic War* (New York: Praeger, 1962).

LAPP, RALPH E. *Kill and Overkill* (New York: Basic Books, 1962).

LEVINE, ROBERT A. *The Arms Debate* (Cambridge, Mass.: Harvard University Press, 1963).

MILLIS, WALTER, HARVEY C. MANSFIELD and HAROLD STEIN. *Arms and the State* (New York: Twentieth Century Fund, 1960).

MORGENTHAU, HANS J. "The Four Paradoxes of Nuclear Strategy," *American Political Science Review,* LVIII (March 1964), 23–35.

NOEL-BAKER, PHILIP. *The Arms Race: A Programme for World Disarmament* (New York: Oceana, 1958).

OSGOOD, ROBERT E. *Limited War* (Chicago: University of Chicago Press, 1957).

ROTHSCHILD, BRIGADIER GENERAL J. H. *Tomorrow's Weapons* (New York: McGraw-Hill, 1964).

SCHELLING, THOMAS C. *The Strategy of Conflict* (Cambridge, Mass.: Harvard University Press, 1960).

SCHELLING, THOMAS C., and MORTON HALPERIN. *Strategy and Arms Control* (New York: Twentieth Century Fund, 1961).

SCHILLING, WARNER, PAUL Y. HAMMOND, and GLENN H. SNYDER. *Strategy, Politics and Defense Budgets* (New York: Columbia University Press, 1962).

SINGER, J. DAVID. *Deterrence, Arms Control and Disarmament* (Columbus, Ohio: Ohio State University Press, 1962).

SNYDER, GLENN. *Deterrence and Defense* (Princeton: Princeton University Press, 1962).

WOHLSTETTER, ALBERT. "The Delicate Balance of Terror," *Foreign Affairs*, XXXVII, 2 (January 1959), 211–34.

WOLFERS, ARNOLD. *Alliance Policy in the Cold War* (Baltimore, Md.: The Johns Hopkins Press, 1959).

# IV THE PROPAGANDA INSTRUMENT

# 31 / Psychological Warfare Reconsidered

ROLAND I. PERUSSE

"Psychological warfare," "propaganda," "international communication"—each of these terms has been used with reference to government-sponsored programs for foreign persuasion. How are these terms best defined? What is the distinction among them? And what is the best label to attach to programs for foreign information and persuasion? These questions are explored in the following selection, which traces the history of the term "psychological warfare" and suggests the abandonment of its use to describe American overseas propaganda efforts.

## Introduction

" 'Cold war' and 'psychological warfare' are unfortunate terms. They do not describe the efforts of our nation and our Allies to build a world of peace and freedom. They should be discarded in favor of others that describe our true goals."

This pronouncement, made in June 1953 at the highest level by a group of the nation's foremost authorities in foreign affairs (The President's Committee on International Information Activities), fell like a bombshell on the elaborate structure of "psychological strategy" theory that had been erected during the preceding decade. The result has been a year of rethinking, reappraisal, and reevaluation of the general technique of influencing foreign peoples. This process of reappraisal is by no means complete; indeed, it is and should be a continuing one. However, a number of significant trends and new philosophies have already emerged, and it may be useful at this time to analyze some of the changes that have taken place in psychological warfare theory and practice since the revolutionary pronouncement of a year ago.

Reprinted from William E. Daugherty and Morris Janowitz, *A Psychological Warfare Casebook* (Baltimore, Md.: Johns Hopkins Press, 1958), pp. 25–35. By permission. Numbered footnotes have been omitted.

Roland I. Perusse has been a public affairs officer with the U. S. Information Agency.

248

## The Setting

For those to whom the subject of psychological warfare is new or who have been confused by the multitude of popular and professional writing and commentary on the subject in recent years, a brief survey of the evolution of psychological warfare as a force in international relations may be helpful as background for understanding the June 1953 pronouncement and the developments that followed. Especially useful, it seems, is some indication as to just exactly what is meant by the term "psychological warfare," and a brief analysis of developments in this field over the years.

### DEFINITIONS AND SCOPE

It is absolutely necessary, prior to any discussion or assessment of psychological warfare as an instrument of national policy, to agree on terms of reference. Most of the misunderstandings that have arisen during the past few years as to the proper role of psychological warfare in a democratic society, and as to its capabilities and limitations in helping attain foreign policy objectives, have arisen as a result of confusion over terminology. Interpretations have varied as to the scope of the field coverd by psychological warfare and as to the relation of this particular discipline to the other, more firmly established fields of foreign affairs activity and knowledge.

The difficulty of defining psychological warfare can be appreciated from the great variety of terms that have come into common usage to characterize the peculiar international crisis in which the US finds itself today, and the more unconventional policies that have been adopted to meet this crisis. A few of the more common terms are:

1. Cold war
2. War of ideas
3. Struggle for the minds and wills of men
4. War for the minds of men
5. Thought war
6. Ideological warfare
7. Nerve warfare
8. Political warfare
9. International information
10. Overseas information
11. Campaign of truth
12. Propaganda
13. International propaganda
14. Propaganda warfare
15. War of words

16. Indirect aggression
17. Agitation
18. International communication

Some of these terms have actually been used as synonyms for psychological warfare by writers on the subject, as for example, equation of psychological warfare with propaganda.

A further difficulty arises from the fact that generally accepted official usage of the term "psychological warfare," in the US underwent rapid evolution and expansion during the 5 years 1948 to 1953, whereas many nongovernmental specialists clung to narrower definitions. The term is not defined in the dictionary, and meanings vary from expert to expert.

Definitions of psychological warfare vary from narrow usage during World Wars I and II as an adjunct to military force in time of war, to the broad concepts underlying establishment of the Psychological Strategy Board by President Truman in 1951, and President Eisenhower's appointment of C. D. Jackson as his psychological warfare adviser early in 1953.

Perhaps one of the best definitions of military psychological warfare has been formulated by Paul M. A. Linebarger, a pioneer in systematizing knowledge on the subject. In his well-known text, *Psychological Warfare*, published in 1948, Professor Linebarger defines psychological warfare in the narrow sense of "the use of propaganda against an enemy, together with such other operational measures of a military, economic, or political nature as may be required to supplement propaganda." Military propaganda he defines in turn as "planned use of any form of communication designed to affect the minds and emotions of a given enemy, neutral, or friendly group for a specific strategic or tactical purpose."

It was at about this time that the term "psychological warfare," was borrowed from the military by civilian proponents for a vigorous peacetime overseas information program by the Department of State. In the years 1945 to 1948, the US had undergone a period of psychological disarmament comparable only to the disarmament that had taken place at the same time with respect to conventional weapons and military manpower. It was an act of overcompensation on the part of civilian information specialists that led to the borrowing of this term from the US military vocabulary and, incidentally, to many of the difficulties that ensued. For purposes of definition, "psychological warfare," as "civilianized," came to take on some such meaning as "the employment of modern media of communications for the purpose of reaching mass audiences in order to persuade them to accept certain beliefs or ideas."

It was not long, however, before "psychological warfare" assumed an even more exalted position. In the broad sense, Linebarger had defined

psychological warfare as "the application of parts of the science of psychology to further the efforts of political, economic, or military actions." Authorities such as Harold D. Lasswell and Edward W. Barrett began to speak of the four arms of US foreign policy (diplomacy, military, economy and propaganda). A "psychological strategy board" was established in the US, directly under the National Security Council, top policy organ of our government, for the purpose of coordinating the policies of the Departments of State and Defense and of the Mutual Security Agency for maximum psychological impact abroad.

Finally, psychological warfare was given the meaning of "the struggle for the minds and wills of men" by no less of an authority than President Dwight D. Eisenhower in his famous 8 October 1952 campaign speech in San Francisco. Said General Eisenhower:

> We must adapt our foreign policy to a "cold war" strategy that is unified and coherent. . . . In spirit and resolve, we should see in this "cold war" a chance to gain a victory without casualties, to win a contest that can quite literally save peace. . . .

Thus, by 1953, psychological warfare had been closely identified with the cold war, i.e., the global struggle between Communism and the Free World. Its supreme status as the governing factor in US foreign policy was exemplified by President Eisenhower's appointment of a personal adviser on psychological warfare matters in the person of C. D. Jackson, publisher of *Fortune* magazine and a "psychological warrior" of renown as Deputy Chief of Psychological Warfare Division, SHAEF, during World War II.

Because of the wide variety of meanings that the term has assumed, as well as changes in thinking that have occurred in the past year (discussed in the next section), no attempt will be made to assign a specific definition to the concept of psychological warfare in this paper. Rather, the term will be placed in context each time it is used, so that the reader may know the particular meaning that is intended in each case.

Before dismissing the question of definition, it may be well to refer once more to the 18 terms listed above and to explore their meanings.

The first five terms (cold war, war of ideas, struggle for the minds and wills of men, war for the minds of men, and thought war) are situational; they describe psychological processes in international relations and very dynamic ones indeed. Cold war would seem to encompass the widest field; presumably, cold war is being waged today by all means short of outright mass military offensive action. The other four terms are descriptive of the ideological part of this struggle.

Ideological warfare, nerve warfare, and political warfare can have both situational meanings, i.e., definition of the existing crisis between Communism and the Free World, and a methodological meaning, i.e.,

description of the techniques being used to meet the crisis. Political warfare is a distinctively British term, used to convey the idea of co-relation of all instruments of policy (diplomacy, economies, arms, etc.) in time of war. It comes closest to the meaning of psychological warfare in the broad sense. Nerve warfare is a more strictly psychological term, and because it entails purposeful heightening of tensions, is usually reserved for operations against an enemy in time of outright hostilities.

The terms "international information" and "overseas information" are applied in the US to the process of distributing facts and knowledge that would help offset misinformation about the US being circulated by hostile groups. Propaganda is defined by Lasswell as "the calculated selection and circulation of symbols with a view to influencing mass behavior." Accordingly, international propaganda can be defined as "the calculated selection and circulation of symbols with a view to influencing mass behavior on controversial *international* issues." Propaganda warfare is merely a more dramatic term for the same process, while war of words would pertain to the selection and circulation of word symbols only.

Indirect aggression is a broad term that embraces concepts of sabotage and subversion as well as the use of information and propaganda for offensive purposes. Agitation is a peculiarly Soviet term, used to describe propaganda conducted among the masses as contrasted to the elite. International communication, aside from its purely technical meaning, is used to characterize *who says what to whom, when, and with what effect* in international relations.

There has been an element of each of the foregoing concepts (depending on the definition of psychological warfare that one accepts) in psychological warfare as waged in the past, and/or psychological warfare has constituted an element of each of the concepts.

BACKGROUND OF PSYCHOLOGICAL WARFARE

Whether considered in the narrow military sense or in the widest possible strategic sense, psychological warfare, in fact if not in name, has been practiced by man since the earliest records of civilization. Linebarger cites the use of panic by Gideon in his battles against the Midianites about 1245 B.C. One of the best-known historical examples is use of the Trojan Horse by the Greeks to capture the city of Troy.

Propaganda was never used on a broad scale, however, until World War I. The first organized effort by the US was the Committee on Public Information (better known as the Creel Committee), which had the sympathetic interest of President Wilson and did an acceptable job from 1917–1919 in rallying morale on the home front and exploiting the Fourteen Points in Europe.

The term "psychological warfare," had its origins in World War II.

German psychologists, anxious to rationalize Germany's defeat in World War I, seized on the Allied psychological attack as an excuse for the military collapse. The Germans proceeded to forge the most terrifying psychological weapons of all time, combining propaganda, fifth-column terrorism, and violence with *blitzkrieg* military action.

The US itself engaged in an extensive program of psychological warfare, principally through the Office of War Information and the Psychological Warfare Division of Supreme Headquarters Allied Expeditionary Forces, Europe (SHAEF). The British program was carried on through three agencies: the Political Warfare Executive, a secret organization for propaganda to enemy and enemy-occupied countries; the Ministry of Information, which dealt with the British public and Allied and neutral countries; and the Overseas Services of the British Broadcasting Corporation, which broadcast to all countries, receiving guidance from the Political Warfare Executive and the Ministry of Information. Psychological warfare was recognized and accepted as a military instrument, sharing honors, powers, and responsibilities with the military, economic, and diplomatic agencies of modern war.

The period 1945 to 1948 marked the virtual psychological disarmament of the US. The American people and Congress failed to appreciate the menace of Communist propaganda to American security and to grasp the possibilities inherent in the psychological approach. The value of propaganda as a wartime instrument was admitted, but its potentialities as an instrument of national policy during time of peace were not generally recognized. There was wide opposition from US commercial press, radio, and film media, which feared government competition abroad. Many of the most able and skilled personnel in the fields of information and psychological warfare left government service. Their loss was tragic and irreplaceable. During this period, the US information program was reduced to little more than educational exchange under the Fulbright Act and cultural exchange with Latin America through the Pan-American Union. The low point was reached in the spring of 1947, when Soviet propaganda was at an all-time postwar high and US world prestige at an all-time postwar low.

The Smith-Mundt Act of 1948 (Public Law 402) gave first Congressional authorization for a world-wide US international informational and cultural program in time of peace. US objectives were to be "to promote better understanding of the US in other countries and to increase mutual understanding between the people of the US and other countries." It remains the basic legislation for the conduct of the US information program today.

By 1950 the US had thoroughly awakened to the Soviet threat. There was no longer any disagreement on the need for a program, and President Truman was given a record appropriation of $121,000,000 to carry on a

"Campaign of Truth" against Communism. An official peacetime role, in name, was assigned to psychological warfare with the creation of the Interdepartmental Psychological Operations Coordinating Committee in the Department of State.

On 20 June 1951, psychological warfare was placed on an even higher plane with the creation, by Presidential directive, of the Psychological Strategy Board, responsible to the National Security Council, the nation's top policy-making body. Its mission was to plan long-term psychological approaches to the nation's problems and to help influence opinions, attitudes, and behavior abroad in support of national objectives. Regular members were the Under Secretary of State, Deputy Secretary of Defense, and the Director of the Central Intelligence Agency. Other agencies, such as the Mutual Security Administration, participated as needed. A representative of the Joint Chiefs of Staff was principal adviser, and the Board's director was appointed by the President.

Dwight D. Eisenhower, as Presidential candidate, gave his views on the scope of psychological warfare in the San Francisco address previously cited:

> Many people think "psychological warfare" means just the use of propaganda like the controversial "Voice of America." Certainly the use of propaganda, the written and spoken word, of every means known to transmit ideas, is an essential part of winning other people to your side. But propaganda is not the most important part of this struggle. . . . There are many peaceful tools that must be used through every medium of communication, mutual economic assistance, trade and barter, friendly contacts through travel, and correspondence and sports—these represent some of the political means to support essential programs for mutual military assistance and collective security. . . .

During the 1952 campaign the Republican party strongly attacked the policy of containment of Communism inaugurated by the Democratic Administration and pledged a "roll-back" of Communist influence and peaceful liberation of peoples enslaved by Soviet Communism.

On 16 February 1953, President Eisenhower appointed C. D. Jackson as his personal adviser on psychological warfare, thereby placing the coordinated direction of psychological factors in US foreign affairs on the highest level of government.

### Reappraisals, 1953–1954

One of President Eisenhower's first acts as Chief Executive was to appoint an eight-man committee to study the problem of psychological warfare. Called the President's Committee on International Information Activities, this group, headed by W. H. Jackson, New York attorney, interviewed over 250 witnesses in the 5-month period, 30 January to 30 June 1953.

The committee's startling conclusion has been cited in the introduction to this paper. In addition, the committee had this to say about "psychological strategy":

> . . . the existing Psychological Strategy Board, established in 1951, does not meet the real need which exists in Government and should be abolished. It is founded on the misconception that "psychological strategy" somehow exists apart from official policies and actions and can be dealt with independently by experts in this field.
>
> In reality, there is a "psychological" aspect or implication to every diplomatic, economic or military policy and action. This implication should receive more careful attention, both in the planning and execution stage of policy, but not to the exclusion of other factors.
>
> Except for propaganda, there are no "psychological warfare" instruments distinct from traditional instruments of policy. Every significant act of virtually every department and agency of government has its effect, either positively or negatively, in the global struggle for freedom. The important task is to build awareness throughout the entire Government of the impact of day-to-day governmental actions and to coordinate and time such actions so as to derive from them the maximum advantages. . . .
>
> The primary and overriding purposes of the information program should be to submit evidence to the peoples of other nations that their own aspirations for freedom, progress, and peace are supported and advancd by the objectives and policies of the US.
>
> The efforts of all media—radio, press, and publications, motion pictures, exchange of persons, and libraries and information centers—should be directed to this end: to show the identity of our goals with those of other peoples. These goals and desires, which we hold in common, must be explained in ways that will cause others to join with us in achieving them.
>
> In carrying out this purpose, American broadcasts and printed materials should concentrate on objective, factual news reporting, with particular selection and treatment of news designed to present a full exposition of US actions and policies, especially as they affect the particular country addressed.
>
> The tone and content should be forceful and direct, but a propagandistic note should be avoided. The information services should not, however, be precluded from making forceful and factual refutation of false Soviet accusations. . . .
>
> New terms are needed (instead of "psychological warfare" and "cold war") to express the solidarity of freedom-loving men and women everywhere.

The announcement should not have come as a complete surprise. There had been earlier indications of such trends in thinking about propaganda and psychological warfare. In fact, as early as 1948, Carroll had used practically the same words as did the committee in presenting his views of what the US overseas information objective should be: "American foreign policy will be successful only to the extent that it can convince the peoples that American aims are in harmony with their aspirations for peace and freedom and personal liberty."

Edward W. Barrett, Assistant Secetary of State for Public Affairs from 1950–1952, had recommended that our information program be persuasive but not propagandistic in tone; that all arguments be supported by facts.

Reports had come in from foreign countries that campaign talk pro and con, about "psychological warfare," "liberation," and "roll-back" had excited apprehensions abroad. In some places it was feared that President Eisenhower, as a former general, would be overly concerned with military matters; and would want to launch another "Crusade in Europe," dragging the Free World into a needless war.

There had already been at least one bit of evidence of changed practices: President Eisenhower's 16 April 1953 speech before the American Society of Newspaper Editors. This speech, in which President Eisenhower called for atomic disarmament and use of funds saved thereby for technical assistance to underdeveloped areas, had profound psychological impact in countries around the world. Yet it was not termed "psychological warfare" except by the enemies of the US, who hoped thereby to distort US intentions.

The findings of the W. H. Jackson committee had far-reaching effects on the reorganization of US "psychological" strategy. Presidential Reorganization Plan 8, approved by the 83d Congress, and made effective 1 August 1953, took the overseas information function out of the Department of State and assigned it to a new and autonomous US Information Agency (USIA). The Director of the Agency was made directly responsible to the President through the National Security Council, and he received foreign guidance from the Secretary of State. The information responsibilities of the Foreign Operations Administration and Technical Cooperation Administration were taken over by USIA, although the exchange-of-persons program was left in the Department of State.

President Eisenhower, on recommendation of the National Security Council, issued a directive dated 22 October establishing the basic mission of the Agency as follows: "To submit evidence to peoples of other nations by means of communication techniques that the objectives and policies of the US are in harmony with and will advance their legitimate aspirations for freedom, progress, and peace."

This mission was to be accomplished by:

1. Explaining and interpreting to foreign peoples the objectives and policies of the United States Government;
2. Depicting imaginatively the correlation between US policies and the legitimate aspirations of other peoples of the world;
3. By unmasking and countering hostile attempts to distort or to frustrate the objectives and policies of the Government of the US;

4. By delineating those important aspects of the life and culture of the people of the United States which facilitate understanding of the policies and objectives of the Government of the United States.

Under the new mission, the agency was to concentrate on objective, factual news reporting, with appropriate commentaries, designed to present a full exposition of important US actions and policies, especially as they affect individual countries and areas. Tone and content of material was to be forceful and direct, but a strident or antagonistic tone was to be avoided.

At the same time the Psychological Strategy Board was dissolved and an Operations Coordinating Board was established. The function of OCB is to coordinate the broad foreign policy of the US in all its aspects—economic, military, and political—with psychological factors being considered in the formulation of all policies.

On 8 December 1953, President Eisenhower made a second major policy speech in keeping with the new concepts of US "psychological" relations with foreign peoples—the famous "Atom Pool" address before the United Nations. Peoples of the world were quick to identify "their legitimate aspirations for freedom, progress, and peace" with the President's proposal—so quick, in fact, that the Soviet Union was obliged to reverse its initial position branding the offer a mere propaganda stunt and at least to go through the motions of entering into negotiations with the US on the matter.

On 1 April 1954, C. D. Jackson resigned as the President's adviser on psychological warfare, having played a vital part in formulating new concepts of the place of psychological factors in international relations.* The position, as carried out by Jackson, was not filled, pointing up once more the readjustment that has taken place: psychological factors are no longer considered in isolation and superior to other elements in foreign policy formulation and execution but are considered a vital and integral part of every action.

### Conclusions

The principal lesson to be derived from the reappraisal of psychological warfare that has taken place over the past year is that the term itself had best be avoided in any characterization of either our informational output or our foreign relations generally. The term has decided negative connotations, both at home and abroad, and warfare of all kinds had best be left to the military. It is no exaggeration to say that the US, by announcing to the world that its policies were governed or would be governed by "psychological strategy" and "psychological warfare," raised

---

*C. D. Jackson served as a member of the W. H. Jackson Committee and had a hand in the preparation of both of the President's atomic energy speeches.

unnecessary fears among peoples abroad and gave grist to the Communist propaganda claim of US warmongering. On the other hand, Soviet propaganda claiming Communist monopoly of peaceful intentions, though transparently fraudulent as evidenced by Soviet actions in Korea, the United Nations and elsewhere, made headway as a result of the failure of the US to identify itself more fully with the universal desire of mankind for peace.

The term "psychological warfare" never did set well with the American people. Military personnel have always been annoyed at the "theft" of this term by civilians in government. Much confusion resulted from the attempt to transfer the concept from its wartime setting to applications of national strategy in time of peace. Political officers of the Department of State resented what they regarded as invasion of a field that has been traditionally their domain. Many persons in and out of government found it difficult to understand how "psychological warfare" could be conducted in time of peace, particularly against neutrals and friendly countries. Foreign countries, in turn, did not enjoy being the object of any kind of "warfare," especially when initiated by a supposedly friendly power.

All these difficulties arose, of course, either through genuine misunderstandings of the concept of "psychological warfare" by friends of US policy or as a result of purposeful distortions by hostile groups. It did not help to explain to people at home or our friends abroad that psychological warfare meant essentially the taking of psychological factors into consideration in dealing with foreign peoples—an objective that the most vehement of critics could hardly condemn. However, the fact remains that words are words, that people are naturally inclined to consider words first and foremost according to their primary meanings, that we have not always had the opportunity to explain that by "warfare" we have meant "peacefare," and we have necessarily assumed a ridiculous posture (something akin to Communist corruption of word meanings) every time that we have made the attempt. In brief, those in the business of explaining US policies abroad through a judicious choice of word symbols had failed to choose an appropriate word symbol to characterize their own operations. To try to confine the term of official usage, "within the family" of persons who do "appreciate" the "true" meaning of the word, did not help; not only did interpretations vary between experts but official terminology inevitably crept into popular usage.

Abandonment of the term, however, should by no means result in the abandonment of any of the processes involved in what has been known professionally as "psychological warfare." There will always be a need for "psychological intelligence," i.e., the kind of information on foreign societies that anthropologists, sociologists, psychologists, and area specialists can provide. It will always be necessary to take psychological factors

into consideration in shaping policies toward foreign nations. Those persons having specialized knowledge about dealing with foreign populations, whether called "psychological strategists," "psychological operators," "psychological warriors," or just plain cultural anthropologists, social psychologists or foreign information and area specialists, will always play a vital role in the conduct of foreign policy in this era of popular government. Even the twentieth century dictator makes no pretense at absolute rule; he is anxious to give his government an aura of "popularity" and so keeps his ear tuned to public opinion, if not to be guided by it, then in order to "correct" it where he deems it necessary. It is the duty of persons cognizant of psychological factors to keep diplomats, political and military officers, economic experts, and others who have dealings with foreign peoples and foreign governments informed of the climate of and changes in public opinion in foreign countries and to let such persons know of the probable public reaction to policies contemplated. In this way, many moves that could cause resentment can be avoided, or if they must be taken, regardless of probable adverse public opinion, because of the other overriding factors, the psychological specialist, if we want to call him that, can offer suggestions as to how effects may be mitigated or cushioned. Such a specialist also has a duty to come up with suggestions for actions that will create favorable public reaction abroad.

Propaganda is another term that is best avoided, again because of negative connotations at home and abroad. Many Americans were shocked when they learned to what extent British propaganda activities in the US during World War I had pushed the US into the war on the Allied side.

Communist world revolutionary propaganda in the US following World War I, together with the activities of Dr. Goebbels and Japanese propagandists, helped reinforce American suspicion and abhorrence of propaganda and propaganda techniques, and to associate propaganda with dictatorship. The use of propaganda by the Communists in the post-World War II period has seemed to confirm the deepest distrust of propaganda and propaganda operations as something basically and intrinsically evil.

It has helped little to point out that propaganda, technically speaking, is essentially a neutral term, that one can have both good and bad propaganda, that the word actually has a religious origin (from propagation of the Catholic faith during Counter Reformation), and that "to propagate" means little more than "to disseminate." (And who is against diffusion of knowledge?) Popular conception has converted "propaganda" from a positive, or essentially neutral, to a negative word, and rather than try to reverse the process, it is better to let the term ride as a proper definition for totalitarian efforts and to characterize the activities of democratic societies as "information." From a strictly academic

point of view, the distinction is not valid; but from a practical and public relations point of view, the entire task of dealing with foreign peoples will be made easier if we go along with the tide of public opinion, at home and abroad, and drop the word completely from descriptions of our own efforts.

The expressions, "psychological strategy," "psychological operations," and "target" should also be avoided. US observers can vouch for the discomfiture of foreign peoples at being considered by us as a fitting subject for manipulation in the interest of achieving certain of our strategic objectives vis-à-vis the USSR. The terms, "foreign policy," "foreign relations," and "foreign peoples" have much longer standing and much more positive connotations.

The announced purpose of the US information program (as seeking to show that the objectives and policies of the US are in harmony with and will advance the legitimate aspirations of foreign peoples for freedom, progress, and peace) should offer further suggestions for substitute terminology. It would seem that such terms as "peace," "security," "prosperity," "solidarity," and "cooperation," when properly compounded with such concepts as "mutuality," "reciprocity," and "collective" or "united action," should provide a more fitting description of what we as a nation are striving for in our relations with other countries.

In summary, then, the conduct of foreign affairs today demands identification and consideration of psychological processes in international relations. USIA, having, as its principal objective, identification of US policies with the legitimate aspirations of foreign peoples, must necessarily be able to identify and assess these aspirations. It must know which psychological approach is most likely to achieve the desired result and to act accordingly. From a strictly professional viewpoint, this is "psychological warfare," pure and simple, as everyone who has engaged in any aspect of such activity will recognize, but for the better chances of its success, it would appear wise not to call it that, but rather, as recommended by the President's Committee, to concentrate on finding other terms that describe our true goals.

# 32 / Information and Cultural Representation Overseas

HOWLAND H. SARGEANT

Overseas propaganda programs on a regular basis are relatively new functions for the United States. Prior to the onset
of the cold war, most American experience in this field had
been with wartime propaganda programs. The background of
the United States in the use of this foreign policy instrument
is detailed in this selection.

ALTHOUGH OPINIONS will differ as to the exact points in time when
the United States government began to embark seriously upon programs
of international persuasion through information and cultural representation overseas, most will agree that World Wars I and II forced us into a
war for the minds of men, for the "conquest of their convictions." The
Creel Committee on Public Information was created and in 1917 and
1918, in the words of George Creel, "not only reached deep into every
American community, but . . . . carried to every corner of the civilized
globe the full message of America's idealism, unselfishness, and indomitable purpose."

The Creel Committee was liquidated on June 30, 1919. Until almost
the time of the Japanese attack on Pearl Harbor, the United States
officially did little or nothing to cultivate the opinions of mankind. It was
true that a few feeble beginnings in the cultural field were undertaken.

The interchange of persons, which has existed for scores of years on
an individual and private basis, became a small part of the conduct of
American foreign relations in 1936, when the United States signed the
Buenos Aires Convention for promotion of inter-American cultural
relations. Congressional action followed in 1938 to enable the United
States to adhere to the provisions of the 8th International Conference of
American States. In 1938 the State Department set up a Division of
Cultural Relations, directed to confine its activities to the Western
hemisphere, and President Roosevelt established under the Secretary
of State the Interdepartmental Committee on Cooperation with the Ameri-

Reprinted from *The Representation of the United States Abroad*, pp. 69–75,
background papers prepared for the Ninth American Assembly, sponsored by The
American Assembly, Graduate School of Business, Columbia University, May, 1956.

Howland Sargeant has served in many important posts in American government
and the United Nations. In 1952 he was Assistant Secretary of State for Public Affairs.

can Republics to plan and execute the program of scientific and cultural interchange. By 1939—largely as a result of the needle of Nazi penetration among our good neighbors to the south—we were carrying out a cooperative program there including exchange of persons and books; maintenance of libraries; distribution of documentary films; aid to binational cultural centers and American-sponsored schools; and the beginnings of Point IV type cooperative projects like developing agricultural experiment stations.

In 1940, Nelson Rockefeller, appointed to a post later known as Coordinator of Inter-American Affairs, undertook a massive program of persuasion through both information and cultural representation abroad, backed by a strong central organization in the United States. Although Mr. Rockefeller had broad programs in economic and political fields, he set in motion some highly important information and cultural representation overseas and through his programs presented convincing evidence of United States power and laid the basis for producing much of the era of inter-American good neighborliness in the 1940's.

Americans were not doing very much however in the rest of the world. In the spring of 1941, Robert E. Sherwood and William J. Donovan developed a "Foreign Information Service"—without any Congressional authorization—but it was not until June, 1942, that the Office of War Information was set up under Elmer Davis, charged with coordinating the government's domestic information activities. Robert Sherwood and his international propaganda team were thrown in under OWI, which also conducted cultural operations, ran United States overseas libraries, and distributed cultural materials.

During the remaining war years, America learned a great deal about the arts of international persuasion. We welded together the eleven private short wave stations then broadcasting to overseas audiences and made them the first official Voice of America. We set up information offices in nearly every country abroad. We sent out Americans to friendly, to neutral, and to military areas. "Psychological warfare" became a common term as civilians using leaflets, loudspeakers and radio broadcasts worked in newly created psychological warfare units in military theaters.

By the end of World War II, Americans were deep in the business of international persuasion. We were using most of the techniques in use today, including documentary films, translations of American books, radio broadcasts, photo displays, American libraries, exchange-of-persons programs, news releases, press photographs, magazine articles, posters, film strips, pamphlets. These techniques were applied by Americans abroad, operating with much assistance from local citizens. They were learning how to represent the United States in ways which were new to us. "Psychological warfare," as an integral part of military operations,

achieved some spectacular results including the mass surrender of complete enemy units; enormous supporting services to the D-Day invasion of Normandy; the broadcasts in the Pacific by Captain Ellis Zacharias which were held by some to have precipitated the final Japanese surrender.

### America Plays Postwar Blindman's Buff with International Persuasion

On August 31, 1945, President Truman's Executive Order 9608 began the disbanding of our overseas persuasion programs at a pace even quicker than our military demobilization. The overseas information functions and personnel of the OWI and the Nelson Rockefeller's OIAA were transferred to an Interim International Information Service in the State Department. The Secretary of State was required to study the problem of whether we needed any kind of permanent activities of this sort although the Executive Order itself said: "The nature of present day foreign relations makes it essential for the United States to maintain information activities abroad as an integral part of the conduct of our foreign affairs."

But Americans weren't so sure as the drafters of this Executive Order that this in fact was called for. Assistant Secretary of State William Benton led the fight during the next two and a half years to win executive, legislative and public support for the necessity in peacetime of a permanent overseas information and cultural representation of the United States. When this finally came with the signing on January 27, 1948, of P.L. 402 (The Smith-Mundt Act), American indecisiveness and perplexity over the significance of these new and strange functions had been amply demonstrated. Out of the long and violent debate, a few of the perplexities emerged in sharp focus. They included:

1. Is it right for the American government to be engaged in "propaganda" which is somehow a dirty business—and is there the danger that a government which propagandizes foreigners may some day attempt to propagandize the American people?

2. Now that the shooting war is behind us, is all of this vast bureaucracy, put together like our military forces in wartime to achieve victory, any longer necessary?

3. Can't we do all that is needed simply by making it possible for peoples to speak to peoples?

Postwar American public support seemed firmest for exchange of persons: If you want to convey an idea, do your best to wrap that idea in a person and send the person to the place where persuasion is needed. We Americans didn't formulate the proposition quite so precisely. We did show that out of our tradition we had acquired and retained a great faith

in the ability of individuals to communicate with each other across the barriers of race, language, religion and national boundaries. Even before it was willing to authorize the rebuilding of an international information program, Congress had acted in response to a ground swell of American public opinion. In 1946, Congress authorized United States participation in UNESCO (The United Nations Educational, Scientific, and Cultural Organization), dedicated to the use of tools of education, culture and science to permit peoples-to-peoples communication in an all-out attack based on the assumption that "wars begin in the minds of men." In 1946 Congress authorized, under the leadership of Senator J. William Fulbright, the use of millions of dollars of foreign currencies to finance the international exchange of students and teachers.

This faith in the concept of peoples-speaking-to-peoples runs like a connecting tissue throughout the whole postwar decade. So strong was this faith that many believe the Congress would have authorized nothing more than cultural relations and educational exchange programs, *excluding* any information service, had it not been for the fact that nearly half the members of the Congress had travelled abroad in 1946 and 1947. Most of them came back alarmed and angry over the Soviet Big Lie technique of misrepresenting and maliciously distorting America and American motives. The United States Information and Educational Exchange Act of 1948 was the result.

The concept of peoples-speaking-to-peoples provided a firm basis for American overseas representation, especially in the cultural field. We sought to provide means by which private American citizens, representing cross sections of these United States, might talk to peoples of other countries. We said that we hoped other peoples might have a chance of coming to know us as we really are. We set up programs of communications supported and facilitated by the government itself. We were trying to wash out age-old jealousies, animosities, prejudices and misunderstandings. We were acting on the premise that we must have an understanding among peoples if we are to have a peaceful world. We were expressing our prophetic faith that in a hydrogen bomb era "truth is no longer merely the first casualty in war; today it must be assassinated before war can be started," as *The Economist* puts it.

We were also saying that for a democracy, no governmental program could by itself do the job. We were saying that we are not like the Soviet Union, which speaks with but one voice—the voice of dictatorship, but that we, like any other democracy, make ourselves known abroad through the student, the tourist, the visiting professor, the soldier, the free press, radio and motion pictures, as well as through our government spokesmen. Where the Soviet Union speaks with but one opinion, we speak with many. If we were to try to do otherwise, we would be imposing on ourselves the very totalitarianism we are struggling to avoid. Deeper

down, and without ever making this specific point, perhaps we were saying that our ability to persuade other peoples can never rise above the level of the behavior and actions of the American government and of the American people themselves.

Certainly these were among the bases for our programs of international persuasion as authorized in January, 1948.

### From the Full and Fair Picture to the Campaign of Truth

At the same time these debates were rumbling through the halls of Congress, officers directing the surviving postwar programs were re-examining their basic assumptions. Our assumption at war's end was that we should present "a full and fair picture of America to make clear our aims and policies." It is probably true to say that from 1946 to 1950, our international information and educational exchange programs were essentially dedicated to meeting the conditions of a peaceful world. But events were moving fast and tended to outrun the policies set for these programs. By the spring of 1947, the United States gave ample evidence of recognizing that we had merely passed from a hot war to a cold war. Greek-Turkish aid was instituted. The Truman Doctrine was proclaimed. The Marshall Plan began. NATO was established.

As early as the spring of 1946 State Department officers in charge of our overseas information and cultural relations activities were beginning to study the ways in which emphasis should be shifted. By May, 1947, one officer wrote: "As long as the objective of an information and cultural program is to present to the world a full and fair picture of the US, we'll be planting flowers in soil chemically unprepared to sustain them, and which has the further disadvantage of being continuously trampled by wild bulls." During 1947 and 1948, policies gradually evolved which more and more made the information programs a part of the free world's recognition that the cold war was a reality. We set about exposing communist distortions and placing United States policies in perspective.

The next step was to be a giant stride, not simply gradual evolution. Under the leadership of Assistant Secretary of State Edward W. Barrett, the Campaign of Truth was planned and initiated in April, 1950. (Up to this point the peacetime program, still under fairly constant attack in Congress, had reached about $30,000,000 annually for its operations in more than eighty countries overseas.) The Campaign of Truth sought to triple the operations, plus a $41,000,000 expenditure for enormous new transmitters for the Voice of America. The invasion of South Korea on June 25, 1950, provided the impetus for Congressional approval of what came to be known as a psychological offensive, aimed at achieving four objectives:

1. To establish a healthy international community by creating a climate of confidence in the free world.
2. To present America fairly and to counter misconceptions, so that other people would want to cooperate with us.
3. To deter the Soviets from further encroachments.
4. To help roll back Soviet influence.

## We Tell Our Neighbors: You and We Share Many Goals and Interests

The installation of the Eisenhower administration brought the latest important phase in national policy towards international persuasion. President Eisenhower's Committee on International Information Activities, a group of distinguished private citizens under the chairmanship of William H. Jackson, made a fundamental study in the early months of 1953. About the time of the Jackson Report, the Senate's Special Subcommittee on Overseas Information Programs, chaired by Senator Hickenlooper, proposed as a result of months of review, certain changes designed to strengthen the foreign information program.

Following and to some extent taking into account the recommendations of both of these groups, on August 1, 1953, all foreign information programs and operations were removed from the State Department and consolidated in a new United States Information Agency, independent of the Department of State. The new USIA embraced the Voice of America, United States libraries overseas, the motion picture service and the press and publications service. The Department of State, however, retained the educational exchange program.

The President's statement of the mission given to the new USIA was "to submit evidence to peoples of other nations by means of communication techniques that the objectives and policies of the United States are in harmony with and will advance their legitimate aspirations for freedom, progress and peace." In carrying out its responsibilities, the USIA would: (a) Explain and interpret "to foreign peoples the objectives and policies of the United States Government." (b) Depict "imaginatively the correlation between United States policies and the legitimate aspirations of other peoples of the world." (c) Unmask and counter "hostile attempts to distort or to frustrate the objectives and policies of the United States." (d) Delineate "those important aspects of the life and culture of the people of the United States which facilitate understanding of the policies and objectives of the government of the United States."

U.S. Information Agency Director Theodore C. Streibert stressed the fact that the new mission given to this agency "embodies the concept . . . that psychological activities and psychological strategy do not exist apart from official policies and actions"—the bedrock of the Jackson Committee

philosophy. As interpreted by Mr. Streibert, American information and cultural affairs officers would now

emphasize the community of interests that exists among freedom-loving peoples and show how American objectives and policies advance the legitimate interests of such peoples. . . . We must make every effort to show the mutuality of our interests and goals with the legitimate goals of other peoples. We must explain those goals in ways that will cause other peoples to join us in achieving them.

By the time the new mission was given to USIA, President Eisenhower had taken three other important steps, designed to serve broader needs but important to American information and cultural programs. He appointed a special assistant to advise and represent him in all matters of this kind. He set up the sub-Cabinet level Operations Coordinating Board to coordinate the plans and oversee the execution of projects in which several government departments shared responsibility for carrying out a national security policy. He placed authority for foreign policy squarely in the Secretary of State and, through him, in the chief of U. S. diplomatic mission of each foreign country. Such actions added support to the President's declaration in his State of the Union Message of February 2, 1953, that we "must make more effective all activities related to international information" and that "a unified and dynamic effort in this whole field is essential to the security of the United States and other peoples in the community of free nations."

# 33 / American Propaganda Abroad: Ends and Means

## EDWARD R. MURROW

**Mr. Murrow, one of the nation's leading radio and television news broadcasters and producers, was persuaded to become head of the U. S. Information Agency in 1961, a post he held until illness forced his resignation in early 1964. In the following selection, he explains the agency's objectives and de-**

Reprinted from *Winning the Cold War: The United States Ideological Offensive,* Hearings, U.S. House Foreign Affairs Subcommittee on International Organizations and Movements, 88th Cong., 1st sess., Part I (March 28, 1963), pp. 2–6.

Edward R. Murrow was with the Columbia Broadcasting System until his resignation in 1961 to become head of the USIA.

scribes the means being utilized as of 1963 to attain those objectives.


WE SEEK to influence people's thinking through the various means of communication—personal contact, radio broadcasting, libraries, book publication and distribution, the press, motion pictures, television, exhibits, English-language instruction, and others. To do this job successfully, our individual country programs are not scattershot efforts but carefully designed to gain support for established U.S. foreign policy objectives relating to the particular country. This requires imagination, sophistication, and flexibility—and means our programs will vary from country to country depending on U.S. policy needs.

There are, of course, many common denominators. Everywhere we seek to encourage constructive public support for what the President has described as "a peaceful world community of free and independent states, free to choose their own future and their own system so long as it does not threaten the freedom of others." We present the United States as a strong, democratic, dynamic nation qualified to lead world efforts toward this goal. We emphasize the ways in which U.S. policies harmonize with those of other peoples and governments, and underline those aspects of American life and culture which facilitate sympathetic understanding of our policies. We endeavor to unmask and counter hostile attempts on the part of Communists and others to distort or frustrate American objectives and policies.

The advisory function is carried out by my senior colleagues and myself at various levels within the Government in Washington, and by our public affairs officers within the country teams at U.S. diplomatic missions abroad. In this connection, I am pleased to report that much progress has been made. Beginning with the Jackson committee report 10 years ago, study groups, advisory commissions, and other experts have repeatedly urged that there be greater consideration of psychological factors in the formulation and execution of American foreign policy. Today these factors are usually given appropriate consideration.

This is not to say that American policymakers decide what to do or what to say on the basis of which way the winds of thought are blowing; foreign affairs cannot, should not, and are not conducted on the basis of a popularity contest. But it does mean that, in this age of swift communication and swift reaction, our Government tries to present its policies and programs in as understandable and palatable form as possible—understandable and palatable to those millions abroad, friend, foe, and neutral, whose lives and fortunes are affected by what we do.

Ours is a pluralistic, not a monolithic, society. There are many voices of America, not just one. But we learned in the 1940's and early 1950's

that a Government information program abroad can be successful only if it speaks with one voice—and that has been the case since Reorganization Plan No. 8 created the U.S. Information Agency and gave it the prime responsibility for overseas information activities. Since 1953, USIA staffs abroad—acting under the supervision of the chiefs of mission—have been responsible for the conduct of public information, public relations, and cultural activities for the civilian departments and agencies of our Government.

To do its job, USIA has 239 offices in 105 countries. In addition, USIA's radio arm—the Voice of America—broadcasts 761 hours a week in 36 languages.

As long as the U.S. Government has been engaged in this activity, and that is more than 21 years, there has been confusion about the role of truth in a Government information program. But there is no confusion within USIA, nor has there been for many years. We operate on the basis of truth. Voice of America news broadcasts are balanced and objective. They cover all the news, even when it hurts.

American traditions and the American ethic require us to be truthful, but the most important reason is that truth is the best propaganda and lies are the worst. To be persuasive we must be believable; to be believable we must be credible; to be credible we must be truthful. It is as simple as that.

Obviously, in our commentaries, films, exhibits, personal contacts, and other activities, we emphasize those aspects of American life and policy which are of greatest significance in furthering our foreign policy objectives. We report events in context; we explain why things happen. But we do not lie, we do not cheat, we do not suppress—and as a result, we are able to obtain a high degree of believability and persuasiveness.

It is this believability and persuasiveness that so enrages the Communists. A recent issue of the Soviet youth newspaper Komsomolskaya Pravda contains a long attack on USIA and its "diverse and abominable" activities. This article also was broadcast by Castro's Radio Progreso. "In the field of propaganda," according to this article, "the ruling circles of the United States certainly occupy first place." The author calls USIA "a truly tremendous monster of the 'cold war' which has no equal in other capitalist countries"—but then says this Agency has been a failure because of "the historical non-viability of anticommunism."

We consider this a compliment, an evidence of effectiveness. But it is very difficult to measure success in our business. No computer clicks, no cash register rings when a man changes his mind or opts for freedom. And, as I have indicated, ours is only one of many American voices. The image of America abroad is molded by countless sources, among them the 4 million American tourists who go overseas every year; a million U.S. troops and dependents abroad; our 33,000 missionaries; Hollywood

movies seen by 150 million foreigners every week; American magazines, newspapers, and TV shows; and letters from the 22 million immigrants who have come to our shores since 1900.

And above all, it is what we do—not what we say—that has the greatest impact overseas. USIA can explain, interpret, clarify, synthesize, and project, but we cannot change the unchangeable or do the undoable. The United States of America cannot and should not try to please everyone on this planet; we have, and will always have, some policies that are unpalatable to some people. We are, then, and properly so, prisoners of policy.

We should understand also that USIA cannot by itself defeat communism, solve the Kashmir dispute, resolve the Arab-Israel quarrel, throw Castro out of Cuba, protect the freedom of Berlin, or defeat the Viet Cong. But given intelligent and effective American policies, supported by Congress and the American people, we can make an important contribution to the achievement of our objectives. In my judgment, we are today making such a contribution.

In recent years, USIA has come a long way in improving its capability and effectiveness as an instrument of American foreign policy. Let me mention some of the recommendations of the Jackson Committee 10 years ago, and the similar Sprague Committee of 3 years ago, which are now standard USIA operating procedures:

Coordinated media activities in support of carefully defined themes;
Decentralization and tactical control in the field;
Greater use of unattributed material and indigenous media;
Greater use of private organizations;
Improved coordination of information activities with our allies;
Better adaptation of Agency films to foreign audiences;
Increased use of research;
Stronger book programs;
Better support for foreign correspondents in this country;
More attention to third-country students in Europe; and
An expanded program in Latin America.

In addition to increasing our effectiveness, we have also come a long way in developing a realistic appreciation of what this instrument can and cannot do—particularly in the face of the monolithic, well-financed worldwide propaganda effort of the Communists. The Soviet Union does have certain advantages: it can conduct its affairs with a minimum regard for public opinion; it can speak publicly with one voice while following contradictory courses of action; it operates in secrecy; it has disciplined fifth columns in the Communist Parties of other nations. But it has its disadvantages, too. For we are in a war not to capture men's minds but to free them—and our free society of free men has a tremendous advantage over the Communist society of coercion.

Nonetheless, there is much still to be done. We need to improve the quality and pertinence of USIA media output. We need to know more—much more—about the people we are seeking to reach: their hopes, their fears, their prejudices, their thinking processes. Electronically, we have made great progress in the techniques of communications; but, like all mankind, we are still in the primitive stage in our understanding of human relations and personal persuasion. USIA officers have developed much professionalism, but if we are to be truly successful we must speak more languages more fluently. We must increase our knowledge of American institutions and American culture. And we must take better advantage of opportunities which present themselves.

With respect to the latter, I am thinking specifically of such things as greater recognition on the part of American commercial media of their impact on foreign affairs; of the conduct of Americans abroad—how they spend their free time, their associations with their foreign neighbors, and their participation in community activities. I am thinking of American tourists who go to the Soviet Union and Eastern Europe—not as spies or propagandists, but as walking, living, breathing, free-thinking, and free-speaking representatives of our open society and our democratic institutions.

The experience of Cuba seems to have demonstrated, at that time and place, at least, that no nation, not even the most belligerent, the most aggressive, dares risk a direct confrontation with America's nuclear might. We hope this will continue to be so. But this does not mean that the forces of aggression will be stilled, only that they will turn to other methods. Persuasion is one of the most important of them, and under these conditions persuasion becomes power. Our arsenal of persuasion must be as ready as our nuclear arsenal, and used as never before.

According to that Soviet writer I quoted earlier, "he is doomed to fail who defends a cause doomed to fail. And USIA," he says, "is doing exactly that."

This angry Communist is, of course, wrong. It is the Communist propagandists, claiming virtue in their system's violation of human dignity, who are doomed to fail. And fail they will, unless we commit the greatest blunder in mankind's history and—through ignorance, blindness, or spite—throw away our triumph.

# 34 / USIA: Uncle Sam's Interpreter Abroad

JOSEPH KRAFT

The principal institution of the United States for overseas
propaganda is the U. S. Information Agency. Created in
1948, the agency has had a checkered career. Frequently its
management and effectiveness have come under Congressional
attack. The following selection traces the ups and downs of
the agency.

"RELEASE THE BERLIN PACKAGE." Edward R. Murrow, Director of
the United States Information Agency, sent that message from Paris to
his headquarters in Washington on August 9, 1961—four days before the
Berlin Wall went up. The Agency responded with a vengeance. At 261
libraries in 80 countries, a shelf of Berlin books was made available
surmounted by pictures of the beleaguered city. A special 20-minute
documentary film—"Journey Across Berlin"—was distributed round the
world, playing, for example, in an Italian version to 5,000,000 persons
watching Rome TV; and in a Portuguese version at 1,400 theaters in
Brazil. A USIA cartoon-strip account of the Wall was used by over 1,000
newspapers in 56 different countries. RIAS, the Radio in the American
Sector of Berlin, interviewed the first 200 refugees to come through the
Wall, and their stories were broadcast back into East Germany, through
the Iron Curtain and around the world by the Voice of America.

The impact of USIA's Berlin effort is impossible to measure. There are
those who believe it played a part in stimulating widespread international
sympathy for Berlin; some of them even believe that public sympathy was
one of the factors that caused the Soviet Union not to press its Berlin
advantage all the way. But whatever its impact in Moscow, the Berlin
performance—like its performance in the Cuba crisis and after John
Glenn's space flight—says something important about what has happened
to the USIA in Washington.

Not many years ago, the agency lay adrift in the bureaucratic
doldrums. It was regularly buffeted by the sharpest winds off Capitol
Hill, including the winds of McCarthyism. Its operations over the years

Reprinted from *Show*, the Magazine of the Arts, June, 1963, pp. 45–47, 89–91.
By permission.

Joseph Kraft, one of the nation's leading columnists and free-lance writers on
national and international affairs, is the author of *The Grand Design* (1963).

1948–61 were successively encumbered by two inappropriate doctrines—first, the Mystique of Truth, i.e., just tell the world what *really* happened and everybody will turn pro-American; then, the Mystique of Superiority i.e., just tell the world how far ahead of everyone we are and they'll all believe us.

Now, as the Berlin package indicates, USIA operations are more or less out of the mystique and operating in the mainstream of American foreign policy. By deliberate play of major episodes and by the tailoring of projects to specific purposes the output of the agency has been brought into explicit relation with this country's overseas objectives. In place of the old mystiques, there has been developed an empirical doctrine—a doctrine in keeping with the pragmatic style of American life—which in effect tunes up the loudspeakers when and where they are needed after a careful reading of the national policy aims involved in each situation. While the sad legacy of an unhappy past still makes itself felt in grievous personnel problems, the USIA has at last found a place in government.

Most of the works in the dreary corpus of literature comprising the bibliography of American propaganda activities commence with a famous phrase from the Declaration of Independence: ". . . a decent respect for the opinions of mankind." There usually follows an excerpt from the instructions given to Benjamin Franklin when, in 1776, he left for Paris on one of the first American diplomatic missions: "You are, by every means in your power, to promote a perfect harmony, concord and good understanding." It is then concluded, as one book claims, "the United States has been in the international propaganda business, off and on, for a long time."

Far more than most genealogies, the ascription of an American pedigree to propaganda is a fraud. The systematic use of information for national purposes in foreign lands, which is what propaganda is, bears only the most rudimentary relationship to Franklin's amiable hypocrisy—or even to Jefferson's conviction that he had a good case for independence. In fact, propaganda activities were originally developed in societies very different from the United States. And the adaptation of their techniques to this country has posed a serious issue between the American ideal of pragmatic debate and the more European tendency to think—and propagandize—in terms of the Big Central Idea. The issue is aptly characterized by the famous prototypes of Isaiah Berlin, the Hedgehog and the Fox.

The Hedgehogs, in Berlin's formula, are those "who relate everything to a single central vision, one system, more or less coherent . . . a single, universal organizing principle, in terms of which they understand, think and feel." It was in Hedgehog societies that modern propaganda first took root. The word itself comes from the Roman Catholic Church and specifically from its *Sacra Congregatio de Propaganda Fide,* or Society for

the Propagation of the Faith. The term was adopted for modern politics by the Communists who assigned "agitprop" work to their foreign agents. It was made famous by the Nazi Minister of Propaganda, Dr. Joseph Goebbels. Historically, and for reasons easy to feel if not to describe, there was a link between the successful use of propaganda and regimes endowed with a received truth, a line or *Weltanschauung*. Initially, at least, only regimes inspired by a distinct creed felt impelled to spread that creed abroad.

The Foxes, on the other hand, are those "who pursue many ends, often unrelated and even contradictory, connected if at all only in some *de facto* way . . . their thought is scattered or diffused, seizing upon the essence of a vast variety of experiences and objects for what they are in themselves, without consciously or unconsciously seeking to fit them into any one unchanging, all-embracing, unitary inner vision." That is not a bad description of the United States. But even to the best Americans, it is not an easy premise on which to found an ideological sales agency. So for years the tension that persisted between the Hedgehog and the Fox impaired the efforts of this country to develop a propaganda program.

Initially, the tension was obscured. The first American flings into the propaganda field came in wartime—George Creel's Committee on Public Information, set up in 1917; and Elmer Davis' Office of War Information, set up in 1942. The exigencies of war channeled the normal diversity of American life toward a single objective—victory—which became the inevitable theme of the propaganda effort. Once peace was established, diversity returned and both organizations withered away. It was, thus, only when the cold war asserted itself that the United States faced up to the task of mounting a propaganda program without the background support of an obvious, immediately unifying national effort, i.e., a war. Twice in these circumstances, doctrines (or rather pseudo-doctrines) were invented and superimposed: the Fox trying to imitate the Hedgehog. Twice the effort collapsed under the force of domestic criticism.

The first failure came in the administration of President Truman with the Mystique of Truth. In 1948, the Congress passed the Smith-Mundt Act, establishing within the Department of State an international information service utilizing press, radio, films and cultural exchange "to promote a better understanding of the United States in other countries." As a means toward achieving that purpose, the new service was given a banner bearing the legend "Truth." President Truman himself called for a "Campaign of Truth." "Truth," said one director of the program, Assistant Secretary of State for Public Affairs Edward Barrett, "is our weapon." And internal directives called for the presentation of a "full and fair picture" of the United States.

But what is truth? and what is full? and what is fair? All things to all men. The new program included accounts of the Marshall Plan, and the

North Atlantic Alliance, and all the elections. It also sent abroad scores of football games in the Midwest, descriptions of pet shops in California, feature stories on department stores in New York. Its broadcasts held the ring evenly between segregationists in the South and integrationists in the North, between expounders of the Administration position and its critics. Slums and suburbs alike had equal time.

A typical example of the Mystique of Truth in action was a 1948 USIA film called "Rural Co-op." The film described the workings of an American producer-cooperative specializing in the marketing of poultry. As a documentary it was not bad, and, as a part of the American scene, the description of the co-op, of course, fell within the bounds set by the mandate to tell the truth. But the film had no clear connection with the American national interest abroad. Neither did it have much relevance for foreign audiences. This interview with a Turkish peasant who saw the movie provides a measure of how little it must have meant to many foreign viewers:

Q: Can you tell what you saw?
A: The factories, the motors for plowing, there was a bottle factory. I saw people who were cleaning the turkeys. It showed the taxicabs and the city. I saw many things, but that's all I remember.
Q: Were the people you saw in the film Turks?
A: Only one or two.
Q: Did the people you saw live in the city or the country?
A: Of course they were city people. They came out of apartment houses and from shops and factories.
Q: Who owned the factories and the shops that you saw?
A: There was a sign but I could not read it. The factory belonged to the American government. I could not understand who the owner of the shops was. I understood the factory. I understood that they cleaned turkeys and crated them.
Q: Can you explain how these films were made?
A: The first time I saw the film, I thought there were real people reflected in the mirror. But my friends explained to me how it worked.
Q: What is a co-op?
A: The boss of a shop is called a co-op, I think.
Q: The film is called "Rural Co-op." Why is it called that?
A: In the film a man got rich in the village, saved his money and became a co-op.
Q: Why do they call him a co-op?
A: To show that he is richer, they say co-op.

Weaknesses so glaring were not lost on the Republicans in the Congress. Sniping, which had begun with the inception of the information program, reached fusillade proportions in a series of investigations launched when the Republicans came to power in 1953. The best known of these was the inquiry conducted by the late Senator Joseph R. McCarthy, with the assistance of that antic pair, Roy M. Cohn and G.

David Schine. Measured against the claim of exposing Communists in government, the Senator's findings were ludicrous: a typical charge was that scripts written by a specialist in Papuan affairs had been criticized by anti-Communists in Papua. Moreover, the Senator did lasting damage to the whole program by forcing the resignation of some 40 percent of the staff, including most of its writers and other creative people.

Still, officials of the program were not able to make clear the rationale for many of the things they did: stocking the overseas libraries, for example, with the mystery writings of Dashiell Hammett, to say nothing of the works of a pro-Communist writer like Agnes Smedley. McCarthy drew most of his information from employees of the program—called, by him, the Loyal American Underground, who, in informing on their co-workers, can hardly be said to have shown a keen sense of the purpose of their work. Indeed, the fact that they were discontented enough to inform was in itself disquieting. Lastly, if McCarthy's hearing drew most of the headlines, sharp criticisms also came from other, more respectable, sources. Secretary of State John Foster Dulles voiced a widespread feeling when, in the spring of 1953, he told the Congress:

*There is no clear purpose that underlies the information program, and the result is that a great deal of miscellaneous information is sent out. Somebody says, "There is a book I like so I will spend a few thousand dollars and send it to all the libraries in the world." Or somebody else says he has a song he likes, and they say, "That is a nice song; let us play it over the Voice of America."*

The Republicans did it differently, but not much better. They did find a sensible bureaucratic slot for the information program; in 1953, under Reorganization Plan 8, it was vested in an independent body, the United States Information Agency, which was to take policy guidance from the Assistant Secretary of State for Public Affairs. They also replaced the Mystique of Truth with a doctrine of their own—the Mystique of Superiority.

The Mystique of Superiority was an obvious reaction to the Mystique of Truth. Instead of presenting to the world an undigested mass of American fact, it aimed to drive home a particular lesson—namely, that the American system was better than other systems and notably better than the Soviet system. Put together mainly by executives from Madison Avenue who figured the cold war as a struggle between two leading manufacturers of competitive products, the new doctrine held that a chief function of USIA was to plug the American wares over the rival Communist brand. The prevailing mood was well represented in this analysis of President Eisenhower's Atoms-for-Peace Plan by Abbott Washburn, a former public relations man who became deputy director of USIA:

*This concept pulls the rug out from under the main propaganda line*

*of the Soviets. . . . It puts the cat on the Soviet's back, either to go along with the thing or not to go along with it.*

In keeping with that "cat on the Soviet's back" attitude, virtually everything American was hawked about as an indiscriminate good. A film on disarmament included numerous shots of American bombers on the grounds that foreigners would be impressed by "this beautiful American plane." Shipments of military aid to Pakistan were lauded in local USIA press releases—without any warning that their purpose was not for use against India. Slanging matches with Russians were a regular feature of the operation. One major project was a traveling exhibit, Peoples' Capitalism, which, by its name, invited comparison between the Soviet and American systems and, by its content, argued that the American system was incomparably better. This Voice of America broadcast, done after the arrest of the late Soviet leader Lavrenti Beria, provides a measure of the caliber of political argumentation under the Mystique of Superiority:

*Oh tender Communists in all lands: If the milk of human kindness has not suddenly soured in your veins, if you would have Lavrenti Beria, you had better move fast. Otherwise he is very shortly going to be a dead duck. Just a word of caution: If you stage any "Save Beria" rallies in the Iron Curtain countries, you are going to be dead ducks.*

Apart from questions of taste, one obvious trouble with the Mystique of Superiority was that it staked claims that events proved false. The first Soviet Sputnik, for example, was a dramatic denial of the claim that this country had an automatic technical leadership in all fields; indeed, the Sputnik looked much better than it really was just because the U.S. claim had been made. Moreover, there was in the Mystique of Superiority a large element of preaching to the converted. The American program found an appreciative audience in Western Europe, which was already strongly anti-Communist, and among pro-Western client leaders and their retinues in the Middle and Far East. But in the "third world" of the Southern Continents, the anti-Communist line evoked little response. Vaunting of the American standard of living excited envy as much as sympathy. And as indicated by the riots accompanying Vice President Nixon's Latin-American tour and preceding President Eisenhower's projected Japanese visit, almost no rapport was established between this country and student or labor groups. Indeed, one USIA official boasted to the Congress in 1955 that material sent to Egypt went to a "list of doctors, lawyers, government officials, educators, prominent people right across the board"—that is, to all the "ins," but not to the "outs"—who have since come to dominate Egyptian life.

Far worse than the trouble abroad, however, was the trouble at home. The Democrats, at least, nursed a suspicion that the Republicans were doing daily propaganda war against the Russians chiefly for domestic

purposes—and, namely, in order to wrap themselves up in the flag of anti-Communism. This exchange between Robert Button, Director of the Voice of America in 1956, and Democratic Congressman John Rooney suggests how little impressed the Democrats were by Administration rhetoric:

MR. BUTTON: *I would like to state at the outset that in my opinion the Voice of America is fully committed, as we sit here, for tactical combat.*
MR. ROONEY: *Mr. Button, please do not take our time with generalities.*

Skepticism turned to positive anger in 1957, when USIA director Arthur Larson merged the propaganda line with a blatantly partisan, political appeal. "Throughout the New and Fair Deals," Mr. Larson told a rally in Hawaii, "this country was in the grip of a somewhat alien philosophy imported from abroad." Not only was Mr. Larson roasted alive in the Senate hearings, but the Democrats cut the USIA budget to ribbons. Not long thereafter, Mr. Larson resigned. The second effort to come up with a propaganda formula had collapsed.

Amidst the ruins there remained something of value. Thanks mainly to Larson's predecessor, Theodore Streibert—director from 1953 through 1956—USIA had been developed into the largest information service in the world. It had a permanent staff of 10,000 people, including a foreign service of nearly a thousand persons trained to serve as public affairs officers for U.S. diplomatic missions abroad. It broadcast short wave round the world, in more than 30 languages, to an audience estimated at 20 million (and including enough Russians to cause the Soviet Government to spend for jamming activities roughly $100 million annually, or the budget of USIA). It had a network of over 150 libraries with 2,500,000 books. It produced daily, and circulated round the world by radio-teletype, a basic news file of 10,000 words. It published at least four magazines—*Amerika and Ameryka,* Russian and Polish language magazines; *Free World,* a Far Eastern magazine published in 14 different tongues; *Problems of Communism,* a scholarly periodical published in English and Spanish—and scores of lesser pamphlets, brochures and newspapers. Larson's successor, the veteran State Department official George V. Allen, had begun to tie the program more closely with the Department's operations and had clipped some of the more egregious edges off the Madison Avenue approach. To be sure, chopping and changing fostered low morale; there was widespread dislike within the Agency for the "European Club," comprising those officers holding down "cushy" posts in London, Paris, Rome and Madrid who were said to dominate the program; and professional standards were generally low. Still, by any standard, the basic machinery was in place. It was on that base that Murrow built when he took over in 1961.

He started off with one unique advantage. Apart from the President himself, Murrow was by all odds the best-known figure on the New

Frontier. Not only was he familiar to millions through his CBS broadcasts, but while most of the new Cabinet and agency heads were strangers to one another, Murrow was at least slightly acquainted with almost all of them. "I am probably the only one around who never had to show his credentials," he recalls.

Moreover, he took on with him at USIA two men with lines of their own into the center of the Administration. Donald Wilson, a former Washington bureau chief for *Life* magazine who had worked for Pierre Salinger during the Presidential campaign, and who had personal ties with Robert Kennedy, became Murrow's Deputy Director. Thomas Sorensen, an old hand at USIA and the brother of the President's Special Counsel, Theodore Sorensen, became Deputy Director for Plans and Policy.

Thus well-connected, USIA has become, for the first time, something more than a stepchild of government. Murrow sits in on nearly all the higher policy councils, including many of the committees of the National Security Council. Though known for spareness in comment, he has not hesitated to say his piece on matters relevant to the propaganda effort. He played a major part, for example, in the decision which held off American resumption of nuclear testing until after the Russians had first broken the test moratorium in September 1961.

Nothing better illustrates the fitting of USIA into the total government picture than the way Murrow himself has settled to his work, for the one authentic glamor boy on the New Frontier has become Mr. Devotion-to-Duty. Over the famous eyebrows the bureaucratic mask has descended, and the well-known voice has been muffled in the interoffice memo. Murrow does almost none of the things that make good copy: he does not Twist, hike 50 miles, live in Georgetown, get pushed into swimming pools, publicly lament the state of American culture or even shovel snow from his walk. Most of his time he spends standing at a special shoulder-high desk in his office, pouring over the enormous volume of USIA traffic, making comments and sending off memos. Lunches he tries to spend with incoming men from the field, culling suggestions and criticisms on the program abroad. Evenings, too, he tends to mix pleasure with business. To familiarize Washington with the work of USIA, he has arranged a series of program showings for Cabinet members, Senators and Congressmen and the press. Because USIA has virtually no funds for entertainment at home, Murrow pays for the food and drink from his own pocket. But apart from that largesse, he is the compleat bureaucrat.

As a result, his own personal influence has become institutional. Murrow was in the hospital with pneumonia during the famous week in October 1962 which preceded the decision to blockade Cuba. But Deputy Director Wilson sat in on almost all of the meetings which followed the discovery of Soviet missile sites on the island. "It would be unthinkable

now," one USIA veteran says, "to have something like the U-2 affair, where, on a matter of great propaganda importance, we had to read about it in the papers." "The psychological arm of foreign policy," another veteran says, "is now as well established as the political arm, the military arm, and the economic arms."

With channels to the seat of policy opened up, it became possible to gear the whole USIA operation to the machinery of government. As Murrow wrote in his year-end report of 1961, "Increasingly, the Agency concentrated its resources in support of specific overseas objectives most vital to the United States." To be precise, two techniques, used sporadically in the past, were systematically brought to bear in order to harmonize the flow of information with the achievement of national policy objectives.

The first of these techniques is "tailoring," or the shaping of the information flow so that it conveys a desired message with maximum force. To that end, Murrow, after consultation with the President and Secretary of State Dean Rusk, has identified as central to the whole propaganda effort five themes: Berlin, Disarmament, the United Nations, the Right of Free Choice and Modernization. These themes, all of them having a generally favorable connotation, are supposed to dominate the whole USIA output; explicitly or implicitly, they are to be inserted into every news account, film or broadcast the Agency produces. Films on Berlin, for example, not only stressed the plight of a beleaguered city but also asserted that the real issue was the right of the West Berliners to have a free choice in their own government.

An equally important aspect of "tailoring" is the emphasis now put by USIA on the Big Event. "When something dramatic happens," Murrow says, "people can be reached." The release of the Berlin package just before the building of the Wall is one example of that technique. Another is the widespread coverage given John Glenn's famous space flight; still a third, the special effort, particularly in distributing pictures of the missile sites, that was made at the time of the Cuba quarantine.

"Targeting" is the other technique. It involves the systematic identification of strategic audiences and of the media that will best reach them. "Where literacy is high," Sorensen explains, "we may stress publication activities. Where it is low we may put special emphasis on motion pictures. The atmosphere in one country may be conducive to a program in schools. In another we may decide to expend most of our effort reaching organizations in provincial cities and towns. The target audiences in each country are carefully defined and ceaselessly cultivated."

In keeping with the targeting philosophy, the "European Club" has been broken. Since 1960, the budget for West European activities has been cut by 12 percent, while the number of personnel working in Western Europe is down by over 300. A big increase has been made in

Latin-American (over 150 new posts) and African (over 250 new posts) activities. Instead of concentrating on established groups already favorable to the United States, USIA is now cultivating groups suspicious of this country which are just coming to power in their own countries. In Japan, for example, contact has been made with the leaders of the Socialist trades unions (Sohyo) which led the anti-American demonstrations of 1960, and a number of its officials have been brought to the United States. In Latin America, most of the new American personnel are labor specialists. An example of the refinement that is possible in targeting comes from one Latin-American country where there are three different labor groups: one Socialist, and basically friendly to the U.S.; one Communist, and irrevocably hostile; and a third that is dominated by loyalty to a former national dictator. USIA calculates that the first group is in the bag; that the second is beyond redemption; and that the top leaders of the third are interested only in bringing back the former leader. Accordingly, it is concentrating its efforts on the younger leaders of the third group—men who can be reached and are worth bringing over for the part they may play in the future.

A more subtle approach demands more subtle material. Probably no government in the world has ever made a better short documentary than a recent USIA film "The School at Rincon Santo." The film describes in great detail the daily life in a remote Colombian village that has never had a school. It shows children idling their time away in the fields. It interviews parents expressing their hopes for a better life. It then depicts the arrival of a government official with a proposal for building a school, which also means a road to bring in materials, and a new town well. The villagers agree, provide land and contribute labor. The film ends on the first day of school, with the children learning the alphabet. Only in a tiny comment, inserted at the end, is there a suggestion that the building of the school is an example of what Latin Americans can do for themselves in cooperation with this country's Alliance for Progress.

The low key of "Rincon Santo" bears Murrow's special brand. In presenting the film at a showing not long ago, he referred to it as "a simple thing which may disappoint many of you." He himself always uses the accents of understatement in describing the USIA program. He has been resisting heavy pressure from Alliance for Progress officials to give the program more publicity on the grounds that, so far, more publicity is not justified. "Before we advertise," Murrow says, "we want to be certain the goods are on the shelf."

Between Murrow's ideals and the actual general practice at USIA, however, there remains an important distance. In the field, USIA personnel have chiefly a contact function: establishing personal rapport with editors, artists, trade union officials, teachers and other opinion leaders abroad. It is of necessity a delicate business. But very few USIA

officers are truly at home in foreign languages or at ease in foreign cultures. Even Murrow acknowledges that "a foreign culture and a foreign language today often shield us from the foreign populace. We do not know the culture well enough; we do not speak the language easily enough." It is regrettable, moreover, that some USIA staffers abroad are not top-caliber newsmen and would probably have trouble finding jobs on U.S. newspapers or the networks.

At home, USIA is a swollen bureaucracy. Eight people, for example, are taken up with the selection and translation that goes into the daily half-hour broadcast in Armenian. There are USIA people, notably in the Voice of America, who have been in the same grade for eight years, but who cannot move up or find places on the outside. One of the lowest turnover rates in Government (eight percent against an average of about 20 percent) suggests that, once ensconced, the mediocrities are almost impossible to unload. "The only way I can open room for younger men coming up," one USIA official says, "is to send old-timers to the War College for a year or so." Morale, in these circumstances, remains distinctly low.

"I have a real case of conscience every time I talk to someone about coming into the Agency," one of its top men acknowledges. "I want to bring in good people. But steering good people into USIA is no service to them."

Such attitudes inevitably find expression in the USIA product. Much of the output is leaden and uninspired. USIA prose reads like a monument to Dr. Arbuthnot, the cliché expert. Here, for example, is a sampling from a pamphlet on exchange students in the United States:

> In their shared life on the American campus, both exchange and American students learn much from each other. One thing becomes clear. This is that, despite differences in cultures, customs, nationalities and backgrounds, basically people the world over are much the same.

And here is an introduction to a Voice of America news report that is admirably calculated to make listeners switch off their sets:

> Federal German Chancellor Adenauer has presented his new cabinet. A Voice of America correspondent says in this report, the settlement of the six-week crisis comes as no surprise.

Murrow is aware of such failings. To correct them, he has devoted a great deal of his time and energy to personnel problems. He has brought in to run the Agency's film program one of the country's most talented young directors, George Stevens Jr., the son of the Hollywood movie-maker. He has got as a USIA news analyst, for a year, anyhow, his former CBS colleague Larry Leseur. He has streamlined operating procedures to free USIA men in the field from the burden of writing long reports on all their activities. He has USIA personnel scouts beating the college bushes

for promising talent. As a boost to morale, he has taken a hand in making one USIA man an ambassador and in getting another the rank of minister. He is an active lobbyist for the proposal (put forward recently by a commission headed by former Secretary of State Christian Herter) that would place USIA under the Foreign Service personnel system, with similar privileges and with the possibility of selection-out, that is, firing those who do not perform.

But at best, improvement in personnel is a slow, long-range business. For the moment, all that can be said is that the conceptual stage has been set for the creation of a professional American propaganda service. If serious problems of execution remain, the problem of developing a USIA creed has been solved. Indeed, a good indication of the change is Murrow himself. At the outset of his term, while still awaiting confirmation, he caused a stir by seeking, unsuccessfully, to suppress a showing in Britain of a CBS documentary he had made which sharply criticized the treatment of migratory workers in this country. Now, however, Murrow takes a relaxed, pragmatic attitude, both as regards praising this country and knocking it. Of the Mystique of Superiority, he says: "We cannot be effective in telling the American story abroad if we tell it only in superlatives." Of the Mystique of Truth, he says: "We tell the truth because we want to be credible. We want to be credible because that is the way to win audiences and to hold them."


# 35 / The Policy of the USIA

CARL T. ROWAN

This selection gives a modern restatement of the principles that guide America's foreign propaganda programs. It helps to answer the question: What does the United States want other countries to know about American aims?

THE [USIA's] responsibility as defined by President Kennedy and affirmed by President Johnson, "is to help achieve United States foreign policy objectives." We have no other business.

Reprinted from *Congressional Record*, 88th Cong., 2d sess. (May 25, 1964), pp. A2750–A2751; an address by Mr. Rowan to the National Press Club, Washington, D.C., April 29, 1964.

Carl T. Rowan, a former newspaperman and United States ambassador, succeeded Edward R. Murrow as Director of the U. S. Information Agency in 1964.

We are instructed to do this, among other things, by influencing public attitudes in other nations. We are the fourth dimension in foreign affairs: to the diplomatic arm, the military arm, and the economic arm has been added the information or psychological or propaganda arm—I let the semanticists choose the precise word.

Let me ask, where would you begin this task? You have a mandate from the President to help achieve U.S. objectives abroad, your field is information, and Congress has given you, in the current [1964] fiscal year, $145 million to do the job.

Before we go on, a word of perspective on these resources. I am not pleading poor mouth, but it should be noted that at our present respective rates, the annual appropriation of the Department of Defense would run USIA for 338 years, or until the Year of Our Lord 2302. The AID budget would carry us for more than 20 years. If we count as our clients all the people of the world outside the United States, which they essentially are, we could not afford to send each one of them one post card a year.

The answer, of course, must lie in selectivity. Selectivity in audience. Selectivity in message. Selectivity in priority. Selectivity in effort. Selectivity in use of media. The same kind of selectivity which writers, editors, directors, and producers apply every day in conveying a message to anyone anywhere.

We are painfully aware of our major public opinion problems overseas. Some grow out of the facts of American life and policy: the problem of race and discrimination, the problem of poverty in the affluent society, the maldistribution of the costs of medical and hospital care, the conflicting voices of a free society. Some grow out of the efforts of the adversary: lies, distortions, misrepresentations, shibboleths actively propagated to undermine our position. Some grow out of the genuine accomplishments of the adversary: the spectacular Sputnik I and subsequent Russian space shots; the irresponsible and unnecessary terror of the 100 megaton bomb.

With its resources—and here I paraphrase Lincoln's famous words— USIA cannot tell all of the truth about the United States to all the people of the world all of the time, however desirable that may be.

We have evolved, therefore, a system of priorities. They reflect official policy, and are periodically examined and revised as required.

Here are the five things we believe the people of the world most need to know about U.S. foreign policy at the present time, if they are to make intelligent decisions:

1. The United States has no more urgent task than the pursuit of peace. In the words of President Johnson, "We will be unceasing in the search for peace; resourceful in our pursuit of areas of agreement even with those with whom we differ." We believe this search for an attainable and honorable peace should be based on a gradual evolution in human

institutions and on a series of concrete actions and effective agreements (such as the limited nuclear test ban) leading to general and complete disarmament. The United States will continue to encourage the settlement of international issues by peaceful means rather than force.

2. The United States, matured and tested under the responsibilities of free world leadership, will maintain its strength in all fields to protect its own freedom and to aid in the defense of other free nations against threats to their independence and institutions. The United States can and will keep its commitments to its allied and to other countries.

3. The United States believes in a peaceful world community of free and independent states, free to choose their own future, free to build and change their own systems so long as they do not threaten the freedom of others. We believe in the dignity of the individual, and will continue to help other nations in their efforts to modernize their societies, to resist coercion, and to construct and maintain free institutions.

4. The fundamental commitment of the United States is to freedom of the individual, of the community, and of the Nation under law. This commitment is the hallmark which distinguishes societies of free men from societies where rule is based on privilege and force. Historically, the rule of law was a commitment of the people of the United States to themselves; today it is the cornerstone of both our domestic and international policies. We will continue to work toward perfecting the rule of law at home and encourage its extension to and among all nations.

5. The United States will continue its full support of the United Nations, seeking in concert with other countries to strengthen the U.N.'s peacekeeping machinery. It will also continue to support U.N. functions which assist all free nations, large and small, to maintain their independence and to move toward political, economic, and social justice.

# 36 / From *Around the Edge of War*

JOHN FORTH AMORY (pseudonym)

**The alleged ineffectiveness of American overseas propaganda
has been the topic of discussion for many analysts. What is**

Reprinted from *Around the Edge of War* (New York: Clarkson N. Potter, 1961), pp. 87–104. By permission.

John Forth Amory is the pseudonym of a person said by his publisher to be experienced in governmental positions in foreign policy and international relations.

the basis for this criticism? If it is valid, how can remedies
be applied? These questions are explored in the following
selection, which cites, among other examples, the failure of
American propaganda in Laos.


IN CONSIDERING the effectiveness of the American propaganda instrument as a means of carrying out a phase of foreign policy in the areas
of upheaval, it might not be amiss to recall a favorite quotation of
Jeffersonian Americans, whose early upheaval turned out quite well
despite the existence of a foreign-linked power elite. Although only one in
seventeen of those earlier Americans was a church member, many were
assiduous Bible readers. In that Book they found what today would be
called "a statement of policy" which American propagandists might
consider:

"I came not to call the righteous but the sinners to repentance."

Along with the rush toward church membership has come a parallel
modern decline in Bible reading, which may help explain modern
aversion to many early American precepts. Our propaganda, to the extent
it has taken people into consideration at all, has been aimed strictly at
leading the "righteous," that is, the ones already on "our side," for economic reasons, to a presumed salvation; the 90 per cent, the huge out-
group majorities in the underdeveloped lands, who are "sinners" in our
eyes, have been left for the Soviet Union to manipulate or, at least,
to infiltrate.

This is particularly so in the critical areas of upheaval, where the
existing power cliques are strongly supported by us and laved by high-
powered propaganda, while the huge popular movements, although really
brought into being by Western economic organization, are forcibly
opposed, even by armed intervention, and left unilluminated by our
message. This apparently enigmatic propaganda policy, which would
seem to be directed at building another barrier against the earth turning,
is in fact logical and even inevitable, given the limited premise on
which it is built.

. . . American foreign policy and therefore its propaganda arm is
determined by the Executive branch of the government, subject to
important influence by only one major pressure group, our overseas
investors. American propaganda thus tends automatically to serve
primarily the interests of the dominant group concerned; and the interest
of this group, quite logically and praiseworthily, is to sell goods and
services and make profits abroad.

What could be less enigmatic, therefore, than a propaganda policy
aimed at the "righteous," at the 10 per cent in the underdeveloped areas
who have wealth and purchasing power? Could one expect it to be aimed

at the 90 per cent who cannot buy? Advertising men, who are commercial propagandists, discovered long ago that if you want to sell something, you make your pitch to the customer with purchasing power, not to someone who is dead broke. The motivation in American propaganda, and much of its content, is thus commercial—and effective within those limits.

Unfortunately, in the confusion between long-range national interests and short-range business interests, our propagandists were unable to recognize that the two do not always coincide. What is good for General Motors in the short run may not be good for the country in the long run. The balance of power in the whole of the underdeveloped world is swinging over rapidly from the 10 per cent to the 90 per cent; and as power goes, so goes the wealth of the nation, including whatever share in it American overseas investors might have.

American propaganda, along with the military and economic instruments of our foreign policy, suffers from the lack of "people power" and "people objective." It is essentially class propaganda; we save the saved and convert the converted. Long before we became so powerful, we did a better job in reaching the people. Our own revolution was the mother of the first great wave of upheaval; all through the late eighteenth and the entire nineteenth centuries documents such as our Declaration of Independence and the Bill of Rights were smuggled from popular leader to popular leader; the great Brazilian patriot Tiradentes was reputedly hanged because a copy of the Declaration of Independence was found in his pocket. Even today the words of Thomas Jefferson, forgotten (and some of them considered subversive) in his homeland, come easily to the tongues of the leaders of the submerged peoples in many lands, quoted often to refute our present-day propaganda.

The advanced, streamlined, efficient and modern techniques used by our principal propaganda agency, the United States Information Service (an agency at home, USIA; a service overseas USIS) must be applied, unfortunately, in areas of upheaval where the local population has not been conditioned to them by Madison Avenue commercials. Laos was a case in point. It was a critical area; hundreds of millions of American dollars had poured into the tiny Buddhist country until the officials of the United States-sponsored regime had accumulated so many luxury cars that more millions had to be sent to build roads for them. The USIS also had available in Laos, because of the emergency circumstances, a much larger allocation than usual; it had enough funds to do whatever the job might require over a critical period.

The first problem faced by USIS was a common one in the upheaval areas: Not more than one out of six Laotians could read; few had radios; none had television. As a noble gesture, however, the USIS turned out something like one million leaflets and pamphlets, forty-eight different varieties, on a specially imported, late-model printing plant. American

planes dropped them over the countryside among the peasants, warning them against the Pathet Lao, the folk-war movement, and lauding the U.S.-sponsored regime in Vientiane, whose representatives 90 per cent of the local peasantry had never seen. The leaflets were turned out by a staff of seventeen Americans and seventy-two Filipinos, Thais and Vietnamese —no Laotians. Laotians were used by USIS for menial jobs only; skilled Laotians were either unavailable or preferred not to get mixed up with the American effort.

It did not take long, however, for USIS, using approved market-survey techniques similar to those employed by McCann-Erickson for its overseas business clients, to discover a degree of difficulty in reaching an illiterate population with its kind of literature. It soon decided to concentrate on movie shorts and features. A total of eighty-three films were prepared for Laotian audiences. Worked in with the subject matter were carefully prepared eulogies of the U.S.-sponsored regime of Prince Boun Oum and devastating attacks on the Pathet Lao movement as Communist.

In at least one of these commentaries the Pathet Lao were presented as possessed of "evil spirits." They were Laotian outside, the film admitted, but inside they were evil spirits who, in accordance with the injunction against allowing witches to live, should be done away with forthwith. This was received with some doubt by the audiences, most of whom were themselves Pathet Lao sympathizers, as evidence of American superstitions foreign to Buddhism. One film, which showed up-to-date American methods of chicken farming, achieved success in the village of Na Nong Buk, near Vientiane. The peasantry was much impressed with the chicken-housing, considerably better than their own: but the commentary to the effect that the Pathet Lao, if they took over, would ban private chicken raising, was received with some wonder. The Pathet Lao had already taken over; every male in the village, most of them chicken owners, was already in the movement except for three new officials sent from Vientiane who had no chickens.

An especially prized film defined communism, which the Laotians had not heard of. "What is it?" the girl heroine asked her boy friend, a stalwart friend of the United States. "Well," the young hero replied, "if I cut my hand off and then make everybody else do the same thing, that's communism." "Oh," commented the heroine, "how frightful is communism." Silly as this sounds, it was an attempt to put across a common *American* idea of communism, that is, a conspiracy by people who have nothing, to take away possessions of those who have something. In the United States, or among Laotian wealthy, this might have been an acceptable, although infantile definition; among Laotian villagers, even if they understood the implication, it would have meant little. They had nothing to lose under any "ism."

The key reason for failure of the "all-out" USIS effort in Laos, however, lay in its basic orientation. This was defined by a top American official on the scene: "Our main effort in Laos," he said, "is to tell the people about their own good government (our Prince Boun Oum regime) and about the dangers of communism."

Even if the United States at one time had a chance in Laos—doubtful at best in view of the side we were on—this orientation would have killed the chance. The first rule in propaganda, when an unpopular government must be praised to its own antagonistic people, is to try to get a popular local figurehead to do the praising; for a foreign agency to do so automatically heightens the antagonism. Just why a group of foreigners should tell a doubtful people how wonderful their own government is, or how bad their fellow citizens are, is a question which has only one answer: The doubtful government is linked with the foreigners. This, of course, was the propaganda objective in Laos, not of USIS, but of the anti-American Pathet Lao. The aim of the Pathet Lao was to paint Prince Boun Oum as a puppet of American imperialists; the USIS achieved the Pathet Lao objective.

Endless poring over of Madison Avenue propaganda techniques by Communist agents could not have produced a better method for the Pathet Lao than the one devised by the USIS in all its innocence. It may be a good thing that most of the upheaval areas have still not been subjected to a "crash program" of American propaganda; the Pathet Lao might now be worldwide.

Apart from propaganda objectives, however, the Laotian fiasco pointed up an aspect of propaganda content. The plain fact was that Prince Boun Oum, however honest, capable or patriotic, was indeed at the time an American puppet, installed by the United States after deposition of a legitimate government—legitimate, that is, in Laotian terms. To presume that any people, even the most illiterate and naïve, would not recognize that fact, indicates a contempt for people by American officialdom, an assumption that American powers of enforcement of policy are so great that people need not be considered. Once again, the basic flaw was demonstrated.

Propaganda, like war, is merely one means of carrying out foreign policy, of trying to impose that policy on others. Success in propaganda, as in war, depends on the use of power (words) at the right time, in the right place, in the right amount and in the right way. In propaganda, as in war, a key element in success is to know the enemy as well as yourself—by no means an easy knowledge to attain—and to know your allies. Words are the weapons in propaganda; but words, unlike bombs, are not necessarily the same for all men.

Propaganda, no matter how true or false, passes through the filter of man's mind; and in the passage it may come to have a wholly different

meaning. American lack of knowledge of how and what the great majorities feel and think in the areas of upheaval—a lack directly traceable to the make-up of our intelligence organization—has rendered our propaganda peculiarly ineffective and even counterproductive among these masses of people, quite apart from its basic flaw, derived from its orientation and content.

An expert propagandist, given a free hand, can convince most people that any object not in their visual range is white instead of dark gray and still adhere strictly to the "truth." He does this by first building in his audience a desire to learn that the object is white, and second, by abstracting from the dark gray its white content and presenting it as white. The technique is easily understood in terms of people: An individual will have, say, four good points, ten bad points and six neutral points; but an expert propagandist can make this mostly bad person seem extraordinarily and humanly good by stressing his four good points and lightly mentioning one or two neutral points for apparent balance. But the technique will work only if this good-bad person is beyond the checking range of the audience. If they see him and know him, the propaganda will immediately be called fake and will backfire. Even if the audience only believes it sees him and knows him as bad, the propaganda will fail.

Propaganda, in other words, must take into account the existing image in a man's mind; it cannot brainwash—this is an individual, not a mass approach. The existing image can be changed somewhat; in some cases a similar but intrinsically different image can be superimposed; but the image cannot be wholly extirpated within the limits of one generation.

This is why American propagandists, no matter how efficiently they try, cannot convince the submerged majorities in the areas of upheaval that the ruling group in their land is good. The existing image is one of a group of corrupt oppressors and overlords; shifts of power within the ruling group, by *coups d'etat* or otherwise, may change the image somewhat; in a few cases another image has been superimposed; but the memory remains and the facts of poverty, disease and exploitation remain. No propaganda can effectively counteract an existing and obvious fact.

To the degree that American businessmen and, through them, America, are associated with the existing image of an exploiting power group, the majorities in the underdeveloped lands will associate America with that group, regardless of propaganda. Before their eyes the people see the American standing at the side of their corrupt rulers; they may even see him calling on his government to bring in planes and guns to save the minority clique from the majority rising. The image and the fact render worthless any contrary propaganda, however suave.

The importance of the existing image is illustrated also by the strictly

relative success of American propaganda in the more developed countries, particularly those peopled or culturally dominated by Western Europeans or their descendants. American withdrawal into nuclear fantasy, the failure to obtain facts and meanings as a basis for policy and its propaganda arm, even mistakes such as the Cuban fiasco, could not wholly erase the image of America that had been built up among these people. In those areas, American propaganda, no matter how poor in content, was filtered through minds which saw America as a land of promise, where kinfolk lived or had gone long before. We were scoffed at by Western Europeans, called childish, or, more pointedly, dreamers, materialists, even warmongers, but the old image of America was still there to transmute the new impressions.

Even in the developed countries of Western European culture, however, American propaganda tends to succeed or fail along class lines; conservative businessmen and most of the middle class are with us; most of the lower-middle class and the urban or rural working people are against us, although hesitantly. The split is sharply illustrated in Brazil, a country which contains one of the world's most highly developed areas, centering around São Paulo, and one of the world's most backward areas in the Northeast. The people of São Paulo, for the most part, think of Americans almost exactly in Western European terms; the people of the Northeast, except for the tiny, exploiting power clique, typical of areas of upheaval, have an attitude almost like that of pro-Castro Cubans.

For the "sinners," for the roughly two-thirds of the earth's population who live in the underdeveloped lands of Asia, Africa and Latin America, the out-groups, our road to salvation seems both hypothetical and hypocritical. Our propaganda has not diminished the interfering image; on the contrary, by the reactive process which obvious falsehood generates, we have magnified it. By our deeds they know us. We can, if we want to, change the deeds; that, after all, is the first step in good "public relations." The second step is to explain our deeds in their terms, not ours, which means that we must first learn how they think and feel.

Soviet propaganda, technically, is far inferior to American. In the underdeveloped areas not yet overrun by folk war, the United States makes use of newspaper, radio and television outlets for its propaganda at a ratio of approximately 500 for any one available to the Soviet Union. Many of the smaller newspapers in Latin America, Asia and even Africa are so swamped with news and feature releases distributed by the United States Information Agency that the local news staff uses the backs for copy paper, a sizable saving in areas where paper is expensive. Few of these outlets have even been offered official Soviet propaganda; and practically none of them would use it if it were offered. Moreover, USIA propaganda is widely printed and broadcast, although not because of intrinsic interest. It is used for the same reason that a newspaper in the

United States, angling for or receiving a big advertisement from a major company, will tend to run news stories about that company. This tendency does not imply direct pressure by the advertiser; it is a more or less "unconscious recognition" of which side of the bread is buttered. American foreign investors and their local representatives, with commendable patriotism, tend to place their advertising with those news outlets which use American propaganda and tend to throw political and economic favors to their owners.

In every technical way, America's official propaganda machinery works far more smoothly than any other. The United States Information Agency, although it may appear amateurish to professional newspapermen or in comparison with major news agencies, is the most efficient propaganda service ever developed, so far as operational procedures go. Propaganda flows smoothly from New York and Washington and local centers overseas to publications around the world. *Official* Soviet propaganda, distributed mostly through the Tass agency, uses techniques which seem almost juvenile in comparison.

Why, then, at every point of critical competition, has Soviet propaganda outpulled the American variety?

There have, of course, been "bad breaks" for American propaganda, such as the U-2 incident, the Cuban fiasco, and the Russian Sputnik or man-in-orbit beats. Of these, however, only the Cuban fiasco was deeply damaging to American interests in the underdeveloped lands; the others did not really have everyday meaning for the masses of people. Bad breaks can come in any propaganda war; they can be overcome. It is not on this level, despite isolated, flashy victories, that Soviet propaganda is winning.

Consistently, American propaganda has met defeat on the "people" level; it cannot penetrate the majorities in the underdeveloped areas and has been especially ineffective among those in or near upheaval. In those areas where the people see Americans aligned with their enemy, the people themselves carry on propaganda which contains much that is anti-American and much that is pro-Soviet or pro-Chinese. Their propaganda is principally word-of-mouth, the age-old method native to the area; but the general illiteracy has not prevented an extraordinarily wide distribution of tiny, four-page pamphlets, handbills and one-sheet newspapers, written simply and plainly in the terms of the average peasant or workman. Where illiteracy is almost total, someone will volunteer to read the contents to small or large groups. Included in this "literature" are millions of copies of tiny pamphlets smuggled in from the Soviet Union and China and distributed and read, not by Russians or Chinese in air-conditioned information offices, but by unpaid native men and women.

In thousands of rural villages throughout the upheaval areas of the world, half-literate peasants are even poring over the complicated

writings of Mao, idiomatically translated. In Latin America, groups have actually gathered to study a rather simple description of a phase of guerrilla warfare written by Ernesto Guevara—indications are that some 100,000 copies have been distributed there, although hardly a bookstore displays them. Why American propaganda fails lies basically in its support of the minority groups, but it fails also because it ignores the problems of change and offers no solutions except a glorified status quo. Even without the interfering image of American business linked with the local power clique, American propaganda could not compete.

Technical facility cannot make up for content; access to the press, radio and television of the ruling clique in the underdeveloped areas does not equal access to the hearts and minds of the people; and, if an old saying may be misquoted, propaganda without works is dead. If we want the people of the underdeveloped world to go with us, we have to go with them, both in words and deeds.

Once again, American technique has produced a pretty package; but it doesn't open for the consumer to get at the contents. Those who accept American propaganda do so because they are already on our side for economic reasons. Those who do not accept it are already against us or at best doubtful of us, for reasons which are also economic in essence.

Our propaganda—like our "little war" ideas, our foreign investors, our intelligence agency, and our entire inchoate foreign policy—goes against the tide. As a "thing-in-itself," our propaganda machinery may be the most streamlined ever developed by artful man; but it is beyond the power of any propaganda to overcome the overwhelming weight of events that are overturning the age-old balances in the upheaval areas.

The effect of American propaganda has been almost as serious at home as overseas, possibly more so in some ways. In this respect American propaganda has, on the whole, had results "superior" to the Russian variety; it is at least believed domestically. No press in the world, except perhaps in China, is as full of propaganda as the American—although the American lead over the Soviet Union in this respect is due to a technical fact: The American press is deluged not only with government propaganda and the angling of the wire services and local editors, but with handouts from private propagandists, flacks and public-relations firms and departments, all promoting some private interest. On a typical day, 75 to 85 per cent of all "news" in two New York afternoon papers was found to be either outright propaganda from one source or another or demonstrably angled—not counting advertisements, which of course are also propaganda of a sort.

It has been the American press, as a vehicle for propaganda—and with a tremendous assist from television—which has pounded home to a credulous public such Orwellian ideas as peace through war with Russia and China; freeing Cuba by conquest; increased defense expenditures

through lower taxes; extending American influence by cutting foreign aid; expulsion from the United Nations of all nations not pro-American; Formosa is China; aid the needy by cutting relief; invade Laos to repel the Laotians; or even Civil Defense against Russian H-Bombs. A complete negation of reality was at times apparent in this propaganda— for example, a general refusal to believe that the Russians had sent a rocket around the moon or a spaceman into orbit. A surprising percentage of these strange unrealisms would seem to be accepted, as a result of the propaganda effort, by a majority of Americans in the metropolitan East and a sizable minority elsewhere.

These American fantasies, among others, have led many foreigners to wonder if Americans are either incredibly naive or verging on a national nervous breakdown. In talking with American "believers," informed Englishmen have reported a sensation similar to that received in an attempt at logical conversation with a member of the world-is-flat sect. An American may test this peculiarity on himself by reading a European or even a Canadian newspaper after a steady diet of, say, the New York *Daily News*.

An indication that this danger of immersion of Americans in fantasy has caused some preoccupation among our policy-makers was contained in a talk in 1961 by President John F. Kennedy before the Society of Newspaper Editors. "The President of a great democracy such as ours," he said, "and the editors of great newspapers such as yours owe a common obligation to present the facts, and to present them with candor and to present them in perspective."

There are, to be sure, circumstances involving national peril in which certain facts, far from being explained with candor, must be withheld from the public lest the enemy also learn them. The decision to withhold facts, in a democracy, is a grave one; and the action is not to be undertaken lightly. The key is correct judgment as to what few facts not already known to the enemy have such extraordinary importance, not how palatable they are for the public.

Censorship—that is, negative propaganda or withholding of danger- ous secrets—can be permitted to a degree by a democracy in times of national peril. Propaganda based on lies, however, can never be justified. No government based on rule by the people can endure if it permits lying, for the reason that a deceived people—who are the source of government—cannot knowledgeably control their elected representatives. By their nature, lies by governing officials in a democracy are expressions of treason against that form of government, which depends on an informed electorate. The security of a nation may require silence in grievous emergencies; but the safety of a democracy cannot be more gravely endangered than by unchallenged lies.

To the degree that American propaganda has a false content, it will

be self-defeating, in the long run, overseas, where contrary views can permeate and where skepticism concerning official propaganda, through centuries of exposure to its falsity, is prevalent; but at home such falsehood undermines the foundations of the Republic. Americans, who have governed themselves and have tended to trust their elected officials, are not yet conditioned to such skepticism; they may prefer to accept falsehoods rather than believe that their own representatives have lied to them. A democracy dare not permit betrayal of that trust; yet the tide of fantasy and falsehood is not receding in the United States—it may be that only an overwhelming force of public opinion can stop it even now. At home, however, America has the mechanisms to bring the pressure of opinion to bear; the problem, grave as it is, will be easier to solve than that of a falsely based foreign policy, on which uninformed or misinformed public opinion and scattered or occasional pressure groups, so far, have had no direct effect. Truth at home must be assured, first of all, to oblige truth overseas.

Perhaps as a first step toward a return to reality, Americans not already prisoners of fantasy might come together, as self-respecting individuals, in community groups modeled organizationally on our Better Business Bureaus—groups which, with due investigation, would challenge fraudulent information practices. Here again American conservatives must in all probability play the key role; not because the conservative has any more understanding of the need for truth, but because the American liberal, ever since the fantasy era of the early 1950's has been afraid to speak up for fear of being tarred with the "egghead" or "red" brush. The desperate need for truth to shed light on American policies, a need which involves national survival, should be great enough to bring together on this point both the liberal and the conservative wings of American thought. Transcending conservative and liberal differences is the common goal of preserving and defending the United States of America, which equals preservation and defense of the truth.

With reality once again shaping our perspectives at home, it would be far easier to evolve an effective propaganda based on the truth, in the great arena of conflict abroad, where the hearts and minds of men must be won or lost.

# 37 / Handicaps of a Democracy in Persuasion

### HOWLAND H. SARGEANT

In utilizing effectively the instrument of propaganda towards foreign policy objectives, can a free and open society compete with closed, totalitarian societies? Does a democracy have any advantages? The handicaps under which the United States tries to operate programs of international persuasion are analyzed here.

CAN A DEMOCRACY use the weapons of psychological warfare and propaganda as effectively as totalitarian countries do? Not in the same sense. The behavior and actions of the American government and the American people themselves create an image that other peoples receive of us. Skillful propagandists can to some extent influence this image but never really produce one basically different from the true picture.

The kind of psychological warfare totalitarian countries carry on is undermined and invalidated promptly in a country where free government depends upon the right of every citizen to ask questions and to receive answers. For example, President Eisenhower's announcement of unleashing Chiang Kai-Shek and deneutralizing Formosa touched off a wave of Congressional debate, "informed" press speculation, and British and French parliamentary questions, which quickly destroyed any favorable psychological effect.

Arthur Schlesinger, Jr. said: "A totalitarian state can use psychological warfare like a sword. For the Communists or Nazis, psychological warfare is automatically unified in concept, ruthless and flashing in execution."

A free society cannot behave in this way. The essential ingredients, as stated by C. D. Jackson several years ago, for making psychological warfare really effective included: "fanaticism—flexibility and maneuverability—money—no holds barred, and—no questions asked."

Our experience shows that these basic ingredients are lacking in democracies. But our persuasion can enjoy the *advantages* of being based on truth and therefore of promising no more than we can perform; of

Reprinted from *The Representation of the United States Abroad*, pp. 111–19, background papers prepared for the Ninth American Assembly, sponsored by The American Assembly, Graduate School of Business, Columbia University, May, 1956. A brief biographical sketch of Mr. Sargeant accompanies selection 32.

having objectives that most foreign peoples hold in common with us. When we forget these basic realities, we often are trapped by glittering fallacies.

### Fallacy No. 1: The Cheap Substitute, or Words Without Deeds

Perhaps the easiest way to deal with this fallacy is to use the military analogy. Although we have psychological warfare and it can hurt enemy morale or induce enemy surrenders, it does not take the place of actual fighting. "Words without deeds" will lead us into the flush of cheap victories which are just propaganda fencing matches, and worse—by our words we *may* push far in advance of action itself (political, economic, military) and thus destroy the whole cause in the minds of those we seek to reach. Our leadership of the free world is impaired whenever we deliberately set out to give the impression we are doing more than we actually are. The "liberation doctrine" as enunciated during the campaign oratory of 1952 had some of these connotations.

### Fallacy No. 2: Press Agent, or Contributor to Policy?

A public relations man who simply hands out canned stories ground out after the fact is never going to be very successful. A central issue in our persuasion programs has been the question: How do you bring to bear on the formulation of national policies those essential elements of public attitudes at home and abroad which ought to be considered when the policy is being made? Since the end of the war, the greatest single advance in our persuasion programs has been the increasing acceptance at the highest levels in the State Department and the Executive Branch of the contribution that can be made by the professional in public opinion and persuasion *at the time that policies are being developed.* Increasingly this is also true for the Public Affairs Officer and his USIS staff overseas in their relationships to the chiefs of United States diplomatic missions. We are learning that American information and cultural representation abroad must do something different than apply the techniques which successfully sell mass-production goods to the consumer. Occasionally we blunder. At almost the same time that Chancellor Adenauer, on his return from his September visit to Moscow, was saying in effect to the press in Bonn that "we were bludgeoned over the head," a press agent approach was being made in Washington to claim a victory for the free world in the results of that trip.

### Fallacy No. 3: Let's Use the Big Lie, Too

Some people think that in a cold war we can't afford to be squeamish.

We must fight fire with fire. If our opponents lie, we'll just lie all the more. This disregards one important fact: democracies are *poor* liars. Although there is of course a basic moral issue at the heart of all this, the plain facts are that a successful propagandist must maintain *credibility*. His ultimate aim is not to affect attitudes, but to cause action. This action must not only be desirable to the propagandist but also seem in the interest of the persons supposed to act—and must appear *feasible* to those persons.

When we see the success of the science-fiction of the enormous germ warfare campaign mounted by the communists—devoid of any shred of actual supporting evidence save that which they fabricated themselves—propagandists of the free world may be sorely tempted to try campaigns of this kind. It is one of the facts of life in a democracy that the conditions simply do not obtain which will permit sustaining any important campaign of this type, except in wartime, successfully.

### Fallacy No. 4: The Short-run Mentality

It sometimes is pretty hard to sustain the concept that the march of freedom has gained the momentum that will make it the wave of the future when the leading member of these free societies—the United States—from time to time behaves as though we really were not involved in a life and death struggle but only in it for the short run. *Symptoms* of this short-run mentality have been the drastically fluctuating appropriation levels for our information and cultural representation programs abroad; a "go-it-alone" philosophy leading to irresponsible calls for dropping the atomic bomb and for preventive war; a preoccupation with the anti-communist crusade here at home to the exclusion and sometimes to the detriment of fighting communism in the rest of the world.

The United Press recently carried under a Dublin dateline an interesting example. "The United States will close its information and library service here tomorrow because it feels it has so many friends in Ireland the service no longer is needed." Does American business stop advertising because it has made so many friends that it no longer needs to tell old ones about its products and to acquaint new ones with them?

### Fallacy No. 5: Let Our Psychological Warriors Strike Out Independently

The U.S. Information Agency today is independent of the Department of State. There are some functional advantages in permitting those who deal with the media of mass communication a type of organization different from that required by those who set our foreign policy objectives and conduct our diplomatic relations. There is occasionally a feeling

expressed that since the USIA is separate from the Department of State, it should abandon the restraints allegedly inhibiting that staid old Department. As an independent agency it should move freely and initiate its own policies. On turning this stone over, one usually finds there is hidden beneath it that hardy old perennial: "Let's have two foreign policies and two Departments of State; if we don't like the foreign policy we've got, we will have a new Foreign Affairs Department but we will call it an Information Agency and it will put out a totally different and more acceptable foreign policy."

Independence which affords flexibility in operation carries with it the duty of strict compliance with United States policies laid down at top levels. The U.S. Information Agency and its overseas representatives have made an excellent record in this respect. The Korean War provided several examples of the importance of observing this principle. A striking one was the discovery that large numbers of Korean and Chinese POW's hated conditions under communism so much they would refuse to go home even if allowed to do so. This was of course a great "break" for psychological warriors. On the other hand, military and political elements had weighty objections to making full propaganda use of this discovery. Why? Premature exploitation might affect the fate of UN POW's held by the communists, and the outcome of the truce talks and the solidarity of the United Nations coalition could be gravely affected.

### Why Does Uncle Sam Sometimes Seem to Have Two Left Feet?

There are conflicts between domestic and foreign policies which sometimes unavoidably make Uncle Sam look abroad as though he has two left feet. When we debate passionately whether we are going to subsidize our surplus farm crops and dump them in the export markets overseas, we may make cotton-producing countries like Egypt or rice-producing areas like Burma or dairy countries like Denmark extremely unhappy. We may put quotas and tariffs on the import of wool and dismay our friends in Latin America who depend upon wool. We may upset our Canadian neighbors by our behavior with respect to our vast wheat surplus. The Public Affairs Officer can only grit his teeth and make the best of such circumstances as these. They are inherent in the working out of the great decisions of a democracy. They reflect the fact that today every foreign policy decision has its domestic counterpart—they're just the inside and the outside of the same glove.

Similarly, life may be difficult for the Public Affairs Officer if our government takes an action which is important to attain foreign policy objectives but which is not really understood by Americans at home. The accompanying clamor and debate may sometimes nullify the effects of a

wise decision from the point of view of strengthening the bonds between us and another country. Delivery by Denmark of a tanker to the Soviet Union in the spring of 1952 required extraordinary efforts here at home to make clear to the Congress—and the American people why this apparent breach of the embargo on delivery of strategic materials to the USSR should not bring an end to American aid to Denmark.

There are other times when Uncle Sam seems to have two left feet for much less respectable and valid reasons. The U.S. Air Force announces the launching of two hundred of the big meteorological balloons from Scotland without mentioning any other European launching site and at a time when the Soviet campaign against balloons of all kinds is getting into full swing. A high official of the Pentagon issues a report on research on bacteriological and chemical warfare at the height of the communist germ warfare campaign and just *before* the President sends his major disarmament proposals to the United Nations.

## *Selling America versus Creating Mutual Understanding*

We have learned painfully and to our sorrow that there are many occasions when Madison Avenue huckster techniques of selling the sizzle and not the steak will boomerang if applied to attaining American objectives overseas. We seem to be slowly groping our way to a firmer and more genuine conviction that we really want the rest of the world to have a much greater understanding of us and of our objectives—and that as Americans we really want to seek a comparably full and fair picture of other nations and peoples. We are learning how to compete with the communists whose messages come primarily through one's friends and neighbors and are often disguised under the slogans of patriotism and nationalism. We are not able to create fifth columns of the communist kind. Our information representatives overseas, however, are learning how to make far greater and more effective use of local citizens on our USIS staffs. This is especially true in the Far East where the concept of Asians speaking to Asians has repeatedly demonstrated its effectiveness. Our Public Affairs Officers are experimenting with books actually written by local Asian citizens about the United States.

Increasingly, Public Affairs Officers are using *unattributed* material in what might be called "indigenous" operations. This really means such things as radio programs going out over local networks or posters issued or pamphlets distributed without an attribution to the United States or any evident American sponsorship. Instead, such material is distributed in the name of local organizations. There is nothing tricky or underhanded about this. It does involve cooperation with like-minded organizations including educators, labor groups, war veterans, religious organizations, which share our views and find that the values and

aspirations of their own peoples have much in common with those of us Americans.

This is a genuinely delicate strategic choice for the Public Affairs Officer in any country to make, intensified by the fact that in our persuasion programs, we are going over the heads of governments to the people themselves. We are handling these choices with increasing success and with fewer backfires, due in large part to the far greater degree of autonomy which is entrusted by Washington to the USIS officer in the field today. The rewards are great when such unattributed locally-sponsored material hits home. The most successful cannot be talked about. One successful example recounted in Edward Barrett's *Truth Is Our Weapon* concerns the Rome Public Affairs Officer's distribution of a flaming red handbill, simulating the Soviet-type, entitled "For a Lasting Peace." Its subheading: "25 years of Soviet Effort towards Lasting Peace." The text specified thirty agreements that the Soviet Union had signed and in a parallel column showed how the Soviets had vetoed, scrapped or ignored each of these. The culmination of this maneuver was the distribution of a million of these handbills through normal Italian labor channels plus the remarkable feat of getting a major Communist Party mailing room in Northern Italy to send out more than 20,000 to the CP membership list in that country. The communists often bungle—and badly—in propaganda!

There will be an occasional backfire. Victor Lasky reports that in Burma a secret subsidy to a Buddhist Conference (where anti-communist sentiment was to be strengthened) was disclosed. A leading Buddhist is reported to have said that while Buddhists have no quarrel with Americans "we may have if they persist in trying to use Buddhism as a weapon against communism."

"You can't generalize!" is the lesson learned in our decade of post-war experience with these programs. The problem in each country is different. The problem is different in each country from time to time. Whether to use an unattributed piece of material or to reveal fully and openly American sponsorship of the information will continue to be one of the key decisions a Public Affairs Officer has to make. Problems not only vary from country to country, but also from region to region. For example in the Far East there is the problem of the overseas Chinese—300,000 in Burma, 3,000,000 in Thailand, and unassimilated minorities of the same nature in other countries—a ready-made fifth column for the communists. Many of these Far Eastern countries are what are called "two-level societies"—with a small elite group who run things but with the vast majority of people in the lower level. A large number of these countries have newly won their independence. USIS officers here will operate far differently than in Western Europe or in many Latin American republics.

The Asia Foundation, whose activities are supported by private American citizens, finds that the best way to fight communism in Asia is to assist the non-communist Asians to find and achieve positive alternatives to communist action. There is no substitute for personal action and no substitute for organized group action on a local basis.

### Lessons We Are Learning

Yes, America is learning. We are learning that words without deeds are ineffective in a democracy's programs of persuasion. We are learning that we must not be too preoccupied with day-to-day events rather than with ultimate purposes, since this is the role of a press agent and not the role of a persuader. We are learning that persuasion must be based upon the true and tried instruments of national policy. A military undertaking such as the Berlin airlift, the commitment of American troops to Europe, or the appointment of General Eisenhower—symbol of victory in Europe —to head Allied forces there. A program like the Marshall Plan or Point IV in the economic field. A statement of policy like the Truman Doctrine or President Eisenhower's appeal for "a true and total peace." The development by diplomacy of NATO or the Pacific Pact. Using these and other instruments a nation can secure support for its national objectives and for the different things that it does day by day. These are the things which give American information and cultural representatives overseas an opportunity to perform effectively.

These front-line representatives of America in a major area of the cold war can hope that in time it will be the policy of the United States government habitually and instinctively to analyze each action that we propose to take in the light of what world opinion will probably think of it. Our representatives overseas can hope that we will automatically and instinctively require that some measures or plan be adopted at that time which will attempt to influence world opinion in its favor and which will form part of the action we finally adopt. They can hope that we will come to agree that taking the right action is only part of the task. We must strive to see that the meaning we want attached to that action shall in fact be accepted by those people who are not Americans.

Under these conditions, an overseas representative can honestly begin to say that we as Americans are presenting some clear hope for a better future. We are not simply presenting a program that will leave room for no one except bigger and better Americans. We will seem less occupied with the immediate present and less in the position of advocates of maintaining the status quo. We will begin to show foreign peoples that the great dynamic qualities of American leadership are in fact leading us somewhere and therefore leading them somewhere that they want to go.

It will no longer be possible to say, as an important paper discussing this topic concluded several years ago, that "the absence of a defined faith in the future deprives us of our best of all possible guides in planning for the future."

We'll also be abandoning the occasional excesses of the skywriting school of international persuasion. There will be greater genuine belief in and less lip service paid to a concept expressed by President Eisenhower once at a press conference—"Manifestly, if we were going to have peace and understanding in the world, we had to know about each other's cultures. There had to be greater information disseminated throughout the world, each about the other." Overseas representatives will no longer be torn between "selling America" and the creation of mutual understanding and the securing of participation by our audiences themselves in the work to be done. We may even move to the position where in each country in which we carry on a persuasion program of our own, we may invite some qualified person to assist the nationals of that country in a flow of information *toward* the United States.

Where might this concept of mutual understanding lead us? As we go on in a genuine belief that we are sincerely trying to understand the ways of life, problems and purposes of other peoples, perhaps our work will become less that of Americans conducting persuasion on a foreign soil and more a partnership arrangement between us Americans and others for the mutual welfare of both of us. We might ask whether this would not lead to a more effective contest with the communists for what has been called "an indispensable basis for credibility"—namely, that the persuasion in each country is carried on primarily by its own nationals. Perhaps at some future time the spokesmen of the free world will in fact appear to be speaking not in the name of some foreign power but in the name of the nationals of their own countries and of their fellow workers and their own neighbors. Perhaps brown, black, and yellow skins can speak to people of similar pigmentation . . . and not in the role of the White Man feared and hated because of his encumbrance of colonial subjugation and exploitation of inferior races.

An overseas representative might even ask the question: Will the American people themselves come to believe so strongly that we are not in this just for the short run but we are in it for keeps, however long that may be, that Americans will be willing to make those same kinds of sacrifices of inclination and personal choice for the purposes of persuasion in the cold war, that all of us have been cheerfully and valiantly ready to accept in a hot war? Will the time then come that every soldier stationed overseas honestly regards himself as a grass-roots ambassador of this country? And will every American tourist feel some responsibility in his actions abroad for reflecting correctly the great traditions and ideals of these United States?

ROBERT J. DONOVAN

*Some Issues for Discussion*

Are we in this cold war for keeps or only for the short run? If we really believe it to be a life and death struggle, what would it be reasonable for Americans to do beyond what we are already doing in American information and cultural representation overseas?

Is there a basic conflict between the concept of peoples speaking to peoples *and* government information and cultural relations programs?

Can a democracy carry out international persuasion on the same basis as a totalitarian power? If not, what is it reasonable to expect that a democracy can do?

What should be the role of cultural relations in supporting United States *government* objectives?

How can American private resources best be employed in supporting American information and cultural representation overseas?

Do we believe that it is better to try and create mutual understanding between Americans and other peoples—or should we concentrate on the use of the proven advertising techniques for selling America? If we want to create mutual understanding, should we be more concerned about how other countries are able to reach American audiences with the story of their cultures, aims, aspirations and values?

*Getting and keeping good people:* Should we have a permanent career service for American information representatives? For American cultural officers? What kind should it be—independent? Part of the Foreign Service of the United States? Should it use a single administrative system at home and abroad? Should we have a national scholarship and training program to commit *early during their college careers* promising young men and women to work as American information and cultural representatives? Do we need a national training center for producing better candidates for such representation—and for providing later training for intermediate and senior officers?

# 38 / U.S. Image Abroad

ROBERT J. DONOVAN

**That the deed is more powerful than the word is an axiom of sophisticated propaganda doctrine. The United States**

Reprinted from *The New York Herald Tribune,* May 13, 1963, by permission.
Robert J. Donovan has for many years been a Washington correspondent of *The New York Herald Tribune.* He is the author of *Eisenhower: The Inside Story* (1956).

must contend with the difficult fact that much of its propaganda effort abroad can be offset by deeds that seem to contradict the words or to blur the desired image. The plural nature of American democracy, particularly federalism, offers special problems for those who would plan and try to implement an information strategy. Some of these problems are acutely illustrated in the following selection.

THESE ARE SOME of the headlines from around the world gathered by the *Herald Tribune* bureaus: "Race Clash—1,000 Children Jailed" (*Daily Mirror*, London); "Explosive Situation in Alabama" (*Unità*, Rome); "Monstrous Crimes of the Racists in the United States" (*Pravda*, Moscow); "Is This America the Beautiful?" (*Times*, Ghana); "Arrests of Schoolchildren Do Not Make a Pretty Picture" (*The Mail*, Kuala Lumpur); "Brutes of Alabama" (*Morning Post*, Lagos); "Savages in Alabama" (*Liberation*, Paris).

This summary of world opinion illustrates what President Kennedy meant at his press conference . . . [May 8, 1963] when he called the racial disorders "a spectacle which was seriously damaging the reputation of both Birmingham and the country."

For two reasons in particular the troubles in Birmingham have been more difficult than even Oxford, Miss., and Little Rock, Ark., were for American officials overseas to explain away.

One reason is that the news photographs from Birmingham—with the dogs, firehoses and arrested Negro children—have been more gripping than the photographs of the Oxford and Little Rock incidents.

The other reason is that in these two previous situations the Federal Government was able to move in with troops to restore order, whereas in Birmingham Federal activity, though intensive and effective, has been hidden and subtle.

In the eyes of other peoples, particularly in Africa, the overt, dramatic Federal intervention in Arkansas and Mississippi compensated for local discrimination against Negroes. The resentment toward the United States that black peoples felt everywhere was assuaged when they beheld the military as well as the moral and legal power of the Federal Government applied to the redress of Negro rights.

In Birmingham, on the other hand, they saw Negroes being checkmated day after day with dogs and firehoses while the Federal Government took no overt action.

The explanation, of course, is that the legal grounds on which the Federal Government intervened in Oxford and Little Rock were absent in Birmingham.

"There isn't any Federal statute that was involved in the last few days in Birmingham," the President told his press conference. "I indicated the areas where the Federal Government had intervened in Birmingham—the matter of voting, the matters of dealing with education and other matters. On the specific issues of the parades, that did not involve a Federal issue."

Even in the United States, where the Federal–State relationship is familiar, this point was widely misunderstood. Mr. Kennedy was receiving stinging criticism from certain Negroes, liberals and others for not going overtly to the assistance of Negroes in Birmingham. Indeed it was a very uncomfortable week for him.

If many Americans failed to grasp the legal distinction, how much more difficult it was for Africans and Asians. Vast numbers of them had no way of knowing that the local disturbances in Birmingham did not thwart the orders of Federal courts as was the case at the University of Mississippi last year and at Central High School in Little Rock in 1957. From their great distances away all that they could see was the sight of Negro masses scuffling with the police in Birmingham.

Press reaction in Ghana and Nigeria, especially, to the supposed lack of Government action was sharply critical.

And the Moscow newspaper *Pravda,* which doubtless knew better, taunted the United States for lack of Federal efforts to settle the troubles. Like certain other papers around the world it linked the Birmingham disorders with the recent fatal shooting of William L. Moore, Baltimore postman, in Alabama while he was hiking across the State to deliver a letter to Gov. Ross R. Barnett, of Mississippi, protesting racial discrimination.

*Pravda* juxtaposed an account of Justice Minister Robert F. Kennedy's recent courtesy visit to racist Governor Wallace in Alabama and the slaying of Mr. Moore. Though known to Mr. Kennedy, the paper said, the murderer was not in jail. More than a week before this article appeared Floyd L. Simpson, a rural store operator in Alabama was arrested on a charge of first degree murder in the case.

A roundup of world opinion as compiled by the U.S. Information Agency shows that up to now, at least, the severest criticism of Birmingham centered in Africa. This was not unexpected. What is more surprising is that so far comment in Western Europe and the Soviet Union has been relatively moderate both in tone and in quantity.

Editorial comment in Western Europe, of which there was little last week, contained less moralizing than heretofore and displayed an understanding of the difficulty of the Negro problem in the United States.

Thus the *Daily Telegraph,* a conservative London paper, noted that the problem is not exclusively an American one but part of a widespread and potentially dangerous condition. "Such scandals of intolerance as these," the paper said, "are not of local but international danger. For

more and more the dark races are conscious of common interests and will support one another's struggles for emancipation."

*La Stampa*, a Liberal paper in Turin, Italy, while deploring the tactics of the Birmingham police, said that the spectacle was not "representative of the true face of the United States."

Remarkably, even *Pravda* said that "to the honor of the American people it must be mentioned that they do not share the view of Alabama's Governor and are deeply disturbed by events in America's South."

Peking news media confined themselves to reporting the Birmingham story and stressing police brutality and the fact that the President had not ordered troops to Alabama.

Cairo papers also singled out police brutality and headlines in Egypt's leading papers called attention to the use of police dogs against Negro demonstrators.

The insidious effect of Birmingham on Africa, in particular, it seems, was to cast doubt on the sincerity of American friendship for the new nations.

Still, while making allowances for the damage done to American prestige last week, USIA reports show that there is now considerably more understanding abroad of the American racial problem than there was when the world was shocked by Little Rock 6 years ago.

Last week, as it had done at the time of Little Rock and of Oxford, the Voice of America broadcast to the world the straight news of the Birmingham disorders. There was no attempt to deny the facts, but drawing on experiences in the two earlier incidents the Voice and other USIA organs did try to put the facts in perspective.

This effort took the form of broadcasts and distribution of commentaries aimed at showing, for example, that:

1. The disorders were greatly deplored by the overwhelming mass of the American people.
2. The problem was primarily regional.
3. Extensive progress in race relations is being made throughout the United States.

The USIA also was making a special effort to make clear to peoples abroad the legal reasons that inhibited the President from intervening in Birmingham. USIA broadcasts have played up the fact that the President and Attorney General Robert F. Kennedy sent Burke Marshall to the troubled city as their personal representative. And attention of foreign audiences has been called to the fact that Mr. Marshall, who is Assistant Attorney General in charge of the Civil Rights Division of the Justice Department, was the man who engineered the settlement that brought the truce Wednesday.

As USIA officials are the first to point out, however, the long-term

307

endeavors to inform public opinion abroad about the progress of race relations in America is at least as important as efforts made abruptly in the midst of a crisis like last week's.

These longer range efforts take such form as circulation of pamphlets and books by Negroes through overseas American libraries, broadcasts by leading Negroes, and trips abroad by authorities on race relations, of whom Ralph McGill, editor of the Atlanta *Constitution,* was one of the most recent.

. . . . .

Despite all their best efforts, however, USIA officials admit that all their pamphlets, all their words and books and motion pictures have not half the impact—or one-tenth—of the reports of the actual events that took place in Birmingham.

And if, as was the case in Birmingham, the problem lay outside the powers of the Federal Government, the only answer is that the responsible people of the community come to the realization of their responsibilities as citizens of the United States, and solve these problems before they explode.

# 39 / Soviet Political Warfare: Strengths and Weaknesses

## FREDERICK C. BARGHOORN

What are the principal features of the propaganda programs of the U.S.S.R.? This is a question to be considered in any study of American efforts in this field, since one inevitable mission of American propaganda programs is to counter Soviet propaganda. Professor Barghoorn traces the history of Soviet propaganda doctrine and analyzes its major features, its strengths and weaknesses.

Reprinted from John Boardman Whitton, ed., *Propaganda and the Cold War* (Washington, D.C.: Public Affairs Press, 1963), pp. 13–24, By permission. Footnotes have been omitted.

Frederick C. Barghoorn is professor of political science, Yale University, and a leading authority on the Soviet Union. He is the author of *The Soviet Image of the United States* (1950), *The Soviet Cultural Offensive* (1956), and *Soviet Foreign Propaganda* (1964).

HOW EFFECTIVE is Soviet propaganda? Not many problems confronting social scientists or men of affairs could be more difficult than those raised by this question. It is equally clear that few problems facing the policy-makers of non-communist countries are more significant and urgent than those with which this paper is concerned. Unfortunately, in the present state of our knowledge it is possible to give only the most general and approximate answers to the questions which we shall raise. This is true for a number of reasons, of which the following may perhaps be singled out for mention. Outside of case studies which may or may not exist in government files, there is an appalling dearth of the descriptive, historical, analytical and statistical data which would be necessary for the appraisal of the effectiveness of Soviet and other communist propaganda activities. Secondly—and this is even more fundamental—the methodological problems involved in relating propaganda to other branches of policy and evaluating the impact of policies upon the situations which they seek to identify and to influence are formidable indeed.

This paper, then, will raise more questions than it can possibly hope to answer. It will present some of the data which have come to the attention of this author in his study of the theory, history, strategy and tactics and organization of Soviet propaganda and which are pertinent to an evaluation of the effectiveness of this propaganda. It will also refer to some of the abundant evidence of the defects and weaknesses of Soviet propaganda. In addition, it will be concerned with the context in which Soviet propaganda has operated, and in particular with the predispositions, especially in the developing areas, which at least in the short run render the task of the Soviet propagandists in some ways an easier one than that confronting western, particularly American efforts to exert influence. It will also seek to perceive meaningful relationships between predispositions on the one hand and Soviet efforts to exploit them, on the other. Finally, it will be concerned to some extent with organizational structures and techniques and with the scope and dimensions of the Soviet propaganda effort.

In their pioneer case study of communist propaganda in Chicago, Lasswell and Blumenstock pointed out that the success of propaganda depended upon "the exercise of skill under favorable circumstances." Lasswell and Blumenstock distinguished between tactics of propaganda involving the two main elements of "distinctiveness" and "adaptiveness," and the strategy of propaganda which required "combination"—more or less synonymous, it seems to this author, with "alliance"—as well as what Lasswell and Blumenstock referred to as "precaution." The propaganda strategist must combine sufficient semantic rigidity and consistency to retain control over his followers, with sufficient flexibility in the choice of terminology and organizational methods to attract new followers. At the same time, he must associate his movement and its goals with other

political parties, movements and associations, and simultaneously be on guard against possible hostile counter-offensives. In this paper, we shall tend to merge Lasswell's concepts of tactics and strategy into one set of maxims, calling for a combination of consistency and flexibility adequate to deal with changing circumstances without running excessive risks of confusion and dissipation of effort.

Another useful organizing principle is the distinction drawn by Dyer between a propaganda policy which seeks "conversion" and one that seeks "relevant political action." Dyer's terms help us to understand the problem of the Soviet leadership in combining long-run ideological consistency with short-run political expediency. This is a problem of all propagandists, and in particular of revolutionary propagandists. A major purpose of communist propaganda is to facilitate the recruitment of party members. As one scholar has written, the technique of attraction and indoctrination involved in this effort "produces revolutionaries and makes possible both the party and its hope for eventual success."

The program of the Communist Party of the Soviet Union adopted by its Twenty-second Congress in October, 1961 identifies "the social revolution" as the party's goal. The program goes on to say that "imperialism is decaying and moribund capitalism; it is the eve of the socialist revolution. The world capitalist system as a whole is ripe for the social revolution of the proletariat." The universalization of the Soviet social-political and economic-cultural pattern remains the ultimate professed objective of the CPSU. However, the CPSU and other ruling communist parties must function not only as revolutionary political movements but also as the directing cadres and controlling elements of governments. This governmental function of ruling communist parties imposes upon them policy and administrative problems and tasks which of course encompass far more than revolutionary propaganda and agitation. The Soviet and other ruling communist parties of the world must develop economic, military, diplomatic and propaganda policies to deal with "capitalist" governments as long as the latter survive and oppose the efforts of communists to subvert them, by effecting what Khrushchev in his political report to the Twentieth Congress of the CPSU in 1956 referred to as the necessary and inevitable "revolutionary transformation of society." The duality of Soviet policy and propaganda resulting from this combination of revolutionary and conventional aspects presents baffling problems both to the Soviet leaders and to non-communist statesmen and political analysts.

Once it became apparent, shortly after the Bolshevik Revolution of 1917, that communist power would not immediately overrun Europe and Asia, the Soviet leaders were confronted with the problem of reconciling the somewhat conflicting interests of the Soviet state and of international communism. Lenin and his successors generally tended to sacrifice the

immediate interests of international communism in favor of those of the Soviet state, rationalizing this practice with the argument that in the long run the two were identical. The development of the "world system of socialism" after World War II of course has further complicated the pattern. We cannot in this paper deal with the impact upon Soviet propaganda of the Sino-Soviet dispute or the problems of "polycentric communism," but it would be unrealistic not to mention them as part of the general political context in which current Soviet propaganda operates. While seeking to influence the behavior both of communists and non-communists in the "capitalist" countries, Soviet propaganda must at all times take into account the problems connected with maintaining the cohesiveness, first of all of Soviet society and secondly of the Sino-Soviet bloc—if indeed one can still meaningfully refer to the various communist-ruled states as a "bloc."

At the same time, the leaders of the CPSU and of other ruling communist parties must at all times be concerned with the relative roles to be assigned, in their total policy effort, to force and subversion, whether exercised directly from the Soviet or Chinese power base or indirectly by means of local subversive and guerrilla activities—and to various forms of diplomacy and persuasion. Propaganda, defined by Lasswell as "the management of mass communications for power purposes," certainly plays an important part in Soviet foreign policy. Communists, clearly, will achieve their objectives by the relatively inexpensive instrument of propaganda, if they can do so. However, their doctrine, as well as their experience, teaches that the outcome of political battles is likely to be decided mainly by superior power. There is no convincing evidence that even the Soviet communists, let alone the Chinese, have repudiated Lenin's dictum that great political problems are decided, in the final analysis, by force. It should of course be emphasized that force does not necessarily mean all-out war, particularly in the modern era of super-weapons. Khrushchev's doctrine, however, does include support of so-called wars of "national liberation."

Perhaps the most striking characteristic of Soviet foreign propaganda, especially since the death of Stalin, has been its alertness and energy in seeking to link up Soviet policies with the dynamic, revolutionary forces of our era. Soviet propaganda seeks to harness to the chariot of Kremlin power the grievances and aspirations of the most diverse social, national, ethnic and even religious groups. Despite certain rigidities, Soviet propaganda has on the whole achieved much of the adaptiveness and flexibility which Lasswell and Blumenstock regarded as essential to propaganda skill and effectiveness. It has often succeeded in more than overcoming the disadvantages of ideological orthodoxy, of totalitarian organizational ponderousness and of the fear of freedom inherent in communism. These and other weaknesses of Soviet communism and its

propaganda behavior have been counterbalanced, at least in many situations and in many parts of the world, by purposiveness, strength of will, energy and scope of effort and above all by skill in selecting and exploiting sensitive propaganda targets.

The foregoing remarks lead us, however, to reiterate once more the enormous importance of certain favorable predispositions in facilitating such propaganda successes as the communists have achieved. Our era is one of social and ideological revolution on a scale unprecedented in the history of mankind. The "deprivational changes"—to borrow a phrase from Lasswell—inherent in this situation have of course been compounded by the effects of two world wars. Add to all this the anxieties induced among all thinking people by the existence of nuclear weapons and one has a situation pregnant with potential for propaganda manipulation.

Our emphasis on the factors in the international environment which may foster susceptibility to the appeals of communism is in no sense fatalistic or defeatist. If we are to cope with communist influence, we must perceive its dimensions and proportions as clearly as possible. Awareness of the predispositions which favor communist influence may, in many instances, stimulate action designed to alter the circumstances which feed pro-communist attitudes. It may also prevent us from falling into the trap—sure to be set for us—of indiscriminately labelling all social protest movements as "communist." Finally, it may facilitate refutation of communist propaganda by enabling us to point to incompatibilities between standard communist operating procedures and the promises communists often make to disturbed persons unaware of the gulf between propaganda and reality.

Soviet propaganda has energetically exploited both the negative and the positive sentiments generated by the revolutionary social-political and psycho-cultural developments of the twentieth century. Paul Kecskemeti has pointed out that Soviet propaganda has been most successful when it has been in a position to protect an image of the Soviet Union as being bent on combating a "manifest evil." In Kecskemeti's opinion, it has been able to make a significant impact only in such situations, when it could win helpers, or at least benevolent neutrality toward Soviet policy, by identifying Moscow with opposition to the effects of (1) the first world war; (2) the rise of Nazi Germany; (3) the fear of war in the late 1940s; (4) the decline of colonialism in Asia and Africa. It will be noted that three of the four situations identified by Kecskemeti as exceptionally favorable to the success of Soviet foreign propaganda were concerned with the effects or the fear of war.

Kecskemeti correctly emphasized the essentially negative character of Soviet foreign propaganda. However, he wrote before the full development of certain major features of post-Stalin propaganda. In the last few

years, Moscow has made increasingly successful efforts to project important positive propaganda themes, especially to the peoples of the less-developed countries and the newly emerging nations of the world. As Dyer noted, in commenting on Soviet propaganda handling of the launching in 1957 of Soviet artificial earth satellites, the Soviet Union "proclaimed a right to leadership on the ground that its knowledge was superior." Soviet propaganda regarding such matters as educational and scientific progress, economic development, and the alleged Soviet solution of the "nationality problem" has, in effect, told the peoples of the developing areas that by following the Soviet path of economic, social and political development, they could most effectively realize their own legitimate aspirations. John A. Armstrong has written that "The old dedication to world revolution as the answer to burning social problems has almost vanished. In its place is the constantly reiterated theme that the USSR must be emulated because it is—aside from 'historical accidents' like the United States—the most successful country on earth."

The remarks of Dyer and Armstrong raise a question to which the student of Soviet propaganda impact must devote attention. To what extent has Soviet propaganda been effective because of the appeals of Marxist-Leninist ideology to disaffected intellectuals, working men and occasional bright and discontented peasants, and to what extent does it owe its appeal to the tangible evidence of Soviet scientific, technical and industrial progress? Khrushchev evidently regards the latter considerations as the most important, to judge by his emphasis, beginning in 1956, on the importance of victory in the "battle of production" as the key to the world triumph of communism. This conviction is also indicated by current stress, in Soviet articles regarding propaganda and ideology, on the central place of the propaganda of production in these spheres.

Soviet propaganda has systematically exploited such major issues as peace, nationalism and the desire of the dynamic elements in underdeveloped societies for "modernization." From the earliest days of the Soviet regime, and indeed dating back to a period several years before the Bolshevik Revolution, Lenin and his followers obviously regarded exploitation of mankind's revulsion against war and hope for lasting peace as a central area of propaganda opportunity. This is one of the areas of greatest continuity in Bolshevik propaganda. There has always been a communist effort to convince intellectuals and others that lasting peace can only be achieved by the abolition of "capitalism" and the establishment of a "socialist" society. Of course, complex tactics have been involved in this effort. While eschewing pacifism, for example, in doctrinal communications to communists, the Kremlin in its communications to "bourgeois" audiences has often sought to exploit pacifist moods and movements. In establishing links with such moods and movements, they have concealed, played down or even blandly denied the class struggle

and violence aspects of their theory. Similarly, while they tell their fellow-believers that disarmament is impossible as long as capitalism remains in power, they seek in their propaganda to non-communists to demonstrate their devotion to disarmament. These are only among the more obvious aspects of the immensely complicated Soviet and communist effort in the field of peace and disarmament propaganda.

In connection with the foregoing it may be useful to note that concealment of certain aspects of communist doctrine and practices is as significant—if negative—a mode of communist communications behavior as is the communists' insistence on bringing their slogans to the forefront of world attention. Just as it is important for opponents of communism not to engage in "red-baiting," so also, in view of communist secrecy, is it important, in some situations, to deprive communists of the advantages of "innocence by association" with respectable symbols, movements and aspirations.

Soviet propaganda has sought to associate its effort to create an image of Soviet peaceful intentions with other major themes. For example, in its exploitation of national sentiments, especially those of colonial and newly emerging peoples, Soviet propaganda seeks to gain favor by arguing that if Moscow's disarmament proposals were accepted, vast economic resources would be freed for use in assisting the economic development of the new nations. This observation leads us into the problem of the uses of nationalism in Soviet propaganda. While in many fundamental ways Soviet communism is exceedingly nationalistic and chauvinistic, it has never abandoned the profession of belief, very useful in a revolutionary era, in "proletarian internationalism." To trace this theme to its origins would require an extensive analysis of Leninist thinking. Suffice it to say here that the communists combine belief in the transitory "bourgeois" character of nationalism as a pattern of beliefs, with immense sophistication in exploiting nationalist sentiments and aspirations for short-run tactical purposes. Perhaps the two major weapons of Soviet propaganda in this area are, first, support for "national liberation" movements in colonial countries, supplemented by support for the aspirations of formerly colonial countries against alleged "imperialist" attempts to impede the economic and cultural development of such countries, and, secondly, propaganda regarding the Soviet model of the solution of the "national problem" inside the USSR. To the dissemination and application of both of these themes Soviet propaganda has devoted impressive energy.

Finally, in this brief survey of Soviet "adaptiveness" in associating the image of Moscow with the legitimate aspirations of mankind, we should say a few words about "modernization," Soviet style. There is no doubt that Soviet success in rapid economic development of a formerly backward society—one which in many ways, especially those pertaining

to the comfort, convenience and dignity of the individual, is still rather backward—made a great impression throughout the world, especially of course in the developing areas, but also to a considerable degree even in the most advanced industrial countries, at least in periods of economic depression. Students of world affairs are familiar with some of the major aspects of Soviet progress, such as spectacular achievements in space technology, very high rates of economic growth, vast efforts in education, especially technical education, and the like. If all of this impresses even sophisticated western Europeans and Americans, it is only sensible to assume that its impact on those in the underdeveloped countries who see in rapid modernization of their societies the path to national and social dignity and salvation, must be immense.

The foregoing remarks relate to the general area of propaganda "strategy." Let us now turn briefly to some aspects of the organization, techniques and dimensions of Soviet propaganda. The major advantage possessed by the communists in their world-wide propaganda activities is, of course, the existence of the international communist movement and the various "fronts" which partially mask and certainly assist the efforts of communist parties to "carry the word" to non-communists. Among the many advantages of Moscow and Peking in possessing a network of international organizations one might mention the useful intelligence activities of members of these organizations, which help to enable the communist leaders to appraise the attitudes of their target audiences, the concealment of ultimate aims made possible when an essentially alien ideology is presented by "natives," and, of course, the unity of command in policy and propaganda made possible by this system of organizations. However, the international, centrally-directed and hierarchical pattern of communist organization for propaganda has its disadvantages too. The tendency to "speak with one voice" can induce monotony and corresponding boredom. If policy at the center is incorrect, so will policy in the field be incorrect. The fact is that it is exceedingly difficult to know whether the advantages inherent in centralism and monolithism—to the degree that it survives—outweigh the corresponding disadvantages.

Much in communist foreign propaganda behavior can be explained by the effort to overcome the isolation from local societies inherent in the centralist communist organizational pattern. In order to link up communist goals with local interests and aspirations, conspiracy and deception must be practiced on a wide scale. While sometimes successful, this effort of course can also arouse mistrust and suspicion. One way of writing the history of international communist propaganda would be to organize it around the exigencies of the problems posed by this situation. It must be admitted, of course, that the communists, particularly since the death of Stalin, have shown ingenuity and skill in overcoming the disadvantages of ideological orthodoxy. Perhaps their most important weapon in this

regard has been the development of "personal diplomacy," as practiced by Khrushchev, for example, on his trips to India, Burma and Afghanistan in 1955, and to India, Burma, Indonesia and Malaya in 1960, and of course during his spectacular and flamboyant appearances before the United Nations General Assembly in 1959 and 1960.

While in New York in 1960 Khrushchev, it will be recalled, went out of his way personally to cultivate Afro-Asian diplomats and heads of state. Besides its obvious relationship to Soviet exploitation of anti-colonialist and even at times "anti-white" sentiments, this tactic illustrates the surprising sensitivity of the Soviet "Marxists" to emotional and subjective factors in politics. In their foreign aid policy, for example, the Russians have displayed not only impressive alertness to opportunities to attract attention to their sometimes spectacular projects but also considerable solicitude regarding the national and cultural pride of recipient countries. In part, their apparent success in these efforts results from the appeal of Soviet poverty in contrast to American affluence, but in part also it reflects good organization, briefing and training in local languages.

Khrushchev's activities, of course, represent only some of the more successful Soviet efforts to solve problems related to what Philip Selznick in his study, *The Organizational Weapon*, identifies as "the strategy of access." Other aspects of Soviet efforts in this direction include infiltration of non-communist organizations, more or less successful concealment, for considerable periods at least, of the ultimate communist identity and control of various "front" groups, etc. It should be emphasized that in their use of face-to-face communication the communists to a considerable degree succeed in overcoming the disadvantages of ideological orthodoxy and organizational rigidity. Especially in talking to non-communist politicians and businessmen, have Khrushchev and other Soviet leaders often been successful in disseminating deceptive and reassuring images of Soviet intentions. A brilliant example of Khrushchev's application of such techniques was his appearance on American television on the "Open End" program in 1960, when Khrushchev, as one observer noted, probably succeeded in conveying to many Americans an image of himself as "peace-loving as any grandfather."

It is plausible to assume that a combination of the predispositions of many audiences in the world today with systematic, large-scale Soviet exploitation of these predispositions, will lead to Soviet propaganda effectiveness. This will be particularly true in the absence of effective free world concern. However, as we pointed out in the beginning, direct evidence of Soviet propaganda effectiveness is extremely scanty. There have been, of course, a few published studies which strongly suggest that certain Soviet activities, particularly in the area of space technology, have had a powerful world propaganda impact. There are also bits and pieces of data regarding the audiences of Soviet exhibitions, especially in under-

developed areas, and for Soviet and other communist radio broadcasts. According to one unclassified United States government report, the Soviets claimed that 1.4 million people attended an exhibition that they put on in Colombo, Ceylon, in 1959 and one million attended a Soviet exhibition in Mexico City. With regard to the audiences for Soviet radio broadcasts, information received by this writer from an authoritative United States government source indicates that Soviet radio broadcasts do not have as large a foreign audience as is achieved by the Voice of America or the BBC. Soviet foreign propaganda efforts have apparently been somewhat more successful in the area of "cultural exchange" and generally in the employment of face-to-face communication than in the use of mass media. It would appear that the impact of Soviet ballet, motion pictures and other artistic productions, as well as the impact of Soviet sports groups, has been considerable.

While such efforts may not convert anyone to communism, they tend to disarm suspicion of Soviet and communist intentions and to convey subtly an image of friendliness, humanitarianism and general good will. This may influence the attitudes of peoples toward their governments and the foreign policies of their governments and it may, in countries such as India, Indonesia and other countries with severe social problems, enhance the respectability both of the Soviet Union and of local communist parties. In connection with Soviet export of motion pictures, it may be of interest to note that according to Reference Paper No. 23, 1960/1961, distributed by the Soviet Affairs Analysis Service of the American Committee for Liberation, such Soviet movies as "The Cranes Are Flying" and "Ballad of a Soldier," which have enjoyed widespread success in the non-Soviet world, do not conform to the orthodox rules of Soviet motion picture art and, despite the accolades which they received in the West, were treated very coldly in official Soviet motion picture criticism. This example typifies a certain degree of success in Soviet efforts to overcome the disadvantages of ideological orthodoxy in the area of foreign propaganda.

The foregoing observation leads us to a few remarks concerning some of the major weaknesses and defects of Soviet and other communist propaganda. Despite the adaptiveness and flexibility to which we have referred, Soviet propaganda still is handicapped somewhat by the rigidity of the categories with which it views the world. In the long run, the ideological rigidity of communism may prove to be its most fatal weakness in its competition with the free world. As Edward R. Murrow recently pointed out, "The Soviet way is the way of required orthodoxy." Soviet efforts to overcome the disadvantages of orthodoxy are tactical rather than fundamental. That this is true is indicated by the failure of the Soviet Union to modify basically its secrecy practices. It is true that there is a considerably greater flow of persons and of information across

Soviet frontiers than in Stalin's day. Even more significant are recent indications that Soviet opinion manipulators are beginning to study and even to apply empirical social science. However, analysis of the Soviet communications pattern seems, on the whole, to indicate continued adherence to a tightly controlled system, in which even intellectuals and creative artists cannot openly or fundamentally question the pattern or orthodoxy at the heart of Soviet culture. While for a long time to come this rigidity may be a source of strength rather than of weakness, no believer in the values of the "open society" can doubt that eventually this pattern must be basically modified or stagnation or revolt will follow. Unfortunately, in many parts of the world where freedom ranks low on the order of priorities of politically active groups, Soviet orthodoxy and secrecy may perhaps not be a great liability, or even a liability at all. Even more unfortunate is the fact that the West has, thus far not made a vigorous and systematic effort to expose the backwardness and ludicrousness of Soviet secrecy. "What are you hiding?" and "What are you afraid of?" are questions we should more often put to the rulers of communist states.

Perhaps one of many sets of questions remaining in the mind of the reader of this paper is concerned with the size and scope of the Soviet communication effort. There is no doubt that the effort is a big one, although not as vast as we sometimes think. According to information received from the United States government source already referred to, it was estimated that as of 1957 the total communist bloc foreign propaganda effort amounted, in terms of American dollars, to something between $475,000,000 and $700,000,000. . . . The Soviet part of this total effort was estimated as about forty per cent. Reflecting the communist fear of free communication was the fact that it was estimated that the USSR alone was spending about $115,000,000 a year, as of 1961, for the jamming of foreign radio broadcasts, a figure in excess of the estimated Soviet expenditure for transmitting radio broadcasts to foreign countries. These latter figures are indicative both of the energy, determination and scope of the Soviet effort and of its grave weaknesses. Certainly Soviet propaganda is not the magic instrument which some alarmists conceive it to be. On the other hand, in some parts of the world, especially during periods of acute instability, it can be a powerful, perhaps at times even a decisive instrument of policy. Further systematic efforts of research and analysis will be necessary before we can rise much above the level of guesses and impressions to which this paper has perforce been confined.

# 40 / The Challenge of Ideological Warfare

GEORGE GALLUP

Are American efforts in persuasion overseas adequately supported? Do the existing programs reach a large enough audience? Is Russia more successful? Opinions on these and related questions are contained in this selection by one of America's leading experts on public opinion.

IT IS MY PERSONAL BELIEF that Russia is a good generation ahead of us in her understanding of propaganda and in her skill in using it. Many people in public life in this country pay lip service to the idea that the great struggle of this era is the battle for the minds of men, they are quite willing to admit that Russia has scored many victories, but they are still unready and unwilling to map out a campaign of the dimensions necessary to match Soviet efforts.

A notable exception to this is Senator Karl Mundt and his committee who have been seeking funds to establish a Freedom Academy.

Some years ago I had suggested to a Senatorial committee that five billion dollars spent on today's tanks, guns, and battleships will make far less difference in achieving ultimate victory over communism than five billion dollars appropriated for ideological warfare.

I do not mean to imply that money alone can do this job. The mere expenditure of large sums of money offers no guarantee of winning the cold war. We must have an effective message, and what is of equal importance, we must make sure that it is effective before we spend the money.

But you can't sell people unless you reach them, and this costs a lot of money. You can't do this job with mirrors. No one has figured out a better formula than the one the communists are presently using.

I once laid down the dictum that the best and the safest principle to follow in fighting an ideological war, at least at this stage of our knowledge, is to follow the rules of shooting war.

We must reach *more people, more often,* and with a *better message* than the enemy.

Reprinted from John Boardman Whitton, ed., *Propaganda and the Cold War* (Washington, D.C.: Public Affairs Press, 1963), pp. 54–56. By permission.

George Gallup is perhaps the most famous of all "pollsters." He is Director of the American Institute of Public Opinion, and as such directs the "Gallup Poll." He is also President of the International Institutes of Public Opinion and the author of many works on public opinion.

One other principle which works in every field—whether it be warfare or business—is to find out what succeeds and then do more of it. It can easily be demonstrated that learning a foreign language pre-disposes one towards that country. We are presently making a small-scale effort to teach people of the world the English language. But instead of teaching thousands of persons, we should be teaching scores of millions. We would be mightily concerned if Russia went all out to teach the people of the neutral nations the Russian language. Yet, we seem to be happy doing a wholly inadequate job of teaching our language, and distributing only a relatively few of the millions of textbooks which students in the underdeveloped nations are eager to obtain from this country.

We should bring all of the teachers of the world to the United States who wish to come. We should work out a carefully guided tour to give them the best possible impression of the country. We should take the same attitude towards these visitors that we do when we invite people into our homes. We don't take our guests immediately to the cellar or to the attic to show them what bad housekeepers we are. We show them what we ourselves are most proud of.

Some people would like to ignore completely this fight for the minds of men. Many hope that if we are strong militarily that somehow strength in this department will solve our propaganda job.

But you can't kill ideas even with H-Bombs. There is absolutely no possible way out of fighting the ideological war. In order to compensate for defense which we are constantly suffering, we naturally tend to lean more heavily on the armed services, appropriating more billions for defense.

So, no matter how you figure it, the most *economical* and most *effective* way to deal with Russia is to try to match her efforts in ideological warfare.

If a country is lost to communism through propaganda and subversion it is lost to our side as irretrievably as if we had lost it in actual warfare.

We often overlook the fact that a good many of our friends and allies can be lost to us almost overnight. All it takes in any of these nations is just one election in which the communists gain enough votes to take control. And we would have to sit by helplessly—unless we renounced the very democratic principles which we espouse.

Another fact which seems to have escaped the thinking of our Congressional leaders is that *total victory* in a new world war would not resolve the ideological war. Just try to imagine the problem this country and our allies would face in trying to police Russia and China and to keep communism from rearing its ugly head again. No, the problem would not only *not* be solved, it would be intensified.

Why have our leaders been so slow in recognizing the importance of ideological warfare?

One argument frequently advanced against an adequate propaganda program is that we don't need propaganda—that deeds speak louder than words. Maybe in an ideal world this is true, but the best proof that this view is false is the very success of the communist efforts at this time in Asia, Africa, and Europe. *Communist deeds are the exact opposite of its words.*

Another argument—akin to the first—is that we have no right to speak out until we, as a nation, are perfect, that we must set our own house in order first. If this rule were applied strictly, we would have no preachers of Christianity—except the saints—and certainly there would be no advertising, because no product or institution has yet reached a state of perfection.

Still another argument is based upon the misconception that propaganda is necessarily based upon lies, and that on moral grounds, if no other, we should not engage in propaganda. The word, unfortunately, has acquired a bad odor, thanks to Goebbels and his modern Russian counterparts. But the most effective propaganda, like the teachings of Christianity, can and should be based upon the truth. A lie, repeated endlessly, can be sold to many; but what is often overlooked is that truth, *by the process of repetition, can be sold more easily than lie.*

A final argument is the one I mentioned earlier. There is no point in spending billions of dollars unless we are certain that we are getting results. With this I am in complete agreement.

And that is where research comes in.

I believe that the only department in which we may have an advantage over the Russians is in our research methods for pre-testing propaganda ideas and for measuring their success in use.

We do not need to spend millions of dollars on ideas or programs which later are discovered to be ineffective. Through research it is possible to find out which of many basic appeals should be incorporated into our propaganda program and to measure the effect of these ideas in changing attitudes.

Through research it should be possible to discover the best way of nullifying the enemies' propaganda. Through research we can know at all times, and in every target area, just who is winning the propaganda battle and we can learn a lot about the why.

# 41 / Strengthening American Information Efforts

## ALLEN W. DULLES

Do we overrate the comparative advantages of the Communists in operating foreign propaganda programs? The Soviet Union has encountered some major difficulties in recent years, according to the following selection.

WE ARE TOO MUCH INCLINED to attribute to the Soviets, and to the communist movement generally, clear-cut blueprints of where they are going and what themes in the propaganda field they propose to exploit over the years. We are too inclined to ascribe to their propaganda the attributes of long range and subtle direction. We are also somewhat too apologetic about our own efforts in this field.

Of course, we must assume that the Soviet, as Mr. Khrushchev has said so often, will continue to preach that communism is the wave of the future; that over the years it will be adopted by all nations, including the United States. In effect they claim that our system will be "buried" by the force and dynamism of the communist movement.

To put matters in perspective, it may be worthwhile to look at the contradictions and failures that the communist world has had to "swallow" in their propaganda over recent months and years.

*First:* They have recently had to return to the charge that Stalin, the head of the communist movement for over twenty-five years and the dictator of the Soviet Union over this period, was a cruel and ruthless man, guilty of repressions and crimes against his own people and wild adventurism in the foreign field. They started this campaign in 1956 with Khrushchev's famous speech to the Twentieth Party Congress. However, they never dared publish this in full in the Soviet Union. Hence they had to substantiate this charge at the Twenty-second Party Congress during 1961 and tell the people that they really meant what they had only partially disclosed more than five years before. The name of Stalin has now disappeared from "Stalingrad" and elsewhere and his body left the tomb he was sharing with Lenin. In fact in their propaganda they have had to try to rewrite or bury the history of twenty-five years, which pre-

Reprinted from John Boardman Whitton, ed., *Propaganda and the Cold War* (Washington, D.C.: Public Affairs Press, 1963), pp. 72–74. By permission.

Allen W. Dulles was Director of Central Intelligence, 1953–62. He is the author of *Germany's Underground* (1947) and *The Craft of Intelligence* (1963).

ceded 1953. This has resulted in some of the silliest bits of historical juggling that the world has ever seen.

*Second:* They have had to explain the brutal repudiation without prior notice of the agreement regarding the nuclear test moratorium. This they flaunted in the face of the meeting of the unaligned nations at Belgrade.

If we, in the United States, had done something of this kind, everybody here would be saying that our propaganda had gone completely mad.

*Third:* They have had to explain why a Berlin wall was required to stop hundreds of thousands of people trying to escape from what they portray as a communist "heaven."

*Fourth:* They have had to admit critical agricultural failures other than those which they could blame on God and the weather.

*Fifth:* They have had to explain their ignominious retreat from Albania.

*Sixth:* Likewise they have had to cover up their failures in the Congo and Guinea in Africa.

Finally, and most importantly, after making the welkin ring with the claim that communist-socialist regimes could be counted upon to lie down together in peace and unity, they have been engaged in an open brawl with communist China, which has reached the point of seriously affecting relations between the two largest communist countries.

In fact, faced with a series of contradictions and failures, they have resorted to the use of tactics in their propaganda that we would repudiate and would consider totally counter-productive. In true Pavlovian style the communists attempt the use of shock treatment, the carrot and the stick—and expect that we and the other people in the Free World will like it. They believe that at times brutal attacks are more productive than honey; that it is better to instill fear than affection.

While we have something to learn from communist propaganda techniques, particularly their willingness to repeat themes endlessly until people begin to swallow them, I see no reason why we should either emulate them, or ascribe to them a power or effectiveness which I do not believe they really have. It is true that they are adept in repeating misrepresentations—as, for example, their charge about our having indulged in germ warfare in the Korean war, and more recently that American agencies supported the plot of the French generals against DeGaulle. Both of these were patent lies, but the latter of these themes was repeated by serious elements of our press as though it were a fact.

We cannot expect that we can make all of the people of the world love us all of the time. In the interest of our security and world peace, from time to time we have to do things that some people do not like.

We must also realize that we cannot penetrate a *closed* society with

its Iron Curtains, its radio jamming and the like, with the ease that the Soviets can penetrate our own *open* society.

I suggest that in our own public posture toward the rest of the world we should have the following objectives in mind:

1. To bring people to respect, but not necessarily to love us.

2. To support all measures which will break down the barriers to the communication of ideas between the Free World and the countries behind the Curtain.

3. To be realistic and hard-headed in our programs of aid.

4. To expand greatly the availability of good English language books and publications throughout the world, particularly taking advantage of the fact that English is the lingua franca of much of the world outside of the Anglo-Saxon nations.

# 42 / From *The Weapon on the Wall: Rethinking Psychological Warfare*

MURRAY DYER

**How can the United States use more effectively the propaganda instrument of foreign policy? This is a sophisticated view of the potentialities and limitations of propaganda.**

IF WE ARE to develop and use the instrument of political communication to an extent commensurate with its potential capabilities, we must realize that a certain pattern has been created by our past history and experiences with the activity and that this pattern requires some alterations in essential particulars.

We have to remember that a considerable amount of our recent experience is rooted in war. Ever since the end of World War II it has been in terms of the cold war that we have resorted to political communication. But if the concept put forward in this book is accepted, political communication is neither solely nor chiefly military in context. It

Reprinted from *The Weapon on the Wall: Rethinking Psychological Warfare* (Baltimore, Md.: The Johns Hopkins Press, 1959), pp. 194–98. By permission.

Murray Dyer is a consultant on international affairs at the Research Analysis Corporation, Bethesda, Maryland. During World War II, he served with the Office of War Information. He has written several essays and reports on propaganda and has had extensive experience in newspaper and radio journalism.

must be regarded, rather, as an integral instrument available to government at all times for the furtherance and attainment of national aims.

On the basis of the premises that govern it, political communication is an honorable and important means, ranking with the instruments of diplomacy, the military art, and economic measures, which can be effectively employed, not intermittently, but as an essential component of the daily practice of government. We are more accustomed to think of it, under the name in current use—psychological warfare—as a military weapon. In time of war this aspect of it assumes prominence. But at all other times political communication possesses a more significant and wider role as an instrument of government for the prevention of hostilities and the preservation of peace.

It is the capabilities and requirements of political communication as an instrument, and not its subordinate aspect as a weapon, that require development. The problem here is one of grasping the distinction between the part and the whole when, in the past, our experience has weighted the scales heavily on the side of its military characteristics.

We have to consider, also, our ingrained reluctance to attempt to influence the thinking of others, except in times of stress. This has been referred to as a business contrary to our ordinary practice. This comment reflects a generally accepted viewpoint. And, indeed, if political communication is thought of as chiefly broadcasting and propaganda leaflets, there is a good deal to be said for it. But political communication is not a matter of slanted or selected information. It is, in essence, as has been said earlier, the interpretation and explanation of a nation's action and policy. If this is accepted, there should be no reluctance to our making the fullest possible use of it. The attempt that is being made, in these circumstances, to influence the thinking of others is not in terms of trickery or only partial revelation of the facts. The objective is the presentation of our national position so lucidly and unequivocally that all who are affected will understand clearly what we mean and what we intend. And it should be our hope that these intentions will affect not only thinking, but decisions, in terms of relevant political action that will accord with our aims. Obviously our aims, in such circumstances, must be congruent with basic desires and aspirations of free men. But this assumption is implicit in any program of political communication undertaken by the government of a free society.

Furthermore, we shall have to stop thinking of this activity as propaganda in an odious sense, and the concept must be broadened to include far more than merely information work. Information work, in fact, which is what is thought of now, for example, when the activities of USIA are considered, becomes of secondary concern. Instead of merchandising American culture, American literature, arts, crafts, and political

325

practices, the task takes on the aspect of militant interpretation of the significance of the actions and decisions of the executive, legislative, and judicial branches of government. To the extent that we can demonstrate that these are consonant with the common desires of mankind, we may hope for acceptance and thinking that generally will support our moves. In the event that we are narrow and chauvinistic in our actions, we ought to expect quick rebuttal and evidence that should, if political communication is to fulfill its function, impel us to reconsider and re-assess our proposed courses of action.

Beyond this, we must also accept the instrument as auxiliary only, never primary. In the past, at times, there has been a disposition to look on it as capable of accomplishing ends by itself and on its own. The evidence for this is slight and the logic for it unconvincing. The minds of men are not changed by words—they are changed under the impact of dynamic ideas translated into concrete action that proves the conviction behind the idea.

In trying to accomplish our purposes by propaganda alone we can be shown largely to have failed, and for reasons previously given. This is a mark of immaturity. In the past, too often, we have been fired with missionary zeal for what we have termed the American way of life, and we have set out to try to convert others, perhaps almost as literally as the missionaries of the nineteenth century tried to convert the "heathen" and this is an impossible and thankless task in which we are vulnerable to the ancient admonition: physician, heal thyself.

We have to remember that both we and those to whom we may be talking still have great gaps in our knowledge and in our practices and that we know nothing that permits us to assume that we can get away with preaching. We can draw, and lead, and assume responsibilities, but we can do this successfully only if we demonstrate that we, too, are learning even while we seek action that accords with our objectives.

A further problem for attention centers on personnel. The history of our experience shows that we have had many unhappy moments involving personnel. In World War II psychological warfare was, essentially, a civilian activity carried on in theaters of military operations. Many of the qualifications for the kind of work that had to be done called for men who, in Sir Robert Bruce Lockhart's words, were prima donnas. The characteristics of military discipline and the antics of prima donnas do not marry well.

As a result of World War II experience, the Army wants its personnel in this field, in any future hostilities, to be in uniform. In the Korean war the Army ran our psychological warfare operations in the Far East. Relatively few civilians were involved, and those who were came under the classification of DAC's (Department of the Army Civilians), which gave the Army the authority and control it desired.

Recently the Army has been tapping men currently engaged in information work and arranging to use them if hostilities break out. This, in effect, is to weaken the national effort. The major pool of competent personnel for this kind of work is USIA. In the event of war, USIA ought to switch its emphasis from information to psychological warfare and carry on its duties. It will not be able to do this if many of its staff are drawn off into the Armed Services for military psychological warfare duties. And furthermore, strategic psychological warfare is not, under the basic premises, the prerogative solely of the military establishment. It is, first and foremost, national and political in character, not military.

# For Further Reading

BARRETT, EDWARD W. *Truth Is Our Weapon* (New York: Funk and Wagnalls, 1953).

BERELSON, BERNARD, and MORRIS JANOWITZ, eds. *Reader in Public Opinion and Communication* (Glencoe, Ill.: The Free Press, 1953).

BLUM, ROBERT. *Cultural Affairs and Foreign Relations* (Englewood Cliffs, N.J.: Prentice-Hall, 1964).

DIZARD, WILSON P. *The Strategy of Truth: The Story of the U.S. Information Service* (Washington, D.C.: The Public Affairs Press, 1961).

DUNN, FREDERICK S. *War and the Minds of Men* (New York: Harper, 1950).

GOODFRIEND, ARTHUR. *The Twisted Image* (New York: St. Martin's, 1963).

GORDON, GEORGE N., IRVING FALK, and WILLIAM HODAPP. *The Idea Invaders* (New York: Hastings House, 1963).

HOLT, ROBERT T., and ROBERT W. VAN DE VELDE. *Strategic Psychological Operations and American Foreign Policy* (Chicago: University of Chicago Press, 1961).

JOYCE, WALTER. *The Propaganda Gap* (New York: Harper and Row, 1963).

LERNER, DANIEL, ed. *Propaganda in War and Crisis* (New York: George Stewart, 1951).

LINEBARGER, PAUL M. A. *Psychological Warfare* (Washington, D.C.: Infantry Journal Press, 1948).

QUALTER, TERENCE H. *Propaganda and Psychological Warfare* (New York: Random House, 1962).

STEPHENS, OREN. *Facts to a Candid World* (Stanford, Calif.: Stanford University Press, 1955).

THOMSON, CHARLES A., and WALTER H. C. LAVES. *Cultural Relations and U. S. Foreign Policy* (Bloomington, Ind.: Indiana University Press, 1963).

WHITTON, JOHN B., and ARTHUR LARSON. *Propaganda: Toward Disarmament in the War of Words* (New York: Oceana, 1964).

WINGENBACH, CHARLES E. *The Peace Corps* (New York: John Day, 1963).

# V THE ECONOMIC INSTRUMENT

# 43 / World Economic Disparities: The Haves and the Have-Nots

## DAVID HOROWITZ

In order to consider the economic instrument as a tool of foreign policy, one must be aware of the major features of the world economic environment. The central fact is that most of the world's population lives at or below the subsistence level. This fact and its ramifications are analyzed here, along with such questions as: Can economic controls be made effective within a democratic framework? How can capital be effectively transferred? Can economic development go forward within a democratic framework?

TWO-THIRDS of humanity today live at or below subsistence level. This is the most crucial problem of our time. It transcends in importance and gravity all other social and economic problems of the century. It is the living symbol of the fact that the disparities in the economy of the world are clearly the most disruptive agents working against the achievement of world order and peace through a world community.

The rift between the two giant power blocs is mainly an ideological one resulting from the different ways in which they view their economies and from the different social patterns that these different economies have created. These economic disparities are a breeding ground for growing world antagonism.

In many of the developed countries class conflicts on a national scale dwindle into insignificance thanks to the Welfare State, built-in stabilizers, fiscal and monetary policies, and so forth. The economic conflicts are now not national but regional. The economic gaps between the

From an address given at the Conference of World Order and Freedom, Athens, Greece, October, 1961. Published by the Center for the Study of Democratic Institutions, Santa Barbara, Calif. Copyright 1962 by the Fund for the Republic, Inc.

David Horowitz, a distinguished international economist, has been Governor of the Bank of Israel since 1953.

developed and the underdeveloped nations are incomparably greater than any that exist between the social classes within the developed countries.

Ideological concepts persist long after the economic basis for their existence disappears. Semantics and intellectual orthodoxy perpetuate them. This is true both of class conflicts in the highly developed Welfare States and of the anti-colonial reactions in the underdeveloped countries to colonialism in its crude form of political domination and economic exploitation.

The disparities that lie at the root of the economic problems of our time are paradoxical. In the highly developed countries lack of demand slows down production and full capacity is frequently not utilized; in the underdeveloped countries production lags behind demand.

The terms of trade favor manufactured products the prices of which rise or at least are maintained, as prices of primary commodities fall behind. Productivity in agriculture is lagging where its increase is most imperative and is relatively lowest where the proportion of agricultural population is greatest. Increase in agricultural production is highest where stocks of food are already excessive. Growth of population and the demographic explosion are most pronounced where malnutrition prevails. Shortage of capital is worst where capital is most needed. The rate of saving is lowest where new investments are most imperative, for the simple reason that saving is lowest where incomes are at or below subsistence level.

The pronounced difference in liquidity between nations, and short-term capital movements, create disparities in the balance of payments among various national economic units, impairing the exchange of goods and services.

The disparities are clearly reflected in the fact that the share of the United States, Western Europe, and Japan in the total national incomes of seventy of the states affiliated with the International Monetary Fund (which represents a large cross-section of the world) is 75 per cent, although these three areas represent only 25 per cent of the population of all of the countries within the Fund.

Demography, terms of trade, difficulty of capital formation in less developed countries, and paucity of capital imports, all combine to aggravate the human, political, and economic implications of the problem.

Despite the technological progress of modern times, there may be more poverty-stricken people in the world today than there were fifty or a hundred years ago.

### Chaining the Malthusian Devil

The disparity in economic standards and in stages of economic

330

development is aggravated by demography. The spectre evoked by Malthus is rising again. Frequently, development is unable to catch up with the rapid increase of population. Standards of life in countries where the population pressure on limited resources is greatest cannot be further depressed without grave consequences. We are living in "the period of demographic explosion." At the present rate of increase, the world population will double every forty-two years, and will total some six billion by the end of the century.

The pressure of growing populations on scarce resources is accentuated in countries that are already densely populated. In 1949 the national income in Europe generally ranged between $350 and $800 per capita, but in Asia it was $50 to $100 per capita.

A paradox appears in this demographic discrepancy: the more extensive and more developed are health services and hygienic progress, the graver the population problem. The main factor in the rapid increase of the population is not a rise in the birth rate but decline in the mortality rate, which in some underdeveloped countries has dropped 30 to 60 per cent in one decade. In some countries with the highest rate of reproduction in human history, the population doubles every twenty-two to twenty-five years. Preventive medicine, more hygienic methods, and the increasing use of vaccination, sulfa drugs, and antibiotics, and D.D.T. as a remedy against the spread of malaria, are radically reducing the mortality rates, particularly among infants. And while the death rate falls rapidly, the birth rate remains high.

This extraordinary increase in population takes place in the underdeveloped nations in spite of the appalling poverty and low standards of life reflected in a life expectancy at birth of 32.5 years for males and 31.7 years for females in India (1941–50), in comparison with some 67 to 70 years in the highly developed countries of Europe and America. In countries in which the decline in the death rate is gradual, it is usually accompanied by simultaneous changes in mental, psychological, and cultural attitudes leading to a declining birth rate. It is obvious, however, that if the process is very rapid and revolutionary, the changes cannot keep pace with the new developments and the decline of the birth rate thus lags behind the decline of the death rate. Production cannot keep up with the rapid increase of population and so living standards of life do not rise in these countries. Moreover, changes in the birth rate through conscious control of procreation are subject to cultural and psychological, as well as social and religious, influences, which are generally rigid and conservative.

The vicious circle of uncontrolled demographic expansion and declining standards of life is thus closing. The imbalance of population on a world scale is being accentuated by growing differences in per capita incomes.

Eugene Black, President of the World Bank, warned recently that all the efforts of industrial countries could be nullified if population in the poorer countries continues to grow at its present rate of 2 to 3½ per cent a year. He maintains that to point to the favorable economic effects of a growing population is "widely irrelevant" to the problems of most developing countries today. "We are coming to a situation in which the optimist will be the man who thinks that present living standards can be maintained."

These circumstances explain the efforts of the underdeveloped nations to chain the Malthusian devil as a precondition to the rise of living standards. Otherwise, an increase of the gross national product may be vitiated by an excessive increase of population.

### Price Pattern

Another disparity is the result of the price pattern and price fluctuations in a modern economy. The changes in prices of primary commodities as a group have been about 50 to 55 per cent greater than those of manufactures as a group. While the prices of manufactured products have been maintained or even risen, the prices of primary products have continuously declined. This fact has created balance of payment difficulties for the primary-producing countries, particularly in view of their fixed obligations. The decline reflects long-term structural trends and is not a problem that arises only in connection with general cyclical fluctuations in the world economy. We are faced with some basic structural changes.

Since 1951, the underlying world trend of prices of primary commodities, measured in the aggregate, has been irregularly but steeply downward. And since 1957 there has been a decline of nearly 5 per cent in the prices of exports of the countries producing primary commodities. The net loss after deducting the decline of prices of imported products in these countries in the year 1958 alone exceeded the total financial assistance received in that year by the less developed countries.

Even in times of boom in the highly developed industrial countries, there was no improvement in the terms of trade for the underdeveloped nations. The decline in prices has a cumulative effect because price declines discourage large stock holdings and the unloading of these stocks further enforces the downward trend of prices. Thus, while the trend of the 1930's was reversed in almost every other respect in the post-war period, surpluses of primary commodities have continued to depress their price levels.

The underdeveloped nations of the world are caught in the scissors of declining prices of primary produce and rising costs of manufactured commodities and of capital equipment required for their development.

### Development and Democracy

The first industrial revolution was based on a very high rate of savings and private accumulation of capital. The distribution of the national income in those times was instrumental in accelerating the formation of capital, by assuring a high rate of profit, and keeping wage rates on levels just sufficient for the maintenance and reproduction of the labor force. These wage levels were possible because there was always a reserve army of unemployed workers to be called on. It was a dismal, grim period and amply illustrated the theory of the iron wage law. The conditions were possible only within the framework of a society in which democracy was in a nascent state and the broad masses of the population were either deprived of political influence or inarticulate.

This performance was repeated in the U.S.S.R. after the 1917 revolution. The very existence of the new regime depended on rapid economic progress. Speedy industrialization, occupational re-shuffles, and large-scale urbanization were possible only by a fast formation of capital through forced savings, and the totalitarian regime was strong, stern, and severe enough to enforce this solution. Today Red China is trying to achieve similar results by lowering consumption and forced saving.

There is one common feature between the early capitalism of the industrial revolution in England and Western Europe on one hand and the Soviet regime and the economic system of Red China in the post-war period on the other. This is a very rapid capital formation through cruel and ruthless restraint of consumption and reduction in living standards. Such an economic policy can be enforced only in a pre-democratic or totalitarian regime. Its concomitants are the appalling poverty and starvation of early capitalism and the extremely low standards of life in totalitarian regimes in the initial period of their development.

The process of primary formation of capital under these circumstances is extremely slow in underdeveloped countries and is made even more difficult by the increasing pressure of population growth. The propensity to save is, of course, reduced if the population expands more rapidly than the national income, so that real income per capita decreases. The rate of saving will be low because of the relatively small excess of real income over and above the subsistence level. The process of accumulation is further retarded by the fact that institutional saving in these countries is in its embryonic stage and the use of money as a medium of exchange is limited.

The margin above bare existence in these populations is so small as to defy any attempt to squeeze out of them savings for capital formation and subsequent investment. They cannot lift themselves by the straps of their own boots. In addition, political and social factors would militate against

a policy of forced savings so long as consumption levels are distressingly low.

Theoretically such a policy could be put into effect by heavy taxation, extremely low wages, and the introduction of what would practically amount to forced labor in village communities, but the resistance to these measures in any but totalitarian regimes would be so formidable as to defeat their ends. They would be even more difficult to apply nowadays because of the "demonstration effect" of Western civilization and living standards. The modern media of mass communication, even the shining car crossing an appallingly poor village in India or Egypt, conjure up the picture of a better life that is not solely confined to keeping body and soul together. This is the new revolution of rising expectations.

Thus, an attempt to execute a policy of rapid capital formation in these countries could only be achieved by coercion, and a totalitarian regime would be much more efficient and effective in it. Under a democratic system, moreover, in an economy run on the basis of a multiplicity of private decisions of employers, factory owners, landlords, and the like, there would be no certainty, and perhaps little probability, that the resources that would be created by depressing living standards and decreasing consumption would be diverted to investment anyway.

The sheer accumulation of capital does not guarantee that it will be used for investment and the promotion of economic growth. In some of the underdeveloped countries a small but wealthy minority at the top of the ladder has considerable resources in its hands and squanders most of them in conspicuous consumption. This is particularly the case in the Middle East, with its immense income from oil royalties. England of the industrial revolution used its accumulated resources for investment in order to expand its production capacity, but this does not mean that the same course of action will be followed in Saudi Arabia. The will to apply resources properly, knowledge, skill, and entrepreneurial initiative are the indispensable prerequisites of economic growth.

### Transfer of Capital

Import of capital and forced accumulation of savings are interchangeable. Help from outside sources is the only possible substitute for forced formation of capital. The alternative to both is economic stagnation. The problem of large-scale capital transfer must be viewed, first and foremost, from the angle of the capital market in countries able to export capital. The worldwide shortage of capital is becoming one of the most decisive and influential factors in the economic pattern of the world. The pressure of demand for capital is accentuated by powerful new economic, technical, political, and sociological developments in this post-war "age of dislocation and experiment."

First, the second industrial revolution. Automation, or the replacement of labor by machines; the electronic industry, spreading out new, hitherto unknown branches, as an auxiliary arm of armament and a source of new needs through communications; the use of atomic energy for industrial purposes, all of these need immense capital investment. They deeply affect general economic conditions because of the competitive advantage possessed by enterprises with a high component of fixed capital and the consequent need of other enterprises to accelerate their pace or re-equipment in order to reach the same objective. Thus, the new industrial revolution works in two directions: quicker obsolescence and a need for re-equipment of whole industries; and a higher unit of fixed capital per unit of production. Re-equipment is being accelerated. The volume of capital to be used for this purpose in the United States alone in 1960 was estimated at 38 billion dollars.

Second, rearmament: The immense needs of rearmament coincide with the new industrial revolution and create an additional claim on existing resources. Moreover, the developments in this field parallel those of industry in general—less manpower, more fixed assets (long-range aircraft, ballistic missiles, etc.), and vast quantities of capital equipment.

Third, the rising curve of world population. The world's 2.7 billion population has almost doubled in the past seventy years and is expected to redouble in the next forty-two years. This stupendous growth generates new needs in housing, schools, roads, and, last but not least, capital equipment for the integration of the population into the machinery of production.

From the supply side, the flow of capital to investment is being diminished by the redistribution of national income, which reduces high-bracket incomes, a large part of which were accumulated and invested, and raises middle and low incomes. This results not only in the elimination of social extremes but also in an increase in aggregate consumption because of the rising living standards of those sections of the population which have a higher propensity to consume. Under conditions of full employment this rise in living standards decreases the share of income saved, accumulated, and invested and increases the share of income consumed.

Thus, the rate of accumulation is decreasing through social progress as a smaller share of income is saved and accumulated. This social transformation has invalidated the nineteenth century prognosis of social polarization. Today the economic and social gap between the worker and the employer in developed countries is much less pronounced than that between the worker in developed countries and the worker in underdeveloped areas.

The supply of capital is also reduced by the bargaining power of trade unions, which affects the internal supply of capital in highly

developed countries and has an even more powerful impact on the export of capital to underdeveloped countries. This leads to a conflict of social and economic interests between the trade union movement in the developed nations and the vast populations of underdeveloped areas. It results in a diminished rate of savings and capital accumulation; higher consumption with a larger internal market and greater and more varied and attractive possibilities of investment in developed countries; accentuation of discrepancies between the prices of primary commodities produced by underdeveloped countries and the prices of manufactured products in the highly industrialized nations; and a rise in the price of capital equipment needed for the development of underdeveloped nations.

Of course, this clash of interests is not conscious and deliberate. The workers in the developed lands are among the ardent supporters of aid to underdeveloped countries. The rather indirect influence on the possibilities of export of capital of rising living standards and increased consumption caused by rising wage levels is too complicated a phenomenon to be understood by many people concerned with their own individual problems. So far as the great mass of people are concerned, the esoteric character of intricate economic processes and the many ramifications and indirect impacts of various socio-economic measures are unknown or ignored. It is impossible to gauge what the attitude of the labor movement would be if the contradiction between ideology and vested interests were raised to the level of political consciousness and action.

The expectation of an easy capital market after a period of reconstruction following the Second World War has not materialized. A chain of technological discoveries and a booming home market in the mature economies of the West claim a growing share of capital for their own investment needs, leaving only small surpluses for export to underdeveloped countries. The annual report of the World Bank mentions the "heavy investment demand which pressed with increasing force on the available supply of savings." The claim of developed countries on existing resources for new investment is expected to increase.

The theoretical assumption that the surplus of capital in the Western economies is attracted because of higher potential returns to countries with underdeveloped resources, cheap labor, and unexploited sources of raw materials has not come true. Insecurity of the capital invested is only one of the factors against extensive exports of capital to underdeveloped countries. The low productivity of the labor force, as well as its lack of skills, likewise discourages foreign investment. An expanding and diversified market, coupled with increasing demand, exerts a pull on capital to invest in already industrialized countries. The existence of auxiliary industries, of scientific institutions, and of all kinds of technical facilities is

an additional stimulant to such investment. Capital is reluctant to break virgin ground in unexplored and undeveloped areas when the lure of profitable investment in developed countries is so great.

Another attraction of the developed and industrialized countries is their money and capital market, with ample credit facilities on the one hand and, on the other, the high liquidity of investment in shares wherever the stock exchange serves as an efficient instrument for shifting from liquid to fixed and from fixed to liquid assets. Except for the capital going to underdeveloped countries to exploit their oil resources, little is flowing according to the natural processes of economic gravitation, and even this amount is affected to some extent by artificial stimuli, such as the activity of the World Bank, grants-in-aid, and so on.

### Limited Use of Resources

Still another disparity making for international economic disequilibrium appears in the under-utilization of productive capacity in highly developed nations at the same time that the demand for capital equipment in the underdeveloped countries remains unsatisfied.

Full use of existing resources in highly developed countries could be greatly facilitated by export of capital. Increasing productivity and far-reaching mechanization and automation are already causing technological unemployment in the United States. Even in parts of Europe, increase in employment lags behind all other economic indicators. The diversion of resources in the developed countries to the production of commodities to satisfy artificially created needs has recently provoked much adverse comment because it is happening where conditions in the underdeveloped nations are desperate and their amelioration should be our paramount interest.

The "bogey of maturity" arises in the highly developed sections of the world with the gradual widening of the margin between production capacity and actual output. Stimulating the export of capital to underdeveloped nations or increasing internal expenditures, mainly through governmental channels, are the alternative solutions to this problem.

Prolonged recessions involving a high rate of unemployment are now being prevented by deliberate stimulation of the domestic market. But even in their present mild form, mitigated by built-in stabilizers, the cost of recessions in terms of underemployed resources is high. The Council of Economic Advisers found that "the gap between actual and potential output for 1960 as a whole can . . . be estimated at 30-35 billion dollars, or 6 to 7 per cent of total output. . . . Even the most prosperous nation cannot afford to waste resources on this scale." [1]

---

[1] "The American Economy in 1961: Problems and Policies."

Banning the "bogey of maturity" and reducing the margin of underemployed resources could be important by-products of large-scale investment in underdeveloped nations.

One suggestion for such investment is to allocate a certain proportion of the Gross National Product of the industrialized countries to that purpose. One and a half per cent of the GNP of the developed nations is about 15 billion dollars. The interest of developed nations in such a plan is reinforced by the structural changes in mature economies.

The most pronounced swings and cyclical fluctuations occur in the production of capital equipment and durable goods. They are the most vulnerable sectors of modern economies and frequently are the sources of recession or economic slack. Heavy industries producing capital equipment and durable goods obviously occupy a key position in cyclical developments. A balanced growth, therefore, depends upon a rising curve of production in heavy industry producing capital equipment. In periods of economic recession in the United States after the Second World War, the decline was most pronounced in the durable goods sector. This seems to be the key to the prevention of cyclical crises and recessions.

However, we are confronted with certain realities. The flow of capital to those areas which are most in need of it is still very limited, as we have said. These are mostly countries with growing populations pressing on limited resources. They are clearly not the most attractive areas for investment of capital and can hardly be expected to compete with more developed economies on the capital market of the world.

## Hot Money

All the disparities that we have described so far are accentuated by disparities in the balance of payments and differences in liquidity among the various countries. They result from the fact that although the supply of money in each country is determined by the fiscal policies of the government of that country and the monetary policies of central banks, no such control exists in the international arena where the flow of capital is erratic and independent of conscious direction. Within a short period of time the world experienced the dollar gap, then the sterling crisis and the dollar crisis, and later the sterling crisis again. The abolition of the gold standard compelled each country to organize its own control of the money supply. But as long as there is no such organization internationally, financial disparities are inevitable.

Short-term capital movements, mostly speculative, that clog the channels of trade and certain internal policies of national units lead to fluctuations and lack of equilibrium in international financial and trade relations. The new method of managed currency encounters the pitfalls of the sorcerer's apprentice. The uninitiated playing with forces and

formulas they do not fully understand can easily and even inadvertently open the Pandora box of inflation. The problem is one of balance between effective demand created by the supply of money and between actual or potential supply of goods and services.

Government-induced monetary expansion is frequently the result of a genuine desire to accelerate the process of badly needed economic development. In a country with dormant factors of production or under-utilized resources, this policy may even be successful in the short run by galvanizing idle capacity. Eventually, however, the acquisition of resources by the State through inflation defeats its own purpose. As the surplus purchasing power spills over into excessive demand for foreign currency with which to buy imported goods because even increased domestic production cannot satisfy the new demand, rising price levels and greater pressure on the balance of payments must lead to a deterioration of the economy. Depletion of the reserves of foreign currency, physical shortages, and unemployment caused by lack of raw materials and other components of production dependent on imports are the inevitable results.

### Summary

The central problem, on which the future of humanity may depend, is to eliminate economic disparities throughout the world. This has become possible in our time because the blind incalculable economic forces are being increasingly superseded by conscious economic policies and controls. Wiser monetary and fiscal policies, the growth and impact of the Welfare State, built-in stabilizers, all contribute to the new pattern of a balanced economy. Modern technology is a great contributing factor in making such control possible.

The three chief predictions of the nineteenth century by both classical and Marxist economists—increasing impoverishment, unavoidable cyclical crises, and the compelling need for economic imperialism—have been disproved by the realities of our time.

The questions we face are these:

How can economic controls be made effective within a framework of free democratic decisions? How can formation of capital be supplemented by transfer of capital? How can short-term movements of capital and difficulties in balance of payments be neutralized by institutional, world-wide arrangements? How can fluctuations of boom and recession be smoothed out on a national and international scale? How can the population explosion be mitigated by family planning?

The tools for answering these questions and for developing a world-wide economic policy are available. The economic forces that caused the 1929 crisis can now be controlled. There is no need for a perilous and

pernicious pessimism. A projection of the Welfare State onto the international scene and transformation of the community of nations into a world welfare community would eliminate the gravest of disparities.

The struggle for world peace is a race against time. Today the rift between the power blocs rooted in differences between their economic ideologies seems to be unbridgeable, but the actual gap between the economic regimes is decreasing all the time. The growing reliance on market forces in the Soviet bloc and the growing consciousness of the need for direction and planning in the Western world are leading to some degree of assimilation of the different economic systems. Some day it may seem absurd to fight wars or to hurl nuclear weapons around because there happen to be technical differences in the methods of economic control between one group of countries and another.

For men who are now reaching for the stars it should not be beyond their power to eliminate economic disparities. Their ability to accomplish it depends only on one simple thing: their will to accomplish it.

# 44 / Economic Assistance in United States Foreign Policy

## CHARLES E. BOHLEN

Extensive programs of financial and technical assistance to the economies of foreign nations—as instruments of foreign policy—are relatively new to the United States. According to this author, such programs since World War II have gone through four identifiable periods, which he traces and succinctly describes below.

IN DISCUSSING the history of assistance to foreign countries and its development as an integral part of our relations with friendly countries abroad, it should be emphasized that this is a comparatively new venture in relations between nations. Prior to World War II, with the exception of wartime loans, certain emergencies, and a modest amount of foreign

Reprinted from U. S. Department of State, *Department of State Bulletin*, XLII (March 28, 1960), 495–98.

Charles E. Bohlen has held many of the top ambassadorial posts in the United States foreign service and has been special adviser to the State Department and the White House.

lending by the Export-Import Bank established in 1934, government-to-government assistance was virtually unknown. To grasp what has happened to the United States position in the world in the last generation, I might mention that, at the time I joined the Foreign Service in 1929, the budget of the State Department for that year was $14.5 million. This appropriation was not only for the administrative expenses of the Department of State, including salaries of its employees in Washington and abroad, but also included the U.S. contribution to existing international organizations such as the U.S.-Mexican boundary committee, the Pan American Union, and the International Fisheries Commission. The State Department budget thus represented, together with some small additional appropriations from other Government departments, the total cost to the U.S. taxpayer of conducting our foreign relations.

Now what is the comparable cost of United States foreign relations today, 30 years later?

For the 1961 fiscal year the Department of State budget is $247 million, 17 times greater than in 1929. But this does not include the cost of our foreign military and economic assistance, which is embodied in the Mutual Security Program. On February 16 the President transmitted to Congress the administration's request for the Mutual Security Program in the 1961 fiscal year of $4.175 billion. There can be no more dramatic indication of the changed role of the United States in the world today than in the comparison with the figure I gave you earlier for 1929—$14 million—and approximately $5 billion. And this of course does not take into account that portion of national defense which supports our military establishments overseas.

What are the reasons for this vast increase in U.S. expenditures in the field of its foreign relations which has come about within the span of one generation? The basic reason, of course, is that the world situation which we face now compared to 30 years ago has undergone its own form of revolution.

I cannot here go into all the vast changes which have occurred in the world during that period or the immense increase in the role that the United States has been called upon to play in these changing circumstances. But it is sufficient to say that in 1929 the United States lived in a state of virtual political isolation from the world. We enjoyed a position of greater security than that of any other major nation in the world. With friendly neighbors to the north and south of us we were also protected, under the conditions of military capabilities then prevailing, by the broad expanse of two oceans. Furthermore—and this is extremely vital to the understanding of what has happened in the world—the great democracies of Western Europe stood guard on the ramparts on our behalf to a greater degree than we perhaps realized at the time. In addition, these democracies governed and controlled large sections of the world in the

shadow of whose authority and policing functions we in large measure lived. In two world wars these countries took the first shock of an onslaught antagonistic to the philosophy of human society and ideals which we had in common and thus afforded this country the priceless element of time in which to mobilize our resources, both human and material, to join in beating back the attack.

Insofar as the United States is concerned, this all changed in a breathtakingly brief period of time. We found ourselves catapulted in the space of some 15 years from a position of relative security, when we could divert our entire energies to our own national development and the advancement of our own society, to a position of responsibility in the world perhaps unequaled in human history. These fundamental changes in the world, and in particular our position in it, underlie the whole question of foreign aid. Having learned, although possibly imperfectly, certain lessons of World War I, we approached the entire problem of the conflagration which broke out in the world in 1939 with a somewhat more understanding attitude.

### The Lend-Lease Program

The beginning of the conceptions which underlie our policies of assistance to foreign countries may in part be found in a specific measure adopted by the United States before it was a belligerent in World War II. I refer, of course, to lend-lease. Although we were not militarily involved in the war, lend-lease was nonetheless a clear expression of the recognition of the United States Government at that time that our interests were vitally and indissolubly bound up with the fate of the Western democracies engaged in a struggle with the Axis powers. Lend-lease was the forerunner of our future aid programs in that it recognized that U.S. contributions to the common cause of national survival could not be treated merely as commercial transactions.

We had learned after World War I that the attempt to collect, on a bookkeeping basis, loans advanced for the prosecution of a war in a common cause was not only morally questionable but also economically and politically undesirable. The idea of lend-lease, which was subsequently carried over into the time when we were an active belligerent in both the European and Far Eastern theaters of war, was predicated on the recognition of these simple facts. We have never, therefore, sought to collect from any of our former allies repayment for the military supplies and equipment, and indeed for any supplies consumed, during the course of the war itself. Lend-lease settlements dealt merely with what is known as civilian inventory with due allowance for depreciation of such items of lend-lease supply as had a continuing and real value to the economy of the recipient country. Although entirely related to the prosecution of the

war, nevertheless lend-lease itself indicated a keen awareness on the part of the United States of the role that it might be called upon to play in the postwar world in the field of foreign assistance.

The second phase of this developing program of assistance was found in our contribution to take care of the immediate human needs of the people who had suffered so heavily during the war. For the Allied and friendly countries this took the form of UNRRA [United Nations Relief and Rehabilitation Administration]. For former enemy countries this assistance went under the name of GARIOA [Government and Relief in Occupied Areas]. It was obvious that the first great task of the postwar period of reconstruction and recovery would be to take care of the simple human wants of the peoples most afflicted by the ravages of the war. This was the essential purpose of UNRRA and GARIOA. However, it soon became apparent that the mere alleviation of human suffering was not sufficient to restore economic health and political stability. Measures of a longer term and more coordinated nature were clearly necessary.

### The Marshall Plan

It was in response to this need that the United States developed the first coherent measure of economic recovery, generally known as the Marshall plan. The aim of this great venture, certainly one of the most successful in U.S. postwar history, was of course to assist European countries which had suffered particularly from the war and which wished to retain their independence and their ability to order their own affairs. It was heavily influenced, however, by one of the central facts of our time. The Soviet totalitarian system and the postwar policies of its leaders had emerged as a new menace to the powers so recently victorious over the Axis coalition. It was this visible threat of unchecked Soviet power, supported by widespread Communist subversion and infiltration, that lent the Marshall plan its urgency.

I might go back here a bit into history and describe to you a single event which had a very important impact on the thinking of General Marshall, then Secretary of State, and therefore on the development of this concept of American foreign assistance. In Moscow in 1947, toward the close of the Council of Foreign Ministers meeting, General Marshall paid a courtesy call upon Stalin. I accompanied him as his interpreter. We were about to terminate almost 6 frustrating weeks of discussion of the central problems of the postwar settlement in Europe, particularly that of German reunification. We had encountered during this time Foreign Minister Molotov's unquestionable skill in obstruction, diversion, and delaying tactics. The conference, as you all know, made no progress whatsoever in the task of postwar European solutions. During this interview Stalin seemed to view with complete equanimity, and even

satisfaction, the prospect of a Europe continuing to flounder in economic disorder and hopelessness. He saw no reason for any urgency in the solution of the problems put to him by the Western foreign ministers. In fact, he very clearly left General Marshall with the impression that he welcomed rather than deplored the prospect of a steady deterioration in the European situation. It was clear that he looked on an enfeebled Europe as nothing but an asset to Soviet ambitions.

Stalin's cynical attitude toward the problem of European recovery made a deep imprint upon the mind of General Marshall. I have always believed that this meeting in the Kremlin convinced General Marshall that some program would have to be devised with the utmost urgency if Europe were to recover and not to drop like a ripe plum into Soviet hands.

Time does not permit me to outline in any detail the various steps which led to the congressional adoption of the Marshall plan in 1948. The speech of General Marshall at Harvard University on June 5, 1947, while very short, nevertheless set forth most succinctly and clearly the concept of this great venture in foreign assistance.

It is this philosophy of self-help and mutual assistance expressed in this speech which has remained at the heart of all our foreign aid programs, whether administered bilaterally or under U.N. aegis.

You all know how brilliantly the Marshall plan succeeded in its original objectives and indeed far surpassed them. Western Europe has now regained its economic vitality and political stability. Mainly Western European countries are beginning to share with us in increasing measure the burdens of economic and financial assistance which the less developed parts of the world so urgently need at the present time. I think it is safe to say that Western Europe, with its enormous productive capacity and skills, has been made secure against subversive activity and penetration by communism. It is sufficient to contemplate what perils the United States would have confronted if Western Europe had passed into the Soviet orbit in the immediate postwar period. At the present time we continue to give some military assistance to the countries of Europe whose economy still does not permit them to incur the vast expense of modern armaments, but U.S. economic assistance to Europe has dwindled almost to the vanishing point. The recovery of Western Europe and the American part therein in a sense brought to a close the third period of the development of American foreign economic assistance.

### Aid to Less Developed Countries

The fourth period, which we are now in, primarily relates to the necessity of affording economic and financial assistance to the less developed countries of the world, as well as to those in close proximity to

the centers of Communist power. In the last few years 21 countries have emerged into independent national life, with 6 more African countries due to assume this status in the next year. These are countries which for one reason or another have entered the modern era at a much lower stage of development than that of the advanced industrialized countries of the world. It is in the area of these less developed countries where very possibly the outcome will be determined of the worldwide contest now going on between the Soviet concept of the organization of society, which we generally and sometimes inadequately describe as communism, and our own complex of beliefs.

# 45 / *The Yearning for Economic Development*

### HARLAN CLEVELAND AND OTHERS

**One of the prime features of the world political environment today is the "revolution of rising expectations." No longer are most of the peoples of the world willing to accept their low economic standards of living as destined by fate. They now actively seek effective leaders and methods for economic betterment. This pits the democratic way *vs.* the totalitarian way. This selection discusses this crucial competition, the strengths and weaknesses of democratic and dictatorial methods, and Russia *vs.* the United States in the *realpolitik* of contemporary world politics.**

ONE OF THE GREATEST social consequences of the technological revolution is the idea that starvation and poverty are no longer inevitable. For most of men's history the welfare of the masses depended on the harvest. If the weather was good, people ate well for that year; if it was

Reprinted from U. S. Senate Committee on Foreign Relations Study No. 6, "The Operational Aspects of United States Foreign Policy," by Maxwell Graduate School of Citizenship and Public Affairs, Syracuse University (November, 1959), in *U. S. Foreign Policy: Compilation of Studies*, 87th Cong., 1st sess., S. Doc. 24 (March 15, 1961), pp. 575–85.

Harlan Cleveland has been a distinguished journalist, dean of the Maxwell School, Syracuse University, and Assistant Secretary of State for International Organization Affairs.

bad, they starved that year. Not their efforts but the will of the gods determined men's lot on earth. The technological revolution has forever banished this passive response to material welfare. Thinking people in all lands start from the assumption that if poverty exists, it is not because of the gods but because of men's ignorance or lack of will. Since it is believed to be within the competence of man to change man's fate, the task of changing it has become one of the deepest obligations of the political and intellectual leaders of every underdeveloped country.

Two grand ideas are competing for the support of the masses in their search for a way to end poverty. In the villages and the cities of Asia, for example, the common people listen to the views of the educated young men who come to talk to them and persuade them. One group points to the way of China and another group points to India. The Communists have the great advantage of pointing to a nation that has indubitably entered the path of rapid economic development and will unquestionably be a great industrial power in the future. They have the disadvantage of supporting ethical, social, and political doctrines that offend the religious and ethical traditions of great masses of people. Those who support the Indian way must still talk in terms of "hope" and "if we all pull together." But they have the great advantage of espousing ethical and social doctrines that are not offensive to the religious and political values of the people. The question which of these two philosophies will win out is of fundamental importance to the future of the United States in the world. If the non-Communist nations fail to achieve adequate rates of economic growth, more and more people will be persuaded by the arguments of the Communists and more and more of the world will fall prey to Communist political systems. It is clear where the obligations of all freemen lie; it is to do everything in their power to help the underdeveloped countries abolish their poverty so that they can choose freedom without having to pay the price of hunger.

## 1. THE FLEXIBILITY OF DEMOCRACY

While the differences between the Communist and democratic philosophies can be expressed with considerable clarity, in practice the range of institutions that might be classified as democratic constitutes a broad continuum. The institutions by which Asian and African nations are striving to create societies of freedom must be expected to be radically different from ours. Just as in the political sphere we cannot expect two-party systems of free elections to spring full blown out of tribal or feudal societies, so in the economic sphere we cannot expect the forms of economic enterprise to be very similar to ours. For reasons that have been spelled out at great length by experts on economic development, we can expect that those governments will exercise a degree of direction over

investment and enterprise which might strike Americans as intolerable in America. For political reasons, economic criteria will often be subordinated to political; in fact, we do this in our own economy in various ways by protective tariffs, housing guarantees, veterans payments, farm support programs, river and harbor legislation. But since the underdeveloped countries will do it in different ways, our initial reaction may tend to be negative. The point of all this is that in our attitude toward the unfamiliar methods by which the less-developed countries, with their different historical and cultural backgrounds, will strive to create economic institutions, we must avoid applying our traditional standards of political, economic, or ethical admissibility. It is well for us to understand this because we are deeply involved in the invention and support of these very institutions.

### 2. INVOLVEMENT VERSUS "INTERFERENCE"

What is required of our foreign policy if we are most effectively to contribute toward the economic development of the less-developed countries? One of the major requirements is the adaptation to the new conditions of modern administrative and technical skills. Unlike the transfer of a shipload of wheat, the transfer of skills is a continuing process of cultural interchange. It is one of the major forms of that deep involvement in other countries' affairs that has become the essence of modern foreign policy.

Such involvement is not only a necessary aid in promoting economic development but it is also an occasion and means for forming favorable associations and attitudes, building the viable institutions required for each society's "success" in its own terms, and deepening our own understanding of other people's felt needs. These new overseas functions require some change in terminology that classifies all forms of participation in other countries' affairs as "interference" and therefore a bad thing. We cannot undertake any significant action without becoming involved in some nation's internal affairs, either in technical assistance, in economic planning, or in military training. Indeed, our very failure to move a hand may, in some cases, constitute an act of profound significance for the internal affairs of another country. The appropriate attitude toward this new role of ours is acceptance of involvement, or joint participation, as a permanent part of our international life and on this basis to participate as intelligently and usefully as we can. As far as our involvement is concerned, this means that our modern "diplomats," whether in suits or shirtsleeves, must be more carefully trained to think realistically about their unavoidable role as participators in internal affairs abroad. For they are that, whether they know it or not. It is better that they should know it before they start.

### 3. AN ATTITUDE OF COMMITMENT

Along with the skills must go the resources. The success of our efforts to promote economic development depends partly on the volume of resources we are prepared to use, but it depends on more than that. It depends on the depth of our commitment to see the thing through to the end. Our major entry into the business of economic assistance was the Marshall plan. We looked upon that great mission as a temporary one, designed to get Europe on its feet in a few years, after which it would no longer need our assistance. And that is how it worked out, although the Korean war extended the period beyond that originally contemplated. This short-run temporary attitude toward economic aid has carried over into our view of the problem of assistance to the underdeveloped countries; while Congress is in session, it is not unusual to read speeches in the Congressional Record calling for an end to it all. But the old attitudes are not at all appropriate to the new task. It is clear by now that if we really mean to see to the end our commitment to economic development, we must learn to think of it as a long-run venture. Only if we learn to cease asking each year when it will all be over, and concentrate on our determination to do everything in our power to bring about the developments we desire, can we fashion institutions and attitudes appropriate to our full and permanent involvement in the lives of other nations.

All change involves dislocation, and in the process someone's interests are often injured. The economic development of the underdeveloped countries (like the recovery of Western Europe) will inevitably entail some injury to the interests of some groups of Americans. As new industries spring up in other countries, they may be expected to hurt the competitive position of some American industries. It is at this point that our attitude toward change may mean the success or failure of American policy as a whole. Powerful interests will form to oppose the process of change and to frustrate those of our national policies that are contributing to that change. In the past the Nation's surrender to protectionist pressures on particular issues was not of very great consequence; our living standards suffered somewhat and some of our trading partners were irritated. But the time is gone when we can indulge our nationalism as we could afford to do in the past. Protectionism is no longer primarily a matter of domestic politics.

Thus, while few Americans would describe themselves as opposed to the promotion of economic development in other countries, when the blue chips are down many will shrink from the costs of seeing that policy through to the end. Political leaders will face difficult choices: how to tell their constituents that the national interest requires higher taxes or that foreign competition cannot be cut off by tariff increases. Our attitude toward economic change may be firmer if the likely alternatives are more

often called to the public attention. We can refuse to give up our wealth for the sake of other countries, and we can refuse to permit any American industry to have to face increasing competition from abroad, but we must be prepared in that case to face the likelihood that our children's America will be a relatively much smaller democracy in an overwhelmingly totalitarian world.

### F. Soviet Power and American Policy

If we have delayed so long before directing attention to the rise of Soviet power as one of the great changes in world affairs, it is not because a lesser degree of importance is assigned to this factor. It is rather to emphasize our view that our differences with the U.S.S.R. are not the exclusive problem of U.S. foreign policy. Much of the preceding analysis would be valid (to use the current cliché) even if there were no Soviet Union, and the appropriate policies would not be very different if there were no Soviet Union. Too often our relations with Western Europe and with the underdeveloped countries are so affected by our preoccupation with the Soviet threat that we subordinate all other considerations to that danger. To the extent that we are mesmerized by Moscow, U.S. foreign policy takes the form of reacting to Soviet initiative.

### 1. THE CHALLENGE OF SOVIET PRODUCTION

But this is not to gainsay the fact that the rise of Soviet industrial might is one of the greatest factors of change that our foreign policy must take into account. If one were to ask, "What more than anything else accounts for the rise of Soviet military and political prowess in the last quarter century?" the answer would be "heavy industry." The rapid growth of Soviet steel, power, and machinery production is the chief contributory factor to the relative decline in the U.S. international position. While specialists disagree over the relative rates of growth of national product in the two countries and over the precise ratio of Soviet to American production, none would disagree that in heavy industrial production alone the gap between Soviet and American production has narrowed dramatically in recent decades.

The rapid growth of Soviet heavy industrial production reflects the power of the Communist Party leaders to impose their own priorities on the population. During the decade of the thirties consumption was deliberately held down to a minimum while all possible effort was mobilized into industrial investment, and particularly heavy industrial investment. In the last decade consumption standards have been permitted to rise moderately, but the priority of heavy industry continues to dictate the direction of the national economic effort. Thus, in the recent past the United States has been investing 17 to 20 percent of its national

product, while the U.S.S.R. continues to devote 25 to 30 percent to investment. If we consider not total investment but investment in heavy industry alone, the difference is even greater. By devoting a larger proportion of their smaller national product to industrial investment, the Soviet Government has been able to achieve an absolute volume of industrial investment approximating that of the United States. Moreover, their investment is, of course, concentrated in growth-inducing industries such as steel and machine tools, and not so heavily in automobiles and washing machines.

There are cogent reasons for believing that in the future Soviet over-all economic growth cannot continue at the same high rates as in the past. But the political objectives and power of the regime are such that we can expect the emphasis on heavy industry to continue. Our long-run foreign policy must take full account of the likelihood that, barring great changes in the character of our own economic system, Soviet heavy industrial production is likely to continue to grow more rapidly than ours. Under such conditions there should be a strong presumption against wait-and-see policies in every field.

These changes focus our attention on the impressive volume of economic and social waste in our own economy. Such waste is no longer a matter of purely domestic concern, but has profound effects on our capacity to conduct a foreign policy that must reckon with the forced-draft growth of the Soviet economy.

The continued waste involved in cyclical recessions threatens not only our pocketbooks but, in the long run, our national security. Only in a vigorous, fully employed economy can we be confident that the people will consent to the expenditures necessary for putting the full weight of our national wealth into the international political arena. A determined resistance to "creeping protectionism," not only in case of the tariff, but of the worker or employer protecting himself from the impact of economic change, or of the taxpayer protecting his income against the local school board, is of vital importance in strengthening our Nation's ability to conduct a successful foreign policy. Soviet economic growth has transformed the issues of domestic economic policy into issues of foreign policy as well.

It is sometimes argued that it is not enough merely to attain a healthy, fully employed economy, but that we must go beyond this and attain a rate of growth at least as rapid as that of the U.S.S.R. The argument raises two questions: first, is it possible for us to attain a rate of growth equal to that of the totalitarian Soviet economy; and second, ought we to make the effort to do so?

There are no economic reasons why we could not keep up with and even outdistance the U.S.S.R. if we thought the emergency desperate enough to warrant the effort. It would require that the Nation place itself,

in effect, on a wartime regime. The tax rate would have to be increased sharply to curb the rate of consumption and the tax revenues would be used to subsidize the construction of new heavy industrial capacity according to some national plan of industrial expansion. Under these grim conditions, our current consumption would decline sharply, but we would have increasing quantities of resources to devote to military, foreign economic aid, and industrial expansion purposes. There is little doubt that we could forever keep ahead of the U.S.S.R. The price of this policy would be enormous, for we should have turned over to the Kremlin and denied to ourselves the power to decide what our economy should produce.

The question, then, is not whether we can match the Soviets, but rather whether we ought to. If the continued gain of Soviet heavy industry were to be judged of *decisive* importance in the future political contest, we should have no choice but to pay the price of staying ahead. But it does not appear to be of *decisive* importance. And therefore we need not match the Soviet Union in the mad race for machines to build more machines at the expense of current welfare. We ought to lament the sacrifice forced on the Soviet people by leaders obsessed with heavy industry, but we need not ape them. With our economy growing at a pace compatible with our large measure of freedom but significantly more vigorous than in recent years, and with our people prepared to devote all the necessary resources to our international political objectives, then the continued Soviet gain in economic growth need not be decisive. The best way to see this clearly is to consider in turn the three possible sources of danger engendered by growing Soviet industrial prowess; they might be termed the military effect, the demonstration effect, and the economic power effect.

Concern over the *military effect* of growing Soviet industrial strength is based on the view that military power increases with heavy industrial power. If this view were correct, it would indeed be of vital importance for us to strive at all costs to maintain our heavy industrial superiority over the U.S.S.R. But given the nature of modern nuclear weapons and their delivery systems, the 1-to-1 correspondence between steel production and military potential no longer holds. The last two World Wars were fought under limited conditions; more steel meant more bombs, meant more destruction. Today we must learn to think in ultimates; a limited number of hydrogen bombs can create total destruction, and more hydrogen bombs cannot do more than that. The military problem is qualitative rather than quantitative; the decision will depend on the laboratory and not the factory. If either nation gains a decisive advantage over the other, it will be based on research and development, and not on mere mass. Since the limiting factor is not steel, but brains and will, the prospect of a continued Soviet gain in industrial prowess is not of decisive

military importance. Even in the case of conventional forces to fight limited war, the present combined economic systems of the free world are likely to be sufficient to provide all the forces needed for such wars. The problem is not in the availability of the resources but in our willingness to provide them and to maintain them through the hot and cold running of our relations with the Soviet bloc.

It has been argued that the more rapidly growing economy is likely to be the more progressive technologically, and therefore the more rapid rate of Soviet heavy industrial growth may indirectly contribute to technological and scientific breakthroughs. While it is true that a stagnant economy is not likely to stimulate technological and scientific progress, it does not follow that the rate of such progress is proportional to the rate of economic growth. As long as our economy is expanding at a reasonable pace, the climate for technological and scientific progress is favorable. If we should lose preeminence in these fields to the Soviet Union, the reason is more likely to lie in the grossly inadequate financing of our educational and scientific efforts. The answer is to find direct ways of increasing national expenditure in these fields, not to try to achieve this indirectly by artificially accelerating our rate of industrial growth to meet that of the Soviet Union.

By the *demonstration effect* of Soviet industrial growth, we mean the force of the Soviet example as a way of breaking out of economic backwardness through Communist revolution. The argument is that as Soviet heavy industry continues to grow more rapidly than ours, communism will become increasingly alluring to the populations of the underdeveloped countries. But we cannot really dispel the allure of communism by demonstrating that we Americans can always produce more steel than the Soviets. Keeping ahead of the Soviets is not the answer. Only if the non-Communist underdeveloped countries themselves succeed in raising their own living standards through non-Communist methods, will communism be rejected. Our present national wealth is such that if we really mean to make the maximal effort in this direction, we already have more than enough resources with which to do it. Moreover, time is of crucial importance. The poverty-stricken peoples of the world will not wait indefinitely. If existing non-Communist governments provide no relief, the desperate masses will turn to communism. Hence, the way to combat the demonstration effect of rapid Soviet growth is to invest extra resources not in our own economy but in the economies of these countries where it is important to prove that free institutions can produce rapid economic growth.

## 2. COMMUNISM AND CONSUMER GOODS

It is sometimes argued that the rapidly growing capital stock of the U.S.S.R. will one day provide the Soviets with the opportunity of turning

to a policy of consumer goods production, and in a short time raise the level of living of their population higher than that of the advanced democratic countries of Western Europe. If the U.S.S.R. could demonstrate that communism can provide not only more heavy industry but also more consumer goods than free economic systems, the appeal of communism will be overwhelming not only in the underdeveloped countries but also in Western Europe. Surely this day, if it ever comes, is very far in the future, certainly further than the day in which Soviet capital goods production rivals that of the free world. But even granting the possibility, it does not mean that we ought to adopt a policy of staying ahead of the U.S.S.R. at all costs. If people anywhere are so devoted to material goods that they would willingly accept the political bondage of communism for their sake, there is nothing we can or ought to do about it. Our task is not to demonstrate that free men can always and in every way outproduce the unfree. The fact is that under modern conditions of mass communications and controls, unfree men may well under certain conditions be compelled to out-produce the free. *Our task is rather to create a world in which people who wish to be free need not accept hunger and poverty as the price.* If we achieve this end, if all men could look forward to a reasonable and rising living standard for themselves and their families under conditions of economic and political freedom, our job is well done. If it then turns out that people value freedom so lightly that they would voluntarily surrender it not for food but for the frills of life, we must concede them this right. In short, if men voluntarily turn to communism out of desperation born of poverty, the fault is partly ours; if they turn to it for other reasons, the fault is mostly theirs.

Finally, by the "economic power" effect of Soviet industrial growth we mean increasing Soviet capacity for influencing foreign governments through trade, grants, and loans. Again, the crucial factors in our ability to engage the Soviet Union in economic warfare are wisdom and will, not resources. It is hard to imagine a hypothetical Soviet maneuver in which we would have to say "we know what we ought to do but we are too poor to do it." Suppose, for example, that a decade or more hence, if Soviet production of a number of heavy industrial commodities then rivals or surpasses ours, the U.S.S.R. should attempt to exert pressure on another country by threatening to cut off its sales of machinery to that country. Our ability to defend that country's independence will surely not be frustrated by our *economic* inability to act. Therefore the answer to the "economic effect" of increasing Soviet heavy industrial prowess is not to stay ahead of them at all costs, but to develop a strategy for meeting a mounting Soviet economic offensive.

Our conclusion is that the answer to the forced rate of Soviet economic growth is not to strive at all costs to stay ahead of it. It is rather

(1) to eliminate the grosser forms of economic waste that we could afford in the past but which are more serious under the new conditions, and (2) to support within the full power of a healthy and growing economy those military and foreign policies of our Government that are vital to our international aims. If we refuse to adopt the attitudes and policies appropriate to the new conditions and if we continue our domestic business-as-usual without regard to the foreign policy consequences, we may well be overwhelmed eventually by a more powerful antagonist. But if we throw the full strength of a prosperous and growing American economy into the task of helping shape the world we want to live in, we have little to fear from the Soviet obsession with forced economic growth.

### 3. SOVIET AID AND TRADE

In the period since the death of Stalin the U.S.S.R. has dealt itself into the game of economic development, and today it is not only the West that has espoused economic development in those lands, but the Soviet bloc as well. The new state of affairs requires that we be clear in our own minds about the attitudes we ought to adopt toward Soviet bloc activity in the underdeveloped countries.

Soviet bloc economic activity has taken the form of an increase in trade and in credits to the underdeveloped countries. The overall magnitudes are not large compared with those of the Western World. For example, total Soviet bloc nonmilitary loan commitments made to all underdeveloped countries amounted by the end of 1958 to about $1.6 billion, of which only about $400 million had actually been disbursed by that date. By comparison the International Bank, in the decade 1947 to 1957, had actually disbursed over $1.5 billion in loans. In 1957 alone U.S. short-term assistance from the sale of surplus agricultural commodities amounted to $417 million. However, such success as the U.S.S.R. has enjoyed has been due to factors other than mere magnitude. Soviet trade and lending has been concentrated in relatively few countries, and in the smaller of them the absolute magnitudes loom relatively large. The program has been managed with great flexibility, and quick advantage has been taken of difficulties that have arisen between the United States and other countries. The novelty of the program contributed to the wide publicity it received, and in the early stages there was not time for the inevitable conflicts to arise. Now, as the program has rolled on, the benefits of novelty have been falling away, and the Soviets have been increasingly involved in the familiar irritations of conducting a foreign aid program.

The U.S.S.R. has not, however, had to confront the full range of problems we have faced in conducting an economic aid program, and for

an important reason. They cannot permit themselves to become as deeply involved in the affairs of the recipient countries as we have and must. They can escape the obligation of involvement because their objective is really not economic development but political gain. But since our objective is precisely to see the job of economic development through to the end, we cannot afford to adopt the standoffish policy of the Soviets. Our objectives demand a full-scale involvement, with all the political frictions it may entail.

We do not need to become overexcited about the "goodwill" that the Soviet Union has gained from its aid and trade initiatives. There is nothing the United States can or ought to do to deprive the U.S.S.R. of the goodwill it earns for copying the kind of thing that we have been doing for a long time. Moreover, such goodwill as can be generated by economic aid does not usually survive a breakdown of general political relations. In fact, since the launching of the post-Stalin policy in 1954, three of the largest recipients of Soviet loans have found themselves on worsened terms with the Soviet bloc (Yugoslavia, Egypt, and India), and the most dramatic Soviet success was scored in a country that had at that time received no Soviet economic aid (Iraq). It is therefore important that we do not fall into the error of ascribing to Soviet economic policy all the successes that ought properly to be ascribed to broader political factors—or of believing that the Soviets can somehow make more political capital out of economic aid than we can.

A greater danger of the new Soviet policy is that countries heavily dependent upon Soviet trade or loans may be subjected to irresistible pressure to adopt policies insisted upon by the U.S.S.R. The single important case in which this has been tried is Yugoslavia, and the result is of great significance: the Yugoslavs chose to go without the Soviet loans, at great economic cost to themselves, rather than knuckle under to Soviet (and in part Chinese) pressures. The intense spirit of nationalism in the newly independent countries is their greatest defense against victimization by Soviet economic pressure. But U.S. policy can assist them in resisting Soviet encroachments by standing ready to ease the economic blows of the withdrawal of Soviet trade or loans. It is therefore of great importance that we do not adopt a policy of hostility toward countries that accept Soviet loans and trade offers, for this might weaken their ability to resist Soviet pressure.

U.S. foreign policy must be based on the likelihood that the use of economic instruments by the U.S.S.R. will increase in the future. Our policies can be so fashioned that their character and timing need not be altered in response to changes in Soviet tactics. A sufficient flexibility permits us to seize quickly advantages that suddenly arise. But the test of how well our policies are conceived is the extent to which we maintain the initiative, instead of reacting to Soviet tactical changes. We must have

sufficient confidence in our own policies to welcome Soviet trade and loans when they do contribute to the economic welfare of other countries, and draw attention to their shortcomings when they do not. We can continue to strive to channel Soviet loans into multilateral agencies or soundly conceived country programs even though the Soviets are likely to continue to pursue their bilateral way. If our programs are well conceived, we need have no fear of matching our contribution against that of the U.S.S.R.

### 4. THE U.S.S.R. AND ITS SATELLITES

In most of the world the U.S.S.R. has an interest in upsetting the *status quo*. The one area in which change would be damaging to Soviet interests is the Communist bloc. It is in this area that U.S. policy is least likely to score significant victories, and in which ill-considered policies are most likely to erupt in the use of force. And yet it is in those countries, particularly Eastern Europe, that the U.S.S.R. is potentially most vulnerable. Nationalism is a force in all of Eastern Europe, and in many of the countries cultural and political sovietization has been bitterly resented. While socialization of the economies has enjoyed support among important segments of the population, in certain segments such as agriculture and trade there exist pressures for more freedom of enterprise. As for the political forms of communism, traditions of individual freedom are deep in such countries as Czechoslovakia, Poland, and Hungary, and the Communist Party monopoly is resented by important segments of youth and the intelligentsia. For these various reasons Eastern Europe would be a very dubious ally of the U.S.S.R. in case of a general war.

At the same time, the people of the area understand the Soviet interest in maintaining control over small countries on her borders, and are aware that the U.S.S.R. will not tolerate anti-Soviet or Western-alined governments surrounding her. The Hungarian experience has driven home the lesson that domestic politics are always conducted under the shadow of Soviet arms.

Nevertheless, in the post-Stalin period the Soviet Government has tolerated some degree of independence of action, at least in Poland. U.S. policy should be prepared to encourage and support the efforts of the East European countries to control their own destinies within limits tolerable to the U.S.S.R. We can do this by encouraging the expansion of trade relations between Eastern Europe and the non-Communist world, and by a vigorous prosecution of cultural exchanges between Eastern Europe and the United States. The recent encouragement of many kinds of relations with Poland, pursued effectively by private foundations as well as by official agencies, may pay great dividends on a very small investment.

5. THE CASE OF COMMUNIST CHINA

The Eastern European countries are too small to threaten the peace, and are in any case dominated by the U.S.S.R. However, the increasing military and economic power of Communist China (not a Soviet satellite) may very well lead to further aggressive adventures for territorial and ideological conquest; it is apparent, moreover, that the U.S.S.R. will have less and less influence over the national-power decisions of China, which may entail more, rather than less, aggressive behavior by the junior partner.

In these circumstances the central issue of American policy has practically nothing to do with the hotly debated question of recognizing the Chinese Communist regime and admitting it to United Nations membership on some basis or other. Neither action would substantially change the present situation, which is the product of Communist China's impressive efforts at rapid modernization. "Recognized" or not, the relative power of Communist China in Asia is in direct proportion to its industrial growth. This growing power now significantly supports Mao Tse-Tung's familiar and effective line against "imperialism" and for his "new democracy." Thus all roads seem to lead back to the importance of economic development in the non-Communist parts of Asia, to serve as an economic and ideological counterweight to China. The economic progress of India and Japan in particular are of vital importance in preventing the "demonstration effect" of economic growth to capture the imagination of the rest of Asia. These countries, as well as the less developed countries of Asia, would benefit from the rise of regional Asian arrangements in which Indian and Japanese successes in the economic field would enable them to serve as an important source of the capital goods and technical assistance needed by the less-developed countries in the area. Whatever is done on the diplomatic level, we cannot be said to have recognized what is happening in China until we are making far more vigorous efforts to produce a contagious success in economic development on freedom's side of the Bamboo Curtain.

# 46 / Economic Development: Rival Systems and Comparative Advantages

## JOHN KENNETH GALBRAITH

Much has been said about the disadvantages of the democratic way in providing rapid economic development of
underdeveloped economic systems. What are the comparative advantages of the major competing systems? Particularly,
what are the advantages of the West in transferring capital
and spurring economic development? These and related questions are discussed below.

ONE OF THE well-observed features of economic development in
the 20th century is the need to choose between two broad political and
economic designs. This choice, one from which developing nations of the
18th and 19th centuries were conveniently exempt, is between Western
constitutional organization on the one hand and Marxian and neo-
Marxian polity and economic organization on the other.

These are not, as everyone knows, homogeneous alternatives. Wide
differences separate a state such as Poland, where the agriculture, and
hence close to half the economy, remains in private hands and subject to
market influences, from the far more completely socialized economy of
the Chinese mainland. There are similar distinctions between the non-
Marxian economies, which, in this case, are enlarged by terminological
preference and political semantics. In Scandinavia, the United Kingdom
and modern India the word "socialism" is politically evocative. As a result
politicians try to find as much of it as possible. In the United States, steps
that would elsewhere be identified with socialist enlightenment—social
security, agricultural price guarantees, even the public development of
public power sites—are firmly for the purpose of making private
enterprise function better.

Also one must be cautious in speaking of a "choice" between the two
designs. Geography and the proximity of military power have had much to
do with the decision. Had Poland, to select a country not unaccustomed to

From U. S. Department of State, *Department of State Bulletin,* XLVII (July 2,
1962), 13–17; an address by Mr. Galbraith to the Commonwealth Club, San Francisco, Calif., June 4, 1962.

John Kenneth Galbraith, professor of economics, Harvard University, served as
U. S. ambassador to India, 1961–63. He is the author of *American Capitalism* (1952),
*The Affluent Society* (1958), and numerous other works.

movement, been radically relocated after World War II to approximately the position of Paraguay, her subsequent economic and political history would have been rather different. Individuals do commit themselves as a matter of free choice to a Marxian political and economic design. But nations have rarely done so in the normal course of unmanaged elections—a reluctance, incidentally, which was foreseen by both Marx and Lenin.

Nevertheless these broad alternatives exist. My purpose is to weigh their advantages and disadvantages from the standpoint of the developing country. I am aware that an American ambassador will not be considered by everyone a wholly impartial judge. And even in this liberal and sophisticated gathering there would doubtless be eyebrow-lifting if any evidence were to lead me to the wrong conclusion.

But the choice merits serious assessment. Much of the present literature consists of declarations of superiority by one side or the other. We share with the Communists a strong faith in the value of robust assertion. Were the advantage all on our side, we would have little reason to worry. But we do worry, and it might be well, accordingly, for us to have a moderately unemotional appraisal of what we have to offer the developing nations as compared with the Communists.

### The Goal of Developing Countries

The goal of the developing country can be quickly stated: It is to bring itself as rapidly as possible into the 20th century and with the apparatus of individual and group well-being—food, clothing, education, health services, housing, entertainment, and automobiles—which is associated in every mind, urban and rural, bourgeois and Bolshevist, with 20th-century existence. Here and there are some that demur. But in my observation the most monastic Christian, the most contemplative Buddhist, and the most devout Gandhian cannot be considered completely secure against the charms of the bicycle, motor scooter, or transistor radio.

The things associated with modern civilization are now denied by backwardness and poverty. The task of the two systems is to overcome this poverty. The causes of poverty, in turn, are not simple—although the problem has suffered prodigiously from oversimplification. One cause, clearly, is an oppressive social structure which channels return from the many to the few and which denies the individual the natural reward of his efforts at self-improvement. Another is a feeble, nonexistent, or corrupt apparatus of public administration which denies to the country the things—law and order, education, investment in roads, power, manufacturing—which are possible only where there is effective public authority. Or poverty may be itself a cause of poverty; it denies the

country capital for investment, revenues for education, or purchasing power for consumer products which, in turn, are an incentive to effort. Thus poverty perpetuates itself. Such are the fundamentals that both systems must attack. It is unlikely that the same causes operate in the same form and with the same intensity in any two cases. An effective attack, therefore, requires not only efficient remedies but effective diagnosis of the condition to be cured.

Both systems agree on a number of important points. It is common ground that a shortage of capital is a likely cause of stagnation. Both agree on the need for a massive volume of investment to initiate and stimulate not only economic but social advance. There is agreement also that this investment should be in accordance with a carefully conceived plan. (Here we have paid the Soviets the compliment of appropriating an important idea.) There is increasing agreement that a principal object of this investment must be in the educational and cultural improvement of people themselves. The visitor to the more remote parts of Soviet Asia is immediately impressed by the volume of resources going into schools, colleges, adult education programs, and other forms of cultural extension as part of the attack on the traditional backwardness of these areas. If, in the years following World War II, we thought too much of investment in terms of physical capital and too little of the importance of a literate and educated populace, this is an error we are now correcting.

There are, however—and this will doubtless come as a relief—important differences between the two approaches, and these are vital. The first lies in the diagnosis of the causes of poverty and the related remedy. The second difference is in the way development is organized. The third is in the political and constitutional environment of development. Let me take up each of these differences in turn.

### Diagnosing the Causes of Poverty

In the Marxian view poverty is principally caused by institutions which chain the country to its past—which hold it in colonial subjection, which exploit and subjugate the masses and deny them the reward of their labor, which make government not the efficient servant of the many but the corrupt handmaiden of the few.

In the predominant Western view the poor are the victims of their poverty. All societies have capacity for growth; the poor society lacks the resources to invest in growth. Having less than enough for its current needs for food, clothing, and shelter, it has nothing for investment in education, improved agriculture, transportation, public utilities, or industrial enterprise.

Each of these views leads naturally to a prescription. If institutions hold a country to its past, the answer is the elimination of these

institutions. If the problem is the self-perpetuating character of privation, the answer is to provide the catalyzing resources—specifically, economic aid and assistance in its use—which the country cannot supply to itself.

This is the first difference. The Marxian emphasis is on the institutions that inhibit progress and the need to eliminate them. Our emphasis is on the self-perpetuating character of poverty and the catalyzing role of aid. It will be noted that each system has a cause and remedy that is not without convenience to itself. The Soviets, at least until recently, were short of capital. They had a revolution which could be exported at moderate expense. Accordingly it was convenient to associate backwardness with colonialism, feudalism, and repressive capitalism, all of which could be eliminated by revolution. By contrast, we had capital. This we could export with greater ease than comprehensive social change.

The second difference is in the way development is organized. Although there is room for some national preference, and heresy cannot be entirely eliminated, the Marxian commitment is still to state ownership of the means of production—of land, capital plant, and natural resources. Private ownership of productive resources and their use for private gain is one of the retarding institutions. Its elimination leaves the state in possession and this continues. Incentives to individual and group effort are strongly supported. But incentives which use the device of property ownership to combine reward for individual effort with reward for management of property are excluded in principle and in large measure in practice.

The non-Marxian design for organizing development is not so easily characterized. In the past many countries—Japan, Germany, Canada, and to a remarkable degree also the United States—have made state ownership of canals, turnpikes, railroads, electric power and other utilities, and even steel mills the fulcrum of development policy. India, Egypt, and some South American countries are taking the same course today. However, the main and indeed overwhelming reliance in non-Marxian development, both in agriculture and industry, is on private ownership of productive plant. This is true of countries, such as India, which choose to describe themselves as socialist.

### Western Advantage in Providing Capital

The foregoing differences are sufficiently sharp so that we can relate them to results. And in Eastern Europe and China, not to mention the much older case of the Soviet Union, there is now an ample experience of Marxian development on which to draw.

Two major advantages lie with the Western or non-Marxian alternatives. There is, we have anciently been advised, a certain physical difficulty in extracting blood from a stone. This, however, is compara-

*361*

tively easy as compared with getting savings out of a poor society. When people do not have enough to eat, they are loathe to forgo any part of their meal in order to eat better in the future. Pleas on behalf of children and grandchildren leave the man of simple, uncomplicated intelligence unmoved; he reflects that starvation will prevent his having children and, *pro tanto*, grandchildren as well. But Marxian no less than non-Marxian societies must have savings; without them there can be no growth. Accordingly, the Western pattern of development, with its prospect of assistance from outside the country, eases one of the most painful problems of development. This is why economic aid has become such an important feature of Western foreign policy. It is the process by which savings are transferred from countries where saving is comparatively unpainful to those where it is very painful. It exploits one of the major advantages of our system.

The Communist countries are not without resources in this respect. The Soviet Union, though its capacity has been far less than ours, has spared some savings for other countries. Communist economic and political organization deals more effectively—or ruthlessly—with unproductive and excessively luxurious consumption, of which there is always some and may be much in the poor country. And Communist organization can, within limits, squeeze blood from its turnip. The penalty is the pain, and this cannot be avoided. The rioting in Poland in 1956 which brought Mr. Gomulka to power was occasioned in large measure by the enforcement of a rate of saving that was too grim for the people to bear. These last years on the Chinese mainland have evidently been ones of serious trouble and tension. Part of the problem is inherent in socialist organization of agriculture to which I will advert in a moment. But some has certainly been the consequence of squeezing a large volume of savings out of a very poor population.

The larger consequence is that Marxian development risks the alienation of the people as non-Marxian development does not. It seems doubtful if a majority of the Chinese people are very pleased with their government and would vote for it in an uninhibited poll. By contrast, in India, after a decade of development, there has been an overwhelming vote for the government that led the task. If the Indian Government had to subtract the $7.3 billions it has received from the West in overseas loans and grants since independence from the meager incomes—an average of about $70 per year—of its own people, its popularity might well have suffered. We see in India, in remarkably clear relief, the advantages of the Western design in providing capital.

### Western Advantage in Agriculture

The second and equally substantial advantage of Western development is in the matter of agriculture. Industry, on the record at least, is

fairly tolerant as to forms of organization. American industry works well under private ownership. Even the most reluctant among us must agree that the Soviets have made considerable progress with socialism. So no decisive contrast can be registered here. But the undeveloped country is, by definition, a pastoral or agrarian community. The agricultural policy is, accordingly, vital. And it is far from clear, as a practical matter, whether it is possible to socialize a small-scale, densely populated, peasant agriculture. Even in the Soviet Union the agricultural problem has not been wholly solved. And here, at least, there is no serious talk of catching up. Each year we insouciantly extend our advantage in manhour productivity without effort and somewhat to our regret. Outside the Soviet Union, agriculture has been even more of a problem. Poland and Yugoslavia have had to revert to private ownership. In China, by all external evidence, the effort to socialize agriculture has brought a serious crisis. Certainly it has forced her to turn to the West for the largest food imports in history.

There are good reasons for this failure. Farmers, when they are small and numerous, cannot be brought unwillingly into a state-run system of agriculture for they can defeat any system that is available for their control. The employees of a factory, like the men of an army, are subject to external discipline. Failure in performance can be detected, judged, and penalized. (The same rule holds for certain types of plantation agriculture.) A scattered peasantry, carrying on the diverse tasks of crop and especially of livestock husbandry cannot be so regimented. As a consequence, productivity falls off. Working for others, the farmer works at the minimum rather than the maximum, and the difference between the two is enormous. He can be made to work at the maximum by giving him land to work and rewarding him with the fruits of his labor or some substantial share to consume or exchange as he wishes. But this is to restore individual proprietorship—private capitalism—which its doctrine excludes.

One day the Marxian economies may succeed in socializing agriculture—no effort is being spared. And the ability of the small man in agriculture to sabotage a system he dislikes or which treats him badly is not confined to communism. It is the reason for the low productivity and backwardness of the latifundia of Latin America and the feudal domains of the Middle East. But the fact that it accepts independent agricultural proprietorship is the second clear advantage of Western development.

### Eliminating Retarding Institutions

I come now to a disadvantage of Western development. The Marxian alternative, I have noted, emphasizes the destruction of the bonds that tie the economy to the past. Our emphasis is on capital, education, technical

assistance, and the other instruments that allow of change. Until recently, at least, we have been tempted to suppose that any society is a platform on which, given these missing elements, development can be built.

In fact, institutions do chain economies to the past, and the breaking of these chains is essential for progress. The promise that this will be done is a valid and an appealing part of the Marxian case. There is no chance of agricultural development in the underdeveloped and hence agricultural country under systems of absentee landlordism, with the workers or sharecroppers confined by law and tradition to a minor share of a meager product. And feudal systems of farming extend their corrupting influence to government, to the provision of public sinecures to those who lack a claim on the land, to the milking of middle-class and industrial enterprise, and to the destruction of incentives and the morale of the society itself. "In our country," a South American guide once told me, "those who do the least get the most. I hear that in the United States it is the other way around. It's a better system." Progress does require the radical elimination of retarding institutions. If elimination can be had from no other source, the Marxian alternative will sooner or later be tried. The revolution they offer here, we should remind ourselves, is less the Russian Revolution than the French Revolution.

### Political Environment

I come now to the final point of comparison—one, unfortunately, which has been much damaged by bad rhetoric. From the earliest days of their development, personal liberty, equal justice under law, and constitutional government have been important to Englishmen and to Americans. They haven't been the concern of everyone, but we have never supposed they were the fad of the esoteric and privileged minority.

And so it is in the undeveloped country today. The Andean Indian and the landless worker in the Indian village do have a preoccupying concern with keeping themselves fed. But the general yearning for the dignity of democratic and constitutional government is very great. No people who live under a dictatorship ever feel themselves to be first-class citizens.

There can be little question that most people believe that liberty and constitutional process are safer with the Western than with the Marxian alternative. We haven't, in my view, made as much of this advantage as we might. But the Communists are under the considerable handicap that their alternative involves a step into the dark. And while the details are obscure, most people know that it does not involve free selection of rulers by the governed, *habeas corpus,* equal justice under law, and a voluntary return to other economic arrangements should the experiment prove unpalatable.

## Making Use of the Advantages

On first assessment, then, the advantage of the non-Marxian alternative for the developing country is considerable. It promises at least a partial avoidance of the pain that for the poor country is inherent in finding savings for investment and growth. It promises an acceptable and viable system of agriculture rather than a certain unpalatable and possibly unworkable one. And it offers personal liberty and constitutional process. Against this the Marxian alternative promises a more rigorous attack on the institutions—the unproductive claims on revenue and especially the feudal control of land—which exclude change.

But this is not a game where one can count the cards and decide the winner. Some cards count for more than others, and there is the unfortunate possibility that some good cards will not get played.

The Marxian promise can be decisive. That is because the things we offer are only effective and attractive after the retarding institutions are eliminated. In a country where land and other resources are held by and operated for the benefit of a slight minority and where the apparatus of government serves principally to reinforce such privilege, aid is not of much use. It will also benefit not the many but the few. Our promise of independent proprietorship is obviously nullified so long as land remains in the hands of the few. And personal liberty and constitutional government have little meaning in countries where government is of the privileged for the rich.

We must, in short, meet the Marxian promise of reform of retarding institutions. We cannot organize revolution. We can place our influence solidly on the side of reform. Having done this, our cards give us a clear advantage. To be sure, we must play them. We must make good with aid on our promise of a less painful savings and investment process. We must give firm support to the small farmer. We must be clear in our commitment to constitutional process and personal liberty. We cannot suppose that these are wanted only by people of Anglo-Saxon origin of good income. And we must not excuse dictatorship on grounds of anticommunism or convenience in the absence of visible alternatives. The price of doing so, as we have so painfully learned, is disaster magnified by postponement.

These are highly practical matters. If there are no advantages in our alternative, it won't be chosen. The first resort to the Marxian alternative in this hemisphere was in a country where the concentration of wealth and land ownership was extreme, where these had extended a corrupting influence to other economic life and to government, and where dictatorship had been endemic. This being the experience with the Western alternative, it was not remarkable that so many were so little perturbed by the alternative. India, in face of formidable difficulties, is

firmly committed to development on the Western model. That is because already in British India and over the whole country at the time of independence there was a strong attack on retarding institutions—especially on the feudal claims of princes, zamindars and great landlords, and government which was an extension of this landed power; because a substantial measure of peasant ownership had replaced the old system; because aid from outside eased the problem of supply capital; and because people felt secure in the protection of constitutional guarantees and representative government.

The lesson is clear. The advantages are with us. We must, however, have confidence in them and exploit them to the full.

# 47 / Foreign Aid: Billions in Search of a Good Reason

## CHARLES J. V. MURPHY

**The following selection was written in a period of widespread reappraisals of foreign aid policy and programs. It reports the thoughts, as of early 1963, of leading bankers, who saw aid turning into an instrument of nationalistic trade rivalry; of a political scientist, who saw it as a traditional cover for diplomacy; and of Congressmen, who demanded more efficiency and results.**

WARMING TO THE CHALLENGE and informality of a question-and-answer session with the Economic Club of New York last December, President Kennedy flashed a hint of his personal feelings about foreign aid. He was discoursing on the costs to the U.S. of shoring up weaker nations with weapons, goods, and money, when he abruptly said, "I would like to cut out foreign aid. It is very unpopular. It is a hard fight every year. President Eisenhower had the same struggle, and so did President Truman." Then, catching himself, he went on to suggest, as do other troubled men inside the government and out, that he did not know what to put in its place.

Reprinted from *Fortune*, March, 1963, pp. 126–30, 205–12; by special permission. Copyright © 1963 by Time, Inc.

Charles J. V. Murphy, of *Fortune* magazine, is one of Washington's ablest and most experienced journalists in the field of foreign and military affairs.

Since that date Kennedy has buckled down to the enormous task of selling Congress and the nation on the need to contribute $4.9 billion more in the coming fiscal year to a program that has already cost about $100 billion since World War II. Yet in his moment of candor he was acknowledging Washington's awareness of an increasingly apparent situation. Whatever good the vast foreign-aid programs may have produced around the world, they have certainly produced at home a consensus of doubt, disillusionment, and distrust, which in itself, considering the bounty pouring out year after year, constitutes as strange an irony as is to be found in the entire range of American action.

In large part the criticism is the familiar faultfinding with specific programs and results, the kind that echoes from congressional hearings —and is no less telling for its familiarity. But a new and formidable criticism is gathering strength in the American business community. That businessmen are critical is not so surprising as the nature of the new criticism; it puts industry itself in a culpable role in foreign aid. This line of attack comes principally from Eugene Black, who retired two months ago as president of the International Bank for Reconstruction and Finance, George Champion, chairman of the board of the Chase Manhattan Bank, and Herbert V. Prochnow, president of the First National Bank of Chicago, himself a former deputy Under Secretary of State for Economic Affairs in Eisenhower's Administration. They note that foreign aid, as it is coming to be practiced on a bilateral basis by this country, Western Europe, and Japan, is rigorously tied to goods and services that can be supplied only by the donor nation. The effects of this intensifying bilateralism, all three are agreed, could mean, especially in the Middle East, Africa, and Latin America, another mischief-making race for markets and political advantage, with the lending governments separately allied with their own export industries to outbid or outsell all rivals. For the recipient nations it could mean—and for many countries already has meant—being lured into costly projects that do not serve their fundamental economic needs, and hence an undermining of the very economic stability that foreign aid is designed to ensure. Many of the central bankers in Europe, together with economists and government officials occupied with foreign policy, are equally sensitive to the rising danger. What they and the three American bankers would like to see, under terms that will presently be spelled out in more detail, is a shift to much more of a multinational approach to foreign aid.

### *"The Bum and Beggar Nations"*

The bankers' attack followed closely on a devasting thrust from the campus that is still having its effects in Washington. The highly respected political scientist Hans Morgenthau of the University of Chicago has

stated his belief that the American public is disenchanted with the foreign-assistance programs because the government is kidding itself and the voters about the true purposes of such programs. Within the Agency for International Development (AID), which Kennedy created eighteen months ago as a sort of holding company for all U.S. foreign-aid operations, Morgenthau finds not one but six wholly different policies, or activities, being carried on simultaneously, and often at cross-purposes, under the assumption that they somehow embody an "intelligible" theory of assistance. In his breakdown, outlined last June in the *American Political Review,* these activities are listed as humanitarian operations (such as famine relief), subsistence (to prevent the collapse of an organized society), bribery (loans and grants, yachts and palaces for local magnates in exchange for military bases and "political services"), prestige foreign aid (uneconomic steel mills and air terminals primarily for show), defense, and, finally, aid for avowed economic development and "social progress."

Morgenthau particularly questions the central proposition that funds for economic assistance (which in one disguise or another now absorb nearly three-quarters of U.S. loans and grants to other nations) are really capable of fostering stability and certain growth among the underdeveloped countries. Few such nations, he argues, have the managerial talents or the political outlook for making profitable use of the capital and technical help flowing to them. ("As there are bums and beggars so are there bum and beggar nations.") What is even more important, in Morgenthau's view, the real impact of economic assistance upon under-developed societies depends not so much upon the validity of one program or another, measured strictly in economic terms, as it does upon the moral, intellectual, and political climate in which the program must operate. ("Foreign aid [is] too important a matter to be left in the end to the economists.") And where the aid is actually intended for straightfor-ward military purposes, as in South Vietnam, or to advance certain political ends, as in the countries of the Middle East, he urges that the programs be honestly labeled, for two reasons. It would compel a more realistic evaluation of the programs in relation one to the other. It would also force the Washington planners to decide the true politico-strategic interests that foreign-aid policy is itself expected to serve, in the vacuum that cannot wholly be filled by traditional methods of diplomacy and military policy.

That some of these same doubts and misgivings have begun to penetrate the New Frontier became evident . . . [in 1962] when Chester Bowles circulated around Washington a paper summing up his reflections in his role of special adviser to the President on African, Asian, and Latin-American affairs. To the astonishment of liberals and conserva-tives alike, Bowles, until then tagged as the principal raider of the U.S.

Treasury for international handouts and giveaways, suddenly called for a thoroughgoing rethinking of the logic and philosophy of the entire foreign-aid operation. Specifically, he proposed that a higher degree of "selectivity" be practiced in determining what countries should get aid, in what amounts, and on what priority. Those countries that are making an honest attempt to put their own affairs in order and whose prospects of improvement are sound would go to the head of the U.S. list of desirable clients. Those that are beyond reasonable rejuvenation, because they either lack inherent resources of their own or are unwilling to put their own societies in order, would bring up the tail end of the queue. In these terms, Bowles has reverted to the fundamental discipline of the Marshall plan, which held that the U.S. would help those who were helping themselves.

### The Man Who Knows Everything

Finally, of course, there is Representative Otto Passman of Louisiana, a man who has made a career of hounding foreign aid. In terms of immediate effectiveness, he is, by reason of his being chairman of the House Appropriations Subcommittee on Foreign Operations, the most powerful critic of all. Last year Passman all but singlehandedly knocked $1 billion from the Kennedy Administration's first request of Congress in this category.

His case against foreign-aid largess is simplicity itself: Too much of it is sheer giveaway; there is shocking waste; aid has debased the tried-and-true principle of trade in the relationships of nations truly bent on self-improvement. While the American substance has been drained off to develop industries in other lands, foreign steel has been landed at our ports at prices as much as $33 a ton less than the U.S. domestic price. The best place to put federal capital to work, Passman argues, is at home, if any gold is to remain at Fort Knox and if the U.S. public debt is to be kept from overwhelming us before Khrushchev tackles the job.

It is easy enough for statesmen, economists, and political scientists to dismiss the fulminations of Passman as the weather-beaten prejudices of an unreconstructed isolationist from the Bible belt in the hill country. The fact is, though, that Passman is a formidable authority on how foreign aid should not be administered. No one else in the government can match his detailed knowledge of hundreds of programs spread among some fivescore client nations. The digging he does day after day, month after month, year after year, is genuinely heroic. Last year he held his fellow committee-men's feet to the fire while, with alternating guile and irascibility, he conducted scores of witnesses through 710 hours of hearings that filled over 3,000 pages of printed testimony, much of it hair-raising.

It may rightly be said of him, given the American situation in the

world, that he misses the forest for the trees. But he certainly knows all about the trees. Passman's trees are the drooping, scraggly growths that bureaucratic bumblers were unable to nourish in outlandish places either because they failed to realize the soil was too thin, or the climate was poisonously corrupt, or because they themselves were disastrously naive. His files bulge with examples of good American dollars wasted on roads in far-off jungles and mountain passes that go nowhere, on schools that are empty of pupils and teachers, and on steel mills and chemical plants and power plants that do not begin to meet their true costs.

Muckraking of this sort does not make for friends among policy makers whose gaze is high-mindedly fixed on the shape of the forest itself. President Eisenhower, after one particular rasping encounter with Passman, gave orders that the man was never to be invited back to the White House. Kennedy, in his turn, now has him there no more often than is demanded by the minimum civilities due a powerful subcommittee chairman of his own party. But for all that, Passman, with no friends in the seats of the mighty, does not lack influence where influence counts. He dominates the deliberations of Congress in his specialty.

The more or less unexpected doubts of Morgenthau and Bowles, of Black, Champion, and Prochnow, really serve to round out Passman's case. Collectively they are saying that what is wrong is that the foreign-aid operation, beginning with the Eisenhower Administration in its later stages and continuing through Kennedy's, has broken away from its philosophical moorings. It desperately needs restatement as a public philosophy—a philosophy that makes sense in the world as we now find it.

### One Percent of the G.N.P.

Kennedy realizes this all too well. In December he appointed a committee of ten, headed by General Lucius Clay, to conduct what is advertised as a "bare-bones" analysis of the entire foreign-aid operation. Among the members of the committee are investment banker Robert Anderson, Eisenhower's Secretary of the Treasury; George Meany of the A.F.L.-C.I.O.; investment banker Robert A. Lovett, who served Franklin Roosevelt and Harry Truman in many high offices; Dr. Edward S. Mason, a Harvard economics professor; and banker Eugene Black. Their charter in general terms is to decide whether these pyramiding programs are really contributing to the national security. Their first conclusions were scheduled to go forward to the White House in time for the President's own detailed message later this month in support of his request for $4.9 billion of new foreign-aid appropriations for fiscal 1964.

The request for fiscal 1964 is just about what Kennedy sought last year, and so seeks to recapture the exact $1 billion that Passman knocked

out of the current budget. The requests themselves figure out at not quite 1 percent of the G.N.P., the percentage the Kennedy Administration early hit upon as a convenient rule-of-thumb index for calculating the amount of capital that the industrial nations—the U.S., the more affluent countries of Western Europe, and Japan—should each set aside annually for grants and loans to the world of the underdeveloped. Nearly $1.5 billion of the $4.9 billion is designated as military aid to other nations, with the largest amounts earmarked for South Vietnam and Korea. The balance, not quite $3.5 billion, is for all the various activities—such as development loans and grants, technical assistance, supporting assistance, investment guarantees, and contributions to the United Nations and other international organizations—that are classed as economic aid.

The President is under no illusion that he will get anything like these sums. Despite whatever endorsement may come from Clay's committee the current corpus of foreign aid is not likely to fare better in the present Congress than the aid program did in the last one. One of the senior Democratic leaders, after smelling the air on Capitol Hill at the end of January, figured that Kennedy would be lucky to end up with $3.5 billion. Even this figure may be overly optimistic if President de Gaulle's go-it-alone policy for Europe should whip up the fury of those in Congress and in the country who have always held that aid only makes ingrates.

### The Three Controlling Aims

Viewed in retrospect, the major reason why Kennedy can expect to have more difficulty in Congress than his predecessors is that there is no longer that imminent sense of Communist encroachment that gave urgency to the developing days of foreign aid. Starting under Truman, U.S. aid went forth in a series of surges, as the world struggle ebbed and flowed. The major considerations that have since entered into foreign-aid policy making—containment of Communism, support of threatened nations, and economic development of the underdeveloped—crystallized between Truman's second and sixth years in office.

In 1947, Truman rushed arms and military advisers to Greece and arms and economic assistance to Turkey. A year later he set in motion the Marshall plan, which provided $13.4 billion in aid, all but 14 percent in outright grants. Its prime purpose was to save the countries of Europe, especially France and Italy, from possibly succumbing to the control of the local Communist apparatus. In 1949, the Soviet Union having in the meantime blockaded Berlin, the Truman approach to foreign aid dramatically widened. The U.S. undertook to rearm its fellow members in the newly formed North Atlantic Alliance.

The determination to defend the free world against Communism achieved the status of a public philosophy in 1951 when the Mutual

Security Act was passed by Congress. The act undertook to lump the economic and military assistance programs into a coordinated whole. Also included was the Point Four program, which committed the U.S. in principle to assisting the underdeveloped nations toward faster economic growth.

These Truman programs succeeded remarkably well, despite the fact that they were riddled with contradictions. When, for example, the Marshall plan was launched to rebuild Europe, the U.S. with its other hand was still doggedly dismantling German industry. In the opening experimental phase, three-quarters of the aid was economic, the bulk of it going to Europe. In the budget for fiscal 1953, the military element had risen to more than 60 percent of the dollar value. Three years later, under Eisenhower, it had dropped back to about 55 percent. None of these programs was intended to become a permanent policy. The Marshall plan, for instance, was specified to continue only four years, and Congress stipulated, in passing the Mutual Security Act, that it would terminate automatically three years later. As for Point Four, it was never projected as a scheme for the rapid and dramatic industrialization of backward nations. Its simple purpose, as then Secretary of State Dean Acheson assured Congress, was "to show other people how to meet their own needs, not to attempt to meet those needs ourselves." At the close of the Truman Administration the technical-assistance cost approached $68 million. It now totals $315 million annually.

### The Emergency Becomes Permanent

When this apparatus came under Eisenhower's responsibility in 1953, it was very much in the back of his mind, as it briefly was in Kennedy's, to get rid of as much of it as he could. But foreign aid was soon enlisted to support Secretary of State John Foster Dulles' politico-strategic drive to complete a ring of strong points around the Communist bloc. The theory was that as the then weak nations on the periphery of the Eurasian continent were rearmed by the U.S., and as Europe recovered the capacity to defend itself, the U.S. could gradually bring home most of its own forces, with a consequent drop in U.S. military outlays overseas. The U.S., of course, was also required to subsidize governments that in most instances could not support military forces. Thus was invented a form of economic aid called defense support, designed to pay all or part of the collateral costs (pay, uniforms, roads, housing) and also to absorb the running foreign-exchange deficits of numerous friendly regimes.

In 1954 Eisenhower was obliged to ask for a four-year extension of the expiring Mutual Security Act. Nevertheless, the following year Secretary Dulles warned our foreign clients that not even the U.S. could "prudently make vast economic grants a permanent part of its policies."

Even then an emergency supposed to be transitory was inexorably congealing into permanence.

### The Soviet Economic Offensive

And Dulles' words were hardly out of his mouth when the Soviet Union, starting in Egypt, got going on what looked to be a massive economic offensive aimed at seeding its influence in countries that styled themselves as neutrals or non-aligned. A prime element in that offensive was Moscow's offer of lines of credit for military gear, machinery, and technical assistance on easy terms (usually 2½ percent interest, eight to twelve years to pay, and local currency often acceptable in repayment). Over the past nine years the Soviet Union and the other Communist bloc countries, including Red China, have extended a total of almost $8 billion in credits to non-bloc countries. (The U.S.S.R. has put up about 70 percent of total economic assistance, Red China about 10 percent, and the East European satellites the rest.) Some $3 billion of the total was represented by arms; the balance of $5 billion was for economic aid.

This Communist economic drive, actually, has proved to be a good deal less ominous than it had first looked; but it had the competitive effect of bidding up U.S. costs. Candidates for credit perceived that their chances of getting American aid rose significantly if they flirted with the Communists.

As dozens of new and poor nations achieved independence and the so-called "revolution of rising expectations" began to be talked about, Eisenhower put more and more emphasis on the economic side. Since Congress was increasingly restive about "giveaways" (in the early 1950's upwards of 90 percent of U.S. foreign aid had been in the form of grants), the Eisenhower planners turned to extensive use of the soft and soft soft loan instead of the handout, founding or setting in train three new international lending agencies:

The Development Loan Fund (DLF), first and most important, was established to provide capital for long-range economic development on easy terms to nations that could not qualify at the World Bank. The capital was to be concentrated in economically plausible projects—highways, chemical plants, agricultural machinery, steel mills, railroads, power plants, and the like—all to be closely supervised by hardheaded U.S. engineers. The first batch of loans were for thirty or forty years, at respectable interest rates of 3½ to 5¾ percent to commence after a ten-year grace period. Since repayment, however, was to be in local currencies and so inconvertible in most instances, the practical effect was to open a portfolio of soft soft loans all but indistinguishable from grants. So many of these DLF dollars began turning up in the European and Japanese markets that the Eisenhower Administration in October, 1959,

ruled that all capital goods and technical services for U.S.-underwritten projects must be purchased in the U.S. The intention of this restriction was to slow the outflow of gold, but it has, as well, turned the DLF into a subsidy for U.S. business—the kind of narrowly self-serving bilateral arrangement that the banker critics of foreign aid view with alarm. Eighteen months ago Congress specified that all DLF loans be repaid (eventually) in dollars, but it reduced the annual interest to a token service charge of 0.75 percent. So far, DLF commitments total $4.5 billion. Kennedy is asking for fresh capital in fiscal 1964 of $1.8 billion, including DLF disbursements through the Alliance for Progress.

The International Development Association (IDA) was an attempt to try to internationalize the DLF burden. It was set up as the "soft-loan window" of the World Bank in September, 1960; the U.S. subscribed $320 million of the $947 million in capital to be provided over five years. Two and a half years after its birth, IDA's credits are running ahead of its hard-currency inflow, and later this year the major nations will probably have to put up additional capital. IDA banks much the same customers as the DLF, on much the same easy terms, but it holds the second lien on its clients' foreign-exchange earnings (after the World Bank), while DLF holds only the third.

The Inter-American Development Bank (IDB) was set up in 1960 to provide Latin America with both hard and soft loan services. It was capitalized at $960 million. The U.S. put up $450 million, of which 22 percent was earmarked for soft loans. The Latin-American countries subscribed the balance, some of it in their own currencies. The bank has a hard-loan section that competes with the World Bank, but with nothing like the same professional competence; its soft-loan window competes with IDA. IDB was a mistake; it is a bank run pretty much by its borrowers and its prospective clients.

Yet for all the foreign-aid waste and miscarriages, the sum of the outpouring has achieved many valuable political and military ends. Without it, Greece and Turkey would probably have passed under Soviet domination, Italy and France might have succumbed to Communism, Iran would have blown up (it may still do so), and much if not all of Southeast Asia would today be under Communist hegemony. India, that best-advertised showcase of foreign aid, probably has been saved from anarchy (although its economic problems have only begun). Formosa and Israel, moreover, by reason of their talented and vigorous populations, have each achieved a phenomenal growth rate and will soon be invited to work their own passage—as will prospering Greece. U.S. aid has succeeded at least in keeping in existence such new and politically inexperienced nations as Korea, South Vietnam, Cambodia, and Laos. Yet these past successes cannot disguise the fact that today in many countries the population growth is outpacing such increased productivity as the

current aid programs from all sources, European as well as American, can stimulate.

### The Newest Director

Kennedy is now in the process of making his third attempt to frame a philosophy that relates U.S. political and military policies to the current disparate and desperate situations. In his first full-dress discussion of foreign aid, two years ago this month, he presented himself as a hard-nosed chairman with a new broom. The apparatus for managing the programs he accurately described as "haphazard and irrational," and the goal which he set for himself in dealing with the underdeveloped world was to foster "self-sustained economic growth," which sounded fine. But somehow the more he changed things the more they remained the same.

The first executive to whom Kennedy handed the broom was Henry R. Labouisse, a Truman protégé, now Ambassador to Greece. Mistrusted by Congress, he lasted only six months. The second, Fowler Hamilton, a first-class Wall Street lawyer, brought to the job a strong determination to squeeze the "water" out of the more dubious so-called economic-development programs. He did succeed in bringing some order into the scattered programs, which Congress meanwhile had grouped under the single roof now called AID, and he recruited from business some promising mission directors and aides . . . . But the billion dollars that Passman struck from Hamilton's first program unsettled the White House, the White House unsettled Hamilton, and last November he returned to private life, after only thirteen months on the job.

The latest recruit, David E. Bell, previously Kennedy's Director of the Bureau of the Budget, has been described as the very model of a New Frontiersman—the liberal who remains a pragmatist. Only forty-four, a former economist at Harvard's Graduate School of Public Administration, he is an attractive, outspoken fellow who begins with at least one advantage over his predecessors: he has had some first-hand experience working in an underdeveloped country. For three years, beween 1954 and 1957, he headed the Harvard team in Pakistan, which helped that country to organize its first long-range economic program.

On returning in January from a quick reconnaissance trip through Asia, from Korea to Pakistan, Bell made a favorable impression on Congress by suggesting that some program reductions were desirable. But he knows, for all the congressional impatience, that not much can be done precipitously. Many nations have grown dependent on a yearly input of dollars (to balance their international accounts) and food and cotton (from the agricultural surpluses) and military gear; so any substantial cutbacks must be preceded by delicate negotiations with the governments involved. In Southeast Asia, moreover, the input for military and economic

support is likely to increase before it slacks off. Military aid to South Vietnam, not counting the direct expenses of the large U.S. military mission there, now costs close to $200 million annually, and an additional $200 million in U.S. money and food goes to support the local forces and to cover the country's balance-of-payments deficit as well. And Thailand, because of the infiltration of Communist forces from Laos and North Vietnam, is again becoming a client for increasing military support. Now neutralist Cambodia, to which the U.S. has given $86 million in military aid over the years, is demanding more arms to counterbalance those we have given these two neighbors.

### Where the Search Begins

Outlays for military aid are not seriously challenged in principle. Over all, they total less than 2 percent of what we are spending on our own forces. And in such strategic places as Turkey, Iran, Egypt, Spain, even Indonesia, politico-military considerations of State and Defense have more to do with loan making than any economic objectives of AID. The Department of Agriculture, moreover, specifies the kind and amount of agricultural surplus distributed under the P.L. 480 "Food for Peace" program. This runs to $1.6 billion a year; much of it is sold for local currencies and is charged off to Agriculture. The Food for Peace program, which AID helps to administer, represents an aggregate outlay of more than $8.5 billion over the years—but at the same time it relieves the U.S. of the expense of storing the surpluses.

Where the Kennedy-Bell search for a rationale must begin is with the $2.4 billion, embodying nearly 50 percent of the fiscal 1964 requests, that covers technical assistance (mostly grants) and soft loans for long-range economic development. This is the area where the vacuum in policy and philosophy exists. Some twoscore countries are presently DLF clients. But in fiscal 1962, 80 percent of the loans (which totaled about $1.1 billion) went to only six "target" coutries—India ($446 million); Pakistan ($208 million); Brazil ($75 million); Ghana ($62 million); Israel ($45 million); and Chile ($40 million). Yet nowhere in the congeries of plants, mills, dams, and irrigation projects being fostered by these loans is there to be found a unifying economic policy other than a wearied assumption that the U.S. must somehow satisfy the universal lust for industrialization and growth. And the process has clearly got out of hand.

India is a case in point. Recipient of some $7.6 billion in various kinds of loans and grants (nearly $4 billion from the U.S. alone up through last June), India already must set aside for debt service 17 percent of the hard money earned from exports. International bankers believe that anything higher than 10 percent usually signals an approaching foreign-exchange crisis. If, when 1966 rolls around, the U.S., Europe,

and Japan are still willing to bank India's fourth five-year plan on anything like the scale presently contemplated, the annual repayment requirements could rise to $500 million a year, and they could amount to as much as 25 percent of annual foreign-exchange earnings. Pakistan's situation is also perilous. And Turkey is worst off of all, with about 29 percent of its export earnings so mortgaged. Nearer home, there are the lurid examples of Brazil and Bolivia.

These societies have already borrowed to the hilt. A recent World Bank survey shows that some thirty-four countries in the underdeveloped world more than doubled their aggregate foreign debts between 1955 and 1961 while their aggregate export earnings were rising only 15 percent. The ironical fact is that a considerable number of the U.S. dollars flowing out in the guise of economic assistance are silently finding their way to the World Bank and other international lenders as debt service. Indeed, without the side flow of federal dollars loaned on soft terms, the World Bank would have faced shattering defaults.

### Postulates for an Aid Philosophy

The fundamental requirements for government-to-government loans for economic development are certainly obvious. First, the society should be inherently stable. Next, the country should possess resources capable of economic development. Finally, the balance-of-payments prospects should be good. Unfortunately, few of the underdeveloped societies meet these criteria. Bell understands this as well as the next man. In a very real sense, his most serious task is to convince the petitioners that in the absence of these conditions the industrialization they crave is not to be—yet. In one direction, this could mean steering clear of elaborate investment in most of Africa, where the U.S. contribution to development should reasonably be concentrated on road building, schools, the education of an effective civil service—the province of technical assistance. Bell has hinted that Indonesia and Iran, which have been notoriously inept in managing their vast borrowings, might be summarily removed from the U.S. remittance list, although the Soviet maneuverings in both nations, each with genuine economic potentials, would make this an extremely chancy action. The beginning of wisdom could surely mean imposing sterner standards for the management of the $10 billion that the U.S. Government has promised the Alliance for Progress in its first decade. No "self-sustained" growth is going to come from the Alianza billions unless the client nations brace themselves for the most elementary fiscal disciplines. Some technicians suggest that without these the most salutary course for the U.S. might be to give no money at all. But because Kennedy has staked so much of his personal prestige on making the Alianza work, it is doubtful that Bell could nerve himself for so drastic an action, even

with governments as profligate as Brazil. Nevertheless, long second-thinking has prompted a basic question: Would it not have been wiser to seek a cure for Latin America's economic woes through an international apparatus that included the major European nations, long bankers to that region and its first market?

### The Case for Multilateralism

This brings us back to the case for multilateralism propounded by bankers Black, Champion, and Prochnow. They begin with a desire for free, orderly, internationally coordinated, and economically effective growth programs. That means, on the one hand, marshaling the aggregate capital and managerial resources of the industrial nations. It also means, on the other, a combined effort to organize the capacity of the underdeveloped countries to produce more and more primary commodities for export, the only path for those countries toward true "self-sustaining" growth and social stability.

Europe and Japan are already lending or granting more money to the underdeveloped world than is generally appreciated by Americans. In 1961 they put up about 43 percent, or $2.5 billion, of all the investment capital issuing from national treasuries, and nearly 60 percent of the private investment, or some $1.6 billion. France, Portugal, Belgium, and West Germany are all making higher per capita contributions (related to national income) than we are, and Britain and the Netherlands lead the U.S. in credits for private enterprises.

Practically all these funds, to begin with, are bilateral in nature—government to government, or industry to industry. But they differ in their terms and purposes. A considerable part of France's aid for economic development is concentrated in former colonies now regrouped in the French overseas community. Similarly, Britain's investments and grants are predominantly focused in regions once within its sphere of influence— India, Pakistan, Rhodesia, Nigeria, Sierra Leone, Ghana, and such. Elsewhere Europe's lending is generally of a commercial character, at interest rates of 5½ to 6 percent and six to ten years for repayment. The U.S. is thus left to underwrite the greater part of the soft investments.

### The Uneconomic Consequences of Diplomacy

Worse still, in the long view, this bilateralism is more and more becoming a device for stimulating exports (and the U.S. with its tied purchases is as guilty as any other country). As a result of the push for trade, the genuine long-range economic interests of many borrowing nations are being subordinated to the desire to latch at once onto some industrial "magnum opus," to use Eugene Black's phrase, irrespective of its eventual cost. Country A wants a steel mill or a hydroelectric plant.

378

The World Bank declines to bank the enterprise; the economic justification is nil. Then a manufacturer from Country B turns up in Country A, signs a contract, and wangles from his own government a guarantee against loss from the sale of machinery. All the industrial nations are doing this. As one French banker notes with candor, "Never forget that so-called foreign aid is not so much for underdeveloped countries as for French industry."

There is, of course, a short-run advantage in all this to the banker exporter. But what worries bankers such as Black, Champion, and Prochnow is that commercial bilateralism, combined with "political" loans masked as economic investment and tied to trade, is beginning to distort the rational flow of trade and to lure the unsophisticated client into "bargains" that may well deepen his destitution. As Black has pointed out, "aid which is at the mercy of the variable winds of diplomacy offers a poor basis for the rational programing of economic development."

Black, Champion, and Prochnow are practical men. They know full well that no government, least of all our own, would ever give up entirely the politico-strategic options inhering in bilateral "development" aid, however bogus the development potential might really be. All they are saying is that the U.S. should join with the other lending countries for the purpose of more internationalizing of the aid. The advantages of a multinational approach are obvious. It would help to bring now fragmented operations nearer to a coherent whole. It would mean a better matching of total resources to the general needs. An international body would be much less vulnerable to political pressures. Being independent in a sense, it could, with grace, impose on the claiming nations higher standards of performance and a more rational order of true development priorities than one country is ordinarily disposed to set for another country in a straight bilateral deal.

### Toward a World Aid Organization?

The germ of such an organization already exists within the Organization for Economic Cooperation and Development (OECD), to which all the Western nations belong. Attached to it is a Development Assistance Committee, a vehicle staffed by thirteen capital-exporting nations, including Japan. The committee reviews and coordinates the capital supply and demand factors as they affect the individual members. It is now trying to organize separate consortiums for financing the long-term economic plans of Turkey, Greece, and possibly Colombia as showpiece examples of well-managed development economics. It is no bank, of course, and has no executive powers. But the committee does reveal a trend, albeit a tentative one, toward what the multinationalists are urging.

379

Black has not spelled out precisely the kind of organization he has in mind. He has intimated that the functions of the World Bank might be expanded. Champion has been somewhat more explicit. His World Aid Organization, as he has named it, while governed by the high managerial and banking disciplines associated with that bank, would be independent of it. Champion would limit membership in his mechanism to the actual principal suppliers of capital; his aid organization would function as an executive committee for these nations and its staff would be drawn not from government bureaucracies but from engineers, business managers, and bankers experienced in foreign development. When one considers the world aid demand being hypothesized for the next two decades—upwards of $20 billion to $30 billion annually in capital and even more for food, textiles, and raw materials—it seems only prudent that the U.S. should begin preparations for starting up this road. The quality of the company that we can recruit for the journey will necessarily depend, of course, on how well we succeed meanwhile in repairing our splintered European alliance.

# 48 / Message to the Congress on Foreign Aid, April 2, 1963

## JOHN F. KENNEDY

As the years have passed, the Chief Executive's foreign aid requests to Congress have encountered increasingly stiff resistance. Foreign aid programs have been under continuing "reappraisals" both in the Executive Branch and in Congress. The following selection is President Kennedy's foreign aid message to Congress in 1963, supporting budget requests for fiscal 1964. It shows the results from rigorous rethinking of the program, including a study by an outside group headed by General Lucius D. Clay. This was the late President's last foreign aid message to Congress.

"PEACE HATH HER VICTORIES no less renowned than war," wrote Milton. And no peace-time victory in history has been as far-reaching in its impact, nor served the cause of freedom so well, as the victories scored in the last 17 years by this nation's mutual defense and assistance programs.

These victories have been, in the main, quiet instead of dramatic. Their aim has been, not to gain territories for the United States or support in the United Nations, but to preserve freedom and hope, and to prevent tyranny and subversion, in dozens of key nations all over the world.

The United States today is spending over 10 per cent of its gross national product on programs primarily aimed at improving our national security. Somewhat less than 1-20th of this amount, and less than 0.7 per cent of our gross national product, goes into the mutual assistance program: Roughly half for economic development, and half for military and other short-term assistance. The contribution of this program to our national interest clearly outweighs its cost. The richest nation in the world would surely be justified in spending less than 1 per cent of its national income on assistance to its less fortunate sister nations solely as a matter of international responsibility; but inasmuch as these programs are not merely the right thing to do, but clearly in our national self-interest, all criticisms should be placed in that perspective. That our aid programs can be improved is not a matter of debate. But that our aid programs serve both our national traditions and our national interests is beyond all reasonable doubt.

History records that our aid programs to Turkey and Greece were the crucial element that enabled Turkey to stand up against heavy-handed Soviet pressures, Greece to put down Communist aggression, and both to re-create stable societies and to move forward in the direction of economic and social growth.

History records that the Marshall Plan made it possible for the nations of Western Europe, including the United Kingdom, to recover from the devastation of the world's most destructive war, to rebuild military strength, to withstand the expansionist thrust of Stalinist Russia, and to embark on an economic renaissance which has made Western Europe the second greatest and richest industrial complex in the world today—a vital center of free world strength, itself now contributing to the growth and strength of less developed countries.

History records that our military and economic assistance to nations on the frontiers of the Communist world—such as Iran, Pakistan, India, Vietnam and Free China—has enabled threatened peoples to stay free and independent, when they otherwise would have either been overrun by aggressive Communist power or fallen victim of utter chaos, poverty and despair.

History records that our contributions to international aid have been the critical factor in the growth of a whole family of international financial institutions and agencies, playing an ever more important role in the ceaseless war against want and the struggle for growth and freedom.

And finally, history will record that today our technical assistance and development loans are giving hope where hope was lacking, sparking

action where life was static, and stimulating progress around the earth—simultaneously supporting the military security of the free world, helping to erect barriers against the growth of Communism where those barriers count the most, helping to build the kind of world community of independent, self-supporting nations in which we want to live, and helping to serve the deep American urge to extend a generous hand to those working toward a better life for themselves and their children.

Despite noisy opposition from the very first days—despite dire predictions that foreign aid would "bankrupt" the republic—despite warnings that the Marshall Plan and successor programs were "throwing our money down a rat-hole"—despite great practical difficulties and some mistakes and disappointments—the fact is that our aid programs generally and consistently have done what they were expected to do.

Freedom is not on the run anywhere in the world—not in Europe, Asia, Africa, or Latin America—as it might well have been without United States aid. And we now know that freedom—all freedom, including our own—is diminished when other countries fall under Communist domination, as in China in 1949, North Vietnam and the northern provinces of Laos in 1954, and Cuba in 1959. Freedom, all freedom, is threatened by the subtle, varied and unceasing Communist efforts at subversion in Latin America, Africa, the Middle East, and Asia. And the prospect for freedom is also endangered or eroded in countries which see no hope—no hope for a better life based on economic progress, education, social justice and the development of stable institutions. These are the frontiers of freedom which our military and economic aid programs seek to advance; and in so doing, they serve our deepest national interest.

This view has been held by three successive Presidents—Democratic and Republican alike. It has been endorsed by a bipartisan majority of nine successive Congresses. It has been supported for 17 years by a bipartisan majority of the American people.

And it has only recently been reconfirmed by a distinguished committee of private citizens, headed by General Lucius Clay. . . . Their report stated: "We believe these programs, properly conceived and implemented, to be essential to the security of our nation and necessary to the exercise of its world-wide responsibilities."

There is, in short, a national consensus of many years standing on the vital importance of these programs. The principle and purpose of United States assistance to less secure and less fortunate nations are not and cannot be seriously in doubt.

The question now is: What about the future? In the perspective of these past gains, what is the dimension of present needs, what are our opportunities, and what changes do we face at this juncture in world history?

I believe it is a crucial juncture. Our world is near the climax of an historic convulsion. A tidal wave of national independence has nearly finished its sweep through lands which contain one out of every three people in the world. The industrial and scientific revolution is spreading to the far corners of the earth. And two irreconcilable views of the value, the rights and the role of the individual human being confront the peoples of the world.

In some 80 developing nations, countless large and small decisions will be made in the days and months and years ahead—decisions which, taken together, will establish the economic and social system, determine the political leadership, shape the political practices, and mold the structure of the institutions which will promote either consent or coercion for one-third of humanity. And these decisions will drastically affect the shape of the world in which our children grow to maturity.

Africa is stirring restlessly to consolidate its independence and to make that independence meaningful for its people through economic and social development. The people of America have affirmed and reaffirmed their sympathy with these objectives.

Free Asia is responding resolutely to the political, economic and military challenge of Communist China's relentless efforts to dominate the continent.

Latin America is striving to take decisive steps toward effective democracy—amid the turbulence of rapid social change and the menace of Communist subversion.

The United States—the richest and most powerful of all peoples, a nation committed to the independence of nations and to a better life for all peoples—can no more stand aside in this climactic age of decision than we can withdraw from the community of free nations. Our effort is not merely symbolic. It is addressed to our vital security interests.

It is in this context that I hope the American people through their representatives in Congress will consider our request for foreign aid funds designed carefully and explicitly to meet these specific challenges. This is not a wearisome burden. It is a new chapter in our involvement in a continuously vital struggle—the most challenging and constructive effort ever undertaken by man on behalf of freedom and his fellow man.

### Objectives

In a changing world, our programs of mutual defense and assistance must be kept under constant review. My recommendations herein reflect the work of the Clay committee, the scrutiny undertaken by the new administrator of the Agency for International Development, and the experience gained in our first full year of administering the new and improved program enacted by the Congress in 1961. There is funda-

mental agreement throughout these reviews: That these assistance programs are of great value to our deepest national interest—that their basic concepts and organization, as embodied in the existing legislation, are properly conceived—that progress has been made and is being made in translating these concepts into action—but that much still remains to be done to improve our performance and make the best possible use of these programs.

In addition, there is fundamental agreement in all these reviews regarding six key recommendations for the future.

### OBJECTIVE NO. 1

To apply stricter standards of selectivity and self-help in aiding developing countries....

Considerable progress has already been made along these lines. While the number of former colonies achieving independence has lengthened the total list of countries receiving assistance, 80 per cent of all economic assistance now goes to only 30 countries; and military assistance is even more narrowly concentrated. The proportion of development loans, as contrasted with outright grants, has increased from 10 per cent to 60 per cent. We have placed all our development lending on a dollar repayable basis; and this year we are increasing our efforts, as the Clay committee recommended, to tailor our loan terms so that interest rates and maturities will reflect to a greater extent the differences in the ability of different countries to service debt.

In the Alliance for Progress in particular, and increasingly in other aid programs, emphasis is placed upon self-help and self-reform by the recipients themselves, using our aid as a catalyst for progress and not as a handout. Finally, in addition to emphasizing primarily economic rather than military assistance, wherever conditions permit, we are taking a sharp new look at both the size and purpose of those local military forces which receive our assistance. Our increased stress on internal security and civic action in military assistance is in keeping with our experience that in developing countries, military forces can have an important economic as well as protective role to play....

### OBJECTIVE NO. 2

To achieve a reduction and ultimate elimination of United States assistance by enabling nations to stand on their own as rapidly as possible. Both this nation and the countries we help have a stake in their reaching the point of self-sustaining growth—the point where they no longer require external aid to maintain their independence. Our goal is not an arbitrary cutoff date but the earliest possible "takeoff" date—the

date when their economies will have been launched with sufficient momentum to enable them to become self-supporting, requiring only the same normal sources of external financing to meet expanding capital needs that this country required for many decades. . . .

The record clearly shows that foreign aid is not an endless or unchanging process. Fifteen years ago our assistance went almost entirely to the advanced countries of Europe and Japan—today it is directed almost entirely to the developing world. Ten years ago most of our assistance was given to shoring up military forces and unstable economies—today this kind of aid has been cut in half, and our assistance goes increasingly toward economic development. There are still, however, important cases where there has been no diminution in the Communist military threat, and both military and economic aid are still required. Such cases range from relatively stabilized frontiers, as in Korea and Turkey, to areas of active aggression, such as Vietnam.

OBJECTIVE NO. 3

To secure the increased participation of other industrialized nations in sharing the cost of international development assistance. . . .

OBJECTIVE NO. 4

To lighten any adverse impact of the aid program on our own balance of payments and economy. . . .

OBJECTIVE NO. 5

To continue to assist in the defense of countries under threat of external and internal Communist attack. Our military assistance program has been an essential element in keeping the boundary of Soviet and Chinese military power relatively stable for over a decade. Without its protection the substantial economic progress made by underdeveloped countries along the Sino-Soviet periphery would hardly have been possible. As these countries build economic strength, they will be able to assume more of the burden of their defense. But we must not assume that military assistance to these countries—or to others primarily exposed to subversive internal attack—can be ended in the foreseeable future. On the contrary, while it will be possible to reduce and terminate some programs, we should anticipate the need for new and expanded programs.

India is a case in point. The wisdom of earlier United States aid in helping the Indian subcontinent's considerable and fruitful efforts toward progress and stability can hardly now be in question. The threat made

plain by the Chinese attack on India last fall may require additional efforts on our part to help bolster the security of this crucial area, assuming these efforts can be matched in an appropriate way by the efforts of India and Pakistan.

But overall, the magnitude of military assistance is small in relation to our national security expenditures; in this fiscal year it amounts to about 3 per cent of our defense budget. "Dollar for dollar," said the Clay committee with particular reference to the border areas, "these programs contribute more to the security of the free world than corresponding expenditures in our defense appropriations.... These countries are providing more than 2 million armed men ready, for the most part, for an emergency." Clearly, if this program did not exist, our defense budget would undoubtedly have increased substantially to provide an equivalent contribution to the free world's defense.

OBJECTIVE NO. 6

To increase the role of private investment and other non-Federal resources in assisting developing nations....

### Alliance for Progress

In a special sense, the achievements of the Alliance for Progress in the coming years will be the measure of our determination, our ideals, and our wisdom. Here in this hemisphere, in this last year, our resourcefulness as a people was challenged in the clearest terms. We moved at once to resist the threat of aggressive nuclear weapons in Cuba, and we found the nations of Latin America at our side. They, like ourselves, were brought to a new awareness of the danger of permitting the poverty and despair of a whole people to continue long anywhere in this continent.

Had the needs of the people of Cuba been met in the pre-Castro period—their need for food, for housing, for education, for jobs, above all, for a democratic responsibility in the fulfillment of their own hopes—there would have been no Castro, no missiles in Cuba, and no need for Cuba's neighbors to incur the immense risks of resistance to threatened aggression from that island.

There is but one way to avoid being faced with similar dilemmas in the future. It is to bring about in all the countries of Latin America the conditions of hope, in which the peoples of this continent will know that they can shape a better future for themselves, not through obeying the inhuman commands of an alien and cynical ideology, but through personal self-expression, individual judgment, and the acts of responsible citizenship.

As Americans, we have long recognized the legitimacy of these

aspirations; in recent months we have been able to see, as never before, their urgency and, I believe, the concrete means for their realization.

In less than two years the 10-year program of the Alliance for Progress has become more than an idea and more than a commitment of governments. The necessary initial effort to develop plans, to organize institutions, to test and experiment has itself required and achieved a new dedication—a new dedication to intelligent compromise between old and new ways of life. In the long run, it is this effort—and not the threat of Communism—that will determine the fate of freedom in the Western Hemisphere.

These years have not been easy ones for any group in Latin America. A similar change in the fundamental orientation of our own society would have been no easier. The difficulty of the changes to be brought about makes all the more heartening the success of many nations of Latin America in achieving reforms which will make their fundamental economic and social structures both more efficient and more equitable. . . .

Since 1961, eleven Latin-American countries—Argentina, Bolivia, Brazil, Colombia, Chile, Costa Rica, the Dominican Republic, El Salvador, Mexico, Panama, and Venezuela—have made structural reforms in their tax systems. Twelve countries have improved their income tax laws and administration.

New large-scale programs for improved land use and land reform have been undertaken in Venezuela, the Dominican Republic and two states in Brazil. More limited plans are being carried out in Chile, Colombia, Panama, Uruguay and Central America.

Six Latin-American countries—Colombia, Chile, Bolivia, Honduras, Mexico, and Venezuela—have submitted development programs to the panel of experts of the Organization of American States. The panel has evaluated and reported on the first three and will soon offer its views on the balance.

Viewed against the background of decades of neglect—or, at most, intermittent bursts of attention to basic problems—the start that has been made is encouraging. Perhaps most significant of all is a change in the hearts and minds of the people—a growing will to develop their countries. We can only help Latin Americans to save themselves. It is for this reason that the increasing determination of the peoples of the region to build modern societies is heartening. And it is for this reason that responsible leadership in Latin America must respond to this popular will with a greater sense of urgency and purpose, lest aspirations turn into frustrations and hopes turn into despair. Pending reform legislation must be enacted, statutes already on the books must be enforced, and mechanisms for carrying out programs must be organized and invigorated. These steps are not easy, as we know from our own experience, but they must be taken.

Our own intention is to concentrate our support in Latin America on those countries adhering to the principles established in the Charter of Punta del Este, and to work with our neighbors to indicate more precisely the particular policy changes, reforms and other self-help measures which are necessary to make our assistance effective and the Alliance a success. . . .

A beginning has been made in the first two years of the Alliance; but the job that is still ahead must be tackled with continuing urgency. Many of the ingredients for a successful decade are at hand, and the fundamental course for the future is clear. It remains for all parties to the Alliance to provide the continuous will and effort needed to move steadily along that course. . . .

## Conclusion

In closing, let me again emphasize the overriding importance of the efforts in which we are engaged.

At this point in history we can look back to many successes in the struggle to preserve freedom. Our nation is still daily winning unseen victories in the fight against Communist subversion in the slums and hamlets, in the hospitals and schools, and in the offices of governments across a world bent on lifting itself. Two centuries of pioneering and growth must be telescoped into decades and even years. This is a field of action for which our history has prepared us, to which our aspirations have drawn us, and into which our national interest moves us.

Around the world cracks in the monolithic apparatus of our adversary are there for all to see. This, for the American people, is a time for vision, for patience, for work and for wisdom. For better or worse, we are the pacesetters. Freedom's leader cannot flag or falter, or another runner will set the pace.

We have dared to label the sixties the decade of development. But it is not the eloquence of our slogans, but the quality of our endurance, which will determine whether this generation of Americans deserves the leadership which history has thrust upon us.

# 49 / From *American Foreign Aid Doctrines*

### EDWARD C. BANFIELD

In the academic community in general there has been strong
support for foreign aid programs as among the most effective
instruments for attaining foreign policy objectives. This selection, however, gives a penetrating criticism of foreign aid
doctrines. It analyzes and seriously questions the rationale
on which foreign aid programs and principles have been
based.

AFTER CONSIDERING all of the arguments that have been brought
forward, a reasonable man might still conclude that we ought to give
extensive aid to certain countries—much more of it, perhaps, than we are
now giving. Any decision must turn on probability judgments and value
judgments that are highly subjective. That a given country will or will not
develop economically, that its development will or will not lead to peace
and democracy, that its government or public opinion can or cannot be
influenced to our advantage—these are all questions about which we may
form judgments more or less intelligently, but they are not ones about
which we can get reliable answers. And even if we knew the probabilities
exactly, we might still differ profoundly about the amount of risk that the
United States should accept.

That many people favor giving extensive aid does not, then, require
explanation. But that almost no "serious" writers oppose giving it or even
have serious doubts about it; that after more than ten years the theory of
aid has not been worked out and the arguments for it have not been
subjected to hard scrutiny, and that (to the extent such a test is possible)
the factual premises of aid doctrines have not been tested—all his *does*
require explanation.

### The Character of the Discussion

The American theory and practice of foreign aid, as Hans J.
Morgenthau has said, "has derived by and large from certain unexamined
assumptions that are part of the American folklore of politics." The most

Edward C. Banfield is professor of government, Harvard University. He is the
author of *The Moral Basis of a Backward Society* (1958), *Political Influence* (1961),
and other works.

influential writings are hardly more than collections of clichés strung together with rhetorical flourishes. They are full of sweeping statements that turn out on examination to be either meaningless or without any supporting evidence. Nevertheless, their tone is always confident and often hortatory or polemical. The authors do not acknowledge that they have nothing but common sense to go on, if indeed they have that, or that reasonable men may hold opinions very different from theirs. Instead of laboring to make complex what appears to be simple, a task scholars should find congenial, writers on aid, including some of the "serious" ones, try to make matters seem simpler than they are.

Most of the "serious" writing does not clarify the ends of policy. We may be told that the end is to promote freedom and democracy, but the concrete meaning of these ends and the relation between them and others like "national interest" or "national survival" (whatever these may mean) is left unexplained. Economists often ignore the political objectives of aid and treat economic improvement as if it were always the only value to be considered. It is especially hard, apparently, for writers on aid to believe that technological improvements may on balance be undesirable. Writers on aid rarely give any consideration to alternative ways of achieving their ends (e.g., "one way free trade" is not considered by those who favor loans and grants). Sometimes they have no means to suggest for attaining ends that they say are crucial (e.g., Millikan and Rostow do not tell how to bring about the social, political, and psychological changes they say are indispensable). They seldom recognize that the ends appropriate in one country or culture may not be in another, and that, even in those instances where the same ends are appropriate in different countries, the means required to achieve them may be entirely different. Nor do they usually acknowledge that in choosing one set of ends and means we forego the possibly greater advantages associated with others that are incompatible, and that therefore we should decide in such a way as to "balance our margins," i.e., secure the greatest *total* return in terms of the several values (e.g., economic development vs. "impact") among which our stock of resources is to be rationed.

The writing on aid not only lacks the systematic relating of means and ends that is the defining characteristic of rational planning, but much of it conceals the hard problems of choice behind a fog of moralizing. By "moralizing" is meant advocacy, as a basis for action, of moral principles that do not take account of elements of the situation which render them inapplicable or inappropriate. The moralizer averts his gaze from those features of the real situation that constitute the crux of the problem and then, unhampered, tells us how to act in a world different from the one in which we must act. For example, he warns severely against extending aid to corrupt tyrannies or reactionary ruling oligarchies. This would be good advice if the choice were really between a corrupt tyranny and an honest

democracy. Alas, this is seldom the choice, and when it is, the advice is usually not needed. The real problem exists when we must choose between a corrupt tyranny and a Communist one—and here the advice of the moralizer is at best confusing and at worst wrong. He refuses, however, to acknowledge the real problem. If it is pointed out to him that supporting a corrupt tyranny may in some circumstances be necessary, he replies blandly that "the proper and the practical courses coincide."

Similarly, the moralizer cannot see, or else refuses to acknowledge, the tension between the goal of world community and the goal of preserving democracy in the West, or the tension between the security interests of the United States and the development needs of the underdeveloped countries. "As long as our policies are designed to help these societies develop in directions which meet the real interests of their own people," he tells us, "our political and our moral interests coincide."

Sometimes moralizing is half hidden behind an affectation of political realism. For example, Eugene R. Black, president of the World Bank, tells us that by sacrificing our present political advantage to promote long-term economic development we will serve our *real* political interests. And Reinhold Niebuhr, who is known as a political realist, explains that the art of statecraft is to find "the point of concurrence" between the national and the international common good; apparently he is confident that there is such a point, for he goes on to say that "this policy means that we must try to persuade the nation that what is good for the alliance of the free nations is good for our own Nation *in the long run*." Such statements conjure the crucial problems of choice out of existence by making it appear that conflicts of interest only *seem* to exist—that "in the long run" there are no conflicts and "the proper and the practical courses coincide," presumably at the "point of concurrence."

This mentality, evident in most of the writing on aid, ignores the very facts that constitute the problem: that vast areas of the world show little prospect of achieving self-sustaining economic growth or of governing themselves reasonably well within the foreseeable future; that development, when it does take place, is as likely to be inspired by blood and hate as by peace and rational management; that the development of the underdeveloped countries may not on balance be in the interest of the United States or, indeed, of civilization; and that the measures most effective in relieving misery and promoting economic growth are in general least effective in serving the urgent necessities of the West. Instead of facing up to these tragic facts and endeavoring to frame a course of action that is workable and represents the least among evils for us and for mankind, writers on aid generally proffer a few sententious principles of everyday morality and issue stern warnings against using aid for political purposes.

When policy based upon such misconceptions fails, the moralizer knows whom to blame. Not, surely, anyone in the underdeveloped countries—not even if the obvious cause of the trouble is there. Still less those like himself upon whose naive and sentimental notions the policy was based. The fault, he says, is with the United States; it was not generous enough, or not tactful enough, or not firm enough, or it did not organize and plan effectively. That the failure may have been unavoidable, the natures of givers and receivers being what they are, is a possibility that escapes him altogether. "Giving and receiving can be attended by increasing self-respect and friendship," he says categorically, and from this concludes that we should "manage to make the receiver feel he is a partner whose growing strength is important to [our] own welfare."

### Why Aid Doctrine Is Confused

The unsatisfactory state of the theory of aid is to be explained in part by the variety of the situations in which it has been expected to play a part. When the war ended, it meant relief to the occupied countries, and its justification was obvious. When hastening the restoration of the European economy appeared desirable, the meaning of aid changed accordingly. The success of the Marshall Plan encouraged efforts to assist the underdeveloped countries, and so there was a further drastic change in the meaning of aid. Before a new rationale for it had been found—indeed, before the necessity of finding one was fully realized—the Korean War broke out and its meaning changed again, this time to "defense support." When the strategic situation was further changed by the development of long-range missiles, the rationale of aid needed to be modified accordingly. Since ideas, as well as the institutions that embody them, often long outlast the circumstances that give rise to them, it is not surprising that present day aid doctrine consists largely of leftovers and hand-me-downs.

This, however, does not entirely account for the deficiencies of aid doctrine. In particular, it does not account for its optimistic, moralizing, self-deprecating, and apolitical (even anti-political) character, or for the absence from it of rigorous criticism and dissent. To account for these deficiencies, it is necessary to look at certain features of our political system.

Most matters are decided politically by competition of interests. The system gives those who have something at stake in a particular matter a great deal of incentive to exert influence. This leads them to work up the strongest possible case for their interest and to assert it vigorously; it leads them also to search for weaknesses in the arguments of their opponents and to call these to public attention. Competition of interests tends, therefore, to bring a wide range of policy alternatives into consideration

and to expose each of them to searching criticism. When, by contrast, principles, as distinguished from interests, are at stake, the incentive to exercise influence is usually much less and the amount of information and criticism generated in the course of discussion is correspondingly less. When the principles are ones about which there is general agreement, the amount of information and criticism is likely to be at a minimum. This has been the case in the discussion of aid. Some interests have indeed been active, but these (mainly farmers and manufacturers wanting subsidized markets) have almost all been in favor of aid and therefore have had no incentive to analyze it critically. For the most part, decisions about aid have been based on principles—principles about which there was general agreement—and not on the outcome of competition among interests. For this reason, aid has not been discussed as informatively as have those other matters—the farm problem, for example—about which a variety of powerful interests contend.

Because it concerns principles much more than interests, aid as an issue is peculiarly serviceable to the President. One of the most conspicuous features of our political system is the necessity for him to gather in one way or another enough influence to mitigate the extreme decentralization of formal authority contrived by the Founding Fathers. In former times, state and local political machines and the patronage and logrolling prerogatives of the Presidency went far toward giving him the influence he needed. These are still important, but much less so, and the amount of power the President needs to govern the country has meanwhile greatly increased. It is becoming ever more necessary, therefore, for him to enlarge his power by appealing directly to the public through press and television. Sir Henry Sumner Maine observed three-quarters of a century ago that to Party and Corruption, the influences which had hitherto shown themselves capable of bringing the masses of men under civil discipline, democracy was adding a third: "generalization, the trick of rapidly framing, and confidently uttering, general propositions on political subjects."

General formulas, which can be seen on examination to have been arrived at by attending only to particulars few, trivial, or irrelevant, are turned out in as much profusion as if they dropped from an intellectual machine; and debates in the House of Commons may be constantly read, which consisted wholly in the exchange of weak generalities and strong personalities. On a pure Democracy this class of general formulas has a prodigious effect. Crowds of men can be got to assent to general statements, clothed in striking language, but unverified and perhaps incapable of verification; and thus there is formed a sort of sham and pretence of concurrent opinion. There has been a loose acquiescence in a vague proposition, and then the People, whose voice is the voice of God, is assumed to have spoken. Useful as it is to democracies, this levity of assent is one of the most enervating of national habits of mind.

As the power of our central government comes to depend more and more upon appeals from the President to the public, "generalizations" must be manufactured at an ever faster rate and on an ever larger scale. Great formulas for solving the nation's and the world's problems are now an indispensable means of generating the popular support that is required to govern the country. The Cold War is, naturally, the principal subject matter about which "generalizations" can be developed. The question of the proper role of our country in world development is another, however, and if the Cold War were to end it would be one of the few good ones left.

It is not hard to understand why generalizations about foreign aid have popular appeal. We are a nation of activists; we see the relative power of our nation declining and great masses of the world's people suffering chronic poverty while we enjoy unparalleled prosperity. Our impulse is to do something at once. Under the circumstances, about the only thing we can do is to give money. There may be little reason to hope that giving it will improve the situation, but doing so to some extent satisfies our urge for action and it also helps to relieve our feelings of guilt at being rich when others are poor. Moreover, it is cheap, since we do not give up anything really valuable—only money.

There is also at work, however, a much more fundamental and pervasive trait of our national mind. We have always believed that we are the fortunate possessors of political truth, and that other nations will, in time, have to imitate us, or be converted by us, in order to be saved. We have, as Kenneth W. Thompson has said, always abhorred force, distrusted diplomacy, and put our faith in comprehensive formulas for solving the world's problems while exhibiting a "deeply ingrained tendency to speak in large and absolute terms" and to take to all questions a good-and-bad, right-and-wrong approach. Our faith that democracy can regenerate the world without coercion has led us to try one legal or institutional gadget after another. As Thompson, describing the American view of the world after 1914, puts it [in *Christian Ethics and the Dilemmas of Foreign Policy*]:

. . . War was widely attributed to the wickedness of governments and, more specifically, to the nefarious role of secret treaties. A philosophy of international relations was born and flourished which because of its simplicity and directness engendered widespread popular appeal—an appeal that continues to the present day. It was a philosophy which in a spirit of buoyant optimism looked to democracy and national self-determination as twin sources of international peace and order. The creation of popular regimes on the Anglo-American model throughout the world was heralded as the sure corrective to those harsh conflicts that for centuries had wracked international life. Once the numerous subject peoples had achieved political societies reflecting the popular will, their ancient rivalries with "oppressor" states and the struggles

between conflicting dominions warring over territorial claims would come to an end. The unquenchable faith of contemporary Western *homo sapiens* in man's potentialities for progress spiraling ever upward found expression in assurances that a brave new world merely awaited the fulfillment of these goals.

However, faith in the future has had its roots not only in democracy and national self-determination; it also resides in the confidence that novel international institutions have rendered diplomacy obsolete. Implicit here is a belief that the certainty of progress is waiting at the other end of a charter, a constitution, or a court judgment. The United Nations emerges in the minds of some of its American champions as an organization that may confidently be expected to do away with alliances, balance of power, secret diplomacy, and state rivalries.

History, Thompson says, has dealt harshly with these views and our faith in them has been rudely shaken. He forgets, apparently, about foreign aid. The same old zeal to make the world safe for democracy is expressed anew in this. Aid is for the 1960's what arbitration and the World Court were for the 1920's, and what the United Nations was for the decade just passed.

### The Dangerous Goodness of Democracy

The reason for our inveterate devotion to these millennial ideas is to be found in the nature of our kind of democracy. Ours is the only country in which the public at large participates actively in the daily conduct of government; it is the only one in which the opinions of amateurs on foreign affairs are listened to by statesmen and taken seriously by them; consequently it is the only one in which the moral standards of the general public are decisive in the making of policy.

The moral standards of a people are necessarily very different from those of its statesmen. A statesman learns early that it is his duty to act according to the rules of virtue, not those of goodness. Goodness pertains to persons, and is expressed in their everyday relations; it calls for (among other things) kindness, liberality, compassion, and the doing of justice. Virtue, by contrast, pertains to statesmen and is expressed in the actions by which they protect good citizens from both bad citizens and foreign enemies. Virtue has little to do with goodness, and may be entirely at odds with it in concrete cases; frequently the statesman must act unjustly or without kindness in order to protect the society—he must, in short, be virtuous but not good. As Churchill has written, "The Sermon on the Mount is the last word in Christian ethics. Everyone respects the Quakers. Still, it is not on these terms that Ministers assume their responsibilities of guiding states."

Nations, the orthodoxy of political realism tells us, do what their vital interests require, however immoral those things may be. This may

395

be true of nations that are governed by statesmen free to act as their judgment dictates. It is not, however, true of those governed, as ours is, by public opinion. A nation governed by public opinion may act contrary to its fundamental moral standards when swept by passion or when self-deceived. But it does not act so from deliberation or calculation. What is more, it is strongly impelled to express in action the *positive* principles of its morality, i.e., its goodness.

American foreign policy has long been heavily tainted with goodness, and our country, consequently, has frequently acted against its own interests. Political realists, overlooking the difference between the morality of peoples and that of statesmen, have usually regarded American goodness as mere hypocrisy and have looked in the usual places for the "real" reasons of national interest that they were sure must exist.

The optimistic, moralizing, and apolitical nature of American aid doctrine is a characteristic expression of this goodness. Goodness inclines men to have faith in each other, or at any rate to give each other the benefit of the doubt; public opinion therefore takes a compassionate and hopeful view of the prospects for growth and development however discouraging may be the underlying realities of the situation. It is by moralizing that one appeals to goodness; the discussion of the truly hard problems of choice, viz., those in which the principles of goodness will not suffice as criteria, presupposes virtue rather than goodness. Action that is apolitical in the sense that it sees in the situation not the necessity of a struggle for power but rather the opportunity to cooperate in the realization of shared ends is consistent with goodness but not necessarily with virtue.

To know when and on what terms to subordinate goodness to virtue requires high intellectual and moral powers as well as much experience in making—and in taking responsibility for—decisions in important public matters. Few citizens can have all of these qualifications. The citizen, moreover, knows that his views will count only along with those of millions of other citizens, and so he may not trouble to go deeply enough into any public question to see its full moral complexity. Hence his confidence that the proper and the practical courses will coincide and that great affairs of states may be decided by the standards that apply in everyday life.

A public, moreover, cannot deliberately transgress the principles of its morality. Societies are held together by attachment to common values, especially ones that are held sacred. To call such values publicly into question, to consider openly the expediency of transgressing them, and then actually to do so (even though in order to realize other values) would profane and destroy the values and so weaken the mystic bonds that hold the society together. Such a thing could happen only if the values of the society had already lost their sacredness, and if, therefore,

the society was in process of disintegration. A healthy society cannot subject its ultimate moral code to detached, rational scrutiny. If its code is to be scrutinized at all, the scrutinizing must be done by an elite set apart for the purpose—one which, like a bomb decontamination squad, possesses both a specialized skill and a willingness to expose itself to risk for the sake of the society. The professional statesman belongs to this elite.

Much as we may wish it, the world cannot be ruled according to the Sermon on the Mount or the principles of the Quakers, and a determined effort to rule it so may lead to disaster. The goodness and optimism inseparable from democracy represent a great peril. The peril would be somewhat less if we gave our statesmen wide discretion in foreign affairs, as the other democracies do. Our statesmen, however, are trained to goodness, and they are selected for it rather than for virtue. Our tradition and the exigencies of our political system, moreover, tend more and more to subordinate them to public opinion. Confident that its goodness is the world's best hope, American public opinion reaches out eagerly for wider power in world affairs ("accepts responsibility for world leadership" is the cant phrase), thereby engendering—the United Nations is a case in point—ever more goodness in places where virtue is required, and thereby increasing ever more the incongruity between the reality of the situation in which we must act and the moral principles upon which our action is based. It is quite possible that the American people may be persuaded that the indiscriminate use of aid is folly (events may persuade them of this even though their leaders tell them the contrary). But this will not necessarily improve our foreign policy very greatly. The millennial and redemptionist character of that policy will not necessarily be changed thereby; if the American people cannot express their goodness through foreign aid they will doubtless find some other way of expressing it. To the extent that public opinion rules, our policy will reflect goodness. This is a cause for concern because goodness is, by its very nature, incapable of understanding its own inadequacy as a principle by which to govern relations among states.

# 50 / The Caricature of Foreign Aid

### HARLAN CLEVELAND

In the following selection, the foreign aid programs are defended. Mr. Cleveland discusses such questions as: Are
foreign aid operations merely attempts to fill bottomless pits?
Is the United States operating alone in this field? Is there
no end to foreign aid? Does public opinion in the United
States oppose it?

ALBERT EINSTEIN used to say that every proposition should be as
simple as possible . . . but not one bit simpler. Foreign aid cannot be
made simple. If you hear anybody say he's going to make it simple for
you, put him down as simple-minded.

International development is an intricate role of international complexity, and our foreign aid, as part of it, is a multi-purpose tool.

This is of course why purposes and limitations of AID are so
widely misunderstood. Everybody's favorite modern language teacher,
Professor Henry Higgins, had a similar problem with grasping the varied
purposes and motivations of one Liza Doolittle. If you think it's hard to
understand the "why" of foreign aid, stop a moment and think whether
you *really* know why any one person of your acquaintance acts just the
way he does. Then multiply your uncertainty by 180 million givers and a
billion recipients of aid. This exercise won't help you understand U.S.
foreign economic policy any better, but it's designed to make you feel
better.

Economic aid is like water coming from a hose. The water can be
used for many purposes—to put out leaf fires, to wash the car, to cool off
the children in summer, to break up a dog-fight, or even to water the
lawn. To ask, "Is the water successful?" is to ask another, preconditioning
question, "What was it being used for?"

Thus, aid is used to relieve victims of disaster, to get a strategic base,
to help allies build their armed strength, to stave off economic collapse.
It is used to promote international development—that is, to help build
free institutions inside other people's countries and help the people there
to make those free institutions work. We should not be disappointed if aid

---

Excerpt of an address by Mr. Cleveland at the annual banquet of the Modern
Language Association, Washington, D.C., December 28, 1962.
A brief biographical sketch of Mr. Cleveland accompanies selection 45.

given to build a military highway fails to raise more rice or reduce the death rate from malaria. We should be disappointed only if aid designed to build free institutions fails to build free institutions.

## IV

The current impression of the foreign aid program, as a hapless, hopeless chore, strikes me as a badly distorted caricature, compounded of five illusions:

*First,* that the task of helping other countries is a lonely burden, borne quite unfairly by long-suffering Uncle Sam.

*Second,* that the very process of economic growth—what starts it, what keeps it going, and how an outsider can help—is an unfathomable mystery.

*Third,* that foreign aid is an endless task at a growing cost to the American taxpayer.

*Fourth,* that the Communists do this sort of thing better than we do.

*Fifth,* that there is no public support for foreign aid.

These impressions are false. Let us look at them with the fishy eye they deserve.

## V

Many people still have the impression that Uncle Sam is carrying the whole load of helping others modernize their institutions, because we were the first to get into the business. That was way back in the dim past—a decade and a half ago—when General Marshall, as Secretary of State, helped start an era of history first called "European recovery," more recently "the Common Market," and soon to be called "Atlantic Partnership."

It is still a fact that the burden-sharing is still somewhat uneven. But certainly we are not alone in the business. We have never been all alone, yet. Until recently, talk of getting others to set up foreign aid programs of their own was met with innocent unconcern, like the young lady (returning from language study abroad, I suppose) who was asked by the Customs inspector if she was carrying any pornography, and replied, "Why, Sir, I don't even own a pornograph!"

Today, ours is not the only government with an overseas aid agency. There are foreign aid agencies now in London and Paris and Bonn and Tokyo and Brussels and Tel Aviv and Stockholm and Copenhagen as well. According to the definition of "foreign aid" adopted by the Organization for Economic Cooperation and Development, which compares aid with per capita gross national product, the United States aid program is proportionately not the largest but the fifth largest in the world today.

And this refers only to national aid programs. As you well know, we also work through big international organizations—the World Bank, the International Development Association, the International Monetary Fund, and all the Specialized Agencies of the United Nations. We are typically the largest stockholder in these enterprises, as we should be and want to be. But hundreds of millions of dollars are put in by other countries—totalling far more than we contribute. Indeed, one of the good things about working at economic development through international agencies is that it helps make sure that others are doing their part, too.

No, we are not in this thing by ourselves. Only if we were out of it, would we be all alone.

## VI

The second component of the caricature is that the whole business of starting and helping economic growth is a total mystery. There is, indeed, much that we do not yet know about it. What is the role of political leadership in creating a national "will to grow"? How does one go about rooting out corruption in societies where it has become part of the national fabric? How and at what pace can one change, without producing social trauma, customs which frustrate growth? There are many tough questions like these; and to all of them must be added the even tougher question: how, in each country, can outsiders help the insiders build their own free institutions—without making things worse?

I sometimes think that stimulating and managing the modernization process is the most complex and delicate task of social engineering ever consciously undertaken by the mind of man. It is full of pitfalls and those who are working at it will surely tumble into some of them. But as our own pioneers learned on the American prairie, it was no good to have the courage to begin without the strength to continue.

We have not been long at this task, but we have learned much— from mistakes, needless to say.

Our first mistake was to set out breezily to transfer wholesale the institutions and ideas of the economically dynamic to the static societies. When it turned out that you couldn't dig a hole and plant there a replica of some European or American institutions, many Americans suffered a sentimental revolution and swung the other way: the developed countries, we were told, should simply do for the less developed what the "people themselves" wanted done.

But there were problems in transforming this idea into action, too. One was that the leaders of the less-developed countries tended to make the same mistake that we did in the earliest period: that is, they tended to think that what *they* wanted was what *we* already had. Another was

the difficulty of being sure, from the outside, who the "people themselves" were. It is not easy to analyze the rapid mutation of political power in somebody else's country.

In the end, it was necessary to learn how to make a creative blend of *our* technology and administrative skills and *their* folkways and workways—building modern-style institutions out of local cultural raw materials.

Our understanding is still primitive. The state of our theory about how to do this—how to transfer and adapt the growth-inducing elements from one society to another—is still woefully short of the practitioners' needs. But at least we know enough about it to check some old ideas. For example:

We know that a few miles of road in the wilderness, an isolated health center, a country schoolhouse, or a clean-up campaign in one village, do not add up to a development process.

We know that it is much harder to grow people than it is to grow anything else—and much more important, too.

We know that we are living in an era of deep mutual involvement in each other's internal affairs—and we know that this raises some interesting policy questions about the role of the outsider and the principle of non-intervention by a nation in the affairs of other nations.

We know now that the most useful measuring rods in development are those which measure the building of institutions, rather than those which measure only production, trade or national income.

We know that technicians who leave institutions behind are good technicians, and technicians who just leave techniques are bad technicians—even if everybody loves them and they are fairly dripping with cultural empathy.

We know that the vigorous effort by almost all technical specialists to exclude politics from their calculations is doomed to failure.

We know, in short, that development is whole.

If this much knowledge does not provide answers to all the problems, it at least helps to define them. And it is quite a lot to learn about so complex a subject in so short a time as fifteen years. If we can apply these lessons astutely these next fifteen years, the foreign aid program will be a success—measured by the number and quality of free institutions other peoples have created with our help.

### VII

The third component of the foreign aid caricature is the impression that the need for aid is a bottomless pit—that the development road runs through a long curving tunnel with no light at the end—that the cost of the thing is beyond measure and the task is without limit.

Of course world-wide development is expensive. And unfortunately

we cannnot today put a price tag on the job of setting the whole world on the road to self-sustaining growth. But that is not because the cost is so astronomical as to be immeasurable; it is simply that we do not yet know enough to measure it with any real accuracy.

Of course, this will be a long-term job. And unfortunately we cannot today establish a terminal date for the whole affair—as we were able to do with the Marshall Plan. But we do know that it will be shorter if we think of it as long-range. It is guaranteed to last forever only if we make the most costly mistake of all—of tackling 20-year problems with 5-year plans using two-year personnel and one-year money.

The point is that there will be a peak after which the load will begin to taper off. There are more than 100 countries and territories in the so-called less developed world. Yet 40 percent of the total population of that world lives in just two countries. Is it beyond the realm of reason that India and Brazil could, with maximum efforts now, reach a stage of growth during this Decade of Development where massive inputs of government-to-government aid no longer will be required? Or, to put it another way: India and Pakistan, sharing a single subcontinent, have more people than all of Latin America and Africa put together. Some 40 percent of our economic aid goes to those two countries. Is it beyond reason that they can, in a decade of hard work, be earning a considerably larger share of their own way toward self-sustaining growth?

In the meantime, there is a limit to the levels of external assistance, especially capital assistance, which can be absorbed effectively by the developing institutions in the developing countries. We do not know just what the global level is, but probably it is not very much higher than the present rate of flow. So the demand is not unlimited—whatever that limit is.

Also in the meantime, the aid-exporting nations will be sharing the so-called burden on, we hope, an increasingly equitable basis. And as the leading countries now in the "less developed" category move toward modernization, they too can begin to share in the common enterprise as Chile, India, Egypt and others are already beginning to do.

In my view, we should work harder than we have before at the job of establishing at least tentative target dates for self-sustaining growth and of estimating the price tag for reasonably well defined stages. But whether we can do this or not with any degree of accuracy in the period immediately ahead, the fact remains that the task is finite in cost and finite in duration.

## VIII

The fourth face of the caricature is that the Communists are better at the foreign-aid business than we are. They are not.

Perhaps we should get a graduate student in a language and area study program to trace the mistakes the Soviets have made in their foreign aid program. They started by making a slavish copy of ours. Then they failed to learn from our trials and errors. They insisted on making all the same mistakes we made in roughly the same order in which we made them—with a time lag of four or five years, of course.

They built large concrete "monuments," and put bronze plaques on them.

They sent "ugly Russians" who lived in haughty compounds.

They made technical errors. The Soviet engineers who sent cement made for dry climates had to watch in despair as it hardened in the humidity of Rangoon.

They reached out into the less-developed nations to grasp the levers of power, not realizing those levers had first to be created before anybody could manipulate them, for good or for ill.

They overplayed their hand repeatedly—in the Middle East, then in Africa, then in Cuba.

They thought, as some Americans still sometimes do, that aid was a road to popularity—not remembering the lesson in the famous story about the rich Bengali who was told a friend of his really hated him and replied, "Why should that man hate me? I never helped him in my life?" Power and popularity don't mix, for them or for us.

Above all, the Communists could never hide their ambition to make every nation beholden to one doctrine and one totalitarian system of power. And that is an insuperable handicap in a world which likes variety, a world peopled by men and women who can easily tell who wants to see them free and who wants to see them enslaved.

Maybe I don't need to labor the point. Maybe the prostitution of Cuba and the invasion of India have settled, for the moment at least, the question of Communist solicitude for the less-developed areas of the world.

### IX

The final illusion in the foreign aid caricature is that nobody really likes it.

The foreign aid program will, of course, remain under attack—and thereby prove it is important enough to be worth attacking. You will surely remember, as I vividly do, that when the Marshall Plan was first proposed, loud voices were raised to proclaim that it would bankrupt the United States, that it would build socialism in Europe, and that if it worked at all it would only add to the strength of the Communist world when the Soviet Union took over Europe. I also remember that when it began to become clear that the Marshall Plan was to be a brilliant

success, everybody and his brother were for it and it turned out that a remarkable number of people had suggested it first. "Ten cities vied for Homer dead, where Homer living begged his bread."

In any case, the fact of the matter is that public opinion polls—whenever the questions were not loaded—have shown consistent majority public support for sharing our prosperity to help other countries develop the economic base without which there can be no political stability. Every year the leaders of an impressive cross-section of the major private organizations of this country parade to Capitol Hill to testify in support of one or another aspect of the bipartisan foreign aid legislation. Every President and every Presidential candidate since the Second World War have come out publicly and repeatedly for continuing foreign aid.

You may have observed that the supporters of aid stress the economics of the poor countries, while the opponents of aid talk mostly about the politics of the poor countries. Thus foreign economic aid is the special target of those who are dissatisfied about the way the recipients of aid talk and act politically.

The foreign aid director can and should control the administration of his own program. He cannot control what this or that political leader, talking for home consumption, may say at Bandung or Belgrade. Surely the antidote to their loose talk is not to justify it by loose talk of our own about other people's affairs—but rather to help national leaders in every free country to concentrate on spurring internal growth and building free institutions in their own backyards.

# 51 / The Problem of International Payments Imbalances

## CONGRESSIONAL JOINT ECONOMIC COMMITTEE

**The economic instrument of foreign policy must be utilized in the broad setting of international economics. The transfer of capital by foreign aid programs has its ramifications on other sectors of the international economy. This selection sets forth the major elements of the broader problems of trade, aid, and international financial arrangements.**

Reprinted from U. S. Congressional Joint Economic Committee, Report of the Subcommittee on International Exchange and Payments, *International Payments Imbalances* (August 23, 1961), pp. 1–11.

## Introduction

The system of international trade and payments among the industrially advanced countries of the free world has undergone a sweeping transformation during the past dozen years. The key changes have been the lifting of restrictions on external payments, resulting in nearly complete currency convertibility, and the removal of import quotas on most manufactured goods and raw materials, though they are still applied to coal, oil, and many agricultural products.

This marked progress toward liberalization of free world trade and payments conforms to a longstanding objective of our foreign economic policy, and it has contributed substantially to the realization of vital U.S. economic and political goals. By exposing previously sheltered national industries to outside competition, it has stimulated management to improve organization, adopt more efficient technology, and develop better products and thereby it has spurred economic growth both here and abroad. By weakening the excessive market power of concentrated industries and strong industrial unions, it has helped to reduce the danger of a recurrence of sellers' inflation. Finally, it has bolstered free world unity by removing the discriminatory bilateral and regional arrangements of the era of inconvertibility and quotas.

The record is not an entirely favorable one, however. Quotas on certain imports remain and interfere with trade. The European Common Market, which represents an ambitious step toward trade liberalization and economic and political integration for its members, has brought about increased discrimination against American and other nonmember exports. And up to the present the United States has borne a disproportionate share of the costs of programs for joint security and economic development.

Nevertheless, the dominant tendency in the free world over the last dozen years has been toward more liberal trading and payments arrangements amongst its advanced economies. Persistence of this trend would make a great contribution to both free world growth and stability, and to its political and economic unity. It is essential that everything possible be done to encourage further progress.

But it is now becoming clear that even past achievements are threatened by the failure of the free world to create an efficient international monetary mechanism. The difficulties which some of the countries of the free world face as a result of its inadequacy are likely to force them toward more restricted and discriminatory trade, to a lower rate of growth, to a reduced contribution toward economic development and joint military security, and away from meaningful economic integration. In short, the economic objectives of the free world are in jeopardy because its international monetary mechanism is inadequate.

One manifestation of the difficulty is the succession of payments crises, which most recently have affected Britain and the United States. But these are only the most spectacular items of evidence. The demands in several countries to raise tariffs, to protect one sector or another of the economy from foreign competition, to reduce commitments to aid underdeveloped economies, to lower the contribution for military defense, are others. And Britain's recently adopted policy of high interest rates, which cannot but discourage economic growth, is still another. These retrograde pressures are the consequence of arrangements under which a country's international reserves may easily become inadequate.

The Subcommittee on International Exchange and Payments of the Joint Economic Committee is naturally concerned when there is any serious threat to major economic objectives of the free world. It is for this reason that it undertook an investigation of the international monetary mechanism, evaluating it for possible weakness, and considering proposals to strengthen it.

### Analysis: Description and Evaluation of Present System

#### 1. NATURE OF THE PRESENT SYSTEM

*The Gold Exchange Standard.* Countries keep their international reserves in two forms. First of all, they hold gold, which of course can be used on specified terms to make international payments. Secondly, they may hold either one or both of the so-called reserve currencies—sterling or dollars, and these are also generally acceptable as means of international payment. Finally, all members of the International Monetary Fund have unrestricted rights to a certain amount of the Fund's holdings of currencies, and in addition, conditional rights to larger amounts. The Fund's holdings of gold and convertible currencies establish the maximum amounts that member countries together can now get; their unrestricted rights, in total, are a great deal lower.

*Quasi-fixed Exchange Rates.* Under the terms of the Bretton Woods Agreement under which the International Monetary Fund was established, member countries set the price of gold (or dollars) in their own currency and this pattern of gold and dollar prices with unrestricted gold movements determines the structure of exchange rates. But the structure can be modified by the unilateral action of any one country if the change is not greater than 10 percent; or if the change is to be larger, by the agreement of the Fund. Thus the structure of exchange rates can be regarded as fixed, until it is changed; and at certain dates, September 1949, for example, or to a lesser extent in the spring of 1961, the changes have been significant.

*Role of Reserves.* The reserves of gold and reserve-currencies, sup-

plemented by what each country can hope to get from the Fund (and other sources), permit it to make payments which exceed its receipts. If a country's reserves are sufficient it is thus able to finance a level of payments that is higher than its receipts; or in other words, its reserves permit it to finance a deficit in its balance of payments.

When trade is relatively free, and currencies are convertible without restriction into others, deficits (and, of course, surpluses) must be anticipated. This follows because under such conditions payments will not invariably be scaled down so as to be no higher than receipts; moreover, funds can be readily transferred from one country (and currency) into another. And with the gradual growth in the level of trade and spread of convertibility, the likelihood that some countries will have large deficits, and others large surpluses, grows.

Summarizing then, the West's international monetary mechanism is a gold exchange standard, with gold and the key currencies serving as the major reserves; with quasi-fixed exchange rates for the various currencies; and with the need for reserves dominated by the likelihood of large deficits in any country's balance of international payments.

## 2. THE WEAKNESSES OF THE PRESENT SYSTEM

### (a) Major Countries Need Large Reserves

Reserves are needed to allow a country to finance deficits until they can be dealt with by acceptable methods. There are several reasons why, under the circumstances of the present day, reserves must be a good deal larger than earlier.

*Growth in Liberalized Trade Raises Need for Reserves.* First of all, as we have already noted, with progress towards liberal trade and currency convertibility and with a gradual growth in the level of trade the likelihood of deficits is increased and thus the requirement for reserves is raised. But this is only a part of the picture.

*Structural Disequilibria Raises Need for Reserves.* A second reason stems from a change in the factors underlying payments deficits. Typically, in the past, they were a consequence of the uneven timing or severity of the business cycle in the various countries. A country in which demand was inflated, relative to others, would experience a payments deficit, as its purchases increased by more than its sales. The cure for a payments deficit caused by domestic inflation is to halt the inflation, and normally this should and can be done quickly. A country in which demand was relatively depressed would experience a payments surplus. The cure for its domestic and international imbalance consists in prompt domestic monetary and fiscal policies to end the decline. But in recent years, payments imbalances have not been of this type. They have had

their origin in dynamic factors which have created structural disequilibria among the various economies and these have shown themselves to be relatively persistent. Shifts in the pattern of demand (from silk to the synthetic fibers, for instance), shifts in technology, or the rapid development of industry in newly competitive economies may cut into one country's export markets, and foster another's. The proper, though not the easiest or the quickest, adjustment for the deficit country is then to build up a new area of concentration, as Britain did when she shifted resources from coal and textiles to engineering; or as Japan did when she shifted from silk to a broad range of manufactures. But these adjustments take a great deal of time, and for this reason the duration of deficit may be great. The reserves needed to finance deficits during the adjustment will accordingly be high.

*Government Commitments and Need for Reserves.* There is a third reason for expecting the need for reserves to be high. The United States and some of the other advanced countries of the West have accepted responsibility to assist the underdeveloped economies. Such assistance has normally required them to make large international payments. We have also been required to make large additional payments in connection with the common military effort. There is as yet no agreement among the members of the Atlantic Community regarding an equitable sharing of these burdens. Until there is, the United States has had to stand ready to meet these pressing needs, which can grow abruptly without regard to our Reserve position.

*Hot Money and Need for Reserves.* Finally, with convertibility, and no sure guarantee that exchange rates will remain fixed, there are powerful speculative motives for the international transfers of funds; transfers may also be influenced by changing differentials in interest rates. And the volume of funds which their holders can seek to move from one country to another is almost limitless. To refer to short-term capital exports from the United States as an example, they are not limited to the $10 billion of short-term dollar assets held by official institutions in other countries, or to the $17¼ billion of such assets in the possession of both private and official holders abroad. They could be increased many times over by efforts of Americans to transfer their liquid assets to other countries, as was demonstrated in the fall of 1960 when Americans acquired large amounts of short-term assets abroad when rumors of devaluation suggested speculative gains from doing so.

Unfortunately recent experience of currency crises and changes in exchange rates such as the upward revaluation of the mark and guilder have undoubtedly made funds far more volatile than they were earlier. Hence the need for reserves to finance such hot money exports must be much higher than before. The overall need for reserves has surely increased sharply in recent years.

## (b) Supply of Reserves Is Likely to Be Inadequate

*Composition of Reserves.* The total supply of reserves is equal to the amount of gold in official holdings, the amount of reserve currencies so held, and the amount of credit that countries can count upon unconditionally, or at least when their need for it is most intense. The first component is equal to the cumulative amount mined minus that part which has gone into commercial and artistic channels or private hoards. The addition to total reserves through official holdings of reserve currencies cannot exceed the cumulative total of British and American payments deficits and will fall short by (1) British and American losses of gold to foreign countries, plus (2) the amount of dollars and sterling absorbed in private balances. Credit availability includes some of the resources of the IMF together with credit made available on an ad hoc basis through central bank mutual support operations, as in the spring of 1961.

*Overall Reserves Inadequate if Any (Major) Country's Reserves Inadequate.* There has been a good deal of discussion as to whether the total amount of reserves (including credit commitments) is adequate. It seems to us that much of this debate misses the point, for whether the total supply is greater than the total amount needed, or not, does not really tell us whether reserves are in fact adequate. There may well be an excess of reserves, in the aggregate, while at the same time some countries may find their holdings too low. And unfortunately then the deficiencies of these latter countries are not offset by the excesses of others. Indeed, so long as there is any deficiency of reserves in any country, there is an overall deficiency, in any meaningful sense.

*More on Inadequacy of Reserves.* If now we seek to determine whether the volume of reserves is adequate or deficient, we must note that no mechanism exists either to keep the total in line with the total of needs, or to keep the reserves of each country in line with its own needs. And while we cannot, in the abstract, decide whether the total is high enough or not, we can agree that it would be a remarkable coincidence if each country's reserves were adequate. More than that, we can detect a good deal of evidence, in recent exchange crises for example, which points to inadequacy in one country or another at the present time.

One of the strengths of the domestic economy consists in its ability to adjust output to changing demand. When more automobiles are wanted, more will be produced. The same responsiveness can be found in the domestic monetary system. When more domestic reserves are "needed" by the banking system, more will normally be made available through the central banks, or, if the deficiency is felt by only some banks, then through the sale of financial assets by them to other banks whose reserves are excessive. But there seems to be no mechanism which insures

the appropriate response of supply to changes in the need for international reserves. In this critical sector, chance, as it helps determine how much gold can be profitably mined, and the combination of forces that influence the balance of payments of the key currency countries, plays the predominant role in affecting the supply. The demand for reserves plays little part. There is, thus, an ever-present danger that a country's reserves will fall below the level it needs, and that its corrective actions will be injurious to the economic well-being of the free world.

*Future Prospects for Reserves.* The prospects that reserves will fall below the amount needed is even more alarming when we look ahead. The reserves of the free world, under present arrangements, will only grow by an increase in the West's official holdings of gold and reserve currencies. In recent years, a significant fraction of newly mined gold has gone into private hoards, or into the Soviet Union's reserves, and it is widely believed that the addition to free world monetary reserves from this source will not come to more than 1 percent a year. Increases in official holdings of the reserve currencies depend in the first instance upon the payments deficits of Britain and the United States; however, they are in fact likely to be smaller for two reasons:

1. Private holdings of reserve currencies may continue to rise, as they have over the last few decades. They are the more likely to rise, the greater is the confidence in these reserve currencies.

2. And if confidence is wanting, official institutions may be reluctant to continue accumulating reserve currencies. Thus, if there is no lack of confidence, official holdings of reserve currencies would be bound to rise by less than the payments deficits of the key currency countries; while if there is not full confidence, the results might be the same, though for different reasons.

Between 1952 and 1960, the cumulative payments deficit of the United States came to $16.6 billion. Gold production (excluding that of the Soviet Union) came to $8.9 billion. The greatest possible increase in reserves of the advanced economies of the free world in these circumstances could have been as much as $25.5 billion. But in fact there were various drains—gold into private hoards, or into other official reserves, and an accumulation of reserve currencies in private hands, offset by small sales of Soviet gold to the West—and as a result, total gold and reserve currency in the West's official monetary institutions rose by no more than $10 billion, an increase of 29 percent in 8 years—or about 2.5 percent a year.

Generally, under the gold exchange standard, there are likely to be increasing difficulties in securing a large enough growth in reserves. Clearly, the output of gold itself is inadequate, for if it were not, a simple gold standard would have sufficed. But the increase in holdings of the reserve currencies runs into this difficulty—the higher the stocks

already held, the more reluctant the holders are to acquire more, except when the gold stocks of the reserve-currency countries are rising about as quickly; and this reluctance would probably be reinforced by the reluctance of the reserve-currency countries to increase their short-term liabilities too rapidly without increasing their gold holdings.

### (c) Special Difficulties for Reserve-Currency Countries

The United States and Britain are placed in special jeopardy by the operations of the present gold-exchange standard. In order that the reserves of the other advanced economies of the West be adequate, their official institutions must hold large amounts of short-term dollar and sterling assets. These holdings must be convertible into gold or other currencies on demand; moreover, there cannot even be serious doubt about convertibility for if there were, holders would rush to transfer their assets into gold or into a preferred currency.

This means that the gold holdings of the reserve-currency country are especially liable to sharp and severe drains. And when it is remembered that foreign official holdings of short-term dollar assets now come to about $10 billion, while the total U.S. gold stock (including the amount required as reserves against the liabilities of the Federal Reserve Banks) comes to $17¼ billion, the position is seen to be somewhat hazardous. Moreover, recorded private foreign holdings of such dollar assets amount to $7¼ billion, and if a suspension of convertibility should be feared, their owners would presumably join the rush, by transferring their dollar assets to a central bank which can demand gold. Finally, and even more important, given these possible claims upon the U.S. gold stock, wealth owners in the United States showed in 1960 that they can become uneasy at times over the possibility that the dollar might have to be depreciated either against gold, or against another currency; indeed they might be unduly fearful of this possibility. Hence, they would be ready, any time they feared a relative fall in the price of the dollar, to transfer their assets into another currency, and the amount of funds subject to transfer for these reasons could be enormous.

The position of sterling is in some respects even more difficult, for although the holders of a large part of outstanding sterling balances have agreed informally to keep a large part of their reserves in this form, the British gold stock is much smaller.

Thus, the probability of large hot money movements from the reserve-currency countries is especially high, simply because a detonator in the form of foreign holdings of the reserve currency is an inevitable feature of the mechanism of the gold exchange standard. And given this high probability of extensive shifts of short-term funds, the reserve-currency countries need to have especially high reserves. If they lack them, they become exposed to all the dangers described below.

In the light of these considerations, it is not surprising that the United States and Britain do not want to rely upon the growth of dollars and sterling assets held as reserves by other countries. Nor is it surprising that these other countries should on their part want to limit their holdings of dollars and sterling, preferring instead, after a certain point has been reached, to accumulate gold. But when this point has been reached— when the resistance of either the debtor or creditor countries or both to further increases of short-term debt becomes evident—then the gold-exchange standard is no longer fully viable. If that situation does not already exist, it seems, unfortunately, to be not far away.

The special weakness of the gold-exchange standard is that it does not provide adequate reserves. Any of the major economies may be exposed to this inadequacy; the reserve-currency countries are particularly liable to suffer its consequences.

### 3. WAYS IN WHICH INADEQUATE RESERVES CAN HURT THE FREE WORLD

A country's international reserves permit it to pay out more than it receives on international account, the deficit being financed from its reserves. When its reserves are "inadequate," it is compelled to adjust its payments to its receipts more speedily than is desirable. Adjustments of this type may harm the deficit economy without contributing to the removal of the factors really responsible for the deficit; they are even more likely to injure other free world economies both as trading partners and, in some cases, as recipients of aid.

#### (a) Traditional Cause of Deficit and Adjustment— Inflation or Depression

In tradition, a deficit in a country's balance of payments is the result of domestic inflationary pressures relative to the situation abroad. The cure for such a deficit would be then either to reverse the inflationary forces in the deficit economy, or if the other "surplus" economies were in depression, to bring about expansion in these latter economies. Monetary and fiscal measures would normally restore equilibrium, and the equilibrium attained would be desirable not only in the international sphere, but also from the standpoint of domestic stability. Moreover, the restoration of equilibrium should be achieved rapidly.

*This Cause Now Less Important.* Most payments imbalance in recent years have, however, not resulted from such forces. The advanced economies have on the whole been successful in preventing either excessive inflation or depression, and there have been few instances when one economy was considerably more active, or less active than the others. The uneven timing of the business cycle accounts for only a minor part of the payments deficits and surpluses which have characterized the last

decade. And it seems likely that this source of payments imbalances will be of secondary importance in the future.

*Other Causes of Imbalances Persist.* A country can, however, be exposed to a payments deficit (or surplus) which has a quite different origin. Neglecting those which are either seasonal or episodic (like Suez) in character, for they raise no special difficulties, there are two which demand close consideration.

### (b) Deficits Caused by Hot Money

One has been already discussed. Movements of short-term funds, looking either to higher yields, or to the possibility of speculative profit from anticipated changes in exchange rates or in the price of gold, can bring about a very large deficit (or surplus) in a country's payments position. And with the possibility of so large a deficit, there is a need for reserves to be very large, too.

*Appropriate Methods for Correcting Deficits Caused by Hot Money.* An important feature of deficits caused by movements of "hot money" is that they may take place not only when the economy is subject to extraordinary inflationary pressures but also when it is faced with deflationary forces. If they stem from a relatively low level of interest rates, they could be stopped by raising them, but to do this when the economy is depressed means foregoing domestic prosperity. In such circumstances, the better policy would be to permit the capital export to continue while efforts are made to improve the coordination of monetary policy among the major countries. But in order to provide enough time for this coordination to take effect, large deficits may have to be financed for some time from preexisting reserves. If the reserves were not large to begin with, there might be no opportunity for these methods, and instead domestic interest rates would have to be raised, driving the economy still deeper into depression.

If the export of short-term funds is a result of speculative expectations of a rise in the price of gold, or devaluation of the exchange rate, the best cure is to show convincingly that these expectations are groundless. This can be done most effectively when reserves are adequate. When they are inadequate, it may not be possible to do this and the deficit country may have to take other steps to close the gap, such as to raise tariffs, or interest rates, to restrict convertibility, or to restrict aid for economic development. We shall postpone briefly the consideration of these methods since they may also be forced upon a country which lacks adequate reserves when its deficit is the result of dynamic factors.

### (c) Deficits Caused by Dynamic Development

In a world of rapid change, equilibrium in any country's balance of payments is not to be expected under conditions of liberalized trade

and payments; on the contrary, relatively large and persistent surpluses and deficits are a natural and necessary accompaniment of such vigorous growth and change. Among the economically advanced countries, it is, generally speaking, those countries whose growth in productivity has been most rapid which have shown large payments surpluses (i.e., Germany, Italy, France); countries in which the gains in productivity have been retarded (the United States, Great Britain) have had deficits.

*Desirable Corrections of Such Deficits.* The process of correcting these underlying imbalances without reversing the trend toward liberalization and without retarding growth has two aspects. From the side of the surplus countries, these surpluses partly reflect the fact that the growth of aggregate domestic purchases of goods and services plus foreign investment and aid are not keeping pace with rising productivity. In other words, these countries are not living up to their growing means. The resulting margin of excess productive capacity finds its outlet abroad, resulting in balances of payments surpluses and a piling up of gold and foreign exchange reserves.

One requirement for constructive adjustment process is that surplus countries live up to their growing means. The correction of the balance-of-payments surpluses of countries experiencing rapidly rising productivity must occur in part through more rapid increases in domestic consumption or capital formation (including, of course, what is imported from other countries), and in part through greater foreign investment, government aid to underdeveloped countries, and acceptance of a larger share of the costs of common defense. Although some of these adjustments are in part automatic, for example through wage increases such as are now occurring in Germany, they require much time for their realization; in part the adjustment hinges upon appropriate government action and this, too, is likely to lag as is shown all too clearly by the no-more-than-modest progress achieved so far in increasing the share of defense costs and development aid borne by the countries whose GNP has shown the largest increases. Meanwhile, delays and lags result in the stubborn persistence of surpluses; countries whose reserves have reached or exceeded the point of redundancy may feel no urgency about taking corrective action. Since surpluses for some countries must have their counterpart in deficits for others, deficits also tend to be persistent.

The other element in the process of correcting structural imbalances requires action by deficit countries. Deficit countries must act to accelerate their growth in productivity, in order to strengthen their position both in foreign markets and in competition with foreign goods in their domestic markets. Measures to raise productivity necessarily take time to bear fruit; the governmental measures which are appropriate to stimulate growth of productivity are often the opposite of those which would be applied to achieve an immediate improvement in balance of

payments. For example, increased investment in modernization of plant and equipment may require lower interest rates and tax incentives; both the lower interest rates and the increase in domestic spending may temporarily worsen the balance of payments until their effects in higher productivity begin to be felt. Moreover, the experience of the European Common Market shows that reduction of trade barriers (and, perhaps even more, the announcement in advance of intended future reductions) is a powerful spur to technical advance. But the immediate, impact effect of a reduction in trade barriers will be to increase the balance-of-payments deficit through larger imports. Thus, the kinds of measures necessary to accelerate growth of productivity and improve the competitive position of deficit countries take time to bear fruit. And, as we shall see, most of the measures capable of bringing about quick improvement in the balance of payments—import restrictions, tight money, deflation—impair economic growth and intensify the underlying structural imbalance, so that the improvement in the payments position will be short lived.

*Harmful Effects of Other Methods of Adjustment.* Deflation: The country might, for example, raise interest rates and adopt other deflationary measures in order to curb its imports and so reduce payments. But a payments deficit of the kind we are now considering is a reflection of a loss of markets, and so is likely to occur when the economy is depressed. To apply further deflationary pressures at such a time would clearly not contribute to domestic equilibrium. More than that, they would scarcely encourage the investment-inducing facilities and techniques that would be needed to raise productivity and so ease the structural problem.

Trade restrictions: The deficit country might, of course, adopt other policies. It could, for example, raise tariffs to restrict imports in order to reduce its payments abroad. But while such measures might ease its international position, and even secure some relief from depression, the gains would be at the expense of other economies. And since other economies could also be expected to pursue their own advantage, they might retaliate and thus render the measures taken by the deficit country ineffective. What is more, even if the measures did succeed, the free world would lose from the raising of tariff barriers for it would not only reduce international specialization and so lower current productivity but it would also weaken competition and so discourage future technological advance.

Exchange rate adjustment: A devaluation of the exchange rates might also be recommended as a measure for reducing a payments deficit speedily. Provided that other countries did not retaliate, such a move would probably prove effective, and at the same time help to restore domestic prosperity; though perhaps at the cost of an adverse shift in the terms of trade. But the gains of the devaluing country would be offset by losses for the others. And there would be a further loss for the whole

Western alliance simply because any change in the exchange rate would surely stimulate speculation on further changes, and thereby increase the likelihood of large movements of short-term funds.

Reducing aid for development or military programs: The deficit country could reduce payments by reducing the size of its programs for aiding underdeveloped economies, or for joint military security. But while these measures would contribute to the restoration of that country's international equilibrium, it would clearly be opposed to the other interests of the free world.

While the conventional weapons, just described, for dealing with a payments deficit can be condemned on certain grounds, some of them are appropriate when the source of the difficulty is not structural imbalance or hot money movements. Moreover, they are likely to produce their effects quickly. It is this latter feature that would encourage a country without adequate reserves to use the conventional measures whether they are appropriate or not. And when the cause of its difficulties is structural, rather than cyclical, they are not simply inappropriate in the sense that they do not strike directly at the cause, but they are likely to interfere with the needed dynamic adjustments, and in addition to harm the free world by slowing its growth, exposing it to the dangers of inflation, and reducing its contribution to economic development and military security.

But this is the threat which the West must face unless its reserves are adequate. At frequent intervals, some of the major countries will be under pressure to deflate when they should do the opposite, raise tariff barriers, cut foreign aid, and perhaps to depreciate simply because their reserves will be too low to allow them to adopt the other, slower-working policies that could restore equilibrium and in addition contribute to the West's economic health.

*The Reserve-Currency Country Exposed to Additional Dangers.* We have already drawn attention to the special jeopardy in which a reserve-currency country may find itself when foreign holdings of its short-term obligations are high. But this means that it may be unduly subject to political and economic pressures imposed by its creditors. By threatening to convert holdings of dollars or sterling into gold, or another currency, an important creditor can exert an influence which may be difficult to resist, unless the reserve-currency country has ample reserves.

In short, then, inadequate reserves may force important sectors of the Western World to adopt policies damaging to its major economic goals. In the interests of maintaining international equilibrium, economic growth may have to be slowed, developmental aid reduced to too low a level, efforts to enhance joint security curtailed, and competitive pressures against sellers' inflation may have to be relaxed unless reserves are generally adequate. And since the weakness of the current international monetary mechanism consists essentially in its failure to provide adequate

reserves, the importance of making the appropriate modifications in it becomes manifest.

# 52 / Questions of Priority in Mutual Security Allocation

### ARNOLD WOLFERS

The bulk of American overseas financial assistance since World War II has been for military equipment and defense-related purchases. A great debate, which is analyzed in this selection, has continued to revolve around the question of relative emphasis on basic economic assistance and strictly military aid.

IT CAN BE ASSUMED that President Eisenhower was prompted to set up the Committee to Study the Military Assistance Program by pressures exerted upon the administration for a shift from the prevailing emphasis on military assistance (including defense support) to a greater emphasis on economic aid.

These pressures—which are not entirely new—are generated by at least three distinct motivations which raise different sets of questions:

1. Many people, both inside and outside of the United States, are disturbed that so much expenditure goes into building up defenses against the Soviet or Communist threat when millions of men and women are living in a state of dire poverty. In terms of American values, or human values generally, they would naturally prefer to see their country engage in economic rather than in military aid—as they would prefer a national budget devoted to social welfare instead of military preparedness. Perhaps Mr. Dulles had this in mind when, on November 26, 1958, he said that "as an abstract proposition, too much throughout the world is being spent on military and not enough on economic."

However, whether the United States can afford to engage in costly humanitarian tasks abroad, given the limited funds likely to be available

---

Reprinted from Supplement to the Composite Report of the President's Committee to Study the United States Military Assistance Program, Vol. II, Annex B, March, 1959 (Washington, D.C.: August 17, 1959), pp. 35–43. This report is often cited as "the Draper Committee Report."

A brief biographical sketch of Mr. Wolfers accompanies selection 7.

for foreign aid even under the best circumstances, depends obviously on the requirements for pressing nonhumanitarian tasks, and on the priorities to be allotted to the various tasks falling under foreign aid.

2. A second motivation behind the demand for a shift to economic aid is less clearly or not exclusively humanitarian. The Millikan-Rostow school of thought argues forcefully in favor of an aid program designed to assist all countries "in achieving a steady, self-sustaining rate of growth" irrespective of the "short-run political interests of this country."

The assumption here is that "self-sustaining growth," once attained, will not merely relieve human poverty, but "resolve the cold war," "render military deterrence superfluous," "convince the Kremlin that the game for Eurasia power hegemony is hopeless" and thus, in the long run, accomplish more effectively the defense task that is presently being assigned to military aid and short-run economic aid.

It is necessary to determine whether the assumptions on which the MIT study rests are valid if a decision is to be reached on the relative emphasis to be placed on short-range military and economic aid, on the one hand, on long-range economic development aid on the other.

3. Pressure comes from a third source: Eight Senators, in a letter to the President on August 25, 1958, criticized the "serious distortion in the present relative importance which is attached to military and related aid on the one hand and technical assistance and self-liquidating economic development assistance on the other." These Senators may have been motivated in part by the humanitarian and MIT arguments mentioned above, but they stated a different reason to justify a shift to economic aid.

The primary task of the aid program in their view consisted in "strengthening the resistance of the other nations to totalitarianism." They see the danger now faced by the United States and the free world as a Sino-Soviet threat to individual freedom and civil liberties, rather than as a threat to the independence of nations from Sino-Soviet control. As a consequence [they] fear that military assistance may increase what they regard as the chief danger, by contributing to the maintenance in power of "regimes which have lacked broad support within the countries we have assisted," by creating "a militaristic image of the United States," and by "creating in them perpetuating military hierarchies . . . which . . . may endanger the very value of individual freedom which we seek to safeguard."

Here the question must be answered whether, in the light of the threat of further Sino-Soviet expansion, the United States can afford to give priority to the promotion of American democratic ideals and to the defense of individual freedom against autocratic government, Communist or other, even where such defense would tend to increase the Sino-Soviet military menace. In any case, it should be asked: (1) Whether defense

aid against Sino-Soviet expansion cannot be administered in a way that will minimize the danger of promoting the type of autocratic or militaristic rule that runs counter to American values; (2) whether it would be wise, anyway, to interfere with the internal development of other countries or to try to insist on democratic institutions where the preconditions for their effectiveness are absent.

The problem here is not whether the development of democracy in other countries is desirable when the necessary preconditions exist—which nobody would deny—but whether in the face of the Sino-Soviet threat the United States can afford to combat non-Communist autocratic government in situations where the short-run result would be to weaken the military defenses against the Sino-Soviet threat.

### Labels versus Purpose

It clarifies the issues under discussion here if one distinguishes the actual purposes for which aid is intended from the labels under which it is presented to the public at home and abroad. At times, it is expedient to speak of military assistance, although the recipient country is actually in need of aid to bolster its economy or to balance its payments; in other instances it is politic to label the aid as economic although the aim is to strengthen the military establishment of the recipient. Usually the terms are almost interchangeable since almost all military aid, whether in dollars or hardware, will relieve the economic strain on the recipient country and allow it to divert more of its own funds from armaments to other uses. Conversely, almost any type of economic assistance gives the recipient country new opportunities to spend more of its own funds on military preparedness if it so desires.

What needs to be decided, therefore, is not under what name to accord aid but to what uses the United States wishes such aid to be put, whether to military use, to economic emergency purposes, or, finally, to the end of long-term economic growth and industrialization.

A division into the two categories of military assistance and economic assistance is not particularly enlightening and may, in fact, be confusing. The chief distinction is between short-run aid, military or economic, both being in the field of defense broadly conceived, on the one hand, and economic development aid that will bear material fruit at best after two or three decades on the other. It should be noted that some sound long-run economic development programs have favorable short-run psychological and political effects that place them in the first or defense category.

The demands for a shift in the U.S. aid program raise two different questions:

1. Has the present struggle between East and West changed in such a

way that the short-run task of defense of the West has come to require more emphasis on economic and less, therefore, on military aid?

2. Has the present danger of the East–West struggle receded to a point where short-run defense efforts, whether military or economic, should give way to long-run efforts at economic development?

### Short-run Defense Needs

The dangers of the cold war are present dangers. To meet them, efforts of the most exacting kind are needed that can be expected to produce results immediately, or within a brief period of time. Only if and after they have been met can there be room for efforts that will bear fruit at best in two or more decades hence.

Concerning the short-run efforts, controversy has arisen as to whether changes in the circumstances characterizing the East–West struggle have not made military assistance less valuable than it was some years ago, and economic assistance more urgent than before. Several arguments have been put forth sustaining this thesis.

1. It is said that the Soviet bloc has practically given up the idea of expansion through military conquest which it tried in Korea, and is now concentrating on gaining control over other nations through economic penetration and particularly through economic aid. The United States must, it is said, be prepared therefore, to meet competition in this new field rather than to emphasize the race for adequate military defenses.

Undoubtedly, East–West competition in economic aid has become a fact, but it may be asked whether it constitutes a substitute for the earlier military competition or has merely added a new dimension to the struggle. It is worth remembering (a) that in the case of all the recent serious cold war crises—Quemoy, Iraq and Lebanon, Berlin—the character of the challenge was military rather than economic, and (b) that the Soviet and Red Chinese Governments can return to the method of military expansion at any time since they have not reduced but continue to increase their military striking power.

2. According to another argument, American strategic doctrine places chief reliance on long-range strategic nuclear striking power rather than on local forces of countries receiving military assistance. Moreover, since allied local military power is alleged to have lost much of its former value, therefore, it becomes more important to supply friends and allies with economic staying power that will help them resist indirect conquest by infiltration and subversion than to assist in building up local forces.

If we leave aside for the moment the question of whether economic aid is regularly a better means of warding off the dangers of indirect conquest, it should be noted that the strategy of deterrence and defense through strategic nuclear power is meeting mounting criticism, with

many experts arguing that, in the light of the high degree of nuclear stalemate, the possibility of limited military engagements that require on-the-spot local forces should in the future be given more attention.

3. The argument of the eight Senators is also relevant to this point. As mentioned above, they assume that the issue today is a struggle between totalitarianism or autocracy on the one hand, and individual freedom or democracy, as we understand it, on the other, rather than a struggle between two antagonistic blocs, one of which is seeking to upset the present world balance of power in its favor. If this assumption were correct, only such aid would be justified as promised to promote democracy and freedom, and it is more likely that economic rather than military aid would serve this purpose, although neither may be able to stem the tide of autocracy in underdeveloped countries.

Against this argument it should be said that if the struggle in fact were essentially concerned with autocracy in all of its forms, and not with Sino-Soviet expansion and control, the United States and its Western allies would have lost the battle for the time being. The West today is a democratic island in a sea of autocracy, though autocracy varying widely in degree and character, Communist here, Fascist or military elsewhere.

The struggle has not been lost for good, however, as long as the Sino-Soviet bloc remains contained within its present borders. In time many of the autocracies may become liberalized. Meanwhile, although foreign aid should be administered in a way that will promote rather than hinder a process of liberalization, democratic values would not be served if the means of containment were neglected and these countries were allowed to fall into the arms of Soviet totalitarianism, thereby becoming the enemies of the West, and losing most of their chance of future liberalization.

### External versus Internal Defense

In the defense field it makes sense to distinguish between aid intended to help countries protect themselves against *external* Sino-Soviet military attack and aid intended to help them withstand *internal* events and pressures that would draw them into the Soviet orbit even in the absence of any external attack. The first, which covers both military deterrence and defense, might be called aid in the context of "hot war strategy," the latter, aid in the context of "cold war strategy."

1. In terms of *hot war strategy*, there can be no substitute for military aid (including defense support) if the aim is to improve the abilities of the indigenous forces of the recipient country to stand up against an external military attack. This is not to say that it would be wise for the United States to try to bolster the military capabilities of

all members of the non-Communist world. Military assistance to the countries that are exposed to Sino-Soviet military attack must be looked at with a critical eye and with regard to a number of considerations: The area of the recipient country may not be worth the costs of its defense; or no amount of aid within reason could build up local forces to a level at which they would be both able and willing to take up arms against a Sino-Soviet attacker; or better military results, dollar by dollar, may come from expenditure on the American Defense Establishment; or the effort required to build up indigenous forces adequate for external defense may wreck the recipient country by destroying its internal political, social, or economic balance. However, where the conditions are favorable, military assistance adds to the defensive power of the anti-Soviet coalition and thus to the security of the United States.

(It might be worth mentioning that on occasion it makes sense to give external military defense assistance to countries that are in no danger from the Sino-Soviet bloc at all but whose survival is necessary to the stability of a regional power balance. Military assistance to Israel or Jordan falls under this heading since it serves the purpose of balancing the military power of non-Communist countries and, by making them capable of mutual deterrence, of pacifying the non-Communist world.)

2. In respect to *cold war strategy* where the issue is internal rather than external defense, the relative merits of military aid, and economic aid and the character to give to either, raise difficult and controversial questions. Unless they are answered, no decision can be reached for or against a shift to more economic aid, or from short-range economic aid to more long-range economic development assistance.

There would seem to be three distinct ways in which countries might fall under Soviet control by events short of war, or at least refuse to be alined with the West:

(a) The government in power may decide to shift the allegiance of its country to the side of the Soviet bloc, or to choose a course of "positive neutrality" favorable to the Soviets or, finally, to give up ties with the West based on collective defense agreements in favor of genuine neutrality.

(b) Opposition parties may come into power and replace a pro-Western or neutral government by a pro-Soviet government.

(c) Communist forces within the country may arise to power, presumably on the basis of considerable revolutionary public support and turn the country into a Soviet or Red Chinese satellite, and people's democracy.

Not all of these dangers are present in each of the countries that are presently or potentially recipients of U.S. aid. The governments of

Syngman Rhee or Chiang Kai-shek will not and, in fact cannot, swing to the Soviet side or turn neutral. In Europe, the only conceivable danger would be a shift of a NATO country from alliance to genuine neutrality which would raise the question of the price it would be worth paying to prevent such a shift.

Almost everywhere, there are opposition forces with more or less anti-Western sentiments but whose ascendancy to power would not everywhere be sufficiently detrimental to free world defenses for the United States to let itself be blackmailed into giving unlimited support to the "friendly" in-group.

The danger of a rise of indigenous communism, supported by the Sino-Soviet bloc, differs greatly from country to country. It, too, is frequently exaggerated by a government in power as a means of obtaining whatever aid it wants. It is also doubtful in many instances whether such aid will stem the Communist tide. Some aid, in fact, tends instead to increase Communist strength in the recipient country, because it bolsters an unpopular regime.

### Stability Aid—Military and Economic

It is often argued that the economic poverty of the mass of the population is the source of the major internal threat to Western interests. The conclusion is that economic aid is the logical answer whereas military assistance tends to burden the recipient country with a military establishment that will reduce the living standards of most of the civilian population and thus, in fact, enhance the internal danger.

However, of the three types of internal threats to the West listed above, none can be definitely and universally traced to the misery or aspirations of the mass of the people though a dissatisfied and rebellious populace may be a factor behind any one of the three threats. As a rule, the most effective type of aid will be aid that promises to give the greatest internal stability to the country and the greatest satisfaction to those elite groups who are eager to keep the country out of Communist or Soviet control.

1. In many instances military assistance may be the best means of bringing about such stability and satisfaction. A strong military establishment can be an element of order; it gives the government authority and prestige; it offers to many a chance of social and technical advancement. However, not all demands for military assistance or for "internal order and immunity against communism through military strength" are justified in terms of the American interest. Military autocracies are not always stable; they may provoke rebellion led by the Communists. They are not always reliable; there have been cases where the leaders of the armed forces or influential junior officers have gone

over to the Soviet camp (Syria? Iraq?). Excessive militarization may break the economies of weak countries, or it may arouse fears in neighboring non-Communist countries, or split the international non-Communist camp (Pakistan–India). Military assistance as a means of stemming the internal dangers should be scrutinized carefully, therefore, country by country, with an eye to any adverse effects it may have in particular instances.

2. Short-run economic aid, or what can be called either economic emergency aid or economic defense aid, has a vital part to play in the defense against the internal dangers mentioned earlier. Here Soviet competition in economic aid becomes a major factor, though it is not the only justification for such aid.

Soviet economic competition or no competition, there is reason to fear that governments in grave financial monetary or commercial difficulties may be overthrown, or may look elsewhere for support, and that economic crises may lead to the kinds of dangerous unrest on which the Communists can capitalize. Therefore, economic emergency aid—short-run assistance to help countries overcome monetary, fiscal or balance of payment troubles—is an important defense tool. Its significance has increased since the Soviet Union entered the economic field and now stands ready to offer emergency aid if help from the West is not forthcoming, or is not adequate.

One should not conclude that the U.S. aid program should provide funds sufficient to meet every emergency. In many instances, reliance on U.S. aid tends to perpetuate the emergency or increase the probability of its repetition—governments that can count on being bailed out have no incentive to raise taxes, reduce spending or do any of the other painful things that would remedy the situation. As a consequence, the dollar gap, the inflationary pressures, the budgetary deficits may continue unabated. In the case of all countries receiving or demanding economic emergency aid, it must be asked, therefore, whether the risks of their alienation or of their acceptance of Soviet aid are great enough to justify an assistance intended to remedy deficiencies caused by their own unsound fiscal or economic policies.

Long-run economic aid, properly called economic development aid, must be treated separately, both because of the large investment of funds it requires and because of its peculiar relationship to the defense tasks of the United States and its allies.

### Economic Development Aid

The idea of long-run economic development aid to underdeveloped countries is not only extremely appealing, because it suggests help to the underprivileged and represents a constructive effort, but also because

it conforms with long-run American interests. It promises advantages to the "haves," the countries of high living standards, similar to those that slum clearance offers to the privileged parts of an urban community. However, the benefits that flow from the actual completion and successful operation of economic development schemes, for which the Aswan Dam can serve as a symbol, are likely to translate themselves into benefits for the mass of the impoverished sections of a people only after decades, as the MIT report emphasizes. Therefore, even if all the assumptions of the MIT report were accepted—that the recipient country will, in fact, devote the development aid to development and not to current uses, that it has and employs the necessary skills to bring the projects to fruition, that it will survive the long interim period as a free country—the material benefits of industrialization which lie in a more or less remote future cannot in themselves remove or lessen the present dangers of the cold war.

In order to serve as an instrument of cold war strategy, here and now, economic development aid must be of a kind that has psychological results favorable to the West long before it produces any material results. Some development aid has this effect, and the Soviets have not been slow to realize it. In the competition for the allegiance of governments and for the preferences of elites and peoples, particularly of the uncommitted nations, the winner may well be the country that can best demonstrate its concern for an underdeveloped country's industrialization and future economic well-being, no matter how remote and uncertain these may be. Victory in this competition may come long before the long-run projects are completed, and in fact independently of whether they ever are completed or ever prove economically sound.

Here one runs into a serious dilemma. From the point of view of cold war strategy, a relatively phony "economic development" project, such as the paving of the streets of Kabul by the Soviets, may be more successful than a very costly but in the long-run sound irrigation project. Yet, it would be tragic if large funds had to be wasted on the type of phony for which the Soviet Union shows a marked preference. Probably, it will be found that the competitive value of the phony is short lived and that sound projects, if properly publicized and attractive to the elites of a country, will pay higher dividends even in the cold war.

What needs to be stressed, however, is the fallacy of thinking that the time has come to shift from "unconstructive" defense aid (military aid and short term economic emergency aid) to "constructive" sound long-term economic development aid. The latter can at best have a psychological side-effect that will be valuable to the present and exacting defense effort imposed by the cold war. It is also likely to have unfavorable effects, like creating social dislocation, increasing a restless industrial proletariat, or undermining an established cultural and religious order.

425

The MIT report takes lightly the probability that the transition period of several decades preceding self-sustaining growth will witness "an increase in the appetites for improvement surpassing the resources for their satisfaction and cause unrest." The authors of the report must assume that the free world can afford to create additional dangers for itself while waiting for the happy outcome of its long-range efforts. If this assumption is not justified, economic development aid must be judged in each instance on the basis of shorter range calculations, which weigh the favorable psychological effects of "holding out the prospect of economic betterment," against whatever unfavorable effects—social disruption or increased political instability—may materialize during the transition period. Only so can the expected net benefit be compared with the advantages that would flow from using the funds for economic emergency aid, military assistance or additional American national armaments.

It may seem out of place to raise doubts about the value of underwriting the economic development of friendly but underdeveloped countries or to suggest limiting such aid, as a rule, to the amounts either needed to meet Soviet competition in development aid or likely to produce short range psychological capital for the donor. Particularly with respect to India, it is argued that unless India, through our assistance, can match Red China's economic development, the cause of the free world and its way of life will be damaged beyond repair throughout the underdeveloped parts of the world. To this, it can be answered, that unfortunately no amount of economic aid will be able to supply India with the equivalent in capital and working hours that the Communist regime can extort from its people. It can also be suggested that if external economic aid by the United States helps India over its short-run emergencies, gives her technical and educational assistance and meets Soviet psychological competition by some striking demonstrations of Western skill, the United States may be doing as much as it can to meet the dangers flowing from a Red Chinese victory in the productivity race. Similar considerations would apply to other countries in which the government like that of India is genuinely concerned with economic development. Where it is not—and cannot be induced to be so concerned— favorable psychological side effects are the only worthwhile results to be anticipated from economic development aid anyway; here even the resort to "phonies" may be expedient.

# 53 / Foreign Aid: The Essential Factors of Success

## CHESTER BOWLES

A leading proponent over the years of foreign aid as an effective foreign policy instrument, Mr. Bowles came to learn what foreign aid can and cannot do. He feels that future public support of foreign aid is vitally important and that full realization should exist of its limitations as well as potentialities. He lists the essential factors for a successful aid program.

. . . A LARGE MEASURE of our success or failure in the next few years will depend on public and congressional understanding of what the [foreign aid] program can and cannot do, on the emphasis within the program itself, and on the extent to which we can relate our efforts abroad to our own traditions and to the essentials of our own society.

### Clarifying Basic Objectives

More specifically, there are six essential elements which will largely shape our capacity to do what we have set out to do.

1. *We must clarify public and congressional thinking as to the basic objectives of the aid program.*

Let us start by making it clear what the program won't do:

It won't enable us to control events in other countries.
It won't enable us to buy allies and votes in the U.N.
It won't insure us first place in a global popularity contest.

The reasons why our development effort won't do these three things should be clear by now; but since it obviously isn't clear to many observers, let us briefly explore the point.

Most of the recipient nations are either recently emerged from colonial rule or striving, as in the case of Latin America, to establish

From U. S. Department of State, *Department of State Bulletin*, Vol. XLVIII (June 17, 1963), pp. 939–45; an address before the National Conference on International Economic Aid and Social Development, Washington, D.C., May 28, 1963.

Chester Bowles has been an advertising executive, a high-ranking official of the Department of State, a Presidential adviser, and in 1963 became, for the second time, United States ambassador to India.

their own proud, individualistic identity. Consequently they are in no mood to jump through political hoops to please any other nation, however rich or right it may be. We may therefore expect to see the emergent nations frequently going out of their way, noisily and sometimes irrelevantly, to assert and reassert their independence.

While this may be exasperating to many Americans, it should be recognized as a human reaction to a long and humiliating colonial experience—a reaction similar in many ways to that of our own young, nationalistic country in the 19th century. When did the founders and early Presidents of our nation ever hesitate to tell the older nations of Europe where to get off?

Nor will our development program ever be fully understood by the Congress and public—nor will it be effective in its operations—if we continue to present it as a negative stopgap effort shrewdly designed to thwart the Communists.

This narrow view implies that if the Communist movement did not exist, there would be no valid reason for the United States to continue to help the less fortunate nations. For the developing countries this, in turn, ironically transforms a noisy Communist minority into an absolutely invaluable natural resource. Indeed, the unearthing of a local Communist underground might be expected in such circumstances to produce more American dollars than the discovery of oil or uranium.

This poses the basic question: If our foreign aid program cannot be expected to buy friends or votes and if its purpose is not simply to combat communism, what exactly is it good for? What will it do?

Although the answer to this question is well known to this audience, it is essential that it be understood in every community in America, as well as in every congressional committee.

Let me state it briefly: A wisely administered U.S. aid program can help create nations that are increasingly prepared to defend their independence against totalitarian enemies—external or internal, overt or covert—and increasingly willing to work with us as partners on common projects which may lead the world a little closer to peace.

Judged against this realistic yardstick, the program has rolled up an extraordinary record of achievement.

Consider Europe in 1945, dispirited, destitute, and totally vulnerable to organized Communist minorities. Today, thanks in large measure to a wisely conceived program of U.S. Marshall Plan assistance, Europe is a roaring political and economic success with a total production second only to that of our own country.

Consider India in 1947, newly independent, fragmentized by deep-rooted internal differences, with a wobbly government, grossly inadequate food resources, a disrupted transport system, and the bare beginnings of industrial development.

In the last 16 years that same India, with a population greater than Africa and Latin America combined, has created a democratic constitution, run three democratic elections, placed three times as many children in school as before, nearly doubled her agricultural production and more than doubled her industrial production, tripled her electric power, vastly improved her transport system, and, above all, has awakened its Indian people so that today they stand united in defense of their nation against the blatant aggression of their giant Chinese neighbor.

In India, as in Europe, American loans, grants, and technical assistance played a major role. Yet here is the essential point: This aid was not given to force either Europe or India into a satellite relationship to the United States or to purchase good will or votes in the United Nations. Naturally, no country—whether India, France, or any other country in Europe—is happy to feel it is in any way dependent on the United States. Rather, the aid program's objective has been to help establish independent countries able and willing to stand on their own feet and prepared to defend what they believe to be *their* interests—interests that by and large coincide with our own.

### "What Happens to People Is Decisive"

2. Now let us consider a second factor which grows inevitably from the first: *The success or failure of an aid program in helping to create independent nations depends not only on the rate of economic growth but at least equally as much on what happens to people in the process of growth.*

Many observers measure the success or failure of "development" by such purely economic criteria as increases in per capita income, in kilowatt-hours of electricity, in miles of railroad, numbers of irrigated acres, and so on. Yet such standards of judgment can lead to some harsh surprises.

Cuba, just before Castro took over, had the third highest per capita income in Latin America. Indeed, when we compare those Latin American countries with the highest per capita incomes, some of which are higher than several European countries, with those that are most politically stable, we find that there is almost no consistent relationship.

A feeling of national purpose and independence can only be created if the people are given a sense of involvement in their own development, a sense of belonging, and a growing sense of justice. Without these *social* gains, a booming per capita income, if badly distributed, can actually widen the gulf between rich and poor and lead to a political explosion.

As a case in point, I recall two letters I received from friends of mine working in Iraq in the spring of 1958. The first was from a young

American engineer in Baghdad, who reported with great excitement his contribution to the damming of the Tigris and the Euphrates. He listed the exciting industrial development that would soon grow from these power projects as an indication of Iraq's successful development.

That same week, by coincidence, I received a letter from a former associate of mine in India, whose letter in effect was a reply to the engineer, although neither one knew the other. "In the Iraqi village where I live," he wrote, "we often hear that things are going remarkably well in Baghdad, that the Tigris and the Euphrates are being dammed, and that great industries will soon be coming into being. Undoubtedly, this is a grand accomplishment. But out here in the countryside, where most of the people of Iraq make their living as farmers and herdsmen, everything remains much the same. Indeed," he continued, "the only evidence of change here is in the fact that the landlords and the money lenders who formerly came riding out on horseback to collect their rent or interest now arrive in Buick cars."

Obviously something must have changed somewhere, but it hadn't affected many of the people of Iraq. I may add that this was shortly before the political explosion of 1958, when the Iraqi Government came apart at the seams.

In our presentations and our speeches I believe that this second point deserves particular emphasis. Economic growth is critical to national development, but what happens to people in the process is decisive.

### Importance of Rural Development

3. Now let me turn to a third basic consideration: *Orderly political growth in the developing nations is impossible unless it improves the living standards of the 80 percent of the people who live in the rural areas and simultaneously gives them a greater sense of personal involvement.*

In November of 1917, when Lenin announced that the great feudal estates of czarist Russia would be divided among the peasants who tilled the land, he knew that the climax of his effort had been achieved. "Now," he said, "the Revolution has become irrevocable."

In China, Mao Tse-tung's primary appeal was to the peasants. Aroused by Mao's false promises of land and freedom, it was they who provided the mass manpower of his Red army.

As long as the rural areas of Asia, Africa, and Latin America are oppressed with poverty, exploitation, and injustice, they, too, will continue to be targets for Communist infiltration.

The need for greater emphasis on rural development, however, is economic as well as political. This is so because no developing nation can increase its industrial output rapidly if the four-fifths of its people who live in the rural areas lack the purchasing power to buy its factory-produced goods.

This means that our aid program should be increasingly related to the improvement of agriculture, the encouragement of land reform, the creation of rural extension services, and the building of rural schools, roads, and clinics.

As this sophisticated audience well knows, such things are easier to say than to do. Most of us Americans are now urban-oriented. Even our farmers, with their advanced soil technology and their thousands of dollars worth of investment in complex farm equipment, are now largely out of touch with the grassroots farming techniques that are most readily applicable to the rural development of Asia, Africa, and Latin America.

In many countries I have seen our people make an earnest effort to develop effective rural programs, only to become bogged down in the face of the practical difficulties. The heat becomes awfully tiresome, the local people appear more and more apathetic, and new ideas are hard to communicate. The most conscientious of AID administrators may thus find themselves wondering if country $x$ is really ready for a rural program; isn't the more immediate need for a cement factory? After all, *every* developing country needs more cement.

Yet the overriding, urgent challenge of rural development in Asia, Latin America, and Africa must be faced and mastered.

The economic interdependence of urban and rural areas has always been basic to every country, including our own. Here in the United States one of the first signs of a national recession is usually decreasing sales of farm and household equipment in our great agricultural States —a decrease that is quickly reflected back into our industrial centers.

Moreover, in line with my previous point, it is essential that the rural majorities be given not only greater economic opportunity but also an increasingly personal stake in national development.

This takes us beyond the simple question of who owns the land. Although in many cases "land reform" may be no more than a political slogan, wisely planned and administered it can open the door to vast new opportunities for the human spirit and for economic, social, and political development.

Let us consider two cases in point: Country $x$, where the original land reform program ran into difficulties, and country $y$, where from every standpoint it was a substantial success.

In country $x$ millions of acres of land were distributed to the former tenant farmers. Although the enthusiasm of the peasants was great, agricultural production in many areas dropped sharply, and soon right-wing groups who opposed broader land distribution were pointing to the reform program as a failure.

That the program did not fulfill expectations was not a result of land distribution to those who till it but rather an outgrowth of the fact that a coordinated rural development program to back up the land

reform measures was missing. What was needed was an extension service, adequate rural credit, rural marketing cooperatives, better transportation facilities, and a massive effort to educate the new landowners in the techniques of farming and community organization.

In country y, in contrast, the land reform program was a comprehensive and, therefore, highly successful effort. As a result, the distribution of land to the farmers led to a sharp increase in production per acre, an increasing measure of political stability among the rural population, and also to a spectacular increase in the prosperity not only of the rural but also of the urban areas where the added rural purchasing power created many additional jobs and large profits.

May I add that a successful, integrated rural development effort also calls for a high degree of local cooperation among the various government agencies involved—the ministries of health, agriculture, education, welfare, transportation, labor, and all the rest. When their lines of communication and administrative control each run straight down to the village, the result is often chaotic, with each ministry competing for the attention of the village leadership in behalf of its particular program.

In my own experience the method which has been most successful in eliminating this confusion is a coordinated community development operation in which the Prime Minister or the President acts as the chairman of a national rural development board which sets priorities as to resources and manpower. The programs agreed to by this board are then assigned to a rural development administrator who sees to it that each ministry gets its full share of resources at the local level and supplies its services at the proper time and in the proper sequence.

Without an integrated administrative organization of this kind, the various ministries are rarely able to agree on anything. The result is waste of both resources and trained people.

Another critically important facet of rural development that has largely been ignored is the function of the provincial towns in relation to the surrounding countryside. The development program for India, for example, which was originally proposed in 1952, called for groups of approximately 300 villages set around a central provincial town. Here it was planned to create a central marketplace with a high school, technical training school, agricultural training centers, and a sizable sprinkling of light industries.

Unfortunately the initial cost of this program was far beyond the resources which were available. And because after 5 years of independence the 350 million Indian villagers could see little improvement in their lot, it was felt that highest priorities should be given to their welfare. The result was a 10-year village community development program which now covers most of India's 550,000 villages. The next step, many

Indian developers believe, is to tie in the provincial towns as centers of consumer industry, education, and administration.

### Realistic Criteria for Economic Aid

4. Let us now consider a fourth major factor which will help determine the success of our devlopment effort: *the need for clearly worded, realistic criteria for the distribution of economic aid which reflect the requirements of the first three factors.*

The need for such criteria was recognized in the Act for International Development itself. Indeed, in this legislation Congress directed us to do precisely what experience has taught us must be done if our overseas assistance effort is to succeed. For instance, the act says:

Assistance shall be based upon sound plans and programs; be directed toward the social as well as economic aspects of economic development; be responsive to the efforts of the recipient countries to mobilize their own resources and help themselves; be cognizant of the external and internal pressures which hamper their growth; and should emphasize long-range development assistance as the primary instrument of such growth.

In the spirit of this congressional mandate and direction, some searching questions are now being asked in regard to all requests for assistance from abroad. These questions relate to:

The applicant's present per capita income and its distribution;

The competence of the government, and its sensitivity to the needs of the population;

The existence of a well-conceived, long-range national economic development plan;

The adequate distribution and collection of the nation's tax burden;

The priority given to the vast majority of citizens who live in the rural areas; the development of equitable land distribution and the creation of an integrated approach to community development;

The existence of a favorable climate and adequate incentives for foreign and domestic private investment; and

The maintenance of effective controls over the expenditure of foreign exchange for luxury imports.

Perhaps most important of all, we are asking ourselves whether a government which seeks our assistance is sufficiently rooted in public support to assure the broad backing of its people necessary for a bold program of economic and social development.

Although no nation on earth could respond affirmatively on all these counts, I believe that these are the objectives we must stress in developing priorities and standards for the distribution of our assistance.

Let us face the fact that, in some instances, courageous adherence to these standards may lead us to refuse aid to friendly governments

which have assumed that their unquestioning support of our political views in the United Nations would assure them, willy-nilly, a continuing flow of U.S. development dollars—even though their persistent failure to put their domestic houses in order means that we are in fact pouring U.S. funds down a rathole.

What is the better alternative? In my opinion there is none. If the economic development effort in Asia, Africa, and Latin America is to succeed, and if our aid program is to maintain the essential support of the American people and their Congress, we must insist as a general rule on the necessary domestic reforms as a precondition of continuing U.S. Government assistance.

There is nothing in what I have said, however, that requires us to be foolhardy. In our complicated and divided world, overriding strategic considerations in specific situations may occasionally cause us to throw away the book, to exercise our own *ad hoc* judgment, and temporarily to relax our pressures for reform.

The important point is that we keep the number of such exceptions to an absolute minimum consistent with our national interests and that we do not allow temporary compromises to become permanent policy.

As for the inevitable charges of "Yankee interference in our domestic affairs," we should take them in our stride. Whatever we do in regard to giving or withholding economic aid constitutes "interference" of one kind or another.

For instance, when the United States Government provides capital and technicians to governments that are unwilling or unable to create the internal conditions necessary for their own economic development, it is in effect subsidizing the forces of the past. This in itself is "interference"—but in this case interference on the wrong side of what history will surely judge to be a central issue of our times.

### Coordinating International Aid Programs

5. This brings us to a fifth consideration: *the need for improvement in the planning and integration of each foreign aid program in which we are involved, not only in regard to the resources provided by our own Government but in connection with the complex variety of international agencies and donor nations that also operate in this field.*

The United States Government provides unilateral aid through the Export-Import Bank, which helps the underdeveloped nations finance the purchase of industrial goods in the United States; long-term development loans on easy terms payable in both dollars and soft currencies; U.S. technical assistance, which offers a wide range of specialists in planning and technology; the Peace Corps, which provides several thousand volunteers trained in teaching, nursing, rural development, and the like; and Food for Peace, which distributes U.S. surplus farm products, including wheat, rice, powdered milk, and cotton.

These U.S. sources of development assistance should be more carefully integrated with the loans and technical assistance available from the international agencies. These include the World Bank, which provides loans payable in "hard currencies"; the International Development Association, which provides "soft loans"; the International Monetary Fund, which helps stabilize currencies; and the so-called specialized agencies of the U.N.—the World Health Organization, the Food and Agriculture Organization, and UNESCO [United Nations Educational, Scientific and Cultural Organization].

Finally, West Germany, France, Britain, Canada, Australia, Japan, Switzerland, and Israel also provide unilateral economic assistance on a generally similar basis.

The staggering number of sources to which the developing nations can turn for assistance inevitably creates confusion and some overlapping of effort. This suggests the need for careful planning to make sure that the right kind of aid is made available and that its use is effectively coordinated with the resources of the developing country itself.

Here the World Bank and the Special Fund of the United Nations can play an effective role.

### Role of Nongovernmental Agencies

6. The sixth and final factor upon which the success of the program depends is the *greater involvement of the American people in the program, together with a bolder and more substantial effort to explain its objectives to an often critical public and to an increasingly antagonistic Congress.*

First of all, it is essential that we speak frankly and clearly to the American people. At present very few of them have a clear idea of what the aid program can do, what it cannot do, and why it is an absolutely essential instrument in creating a more rational and peaceful world.

In the last 10 years I have discussed this program in detail before audiences in 42 of our 50 States. As a result, I am convinced that once the people are given the basic facts, once they understand the principles which Congress has laid down and the ways in which the President and AID are carrying out Congress's wishes, they will give this effort the support that it deserves and must have if U.S. policy is to be effective in today's world.

Yet we face a serious roadblock: In this effort to explain the program on a mass basis the public information unit of the foreign aid agency has been refused the funds necessary for its task. As a result, it has been able to provide no more than a bare minimum of the information to which all of us as citizens and taxpayers are entitled.

More than that, our congressional and public presentations through-out the 1950's were in large measure negative and in disregard of the factors which I have described. Too often false and expedient reasons were advanced by the administration in power in a desperate effort to gain the necessary votes—only to find themselves forced at a later date to defend the program when it failed to achieve what the public and Congress had been led to expect of it.

In this regard our task will be made easier by a greatly expanded people-to-people effort by nongovernmental agencies to assure much greater involvement of individuals and organizations, both in the recipient countries and in the United States.

For instance, Rotary International, the League of Women Voters, Lions, parent-teachers' associations, labor unions, chambers of commerce, and similar organizations have even greater contributions to make in the process of overseas nation-building than they are now making. There are 1,150 Rotary Clubs in Latin America alone.

U.S. business and labor groups have a particularly important role to play in helping to shape development plans on terms acceptable to the developing countries and profitable to the individual corporations.

In addition the spectacularly successful Peace Corps can be an increasing factor in creating the necessary basis of understanding, not only in the recipient countries but in the United States itself, as a steady stream of volunteers return.

## The Challenge to American Leadership

The task of our foreign aid program is to help release the energies of the people of the developing nations so that they can work effectively toward economic progress, increased justice, and a sense of individual fulfillment and participation.

Its purpose, in other words, is to help them create prosperous societies which they are willing and able to defend. Only in such a world can we ourselves be safe, happy, and secure.

The constructive leadership of America is therefore challenged to understand the nature of the revolutionary forces that are reshaping our world and to put ourselves in touch with the aspirations of the vast majority of mankind who see this planet as something more than an arena for the Soviet-American conflict or the maintenance of an American way of life which is remote from their own.

If civilization is to mean anything, it must be bolstered as well as protected by democratic people with dynamic ideas and the skill and boldness to put those ideas into effect. The future of all mankind may depend on our willingness to accept this challenge which our hungry, chaotic, but infinitely promising world presents to us.

# For Further Reading

ALEXANDER, ROBERT J. *A Primer of Economic Development* (New York: Macmillan, 1962).

ALMOND, GABRIEL, and JAMES S. COLEMAN, eds. *Politics of the Developing Areas* (Princeton: Princeton University Press, 1960).

AUBREY, HENRY G. *The Dollar in World Affairs* (New York: Harper and Row, 1964).

BLACK, EUGENE R. *The Diplomacy of Economic Development* (Cambridge, Mass.: Harvard University Press, 1960).

FEIS, HERBERT. *Foreign Aid and Foreign Policy* (New York: St. Martin's, 1964).

GALBRAITH, JOHN KENNETH. *Economic Development in Perspective* (Cambridge, Mass.: Harvard University Press, 1961).

GOLDWIN, ROBERT, ed. *Why Foreign Aid?* (Chicago: Rand-McNally, 1963).

HEILBRONER, ROBERT. *The Great Ascent* (New York: Harper and Row, 1963).

HIRSCHMAN, ALBERT O. *The Strategy of Economic Development* (New Haven, Conn.: Yale University Press, 1958).

JORDAN, AMOS A. *Foreign Aid and the Defense of Southeast Asia* (New York: Praeger, 1962).

KINDLEBERGER, CHARLES P. *Foreign Trade and the National Economy* (New Haven, Conn.: Yale University Press, 1962).

LISKA, GEORGE. *The New Statecraft: Foreign Aid in American Foreign Policy* (Chicago: University of Chicago Press, 1959).

MASON, EDWARD S. *Foreign Aid and Foreign Policy* (New York: Harper and Row, 1964).

MONTGOMERY, JOHN D. *The Politics of Foreign Aid* (New York: Praeger, 1962).

MORGENTHAU, HANS J. "A Political Theory of Foreign Aid," *American Political Science Review,* LVI (June 1962), 301–9.

MORLEY, LORNA, and FELIX MORLEY. *The Patchwork History of Foreign Aid* (Washington, D.C.: American Enterprise Institute, 1961).

MYRDAL, GUNNAR. *An International Economy: Problems and Prospects* (New York: Harper, 1956).

ROSTOW, WALT W. *The Stages of Economic Growth: A Non-Communist Manifesto* (New York: Cambridge University Press, 1960).

SILVERT, K. H., ed. *Expectant Peoples: Nationalism and Development* (New York: Random House, 1963).

STALEY, EUGENE. *The Future of Underdeveloped Countries* (New York: Harper, 1961).

TRIFFIN, ROBERT. *Gold and the Dollar Crisis* (New Haven, Conn.: Yale University Press, 1960).

WARD, BARBARA. *The Rich Nations and Poor Nations* (New York: Norton, 1962).

# VI SECRET INTERVENTION AND UNCONVENTIONAL WARFARE

## 54 / OSS

### JOHN CHAMBERLAIN

The immediate ancestor of contemporary United States strategic services is the Office of Strategic Services of World War II. What was the nature of this organization and the scope of its activities? Although no official or authoritative history of OSS has been published, the following selection, written shortly after the end of World War II, is a good descriptive analysis. The question remains open as to how relevant the OSS experience is to contemporary requirements in this field.

IN 1941, long months before Eisenhower's and Mark Clark's men started piling ashore on the Moroccan and Algerian beaches, the quality of the U.S. commercial agents in North Africa underwent a sea change that might have perplexed even such a connoisseur of pixies as Barnaby's fairy godfather. If you had gone to one of the new agents on a business matter about the distribution of food from the U.S., you might have got satisfaction. But if you had probed hard on any special business angle you might have discovered that the agent knew considerably less about commercial matters than about the customs of Saudi Arabia or the significance of the brachycephalic head. If, by chance, you happened to have been well-acquainted in U.S. academic circles, you might have been startled to see peering from behind the pepper-and-salt habiliments of the businessman the visage of Carleton Coon, a well-known Harvard anthropologist. And the man who limped, the tall thin, determined fellow who spoke Arabic—was it possible that he was Marine Colonel "Bill" Eddy, the missionary's son and World War I veteran who had become president of little Hobart College back home in upstate New York?

Reprinted from *Life*, XIX, 21 (November 19, 1945), 119–28. Copyright © 1945 by Time, Inc. By permission.

John Chamberlain is a well-known journalist.

In Washington, where the intelligence-gathering Office of Strategic Services was even then a-borning under the deft obstetrical touches of Major General William J. ("Wild Bill") Donovan, a few people who were in on the secret of Colonel Eddy's commercial agents spoke cryptically of our "12 apostles" in North Africa. And, indeed, the 12 apostles were the missionaries of a savior. When the savior, in the collective person of Eisenhower's armies, eventually landed in North Africa in November of 1942, signal lights guided him ashore, guns of Vichy shore installations were spiked, the state of harbor facilities and German troop dispositions was well known and the French officers were in many instances quite ready and willing to "sell the pass" to the invaders. Colonel Eddy and his agents, working for Donovan on a loose rein that permitted full cooperation with Robert Murphy and the U.S. State Department, had done the job.

It was a job for which little public credit could be given or taken at the time. Unable to remove its light from beneath the bushel, the Office of Strategic Services suffered throughout the war from the jibes of columnists who chattered about OSS standing for "Oh So Social," "Oh Shush Shush" and "Oh So Secret." But now that the war is over, it is possible to look into OSS's activities and assess its worth. On the whole the record is impressive. OSS contributed measurably toward victory and in some instances—as in the wangling of German surrender in North Italy—it was a decisive factor. The very fact of OSS successes raises important questions. Why did we have to call on amateurs from scratch to do OSS's job? And what kind of security policy should we now adopt to keep from being caught next time?

Before 1941 the U.S. had no intelligence service worthy of the name, nothing comparable to the 400-year-old British service that currently operates on a free mandate and with unvouchered funds under the Foreign Office, and nothing the equal of the German ABWEHR, whose mysterious Greek head, Admiral Canaris, reported directly to the German General Staff. Nor, on the secret operations side, did we have anything remotely resembling that natural complement to the ABWEHR, the Nazi fifth column, which softened up the European democracies as scurvy softens up the teeth of an arctic explorer. If you wanted a Michelin road map of the Vosges or Haute Savoie in the Washington of early 1941, it was a hundred to one that you could not find one. Nor could you successfully apply to any government agency for the gauge of an Algerian railroad track, the kilowatt-hour supply of the Japanese power grid, the number of wharfside cranes in Casablanca, the quality of drinking water in Tunis, the tilt of the beaches off Kyushu or the texture of the Iwo Jima soil. Our friends in Germany and Japan and adjacent territory were either dead or in jail or unknown to us. The barbed wire was up everywhere, and the few listening posts that we did have—at Vichy, at

General Weygand's North African Headquarters—were in perpetual danger of sabotage by the well-meaning but essentially stupid remonstrances of the more emotional Left press. Even the facts of prime importance that we did possess remained uncoordinated, unevaluated, uninterpreted and generally in the wrong hands. There was no one in Washington charged with putting the jigsaw pieces together to see what pictures would develop or what pieces of the puzzle were missing. The reason was simply that the government—and country—was not security-minded, perhaps a corollary of life in a free-wheeling, ocean-girded, peace-loving democracy. At any rate, while there were intelligence organizations in Army, Navy, State Department and FBI, there was no broadly organized intelligence.

That was in early 1941. By 1945, during the span of time it ordinarily takes a young man to go through college, OSS had beaten Haushofer's Nazi geopolitikers and Admiral Canaris' secret operatives at their own game, and the work done by OSS in foreign lands to counter the fifth column had helped prepare the liberation of a world. Although OSS's freshman exploits were frequently in a highly romantic vein that came to little or nothing, by senior year the processes of learning had begun to pay off in quantity: in 1945, for example, in the China theater 9,000 Japanese died as a direct result of OSS spy work and behind-the-lines killing.

Lieut. Colonel Ilya Tolstoy's visit to "Shangri-La" in 1942 and 1943 is the type study of OSS freshman exploit. When the great German pincers, with one arm clamped on the Volga and the other pressing at El Alamein, threatened to snap shut somewhere east of Suez, the joint high command in Washington began worrying about a last-ditch defense of middle Asia. With the Japanese and the Germans threatening to meet in India, even the Dalai Lama, the high priest of Tibet, had become an important pawn in the game of conquest. In Ilya Tolstoy, the grandson of the Russian novelist, OSS had an adventurous character who was willing to dare the fastnesses of Tibet and the portals of the Forbidden City of Lhasa. With Lieut. Brooke Dolan, Tolstoy set out from India, carrying with him presents to the Dalai Lama from Franklin D. Roosevelt. The two men crossed the mountains, traveled through places that had never before echoed to the foot of a white man, bluffed their way past surly and uncomprehending tribesmen and finally reached the Forbidden City. Tactfully the two explained themselves; they had come seeking goodwill, they wished to convey the personal greetings of the head of a country far across the mountains and the sea—a country, parenthetically, that had no designs on anything that was sacred to the Dalai Lama. But just in case the Japanese hoped to knock China out of the war by cutting the line from eastern India to Chungking, they wished to judge the feasibility of a new supply road to China through Tibet. From Lhasa, Tolstoy and

his companion went on toward Chungking, climbing the goat-track passes, plodding on through the deserts. Whenever they noticed a good site for an airfield, they jotted it down. Eventually they reached Chungking, where they learned that the threat to Suez and India had already been turned back at Stalingrad and El Alamein. Their expedition had been militarily superfluous.

### In the Burmese Jungle

The final OSS work in behalf of China was far from superfluous. In the autumn of 1942, when Tolstoy was setting out for Tibet, 20 OSS men, led by Colonel Carl Eifler, jumped from a plane into the north Burmese jungle, seeking contact with the naked, monkey-eating tribe of the Kachins. Eifler had it on the word of a missionary, Father James Stuart, that 250,000 Kachins were ready to fight the Japanese, whom they hated far more than they had ever hated the British. Eifler's work in organizing the Kachins was OSS's bow in the China-Burma-India theater; it paid off in the successful consummation of the campaign that brought General Merrill and his Marauders to the key airport of Myitkyina in 1944. The OSS-led Kachins accounted for 5,447 Japanese in the guerrilla warfare that took the pressure off the Assam–Chungking supply route. And while the Kachins were sniping and spying and tipping off the air force to easy Jap targets, OSS men were busy organizing the intelligence and special operations groups that Wedemeyer was to depend upon so heavily in China itself.

In Europe OSS teams played a ponderable part in preparing ambushes for the Germans. But in China a handful of OSS men did the work of a small army. In July of 1944, OSS Private X was ranging the contested country to the west of Changsha where Japanese units were maneuvering to expel the Chinese from the rice bowl and to cut the north-south railroad to Canton. Near the town of Yiyang, Private X peered out from his hiding place to see the advance units of a Japanese cavalry patrol moving toward a river. For minutes the Japanese rode on; Private X estimated there must be 10,000 of them. Since batteries are practically useless in the damp heat of central China, Private X pumped at his 20-pound portable hand generator to get up the current to flash a message to Chennault's airmen. Frantic with worry because his code signals did not seem to be getting through, Private X repeated his information again and again in "clear." For eight hours he ground away at the hand generator, powering the trim 31-pound waterproofed special OSS sending and receiving set. Suddenly he was rewarded by the roar of Chennault's planes; a 14th Air Force mission had come from Kweilin. The planes caught the Japanese cavalry just as it was entering the river and 9,000 of the Japanese were killed.

Between the exploits of its freshman and senior years, OSS men covered the world to fill the gaps left by the specialized intelligence officers of the Army's G2, the Navy's ONI (Office of Naval Intelligence) and the Army Air Force's A2. In Washington, in 1942, OSS men Edward Mason and Walt Rostow assembled the figures to prove that Russia would hold, thus providing a statistical underpinning for the hunch of Harry Hopkins and the on-the-spot minority report from Moscow of the Army's Colonel Faymonville. In Washington, in 1942, Sherman Kent, a Yale academician with the forward slouch of a ready prizefighter, drove through a study of North Africa which the Army found quite useful in planning the operation then known as Torch. It was OSS that finally convinced the Army and State Department that the French resistance forces constituted a valuable D-day and pre-D-day fighting army as well as a source of mere annoyance to the Nazis. In the field OSS men jumped at midnight from planes, landed on hostile coasts from rubber boats, swam underwater to attach explosive "limpets" to enemy ships, infiltrated past sentries to carry radio sets to Maquis and guerrillas, set up high-powered telescopes on mountainous Mediterranean islands and slipped into German Paris with a pistol in one hand and cyanide pills in the other.

### Professors, Stockbrokers, Screwballs

Critics of OSS in the other services claim a high percentage of Donovan fumbles. Certainly OSS had its failures. It botched a behind-the-lines expedition into Hungary, it put men ashore to almost instant death on the Italian coast, and some of the $100,000,000 it spent during the war may have gone down the drain. Since the 22,000 people who worked for OSS at one time or another ranged from professors to screwballs, movie producers to Communist fellow travelers, missionaries' sons to stockbrokers and millionaires, college presidents to ex-governors of states, and charwomen to the left-at-home wives of servicemen, there was plenty of room for a wide variety of personal performance. But as a team OSS batted at least .260 in General Donovan's estimation, which is a good team figure in any league.

OSS grew out of the character of ruddy-cheeked, soft-spoken Wild Bill Donovan, whose whole life prior to 1941 was an unconscious preparation for the job of World War II U.S. spymaster. Donovan proved his strategic brains when he quarterbacked a good Columbia football team; he proved his fantastic courage in the course of a volunteer career in World War I that won him the DSM, the DSC and the Congressional Medal of Honor. In France he became a close friend of Colonel Ned Buxton, a newspaperman from Providence, R. I., who was Sergeant York's commanding officer. Buxton had a passion for studying the wiles

of Hannibal, the Carthaginian general whose G2 produced the intelligence that lured the Romans to destruction in the "perfect" battle of Cannae, and he lost no time in communicating his ardor to Donovan. After World War I, Donovan, with Buxton to whisper in his ear, kept a geopolitician's idea of the globe suspended in the back of his mind, rising superior to the traditional rebel Irish view that world strategy is a racket practiced by and for the benefit of the British Empire. When the Reds and Whites were tangling in Russia, Donovan went all the way to Siberia to watch Admiral Kolchak's rear-guard action against the Soviets; then he came home to become an antitrust prosecutor for the Department of Justice and to make an unsuccessful bid for the New York governorship. His legal work taught him how to employ academic experts and gumshoe artists, stool pigeons and idealists. Meanwhile he indulged a personal hobby of reading about colonial guerrilla warfare and the use of Pawnee spies by whites in the wars against the Sioux.

The minute the Japanese attacked in Manchuria in 1931, Donovan knew that his job was to scout the globe as an unofficial spy for his country. With Buxton at his elbow he cooked up a way to bait Mussolini into sending him to Badoglio's headquarters in Ethiopia. "Your excellency," said Donovan to Mussolini in Rome, "if your troops are no better than they were in the last war, then this Ethiopian war is only a small colonial affair. But if you've created a new sixth or tenth legion, then the balance of the world may be changed." Mussolini, falling for the ruse, bridled and said, "You'll see; I'll send you there." From Ethiopia, Donovan went on to watch the "laboratory" war in Spain; after Dunkirk he made an on-the-spot investigation of the staying power of Britain before moving on to Belgrade and the menaced Balkans.

During his English mission he made a detailed study of British secret intelligence and the "special services" that had to be developed to keep the flame of resistance alive in German Europe. When he brought the story of British intelligence and secret operative work home to Washington, President Roosevelt made Donovan Coordinator of Information and told him to go to work on the job of pulling together and supplementing the facts turned up by the routine government intelligence agencies. A year or so later, in June of 1942, the office of the COI became OSS, an organization that was responsible not to any single governmental department but to the all-embracing body of the Joint Chiefs of Staff.

### OSS a Catchall

Functionally speaking, OSS was a catchall organization which, like John L. Lewis' famous District 50 of the United Mine Workers, grew in unforeseen directions to meet unpredictable emergencies. Before it finished it was doing sabotage, organizing undergrounds and doing haz-

ardous spying from Brittany to Korea. But when it began its work in 1941 it consisted largely of the so-called "100 professors"—a group of middle-aged specialists in anthropology, economics and a dozen other fields, plus a few young instructors who had had Ph.D. training in applying the seat of the pants to the seat of the chair in libraries. The 100 professors became the backbone of a fact-grubbing research and analysis department which proved that libraries and microfilmed German magazines could reveal more relevant facts than a whole platoon of Mata Haris.

Donovan picked his administrators for OSS from among his own personal acquaintances in civil life: Buxton naturally became his chief assistant, with able support coming from "Oley" Doering and Ned Putzell, who left the Donovan law firm in New York to follow their chief to Washington. Although the old-line Washington bureaucrats resented the administrative presence in OSS of Financiers Charles Cheston and Russell Forgan, International Lawyer Allen Dulles, ex-Governor Bill Vanderbilt of Rhode Island, Louis Ream of U.S. Steel, Atherton Richards of the Hawaiian Pineapple Co., Cotton Textileman John Hughes and David Bruce, an in-law of the Mellon clan, the fact that Donovan had his own personal machine made for tight loyalties and smooth operating efficiency.

As the war progressed and as the Army and Navy started flying hundreds of reconnoitering flights over enemy territory from advanced bases, the OSS research and analysis branch continued to do the drayhorse work that was the main contribution of OSS; government policy makers depended on its thousands of background studies. The OSS map division, making topographical maps for General Marshall a specialty, turned out 8,000 map titles from 1942 to the war's end in 1945. Churchill preferred OSS maps to all others; at the Quebec Conference he called Roosevelt to his room, pointed to his wall and said, "See, I've got them, too." But since the executive order creating OSS had made provision for a secret intelligence service working behind enemy lines and for special strategic service operations in sabotage, morale subversion, guerrilla organization and aid to partisan resistance, there was plenty of room for OSS to grow in new directions as the character of the war changed. Even the research and analysis functions became more venturesome: an economic objectives unit in London helped the air forces work out the "optimum maturity" schedule for strategic bombing of ball-bearing, fighter-plane and oil-production targets, and in the field OSS agents pieced together enough information from captured enemy units to arrive at a remarkably accurate estimate of German armament production.

Once in a war theater, an OSS operator was sometimes hard put to it to determine whether he was doing research and analysis work, secret intelligence or any one of a number of strategic service operations. Take the OSS career of Peter Karlow, for instance. Karlow began his OSS life as a field staff man in New York City, later, in the Mediterranean, he

examined German armor, a dangerous job when the Nazis were using burned-out tanks for booby traps. In Corsica, Karlow found himself helping OSS guerrillas to improvise a maritime spying operation. Through Leghorn on the Italian coast the Germans were shipping supplies to their armies below Rome. Twenty-one miles southwest of Leghorn the 837-foot island peak of Gorgona rises out of the Mediterranean, and from a high-powered telescope set up on the peak OSS watchers could peer into Leghorn harbor. Another telescope was put ashore on the island of Capraia, farther to the south. From Gorgona and Capraia and Elba, advanced spy units tipped the Allied air forces off to German ship movements and directed the bombing of oil installations on the Italian mainland. Karlow was badly wounded when his Italian PT boat struck a mine; he returned to the U.S. to do less arduous OSS work.

### Radiomen in France

From the "great empty lot" of French North Africa, OSS discovered it was comparatively easy to infiltrate secret intelligence agents into France. And so it was in France that secret intelligence really began to pick up where common research lagged. When the French gave the order to scuttle their fleet at Toulon, one of the escaping submarines, the *Casabianca*, joined the Allies. Although he was suffering from a leg malady that grew progressively worse as the war went on, Commander L'Herminier of the *Casabianca* ran OSS radiomen into southern France to help organize the 28 active radio chains that were working for us below the Loire prior to D-day. One secret intelligence agent, a French Jew who posed as a fur merchant, mapped three fourths of the French Mediterranean coast for Patch's invasion army. His astounding reports insisted that many of the German coastal "defenses" were protected by wooden guns which air reconnaissance could not distinguish from the real thing. Another OSS agent, posing as a recruiting official for the Vichy militia, learned the range, trajectory and location of 20 batteries on each side of Marseilles; he also learned the whereabouts of German observation posts and electric controls. Such information, reaching North Africa by radio, by carrier pigeon, by pick-up plane and by couriers slipping across the Pyrenees and through Spain, helped make the invasion of southern France a comparatively painless operation.

To provide a central nervous system for secret intelligence, OSS built up an elaborate radio network that kept secret information flowing from the field to theater headquarters and Washington: operatives received their instructions and sent back data over 1,126 radio circuits established in enemy-occupied areas. At peak operations during the Battle of France, some 90 OSS agents, aided by 500 French accomplices, were busy radioing out information on troop movements, the location

of munitions dumps, the condition of factory production and transportation, the movement of German secret-service personnel.

The job of penetrating Central Europe with secret intelligence agents was far more difficult than working with the French resistance forces, but OSS found that it could be done. In Switzerland, where John Foster Dulles' brother Allen sat with ready ears, there was a vast coming and going of agents from Germany and Central Europe. Allen Dulles caught echoes in Bern of the Nazi V-weapon developmental program that was being carried out at Peenemünde on the Baltic coast. With his information added to items that had been gleaned from refugees and British aerial photography, the Allied air command was enabled to blow Peenemünde off the map. The bombing of Peenemünde set the German V-weapon program back from six to nine months and probably saved England as an invasion base for D-day. Later on Dulles used his Switzerland post as a focal point from which to wangle the surrender of the Nazi armies in North Italy.

Since a spy needs a "friendly house"—*i.e.*, a place to sleep, eat and set up a radio—the job of keeping an agent going inside Germany required considerable craft when the Gestapo was riding high. But when German internal security began to break down amid the chaos of the bombing and the influx of the six to eight million Poles, Russians, Czechs, French and Belgians who were conscripted for labor, the job of keeping cover and manufacturing a convincing background was made relatively easy. OSS had some 250 agents in Germany and Austria from September 1944 until the end of the war, and one man even managed to penetrate the Gestapo. This "double agent" fed misinformation to the German General Staff that brought about the deployment of 30,000 German paratroopers in the Low Countries at a time when it was important to keep Nazi divisions from reaching the Normandy invasion coast. Other OSS men kept themselves alive in Germany by pretending to be traitors; the cream of the double agent jest came when three OSS agents were actually awarded the Iron Cross.

### Rescuing Downed Airmen

The kindlier manifestations of secret operations resulted in the rescue of more than 5,000 downed Allied airmen from behind enemy lines. Some 3,000 of these were spirited out of the Balkans by various underground channels. OSS's Major Lynn Farish, the originator of the Balkan escape network, parachuted into the Balkans three times and journeyed thousands of miles on foot in search of downed fliers before meeting his death in a plane crash.

The job of recruiting and training an OSS secret agent was something to daunt a republic that had never in its history gone in for large-scale organized secret intelligence and sabotage operations. In the early days

of OSS, recruitment was done on a personal basis; the fact that it was well done is proof either of our luck, the bracing circumstances of American life or the quality of Wild Bill Donovan's connections. OSS's "eager beaver," Lieut. Colonel "Jerry" Sage, who became famous as "Jerry Dagger" and "the Big X" because of his harum-scarum escapes from German prison camps, was picked to join OSS as a behind-the-lines demolition artist on the suggestion of an FBI acquaintance. Jerry, a Procter and Gamble soap salesman, had been a football star and Phi Beta Kappa man at Washington State College; as a boy he had shot ground squirrels and as an early inductee from the ROTC he had learned something about demolition and silent killing, or judo. Jerry went into OSS with no psychiatric screening, and he proved an accession in every way.

The professional recruitment touch, however, was soon applied by psychiatrists working under James McConaugh, former president of Connecticut's Wesleyan University. Whether the prospective OSS overseas candidate was a Norwegian sailor, a Greek refugee, the daughter of a missionary to China, an Italian schoolteacher or simply a halfback from an American college campus, he (or she) was put through an elaborate screening operation to test emotional stability and qualities of leadership under stress. On a property in Fairfax County, Va., Major Henry Murray, a Harvard psychologist, and his screening board put groups of 20 through a three-day grilling that often had the candidates goggle-eyed with incomprehension. One of the group assignments was to move a cannon across a brook, a job designed to winnow natural bosses from natural followers. On one of the evenings at Fairfax a group would be allowed plenty of alcohol, the aim being to test the men on their power of discretion when drunk. After the screening, operatives were trained intensively in such edifying things as gutter fighting, radio operation and repair, coding and decoding, foreign languages, mapping, jugular slashing, the use of explosive "pencils" and other easily concealed demolition devices, and the keeping of cover under the most impossible circumstances. The art of keeping cover was perhaps the most difficult thing OSS had to teach; men might have gone to their deaths if they had been caught in Germany or France with English tobacco grains in their pockets, or shoes that weren't cobbled according to local standards, or laundry marks that were demonstrably Anglican or American, or hair oil with an Oshkosh smell.

The present plans for conserving the assets of OSS are somewhat nebulous. One plan is to bestow the research and analysis functions and membership upon the State Department and to hand over to the Army the clandestine operations files and personnel. Another plan is to set up secret intelligence under the State Department. But this is going back to the very fragmentation and compartmentalization of intelligence that so bedeviled us in 1941.

An intelligence service should derive from the nature of the country it is intended to serve. The Germans could entrust their intelligence to their army's general staff and its ABWEHR, for Germany was a military nation in the heart of a militarized continent. The British can put their intelligence under their Foreign Office, for the immemorial British instinct for keeping tabs on the balance of power renders British Foreign Office employees peculiarly immune to the blandishments of ideology. But the U.S. Army, unlike an army in continental Europe, is not the nation's first line of defense, and the U.S. State Department, which is enmeshed in protocol and officially devoted to the promulgation of justice and good works, lacks the operating coolness and objectivity needed in the gathering of strategic intelligence.

### Our Future Intelligence

If we had a unified Department of Defense, then there would be a good case for putting any successor organization to OSS under the jurisdiction of a Secretary for Defense. As a service department working for a unified command, the reports and evaluations of such an intelligence-gathering and intelligence-pooling agency would be impartially available to Navy, Army, Air Forces and President. But as long as our military arms are compartmentalized, intelligence under any one of them will remain compartmentalized, too. It is the nature of the compartmentalized beast to be jealous of its own files and to fall into the habit of thinking facts are something to be kept out of circulating use.

General Donovan, who bowed out of the picture when OSS was deprived of its autonomous existence on Oct. 1 [1945], would like to see a permanent fact-gathering and fact-pooling organization set up under the control of the U.S. President, who is the sole administrative officer capable of coordinating the work of Army, Navy, Air Forces and State Department. And, since you cannot run a spy service with its financial books open to inspection, he would trust the President to see to it that an intelligence agency's funds were well spent. If Congress, however, objects to putting intelligence under the President, a permanent OSS could be made responsible to an Army-Navy-State interdepartmental committee.

Certainly the republic needs its sentinels. Pearl Harbor resulted from bungled intelligence pooling. The blunder wasn't fatal, but if our next Pearl Harbor comes in the guise of atomic explosions set off by time fuses in the New York, Pittsburgh, Detroit and Chicago consulates of a conspiratorial foreign power, there will be no recovery from it. The *next* time our intelligence service must do its big job *before* the war. We need our new OSS, our new General Donovan, now.

# 55 / Unconventional Warfare

## FRANKLIN A. LINDSAY

American foreign policy objectives have been increasingly
thwarted in recent years by methods of adversaries that
could not be successfully countered by the standard actions
of diplomacy or traditional military means. The nuclear
"balance of terror" has made the situation a revolutionary
one for foreign policy and military planners. Consequently
a great amount of thought and attention has been given to
what is generally called "unconventional warfare." Some of
the dimensions of this problem are discussed in this selection.

### I

UNCONVENTIONAL war is the war that is being fought today in
Laos and South Viet Nam; it is the war that the French fought in Indochina and are now fighting in Algeria. It is a form of warfare the Communists have learned to employ with great effectiveness, and one which
they will continue to exploit to the maximum in furthering their long-
range objectives.

Unconventional warfare differs profoundly from warfare in which
regular armies are openly engaged in combat. The objective of such
conventional combat is to win control of a state by defeating the enemy's
military forces in the field. In contrast, the strategy of unconventional
forces must be to win control of the state by first winning control of the
civil population. For without the disciplined support of the civil population, militarily inferior guerrilla forces can have no hope of success.

As yet the West has not developed a form of defense that is adequate
against this form of warfare. And even where the defense has been effective, the costs to the West of suppressing such attacks have been many
times the costs to the Communists of mounting them. In Greece between
1945 and 1948, for example, Communist guerrilla forces, numbering less
than 20,000 armed men, successfully cut the country in two so that the
only communication between north and south was by sea and air. A

---

Reprinted from *Foreign Affairs*, XL, 2 (January, 1962), 267–74. Copyright 1962
by the Council on Foreign Relations, Inc., New York.

Franklin A. Lindsay is a vice-president of ITEK Corporation. He was a member
of the Gaither Committee on National Security Policy, 1947; he prepared a National
Security Council study for the second Hoover Commission; and has published a
number of essays on military and economic affairs.

Greek army of several hundred thousand men, heavily supported by the United States, was required to contain the very much smaller guerrilla force. The total cost of military and political pacification, and of economic reconstruction, was about $2 billion—or somewhere between 100 and 1,000 times what the Communists had spent. The fortuitous defection of Jugoslavia from the Soviet bloc, and the consequent loss of guerrilla bases in Macedonia, caused the Communists to call off their attack. Had this not occurred, the costs in men, money and material needed finally to subdue the Communist rebels would have been many times greater. And the outcome would not have been certain.

The essential reasons the Communists have been able to do so much with so little in many areas of the world are four:

1. They have learned thoroughly the techniques of gaining control of the civil population by combining effectively the positive incentives of a political doctrine, applied meticulously from the grass roots up, and the negative pressures of a terrorism applied against those who refuse to accept their leadership voluntarily.

2. They have mastered the principles and techniques of guerrilla warfare, a form of warfare quite apart from regular or frontal warfare.

3. They have directed their most determined attacks against countries whose territory is contiguous to the Communist empire so that safe haven and training areas can be provided for guerrillas and so that supplies can be provided clandestinely.

4. They have also been able to exploit effectively the pent-up hatreds against former colonial powers and pent-up frustrations with the slow pace of economic advancement.

In most cases these have proven to be unbeatable combinations.

To gain control of a key part of the civilian population is an absolute prerequisite for further action. Having gained this control, the Communist leadership is then in a position to use its guerrilla force with great advantage against equal or superior forces supporting the government in power.

A guerrilla force is like the top of an iceberg; the supporting civilian organization, without which it cannot survive, is the much larger part that can't be seen. Just as control of the air has become a prerequisite for successful frontal warfare, so control of the population is a prerequisite for successful unconventional warfare. From the outset of conflict, a major struggle for control over the civilian population will take place and it will continue throughout the entire course of the war. Each side must try to organize the civil population into a tightly disciplined force, and, through propaganda and police activities, try to break the grip exercised by its adversary.

In Viet Nam, for example, the defeat of the French was due primarily to the Communists' success in this regard. It made it possible to trap

French forces in one bloody ambush after another until the French were so weakened they could no longer keep open supply lines to their fortified outposts. Once the fortified outposts were isolated and could no longer be supplied, except in driblets by air, the Communists were in a position to complete the establishment of political and military control over the rest of the country. With their base of operations thus secured, they could safely convert their guerrilla forces to regular assault forces equipped with heavy artillery and a supply system to back it. The final phase was to launch massive frontal assaults against these weakened fortresses.

Thus the French and their local supporters were progressively driven from the country into the villages, and from the villages into the cities until, at the end, they held in the north of Indochina only the heavily fortified perimeter immediately surrounding Hanoi. In the areas from which they had withdrawn, the Communists erected a political structure which exacted the positive loyalty of every peasant and his family by the stark example of violence to some and the threat of heavy punishment or death to others.

The key to the successes of the Communist guerrillas in Viet Nam and elsewhere is found in the fact that they had established control over the rural population as a first step. For every man in a guerrilla force carrying a rifle there must be a large number of civilians who provide the support he must have to survive and fight. They are the source of food, clothing and recruits. Even more important, the civilian organization must supply the guerrilla force with constant operational intelligence on every movement of the enemy. Only with such information can a militarily inferior guerrilla force be forewarned of an encircling trap, a planned offensive or an ambush. This intelligence net embraces not only the peasants who observe military movements but also spies in enemy headquarters who provide advance warning of intended offensives.

The cause of the French defeat in Viet Nam can be traced to their loss of the support of the civilian population. Here, as elsewhere, the Communists had been able to capitalize upon a basic anti-colonial feeling and to harness this antagonism into an effective tool for political indoctrination of the population. But in order to obtain effective control, the Communists go far beyond political indoctrination. Once they have a fanatically dedicated minority, they begin the application of systematic terror to ensure that the masses of the people will be brought under, and kept under, complete Communist control. Their objective is to build in each village—even though it may be under nominal control of the legitimate government—a shadow government completely controlled by the local Communist representative. It has often happened that in a single village two governments exist simultaneously, one the official and open government representing the anti-Communist central govern-

ment, the other the secret government which, in fact, exercises complete control over the actions of every member of the village.

The use of terror to form a secret government under the nose of the enemy has long been a Communist technique. In some of the worst German concentration camps, a secret Communist government was often sufficiently powerful to bring about the execution, through clandestine manipulation of Gestapo records, of those prisoners who failed to accept its control.

The French were defeated in Viet Nam because they were fighting blind. They never knew where the enemy was. They were repeatedly caught on the march in the most indefensible positions where, without warning, they were subjected to murderous rifle, machine gun and mortar fire from concealed positions on both sides of the track. The surviving remnants of one ambush lived only to be cut down the next day by the same Viet Minh force, which held them constantly under surveillance, and moved through the jungles on foot to prepare the next ambush on the expected line of march. When the French undertook mop-up operations in areas known to be harboring guerrilla forces, the Communist-controlled civil population collaborated in warning the guerrillas, and in helping them to hide or escape.

The pattern of, first, political organization, second, guerrilla warfare and, finally, frontal assault was followed in Jugoslavia during World War II, in China from the thirties until the Communist victory in 1950, and in Viet Nam prior to the partition of the country in 1955. Now it is being followed in South Viet Nam, where Communist organizers have been increasingly active in building clandestine organizations in the rural areas. During the last year, guerrilla activities were stepped up with the objective of forcing government troops to withdraw from the villages into the larger towns and into fortified positions. Now it appears from reports from Saigon that the Communist leaders have decided that their control of many areas outside the cities is sufficiently firm to permit the use of regular military units trained in North Viet Nam. If their judgment is correct, the war for South Viet Nam has entered the third, or final, assault stage.

Because the Communists have been permitted to consolidate their hold over most of the country, the forces of the government, supported by the United States, find themselves in a very precarious position. They can be extricated from the situation only by an extraordinary military effort coupled with a major effort to free the rural areas from the pressures of Communist terror.

In Malaya and in the Philippines are found two examples of the successful suppression and ultimate defeat of Communist guerrilla forces. In both cases, the heart of the Western strategy was twofold: (1) a vigorous and aggressive pursuit of the Communist guerrillas into their

own territory while maintaining constant pressure on them so that they were denied the initiative and the ability to launch attacks on their own terms; (2) a major political program undertaken to win back the population, to protect it against the violence and reprisals of the Communists, and to match force with force.

The second of these represents one of the West's most difficult problems, for it is obvious that when two forces are contending for the loyalty of, and control over, the civilian population, the side which uses violent reprisals most aggressively will dominate most of the people, even though their sympathies may lie in the other direction. Communist efforts to dominate the population must be frustrated before their control has become strong enough to support guerrilla operations. If the Communists are unopposed in their initial application of force against the civilian population, and thereby gain control, the counterforce which must be applied finally to break that control will be far greater and the population will suffer far more than if action had been taken resolutely at the outset.

In 1945 in Rumania, for example, a broad popular feeling of support for the monarchy had developed spontaneously. As evidence of this loyalty, people wore badges with the royal coat of arms. Communist thugs began systematically beating up people wearing the monarchist symbol whom they were able to catch alone in back streets after dark. There was no reaction from the population other than to stop wearing these pins when they were alone at night. Thus emboldened, the Communists became more aggressive until they beat up, in broad daylight and in the open streets, those who still wore the monarchist pins. Finally the pins were driven completely from the streets; the will of the people had been broken and the first step in the Communist takeover had been accomplished.

The way in which force is applied to counter Communist terror is nevertheless all-important. The strategy of the Communists may be to use acts of terror and sabotage to goad the government into repressive counter-measures and thereby widen the split between the population and the government. Thus when the government and its security forces use force to meet the Communist terror they must do so resolutely, but with great selectivity and only against those who are directly responsible.

## II

The first step in mobilizing a civilian population against Communist subversion and guerrilla attack is to establish a set of political goals expressed in terms that the average person can understand. They must be goals that strike a sympathetic response and that aim to remove the inequities in the existing society and the grievances which they have caused. Through mass communications these reform programs

must be communicated effectively, and repeatedly, to the population.

But this is only the beginning of the task. Political organizers must be recruited and trained in sufficient numbers to reach by direct contact nearly every family in the land. They must be as thorough as the best of ward or district leaders in American politics. The organizer must know everyone in his village. He must know who are the Communist sympathizers and who are the secret Communist organizers. He must know who comes and goes in the village and what their business is. He must build a core of persons loyal to himself and to the government. Through these people he must be constantly informed of the activities of the Communists and the pressures they are placing on villagers to gain their secret help. Above all, he must be able to provide effective protection to those who, against their will, are being forced into Communist collaboration by threats of violence against themselves and their families. To accomplish this, he must have the support of his own government and of the West; he must be able not only to provide physical protection but to alleviate the legitimate economic and political grievances of his village. More than anyone else, the local political organizer holds the key to success or failure. If he is successful in his task, he will hold the loyalty of his village and will be able to integrate its people and resources into the effort to defeat the Communists.

If he is not successful, the shadow of Communist control will gradually be extended and consolidated until the village is organized entirely in support of the Communist forces. Food and money will regularly be collected for that purpose. The entire village will become part of the Communist intelligence network, reporting to the guerrilla commanders every movement of the government security forces. At the same time the government will be totally cut off from information about the guerrillas—their strength, their movements and their intentions.

The organization of the civilian population will require months, if not years. But where control by the Communists has already progressed to the point where they are able to launch guerrilla war, military operations must be conducted aggressively against them, regardless of the disadvantage at which government forces will be operating. Government patrols must push vigorously into Communist-dominated territory, try to contact the guerrillas and force them into open combat. Lacking the intelligence that the civilian population might have provided, the defending forces must employ to the fullest all other means, such as air reconnaissance. The United States has effectively applied its advanced scientific skills to the solution of major problems in the missile and space fields. There is now the opportunity, as yet largely untried, to apply these same scientific capabilities to the development of modern equipment designed to help meet the special problems of guerrilla and counter-guerrilla warfare.

The basic principle of counter-guerrilla military operations is to maintain the offensive and thereby deny the guerrillas the initiative. The Communist guerrilla strategy, in turn, will be to attempt to seize and hold the initiative by mounting a variety of attacks against fixed installations so that large government forces are pinned down defending towns and villages, rail lines, power lines, ports and other vital installations. A counter-guerrilla offensive, then, will have these objectives:

To keep guerrilla units off balance at all times; to force them to flee continuously from attacking government units, and thereby to minimize their opportunities to mount attacks on vital communication lines and military installations or to lay ambushes.

By maintaining the initiative, to force guerrilla units to overrun their intelligence screens, and thereby to deny them the protective cover they need to survive against superior military forces.

To prevent guerrilla forces from grouping for strong attacks against isolated points.

To tire them out, and keep them tired out, through constant offensive action against them; to force them into more isolated hinterlands where food supplies are less and less available; to force them through constant offensive action to expend their limited ammunition.

Whatever the means used to carry out this offensive strategy, the basic and overriding necessity is that counter-guerrilla forces be organized early enough and strongly enough so that they are able to meet and contain, at the outset, the attacks of guerrilla forces. *Too little and too late* has been the normal reaction of governments to the development of such forces.

The core of the counter-guerrilla troops must be a highly mobile attacking force. Normally it need not be substantially larger than the guerrilla elements opposed to it. It should be able to meet and defeat guerrilla forces essentially on their own terms, that is, with small mobile units capable of moving in patrols over extended periods in enemy territory. As soon as one patrol is withdrawn for rest, another should take its place.

Mobile counter-guerrilla units should operate without fixed plans, and with the ability to modify their operations quickly, in order to take advantage of unforeseen targets and to concentrate superior forces against guerrilla units that have been located and brought to combat. In contrast, the government force that relies on "set piece" offensives, based on plans drawn up days in advance, will always be at a disadvantage. Even before the operation is launched, such plans may find their way into the hands of the guerrillas, who will have moved meanwhile to another area. Periodic offensives of limited duration have the further disadvantage of permitting the guerrillas to hold the initiative between offensives. A strategy of constant offensive can effectively de-

prive the guerrillas of the opportunity to conduct the war on terms favorable to themselves.

It will also be necessary to provide defensive forces to guard key installations. Care must be exercised, however, that these forces are not spread out beyond all reasonable bounds in the attempt to defend an increasingly large number of fixed installations. A French military commentator has written, "There should be no fortified posts except those necessary for promoting mobility."

### III

In a broader sense the dilemma of the West is that, even if we can develop a more effective strategy for defending countries against unconventional Communist warfare it can at best only limit further losses. When one considers a strategy for liberating areas over which the Communists have gained control, the difficulties are seen to be very great. The organization of clandestine activities in a Communist state faces extraordinary obstacles. It is, for example, common practice for the Communists to undertake provocative activities designed to test the loyalty of each individual in the régime. A person may at any time be contacted by someone purporting to represent a clandestine organization. Even though the sympathies of the person approachced may be strongly anti-Communist and his fondest hopes that the Communists be overthrown, he must assume that this is not a genuine resistance movement but rather one conducted under the control of, and at the direction of, the secret police. To prove his loyalty he must not only refuse to join the purported clandestine organization, but must also inform the police. If he does not, he will have failed to demonstrate his positive loyalty to the régime and will be subject to reprisals and imprisonment. Thus a clandestinely organized resistance within a consolidated Communist régime is not likely to get very far before someone has, out of fear, reported its existence to the police.

A second device used by the Communists is to form a clandestine anti-Communist organization under their own secret control, to encourage its growth by recruiting unwitting members, and to permit them to conduct actual operations against the régime until finally, having attracted a large number of the most aggressive anti-Communists, its entire membership is arrested.

The communes and collective farms provide other means of containing potential resistance operations, by centralizing food supplies, rather than allowing them to remain under the control of individual peasants. It is thus extremely difficult to obtain locally the food needed to support a guerrilla force. Similarly, the Communist practice of issuing new currency from time to time minimizes the opportunities to build up currency reserves to finance resistance operations.

Because of these techniques, a Communist dictatorship probably can be overthrown from within only in an area in which the Communists have not yet consolidated their control, or in which their control has been seriously weakened by other events. It is therefore of the utmost importance to move quickly to prevent the total consolidation of a nation into a completely controlled police state. This struggle will take place at a very personal level, and the final outcome will depend on whether the individual, faced by the Communist instruments of terrorist control, can, in the face of this force, be given a viable alternative to complete surrender.

Where the effective political control of the country has passed to the Communists, it will not be enough to conduct long-distance propaganda activities or to make plans on the assumption that the very real and very considerable dissatisfactions with the Communist régime will automatically result in a popular uprising as soon as the guerrilla forces appear. Clandestine support of at least a part of the villages and the countryside is an absolute prerequisite to the employment of guerrilla forces, for they must have local intelligence support and supplies if they are to survive in areas in which superior enemy forces are openly in control. In Jugoslavia, for example, in World War II, the Communist partisans had in many ways as favorable a situation for guerrilla warfare as might be expected anywhere. The main German forces were engaged by powerful allies on other fronts. Tito's partisan forces had as overt allies not only the Soviet Union but the United States and Britain. And from the latter two they received massive air support. In Slovenia, where there were no Cêtnik forces of Mihailovich to contend with, the political commissars of the Communist-established National Liberation Front could represent themselves to the people as the only force fighting the invader, and as having the complete support of all the major powers fighting the Germans. Yet they still found it necessary, in the words of one commissar, to "prepare the area intensively by the introduction of clandestine political organizers for a period of several months before we dared to introduce guerrilla forces."

It is not merely with benefit of hindsight that one can say it would have been a better strategy in Cuba to have built organized support in the villages and rural areas of Cuba and to have organized widespread guerrilla activities rather than to have risked all on a spontaneous uprising following a single assault landing. By far the largest part of any population will not voluntarily risk reprisals even though their sympathies may be strong. Instead, they will sit on the sidelines while others battle it out, joining in only when the outcome becomes a foregone conclusion. The political organization of each village must be undertaken under the nose of vigilant Communist political and security services. This is not easy. It requires unusual men possessing great personal

courage and high motivation as well as superior political organizing skills. They must be thoroughly trained and then supported to the fullest extent possible under the circumstances. Guerrilla operations can be initiated only as the Communist control at the village level is loosened so that clandestine support to guerrillas can be provided.

The West needs to acquire the ability to conduct unconventional warfare successfully, and it must do so quickly. The Communists have evolved a highly effective strategy combining grass-roots political organization and guerrilla warfare which they are employing against the non-Communist world. They have devised a totalitarian political structure that is highly resistant to counter-attack. The creation by the West of an adequate defensive and offensive capability for political and guerrilla warfare will require time and effort. It must be pursued vigorously and without further delay.

The United States has expanded significantly its military capabilities and, in the Army's Special Forces units, is creating a highly competent corps of guerrilla and counter-guerrilla fighters. This capability must be quickly matched with the political skills to conduct unconventional warfare at the village level. This will require training in depth and an extraordinarily high level of individual aptitude and competence. Specifically, we require a system of training—both for our own personnel and for those we are aiding—comparable to that for an army officer, a physician or an engineer. A national institute or staff college comparable to those of the Army, Air Force and Navy is needed to provide a center for training of United States and possibly foreign personnel and for elaborating strategic concepts of unconventional warfare and developing practical and effective tactics to meet the operational problems we now face in many parts of the world. Similar institutes should be established jointly with our NATO partners and in the countries lying across the Communist lines of attack.

The Communists have allowed themselves lead times of as much as 10 to 20 years in training revolutionary leaders. One can only hope that the free world yet has time to build the political leadership, both abroad and at home, to meet their threat successfully.

# 56 / Unconventional Warfare in Communist Strategy

RAYMOND L. GARTHOFF

Unconventional warfare as an instrument—or problem—of American foreign policy should not be considered in a vacuum. For, in fact, most of this activity has been and will be, from the American point of view, counterinsurgency, designed to protect the independence of a threatened area. But what of Communist doctrine on this subject? The following selection addresses itself directly to this question.

## I

UNCONVENTIONAL WARFARE has become all too conventional, even if it is not yet adequately understood. It is paradoxical that the coming of mighty engines of war that literally extend war "out of this world" and threaten violence measured in megadeaths should, in fact, lend strength to the resurgence of a kind of hostilities marked by poisoned bamboo spears, bazooka ambushes and civil war. In a recent article in these pages, the nature and dimensions of the problem have been thoughtfully analyzed.[1] In the present discussion, I should like to focus attention on a series of 12 propositions derived from study of Communist theory and practice regarding the seizure of power by unconventional warfare.

Our starting point should be the fundamental role that internal war and unconventional warfare play in general Communist world strategy. On that foundation, we can examine Communist views on the expediency of waging unconventional warfare under various conditions, and on operational strategies likely to be used in cases where it is deemed feasible and desirable. Finally, it will be useful to take a closer look at guerrilla warfare in particular as a technique, in past and future Communist practice, for waging internal war. Thus we shall move from

Reprinted from *Foreign Affairs*, XL, 4 (July, 1962), 566–75. Copyright 1962 by the Council on Foreign Relations, Inc., New York.

Raymond L. Garthoff, a leading authority on Communist military doctrine, has been on the staff of the RAND Corporation. More recently he has been an adviser to various American government agencies, including the Department of State. His works include *Soviet Military Doctrine* (1953) and *Soviet Strategy in the Nuclear Age* (1958).

[1] Franklin Lindsay, "Unconventional Warfare," *Foreign Affairs*, January 1962, p. 264–274, [which is selection 55 in this volume].

looking at unconventional war in Communist doctrine to looking at Communist doctrine on unconventional warfare.

## II

Very simply, "internal," "unconventional," "irregular"—"class"—war is of the essence of Marxist-Leninist theory, hence at least theoretically at the base of Communist strategy. We became so accustomed to Stalin's reliance on the Red Army and the Soviet intelligence services as the most conspicuous elements of force in international politics that it takes a moment to place in focus the older—and newer—more fundamental Communist reliance on maneuvering and manipulating power on an indigenous political fulcrum. This is my first proposition.

Unconventional warfare—our very use of this expression jars one by its contrast to the Marxist-Leninist conception of the conventional nature of internal warfare—may assume various forms, depending on the concrete situation, its opportunities and constraints. Although in other areas the Communists may resort to rigid design or overcentralized planning, when it comes to the application of force they show an acute awareness of the wide range of kinds of unconventional warfare available to them. This is the second proposition I would raise. To rephrase the point: Communists are flexible in waging varied forms of internal war, and irregular warfare is but one of the means.

Not all activity of Soviet, Chinese or indigenous Communists should be considered a form of internal war—though one can define the term broadly enough to encompass most of it. But the Communist leaders do assign a major role to active civil violence at a certain stage of development of the class conflict. For such countries as the United States, that stage may be seen only very dimly—or perhaps merely assumed—in a vague and distant future. But in volatile and unstable societies emerging from colonial rule or undergoing modernization without adequate tools for the job, internal war is expected to have a future— if it is not already present. Thus my third proposition is that the Communists expect, plan and wage internal war as the final stage of class struggle leading to the seizure of power. Internal unconventional war is above all *revolutionary* war.

## III

Bolshevism arose as a revolutionary movement with international pretensions; its fundamental outlook was hostile to the existing international order. None the less, after a number of unsuccessful attempts to wage revolutionary war beyond the borders of the old Russian Empire, in the period from 1918 to 1923, Soviet leaders began to recognize the

need to be more selective in choosing the time and place to conduct revolutionary war. Also, as the years went by, they directed their energies increasingly to internal matters. The building of "socialism in one country" marked an indefinite extension of the original compromise by which the Soviet Union proposed to coexist with the outside world. The avowed revolutionary ends have continued unchanged, but means have become increasingly important in themselves. As occasions arose calling for sacrifice either by the Soviet State or by the forces of the Revolution abroad, Moscow's decision has invariably been at the expense of the latter. The subordination to Moscow of Communist Parties everywhere meant that the suitability of local internal war was defined in terms of the prevailing foreign policy objectives of the Soviet Union. And as a consequence, for over two decades Communist "internal war" boasted few campaigns and no victories. Only in China did an active revolutionary war even stay alive, and it did so by liberating itself from Moscow's strategic direction.

World War II brought new opportunities for building undergrounds and waging partisan warfare in many countries occupied by an alien invader. Local Communists (as well as other resistance elements), aided by the Allies, established strong forces in several countries. The Soviets themselves built up sizable guerrilla forces on their own German-occupied territory. At the close of the war, the Jugoslav and Albanian partisans were able to seize power with little opposition. The Chinese Communists were also immeasurably aided by the course and outcome of the war.

In the early postwar period, the sudden shift in the balance of power in areas on the Soviet periphery, and the not accidental projection of the Red Army into many of these areas, led to new opportunities for expansion of Communist rule by various means including internal war. Where Soviet occupation was prolonged, political and subversive techniques were used effectively to establish puppet Communist régimes. But beyond the shadow of the Soviet Army the story was quite different. A wave of attempts at subversion, rebellion and revolution struck in 1948–1949. Success in Czechoslovakia by a subversive coup was not matched in Finland, and not even tried in France and Italy. In China, the Communists—against Stalin's advice—pushed on to take all continental China. But the revolutionary guerrilla campaigns in Greece, Malaya, Burma, the Philippines and Indonesia ended in failure; only in Viet Nam did such a campaign drag on to an important partial victory in 1954. Causes of failure varied, but one important general one was that the balance of power in the world had become stabilized anew.

In the current phase, since about 1960, there has been a new wave of Communist guerrilla efforts in Laos and South Viet Nam, a failure in the Congo, and a seizure from within of the successful guerrilla move-

ment in Cuba. Similar efforts to take over other native, non-Communist rebel forces, for example in Angola and Colombia, are at present under way.

In summing up this brief historical review, we reach a fourth proposition: One of the key conditions for resort to revolutionary war, in Communist eyes, is the general world situation (as well as the local situation). And as a related fifth proposition: While the general strategic balance of terror today increases the dangers to the Communist bloc of resorting to direct aggression and creating Soviet-Western military confrontations, it reduces the risks involved in indirect, unconventional war.

## IV

Communist strategies for waging revolutionary warfare place a high premium on the political content and context of a campaign. Some strategies, beyond the purview of this article, involve exclusively political action. Others involve infiltration and subversion, where the political vulnerability of the opponent is of cardinal importance. Subversion (which should be distinguished from agitation, propaganda, troublemaking and other overt or underground Communist activities) can be either a substitute for a revolutionary war or a complementary tactic in it, but in general it has not proven nearly as versatile a Communist tool as many of us tend to think. Subversion is usually directed against existing governments, but it may be directed against indigenous revolutionary movements, as in the Cuban case. Infiltration and subversion, political isolation and manipulation, and economic penetration all ultimately should—in the Communist strategy—lay the groundwork for the seizure of power either by coup d'état or by revolutionary war.

As my sixth proposition, I would advance the hypothesis that the Soviet leaders generally prefer the use of subversion, or other non-violent means, to the use of guerrilla war, because the seizure of power by indigenous revolutionary forces tends to make local Communist rulers too independent of Moscow's control. The only countries other than Russia where local Communist forces fought and won their own victories are China, Jugoslavia, Albania and Viet Nam (with Cuba as a quasi-fifth). All, with the uncertain exception of North Viet Nam, are today serious problems for the Soviet Union.

The Chinese—absorbed by their own internal problems and struggles with the Russians, smarting over the frustration of continuing irredentist claims, and "on the make"—have not developed the qualms or subtle calculations which mark the Soviet attitude toward the means of extending Communist power. Maoism as an export item has done well in Indochina; a number of other Communist Parties—especially, but not only, in Asia—are turning to China in the course of the growing

division within the Communist movement. The Soviet leaders do not, of course, turn their backs on the theory or even the practice of national-liberation revolutionary war. None the less, my seventh proposition—companion to the sixth—is that the Chinese Communists are likely in the future to be the guiding spirit in most Communist revolutionary guerrilla wars.

In further support of this conclusion, I offer as my eighth proposition that Soviet experience in 1941–44 (and 1918–20) is not really relevant to the current problems of Communist revolutionary war. In Russia, guerrilla warfare was supplementary and distinctly subordinate to the actions of regular armies; it was national rather than class, and defensive rather than offensive in character. Communist revolutionaries today are aware of this inapplicability of the Soviet experience. Che Guevara states, early in his book "La Guerra de Guerrillas," that:

> For the proper analysis of guerrilla warfare, it should be noted that there are two different types: first, the guerrillas supplement the effort of a large regular army as in the case of the Ukrainian guerrillas; second, an armed group is fighting against an established government. We are not interested in the first type. We are interested only in the type where an armed group is carrying on a fight against an established colonial (or other) power.[2]

While Mao in the 1930s paid tribute to the Russian experience and to the theoretical contributions of Lenin and Stalin, he stressed that they could not simply be transferred to the Chinese scene because, as he put it, "there are a great number of conditions special to the Chinese revolution and the Chinese Red Army." The "laws of war and military directives in the Soviet Union embody the special characteristics of the civil war and the Red Army of the Soviet Union; if we copy them and apply them mechanically and allow no change whatsoever, it will also be like whittling down our feet to fit the shoes, and we shall be defeated."[3] (A curious figure of speech, by the way, suggesting that the Russians couldn't fill the shoes of the Chinese.) Indeed, Mao had won leadership of the Chinese Communist Party in a bitter contest over the very issue of independence from Moscow. He therefore insisted that the Chinese experience in revolutionary war included important features and even "laws" of its own. This, it should be noted, also carries implications for the transferability of Mao's thought and Chinese experience to other countries.

The Sino-Soviet dispute has brought to the surface significant differences in the current Chinese and Russian approaches to revolutionary war. The Soviets have explicitly granted priority to the task of prevention of "war," for which the Chinese have attacked them. Under the pressure

---

[2] Translation in *Army*, March 1961, p. 24.

[3] Mao Tse-tung, "Strategic Problems of China's Revolutionary War" (December 1936). Peking: Foreign Languages Press, 1954, p. 3–4; see also p. 2, 5, 18 and 31.

of polemical controversy with the Chinese Communists, the Soviets have refined their own conceptions and have been led to distinguish three different "categories" of war: world war, limited or local wars, and "national liberation wars and popular uprisings." Recognizing the disastrous consequences of general nuclear war, and the risk of such war in direct Western-Communist confrontation in limited wars, they oppose local as well as world wars. The Chinese are not wholly insensitive to the dangers of nuclear war, but they stress the "inevitability" of local wars in contrast to Soviet emphasis on "averting" them. The Soviets as well as the Chinese of course favor internal "wars of national liberation," so long as they are against the West. The divergence between them arises from the fact that the Soviets are more cautious than the Chinese in evaluating the risks that they believe the Communist bloc should assume in overt support of revolutionary wars.

In the most explicit and authoritative Soviet pronouncement on revolutionary war, Khrushchev declared, in 1961: "Liberation wars will continue to exist as long as imperialism exists, as long as colonialism exists. These are revolutionary wars. Such wars are not only admissible, but inevitable, since the colonialists do not grant independence voluntarily. Therefore, the peoples can attain their freedom and independence only by struggle, including armed struggle."[4] But it is clear from Soviet discourse and action that, while they surely favor such wars in principle and do support them in some concrete cases, this support is not unqualified or universal.

It would be incorrect to write off Soviet influence, interest and impact on Communist revolutionary war and warfare. Many well-developed techniques of Communist conspiracy are useful in this kind of activity. The Soviets have substantial relevant assets, and they have not forsworn all violence. None the less, for guidance on the tactics and operations of revolutionary guerrilla warfare, and for direct support, the Soviets do not have the experience, the doctrine, the cadres or the missionary zeal of the Chinese Communists.

## V

The leading Communist theoretician of guerrilla warfare is Mao Tse-tung; the other two most influential writers are the Vietnamese General Giap and Che Guevara of Cuba. Without summarizing the development of Mao's doctrine on guerrilla warfare, nor reviewing in detail the Chinese Communist and Vietnamese experience, we should note some of the key political aspects of Communist doctrine for waging guerrilla warfare, and also some of the key related military tactics.

---

[4] N. S. Khrushchev, speech of January 6, 1961, in *Kommunist*, January 1961, p. 19.

Almost all Mao's writings on military matters date from the period 1936–38. But in 1929, in one of his earliest pieces, he succinctly stated the political purpose of irregular, internal war: "When the Red Army fights, it fights not merely for the sake of fighting, but to agitate the masses, to organize them, to arm them, and to help them establish revolutionary political power; apart from such objectives, fighting loses its meaning and the Red Army the reason for its existence." [5] One of the best known of Mao's dicta is the statement, "Every Communist must grasp the truth: 'Political power grows out of the barrel of a gun'." [6] It is instructive to note the context of this statement, as it is not that usually assumed and ascribed in Western commentary. The gist of Mao's thought was that it was necessary in a revolutionary class war to implant and cultivate in the masses of the people awareness that they could, with gun in hand, seize power. Naturally, the Communist Party would lead them in this effort and harvest the result. But the idea was not simply that with military might one could take power; it was that the very process of revolutionary mass warfare could give invaluable political impetus to the military effort. This, then, is my ninth propostion: the Communists see revolutionary war not only as a means, expedient under some conditions, to *seize* power, but also as a means of building political support which will *sustain* power.

General Giap, in his recently published "People's War, People's Army," stresses that guerrilla war is waged for people, not for territory. [7] Space is often traded for time, and time used for political advance. The "high ground" of most importance is popular support, or at least popular non-support of the incumbent authority. Mao considered this as cardinal. As he put it, "Without a political goal, guerrilla warfare must fail, as it must if its political objectives do not coincide with the aspirations of the people." [8] This is probably true, with the important qualifications that the political objectives must *appear* to coincide with the aspirations of the people—even if they do not—and that the people compare the revolutionaries with the incumbent régime on the basis of both their own experience and the net image that propaganda and information from all sides convey. Finally, apart from "aspirations," the popular reaction is strongly influenced by expectations as to who is winning.

Mao, Giap and Guevara all stress the importance of exemplary

---

[5] Mao Tse-tung, "On the Rectification of Incorrect Ideas in the Party" (December 1929), "Selected Works," v. I. New York: International Publishers, 1954, p. 106.

[6] Mao Tse-tung, "Problems of War and Strategy" (November 6, 1938), "Selected Works," v. 2, p. 272.

[7] General Vo Nguyen Giap, "People's War, People's Army." Hanoi: Foreign Publishing House, 1961, p. 48 *et passim*.

[8] Mao Tse-tung, "Guerrilla Warfare" (1937), quoted by Brig. Gen. S. B. Griffith, U.S.M.C. (Ret.), in "Mao Tse-tung on Guerrilla Warfare." New York: Frederick A. Praeger, 1961, p. 43.

conduct in relations with the population. Mao, especially, warned against excessive or indiscriminate repressive measures. Ten years ago Giap repeated this Maoist doctrine, but gave attention also to a minor-key Maoist theme recommending selective terror against local representatives of the incumbent régime in order to destroy its control. In South Viet Nam, the Communist-led Viet Cong have in recent years turned to systematic selective terror against local government officials on a large scale. They seek by this means to intimidate those who could organize opposition to their activities, and to paralyze the existing administration of the countryside at its very base.

Turning now to the military tactics of revolutionary guerrilla warfare, my tenth proposition is that the Communists have no "secret" doctrinal formula for success, but they do have considerable experience and a basically sound theoretical expression of their doctrine for waging guerrilla warfare. It is very difficult to summarize usefully the many relevant tactical concepts, especially those in the writings of Mao Tse-tung, but also those of Che Guevara. In 1942, the Soviets prepared a manual on partisan operations, and in 1944 added a chapter on the subject to their regular army "Field Regulations." But except for doctrine on combined and supporting operations for regular war, these are strictly technical and of little relevance to Communist guerrillas in other countries. Incidentally, Mao's chief military writings, and Guevara's, have only recently appeared in Russian translation.

Mao proceeds from the premise that "The principle of preserving oneself and annihilating the enemy is the basis of all military principles."[9] Measures to achieve flexibility and adaptability include dispersion and temporary concentration to achieve local superiority for sharp attacks before shifting to another point of pressure. The enemy is thus forced to disperse and is kept off balance. Guerrilla campaigns must be carefully planned and purposeful in terms of a broad strategic design, and yet susceptible to alteration in order to meet changed conditions. Bases should not be established if it involves pitched battles and position warfare to defend them. Surprise, speed, secrecy, deception, initiative and reliable intelligence are all at high premium. Guerrillas, said Mao, should be "as cautious as virgins and as quick as rabbits."[10] Mobility, maneuverability, ability to melt into inaccessible terrain or into the peaceful population are important qualities in an effective force. I have already discussed morale and rapport with the population. Other necessary characteristics are discipline, ingenuity, Spartan living, ability to

---

[9] Mao Tse-tung, "Strategic Problems of the Anti-Japanese Guerrilla War" (May 1938). Peking: Foreign Languages Press, 1954, p. 6.

[10] Quoted by Lt. Col. Robert Rigg in "Red China's Fighting Forces." Harrisburg: Military Service Publishing House, 1952, p. 226.

live off the land without excessive requisitions, and substantial reliance on captured arms and equipment.

Mao's concept of "protracted war" is now widely, if not always well, known. He advanced the thesis in order to explain the particular situation in China in the 1930s (though on occasion he also did assume a wider applicability), when neither the government forces nor the guerrillas were strong enough to annihilate the other. A protracted period was necessary to shift the balance to the revolutionaries.[11]

The eleventh proposition: Guerrilla warfare, in Communist strategy, is only a stage in the growth of the revolution in a particular country. Usually it must be succeeded by regular civil war before power can be grasped. Mao categorically stated that "guerrilla operations must not be considered as an independent form of warfare."[12] 'In the course of the prolonged, ruthless war," he explained, "guerrilla warfare should not remain its old self but must develop into mobile warfare. Thus the strategic role of guerrilla warfare is twofold: supporting regular warfare and transforming itself into regular warfare."[13] Guevara likewise holds that "guerrilla combat is a phase of warfare that cannot of itself attain complete victory; it is important to remember that guerrilla fighting is only a beginning or preparation for conventional warfare."[14]

In conclusion, I would note as my twelfth and final proposition: The future role of revolutionary guerrilla war in Communist strategy is probably more dependent on local opportunity than on anything else. The politico-military premises of Communist—chiefly Chinese—thought on revolutionary warfare is basically sound, as is their tactical doctrine for such operations. The most vulnerable point, then, is the local societies and polities which may be threatened. This is not a novel idea, but if our analysis of Communist thought and action brings us back to this point, we have at least discovered that there are no short cuts for either side—no basic flaws in the Communist approach, but also no secret weapon in their arsenal.

---

[11] See, in particular, Mao Tse-tung, "On the Protracted War" (June 1938), in "Selected Works," v. 2, p. 157–243.

[12] In Griffith, *op. cit.*, p. 41.

[13] Mao Tse-tung, "On the Protracted War." "Selected Works," v. 2, p. 224.

[14] Guevara, in *Army*, March 1961, p. 24.

# 57 / Working With the "Next Government"

## HARLAN CLEVELAND AND OTHERS

The operational requirements of American foreign policy have changed radically since World War II. But are our policy planners adequately calculating the accelerating change and increasing involvement of every nation in every other nation's internal affairs? Too often foreign policy goals are stated as abstractions: "to encourage the growth of democracy in newly independent nations." What are the concrete operational dimensions toward attainment of such an objective? This selection addresses itself to such a question, with emphasis on the emergent countries of Asia, Africa, and Latin America. How can the United States be prepared to get along with the "next government"?

REGARDING any contemporary government one statement can be made with fair certainty: the "ins" are on their way out. In some countries the chronological age of certain strong rulers makes this easy to perceive, and although such rulers have achieved a certain immortality as far as historians are concerned, their span as political executives has but a few years at most to run. Other societies are subject to such political turbulence that violent upheavals are predictable—even though, like active volcanoes, the degree and timing of eruptions cannot be foretold. Most of the artificial, war-created Arab nations of the Middle East are in this volcanic category; racial strife and class struggle in East Africa, South Africa, and some countries of Latin America create similar prospects for impetuous alteration of the status quo. Some "nations," like Burma and Indonesia, are so rent by internal tensions that violent political change seems a continuous process. Colonial areas look forward to casting off the chains which, however oppressive, did make them effective political units; their future is predictably full of surprises. In the more stable countries of Western Europe, and such semimodernized polities as Brazil and Turkey, elections and constitutional prescriptions guarantee a relatively frequent turnover among the policymaking

Reprinted from U. S. Senate Committee on Foreign Relations Study No. 6, "The Operational Aspects of United States Foreign Policy," by Maxwell Graduate School of Citizenship and Public Affairs, Syracuse University (November, 1959), in *U. S. Foreign Policy: Compilation of Studies,* 87th Cong., 1st sess., S. Doc. 24 (March 15, 1961), pp. 590–600.
A brief biographical sketch of Mr. Cleveland accompanies selection 45.

executives of government; in the United States such turnover is now made mandatory by the 22d amendment to the Constitution. Even in the totalitarian countries the insurrection in Hungary, the liberalization of Polish communism, and the recent abbreviation of tenure for such Soviet leaders as Molotov, Zhukov, and Malenkov, suggest the presence of a principle of political change more fundamental than any doctrinal "ism."

While the United States was a more youthful nation, the slower changes then typical in most parts of the world gave us little concern. Indeed, the idea of continuous progress crept into European and American literature and deeply affected our expectations about the performance of our economy: if things were not constantly getting better and fashions constantly changing, most Americans felt restless and dissatisfied. But when a nation reaches the head of the queue in economic satisfactions, any relative increase of power or wealth elsewhere can easily come to resemble retrogression. Thus it is that the image of an America which believes in constant progress has come to be blurred, especially since World War II, by another image of undiscriminating support for existing governments, of resistance to change by supplying resources, often including arms, to monarchs, dictators, and landowning politicians who, whatever their short-term value as dependable military allies, have often proved insecure in their tenure.

In the emerging countries of Asia, Africa, and Latin America this has been especially serious. Where the status quo is regarded as intolerable, the elements resisting change are seen as the common enemy. For example, most of the poorer countries identify progress with industrialization. To the leadership of these countries, the construction of factories is not only a way of increasing productivity and thus raising both consumption and investment, but also a matter of national prestige; as a consequence, modern plants have sometimes been "parachuted" into underdeveloped areas without provision for the small-industry support and urban services essential to the operation of a large industrial enterprise. U.S. experts, reflecting their more jaded view of the still somewhat mysterious processes of economic growth, have often said out loud that industrial projects are neither a panacea for poverty nor a royal road to better living, that they can be so ill-timed as to be wasteful of the limited capital available, and that they must be weighed against the advantages of other types of projects. Such U.S. attitudes have been reinforced by the sincere desire of many Americans to stimulate the private sector in underdeveloped economies—often, in fact, by an ill-concealed conviction that it is immoral for a government to establish a factory that might conceivably be developed by private industry. The result is a widespread feeling, especially in Asia and Africa, that the United States opposes the industrialization of the less developed countries, and this in spite of the hundreds of substan-

tial factories that have sprung up around the world in direct response to the stimulation of American private and public enterprise.

There are ironies here aplenty, for the expectation of change is partly the result of our own well-advertised demonstration that people can live better if they organize to produce more and divide it up more equitably. The changes that undermine the political "ins" are, in fact, partly the product of stimulation by U.S. action programs—technical aid that remolds institutions and mixes new cultural traditions with the old, dollar investment that changes the rate and direction of a government's use of its own resources, military training that is designed as preparation for troop command and turns out to be education for the exercise of civilian governmental responsibility. Yet because governmental leaders in many of the "underdeveloped areas" come from the wealthier classes and resist rapid social change once they get to the top, U.S. programs in support of their governments have been widely (if often falsely) identified as opposing change and as designed to shore up a crumbling status quo. The consequence is that when inevitable change does occur, the mere fact of change appears to be a U.S. "failure"—and sometimes, indeed, is embalmed in our domestic politics as such.

Can something be done about this state of affairs besides describing and deploring it? Two kinds of foreign operations are surely indicated. The U.S. Government is engaged in both, to some degree unconsciously:

We need to keep effectively in touch with every element of real power, across the whole spectrum of non-Communist politics, in every foreign country to which we have access.

We would do well to concentrate our major foreign operations—economic aid, military assistance, technical advice, public and private investment, information and cultural activities, educational exchange, and relief work—in support of those *institutions and programs,* existing and new, which promise to survive the transitory ambitions of individual regimes. And we may as well face frankly the truth that this goes far beyond "keeping in touch," for in prosecuting such programs and building such institutions we help induce social, economic, and political change and actually speed up the already breathtaking pace of events.

### 1. "Keeping in Touch"

An operational view of political change in foreign countries does not, of course, require us to abandon the traditional diplomatic practice of accrediting our Government's official representatives to contemporary governments in other nations. It is not here suggested, for example, that the U.S. Ambassador to the Cuban Government of Fulgencio Batista should have been spending half his time up in the hills of Oriente Province with the brothers Castro. But *somebody* should have been doing so. There is now no country in the world whose changing internal

"power structure" is irrelevant to United States foreign policy.

The means of getting acquainted with political "comers" and potential "next governments" are ready at hand. Any "next government" must demonstrate a lively interest in a better life for all, and must also possess the organized security forces to maintain a reasonable degree of domestic tranquility. Consequently, the two main ladders of power in most of the emergent societies are economic development programs and military organizations. If we had set out to find the best ways to relate the United States to the forces most likely to ride on the wave of the future, we could hardly have done better than to have established wide-ranging programs of economic, technical, and educational assistance, and (in avowedly friendly countries) cooperative arrangements for the provision of weapons and the training of military personnel.

An American technician assigned to work with a minister of agriculture or a provincial governor may be getting on a first-name basis with the next prime minister; an American colonel working with his opposite number in a local military establishment may (whether he knows it or not) be molding the attitudes toward political or economic institutions of the next military dictator—or the power behind the next civilian cabinet. The fact that most technical advisers and Army officers do not see themselves in this larger role does not make the relationships they establish less important to "American foreign policy." Ignorance, the absence of "a sense for politics," and the lack of training and instructions appropriate to the role have caused the missing of many opportunities in recent years; recent events in Egypt, Iraq, and Burma come readily to mind.

Outside the official channels (including the "officially unofficial" operations of the intelligence agencies) there is a vast range of contacts by organizations and individuals which can often, with modest encouragement from those in charge of official foreign relations, reach into strata of a society which cannot as easily be penetrated by a diplomat or USIA official or even an ICA engineer in his shirt-sleeves. Of the 1,590,000 Americans abroad at the end of March 1959, more than half a million were connected neither with the military nor with civilian Government agencies but with private enterprises ranging from business firms to mission boards.

In trying to reach "next governments," therefore, we have the incomparable asset of our own pluralism. The businessmen, missionaries, teachers, students, relief workers, journalists, and even the hundreds of semiprivate enterprises (consulting firms, universities, and others) that subsist on U.S. Government contracts abroad, are all free to widen their contacts beyond the Capital City cocktail circuit—though many of them do not. The New York Times editor who visited Fidel Castro in the hills; the Fulbright scholar who got acquainted with General

Kassim before the bloody revolt in Iraq; the labor union official who helped build up the non-Communist trade union movement in Italy; the agricultural expert from an American foundation who managed Guatemala's land reform program; the professor on a foundation grant who helped India's civil servants strengthen the professionals' hold on the machinery of government in New Delhi—all these and thousands more established relationships which would have been inconceivable for a Government official. The Soviets have reason to envy us our pluralistic ways. They cannot honestly draw even a fuzzy line between the actions of private persons and those of public officials abroad—even though Khrushchev rather wistfully announced, on arriving at an industrial fair in Eastern Germany some months ago, that he came representing "business circles in the U.S.S.R." He surely wishes he had available such a range of private contacts, such an infinite crisscrossing of lines of interest and influence, such a remarkable variety and extent of channels of communications, as we have. But sometimes we seem hardly to know we have them.

To overorganize our plural contacts abroad, assuming that were possible, would immediately destroy their usefulness. But a better official recognition of the relevance to U.S. foreign policy of this web of communications, and its greater use and encouragement by U.S. officials, would result in improved relations with the "next government."

The operations implied here are quite different from taking part in a foreign country's political struggles, openly supporting one faction or another. Experience has shown that such support by the U.S. Government, or even by a large American business firm, is often a political liability to the faction supported, and likely to result in our being cut off from effective contact with any "next government" composed of elements opposed to the "American party." Our cue is precisely *not* to have an "American party," to position our foreign operations so that they can constitute a basis for mutuality of interest between the United States and a wide variety of social philosophies, institutional forms, and political personalities. The Communists have no such freedom of movement in establishing relationships with the emergent countries. Their apron strings are tied to local Communist parties no matter how incompetent or overanxious those parties may be; the disadvantages of this arrangement recently became clear in the Kerala Province of India, where the local Communists overplayed their hand and were displaced by action of a vigilant central government.

## 2. Supporting Programs Rather Than Regimes

While U.S. foreign policy must avoid taking sides in the formal politics of a foreign country, it must also take into account the obvious fact that U.S.-supported programs have significant political effects. What

472

is needed is a careful analysis of the direction of internal social and political change in each country and region, and a deliberate effort to help each country develop the institutional structure most conducive to effective self-government and cooperative participation in building a world order in which change can take place without major violence. The U.S. operations resulting from such an analysis should have a common characteristic, that they not merely resist types of change we do not like but induce the kinds of changes we do. A few examples will illustrate the point.

*Land reform programs* often induce changes that are both economically important and politically popular; their consistent support in many places would help identify the United States as promoting progress rather than defending the status quo. "Land reform," of course, has different meanings in different contexts, ranging from mild reduction of rentals to drastic changes in the ownership of land; but by and large the desirability of enabling the land to be owned by the men and women who work it would gain wide acceptance as a principle of U.S. foreign operations. The United States might well plan to commit a sizable sum each year to help reorganize land use in the world's less developed areas, and entrust to the United Nations (through the Food and Agricultural Organization and the U.N.'s regional economic commissions) the working out of detailed plans for the application of these funds.

*U.S. support for schools and colleges* likewise represents a wager on the future of the nation in which they are built. An education program should, of course, be accompanied by development activities which put the newly educated youngsters to work; we have witnessed enough examples already, in pre-Communist China and elsewhere, of U.S. help in producing a new class of well-educated unemployed. But basic educational institutions have the double advantage, as a target for U.S. foreign operations, that they tend to survive changes in political leadership and can also be expected, over time, to train more responsible leaders for the "next governments" of the future. The several American colleges and universities in the Middle East have had a profound influence on the outlook of two or three generations of national leaders in that region.

In many countries, also, university students play a leading role in national politics even before they finish their formal education. Some universities, indeed, serve as incubators for revolutionary movements not only in their own country but in others, through organizations of refugee students from neighboring dictatorships; this is notably true in Latin America. U.S. educators associated with foreign universities as visiting professors, administrators, or advisers may thus be advantageously situated for establishing political rapport and influence with the leaders of the future; politically mature exchange students from the United States have a similar opportunity.

*Health programs* have traditionally been a popular form of technical assistance. In this field the dilemmas produced by rapid technological change and deep involvement in other people's internal affairs will soon be well illustrated by the coming debate about support of population control programs by the U.S. Government. A few experiments have already tested the feasibility of spreading birth control information in areas where population growth (partly resulting from the very success of past efforts in public health and sanitation) presses unduly on the supply of food. The President's Committee To Study the U.S. Military Assistance Program (the Draper committee), in its report of July 13, 1959, on "Economic Assistance Programs and Administration," has already dipped its toe into this boiling water by proposing that the United States cooperate officially with other nations "in the formulation of practical programs to meet the serious challenge posed by rapidly expanding populations." It is especially important, in dealing with such a topic, for the United States to be able to work with and through international organizations in order to minimize the pressures of national politics in such a matter.

*Military training,* in some countries, is virtually the only major means of education for public responsibility. In the past few years, more than a dozen national governments have been taken over by the armed forces; in several others there were abortive military coups. One way or another, the military are a major factor in the politics and government of most Asian, Middle Eastern, and Latin American nations. Americans, in whom the principle of civilian control over the armed forces is deeply ingrained, tend to deplore such military intervention in politics. But given the conditions that prevail in many newly emerging nations, it is to be expected, and sometimes may be an instrument of progress. Institutional weaknesses, governmental irresponsibility, lack of political traditions, and deep social divisions—often aggravated by the need to contend with almost insuperable economic pressures—may produce an intolerable degree of governmental instability, threatening major disruption of the social order. The apparent unity and discipline of the army stand out in sharp contrast, and a military regime is likely to seem an acceptable, even an attractive, alternative to the prevailing chaos.

In a number of countries, moreover, where wealth and family position offer the only keys to advancement in most fields, a military career may enable young men of the lower classes to gain an education, and achieve positions of responsibility and command, largely through merit. It is not surprising, therefore, that where no strong tradition of representative government exists, the armed forces may come to regard themselves (and often to be regarded) as an essentially democratic institution, as the guardian of national integrity, the scourge of corruption and injustice, and a principal force for social progress. These

sentiments, reinforcing and justifying the human urge for power, afford constant temptations to seize the reins of government—and, of course, if the military are reasonably united they can readily do so in the absence of restraints by more powerful forces from the outside. They may well succumb, to be sure, to the same pressures that discredited their predecessors, but sometimes a military regime has introduced, at least temporarily, greater order and integrity into the government of its country. In any case, the military remain, for good or evil, a force to be reckoned with. Key military leaders, even if they do not dominate the current government, are generally a major factor in the political equation, and they may well control or constitute the next government, and the one after that.

Thus trained officers often find themselves projected into civilian government responsibilities because they are among the few leaders who are at home with the complexities of large-scale public management. But managing a government, including its foreign relations, is a far cry from commanding troops; it requires, for example, some sense of the nature of economic growth, some exposure to the mysteries of public finance, some experience with international as well as domestic politics. By and large U.S. military training skips these chapters of human experience; even in the U.S. Defense Department's training program for American officers assigned to the military assistance advisory groups abroad, there is a striking emphasis on learning the details of MAAG procedures, at the expense of time for discussion of the military's political role in foreign operations. A serious review of our own training programs for foreign military personnel might suggest the assignment to our own MAAG's of officers with civilian government experience who are competent to deal with the political executives and civil administrators of the future.

To sponsor activities in each country which promise to commend themselves to the "next government," to build institutions and programs rather than merely formal intergovernmental relationships—these modern ways of carrying out a foreign policy do not require the snubbing or ignoring of existing governments. Quite the contrary; all U.S. foreign programs operate with the approval and support of existing governments. The latter request and approve projects, regulate the flow of Americans in and out of their country, and accept many of the resultant financial and administrative burdens. What a modern foreign policy does suggest is—

(*a*) The avoidance of "shadow projects" that advertise improvements but are designed primarily to benefit groups in power;

(*b*) An emphasis on a few long-term programs of major significance, rather than a host of miscellaneous small projects which may fit some theory of "program balance" but make it hard for people at large (whether in the foreign

country or in the United States) to form any clear image of the purposes of U.S. participation;

(c) The value of working through multilateral organizations which when astutely managed can become deeply involved in the touchiest "domestic" decisions of member countries without raising issues of national sovereignty. The importance of this last point is so great as to justify a further word on the subject.

### 3. The Advantages of Multilateral Management

Economic development, with all that it implies in terms of increased welfare, security, and status, is the universal aspiration of the emerging nations of the world. To associate U.S. policy with progress toward this objective offers the broadest and best means of identifying ourselves favorably with the flow of change, and at the same time of influencing its direction and emphasis. Our involvement in economic development activities should bring us into constant, intimate association with the actual and (even more) the future leaders of these countries, providing countless opportunities to foster a sense of identity between their national aims and ours, and to transmit to them something of the spirit and value of our way of life. This has been a principal purpose, and a very sound one, of our espousing the "principle of jointness" in our economic aid programs. There is no doubt that many of the binational agencies which the United States has sponsored—such as the Joint Commission on Rural Reconstruction in Taiwan and the many different types of *servicios* in Latin America—have contributed substantially to this purpose.

But there should likewise be no doubt by now, after more than a decade of experience with foreign aid, that the bilateral relationship seriously limits the effectiveness of such an association, especially when it touches on the central issues of economic and social policy that underlie investment programs or technical assistance projects. The decisions taken on these questions, by some twoscore countries in Asia, Africa, and Latin America, may determine for the indefinite future whether or not we can achieve a truly viable relationship with a third of the world. But we are gravely handicapped—in some countries, indeed, we are effectively debarred from participation and influence in these decisions—by the bilateral groove in which most of our efforts in support of economic development have been caught.

The essential reasons are not difficult to see—

(a) The crucial policy and programing decisions in economic development raise touchy political issues, vitally affecting local special interests, in which it is wholly inappropriate, and would often be unwise, for the United States as a government to be directly involved.

(b) Self-respecting sovereign nations, especially if they are new and insecure in their sovereignty, will normally be afraid to let a powerful foreign government participate in considering such basic questions.

There are two means of escape from this predicament. One is to give maximum encouragement to nongovernmental organizations such as business firms, universities, and private philanthropic foundations. Organizations such as the Ford Foundation's office in India can often establish more intimate and effective relationships with foreign governments than a U.S. Government agency could possibly do; sometimes this principle holds even when the "private" agency is working under contract to an American Government agency.

The other escape, valid for the wide range of activities which can only be carried on at the government level, is to work with and through international agencies. There is a strong case for making an effective multilateral organization our agent for economic development and doing our best to persuade like-minded industrial countries to use the same agency for promoting sound progress in the emergent countries.

Such a multilateral framework would help substantially to reduce the political and psychological barriers to intimate collaboration, to deflate the issue of "intervention," and to permit basic development problems to be considered and worked out between the emerging countries and ourselves in reasonably objective fashion. An international agency for promoting economic development—in whose establishment the countries of Asia, Africa, and Latin America have taken part, whose terms of reference they have explicitly approved, and in which they are effectively represented—cannot be regarded by them as "foreign" in the same sense as a U.S. Government organ. Nor can such an agency reasonably be excluded from concerning itself with its members' domestic policies and programs, for such concern is the essence of its agreed function of promoting sound development. These may appear somewhat abstract, verbal distinctions—and it is not suggested that they are absolutely or universally applicable—but they have very real and wide significance in practice; the experience of every international agency bears witness. A number of American staff members of the World Bank, for instance, have found that their international sponsorship permits them to work in relationships of trust and influence with the local government that they could never achieve working out of the embassy or the ICA [foreign aid] mission.

Other considerations also weigh heavily in favor of using multilateral channels in this field. There is no reason why the Americans should bear the whole burden and responsibility of assistance to development; in fact, there is every reason why we should not. The Western European countries, Japan, Canada, and some others have

the same stake as we in keeping the free world free and increasing its strength and unity; and they have substantial resources of capital, skills, and experience that should certainly be enlisted in the common effort. A multilateral approach, moreover, provides a tangible demonstration of the free world's unity of interest and purpose; minimizes the danger of "development" programs being twisted into instruments of commercial rivalry among the industrial nations outside the Soviet bloc; and offers a challenging outlet for the energies of these nations, a lift for their morale potentially comparable in psychological significance to the settlement of frontier areas in the 18th and 19th centuries. The multilateral approach also serves to discredit suspicions that persist in some circles in Europe, as well as in the underdeveloped world, that our aim is to substitute an American imperialism for European colonialism.

This argument for multilateralization of assistance to economic development runs counter to the widely held view that all economic aid, like our other overseas operations, should be kept available for the managers of our foreign policy to bring to bear on the issues or negotiations of greatest current importance. But this is to mistake the purpose and value of our participation in economic development. If it is to express the genuine mutuality of interest between our national interest and the interests of the emergent countries, this participation of ours must be conceived as an instrument of long-range strategy. The indiscriminate use of economic aid as an all-purpose tactical weapon, in every crisis and for all sorts of short-term ends, blunts and discredits it for its proper function. Both the Soviets and ourselves have found it difficult to "cash" economic aid in terms of short-range political benefit. It has been of doubtful, even negative, value in many of the situations to which it was casually applied, and its availability in such situations may have prevented or delayed consideration of real issues and possible solutions. A most distressing instance of this kind was the Aswan Dam incident and its aftermath, the Eisenhower Doctrine; the Soviets had an equivalent (and evidently more lasting) failure in Yugoslavia.

The case seems clear, as a matter of policy, for multilateralizing U.S. efforts (and those of other industrial countries) to promote world economic development, insofar as possible. But we cannot put the United Nations machinery to work on a large scale unless and until it is organized for the job. It is not now so organized. . . .

# 58 / Reflections on Cuba: Confessions of an Interventionist

## JOHN P. ROCHE

Is political intervention in the domestic affairs of other nations compatible with American values and tradition? Some argue no; others yes. What are the policy consequences of intervening or not intervening? This discussion was written just after the ill-fated, American-sponsored invasion of Castro's Cuba by Cuban exiles in April, 1961.

IT IS DISTRESSING to note the way some respected liberal and Socialist figures have reacted to the Cuban debacle. Norman Thomas, for example, circulated an elaborate statement, the gist of which was, first, that the Central Intelligence Agency (CIA) support for Batista elements was immoral; second, that American support for anybody in these circumstances would risk world war; and, third, that we have only ourselves, and our foolish past policies in Latin America, to blame anyhow, since Fidel Castro was virtually our creation.

It is hardly necessary here to note my respect and admiration for Norman Thomas, but in reading this statement I had the curious feeling that I had been here before. And in fact, I have: The first time I heard Norman Thomas speak was in 1939, and the substance of his speech was that collective security was "collective suicide." I was completely convinced of the correctness of this position and until Pearl Harbor was a dogged activist in the "Keep America Out of War Congress" youth movement.

I have never had much truck with confession, and I know that I can no more "repudiate" my past than I can cut off my arm. The years in the "Youth Committee Against War" are part of that past. But I have since become convinced of the fundamentally wrong-headed character of the non-intervention position in 1939–41, and I deplore the contemporary revival of what can only be called "liberal isolationism." Nuclear devastation terrifies me as much as anyone else; yet, in realistic terms, to run away from risks is not to eliminate them. On the contrary, it may well exacerbate the dangers.

Reprinted from *The New Leader*, May 15, 1961, pp. 5–6. By permission.

John P. Roche is Morris Hillquit Professor of Labor and chairman of the Department of Politics, Brandeis University.

Let me make it perfectly clear that in my mind the CIA operation in Cuba was a piece of immoral folly. But it was not immoral because it was intervention, but because it was folly: The character of the intervention was such as seriously to compromise our democratic integrity. The CIA's addiction to right-wing anti-Communism put us in a hopeless position in the eyes of our democratic allies while providing the Soviet Union with a superb propaganda motif. The operation could not have worked out better for the USSR had it been executed by Soviet agents.

Moreover, the *new* Cuban situation, the result of the CIA's abortive scheme, calls for enormous prudence and self-restraint on the part of the United States. At this point, it seems to me that we have to write off our liabilities, put logic in irons and realize that if the USSR can afford Yugoslavia, Turkey and Iran, we can afford a Communist Cuba.

In short, a moratorium on Cuba seems to me in order. But this is a very different thing from asserting that American intervention in general is bad. The liberal, social democratic tradition is one which makes intervention in the internal affairs of all dictatorships obligatory. It postulates the absolute value of certain fundamental principles and combats every attempt to destroy them.

As Sidney Hook has often pointed out, we cannot employ a double standard. We must be willing to "intervene" in the domestic affairs of all unjust regimes, whether they be dominated by Communists, fascists or non-ideological gangsters like Rafael Leonidas Trujillo. The liberal must assert the same moral position in all areas of the world; in the same way that he fights white supremacy in the American South, he must combat it in South Africa.

As one who grew up with the slogan "Keep Out of War"—*i.e.*, "Hands Off Nazi Germany"—on his lips, I cannot accept a policy of "Hands Off Cuba" except on prudential grounds. We must be prepared to take action of one sort or another to help realize our dream of freedom in this unhappy bi-polar world. To suggest, as Norman Thomas and others have, that Castro is our creation seems to me irrelevant on the level of principle—as irrelevant as the alleged injustices of Versailles were to the evils of Nazi Germany.

The brutal fact is that, however historically occasioned, our allies in vast areas of the world are suffering and dying for our common principles. For us, of all people, to write them off to the enemy because we dare not joggle the balance of terror would be an act of moral cowardice. Such a policy would inexcusably lead to a liberal version of "Fortress America," in which we would stand paralyzed and transfixed because any action we take in the world might lead to devastation. A similar policy of ideological paralysis in the 1930s contributed to the murder of six million Jews and millions of others.

Our moral obligation to help our allies must, of course, be tempered

by counsels of prudence. While we should not allow our obsessional fears of annihilation to freeze us in a posture of impotent immobility, we must take every possible step to avoid war. The key to the U.S. failure in the past eight years was the enshrinement of immobility as our national policy: "Massive retaliation," John Foster Dulles' version of the Maginot Line, served as a substitute for any flexible tactics of a limited character. Actuated by a profound pessimism about the future of the West, we took refuge behind the big bomb.

However badly the Cuban expedition may have been botched, it did mark an emergence from this chrysalis of pessimism, an effort to introduce flexibility into our world policy. President Kennedy is not one to make the same mistake twice, nor is he one to panic in a crisis. The Cuban affair was a beginning of the effort to compete with the Soviet Union on the level of ideological operations; it failed because the CIA is an inadequate tool of liberal policy.

The liberal effort thus should be concentrated on devising appropriate and effective means of intervention, not to attacks on the principle of intervention. There should certainly be no moratorium on criticism of the CIA or the President: Kennedy should be encouraged, pressed and harassed until this *imperium in imperio* is brought to heel. To argue that we should not "rock the boat" is absurd; unless significant changes are made, it could well be the equivalent of "Don't rock the hearse."

To adopt the policy of "liberal isolationism" may provide a tempting escape from the perils of commitment, but it is a betrayal of the deepest values of liberal civilization. There is really no such thing as "nonintervention"; the very existence of a free society is a form of intervention in the internal affairs of dictatorships. In *Arrival and Departure* Arthur Koestler evoked a dream sequence reminiscent of Kafka: A man, brought before a judge and jury in his own likeness, claims that he "never killed a fly," and the remorseless prosecution replies, "Yes, and the flies he didn't kill brought pestilence to a province."

For liberals to stand silent and frozen in the face of injustice is to reject the obligations of their values; it also is a form of intervention in behalf of immobility at a time when we must move. It is our task to help formulate and implement a viable liberal policy which will give the ideals of freedom and justice a chance to win the day without disaster. Our dreams may turn to radioactive ashes, but we must have the "nerve of failure," the dedication to try, even though we have no guarantee of success or survival. To flee from all risk is to elect moral bankruptcy.

# 59 / From *Special Message to the Congress on Urgent National Needs, May 25, 1961*

## JOHN F. KENNEDY

**In the spring of 1961, President Kennedy delivered a second State of the Union message in which he called for the development of military instruments suitable to cope with "wars of national liberation" that seem to threaten United States security. Excerpts from this message follow.**

. . . I HAVE DIRECTED a further reinforcement of our own capacity to deter or resist nonnuclear aggression. In the conventional field, with one exception, I find no present need for large new levies of men. What is needed is rather a change of position to give us still further increases in flexibility.

Therefore, I am directing the Secretary of Defense to undertake a reorganization and modernization of the Army's divisional structure, to increase its nonnuclear firepower, to improve its tactical mobility in any environment, to insure its flexibility to meet any direct or indirect threat, to facilitate its co-ordination with our major allies, and to provide more modern mechanized divisions in Europe and bring our equipment up to date, and new airborne brigades in both the Pacific and Europe.

And second, I am asking the Congress for an additional $100 million to begin the procurement task necessary to re-equip this new Army structure with the most modern material. . . .

Third, I am directing the Secretary of Defense to expand rapidly and substantially, in co-operation with our allies, the orientation of existing forces for the conduct of nonnuclear war, paramilitary operations and sublimited or unconventional wars.

In addition, our special forces and unconventional warfare units will be increased and reoriented. Throughout the services new emphasis must be placed on the special skills and languages which are required to work with local populations.

Fourth, the Army is developing plans to make possible a much more rapid deployment of a major portion of its highly trained reserve forces. . . .

Fifth, to enhance the already formidable ability of the Marine Corps to respond to limited war emergencies, I am asking the Congress for $60 million to increase Marine Corps strength to 190,000 men. . . .

Finally, to cite one other area of activities that are both legitimate and necessary as a means of self-defense in an age of hidden perils, our whole intelligence effort must be reviewed, and its co-ordination with other elements of policy assured. . . .

# 60 / *What Happened When the C.I.A. Won*

### C. L. SULZBERGER

The Central Intelligence Agency is known to have played a major role in the ouster in 1954 of a government seen to be unfriendly to the United States in Guatemala. Was this action a solution to the problems in that Central American republic? This exploration of that question illustrates an episode in recent American interventionism.

THE C.I.A. has come to be regarded as the physical agent of United States Latin-American policy when that policy is expressed by force. In cruder days this role was reserved for the Marine Corps whose Major General Smedley Butler confided in his memoirs: "I helped make Mexico and especially Tampico safe for American oil interests in 1914. I helped make Haiti and Cuba a decent place for the National City Bank boys to collect revenues in . . . . I helped make Honduras 'right' for American Fruit Companies in 1903."

The era of rough, tough capitalist imperialism is happily past. The Marines are now confined to watch-dog duty in embassy code rooms. And the only kind of active role the C.I.A. seems engaged in is the effort to keep communism from establishing Latin-American bridgeheads.

Events in Ecuador may yet remind us again of the need to face this problem, although by what means is not easily decided. Events in Cuba show how embarrassing miscalculated action can be.

Guatemala, however, presents an instance where the C.I.A. won. In 1954 it helped a group of Guatemalans, based in Honduras and Nicaragua, to overthrow a fellow travelling regime here and evict its leaders in humiliating circumstances.

Reprinted from *The New York Times*, November 15, 1961. Copyright © 1961 by The New York Times Company. By permission.

C. L. Sulzberger is the writer of the column "Foreign Affairs," which appears regularly in *The New York Times*.

What has happened since? How has the United States used the opportunity presented by the C.I.A.? Have we employed these seven years to turn Guatemala into a Central-American showcase? The answer is a rather dim no.

President Arbenz Guzman, shoddy figurehead of the pro-Communist Government ousted in 1954, is now a refugee in Havana and his promises to return arouse scant enthusiasm. But his predecessor, the Leftist liberal Juan Areval, makes bigger noises from a Venezuelan haven.

The man we assisted to power in their wake, Castillo Armas, was murdered in 1957 by persons still uncaught.

An election to find his successor was cancelled as corrupt but in a subsequent vote General Miguel Ydigoras, openly opposed by Washington, came to power and still rules. Our own candidate's pride was assuaged with subsidiary office and a financial gift. By careful diplomacy we have since patched up relations with Ydigoras who has shown some unexpectedly democratic traits combined with lack of administrative talent.

### American Gains Noted

United States ascendancy has been re-established. We were able to train anti-Castro forces in obscure jungles and to de-nationalize vast properties of United Fruit Company, seized by Arbenz.

This concern and the powerful Electric Bond and Share subsidiary have since shown they at least dimly perceive the light. United Fruit is trying to sell out and Electric Bond has greatly improved the status of its workers, making them justly envied by much of an impoverished proletariat. Nevertheless, unhappily, we still look like champions of the rich and the status quo, $100 million dollars in aid has had dismally insufficient public impact.

We are trying to help Ydigoras guide a new income tax law through his bickering Congress. We have interesting plans for mass education and have done much to improve health. But if one considers our seven-year influence one must reluctantly conclude we might have done far better. Guatemala's craving for dynamic change has not been met. We have helped initial industrialization and emergence of a rudimentary middle class. But seventy per cent of Guatemalans are still illiterate and a large number hungry.

Students and intellectuals look leftwards. They see corruption among our known friends and therefore link us with it.

It is hard for the United States, with all its benevolent aspirations, to make administrative bricks without administrative straw. Yet we have failed to find guaranteed market outlets for basic agricultural products [on which this country lives], to assure honest government or requisite

sweeping reforms. We have shown decency, sympathy and good intentions. But one knows where mere good intentions lead.

Guatemala's illiterates remain disgruntled and its literates remain substantially unimpressed with our claims to represent the future's wave. When these literates view the tide of avowedly anti-American infiltration from Cuba to Ecuador, they imagine we lack strength. Strength is admired.

# 61 / Footnotes on Revolutionary War

### GEORGE A. KELLY

Semantic confusion on the subject of revolutionary war has been widespread. Are such terms as "guerrilla," "sublimited," or "internal" warfare synonymous? Is there a way out of this conventional confusion about unconventional warfare? The author of this selection uses the concept "revolutionary war" in an attempt to bring some order out of the confusion about "irregular warfare."

. . . MUCH HAS BEEN WRITTEN on the subject of wars of the character of those in Laos and South Vietnam; and not a little has been learned from observing or participating in the battle. But the mountains of theory and data remain, to a certain degree, incoherent and confusing. This is natural while we are in the laboratory or planning stage of guiding our responses to these difficult challenges. At such a time, though, there is always the danger that our unorganized ideas may run away with us.

It scarcely befits an armchair analyst to try to take possession of the laboratory. At best, he is qualified to exercise the function of a critic. But there is room for criticism and clarification in our conception of what will be referred to here as "revolutionary war."

At the outset, we are obviously plagued by the problem of terminology. Various terms have been put forward to describe this type of

Reprinted from *The Military Review*, September, 1962, pp. 31–39. Published by the United States Army Command and General Staff College, Fort Leavenworth, Kansas.

George A. Kelly is associated with the Center for International Affairs, Harvard University.

conflict—"guerrilla," "irregular," "subversive," "internal," "sublimited," and so forth. All of the words will be found wanting in some salient particular.

This is not only semantically distressing; if one cannot describe a conflict properly, one may not be able to fight it properly. To illustrate, irregular is a negative description because it tells us only that the conflict is not regular. Internal may be incorrect because such wars, if germinated internally, frequently cross borders with disarming regularity: this has been true in southeast Asia, where the violability of frontiers has been a significant characteristic of the struggle.

Guerrilla, at best, describes only that part of the conflict which is clearly above the threshold of violence; subversive only that part which lies below. Sublimited, the latest in our galaxy of terms, is palpably incorrect because these wars are not only expansive and expansible in many ways; they are also alarmingly total in their manipulation of resources within a limited area, and they have many efficient, if subterranean, contacts with the outside.

### Types of Revolution

I have chosen to employ the word "revolutionary," recognizing that it has its own defects. (One defect surely is that it has already been used to denote a presumed nexus of wars deriving from a single revolutionary inspiration, an interpretation which I reject.) However, none of the defects seems essentially misleading with reference to the inner nature of the conflict. Revolution is a principal and constant fact of these wars, and it is at the core of our understanding of them. "Revolutionary" has the virtue of comprehending the source and personality of this kind of conflict, as well as its techniques. It is not apt to guide us in the wrong direction.

Now, what kind of a revolution are we attempting to define? Actually, it is many revolutions at once, some of them endemic in the worldwide problem of colonial withdrawal, some of them the instruments of relatively obscure factions, some of them traditionally "nationalist" at base, some of them deriving from civil discontent in established states, some of them notably inspired by foreign, and especially Communist, sources in the pursuit of regional or global policy. The mixtures of these types of revolution are bewildering. But all are aimed, consciously or not, at interfering with a certain political and, more especially, strategic balance in the world today.

Since their interference with this balance will, in the large majority of cases, act to the detriment of the power position of the West— because the Western nations were the colonial powers—unless new weights can be added to redress the equilibrium, our response to this phenomenon has been, to say the least, rather panicky. There is really

more cause for concern than panic, and there is room for some long, hard thinking.

The occasional disputes with our European allies in interpreting these issues are notorious. What is less recognized is that we are divided in our own mind regarding the significance of revolutionary war and the responses it should call forth. Let us make no mistake: a critical paradox is involved. If revolutionary war often acts to the detriment of Western strength, the inference then is that it must be deterred, or fought and won, or at least stalemated, if our positions are to be protected. If others will not make the requisite effort to defend common positions, it seems inescapable that we will sometimes be called on to do it ourselves.

Presumably, in a world of relative international amicability that featured no harsh ideological clashes or armed threats, we would approve unreservedly of today's progress away from colonial dependence. We would welcome the multiplication of new nations without apprehension, so long as they represent the desires of their peoples. Even in a time of peril, our political reflex is still to extend such a welcome.

### Strategic Security Estimates

But our deeply ingrained commitment to liberty and pluralism has clashed harshly at moments with our estimates of strategic security. For example, a neutral Algeria poses no threat to the West, and is undoubtedly a fulfillment of the wishes of the majority of her people. A neutral Algeria, though, might subtract drastically from Europe's capacity to defend itself against a stronger aggressor. And if the new Algeria should slide toward the Eastern bloc, she would become a potential base outflanking Western Europe and pointing toward the Atlantic itself.

Political-strategic paradoxes of an analogous nature plague us in our reactions to many current or future revolutionary situations. This is a factor which has to be weighed in advance of decision and commitment, and, indeed, in advance of operational planning. Unfortunately, the choices are rarely very clear-cut, and, being qualitatively different, they sometimes cannot be meaningfully compared, at least in the short run.

### Guides to Follow

Two conclusions emerge from this analysis. First of all, if it is recognized that revolutionary war, either in its occurrence or in its result, may be calculated to injure the West strategically, it then follows that certain determinations must be made:

Will the political consequences be more abusive than the advantages

gained by military opposition to the revolution or a conceivable escalation of the conflict?

Is the issue central or peripheral to the strategic design in the area? Moreover, can the balance be redressed by other counterweights that might be more sagacious in the long run? For example, could the sacrifice of a Western base in a given area be compensated by an alternative deployment or by some strategic revision that would not sacrifice existing power?

Is the situation at the time of commitment genuinely salvageable, both in its own terms and in the relative allocation of strategic resources?

Have we a moral commitment to intervene? This will depend partly upon our treaty obligations and assurances, partly on the psychopolitical effects of our intervention or lack of it, partly upon our ability to identify the nature of the "revolution." For example, there can be little doubt that we are committed to the preservation of an independent South Vietnam or that the "revolution" which menaces her is of direct Communist inspiration. But as the years pass, we are certain to confront more ambiguous cases.

The second conclusion is that we must be much more sensitive to gathering signs of disturbance leading to a revolutionary situation, and that we must be quick to assess the character of the revolution once it breaks out. This, in turn, leads to the unmistakable corollary that we must exert whatever pressures we possess to prevent the capture of revolutionary movements in their early stages by the designs of Communist expansion.

Success in this objective will involve acute recognition of the trouble spot and a considerable degree of pragmatic adaptation to the needs of the situation. It will be best accomplished by discerning when a situation is incipiently revolutionary, and by preparing adequate countermeasures in advance. This can be done if the proper skills are organized; it amounts to a kind of intellectual spotting technique performed by military personnel and social scientists familiar with the area.

Our response cannot afford to be deformed or paralyzed by initial misinformation about a civil crisis, a so-called war of liberation, or the like. We must treat the traditional bogey-words "Socialist" and "Marxist" with discernment. On the other hand, we must be ready to defend what we are bound to defend even if transient opportunism should argue otherwise. A revolutionary situation can best be influenced in its infant stages. This involves swift recognition and the weighing of possible courses of policy action. A major concern is to keep a budding revolution from becoming an extension of Communist power.

### Difficult to Classify

What is most likely to be the character of this type of conflict? In attempting to answer this question, we risk the pitfalls of oversimplification. In the definition process we may easily sacrifice components that

loom large in any particular war. As we draw closer to refining ideas about this type conflict, many useful details will escape us.

Because a revolutionary war is usually historical in its germination, partly subterranean, and susceptible to many kinds of expansion, it is difficult to classify as a type. This is not simply an academic problem. It is a policy problem and a military problem in the most fundamental sense. Comprehensive doctrines can lead to deep trouble. Observers perceiving that Communist strategy places heavy reliance on techniques of guerrilla and subversion may too often be tempted to conclude that where these elements show their face the hand of communism is always present. In a given situation the truth of the matter may well be either that the issue of communism is chiefly extraneous, or that the aims of the revolution and of communism are tactically joined. In the second instance, the West has the choice of either treating the revolution as a Communist ancillary and combating it on those terms or of adopting tactics designed to sabotage the alliance.

### Other Factors

Many other factors enter the picture. As already pointed out, one of these is the fundamental character of the revolution—the "mix" of elements. Obviously, another, in the military sense, is the relation of the revolution to national and Western strategy. A third important consideration is the distinguishing features of the regional setting which have given birth to and sustained the revolution. For example, certain French analysts have felt that populations in the battle zones could easily be brought under the sway of more or less standard slogans, psychological techniques, and manipulative devices in order to assure their adhesion and deny their support to the revolutionary enemy.

Another, wiser French critic, General Nemo, who himself commanded a unit in Indochina, has properly countered this facile assertion:

> This mobilization of the crowd cannot follow uniform rules. If the objective is the same everywhere, one cannot universally apply like techniques. For the system to be adopted depends on very disparate and varied factors according to the country, composition of the body social, state of opinion, individual and collective psychological reactions to events, ways of life depending on the average level of material existence.[1]

In other words, in revolutionary war "milieu" is incalculable as a component of general theory. In each case the counterforces will need to be well informed as to particulars and will be committed, to a certain extent, to playing by ear. This suggests that doctrine, too, will have to be highly flexible.

---

[1] "La Guerre dans la Foule," *Revue de Défense Nationale,* June 1956, p. 728.

## Common Definitions

We could go on to list other elements of discrimination in revolutionary conflict. But since this article makes no claim to being exhaustive, it seems worthwhile to consider points of common definition as they may pertain to this type of struggle.

### COUNTERREVOLUTION

First, a revolutionary war generally will be a struggle of total commitment of resources by the insurgent forces within a limited sphere of operation. Within the area controlled by the rebels, all social, economic, and political levers will be mobilized to advance the potential of the revolution. The counterrevolution, if it is wise, will have to make a corresponding commitment—or, in the case of counter-guerrilla forces, a much superior one—but there will be a threshold beyond which the commitment of resources will seem implausible or useless. Aside from the effects of this mechanism on the operational dynamics of the war, it will have the psychological result of emphasizing the dedication, tenacity, and solidarity of the revolutionary forces. The forces of order may seem, by contrast, morally weak and flaccid because of the reduced percentage of their commitment.

### IRREGULAR AND GUERRILLA TACTICS

Second, although irregular war has a virtually millennial history and guerrilla war dates at least from the first use of the term in the Peninsular War of 1808–14, the generating feature of modern "revolutionary" war would seem to be the combination of these previous tactics with a totalist ideological inspiration exceeding the common fervor of nationalism. This point is debatable in certain instances. But where it is true, it is the normal connecting link between a revolution of local origin and the dynamism of the Communist thrust.

As we have seen on numerous occasions, the most basic and homely slogans such as "bread" and "land" are highly susceptible to this kind of "ideological escalation" wherever social demands and pressures cannot be fulfilled. Revolutionary war, then, against the novel backdrop of nuclear weapons and global ideological conflict, customarily adds a new dimension to past experiences of unconventional warfare.

### CIVILIAN SUPPORT

Third, it is now broadly recognized that revolutionary war is not so much a struggle for terrain nor even for victory in battles and skirmishes,

but rather a close competition by all existing means for the support of the surrounding civilian population. Mao's "fish in water" principle is now widely quoted. But this dawning came late to many in the West, particularly the United States, where wars of revolutionary character had often been naively dismissed as "brushfire wars." A few more acute critics drew lessons from the Philippine insurgency and other cases. James E. King, Jr. wrote six years ago:

> In combating guerrilla actions against us, our aim should be primarily at the population, and only secondarily at the guerrillas, as Magsaysay so brilliantly demonstrated in the Philippines.[2]

These scattered warnings went largely unheeded until events brought revolutionary war to our doorstep.

Control the population, enlist its support, yes; but how? One can hardly wave a wand, and make several million peasants rich and contented. The French Army went to the extreme of dislocating or causing the resettlement of two million Algerian Muslims, without, as we know, being able to perpetuate the French presence in the territory. A whole range of different answers was possible, and many methods were tried, some wasteful and others bizarre and degrading.

In discussing the problem of controlling populations, the famous Marshal Louis Lyautey had written 70 years ago: "Their faithfulness is based only on our ability to apply force." In the 1950's force was still not perhaps a totally useless instrument in this kind of conflict situation. But with the disappearance of colonialism the benefits of force would have to be described as short-lived. For strategy itself demands, in the last analysis, that one must be prepared to reckon with history rather than fly in the face of it.

#### INTIMIDATION

On occasion, intimidation has been a successful revolutionary technique—especially for proving the weakness of the existing administrative apparatus—but it has not worked well on behalf of the forces of order. Consequently, the perspective has shifted in favor of some form of social action that will be progressive and ameliorative.

The difficulty is in defining the proper mode of social action. Mere largess has a tendency to be dissipated without visible effect. Even if prudently administered, it may create new social imbalances that raise more problems than they solve. Reforms must be psychologically suitable to the customs of the area and compatible with the possibilities of the battle situation if pronounced guerrilla activity is in progress. A

---

[2] James E. King, Jr., "Limited War in an Age of Nuclear Plenty," L57–154, Industrial College of the Armed Forces, 1956–57, p. 15.

judicious land reform may do no good at all if the forces of order cannot protect the crops from being seized or destroyed.

### POLITICAL FREEDOMS

Finally, increased political freedoms, which have a tendency to become a *sine qua non* for the West, may be illusory, incompatible, or unworkable for somewhat the same reasons. Taking care to draw just limits, we may say that greater political license is customarily demanded by the urban intelligentsia and is of comparatively little interest to the peasant, at least while things closer to his livelihood are in jeopardy. Social action, intelligently undertaken, may net great gains by giving the peasant something he is in a mood to protect; political liberty may prove an empty rallying cry.

Few will quarrel with the assertion that the regime of Ngo-dinh-Diem is far from being a model democracy. Yet few also contemplate what kind of regimentation we might have to impose on the United States if the country were guerrilla-ridden and if one out of every four citizens had aggressive Communist sympathies. The casual assumption that democratic reform is the path to triumph in a beleaguered state that has the most transient experience with this kind of institution is a notion that needs to be dispelled. Yet the demands of social justice are constant, cannot be ignored, and should be fulfilled within the capacities indicated by the situation.

A counterpolitics is not a primary component of revolutionary war, except insofar as it can be seen to drag tangible social benefits in its wake. Again, we emphasize that these benefits must not be in harsh conflict with the affected milieu in particulars of custom or indicated evolution. This is the special danger of involuntary resettlement; all the relevant factors, military and social, must be weighed before such a policy is set in motion. The choice here generally will be between the perils of upsetting the social balance and the advantages of denying the enemy a fixed base of support or the easy prey of an unprotected population.

Admittedly, I have only scratched the surface of this question. I will conclude with the premise that the support of the civilian population is capital in a revolutionary struggle. By no other means can the conflict situation be effectively eliminated and real order restored.

The conflict is bound to continue if significant parts of the population are hostile or intimidated by the revolution. The strictly military outcome of the conflict is heavily determined by the role of the civilians, who are the essential intelligence-gatherers and intelligence-furnishers in a type of war where swift and accurate intelligence is virtually the key to the outcome. A sympathetic and confident population can ensure

the issue. This was an important component of the government's victory in the Greek Communist insurrection in the late 1940's.

### Essential Elements

Let us further anatomize revolutionary war. It has two essential elements: *guerrilla,* which we shall describe as the military action of the revolutionaries that is clearly above the threshold of violence; and *subversion,* which, although it may resort to violence in the form of terror or industrial turmoil, is generally restricted to the subterranean vitiation of the existing forms of order.

American military writers have devoted a great deal of attention to guerrilla warfare and its salient features—which it would be folly for a civilian writer to try to improve upon—but they have dealt with subversion in an extremely desultory fashion. It is crucial not only to understand both components, but to have a highly sophisticated impression of their interaction. The fact is that in a revolutionary situation, even though both the guerrilla and subversion elements are customarily present, certain cases may reveal subversion alone. It is doubtful whether overt military violence can exist without the support of subversion, but subversion may enter the picture exclusively in an earlier phase as a prefiguration of the total effort.

### Techniques of Subversion

What are the techniques of subversion, how are they identified, and how are they countered? Unfortunately, far too little attention has been given to this problem. The terrain of subversion is not only the population at large, but specifically the existing government apparatus. Subversion, if skillfully managed, can conceivably enable a belligerent political faction acting on its own behalf or on behalf of a foreign power to come to power by *coup d'etat* without guerrilla action. The aim of subversion is to sap the credit and resources of the legitimate power by a variety of means. Among these are:

Infiltration of agents into the public services.

Inflection and, finally, conquest of certain public and private agencies and their policies.

Agitation and manifestation against the existing authority, often for obscure causes.

Creation of friction and factionalism within all possible elements of the society, so as to weaken them *per se.*

Demoralization and sabotage of legal institutions and their capability of enforcing justice.

Character assassinations of adverse political figures.

Administrative and economic sabotage.

Dramatic instances of civil disobedience.

Provocations, leading to government repression, followed usually by the attempt to enlist the sympathies of political persons in front organizations.

Propaganda of all types.

Interception of communications to gain intelligence and to elicit apprehension.

Encouragement of corrupt practices in the political and legal systems, followed by blackmail or opportunistic exposure.

Creation of efficient information networks and, ultimately, a kind of shadow administration capable of gradually usurping power from the legitimate authority.

### Countersubversion

Obviously, the task of countersubversion will be as difficult or even more difficult than that of counterguerrilla. Unfortunately, whereas the problem of counterguerrilla is partly one of improved materiel, that of countersubversion can scarcely be. The best method is probably the most positive: that of strengthening the basic support of the existing state, its policies, and its functions. But the subversives, like the guerrillas in the field, will have the advantage of surprise and the tactical offensive. In this brief survey we can only open up some avenues of fruitful thinking which persons on the spot are best equipped to pursue in the light of the surrounding circumstances.

The foregoing catalog is deplorably impressionistic. This is why it has been titled "footnotes." The hope is that I have succeeded in stimulating the more concerted and topical thinking of others. The cardinal point is that revolutionary war is as subtle and varied as the colors of a large-size paint box, and that a synthesis is hard to achieve, either in terms of general policy or military doctrine. But we may reasonably expect that in the coming years this many-sided challenge will continue to confront us.

Today, the real revolutionary trouble spots may be numbered on our fingers; tomorrow, fingers may not be enough. We can scarcely foresee the ordeals which parts of Latin America, aroused from its oligarchical slumber, or the new states of Africa, thrust violently into the second generation of nationalism, or the ever-turbulent Middle East may be called upon to endure. But we may guess that the specter of revolutionary war may materialize many times before any genuine passage into calmer weather. And for this, all of our knowledge will not be too much.

# 62 / Internal War — The New Communist Tactic

ROGER HILSMAN

Has the United States any meaningful experience in counter guerrilla operations? Is this experience relevant directly to conditions that face the United States in various parts of the globe? In this analysis of Communist tactics in "internal warfare" there is also a brief account of some of the past experience of United States forces with this kind of warfare. What new conditions do we now face, and how can we improve our capabilities?

... THE COMMUNISTS have found what they regard as a new chink in our armor. The new tactic is internal war—using military force not across national boundaries, but inside them.

This newest concept is guerrilla war—or, to use a more accurate term, *internal* war. It was this that President Kennedy had in mind in his speech to the Nation when he said:

> We face a challenge in Berlin, but there is also a challenge in southeast Asia, where the borders are less guarded, the enemy harder to find, and the dangers of communism less apparent to those who have so little. We face a challenge in our own hemisphere.

Thus even while reheating the Berlin crisis, Khrushchev has stressed this third approach of internal war over and over again. He sees the possibilities for internal wars in Asia, Africa, and Latin America as the best way of using force to expand the Communist empire with the least risk. He argues that nuclear war is too disastrous even for Leninists. Apparently he has begun to have his doubts about even limited war on the Korean model.

We can take some credit for Khrushchev's change of heart. Our strategic force to deter nuclear war has paid its way. Our efforts to build

Reprinted from *The Military Review*, April, 1962, pp. 11–22. Published by the United States Army Command and General Staff College, Fort Leavenworth, Kansas.

Roger Hilsman is professor of public law and government, Columbia University, and a former Assistant Secretary of State for Far Eastern Affairs. He has also been director of the State Department's Bureau of Intelligence and Research. A West Point graduate, he served in Merrill's Marauders and in the Office of Strategic Services in World War II. He is the author of *Strategic Intelligence and National Decisions* (1957) and numerous essays on military and foreign policy.

ground forces, our alliances, and our sacrifices in Korea—the fact that we stood and fought—have all paid off.

In retrospect we can be proud of all this, though our pride should not lead to overconfidence. Moreover, we must beware of thinking that these different tactics were separate or unrelated.

Even in the early stages of the cold war, the Soviets manipulated internal wars in southeast Asia, Indonesia, the Philippines, India, Guatemala, and in vulnerable states in the Middle East. The Soviet leaders, bred as they were in an atmosphere of urban-based intrigue and revolutionary plotting, were pushed further in their thinking by the success of Mao Tse-tung's peasant-based Chinese Communist revolution.

### New Developments

The result is that recently internal warfare has gained a new prominence in Soviet dogma. What Khrushchev calls "wars of liberation" or "just wars" are now considered the most promising paths to further expansion. The theory enables Moscow and Peking to manipulate for their own purposes the political, economic, and social revolutionary fervor which is now sweeping much of the underdeveloped world.

Since many governments are weak; since some are corrupt; since there is much injustice in the world; and since the Communist conspirators are well-trained and supplied, it is usually fairly easy to start or take advantage of an internal war and to claim that years of blood and terror are in the people's interest. Even when a government tries to undertake reform and keep the peace—as in Venezuela or Colombia—the Communists chant that the government is "repressive" and redouble their efforts.

A second development is the flexibility and sophistication in tactics of guerrilla terror and subversion. The Soviets continue to sponsor Communist rebellions overtly wherever possible. They also do their best to infiltrate nationalist movements against colonialism. They try especially hard to capture the extreme nationalists like Lumumba. They sponsor radical nationalism wherever they can find it, for the more violence there is in a country, the greater the Communists' opportunity.

If a democratic nationalist government is in power, Communists will advise that it separate itself from the West and permit the Communists to have "equal democratic rights"—that is, positions of power in the government, freedom to propagandize, and the right to officer regular forces or their own militia.

### Discontent and Strikes

If a colonial or reactionary government is in power, the Communists direct efforts along the entire spectrum of subversion. They foster discontent in the cities, leading to demonstrations and strikes, per-

haps to riots and mob action. Here their targets are student groups, labor unions, and leftwing intellectuals. In the countryside, they establish guerrilla forces in inaccessible regions, move to peasant areas, and, through a judicious mixture—on the Chinese Communist and Castro Cuban patterns—of social reform, administration, and sheer terror, establish a base of political rule.

Whenever possible, in both urban and rural sectors, they endeavor to create "people's militias" as a device for organizing mass support to supplement their full-time combatants. Thus they operate continuously to undermine an unfriendly government, and differ in their handling of popular nationalist regimes only in the degree of their effort to influence the government directly and infiltrate its power centers.

Let me repeat that this new Soviet emphasis on internal war does not mean that we can forget about the other, greater levels of war. Moscow's willingness to raise the Berlin issue indicates that their so-called "peaceful coexistence" does not rule out manufactured crises that run the risk of conventional or even nuclear war. In fact, they could not get away with internal war, except for the inhibitions imposed by these other two possibilities.

The great advantage of internal war is that it is less risky and less conspicuous than the more violent wars. It also involves techniques that the Communists feel they have mastered and we have not. We must also remember that Khrushchev is using his recently increased capacity to wage the more violent kinds of war to expand his freedom of maneuver in guerrilla war and to threaten escalation if we try to stop him.

In short, the so-called nuclear stalemate has not served to inhibit violence. If anything, it has enabled the Communists to resort to a wider variety of force. Their new strength in nuclear weapons makes them all the more tempted to adventure with internal war.

How can we help stop the Communists from destroying independent states from within? At President Kennedy's direction—as outlined in his second "state of the Union" message—steps have been taken in several parts of the Government to meet this threat. The people in the Pentagon and we in the State Department have devoted special attention to it.

Let me take up the question of how we stop the Communists from destroying independent states from within under three headings: Military Security; Modernization and Reform; and Political Factors, especially those unique political factors undercutting a regime's stability. Here we must be very hardheaded—for there are several all-too-popular misconceptions.

### Military Security

In my judgment, it is nonsense to think that regular forces trained for conventional war can handle jungle guerrillas adequately. Yet in spite

of some very hard lessons—Magsaysay in the Philippines, the British in Malaya, and the French in Indochina and Algeria—we have been slow to learn.

Regular forces are vital to resist external aggression. However, we must not be deluded by the desire of local generals for "prestige hardware" or by the traditionalists' belief that well-trained regulars can do anything.

Regular forces are essential for regular military tasks, but guerrilla warfare is something special. Conventional forces with heavy equipment in field formation tend to cluster together, centralizing their power on terrain that allows rapid movement. They rely on roads, consider strongpoints and cities as vital targets to defend, and so, when they do disperse, it is only to get tied down in static operations. In combat, rigid adherence to the principle of concentration keeps units at unwieldy battalion or even regimental levels, usually with erroneous stress on holding land rather than destroying enemy forces.

It is ironic that we Americans have to learn this military lesson again in the 20th century. Have we forgotten that we were the ones who had to teach the British regulars "Indian fighting" back when we were still a colony? Have we forgotten that we taught the British regulars another kind of lesson in "Indian fighting" during our own Revolution?

### EXPERIENCES IN THE PHILIPPINES

We Americans have also forgotten that it was we who fought one of the most successful counterguerrilla campaigns in history—in the Philippines back at the turn of the century. We learned some fundamental military lessons then, and it is time we remembered them.

After Aguinaldo's army was defeated and Aguinaldo himself captured, some of the extremists took to the hills to become guerrillas. They were not alone. For 300 years the Spanish had been fighting a guerrilla war with bands of religious fanatics in the southern islands. Further south, in Mindanao, the Moro remained unconquered. All these roamed the jungles and mountains—raiding, ambushing, killing, and pillaging.

The army tried to fight the guerrillas, but with little success. The enemy faded into the jungle, and the unwieldy regular units were too burdened with equipment, too slow to follow. Regulars needed supply lines. They could not live off the country or do without ammunition trains or hospital corps.

The regulars tended to establish a fixed base from which they sallied out. Thus the guerrilla always knew where they were and when their guard was lax. The stage was set for surprise attacks and massacre.

In fact, one of these massacres was famous in the old Army—second only to Custer's last stand. It occurred at Balangiga on the island of Samar and involved Company C of the 9th Infantry, one of the finest regiments

in the Army. At 0640 the men were lined up before the cookshack, the opposite side of the parade ground from where their rifles were stacked. Suddenly, the jungle came alive as 450 guerrillas charged. The regulars of Company C never had a chance. They fought barehanded. One soldier killed several men with a baseball bat before he was overwhelmed. The cook accounted for several more with a meat cleaver. But soon it was all over. Twenty-four men escaped. The rest were killed and mutilated.

Finally, the United States found the solution to the guerrilla problem in the Philippines. We recruited native Filipinos—men wise to jungle ways, men who knew the trails and mountains as their own backyard. These were divided into small groups of 10, 15, 20, or 50 men, and over each group we put a trained American officer—a bold and determined leader.

This was the famed Philippine Constabulary and the history of their fabulous exploits is well worth reading. The story is told—and very well —in Vic Hurley's book, *Jungle Patrol,* published about 30 years ago.

The trick was constant patrolling over every trail, and careful attention to intelligence work. The jungle, nighttime, and surprise attack are the guerrilla's weapons. The solution is to adopt the same weapons to fight them.

### THE OSS IN BURMA

During World War II our Office of Strategic Services (OSS) guerrilla battalion operated behind the enemy lines in Burma. Nothing pleased us more in those days than to have a regular Japanese force take out after us. They operated in large unwieldy units that were easy to ambush. Their movements were simple to follow through the mountains and jungle. We felt that our own existence was well justified when the Japanese had to take regular forces from frontline fighting to chase a guerrilla unit.

At one stage, my outfit—consisting of four Americans and about 200 Burmese—kept a whole Japanese regiment of 3,000 men marching and countermarching over the mountains far away from the frontlines. What we would have feared far more were smaller groups patrolling steadily—especially cavalry.

In many parts of the world today counterguerrilla operations conducted by regular troops rely on the tactic of sweeps through the countryside like those of the Japanese regiments that chased our guerrilla battalion in Burma. The sweeps are too well publicized and too cumbersome to bring results. This tactic leads to antagonism between the regular troops and the population. Villagers fear reprisals and refuse their help. Soldiers sense they are in guerrilla territory and act accordingly toward the people. Military inadequacy leads to failure and so to defeat.

## WEAPONS AND ENVIRONMENT

I also fear that in the past our military aid programs for countries fighting against guerrillas have often followed the mistaken assumption that all war is similar to the large-scale tank and artillery engagements so familiar in western Europe. The tactics of guerrilla warfare and the customs and culture of the peoples, it seems to me, should determine the proper weapons for counterguerrilla forces.

For instance, the mountain tribes of Burma prior to World War II conducted their wars with long knives—a kind of sword called a "dah" —and with one-shot muzzle-loading flintlocks. Burma's mountainous regions are sparsely settled and the seminomadic inhabitants constantly move from one mountain valley to another when the soil begins to wear out. Consequently, they see no point in holding ground or in taking ground, and their whole history in war is one of lightning raids, sneak attacks, and ambushes.

Those of us in OSS who tried to make our guerrilla troops attack a defended position or to stand by their own positions reaped only disaster. We had to adapt our weapons and our tactics to the terrain and to the customs of the people. I found that my own troops, accustomed to fighting with knives, would wait until the enemy was within arm's reach before firing their guns.

I also found that they saw no point in sticking around after exhausting the first clip-load of ammunition. They were brave in sneaking up on an enemy; they were brave in holding their fire in an ambush until an enemy was upon them; but their fundamental maxim was that the wise soldier lives to fight another day. The Americans who thought their purpose was to stand and hold found themselves all alone in standing and holding.

The lesson was obvious, it seems to me. I equipped my men with submachineguns of .45 caliber. The men wanted to wait until the enemy was close before opening fire, and the jungle itself rarely permitted a shot ranging more than a few yards. I needed weapons with a large volume of firepower but neither range nor accuracy. I equipped my eight-man squads with seven submachineguns and one light machinegun. One squad had 60-millimeter mortars to lay down an umbrella of fire to cover our withdrawal.

Our tactics were traditional for guerrillas—we ambushed, we hit, and we ran. This particular unit, operating behind the enemy line for six months, killed over 300 of the enemy, blew up many bridges and ammunition and supply dumps, and yet suffered less than a dozen casualties.

### ORGANIZATION AND DOCTRINE

For effective counterguerrilla operations we need radical changes in organization, combat doctrine, and equipment. Our key units might be

decentralized groups of 50 men, self-reliant and able to operate autonomously, fanned out into the countryside. The premium is on leadership, for only men of courage and great skill can make this system work; with such men, plus decent pay and training, counterguerrilla force should not be difficult to maintain.

The operational concept is as follows: A guerrilla-infested part of the country is marked off and divided into sections. Each section is patrolled by one of these units, but all are in contact with a central headquarters which, in turn, has a reserve force at its disposal. Upon contacting guerrillas, a patrol alerts headquarters and adjacent patrols. As the latter converge, headquarters dispatches paratroops or helicopter transports behind the enemy, who is surrounded and destroyed. Once an area is pacified, the government consolidates its control and moves its forces on to the next section of land to be cleared. The main ingredients then are constant patrols, good communication facilities, rapid mobility, and a capacity for rapid concentration.

One further point. The operations must cause minimum harm to the people, lest they become antagonistic to the government. The troops must be highly disciplined to respect civilian rights and property. Cargo planes should carry in supplies so that the forces do not have to live off the countryside. The onus for anticivilian behavior should be diverted squarely to the guerrillas themselves. They are the ones who are compelled to take to repressive measures, seizing rice or conscripting men in their desperation. As they lose popular support, they will have nothing to fall back on as they suffer military defeats.

### Modernization and Reform

I hope that this last point indicates my awareness of how important it is to have popular support in conducting an internal war. Many observers argue that stability and physical security are basically political issues, depending on the popularity of governments. To this they add that economic development is the key to popular support, and the criterion by which regimes will be judged.

In the long run, popular support is essential for stable governments and a stable world. There is no question that economic development, modernization, and reform are key factors in creating popular support and stable governments. However, in my judgment it would be mistaken to think that guerrillas cannot thrive where governments are popular and where modernization, economic development, and reform are going forward. And the usual corollary to this thought—the notion that the existence of guerrillas is proof positive that the government is unpopular and, therefore, not worth supporting—is even more mistaken. It is, in fact, defeatist. We need modernization, economic development, and reform to defeat guerrillas, but other things are also needed.

Let me draw on my personal experience once more. When we fought in Burma, about 10 percent of the people were pro-West, another 10 percent were pro-enemy, and the rest were indifferent or turned inward toward their own family and village. Yet our guerrilla group performed with great success. We recruited men not only from the 10 percent who were pro-West, but also from the 80 percent who were indifferent.

We gave no quarter to the enemy and his supporters, but we did everything we could to avoid creating hardship for the rest, and to help them when we could. We were careful to move around their growing crops. When we had to ask them for food, we paid or arranged an air-drop of double the amount of rice we took. Before the war was over, it was the enemy and his supporters in the puppet government who appeared oppressive to the people—and not we guerrillas.

### CIVIL GOVERNMENT AND GUERRILLAS

The idea that guerrillas thrive only where the government is unpopular may apply to the more developed parts of the world. But in many parts of the world, states are underdeveloped in the politico-administrative sense as well as economically. The number of people are few who have the training to perform the standard civil service jobs that we take for granted. Lacking that "steel frame" in which India takes such pride, a government appears as a weak and distant entity to most villagers, except when it serves as a burdensome tax collector. In most lands, at least half the people are indifferent to a government. Even the active elements, ranged for or against the regime, are not too set in their political commitments.

In these circumstances, maintaining the bare minimum of national services is enough to determine a nation's fate in the short run. In the Congo, the collapse of two supports—the military *Force Publique* and Belgian technical service—revealed how far the state has to go before becoming an administrative entity.

By contrast, the Somali Republic, which gained its independence at the same time in 1960, also faced a potentially difficult situation—keeping newly joined regions and powerful tribal groups satisfied. As matters developed, no pseudopopular manifestation of discontent emerged, thanks in part to a small but efficient Western-trained civilian police force.

As for modernization, although essential for the long haul, it cannot help much in a counterguerrilla program. Modernization inevitably uproots established social systems and produces political and economic dislocation and tension. It cannot deliver results quickly enough to relieve these short-term pressures.

However, there is mounting unrest in rural areas all over the world. What peasants increasingly crave is social justice and reform—at a minimum, the old way of life with the cruelties removed.

This includes reform of land tenure arrangements, reasonable rent, credit, market facilities, and simple modern tools. They may see ahead to the value of urban centers that buy their produce—instead of importing from abroad and forcing them to raise crops for export—and, in turn, manufacture for their simple needs. Finally, they crave peace and physical security.

Yet there is a growing link between urban and rural unrest. As modernization begins, the poorer farmers drift to the city, there to form the hard core of the unemployed slum dwellers who overtax the rudimentary metropolitan facilities. These unfortunates form the recruits for the city mobs that Communists and demagogues have been turning out in the Middle East and Latin America for the past 15 years.

The political link between the two becomes clear when we see how the very poor are used as recruits for guerrilla forces in the rural areas and for "people's militia" in the urban regions. Communists have long made use of the former in sustaining a rebellion; Castro and "Che" Guevara have become adept at using both groups to support the present Cuban regime. In Latin America alone, Venezuela, Bolivia, Colombia, and Peru come immediately to mind as countries where the combined urban-rural problem exists.

### BASIS OF SOCIAL REFORM

What is required first is a program of social reform. Very often the conservative element in a community will struggle irrationally against all reform. As a consequence, we have encountered in several parts of the world the amazing and suicidal spectacle of conservatives giving secret aid to the Communists in order to undermine modest reformist efforts.

Equally important is the need to indicate some effort and progress on the long path to modernization. Small results, if they prove the intent of a regime, can inspire faith that will outlast the distress of early change. Finally, where these efforts are combined with democratic government and mass party organization, the government can broaden its base of physical power.

In Venezuela, for example, the ruling party has been fostering reform and change. It also has created a national organization, with loyal popular militia elements to support it. Though not professionals, militiamen can keep the peace in the face of provocative demonstrations and can perform useful services in supplementing the work of regular forces. A

government that cannot get its image across to the peasantry or mobilize peasant support will find its functions in both these endeavors usurped by the Communists.

To summarize my feeling of popularity, reform, and modernization:

1. They are important ingredients but are not the determinants of events.

2. Their role must be measured more in terms of their contribution to physical security than we generally realize.

### Other Political Factors

Let me hurriedly refer to several other variations on the theme of internal security—the political factors that threaten the stability of new states. So far we have noted primarily the nature of the Communist threat and the issues of good government and economic development. Unfortunately, on top of these universal problems, most states have to grapple with specific difficulties that create further divisions, induce tensions, and propel even the best intentioned regimes to violence. Among these difficulties are the following:

*Antagonisms* between underdeveloped states. The familiar pattern of rivalry between neighbors, as old as history itself, exists with even greater intensity today because so many new states have suddenly sprung into being. Territorial claims and other sources of friction are still fresh, as in the Persian Gulf or India's northern border regions. Such difficulties generate tensions, arms races, and nationalistic fervor that Communists try to exploit.

*Disagreements* between regions of a state or between a region and the center. The issues of regionalism in India; separatist movements in Indonesia, and tribalism in the fragmented Congo are examples of serious challenges to governmental authority and stability.

*Social class antagonism.* It is characteristic of established economic elites that they feel themselves threatened from below and refuse to countenance the very reform that would ease the real dangers that they face. The great failures of old regimes in France before 1789 and Russia at the start of this century are but the outstanding instances of this historic problem that presents itself on almost every continent today.

*Intense disagreement over foreign policy.* Radical-nationalist African states accuse their neighbors of following a colonial, subservient line. In trying to get them on a comparable course, radical states engage in clandestine operations to subvert neighboring regimes or support opposition factions whose ideology resembles their own.

*Traditional political rivalries within a social class.* Colombia offers the leading example of two parties that, without basic social or ideological differences, became embroiled in a long civil war, so bitter as to

cause over 250,000 casualties. This war [1] literally superimposed itself on all the other problems of security that normally confront a developing state. The ruling party in Burma split into hostile factions in 1958 and the army had to act to keep that situation from fragmenting the country.

*Lack of popular belief in the state as a sovereign entity.* In large areas of Africa and the Middle East, normal loyalties follow either tribal and provincial lines or grand dreams of regional African or Arab unity. The state does attract some loyalty because it is a going concern, one that can be used as a lever of power at both these other levels. With this overlapping of loyalties, it is only too easy for a government to meddle in the affairs of its neighbors and further weaken their internal cohesion—always, of course, in the belief that its cause is just.

*Ethnic or racial issues.* Rebellious tribesmen are constant drains on national military power in various states throughout Asia and Africa. The Communists found in Malaya's Chinese community ready hands for their bloody insurrection, partly because of interracial political rivalries. Indians in some Latin American countries are living at very low standards, are beginning to stir, and are potential bait for a Communist ethnic-economic appeal. Central African pagans have strained relations with Moslem Arab northerners in a crossroad land that is beset by outside pressures.

*Banditry* is a cultural inheritance in many parts of the world. Bandits (or armed rural gangs) who flout the authorities and exploit local neighbors have long existed in many parts of the world—colored perhaps with varying degrees of political or ideological overtones, but essentially dedicated to violence. One thinks of recent illustrations in the Philippines, of traditional sporadic outbreaks in Java, and of troubles experienced by the new state of Burma. These actions impoverish the peasant, ruin the government's authority, paralyze public morale, and open the path to similar Communist tactics or, conversely, to establishment of Communist authority in that region.

*Constitutional crises.* Unconstitutional extension of presidential power, so often exemplified in the history of Latin America, is one example of a constitutional crisis that may lead to political turmoil when such excesses are traditionally resented and countered by violence. The seizure of power by a military junta is another.

There are other obvious factors, such as the outburst of nationalism that may follow independence, proximity to Sino-Soviet territory, the existence and strength of a Communist Party and its orientation toward Moscow or Peking, and, of course, revolts against colonial rule and white-minority rule in certain areas.

---

[1] The Colombian struggle occurred between April 1948 and May 1957. It was terminated as a result of a reconciliation between the Liberal and Conservative factions effected by a military junta in 1957.—Editor.

The addition of just a few of these special hazards to the basic difficulties I described earlier places a tremendous strain upon a government's staying power. You can clearly see why I believe that internal security is a problem in its own right and not simply a function of good government or economic growth.

### Conclusion

There are many things we can do to help responsible and friendly governments attack this problem all along the line. I have already illustrated how the training of armed forces can be better geared to the specific war against guerrillas. Equally important is the training of police and other forces to cope with the lesser manifestations of violence, not only in detection and surveillance, but also in handling actual outbursts.

We may find ourselves encouraging reformers to organize mass parties, and in certain tense circumstances we may need to help create citizens' militia forces. We are seriously interested in broadening the will and capacity of friendly governments, to augment social and political reform programs as a basis for modernization.

We must also look for ways to ease the access of beleaguered states to outside assistance. The Communists use the concept of state sovereignty as a device to seal off a land from "intervention" once they have made sufficient inroads. They use international law, appeals to neutralist neighbors, the unpleasant reactions to what is called "Western imperialism," and the threat of force in this effort.

We must foster the growth and use of international organizations as sources of help—help on all the problems I have mentioned, and help that can be on the scene and in action before the crisis reaches its peak. In this way we may ward off a showdown or at the very least have elements there to indicate outside support in being and on the way.

In any event, the United States must be prepared to become deeply involved. This effort may be costly, but careful and early involvement is far less expensive or dangerous than a crash program. The Communists are already committed everywhere, and unless we approach the problem in a systematic way, with considerable thought, we will simply be paving the way for Mr. Khrushchev in his new and potent tactic—internal war.

# 63 / Guerrilla Warfare in the Underdeveloped Areas

## WALT W. ROSTOW

**What are the conditions in which guerrilla warfare becomes a useful, even necessary, instrument of foreign policy? How may we compare Communist and United States objectives in underdeveloped areas? How can the United States protect the independence of the revolutionary process? These and related questions are discussed here by Professor Rostow.**

IT DOES NOT REQUIRE much imagination to understand why President Kennedy has taken the problem of guerrilla warfare seriously. When this administration came to responsibility it faced four major crises: Cuba, the Congo, Laos, and Viet-Nam. Each represented a successful Communist breaching—over the previous two years—of the cold-war truce lines which had emerged from the Second World War and its aftermath. In different ways each had arisen from the efforts of the international Communist movement to exploit the inherent instabilities of the underdeveloped areas of the non-Communist world, and each had a guerrilla-warfare component.

Cuba, of course, differed from the other cases. The Cuban revolution against Batista was a broad-based national insurrection. But that revolution was tragically captured from within by the Communist apparatus; and now Latin America faces the danger of Cuba's being used as the base for training, supply, and direction of guerrilla warfare in the hemisphere.

More than that, Mr. Khrushchev, in his report to the Moscow conference of Communist parties (published January 6, 1961), had explained at great length that the Communists fully support what he called wars of national liberation and would march in the front rank with the peoples waging such struggles. The military arm of Mr. Khrushchev's January 1961 doctrine is, clearly, guerrilla warfare.

Faced with these four crises, pressing in on the President from day to day, and faced with the candidly stated position of Mr. Khrushchev, we have, indeed, begun to take the problem of guerrilla warfare seriously.

Reprinted from U. S. Department of State, *Department of State Bulletin,* Vol. XLV (August 7, 1961), pp. 233–37; excerpt from an address by Mr. Rostow at graduation ceremonies, United States Army Special Warfare School, Fort Bragg, N. C., June 28, 1961.

A brief biographical sketch of Mr. Rostow accompanies selection 9.

## Revolutionary Process in Southern Hemisphere

To understand this problem, however, one must begin with the great revolutionary process that is going forward in the southern half of the world; for the guerrilla warfare problem in these regions is a product of that revolutionary process and the Communist effort and intent to exploit it.

What is happening throughout Latin America, Africa, the Middle East, and Asia is this: Old societies are changing their ways in order to create and maintain a national personality on the world scene and to bring to their peoples the benefits modern technology can offer. This process is truly revolutionary. It touches every aspect of the traditional life—economic, social, and political. The introduction of modern technology brings about not merely new methods of production but a new style of family life, new links between the villages and the cities, the beginnings of national politics, and a new relationship to the world outside.

Like all revolutions, the revolution of modernization is disturbing. Individual men are torn between the commitment to the old familiar way of life and the attractions of a modern way of life. The power of old social groups—notably the landlord, who usually dominates the traditional society—is reduced. Power moves toward those who can command the tools of modern technology, including modern weapons. Men and women in the villages and the cities, feeling that the old ways of life are shaken and that new possibilities are open to them, express old resentments and new hopes.

This is the grand arena of revolutionary change which the Communists are exploiting with great energy. They believe that their techniques of organization—based on small disciplined cadres of conspirators —are ideally suited to grasp and to hold power in these turbulent settings. They believe that the weak transitional governments that one is likely to find during this modernization process are highly vulnerable to subversion and to guerrilla warfare. And whatever Communist doctrines of historical inevitability may be, Communists know that their time to seize power in the underdeveloped areas is limited. They know that, as momentum takes hold in an underdeveloped area—and the fundamental social problems inherited from the traditional society are solved —their chances to seize power decline.

It is on the weakest nations, facing their most difficult transitional moments, that the Communists concentrate their attention. They are the scavengers of the modernization process. They believe that the techniques of political centralization under dictatorial control—and the projected image of Soviet and Chinese Communist economic progress— will persuade hesitant men, faced by great transitional problems, that

the Communist model should be adopted for modernization, even at the cost of surrendering human liberty. They believe that they can exploit effectively the resentments built up in many of these areas against colonial rule and that they can associate themselves effectively with the desire of the emerging nations for independence, for status on the world scene, and for material progress.

This is a formidable program; for the history of this century teaches us that communism is not the longrun wave of the future toward which societies are naturally drawn. On the contrary. But it is one particular form of modern society to which a nation may fall prey during the transitional process. Communism is best understood as a disease of the transition to modernization.

### America's Purpose and Strategy

What is our reply to this historical conception and strategy? What is the American purpose and the American strategy? We, too, recognize that a revolutionary process is under way. We are dedicated to the proposition that this revolutionary process of modernization shall be permitted to go forward in independence, with increasing degrees of human freedom. We seek two results: first, that truly independent nations shall emerge on the world scene; and, second, that each nation will be permitted to fashion, out of its own culture and its own ambitions, the kind of modern society it wants. The same religious and philosophical beliefs which decree that we respect the uniqueness of each individual make it natural that we respect the uniqueness of each national society. Moreover, we Americans are confident that, if the independence of this process can be maintained over the coming years and decades, these societies will choose their own version of what we would recognize as a democratic, open society.

These are our commitments of policy and of faith. The United States has no interest in political satellites. Where we have military pacts we have them because governments feel directly endangered by outside military action and we are prepared to help protect their independence against such military action. But, to use Mao Tse-tung's famous phrase, we do not seek nations which "lean to one side." We seek nations which shall stand up straight. And we do so for a reason: because we are deeply confident that nations which stand up straight will protect their independence and move in their own ways and in their own time toward human freedom and political democracy.

### Protecting Independence of Revolutionary Process

Thus our central task in the underdeveloped areas, as we see it, is to protect the independence of the revolutionary process now going

forward. This is our mission, and it is our ultimate strength. For this is not—and cannot be—the mission of communism. And in time, through the fog of propaganda and the honest confusions of men caught up in the business of making new nations, this fundamental difference will become increasingly clear in the southern half of the world. The American interest will be served if our children live in an environment of strong, assertive, independent nations, capable, because they are strong, of assuming collective responsibility for the peace.

The diffusion of power is the basis for freedom within our own society, and we have no reason to fear it on the world scene. But this outcome would be a defeat for communism—not for Russia as a national state, but for communism. Despite all the Communist talk of aiding movements of national independence, they are driven in the end, by the nature of their system, to violate the independence of nations. Despite all the Communist talk of American imperialism, we are committed, by the nature of our system, to support the cause of national independence. And the truth will out.

The victory we seek will see no ticker tape parades down Broadway, no climactic battles, nor great American celebrations of victory. It is a victory which will take many years and decades of hard work and dedication—by many peoples—to bring about. This will not be a victory of the United States over the Soviet Union. It will not be a victory of capitalism over socialism. It will be a victory of men and nations which aim to stand up straight, over the forces which wish to entrap and to exploit their revolutionary aspirations of modernization. What this victory involves, in the end, is the assertion by nations of their right to independence and by men and women of their right to freedom as they understand it. And we deeply believe this victory will come—on both sides of the Iron Curtain.

If Americans do not seek victory in the usual sense, what do we seek? What is the national interest of the United States? Why do we Americans expend our treasure and assume the risks of modern war in this global struggle? For Americans the reward of victory will be, simply, this: It will permit American society to continue to develop along the old humane lines which go back to our birth as a nation—and which reach deeper into history than that—back to the Mediterranean roots of Western life. We are struggling to maintain an environment on the world scene which will permit our open society to survive and to flourish.

### U. S. Responsibilities

To make this vision come true places a great burden on the United States at this phase of history. The preservation of independence has many dimensions.

The United States has the primary responsibility for deterring the use of nuclear weapons in the pursuit of Communist ambitions. The United States has a major responsibility to deter the kind of overt aggression with conventional forces which was launched in June 1950 in Korea.

The United States has the primary responsibility for assisting the economies of those hard-pressed states on the periphery of the Communist bloc, which are under acute military or quasi-military pressure which they cannot bear from their own resources; for example, south Korea, Viet-Nam, Taiwan, Pakistan, Iran. The United States has a special responsibility of leadership in bringing not merely its own resources but the resources of all the free world to bear in aiding the long-run development of those nations which are serious about modernizing their economy and their social life. And, as President Kennedy has made clear, he regards no program of his administration as more important than his program for long-term economic development, dramatized, for example, by the Alliance for Progress in Latin America. Independence cannot be maintained by military measures alone. Modern societies must be built, and we are prepared to help build them.

Finally, the United States has a role to play—symbolized by your presence here and by mine—in learning to deter guerrilla warfare, if possible, and to deal with it, if necessary.

### Local and International Responsibilities

I do not need to tell you that the primary responsibility for dealing with guerrilla warfare in the underdeveloped areas cannot be American. There are many ways in which we can help—and we are searching our minds and our imaginations to learn better how to help; but a guerrilla war must be fought primarily by those on the spot. This is so for a quite particular reason. A guerrilla war is an intimate affair, fought not merely with weapons but fought in the minds of the men who live in the villages and in the hills, fought by the spirit and policy of those who run the local government. An outsider cannot, by himself, win a guerrilla war. He can help create conditions in which it can be won, and he can directly assist those prepared to fight for their independence. We are determined to help destroy this international disease; that is, guerrilla war designed, initiated, supplied, and led from outside an independent nation.

Although as leader of the free world the United States has special responsibilities which it accepts in this common venture of deterrence, it is important that the whole international community begin to accept its responsibility for dealing with this form of aggression. It is important that the world become clear in mind, for example, that the operation run

from Hanoi against Viet-Nam is as clear a form of aggression as the violation of the 38th parallel by the North Korean armies in June 1950.

In my conversations with representatives of foreign governments, I am sometimes lectured that this or that government within the free world is not popular; they tell me that guerrilla warfare cannot be won unless the peoples are dissatisfied. These are, at best, half-truths. The truth is that guerrilla warfare, mounted from external bases—with rights of sanctuary—is a terrible burden to carry for any government in a society making its way toward modernization. As you know, it takes somewhere between ten and twenty soldiers to control one guerrilla in an organized operation. Moreover, the guerrilla force has this advantage: its task is merely to destroy, while the government must build and protect what it is building. A guerrilla war mounted from outside a transitional nation is a crude act of international vandalism. There will be no peace in the world if the international community accepts the outcome of a guerrilla war, mounted from outside a nation, as tantamount to a free election.

The sending of men and arms across international boundaries and the direction of guerrilla war from outside a sovereign nation is aggression; and this is a fact which the whole international community must confront and whose consequent responsibilities it must accept. Without such international action those against whom aggression is mounted will be driven inevitably to seek out and engage the ultimate source of the aggression they confront.

. . . . .

### Learning to Prevent Guerrilla Wars

In facing the problem of guerrilla war, I have one observation to make as a historian. It is now fashionable—and I daresay for you it was compulsory—to read the learned works of Mao Tse-tung and Che Guevara on guerrilla warfare. This is, indeed, proper. One should read with care and without passion into the minds of one's enemies. But it is historically inaccurate and psychologically dangerous to think that these men created the strategy and tactics of guerrilla war to which we are now responding. Guerrilla warfare is not a form of military and psychological magic created by the Communists. There is no rule or parable in the Communist texts which was not known at an earlier time in history. The operation of Marion's men in relation to the Battle of Cowpens in the American Revolution was, for example, governed by rules which Mao merely echoes. Che Guevara knows nothing of this business that T. E. Lawrence did not know or was not practiced, for example, in the Peninsular Campaign during the Napoleonic wars, a century earlier. The orchestration of professional troops, militia, and guerrilla fighters is an old game whose rules can be studied and learned.

My point is that we are up against a form of warfare which is powerful and effective only when we do not put our minds clearly to work on how to deal with it. I, for one, believe that with purposeful efforts most nations which might now be susceptible to guerrilla warfare could handle their border areas in ways which would make them very unattractive to the initiation of this ugly game. We can learn to prevent the emergence of the famous sea in which Mao Tse-tung taught his men to swim. This requires, of course, not merely a proper military program of deterrence but programs of village development, communications, and indoctrination. The best way to fight a guerrilla war is to prevent it from happening. And this can be done.

Similarly, I am confident that we can deal with the kind of operation now under way in Viet-Nam. It is an extremely dangerous operation, and it could overwhelm Viet-Nam if the Vietnamese—aided by the free world—do not deal with it. But it is an unsubtle operation, by the book, based more on murder than on political or psychological appeal.

When Communists speak of wars of national liberation and of their support for "progressive forces," I think of the systematic program of assassination now going forward in which the principal victims are the health, agriculture, and education officers in the Viet-Nam villages. The Viet Cong are not trying to persuade the peasants of Viet-Nam that communism is good; they are trying to persuade them that their lives are insecure unless they cooperate with them. With resolution and confidence on all sides and with the assumption of international responsibility for the frontier problem, I believe we are going to bring this threat to the independence of Viet-Nam under control.

My view is, then, that we confront in guerrilla warfare in the underdeveloped areas a systematic attempt by the Communists to impose a serious disease on those societies attempting the transition to modernization. This attempt is a present danger in southeast Asia. It could quickly become a major danger in Africa and Latin America.

# 64 / *That Massive Hidden Apparatus*

GILBERT A. HARRISON

Few foreign policy subjects must be considered from such an extraordinarily partial view of the facts as secret "intelli-

Reprinted from *The New Republic*, June 27, 1964, pp. 19–22. Copyright 1964 by Harrison-Blaine, Inc. By permission.

Gilbert A. Harrison is editor-in-chief of *The New Republic*, a journal of opinion.

gence" and clandestine operations overseas. Strictly speaking, the term "intelligence" should refer only to information, but in general usage it has come to mean both information and political warfare overseas. Much of the literature on the subject is inevitably speculative or undocumented. Yet this important function of government cannot be ignored, because it has become a major foreign policy instrument and promises to become increasingly important in an age when general war is not a rational choice. One of the most revealing books on the subject is *The Invisible Government* (1964) by Washington journalists David Wise and Thomas B. Ross. The following review of this journalistic and somewhat sensationalized book gives insight into some of the major dimensions of this foreign policy instrument.

YOU *can* tell a CIA man; you can tell him off; and the authors of this book more or less do, though they don't tell him or us much that wasn't known before. David Wise, chief of the Washington Bureau of *The New York Herald Tribune*, and Thomas B. Ross, a member of the Washington Bureau of *The Chicago Sun-Times*, have written no exposé. They peddle no secrets. Still their book is not without surprises. The US Intelligence network, they report, has become a "massive, hidden appartus, secretly employing about 200,000 persons, and spending several billion dollars a year." Congress provides money "without knowing how much it has appropriated or how much will be spent . . . [since CIA's] budget is concealed in other appropriations." They quote a Senate committee's judgment that the US ambassador's authority is a "polite fiction." (Secretary of State Rusk stated in June, 1961: "We expect our ambassadors abroad to take charge of the relations of the United States with the country in which they are posted, and if necessary to take charge of all the officials who are there working with them.") They claim that Intelligence activities are "never discussed in the [National Security] Council" but are "handled by a small directorate, the name of which is only whispered [the Special Group]."

They then offer a few case studies. The CIA (as every taxi driver in Beirut knows by now) directed and financed the Cuban invasion, and so secret was it that "many high officials of the government were not let in on it," including CIA's Deputy Director for Intelligence and the Director of the State Department's Bureau of Intelligence and Research. (And so secret was it that diligent newsmen were writing about it before it happened.) Despite a US pledge that no US armed forces and no Americans would be involved, "American CIA pilots were flying in the invasion and Navy jets were to screen them against attack." . . .

It was the CIA, too, that provided men and equipment to the rebels who tried to overthrow President Sukarno in 1958; the CIA plotted to overthrow the government of Iran in 1953; the CIA secretly supported 12,000 Nationalist Chinese rebels in Burma a decade ago, much to the annoyance of the Burmese government; the CIA engineered a *coup d'etat* in Guatemala in 1954; the CIA tried to "promote the ouster of José Figueres, the moderate Socialist who became President [of Costa Rica] in a fair and open election in 1953"; the CIA conceived of and ran the U-2 flights; the CIA "poured millions" after World War II into an espionage apparatus in West Germany headed by CIA-picked General Gehlen, a member of the General Staff under Hitler; the CIA (and the Pentagon) "at a cost of $300 million" invented and propped up a right-wing military government in Laos, and when it was overthrown and succeeded by the government of "neutralist" Souvanna Phouma, the CIA continued to give substantial support to its original chosen instrument; the CIA organized an elite corps in Vietnam and supported it at a rate of $3 million a year; the CIA got rid of the regime of President Jacob Arbenz Guzman in Guatemala. And so on.

The Agency has a home program too. Tax-free American foundations are used by CIA as "cover." Academic institutions receive CIA subsidies—for example, the Center for International Studies at MIT, founded by Walt Rostow, now Chief of the State Department's Policy Planning staff. Like General Motors, but less openly, the Agency recruits staff from the universities. It finances a number of refugee organizations: "For a decade a $100 million fund was available for this type of activity." The CIA, Wise and Ross conclude, "is not simply an agency that gathers foreign intelligence for the United States in far off corners of the globe. It is deeply involved in many diverse, clandestine activities right here in the United States in at least 20 metropolitan areas. It can and does appear in many guises, and under many names—Zenith, Double-Chek, Gibraltar Steamship, and Vanguard in one city alone. On university campuses and in the great urban centers of America, the foundation, the cultural committee, and emigré group, the Cuban exile organization, the foreign affairs research center, the distinguished publishing house specializing in books about Russia, the steamship company, the freedom radio soliciting public contributions, the innocent-looking consulting firm —all may in reality be arms of the invisible government."

They tell us something about the CIA-run radio stations that beam propaganda around the world—Radio Free Europe; Radio SWAN in the Caribbean; Radio Liberation (now Radio Liberty), which "broadcast exclusively to the Soviet Union 24 hours a day, from 17 transmitters in West Germany, Spain, and Formosa."

I want to repeat, however, the authors' claim that their book contains only the news that someone, somewhere, has already seen fit to print.

They do not (with one exception) describe any current "black" operations; they don't identify any agent whose name has not already been published. They could, of course, have accepted the line that nothing should be written about CIA of which CIA does not approve; in which case they would have been wasting their time and the readers'. Or they could have decided to tell all. But that, they clearly felt, would have opened them to the charge of something like treason. Even so, their circumspection has been cruelly rewarded by William F. Buckley, Jr., who believes that they "verge close to unpatriotism."

If we push on and ask ourselves what, precisely, the authors find defective in CIA and how they could correct it, visibility drops sharply. They don't question that the national interest requires lies and bribes (though officials ought not to be *caught* lying). They might have come to the opinion—some have—that the primary danger in so powerful, highly centralized and hidden an operation as CIA lies in the temptation it offers a few people to conduct their own foreign policy, irrespective of official policy. And although they do concede that "this accusation contains some truth," they're mindful that "there are procedures which call for the approval of any major special operation at a high level in the executive branch of the government." They say that "the CIA and other agencies of the invisible government are free to shape events in the field," but they give no proof. Instead, there are some illustrations of poor coordination, either by design or inadvertence: thus, in Costa Rica, "CIA officers did not see fit to inform the State Department when they planted a fake Communist document in a local newspaper." Nowhere do they suggest that large amounts of money have been wasted, or that the secret operations which they describe ought not to have been undertaken in the first place.

One trouble with this spy business seems to be that "major decisions involving peace or war are taking place out of public view." And so they often are, and would be if there were no CIA. I cite in evidence, one report of a "news briefing" given last week [June 1964] by the White House press secretary, George Reedy. "After failing to obtain an elucidation of American policy in Southeast Asia," wrote Carroll Kilpatrick in *The Washington Post,*

". . . a reporter asked whether the Administration had imposed a lid on such discussions. 'I don't know that there is any official lid, as such,' Reedy replied."

"Finally a reported asked: 'George, is there any policy, procedural or operation question that you can comment on off the record, on the record, for background or deep background?'"

"'I will just go back to what I have said before,' Reedy replied."

"Reedy opened his morning briefing . . . by announcing that Alexander A. Matsas, the Greek Ambassador, was scheduled to see the President at 12:30.

The following exchange took place:
"Q. 'Did he request the appointment?'
"A. 'I am not certain who requested it.'
"Q. 'What will they talk about?'
"A. 'I don't have any comment on what they will talk about.'
"Q. 'Is it fair to assume that Cyprus will come up?'
"A. 'I would not want to be setting the rules of fair play.'"

Mr. Reedy deserves our sympathy, not our censure. "Invisible government" is a large part of government and setting the rules of fair play is far trickier in the field of Intelligence than elsewhere. When the authors report that "critics of the CIA have been hobbled by a lack of sure knowledge about its activities," they are on solid ground. But do they mean this in derogation or in approval of CIA? Probably the former, though we cannot be sure. For frequently in their book they seem to regret that the Secret Society isn't secret enough—which is essentially an allegation of inefficiency.

There has been discussion recently of whether CIA's two functions of Intelligence-gathering and "black" operations should reside in the same agency. The authors seem inclined to think a separation of these functions would not be desirable: "If the CIA were to be prohibited from carrying out secret operational activity, and that task were to be turned over to another agency, it might be necessary to create another set of secret operatives in addition to the large number of CIA men already at work overseas. Such a situation would probably reduce efficiency, raise costs, and increase the danger of exposure."

CIA has "quasi-independent status," we are informed. Is that good or bad? I *think* Mr. Wise and Mr. Ross think it's bad. But if the Agency were less independent (more responsible to more outsiders) would there not inevitably be more "leaks," more danger of compromising the secret purposes for which CIA was established? Their recommendation that "if . . . it becomes necessary to undertake a secret operation, it is imperative that the long-range repercussions be weighed fully in advance" will be disputed by none.

Yes, our ambassadors abroad should know what's going on, should be in charge of their posts. The point was made firmly by Chester Bowles as he traveled about from embassy to embassy in the early days of the Kennedy Administration. President Kennedy and Secretary Rusk backed him up. Nevertheless, as Wise and Ross imply, things go on much as before. CIA agents "maintain communications and codes of their own"; they have money to spend, and they are not financially accountable to the ambassador. Is there any remedy for that—except the appointment of ambassadors who can spot foolishness when they see it, and who don't mind treading on toes, even the toes of CIA's powerful friends in key committees of Congress?

Perhaps funds for CIA should *not* be concealed in the appropriations of other departments, but if the amount and nature of these funds is to be kept secret, how can they be made more public in the Budget? And anyway, the present director of the international division of the Budget Bureau, under whom "all of the budgets [for Intelligence] are pulled together," is the former Deputy Director of CIA.

The authors argue plausibly for a joint, watchdog committee of Congress with lively, independent members who will spend more time looking more carefully into the details of Intelligence. But they stop short of outlining the rules under which such a committee would operate, the means by which it could learn any more than CIA wished to tell it.

Perhaps the best defense of CIA is that in this age of conspiracy, it does what no other group—public or private—can do, and that what it does is necessary; that only a clandestine elite, freed from the drag of public scrutiny or bureaucratic timidity can effectively counter Communist subversion abroad. Had Mr. Wise and Mr. Ross explored that proposition in depth, they would have deserved our gratitude. They deserve it anyway. Their dramatic story reminds us, again, of the need to keep this "dirty business" under wraps as well as under adequate control. Some will be alarmed by what they reveal; some will be annoyed. The Director and the Deputy Director of CIA some weeks ago personally contacted Random House, and let it be known that the book should be revised, or possibly withdrawn.

# 65 / Secret Mission in an Open Society

## HARRY HOWE RANSOM

If secret political or paramilitary intervention is, in terms of national interest, a legitimate foreign policy instrument, its role and control confront a democracy with serious dilemmas and practical management problems. Secrecy may be a requirement for successful use of this instrument, yet democracy in general requires publicity in the government's exercise of power. The nature of this dilemma and how the United States has dealt with it are considered here.

Reprinted from *The New York Times Magazine*, May 21, 1961, pp. 20, 77–81. Copyright 1961 by The New York Times Company. By permission.

Harry Howe Ransom is the editor of this reader and professor of political science, Vanderbilt University. His publications include *Central Intelligence and National Security* (1958) and *Can American Democracy Survive Cold War?* (1963).

SILENCE is the golden word of intelligence. Recent events, however, have trumpeted United States foreign intelligence activities at full volume and high fidelity for all the world to hear. What has come through is disturbing.

The Central Intelligence Agency's misfortunes have engendered the publicity which an efficient intelligence system always seeks to avoid. The fact that disclosures have been made in itself represents a failure. The nature of the disclosures raises troublesome issues, but the central question in the current White House and Capitol Hill investigations is, what is the role of a secret intelligence apparatus in a democracy?

Few would deny the necessity of intelligence activities. After the American U-2 aircraft was downed in Russia last year President Eisenhower publicly confessed to the world that the United States—pursuant to authority granted in the National Security Act of 1947—seeks intelligence "in every feasible way." The espionage side of this activity he described as a "distasteful but vital necessity" for security against surprise attack and for effective defense planning.

The Cuban fiasco, however, has revealed in unprecedented detail another side of C.I.A. activities—clandestine political operations designed to subvert an unfriendly government.

Central Intelligence today has three principal functions: intelligence collection, its analysis and communication to policy makers, and clandestine foreign political operations. The increasing necessity of these activities is attributable to three major reasons.

From earliest times, an intelligence apparatus has been an indispensable part of the paraphernalia of a great world power. The world-wide responsibilities of the United States today require both a system for keeping the complex details of world politics under constant surveillance and an instrument for secret foreign political action.

A second reason is that national policy decisions are based, increasingly, upon predictions of foreign political, economic and military developments five to ten years hence. This fact is a consequence of the long lead-time in developing weapons systems and of the need to make economical use of finite resources to implement long-range foreign policy objectives.

Consequently, an intelligence system today is asked an incredibly wide range of urgent questions, answers to which can be obtained sometimes only by devious methods. When will Communist China test an atomic device? What future has the economic integration of Europe? How stable is the government of South Vietnam? What course will Sino-Soviet relations take?

A third reason derives from modern military-technological developments. Intelligence, it often is said, has become the first line of defense. Accurate and rapidly transmitted information is an absolute requirement

for an effective strategy of deterrence. Strategic striking forces must have an accurate dossier of potential enemy targets. And "essential elements of information" always must be available to thwart an enemy's possible surprise knockout blow.

Much of such information is held in tightest security by the Iron Curtain countries, requiring a systematic effort to ferret it out. Similar information is freely available to the Communists from our open society.

Americans have not flinched at espionage or underground political action in wartime. A favorite national hero is Nathan Hale, who spied in the American Revolutionary cause. In World War II, the Office of Strategic Services was, deservedly or not, considered most romantic.

Short of declared war, however, secret operations are widely regarded as a "dirty business," unfitting America's open, democratic—and formerly isolationist—society. Events of recent years have, nonetheless, revealed to the public at least the top of the iceberg of a vast secret intelligence program.

Distasteful or not, secret operations have become a major underground front of the cold war. The accelerating pace of cold warfare in Laos, South Vietnam, Thailand, the Congo, Latin America and elsewhere increases the pressure for greater American involvement in the secret "black arts."

One's attitude toward these activities will depend, finally, upon one's assessment of contemporary international politics and of the requirements for the common defense. President Kennedy recently declared that the cold war has reached such a stage that "no war ever posed a greater threat to our security." If they take that as a valid assessment, most Americans will assume, although doubtless with misgivings, a wartime attitude toward secret operations.

Whatever one's view, the existence of a secret bureaucracy poses special problems in the American system of government. Knowledge is power. Secret knowledge is secret power. A secret apparatus, claiming superior knowledge and operating outside the normal checkreins of American democracy, is a source of invisible government.

The American democratic system, however, is based upon the concept of visible, identifiable power, subject to constitutional checks and balances. One important check is the citizen's right to know what his Government is doing. Another is the existence of a free press to inform him.

How, then, can the controls of a democratic system be imposed upon the intelligence system while maintaining the secrecy required for its successful operation? Secret operations must remain immune from some of the normal checks, especially publicity. Heavy dependence must be placed upon politically responsible officials to exercise control.

In a parliamentary democracy, such as Great Britain, the problem is less acute. The difference is attributable to four factors.

First, Britain has been a world power for several centuries. Over the years a degree of confidence in the professionalism of secret operations has developed.

Second, parliamentary government unifies executive and legislative responsibility under majority-party leadership. When Ministers are also Members of Parliament, responsibility for management of secret functions is reinforced.

A third mitigating factor is "The Establishment." That political leaders, intelligence chiefs and lords of the press often have common social ties facilitates consensus on necessary secrecy.

Fourth, the existence of the Official Secrets Act inhibits the publication of secret information by imposing legal sanctions on the press. Additionally, a special Government-press arrangement exists under which British editors are sometimes asked, upon receipt of Government "Defense Notices," to refrain voluntarily from publishing specified sensitive information.

British intelligence services, too, are so organized that secret political operations overseas are entirely separate from political and military intelligence functions. An agency for secret operations is supervised by a special Cabinet subcommittee. The point is that all are under firm political authority.

Totalitarian regimes, with their absolute control of the press, suppression of opposition and centralized government, have few of the problems of disclosure and control experienced by open societies. The Soviet Union is thought to possess the largest intelligence system in the world; its existence is never avowed by Communist leaders.

Even in dictatorships, however, problems exist. The interpretation of foreign intelligence doubtless is often distorted by the rigid ideology. And it is also a fact of history that the secret intelligence apparatus often has been a vehicle for internal political conspiracy. Invisible power is a potential threat to constituted authority whatever the form of government.

Aware of the danger of secret power within government, the President and Congress have attempted to surround the C.I.A. and related secret apparatuses with controls. These are designed to reconcile the conflicting requirements of secrecy and of democratic control.

The first of these mechanisms derives from the fact that the C.I.A.'s functions are specified, broadly, by Federal statute, defining the agency as an instrument of the Presidency. The C.I.A.'s operational guidelines are some two dozen codified National Security Council intelligence directives, approved by the President. Actions such as the U-2 flights and the Cuban expedition must be approved specifically by the President. In the past he has had the advice on such matters of a special N.S.C. subcommittee on clandestine operations.

A second potential check has been the President's eight-man Board

of Consultants on Foreign Intelligence Activities. This was established early in 1956, after a Hoover Commission study expressed concern about "the possibility of the growth of license and abuses of power where disclosures of costs, organization, personnel and functions are precluded by law."

The first chairman of this group, composed largely of distinguished industrialists and former armed-services officers, was James R. Killian Jr., then president of the Massachusetts Institute of Technology. President Kennedy recently reappointed Dr. Killian to the chairmanship of a reconstituted board after a two-year interval in which Gen. John E. Hull, retired Army officer, presided.

While the C.I.A.'s huge annual budget—estimated at more than half a billion dollars—is not subject to normal legislative review, three Congressional standing subcommittees on central intelligence in fact exist as a third potential checkrein.

The Senate and House Armed Services Committees both have sub-units assigned as watchdogs over the C.I.A. The Senate subcommittee combines senior Senators from the Appropriations and Armed Services Committees. The House maintains a separate Appropriations subcommittee, some members of which have been privy to such secrets as the atomic-bomb (Manhattan Project) appropriations during World War II.

The working principle of the intelligence system in the United States was expressed some years ago by Allen W. Dulles, Director of Central Intelligence:

"In intelligence you have to take certain things on faith. You have to look to the man who is directing the organization and the result he achieves. If you haven't got someone who can be trusted, or who doesn't get results, you'd better throw him out and get someone else."

Central Intelligence is subject today to three major criticisms. They involve questions of control by responsible authority, the efficiency of existing organizations and the problem of secrecy.

True, the C.I.A. operates under Presidential directives, and inter-departmental groups from the National Security Council downward participate both in interpreting intelligence data and in authorizing covert operations. Yet the principal intelligence adviser to the highest authority remains the Director of Central Intelligence, armed with extraordinary secrecy inside the Government and with a secret budget.

In a complex world of fast-moving events and in a Washington "intelligence community" where C.I.A. professionals are increasingly influential, too few sources of countervailing power exist. This particularly is a problem with covert operations in which the Presidency is largely dependent upon the C.I.A. for information on what is being done or what needs doing. The danger of self serving by the agency is

great. C.I.A. may, without careful policy guidance, write its own ticket.

In its six years of existence, the President's Board of Consultants on Foreign Intelligence Activities, recently renamed the Foreign Intelligence Advisory Board, has functioned more as a polite alumni visiting committee than as a vigorous watchdog. With one professional staff assistant and a single secretary, the board has been able only sporadically to oversee the 15,000-man C.I.A.

Congressional surveillance has been much the same: infrequent meetings of uncommonly timorous subcommittees. The attitude of veteran legislators assigned to these units is exemplified by one who declared:

"It is not a question of reluctance on the part of C.I.A. officials to speak to us. Instead, it is a question of our reluctance, if you will, to seek information and knowledge on subjects which I personally, as a member of Congress and as a citizen, would rather not have."

As astute politicians, members of Congress realize the possible national embarrassment if they formally approved espionage or covert political action that fails and is disclosed. Yet even were Congress less inhibited about monitoring secret operations effectively, none of the subcommittees has adequate staffs today for thorough surveillance.

Persuasive reasons possibly can be advanced for not placing covert foreign political and intelligence (informational) functions under separate agencies. If so, the dangers inherent in combining them should be recognized and appropriate safeguards provided.

A third and related criticism involves secrecy. Democracy cannot work without a free press. Expanding Government secrecy increases the danger of official manipulation of opinion and concealment of shortcomings of an incumbent leadership. Secrecy also vitiates the party and electoral system and reduces the meaningful autonomy of Congress. Yet certain intelligence activities by definition require secrecy.

In the face of this dilemma, C.I.A.'s secrecy today has become ambiguous. This may be the fate of any secret apparatus within America's open society. But only in America have intelligence officials become famous personalities eager to mount the public rostrum. The director, deputy director and other C.I.A. officials in recent years have made frequent public speeches, some containing implicit policy recommendations. The C.I.A. leadership should become again publicly silent and unquestionably non-political. Anonymity is the only proper role.

Another aspect of the C.I.A.'s ambiguous secrecy is that major operations that fail often produce, as we have seen, public confessions from highest authority. On the other hand, secret missions that succeed often are known to the press but voluntarily censored.

For example, the C.I.A. played a dominant role in the overthrow of Premier Mossadegh in Iran in August, 1953, after his abortive attempt,

in league with the Communist Tudeh party, to exile the pro-Western Shah. This role has never been officially admitted.

Secret intelligence must never be more or less than an instrument of national policy. Its control should remain primarily a responsibility of the Presidency, but Congress also must assume a more carefully defined and active surveillance role. And the Department of State, particularly, must be aggressive in weighing gain from success, against cost of failure, in every proposed major secret operation.

A second major criticism is that the C.I.A. places under one roof the separate functions of intelligence collection, its analysis and underground foreign political action.

Those who would organize and carry out a proposed secret operation should be separated in the decisional process from those who supply and interpret information to justify the plan.

This unification appears to have been a major defect in the Cuban misadventure. It may explain both the prediction that Cubans would rise to assist the exiles in overthrowing Castro and the policy decision that the venture was feasible.

Planners and operational commanders notoriously come to view the plan as an end in itself. They gradually develop a state of mind that is receptive only to intelligence data that justify the plan's practicability. A distorted view of reality often results.

Another example is the unexpected intervention of the Chinese Communists on a large scale in the Korean War in November, 1950. Hard intelligence was available that the Chinese Communists were infiltrating North Korea, with a strong possibility of major intervention. Yet the operational plan of General MacArthur's forces to drive north to the Yalu went ahead disastrously in disregard of available information that should have given pause. The decisional system should be insulated against this common cause of self-delusion.

Another example is C.I.A.'s involvement in the 1954 Guatemalan episode. In an operation resembling on a smaller scale the recent Cuban expedition, the C.I.A. aided the successful counter-revolution against the regime of Col. Jacobo Arbenz Guzman, which the United States Government regarded as Communist-dominated. The American press remained silent. Perhaps the inevitable penalty for failure is disclosure.

Self-restraint on the part of the press and of Congress in dealing with justifiably secret information will come at that point when confidence is restored in the professional quality and unquestioned subordination to political authority of secret operations.

It remains to be said that America's foreign policy headaches around the globe today stem less from information or organization deficiencies than from lack of clearly articulated foreign policy objectives beyond anti-communism. Many of the aforementioned problems of the intelli-

gence system would solve themselves, given a clearer consensus about America's world purpose and specific policy objectives.

No greater challenge confronts American society than responding to the question of how the United States can engage successfully in protracted cold warfare without sacrificing the principles defended.

As an open democratic society, the United States has to recognize its handicaps in some form of competition with the closed societies of totalitarian regimes. It would be unwise to attempt to match the proficiency of Communist regimes in subversion as the main avenue to the attainment of national objectives. There is no point in America's fighting totalitarianism by imitating it.

It is equally as important to recognize that any Communist competitive advantage in cold warfare comes not alone from centralization, secrecy and rigid discipline. More important is the existence of a Communist purpose, clear objectives and refined doctrines for implementing them.

In a world still lacking universal acceptance of law and order based upon government by consent, the United States will sometimes face compelling requirements to engage in distasteful—indeed, illegal—secret operations. What is crucially important in a democracy is that plans, policies and programs for such reflect the deliberate, informed and purposeful decisions of responsible political authority.

# For Further Reading

American Academy of Political and Social Science. "Unconventional Warfare," *The Annals*, May 1962.

BLACK, CYRIL, and THOMAS P. THORNTON. *Communism and Revolution: The Strategic Uses of Political Violence* (Princeton: Princeton University Press, 1964).

BLACKSTOCK, PAUL W. *The Strategy of Subversion* (Chicago: Quadrangle Books, 1964).

CROZIER, BRIAN. *The Rebels: A Study of Post-War Insurrections* (Boston: Beacon Press, 1960).

DULLES, ALLEN. *The Craft of Intelligence* (New York: Harper and Row, 1963).

ECKSTEIN, HARRY, ed. *Internal War: Problems and Approaches* (New York: Free Press of Glencoe, 1964).

FELIX, CHRISTOPHER. *A Short Course in the Secret War* (New York: Dutton, 1963).

GRABER, D. A. *Crisis Diplomacy: A History of U.S. Intervention Policies and Practices* (Washington, D. C.: Public Affairs Press, 1959).

GRAMONT, SANCHE DE. *The Secret War* (New York: Putnam, 1962).

KURZMAN, DAN. *Subversion of the Innocents: Patterns of Communist Penetration in Africa, the Middle East, and Asia* (New York: Random House, 1963).

OSANKA, FRANKLIN MARK, ed. *Modern Guerrilla Warfare* (New York: Free Press of Glencoe, 1962).

PARET, PETER, and JOHN W. SHY. *Guerrillas in the 1960s* (New York: Praeger, 1961).

RANSOM, HARRY HOWE. *Central Intelligence and National Security* (Cambridge, Mass.: Harvard University Press, 1958).

SCOTT, JOHN. *Political Warfare* (New York: John Day, 1955).

STANGER, ROLAND J., ed. *Essays on Espionage and International Law* (Columbus, Ohio: Ohio State University Press, 1962).

THAYER, CHARLES W. *Guerrilla* (New York: Harper and Row, 1963).

TULLY, ANDREW. *CIA: The Inside Story* (New York: Morrow, 1962).

WISE, DAVID, and THOMAS B. ROSS. *The Invisible Government* (New York: Random House, 1964).

# 66 / The Decline of Classic Diplomacy

QUINCY WRIGHT

What is the nature of classical diplomacy and what are its
origins? How has it been related to the balance of power
concept? What has been the impact on traditional diplomacy
of democracy, of technology, of the growth of international
organizations? Has "classical" diplomacy a future? These and
related questions are discussed in this selection.

FOLLOWING THE BREAKUP of Medieval Christendom in the 15th
century, classic diplomacy developed in Europe amid conditions of
anarchy and continuous hostility among sovereign princes struggling
for power by the methods advised by Niccolò Machiavelli early in the
16th century.

## Origins of Classic Diplomacy

In the religious struggles of the 16th and 17th centuries which cul-
minated in the Thirty-Years War, the territorial monarchs, having gained
general recognition of their sovereignty, accepted the peace of Westphalia in 1648. Central Europe had lost a quarter of its population in
a war which saw the Holy Roman Emperor, who had tried to restore
the unity of Christendom, defeated by a combination of Protestant princes
and Catholic France. The peace of Westphalia was based on the principle first suggested at the Augsburg Conference of 1555, *Cuius Regia
Eius Religio* (whoever is the prince, that is the religion), thus relegating
the religious struggle to the domestic jurisdiction of each prince. The
relations of the princes came to be regulated *theoretically* by a law of
nations set forth in 1625 by Hugo Grotius, and *practically* by their mili-

Reprinted from *Journal of International Affairs*, XVII, 1 (1963), 18–28. Published
by the School of International Affairs, Columbia University. Reprinted by permission.

Quincy Wright is professor emeritus of international relations, University of
Chicago, and has been professor of foreign affairs, University of Virginia. He has
written *A Study of War* (1942), *The Role of International Law in the Prevention of
War* (1961), and numerous other works.

tary rivalry which tended toward a balance of power maintained through diplomatic intercourse.

This "classic diplomacy" assumed the coexistence of many sovereign states each respecting the territorial integrity and political independence of the others. These states dealt bilaterally with controversies about territorial limits, maritime navigation, commercial intercourse, and other issues by means of the exchange of diplomatic representatives. Diplomats were guaranteed immunity from the jurisdiction of the local sovereign, thus enabling them to conclude treaties under the sole instruction of the prince they represented. Through these treaties, a network of obligations arose which confirmed the sovereignty of states, the immunity of diplomats, the freedom of the seas, the sanctity of treaties, and the rights of belligerents and neutrals in time of war. The system recognized that the rights of princes to initiate war, *ultima ratio regem*, was implicit in their sovereignty, as was their right to keep out of the wars of others so long as they observed an impartial neutrality. This conception of war as a duel of princes superseded the medieval concept that the right to make war depended on the justice of the cause and that non-belligerents should not be neutral, but should help, or at least not hinder, the just cause and should hinder, or at least not help, the unjust.

### The Balance of Power

Although the diplomacy which operated under this concept was basically bilateral, power rivalries and the right to initiate war nevertheless made it clear that if a state conquered a neighbor, it would be likely to attack another neighbor. Thus all states were interested in maintaining the "balance of power" by ganging up against any one who was becoming too powerful. The reconciliation of the precepts of power politics, which urged attack on the overly-powerful prince, and the precepts of international law, which required a non-belligerent to be neutral unless one side violated its own rights under international law, was considered by international jurists such as Gentili and Vattel. They concluded that maintenance of the balance of power was essential to the stability and security of all, but in deference to international law, a threatened state should not attack an overly-powerful state until the latter had violated that law. This contingency, they thought, would occur because the overly-powerful state would soon commit aggression.[1,2]

In times of great emergency, especially after major wars, it was not possible to maintain the bilateralism of international relations, so that, following the precedent of Westphalia, multilateral congresses met to

---

[1] Alberico Gentili, *De Jure Belli* (1585) (London: Milford, 1933), chap. xiv, p. 66.

[2] Emerich Vattel, *Le Droit des Gens* (1758) (Washington: Carnegie Institution, 1916), Bk. III, chap. iii, pp. 248–249.

consider the general interests of Europe. But the treaties which emerged were more likely to be bilateral than multilateral. The Treaty of Utrecht in 1713 was based explicitly on the principle of the balance of power. The treaties of Paris in 1763, Vienna in 1815, Paris in 1856, Berlin in 1878 and 1885, Peking in 1901, and Washington in 1922, though less explicit, also sought to maintain the existing balance. The 19th century conferences were products of the Concert of Europe which originated in the post-Napoleonic conferences and which induced the five, later six, great powers to harmonize their efforts to settle European problems such as those which developed from the separation of Belgium from the Netherlands, the independence of the Balkan states from the Ottoman Empire, the colonization of Africa, and rivalries for spheres of interest in China.[3] However, classic diplomacy assumed (a) that the dominant interest of states was the preservation of their independence and territorial integrity, (b) that bilateral diplomatic negotiations of war were the means of maintaining rights or promoting interests, (c) that international law and treaties would be respected, at least verbally, but (d) that wars would recur and threats, subversion, and duplicity would be used within an atmosphere of secrecy. It also assumed, somewhat inconsistently, that stability, peace, and plenty were desirable and possible for considerable periods of time if the balance of power were maintained.[4]

Such maintenance was facilitated by the existence of a balancing state, itself relatively invulnerable and able to shift its support to the weaker side in a crisis, thus preventing the most powerful state from establishing a new Roman empire, the possibility of which was in the mind of each statesman whether his immediate object was to build such an empire for his prince or to prevent its building by another. Great Britain served as such a balancer after it had abandoned continental conquests and devoted attention to overseas colonization, trade, and the defeat of any power which threatened to unite Western Europe. Britain followed this policy for its own security and was successful for several centuries, because seapower and geography made it relatively safe from invasion, and it could rely on the cooperation of many continental states, equally anxious to frustrate the overly powerful in a given emergency.

### Diplomacy in the 20th Century

The late 19th century witnessed changes no less momentous than those of the 15th and 16th centuries. These changes have greatly modified, if not displaced, the practice of classic diplomacy in the 20th cen-

---

[3] Sir Charles K. Webster, *The Art and Practice of Diplomacy* (London: Chatto, 1961), pp. 55ff.

[4] Hans J. Morgenthau, *Politics Among Nations* (3d ed. rev.; New York: Knopf, 1960), pp. 178ff.

tury.[5,6] Science and technology have greatly augmented industrial production, transportation, commerce, and the dependence of most states on international trade for raw materials and markets. The range, speed, and destructiveness of weapons have made nations vulnerable to sudden and unbearably destructive attack from the most distant parts of the world. The airplane destroyed the security of Britain, and the missile that of the United States. The speed and destructiveness of a nuclear attack promises to leave no time to mobilize traditional alliances, resources, and counterattacks which in the past assured the eventual defeat of the aggressor even though he was usually better prepared on the opening of hostilities and won the first battles. No state could any longer be an invulnerable and effective diplomatic balancer, and war was not likely to restore a shattered balance.

Science and technology, in addition to shrinking the world and making war suicidal, have accelerated the rate of change, making custom and tradition less useful guides to action, reducing the predictability of the intentions—and the calculability of the offensive, defensive, and deterrent capability—of the powers, and therefore increasing the difficulty of maintaining a stable balance of power.

In the past, power relations have been more stable when there has been a large number of states with relatively equal power. There has, however, always been a tendency for more powerful states to absorb their weaker neighbors, for permanent alliances to be formed, and for the balance of power to become bipolarized and unstable. Formerly, these tendencies have led to war, as illustrated in the situation before the two World Wars. Once power became bipolarized, each side regarded eventual war as inevitable, and if the course of events seemed to favor one side, the other was likely to start war immediately rather than wait until its relative power position deteriorated further. In a multipolar balance of power, on the other hand, uncommitted states rapidly shifted their positions by opposing the most powerful state, thus making it possible to maintain the equilibrium by diplomacy for some time. Because of this tendency, the balance of power has usually broken down at intervals of roughly fifty years into general wars, such as those against France in the times of Louis XIV and Napoleon, and against Germany under the Kaiser and Hitler, with lesser wars midway between. However, in the experience of Europe during the past three centuries, equilibrium has been re-established after such wars. The new military, political, and economic conditions arising from the new technology have, however, rendered the balance of power system chronically unstable.

Other factors militating against a stable balance of power have been

---

[5] Webster, pp. 13ff.

[6] Quincy Wright, *A Study of War* (Chicago: University of Chicago Press, 1942), pp. 647ff, 760ff.

the rise of great powers outside of Europe, such as the United States, Japan, and China, and the break up of empires by defeat in war or by independence of their former colonies. The dismemberment of the Ottoman and Hapsburg Empires in the Near East and in Europe, and of the British, Spanish, Portuguese, French, German, American, Japanese, Dutch, and Belgian Empires overseas, have proceeded since 1776 and at an accelerated rate since World War II. The behavior in times of crisis of non-European states, unfamiliar with the European diplomatic system, is difficult to calculate. The new states of Asia and Africa continue to be suspicious of an international law based on European ethical standards which allowed these states to become victims of European colonialism.[7, 8, 9]

Finally, the spirit of Westphalia, calling for the coexistence of territorial states, each unified by an absolute monarch, was affected by democratic ideals springing from the British, American, and French Revolutions and set forth in the writings of Locke, Jefferson, and Rousseau. The philosophy of free trade, free enterprise, and free communication springing from the British liberalism expounded by Adam Smith and John Stuart Mill was also rooted in these revolutions. Freedom of the nation, however, was never reconciled with freedom of the individual. The ideology of communism, initiated by Marx (who was familiar with the ideas of the British economists, French revolutionists, and German Hegelian philosophers) and developed into a strategy of action by Lenin, was emphasized by the Russian and Chinese Revolutions of the 20th century. These philosophies and ideologies, creating missionary zeal to convert peoples, to emancipate colonies, or to remake boundaries raised serious doubts about the Westphalian principle of coexistence of independent states, each competent to regulate its own political philosophy, economy, and government.

### Diplomacy and International Organization

The consequences of these changes have been the incapacity of bilateral diplomacy to maintain a stable balance of power or general respect for international law, the occurrence of two world wars of unparalleled destructiveness, and the emergence of a Cold War in a world tending toward bipolarization where the precipitation of a nuclear holocaust might destroy the human race.

---

[7] R. P. Anand, "Role of the New Asian-African Countries in the Present International Legal Order," *American Journal of International Law (AJIL)*, Vol. LVI (April 1962), pp. 387ff.

[8] Quincy Wright, "The Goa Incident," *AJIL*, Vol. LVI (July 1962), pp. 629ff.

[9] Quincy Wright, "Asian Experience and International Law," *International Studies* (New Delhi: Indian School of International Studies), Vol. I (July 1959), pp. 71ff.

The emergence of these forces was dimly foreseen in the late 19th century when efforts were made to build a new international system. Public international unions were established to administer common interests of all states in such matters as communication, transport, trade, and health. The Hague Conferences of 1899 and 1907 met to prevent war, promote disarmament, codify international law, and establish institutions facilitating arbitration and conciliation of disputes. The League of Nations was established after World War I to promote international cooperation and to prevent hasty resort to war by putting teeth into the Hague System. The Kellogg-Briand Pact of 1929 was initiated by the United States, ratified by nearly all nations, and enforced against individuals by the Nuremburg and other war crimes tribunals. The Pact outlawed war as an instrument of national policy and required the settlement of all international disputes and conflicts by peaceful means. The United Nations was established after World War II to fulfill the purposes of the League and the Pact more effectively.

These instruments and organizations were not designed to supersede classic diplomacy, but to supplement it with permanent multilateral obligations and institutions for collective security and cooperative betterment of human welfare. They were not designed to supersede traditional international law, but to supplement it with principles outlawing war and recognizing the rights of man and of the organized international community. The scope of state sovereignty was, therefore, to be limited by requiring each state to settle its international disputes by peaceful means, to abstain from the threat or use of force in its international relations, to assist the United Nations in ending hostilities, to cooperate in general and regional agencies for social and economic progress, to promote the protection of human rights, and to accept the status and the operative authority of the United Nations and the Specialized Agencies.

These efforts have been only partially successful because of the prevailing sentiment demanding the complete sovereignty of the nation-state and because of the influence of zealous ideologies. The conflict between democracy and communism has led, since World War II, to a situation similar to that of the century of religious wars before Westphalia. The principle of coexistence of sovereign states which ended that period has not been fully re-established among adherents of the new "religions." (It is worth noting that the militancy of these new "religions" appears roughly proportionate to the recency of the national revolutions from which they stemmed.) In spite of the assertion in the Charter of the United Nations of the sovereign equality of states, of the assertion by the Soviet Union of the principle of peaceful coexistence of sovereign states of different ideologies,[10] and of the affirmation by the United States

---

[10] Nikita S. Khrushchev, "Peaceful Coexistence," *Foreign Affairs*, Vol. XXXVIII (October 1959), pp. 1–18.

of the right of every state to enjoy security and self-determination within its domestic jurisdiction,[11] each side in the East-West conflict has been convinced that the other is less interested in stabilizing peaceful coexistence in accord with the United Nations principles than in establishing its own ideology throughout the world by using deceptive propaganda, subversion, or even military force, if debate in the forum of world opinion proves unsuccessful.

Classic diplomacy cannot deal adequately with the problems of a world with more than 110 states of diverse culture and ideology, militarily dominated by two great alliances competing for superior nuclear power in an unstable balance of terror, and for support of the militarily weak but heavily populated uncommitted half of the world. The complexity of the situation is compounded by small wars erupting sporadically in areas such as China, Vietnam, Korea, Germany, Berlin, Kashmir, Israel, and the Caribbean. Peace is threatened by accident, miscalculation, or escalation, if not by design. All states are militarily vulnerable, most are economically dependent on each other, many have extensive political and military commitments, and few are inapprehensive that border hostilities may escalate into global thermonuclear war.

If there is to be stability under such conditions, the vision of major decision-makers must not be limited to the parties to a conflict or a negotiation; it must not be limited to the parties to a defensive alliance, a regional arrangement, or an ideology; it must be world-wide. Decision-makers must be aware that the security and progress of each state is dependent upon the security and progress of all states. Such decision-makers require contacts and information beyond that which classic diplomacy can provide. They must be able to initiate action for collective security and international cooperation by agencies of more extensive competence than diplomatic negotiation. They must be prepared to subordinate regional and defense organizations and a considerable measure of sovereign initiative to universal institutions guided by international law. Such a world was formally accepted by all United Nations members when they ratified the Charter.

Whether the world will actually develop in accord with the needs of the 20th century cannot be predicted, but if general war can be avoided, it seems probable that technologies will spread, that tensions will be reduced, and that ideologies will converge.[12] While in the past, the immediate effect of increased contact among divergent cultures has been conflict, the long-run effect has been peaceful competitive coexistence,

---

[11] Quincy Wright, "Maintaining Peaceful Coexistence," *Preventing World War III*, ed. Quincy Wright, William M. Evan, and Morton Deutsch (New York: Simon & Schuster, 1962), pp. 414ff.

[12] Pitirim A. Sorokin, *Mutual Convergence of the United States and USSR to the New Mixed Socio-Cultural Type* (Mexico City, 1961).

with increasing cooperation as common values and interests were perceived. [13, 14]

The progress toward such a realization should not be minimized. The United Nations has promoted cooperation in many fields and has helped to stop incipient wars in Greece, Indonesia, Kashmir, Palestine, Korea, Suez, Lebanon, and Cuba. Its action in the Congo appears promising at this writing. It has organized United Nations forces and has mediated or otherwise settled more than a score of disputes. Since World War II it has, on the whole, been more successful than has classic diplomacy which has attempted to deal with the problems of Vietnam, China, and Germany. This progress gives hope that classic diplomacy, while operative with considerable success under the conditions of the 17th, 18th, and 19th centuries, will subordinate itself to universal institutions better adapted to the conditions of the 20th century.

### Diplomacy and Democracy

Classic diplomacy faces particular difficulties in democracies because of their inherent incapacity to adapt themselves to the secrecy, rapidity of maneuver, and freedom from public opinion regarded as essential for its operation. All governments in the age of absolute monarchy could, and totalitarian dictatorships in the present period can, operate with more secrecy, freedom, and dispatch than can constitutional democracies. For this reason, Alexis de Tocqueville [15] was convinced that the American democracy of which he wrote in the 1830's could not play the game of power politics successfully.

Secret diplomacy was regarded by many as a contributing cause of World War I. President Wilson called for its termination in his Fourteen Points. The League of Nations Covenant and the United Nations Charter called for the publication of treaties. The practice of recent diplomatic conferences, such as that at San Francisco, has been to give much greater facilities to newsmen to broadcast the proceedings than was usual in earlier history. Statesmen have frequently practiced "diplomacy of the housetops," publishing diplomatic communications to the world simultaneously with their delivery to the government addressed.

There has been vigorous criticism of these practices. Walter Lippmann [16] asserted that President Kennedy should have communicated his

---

[13] Malcomb M. Willey and Stuart A. Rice, "The Agencies of Communications," *Recent Social Trends in the United States,* ed. William F. Ogburn (New York: McGraw-Hill, 1933), Vol. I, p. 217.

[14] Harold D. Lasswell, *World Politics and Personal Insecurity* (New York: McGraw-Hill, 1935), pp. 203ff.

[15] *Democracy in America* (1834) (New York: A. S. Barnes, 1862), Vol. I, p. 254.

[16] "Blockade Proclaimed," *New York Herald Tribune,* October 25, 1962, p. 20.

information about missile bases in Cuba to Soviet Foreign Minister Gromyko, and entered into bilateral diplomatic negotiations before establishing a unilateral quarantine of Cuba on October 22, 1962. There can be no doubt that classic diplomacy still has a role to play. Conflicts can sometimes be resolved at private negotiations in which neither side loses face. Publicity may arouse public opinion within the disputing states, preventing either side from making the concessions necessary for peaceful settlement. Private negotiation is important among party leaders in parliaments and nominating conventions if the processes of election and legislation are to proceed within democratic states. Such negotiation can be no less important in international relations.

It seems unlikely, however, that people who have a voice in the selection of major officials and the processes of domestic government will, unless faced by military necessity, abandon that voice in the making of a foreign policy which involves problems of war and peace more vital to them than domestic legislation. It is true that in England during the 19th century the public understood tacitly that foreign policy should be left to the government and should not become a subject of public agitation in parliament and elections. The concept that politics should end at the water's edge in times of crisis and that the nation should support the government "whether right or wrong" expressed this idea. These prescriptions have never been entirely carried out: in England this concept could not withstand the rise of the Labour Party and of a more egalitarian democracy in the 20th century. The governments of democratic countries have found it necessary to inform and, to some extent, be guided by public opinion in foreign policy. Even modern dictators have found it necessary to gain the support of public opinion, although their control of communications allows them to mold public opinion in support of their policies more easily than can leaders of democracies who must face a free press and free radio and television.

All genuine democracies impose constitutional limitations upon the freedom of the executive to conduct foreign policy, usually requiring that major international commitments and major uses of force have the consent of one or both houses of the legislature. Also, consent is required for appropriations which today are a vital element in military preparations, alliance commitments, economic assistance programs, and participation in international organizations.

Noting the frequent misinformation and prejudice of public opinion and legislative bodies, the limitations which obedience to public opinion imposes on the flexibility of governmental response to foreign attitudes and conditions, and governmental inability to initiate action, some students of international relations have urged an abandonment of democratic methods in the conduct of foreign relations and a return to a system of government that would be free to employ secrecy, to act rapidly, to

make threats, to utilize deception, and to retreat if necessary without loss of face.[17] However, if governments abandon democracy in making foreign policy decisions, they are likely to abandon it also in other decisions. They will find it necessary to support threats with espionage and military action, to develop defense forces by rapid coordination of national arms, economy, and morale, and to gain allies and foreign bases by concessions and bribery, all by secret executive action.

These tendencies of democracy are to be observed in periods of war and crisis. All democracies in such situations tend to abandon democratic methods, to curb civil liberties, and to exercise wide authority not only in recruiting the population for war but also in controlling the economy and opinion. In times of prolonged international crisis, all states tend to become "garrison" or "warfare" states embracing certain totalitarian principles. Such states have an advantage under the conditions of classic diplomacy as Machiavelli and de Tocqueville observed. The prince, according to Machiavelli, must pay major attention to his arms, must practice duplicity, and must keep his movements secret.[18,19] For these reasons democracy has developed only in countries which for long periods have felt relatively secure from invasion, as did England and the United States when sheltered by seas and navies, and states of Western Europe when protected, as in the 19th century, by a relatively stable multilateral balance of power and a viable international law.

While the functioning of democracy through classic diplomacy may be assisted by better education of the public on the realities of international politics, on the precepts of international law, and on the need for secrecy and freedom of action by governments in many circumstances, its survival in the long run may depend not only on such education but on the creation of conditions in the international community favorable to democracy.

These conditions include publicity for all basic decisions in the international field, universal forums in which representatives of all interested parties can participate in such decisions, elimination of war and threat of war making possible the deliberation and publicity basic to democracy, development of basic rules of order and principles of justice adapted to changing conditions of technology and ideology, and maintenance of these conditions by a world public opinion operating through universal institutions able to organize collective security and enforcement of international court decisions.

---

[17] Fred. J. Cook, "The Radical Right," *The Warfare State* (New York: Macmillan, 1962), pp. 260ff, 318.

[18] Niccolo Machiavelli, *The Prince* (1513) (New York: Dutton, 1948), chap. xv.

[19] Harold D. Lasswell, "The Garrison State," *American Journal of Sociology,* Vol. XLVI (January 1941), pp. 455–469.

### Conclusion

Classic diplomacy faces great difficulties because of the instability of the balance of power, because of the vital interests of many states in major decisions, because of the rapidity and pervasiveness of change, because of the enlarged and possibly catastrophic consequences of single decisions, [20, 21, 22] and because of the zeal of crusading ideologies. While useful in limited circumstances, classic diplomacy cannot establish conditions suitable for the functioning of democracy in a world in which the use of force may become an instrument of suicide rather than of policy. Such conditions can spring only from successful efforts to reduce tensions, to eliminate the threat or use of force as an instrument of national policy, to achieve a spirit of tolerance among diverse ideologies, to develop among states a modicum of mutual trust and confidence in agreements, and to develop in the minds of men everywhere the image of a world of peacefully coexisting states, each confident that its territorial integrity and political independence will be respected and that it will be free to experiment with its system of economy, culture, and politics within its own borders.

The changed conditions of today's world call for less emphasis on classic diplomacy and more on international law and on international institutions able to deal with problems not only of nations, but also of Mankind.

---

[20] John von Neumann, "Can We Survive Technology?," *Fortune,* Vol. LI (June 1955), pp. 106ff.

[21] Adlai E. Stevenson, "My Faith in Democratic Capitalism," *Fortune,* Vol. LII (October 1955), pp. 126ff.

[22] Quincy Wright, "The Human Spirit in the Atomic Age," *Contributors to Synthetic Jurisprudence,* ed. Minocher J. Sethna (Bombay: Tripath, 1962), pp. 69ff.

# 67 / *Diplomacy in Transition*

### CHARLES BURTON MARSHALL

**The term "diplomacy" is commonly used loosely, surrounded as it is by a romantic aura. In strict usage the term means official communications among governments. Was there ever**

---

Reprinted from *Journal of International Affairs,* XVII, 1 (1963), pp. 9–17. Published by the School of International Affairs, Columbia University. Reprinted by permission.

A brief biographical sketch of Mr. Marshall accompanies selection 6.

a "golden age" of such communications? Or is this a myth?
This debatable question is explored below by a leading American commentator on diplomacy and American foreign policy.

IN CONVERSATION a while back a lady of high civic zeal referred
to her experiences in diplomacy as constituting the pleasantest way of
spending a summer within her recollection. To my query for details, she
told of a trip abroad. Along with her passport, she had been handed a
brochure on proper conduct in foreign lands and had taken its hyperboles
at face value and to heart. I have seen or heard the word *diplomacy*
used and its cognates similarly invoked in relation to men of the fleet
in a port of call, American lawyers in England for a professional conclave,
touring glee clubs, Fulbright scholars, and foreign guides at a fair. A
pianist recounts his experiences in concertizing abroad under the heading
"Diplomacy by Keyboard."

With a rigor unfashionable in a time abundant with such notions as
"people-to-people diplomacy," I prefer to use the term not to denote
geniality among strangers but to refer to official representation and
communication among governments, associated methods and conventions,
the vocation devoted to them, and accumulated relevant lore.

Such are the senses intended when someone represents diplomatic
style as determining the character of relations among governments or
cites relevant proprieties as a remedy, even *the* remedy, for the troubles
of world politics. Usually the appeal couples diplomacy with a modifier
denoting orthodoxy—some reference to standards presumably once
upheld, then abandoned, and now requiring only to be embraced anew
in order to move the world into safer, happier courses. The appeal to
experience gives the idea an advantage of plausibility. Characteristically,
also, the proponents are men of scholarship and pertinent experience, not
lightly to be disputed.

With George F. Kennan, for example, the matters wished for are
"more effective use of the principles of professionalism" and "diplomacy
in the most old-fashioned sense of the term." Sir Harold Nicolson,
regarding a troubled world, has asserted belief "that the principles of
sound diplomacy, which are immutable, will in the end prevail, and
thus calm the chaos." Seeking a way to "disentangle the skein," former
Ambassador John Wiley has urged a return to "conventional diplomatic
framework." Senator Mike Mansfield pins hopes on "the quiet art" of
"traditional diplomacy." Sir Ivone Kirkpatrick recommends "the classical
method of successful diplomacy." With Louis J. Halle—to name another
from a legion of examples—the prescription calls for restoring "the
practices associated with the Golden Age of Diplomacy."

When, if ever, did such a Golden Age occur? Traditionalists are wont to date the unfolding of a diplomatic Golden Age to the second quarter of the 17th century, roughly two hundred years along from the origin of the modern state system. Some identify it specifically with the tenure as France's chief minister of Cardinal Richelieu, who, as Nicolson notes, "first laid it down as a definite precept that diplomacy was not a mere *ad hoc* operation but a continuous process . . . , surely . . . an important concept to have originated." Others—Halle, for example—place the time in 1642, when at last, in the Peace of Westphalia, governments foreswore trying to do each other in for the glory of God.

Both versions are unconvincing. The Thirty Years' War went on undeterred by Richelieu's innovations. The accommodation at Westphalia brought two dozen years of peace. Then Louis XIV began his onslaught against the state system. For forty-one years institutions of diplomacy were in virtual abandonment. Twenty-seven years without war on a grand scale followed before the launching of the three Silesian wars, the last of them known as the Seven Years' War, persisting until 1763. The three following decades were an interval of relative peace, with struggles marginal and formally unacknowledged. Then in 1792 gigantic hostility was resumed with the French Revolutionary Wars, which merged into the Napoleonic Wars ending with Waterloo. Only then did Europe's rulers, chastened by twenty-three years of conflict, begin giving persistent heed to keeping peace. Notions of Europe's having been, in an antecedent phase of the modern age, "a society of states, regularly constituted, in which each conformed its conduct to principles generally recognized by all," reach back, in George Sorel's phrase, to "one of the beautiful theories of philosophy in the 18th century."

The contrasting apparent stability of the ninety-nine years following Waterloo is reflected by the identicalness of the great powers involved in the deliberate construction of peace in 1815 with those participating in the precipitate dismantling of the structure in 1914—save only for one's change of name from Prussia to Germany. The near-century had been relatively peaceful. Most of its wars were fought away from centers of world politics. Issues at stake and destruction incurred in the brief, infrequent central wars were modest. Tranquility and continuity rested on general agreement among powers counting for much. Their regimes drew on a generally common fund of history. The frame of discourse among them was unified to a degree permitting any government participating significantly in world affairs to be confident of having its utterances understood by others in the sense intended. None was a revolutionary power. Ideologies were "a minor theme" through most of the period, and balance of power "seemed to be the political equivalent of the laws of economics, both self-operating," as A. J. P. Taylor puts it. The basis of general order was not at issue. A common notion of legitimacy prevailed.

Looked back upon after an interval sufficient to soften details of enduring suspicions, recurring tensions, and occasional violence, the time, as no other, deserves celebrity as a Golden Age of Diplomacy.

Under precepts of the time, governments were normally to seek concord, finding ways of making purposes compatible through methods of discreet bargaining looking to contractual results. Participants in this distinctly rational way of conducting affairs did not delude themselves into regarding consent and coercion as disjoined. Some factor of constraint invariably underlies assent. Awareness of penalties of not agreeing is invariably a condition of agreement among governments. Recognizing these concepts, those handling policy had possibilities of resorting to force generally in back of their minds and sometimes in front. Though regularly involved in calculating relevant capabilities, they ordinarily refrained from flaunting the circumstance. "'The rapine underneath was there,'" as Lord Vansittart has observed, "but relatively it was war in lace."

Bargaining and consent rested on a canon of equality, measured not so much in calculable strength, resources, size, or technical achievement as in autonomous right to define one's interests and to make up one's own mind and of capacity to enter into contract. Participation in the pattern signified statehood. It denoted capacities to make and to effect decisions, to meet obligations, and to keep order within one's domain—capacities summed up as sovereignty, carrying title to be left alone by outsiders under a precept as stated by Kennan: ". . . once a state had been recognized as a sovereign entity, one did not attempt to extinguish it entirely, or to deny it the basic right to order its own internal affairs in accordance with its own tradition and ideas."

What regimes needed to say to each other was supposed to be appropriate to, and confined to, channels provided by reciprocal presence of envoys. A deviation, such as an appeal by a government to another nation directed past a regime to its people, was regarded as an unstately trenching upon sovereignty.

As privacy was part of diplomatic usage, so circumspection, along with a stylized sort of courtesy, was a supposed quality of practitioners. It was considered fitting to appoint to diplomatic missions, and to use in foreign offices, men of aristocracy schooled to appropriate attitudes and well reputed. Professionalism thus developed in step with permanence of representation. A practitioner might meet his opposite number of the moment, and need his good will, at later stages in his career, and accordingly it was prudent to give heed even to an adversary colleague's interest in preserving standing with his principals and thus to avoid pushing too harsh a bargain. A practitioner owed obligations to his vocation as well as to his regime. Duality of obligation was supposed to enable a diplomat, dealing with his kind, both to advocate for his

principal's interests and to mediate between them and rival interests. The extremes of policy were thus mitigated by negotiation, easing compromise much as in the manner of attorneys working out terms of agreement beyond reach of their principals in direct encounter. The profession was thus set apart—not only by a right of protection from local harassments and exemption from coercion by host regimes but also by attributes of "a certain freemasonry of diplomacy," in François de Callières' phrase, transcending locality "like the knights of chivalry in the Middle Ages."

With eloquent emphasis, Kennan has embellished this view of the profession in an idealized interpretation of diplomatists as men rising above foibles otherwise affecting state business, spared of prejudice and ambition, guided only by reason, vouchsafed insights not accessible to other mortals concerned with public affairs, and standing superior and patronizing in relation to the sorry apparatus of the state much as physicians stand in relation to wayward patients or expert mechanics to outmoded and balky cars. In the tradition as celebrated for example, by Kennan, a government's will in external affairs and the processes of striking balance with external interests by negotiation tend to merge. The blending is as if the negotiators' role were, or should be, pre-eminent in setting policy and as if skill in parleying and reporting constituted the total requirement. The political character of foreign affairs, the element of conflicting purpose, fades into quiet professional interchange. The notion of rectifying a world through diplomacy amounts to having it regulated by diplomats.

If an accessible but overlooked set of techniques and a willing but slighted profession do indeed harbor workable but neglected solutions for otherwise obdurate and perilous international issues of our time, it is obviously urgent to make avail of them. The question entailed, whether the prescription of orthodox diplomacy is of practicable import or merely reflects a hankering for paradise lost, is easily disposed of.

Celebrators of a diplomatic Golden Age have, according to Robert W. Tucker, built the tradition into something "at times amounting almost to *mystique*." It is worth a moment to examine the mystification. In its time of celebrity professional diplomacy was a bureaucratic expression—elegant but still bureaucratic—of a political concord seemingly firm and universal but actually neither. "Every bureaucracy . . . , in accord with the peculiar emphasis of its own position," Karl Mannheim has observed, "tends to generalize its own experience and to overlook the fact that the realm of administration and of smoothly functioning order represents only a part of the total political reality."

Thus it is with the tradition surrounding diplomatic bureaucracy. Diplomacy, as Sorel made clear, "is the expression of political customs," not itself determinative of the character of political relations. The techniques of diplomacy did not create the Golden Age. Rather, the conditions

of the time—with Europe ascendant and superficially tranquil for the time being—provided opportunity for diplomacy and its practitioners to seem prodigious. The circumstances, while they lasted, were bound to be flattering to diplomats. Elements of success were in the environment, like a rainy spell for forest rangers or an abundance of duck for hunters.

The glow of diplomacy was but a reflection of assumptions prevailing within the societies mirrored in it—those of the West, especially Europe, in an auspicious time. Alfred North Whitehead recalled the latter decades of the period as one of "the happiest times I know of in the history of mankind," filled with "a sense of purpose and progress in the world." As Sir David Kelly reminds us, "Western man . . . regarded as obsolete the tendency to sheer wickedness. . . . Evil was associated with Nature, pestilence and earthquakes, and primitive man shared in the cruelty of Nature because he was still half-animal—but civilized man was envisaged as the innocent victim of evil and advancing rapidly to its conquest." The era, again in Sir David's phrase, was marked by "two obsessions—a dogmatic theory of linear progress and a belief that the local temporary conditions of Europe in the nineteenth century were final and stable."

Those conditions were indeed local and temporary. It is important to have clear in our minds the circumscription of the diplomatic order at the very high point of its contingent celebrity. Diplomacy and its equalitarian usages were strictly limited in application. Their time of eminence coincided with the heydey of empire—a general term summing up a variety of inequalitarian arrangements, accepted then as normal for handling relationships between governments within the Europe-centered state system and peoples of divergent cultures in remote areas.

The ranges both of diplomacy and of empire grew with the extension of European influence outward to other continents, beginning with what Halford Mackinder called "the great adventure on the ocean that was to make the world European." The respective scopes altered from one juncture to another. Fastening of imperial arrangements onto one area might accompany a modification in the direction of diplomatic usages with respect to another. Sometimes—this happened especially as to parts of Africa—outlying areas and peoples might be brought tentatively and ambiguously within the diplomatic nexus only to be subjected later on to outright imperial domination. Again, forms of diplomacy might be applied but mitigated by inequality of privilege. The distinctions between equalitarian diplomacy and inequalitarian empire were not always of litmus-paper absoluteness. The point essential here concerns a misproportion involved in picturing a globe formerly ministered by diplomacy, while overlooking the complementary and no less significant role of imperial office—colonial ministers, viceroys, proconsuls, captains-general, and colonial governors—in holding together what there used to be of a world order in times now recalled as a Golden Age of Diplomacy. The

oversight is of a bureaucratic sort, arising from tendencies to interpret realities in correspondence to departmental pigeon-holes.

Indeed, diplomatic functions have suffered no reduction of scope or curtailment of numbers. Quite to the contrary, diplomacy has undergone sudden enormous extension—demonstrable by a visual count of automobiles illegally parked with legal impunity along Washington's curbs any day or by such a datum as a *Washington Post* news item placing at "more than 6,000" the number of persons enjoying diplomatic status in our national capital. Emissaries and their staffs abound and are kept busy far beyond past measure, and the work of burgeoning missions goes on at a volume and pace undreamt-of even a lifetime back. Surely not diplomacy but rather the imperial order has shrunk. The rate and sweep have been such as to make the change a major historic phenomenon.

With Americans, the characteristic relevant feeling is gratification, susceptible of being carried rather far in some cases. I recall once having read a woman journalist's account of being ordered at gunpoint to get off a sidewalk so as to make way for some passing minor functionaries in a newly independent Oriental land and of complying in thankfulness for opportunity thus to be demeaned in atonement for past imperial inequalities. I, for one, should find it difficult to summon up such large contrition for the circumstance that some governments, in whose acts neither I nor anyone of my acquaintance had a part, found it necessary, profitable, or convenient to interpose authority in other lands and over other peoples in times past. A more typical attitude toward proliferating new states would be a measure of misty pride in having other peoples in their fashion follow in our national footsteps.

Myriad factors, to be sure, must be added up as causes to balance against historic results of such scope as the wholesale movement into juridic independence in our time. A full accounting would encompass a complex of causes traceable over many centuries. Without the power of examples set at Concord, Philadelphia, and Yorktown, would the ideas carried far and wide by the thrust of empire—national identity, authority pervasive over a defined area, and a general will to make a place in history—have produced their now manifest consequences? No one can say for sure, but Americans are entitled to feel self-congratulatory for the nation's having got in on the start of a big trend—for having created, if not a model, then at least a precedent.

With ours, in Raymond Aron's phrase, "a world in which the grand principle of self-determination has somehow become an absolute," it is a prerogative of a multitude "to assume, among the powers of the earth, the separate and equal status" and to participate in diplomatic interchange. The novelty and anomaly of the resulting situation do not lie altogether in the multiplicity of participants, in the diminutiveness of a portion of them, or even in the meagerness of many of them as polities.

One should have to turn back over less than a century to find a redundancy of states taking part in diplomacy, owing to the honeycombing of Central Europe and the Italian peninsula. Cyprus, Gabon, or Burundi has its numerical counterpart in Iceland or Honduras. The Balkans and Central America come to mind as examples of historic clusters of states with thin endowments for political life. What most of all distinguishes the present is a combination of unprecedented universality with unprecedented cleavages within the diplomatic framework—and therein lies a central part of the problem of order confronting diplomacy in a world "for the first time presented with a closed system," in Mackinder's phrase.

Whatever its contingency and injustices, the unequal imperial structure did serve a use in providing a frame of relationship among highly diverse entities.

> *How could communities . . .*
> *But by degree, stand in authentic place?*
> *Take but degree away, untune that string,*
> *And, hark, what discord follows!*

Those lines from *Troilus and Cressida* are relevant. Filling in behind vanishing empire and for the first time being stretched to encompass a globe, the diplomatic nexus is called upon to join diversities hugely beyond what it enclosed in its eminent century. It has become surrogate to the imperial dispensation—under different and often inapposite rules. In comparison to its Golden Age, diplomacy is not so much neglected as baffled. It has no unified order matching its scope to stand upon, to minister, and to reflect.

The approach to realization of "a whole world consisting of peoples who have in the fullest sense entered history and become the concern, no longer of the colonial administrator or the anthropologist, but of the historian"—I quote Aron—implies universalization in a sense that every view of nationhood and history, whatever its quality, comes to count in the problem of order; but it does not mean universalization as an engrossing unity underlying order.

Of the multiplicity of states in the increment, some are only nominally qualified—scarcely endowed with that unified view of will, action, and reality called a sense of history. "Man makes history," according to José Ortega y Gasset, "because, faced with a future which is not in his hands, he finds that the only thing he has, what he possesses, is his past . . . ; this is the small ship in which he sets sail toward the unquiet future. . . ." Yet, as Robert L. Heilbroner has emphasized, "it can fairly be said that most of the underdeveloped world had no history" in the sense "of a shared political and social and economic self-consciousness which become part of the biographies of millions of human beings, help-

ing to shape these biographies and to give them a common purpose." It is awesome for a people to be, in a phrase from Edmund Burke, "in so deep a play without any sort of knowledge of the game"—assuming nationhood and attempting a role in history without much of a grasp of either, trying to create a future with only a set of clichés for a past.

This proliferation of states without determined political character but with ambition to play a role in history occurs in a world already deeply riven over the meaning of history and, therefore, of the character of a legitimate order. I refer to the confrontation called the Cold War. The interplay between that division and the sudden vast extension of diplomacy—a unification without unity—is truly unprecedented. "Never before have states belonging to the same diplomatic system differed as they differ today," according to Aron. "Never before have people involved in a common enterprise been so disunited on fundamental issues."

# 68 / The U. S. Government Organization Overseas

## HARLAN CLEVELAND AND OTHERS

**The foreign policy objectives and commitments of the United States and the realities of technology and world politics place enormous requirements on contemporary American diplomacy. These modern conditions have created what is commonly called the "new diplomacy." This confronts the American foreign service with formidable challenges and problems of administration, recruitment, and training. But what, concretely, is required of the modern "overseas American?" This important question is explored in the following selection.**

THE ADMINISTRATIVE PROBLEMS of our own Government's foreign operations are perhaps more complex, because our purposes are more

Reprinted from U. S. Senate Committee on Foreign Relations Study No. 6, "The Operational Aspects of United States Foreign Policy," by Maxwell Graduate School of Citizenship and Public Affairs, Syracuse University (November, 1959), in *U.S. Foreign Policy: Compilation of Studies*, 87th Cong., 1st sess., S. Doc. 24 (March 15, 1961), pp. 615–21.

A brief biographical sketch of Mr. Cleveland accompanies selection 45.

diverse. But we can start with a simple fact: that the objects of foreign policy are located abroad—in the 86 countries where we maintain diplomatic or other missions, whose policies and actions may significantly affect our political, economic, or security interests, with whose governments we are negotiating, whose people we are seeking to influence, and whose national purposes we are trying to reconcile with our own. The test of the effectiveness of any nation's foreign policy administration is how well it works in the field.

This truism suggests that, within the framework set by our global objectives and strategy as defined by the President and Secretary of State, the day-to-day (and even, for most purposes, the year-to-year) conduct of foreign relations with each country should largely be determined by the complex of aspirations, interests, and forces at work in each society with which we have dealings. The shifting factors can best be appraised, the tactical situation most accurately judged, and the use of our various instruments of foreign policy most flexibly coordinated in the field. Further, the responsibility for coordination of U.S. bilateral activity in each country should be centered, insofar as possible, in the U.S. Ambassador in each country. In practice, however, the emphasis in making of policy, and of many detailed decisions, has tended in recent years to gravitate toward Washington. The effect has been to introduce distortions and irrelevancies into some programs, notably those for promoting economic development, and generally to make our policy excessively rigid and cumbersome.

The causes of this defect are complex, and include the following:

(a) Modern communications make it possible to exchange messages, at great length and detail, and get a quick reply. (To be sure, the ease of communications is partly self-defeating. The volume of messages swamps the recipients, requires more staff to draft replies, and hence further slows and complicates the decisionmaking progress. Even the mechanics of handling cables—coding, for example—are affected by the glut; American cables notoriously take much longer to reach their addressee than parallel messages through British channels.)

(b) Our main foreign policy concerns are global in character, and this appears to necessitate more coordination of specific decisions in the light of worldwide considerations. Before World War II, our policies in the Caribbean, China, and Czechoslovakia were, by the large, in separate compartments. We can no longer so regard them.

(c) There has been an extraordinary proliferation of U.S. agencies concerned in some way with foreign affairs, requiring more coordination both at headquarters and in the field. But since the final word rests with Washington, a very large number of questions involving interagency differences or understandings, rather than real policy, get referred to Washington for interagency brokerage.

(d) There has been a striking growth in congressional intervention in

general, especially through its appropriations and investigative processes. This
is a government wide phenomenon; but the foreign affairs agencies, because their
operations are well publicized, are particularly sensitive to detailed congressional
review.

## 1. The Executive Ambassador

The ambassador represents in his person the authority of the President. In the era of foreign operations that is now upon us, his constitutional position must now be reinterpreted to include the task of presiding over the whole range of U.S. governmental activities in the country to which he is assigned. The most important and difficult parts of his job are likely to be not the traditional State Department functions of *foreign policy* and *foreign relations,* but *foreign operations* which in some countries are virtually as broad as those of the government to which he is accredited.

The effective ambassador must have, then, not only diplomatic but also executive qualities of the first order. Although the presumption in filling top embassy posts should certainly favor the career service, it would be a mistake to regard ambassadorships as its exclusive prerogative. It cannot be assumed that the experienced diplomat, however able in his field, will always have executive abilities, any more than an experienced administrator will necessarily possess the diplomatic qualities that are required—or that a successful politician will necessarily have either.

On the other hand, an increasing share of our foreign relations is now conducted in various international frameworks—the U.N. organs, the specialized agencies, NATO and other treaty organizations, the Organization of American States, etc. The duties of our representatives in these bodies are not mainly the coordination of operations but diplomatic negotiation, considerably complicated by the multilateral context in which it is conducted. Here is where the experienced Foreign Service officer can show to best advantage. Yet the major posts in our delegation to the U.N. General Assembly—and many other positions requiring special background in international politics and experience of diplomatic infighting—are often filled with estimable Americans trained in such dubiously relevant specialties as manufacturing, scientific research, teaching, singing, or organizing civic clubs.

Some of the amateur diplomats soon develop the requisite political sense and some FSO's make first-rate executives. But we could enhance the prospects of success by using men with demonstrated diplomatic skill for professional diplomacy and appointing as country chiefs of mission men with proven capacity as Government executives, as well as extensive overseas experience—from the career service if available, from

outside if not. Perhaps the prime qualification for an effective ambassador, career or noncareer, is a strong sense of policy: an understanding of the objectives that the United States is trying to achieve in the country to which he is assigned, the ability to grasp the significance of the politico-economic-social forces at work there, and the imagination to see how some of our specific aims might be adapted to harmonize with local aspirations without prejudice to our essential interests.

The pool of potential executives, from which a sufficient number of ambassadorial candidates can be selected in the future, might be enlarged in several ways:

(*a*) By widening the Foreign Service to take in more of the "generalists" (e.g., the program officers and general administrators) from ICA and USIA.

(*b*) By insuring that members of such a combined Foreign Service have opportunities during their careers not only to handle visas and do politico-economic reporting but also, for example, to work in a foreign aid program, as a public affairs officer, with the ICA or as liaison with a MAAG.

(*c*) By urging our national political party leaders to endorse for Presidential and congressional consideration only those political candidates for embassy service who have already had successful executive and international experience.

The modern embassy is not, of course, concerned only with coordination of field operations. No less important is the characteristic foreign relations function—of negotiating, reporting, "keeping in touch." But the nature of this function has also changed; as indicated above, it involves making sure that we have some U.S. elements in close and friendly contact with all important forces in the country. The effective use of our plural contacts, official and nonofficial, in each country, however, requires that ambassadors and embassies recognize, as regards the diverse unofficial contingent, the inexpediency of trying to impose conformity to the current official line out of fear that deviations might "embarrass the United States." Coordination in this regard can better be informal rather than explicit, by leadership rather than by direction.

If recent history is a guide to the future, there is a good chance in many countries that the "next government" will be a military or a military-dominated one. The closest previous contacts that these new rulers are likely to have had with Americans are with the military personnel attached to our diplomatic missions and to MAAG's. This fact should be an important consideration in our selection and training of officers for such posts abroad. Apart from their competence in their several military specialties, the key members of our military aid missions should above all possess a "sense for politics," and be encouraged, under the ambassador's supervision, to cultivate politically minded leaders of the local armed forces, who may control the next regime. For this purpose

it may be useful to call up for MAAG assignments some civilians experienced in Government who happen to be reserve officers.

In summary: The flexible, effective administration of foreign affairs requires a true delegation of responsible authority to the field. Within broad limits we need to get back to the concept that the ambassador is the President's representative, that he is "plenipotentiary." But such a delegation is acceptable only if we revert, in the selection of ambassadors, to standards closer to those observed in the earliest days of the Republic. Then our foreign relations were vital to survival, and we were on occasion represented by men of the caliber of Benjamin Franklin, Thomas Jefferson, John Jay, and John Quincy Adams. In this time of rapid change and deep involvement, the challenges we face cannot be met with money or armed power or technical skills alone; statesmanlike leadership is needed, and scope for its exercise.

### 2. Training for Oversea Service

An examination of Americans at work abroad reveals some uncommon qualities of mind and spirit which seem to be common to most of our citizens who have made successful careers abroad, whether in Government or with private business firms and voluntary agencies. These elements of effective oversea performance appear to be generally applicable to Americans in responsible positions abroad regardless of the kind of work the American is doing or in what foreign country he is doing it. Five of these elements stand out:

1. Technical skill: The versatility and willingness to improvise that requires both a thorough knowledge of a specialized field, but the attitude toward it of a general practitioner rather than a narrow specialist.

2. Belief in mission: A dedication to his work regardless of geography that enables a man to survive repeated frustrations and still retain a zest for the job.

3. Cultural empathy: The curiosity to study and the skill to perceive the inner logic and coherence of the other fellow's way of thinking; and the restraint not to judge it as bad just because it is different from the American way.

4. A sense of politics: The sensitivity to see oneself as a "political man" whose action (or inaction) affects the power structure around him; the ability to do one's work despite being conspicuously the object of curiosity, envy, or opprobrium; and the understanding of American civilization that qualifies a man to represent not only himself but the culture and society from which he comes.

5. Organization ability: A tolerance for large-scale organization and an understanding of complicated headquarters-field relationships; and a special talent for building social institutions and teaching others to manage them.

No individual can be expected to possess, all by himself, just the

proper "mix" of all the ingredients of effective oversea performance. But every American organization which operates abroad can be guided by these qualifications in trying to locate the proper people to mix together in carrying out its mission.

Now that nearly one percent of the U.S. population lives and works abroad, it is clear that the American educational system is not providing a sufficient number of Americans who, in addition to their vocational skills, have the necessary attitudes and kinds of understanding for useful oversea service. The best recruiting device is an educational program. If the colleges and universities can be induced to do more preparation for oversea life and work, the hiring agencies (in and out of Government) will be able to recruit from a pool of tested professionals, instead of (as at present) doing most of the weeding out of misfits and most of the relevant training for oversea service on the job, after the American has arrived at his post abroad.

The new importance of our deep involvement with other societies calls for some shifts in educational emphasis. For example:

(a) Immersion in an alien culture prior to the first oversea assignment is so important that colleges and universities should make it a live option for every interested student to spend at least a semester abroad under competent academic supervision.

(b) University area and language programs should be expanded to serve all three of the markets for regional studies. The first of these is the scholar who plans to make a career as an area expert. But the professional in a subject matter field who expects to work in the area also needs an academic haven to which he can repair for intensive language training closely associated with the study of cultural history and contemporary social and economic trends, geographic and military facts—a training that can help him face frankly, before he goes abroad, the nature of his role in speeding and influencing rapid social change. Area programs might also take on the task of organizing, for regular undergraduate and graduate students, a brief but intensive exposure in one country, as a practical introduction to cultural empathy.

(c) Every professional school, and graduate program in the social sciences, should reflect in its curriculum the certainty that some of its students will practice their profession abroad. In every American professional and graduate school the next revision of the curriculum should give prominent place to that disturbing and useful question: "What is universal about the rules and standards of our profession, and what is merely American practice?"

## 3. Foreign Aid Operations

Among the most difficult responsibilities for our ambassadors is the direction of U.S. aid operations—economic, technical, defense-supporting and military. Their size and technical nature requires a wide delegation of authority to subordinates. The people engaged in them are generally

more numerous, less homogeneous in background, and in closer contact with the local administration and people than most of the embassy staff. U.S. operations involve very large sums of money, and may offer vast opportunities for corruption, patronage, or special advantage to political or economic interests. They are inordinately subject to functional parochialism, with experts in different fields promoting the development of specialized facilities and services with little regard to budgetary or program balance or to political side-effects. And these activities are concentrated mainly in the emerging countries that are least able to cope with the resulting administrative problem.

Moreover, a number of non-U.S. agencies have a position in this field of economic and technical aid—the World Bank, the several U.N. specialized agencies, the Colombo Plan and other regional organizations, and the export credit institutions of a half-dozen other Western industrial countries, to say nothing of the Soviet bloc. In southeast Asia there may be nearly 20 autonomous agencies operating in any one country; in Latin America as many as 25 or more. The possibilities for duplication, inefficiency, and misdirection of effort are obvious—and have been extensively realized. Local governments, naturally, miss few opportunities to play one off against another.

The sensible solution, of course, is a soundly conceived country program. As we have seen, the emerging nations on which our variegated aid programs are focused are not equipped to shape up or carry out such a program, and the United States, as a foreign government, is disqualified, as a rule, to do it for them. Thus, it is not only from the standpoint of policy that it makes sense to shift both the programing and administration of development assistance as fully as possible to international auspices; the case is equally strong on administrative grounds. From this point of view, such a transfer would—

(*a*) permit more effective integration of American technicians and financial resources with those supplied from other like-minded countries (and thereby help to elicit greater contributions from these countries to the common effort);

(*b*) join administrative control of most external assistance with the development programing function in which we would be jointly engaged;

(*c*) reduce the number of U.S. Government personnel abroad (although Americans as individuals would doubtless make up a large contingent of the multinational staff, as they do in the World Bank and the U.N. technical assistance programs); and

(*d*) reduce the housekeeping functions of the embassy, leaving its staff freer to concentrate on its other responsibilities—including the task of keeping a sharp eye on the operation of multilateral aid programs in the country in which it is situated.

Our embassy could not, of course, direct this international team, but it would certainly be in a position to make its influence felt, as repre-

senting the most important participant in the joint program. Its representations to the local government, in support of the multilateral agency's line on important policy issues, would carry independent weight, no longer pressing a purely American position. On the other hand, the embassy might well be glad to avoid having to take a stand on certain issues, and to let the international team discuss them with the local government.

Military assistance could not, of course, be correspondingly multilateralized. Although the administration of this function may perhaps be shifted in some part of the regional treaty organizations, this could only be a gradual process, at best, outside the NATO area. Similarly the provision of defense support—the provision of economic resources to enable an ally to maintain larger armed forces than it could otherwise afford—must be weighed on essentially military grounds and administered on a bilateral (or very limited multilateral) basis.

Finally, direct assistance to the "wards" of the United States (Korea, Taiwan, South Vietnam, etc.) and to some other countries of special political or security importance (e.g., Jordan) may have to continue for some time to come. In these countries, the resources we provide are essential to their survival; the extent of our commitment to them permits and requires more unilateral operations than would be prudent, or even tolerable, in most other countries. (The fact that they occupy this dependent status is an important reason why other nations, in a position to assert their independence, so strongly resist a comparable donor-client relationship.) We will expect to continue this kind of involvement in these countries; and routine assistance and guidance for development, through multilateral agencies, could be of only secondary importance. Even in these cases, however, it will often be useful to seek active international cooperation in the fields where it is appropriate to do so, in order to help ease political friction and prepare for orderly transition to a less dependent status.

In these countries, where security considerations are overriding, military programs have a tendency to get out of hand. There is increasing recognition of the fact that our short-term military and economic objectives may contradict each other—that the added efficiency of the armed forces, gained through military assistance, may be more than offset by a consequent weakening of the political and economic foundations in some countries. This can be seen, in retrospect, to have been the case in such varied situations as Turkey and Laos. But the gains and losses can only be weighed intelligently country by country.

# 69 / Diplomacy Then and Now

## HAROLD NICOLSON

The rise of democratic government and mass communications,
the dynamics of Communism in its various national forms,
and the complexity of modern international relations—all
pose a great challenge to the diplomat and his trade. In the
following selection, one of the world's foremost authorities on
diplomacy—old and new—deals with the question of what is
required of the modern diplomat.

## I

SINCE 1914 the structure of the world has changed. Compared to
the present struggle between West and East, the rivalries of the eighteenth
and nineteenth centuries sink into insignificance. Today we are faced,
not with a clash of interests, but with a fight between ideologies, between
the desire on the one hand to defend individual liberties and the resolve
on the other hand to impose a mass religion. In the process the old
standards, conventions and methods of international negotiation have
been discredited. Had it not been for the invention of the atomic bomb,
we should already have been subjected to a third world war.

Members of the Communist bloc today are convinced that sooner or
later they will acquire world dominion and will succeed in imposing
their faith and their authority over the whole earth. They strain towards
this objective with religious intensity and are prepared to devote to its
achievement their lives, their comfort and their prospects of happiness.
Anything that furthers their purpose is "right"; anything that obstructs
it is "wrong"; conventional morality, even the creation of confidence, has
no part in this scheme of things. Truth itself has lost its significance.
Compared to the shining truth of their gospel, all minor forms of veracity
are merely bourgeois inhibitions. The old diplomacy was based upon the
creation of confidence, the acquisition of credit. The modern diplomatist
must realize that he can no longer rely on the old system of trust; he
must accept the fact that his antagonists will not hesitate to falsify facts
and that they feel no shame if their duplicity be exposed. The old

Reprinted from *Foreign Affairs*, XL, 1 (October, 1961), 39–49. Copyright 1962
by the Council on Foreign Relations, Inc., New York.

Harold Nicolson is a former member of the British diplomatic service, a former
Member of Parliament, and has published, among other works, *Diplomacy* (1939),
*The Congress of Vienna* (1946), and *The Evolution of the Diplomatic Method* (1954).

currency has been withdrawn from circulation; we are dealing in a new coinage.

This transformation of values has been aided by a new or "democratic" conception of international relations. In the old days the conduct of foreign affairs was entrusted to a small international élite who shared the same sort of background and who desired to preserve the same sort of world. Today the masses are expected to take an interest in foreign affairs, to know the details of current controversies, to come to their own conclusions, and to render these conclusions effective through press and parliament. At the same time, however, current issues have been rendered complex and inter-connected; it is not possible to state issues, such as the Common Market, in short and simple terms. Thus, whereas the man in the street is expected to have an opinion on international problems, the very complexity of these problems has rendered it difficult to provide him with the information on which to base his judgment.

A further difficulty arises over the contrast between "secret" and "open" diplomacy. This stems from the misuse of the word "diplomacy" to signify both foreign policy and negotiation. Foreign policy should never be secret, in the sense that the citizen should on no account be committed by his government to treaties or engagements of which he has not been given full previous knowledge. But negotiation must always be confidential. Very often, these days, negotiations are hampered or even frustrated by leakages to the press. Breaches of confidence are always news.

A further democratic myth is that of egalitarianism. Every country, however small its power, however restricted its resources, is regarded as the "equal" of every other country. Important decisions are taken, not owing to the strength of those who support those decisions, but according to the voices of the weak.

The Soviet Union, moreover, while itself destroying the freedom of several formerly independent countries, has managed to create the myth that it is the champion of the oppressed in their struggle against "colonialism." Preferring as it does ideal to actual truth, it manages to persuade the once subject races of the world that Communism is bound to become the universal religion of the future and that under Communism they will be able to divest themselves of their former inferior status and become the rulers of their section of the world. Thus, for the present at least, Communism is identified with nationalism, and nationalism with ambition. The wind of change howls like a hurricane across Asia and Africa. Everything associated with the past is represented as iniquitous, everything that looks to the future is colored with glamor and glory. The West is associated with the past; the East with the future. It might be said, therefore, and has often been said, that the West is fighting a losing battle. This is a fallacious proposition. If we can avoid committing

arrant mistakes—such as the mistake of Suez and the mistake of Cuba—
we can maintain a defensive position for the next 50 years. Meanwhile
the massive front of the Communist world may have started to disinte-
grate. The Marxist view of society and of the inevitability of history
assumes that the masses can be conditioned to believe eternally in the
same creed. That is a misconception of human nature; always there will
be heretics and the more they are repressed the more ardent and convinced they become. The West in the end will be rescued by the heretics
of the East.

## II

I was reading recently an interesting book called "The Ugly American" in which the failure of the West to stem Communist infiltration into
Southeast Asia is ascribed to the old-fashioned conception of diplomacy
which prevails in Washington. Whereas the Soviet authorities concentrate on winning the support of the masses, the Americans are said to
be concerned mainly with winning the support of the governing classes.
A symptom of this difference of approach is that, whereas American diplomatists seldom can speak any language other than their own, Soviet
diplomatists are chosen because of their familiarity with the language
and dialects of the countries to which they are sent.

This is a specious contention. Governments, even in new or backward
countries, are composed of the more educated people who, in Southeast
Asia, are usually able to speak English or French. Such people take
pride in their linguistic attainments and would be hurt if addressed in
their native language by foreign diplomatists. Even as in the old days
M. Isvolsky, the Tsarist Foreign Minister, would have been outraged if
addressed in Russian by a foreign ambassador, so also in Saigon today
would the foreign minister expect to be addressed in French. In theory,
of course, it appears illogical that the American ambassador at Oslo
should be unable to speak or even read Norwegian. Yet in practice those
with whom he negotiates can all speak English and he has on his staff
translators who provide him daily with an accurate summary of the
Norwegian newspapers.

A diplomatist, moreover, should not concentrate solely on conditions
in the country to which he is accredited. He must at the same time be
aware of conditions and opinions in his own country. Really to know the
language, traditions, prejudices and inhibitions of a country such as Laos,
for example, entails years of study and long residence. A man by such
methods may learn a great deal about Laotian opinion but in the process
he gets out of touch with opinion in his own home country. He is apt to
"go native" and his judgment may be warped by purely local sentiments.
It may be that the Russians, with their uniform policy of destroying the

influence of capitalism everywhere and by any means, can afford to send agents into every Laotian village to persuade the headmen of the philanthropy of the Soviet creed. It may be that by the "cell" method they are able to create disturbances, organize riots and demonstrations, and even overturn governments. Yet in the end their methods may land them in an illogical situation. They may find that in preaching self-government they lose control of the governments they have themselves created. An ambitious politician may be glad to have been brought to power by a students' demonstration; but he will see to it that no students' demonstrations recur.

Although policy should be directed and controlled by the ambassador himself, and although it does not matter much if the ambassador cannot himself speak a difficult local language, it is essential that he be aided and advised by a staff of permanent officials who have lived for long in the country, have studied the local traditions and character, and are acquainted with the background and temperament of those having local influence. Such a staff of experts exists in all well-founded embassies. In the British Foreign Service there existed in the old days the Levant Consular Service and the Chinese Consular Service, which provided the embassies with a pool of experts from which they could draw their advisers. These men were honest patriots; there is no need to suppose, as the authors of "The Ugly American" imply, that they had all gone so native as to become spies. On the other hand, to know everything about a foreign country requires at the very least a lifetime of experience. And if a man spends his whole life in any given community he is bound to develop affections and prejudices which distort his evidence. It is difficult to conceive of a person so circumstanced who would be so objective as to be immune to all subjective impulses. My own experience of such local experts is that they become either so gullible as to believe whatever they are told, or so suspicious as to doubt the veracity of even the most honest. If ambassadors were required to become experts, then surely great confusion would arise.

So strongly is this danger anticipated by the British Foreign Office that it is their habit, when a man has been too long in the Far East, to appoint him somewhere in Latin America. Such mutations are often resented by the official himself and cause surprise to the public. "How odd," people exclaim, "to send to Montevideo a man who has lived for years in Indonesia! How like the Foreign Office!" It is not so odd or irrational as all that. The business of a diplomatist is to represent his own government in a foreign country; if he lives too long in a foreign country, he may lose touch with his own home opinion and his representative value will be diminished. Expert knowledge is essential to judgment; but such knowledge can be obtained from experts whose business it is to advise and inform, not to judge or decide.

### III

A second aspect of American diplomacy as criticized, and indeed ridiculed in "The Ugly American" is the social aspect. The authors of this engaging book imply that American officials abroad are not democratic enough.

I admit that all Foreign Services possess their cocktail side. In the days of the old diplomacy, when foreign affairs were a class specialty, the social element was assuredly important. In Tsarist Russia, for instance, or in Vienna, where the top ranks of society did in fact exercise a great influence over ministers and cabinets, it was highly important for an ambassador and his staff to be socially acceptable. The French Embassy, for instance, some of whose members were deficient in social polish, found itself at a disadvantage in snobbish posts such as St. Petersburg or Vienna when in contact with the local society. The leaders of these societies regarded themselves as the cream of European aristocracy and did not enjoy mingling with people whom they regarded as bourgeois in their origins and manners. Stupid though they may have been, they yet were people of influence in governmental circles and thus it was essential that they should be entertained and consoled. Now that these aristocracies have either been eliminated or have lost all political influence, this necessity no longer exists. Why, if this be not so, should ambassadors be provided with large houses and an entertainment account? Yet whom are they supposed to entertain?

These questions are more pertinent than they seem. In totalitarian countries the names of those who visit foreign embassies are reported to the police. Those whose ambitions or livelihood are dependent on the favor of their superiors do not wish to fall into disfavor by frequenting foreign embassies. Therefore the operative people hesitate to attend embassy parties, or if they do so, arrive in a gang, so that they can all watch each other. Conversely, the ambassador, being anxious to cultivate the good will of those in power, is afraid of seeing too much of the Opposition. In Tsarist Russia, for instance, an ambassador could not ask the liberal leaders to dinner without risking the displeasure of the Court. In free countries this danger does not occur and the members of the government neither know nor care who dines or lunches at the French, Russian or German Embassies. It may arise, however, especially in totalitarian countries, that only unimportant people go to the embassy parties and that these parties tend to degenerate into stagnant pools in which the same old carp circle round and round gazing at each other with lacklustre eyes. Yet the theory persists that a great country should possess a great embassy; that the greatness of that embassy can be assessed by the size of its entertainment; and thus the dreary old round continues to persist, whether those who are entertained are influential

or not. Diplomatic parties are invariably dull parties, since they lack spontaneity. Ambassadors, I suggest, would be well advised to invite important people to small parties of five or six, and to satisfy the multitude by large occasional receptions to which numbers of people can boast of having been asked.

Should the junior members of the staff confine themselves to the accepted circle of embassy guests or should they go out into the wilds? It may require deep devotion to his profession, or a passionate interest in the works of Ibsen, to persuade a young man at an embassy in Oslo to mix with Norwegian society. My own advice to the junior diplomatist is not to confine himself lazily to the easy circle of his own embassy but to cultivate the society of journalists both foreign and native. It is from them that he will derive useful advice and commentary. When I look back on the years before Hitler that I spent in the British Embassy at Berlin, I am grateful for the hours I devoted to talking to journalists in the Adlon Bar. I learned more from them than I did from any other form of social relations. Had I spent an equal amount of time discussing the future with trade-union leaders or factory workers, I should have derived false impressions. Nobody could then have foreseen that the trade-union movement with its elaborate organization could have been swept aside by Hitler's rhetoric in the course of a few days. It was the journalists of the Adlon Bar who first warned me of the coming of the Nazi movement. Diplomatic field work often misleads.

While I contend, therefore, that an ambassador and his senior officials need not, and indeed ought not, to be too closely identified with the country to which they are accredited, and while I agree that the social or representative aspect of diplomacy needs to be reëxamined and possibly revalued, I assert that the old principle that the art of negotiation depends on reliability and confidence is an eternal principle, however much one's antagonists may profit by temporary tricks. I have frequently written that good diplomacy is akin to sound banking and depends on credit. Even if your opponent scores a trick or two by sharp practice, you should yourself abide by the rules of the game. I remember once, when appointed to the Middle East, asking my father, who had had great experience of the problem, by what means one could ascertain what went on at the back of the oriental mind. "Never worry about that," he answered. "There may be nothing at the back of his mind. Concentrate on making quite sure that he is left in no doubt as to what is at the back of *your* mind." That was good advice. The twists and turning of an oriental mentality constitute a labyrinth which it is useless to penetrate or explore; let the straight and simple lines remain on your side of the argument; however much you may try, you will never be able to weave a pattern as intricate as theirs. There will always be an area of deception into which the Westerner will hesitate to enter; it would be like playing

poker with a man a hundred times richer than oneself; it is advisable therefore for the Westerner to stick always to truth, in the expenditure of which he possesses ample reserves. His actions will in any case be misrepresented; if they be based on demonstrable truth, then the misrepresentation will be apparent even to the least educated.

### IV

It is often said, again, that with the development of communications the role and function of an ambassador have been much diminished and that the diplomatist today has been reduced to the status of a clerk at the end of the telephone line. In the first place, the telephone is a dangerous little instrument through which to convey information or to transmit instructions. One of the most important assets of sound diplomacy is precision; the telephone (as was demonstrated by the U-2 incident) is an imprecise instrument, and liable to create misunderstanding.

Moreover, a moment's reflection should convince people that the gibe about "a clerk at the end of the telephone" is an empty gibe. It may be true that it is no longer possible for an ambassador at some distant post to create situations that may lead either to his repudiation or recall, or else to war. That is a great gain. It may be true that the independence of his action may be curtailed, and rightly curtailed, by the fact that his own chief in London or Washington can reach him on the telephone or, if the worst comes to the worst, can descend upon him in an airplane. But the fact remains, and will always remain, that the man on the spot is in a key position and that no action should be taken at headquarters without his advice being sought. No large business undertaking, no newspaper, would be represented in a foreign capital by a man whose stature was no higher than that of a clerk at the end of a telephone. It is the business of a representative abroad to study local conditions; to assess the areas of local susceptibility; to cultivate the acquaintance of local politicians, and thus to be in a position to advise his own minister how far he can go and how far he can trust those with whom he is negotiating. In offering such advice he will rely on the information furnished him by his own experts, upon his personal contacts with local politicians, upon a careful study of the local press, and upon exchanges of views and information with his diplomatic colleagues and resident press correspondents. Again and again have I heard the slogan that ambassadors today have ceased to count. I do not hear a similar statement applied to the local representatives of large firms or newspapers. Yet the position is identical. You do not send abroad a clerk to represent you; you send a man in whose intelligence, initiative and integrity you place full confidence. The only difference today is that things move with great celerity. There is less time for reflection.

Another element of change is the use made today in international negotiation of the weapon of propaganda. In the old days when foreign affairs were recognized to be a specialized study and when their conduct was left to the experts, the element of propaganda scarcely entered into consideration. Today it is sometimes preponderant. It is a dangerous weapon, being all too apt to backfire or recoil. It is one which our antagonists, by concentrating on the shadows of the past and by indicating the sunshine of a Communist future, can employ with great effect. There is, moreover, always an element in propaganda which is exaggerated and untrue; the West finds such assaults more difficult than does the East. Yet here again truth will prevail in the end. Our attitude toward propaganda must always remain a defensive attitude; we must content ourselves with being scrupulously careful not to present our antagonists with propaganda weapons against us. It is admittedly unfortunate that in the propaganda war the East appears to win all the battles all the time. Owing to a series of small successes, of accidental triumphs, they build up an aggregate impression of invincibility and inevitability. This is the impression which they desire to convey and we desire to avoid. It is a difficult task but not one that can be accomplished by telling untruths. The Communists are convinced that there is a "glorious lie," or a "mass untruth," which "becomes true" since it serves the cause of Communism. Yet the saying of Abraham Lincoln remains true: you can't fool all the people all of the time. The misfortune is that one can fool a large number of people for sufficient time for great damage to be done. I admit that the introduction of the propaganda element has greatly complicated the task of Western diplomacy. It is easy enough to convince uneducated people that they are being exploited or suffering humiliations and oppression. It is more difficult to preach to them the rewards of freedom. People who have been convinced that their rights have been disregarded will be glad to throw stones at windows or to overturn motorcars; the doctrine of individual liberty inspires no such acts of passion. We are at a disadvantage when it comes to applying propaganda to the have-nots. Dollars are not always enough; and the fact that our doctrine appeals more to the privileged classes is a fact which cannot be exploited or even avowed.

The principle of egalitarianism has altered the balance of diplomatic power. Even within my own lifetime the affairs of the world were dominated by the eight great powers, whose strength, when it came to a conflict, was overwhelming. The British Government, for instance, could change the whole balance of the Eastern Question by dispatching three frigates to Besika Bay. Today action on the part of the great powers could, even if they were united, be blocked by the votes of the small powers. The Security Council of the United Nations was intended to be a sort of cabinet of action. Its decisions are negatived,

however, by the veto of the Soviet Union, a veto which to date has been exercised 95 times. Thus the power of decision has been to all intents and purposes transferred to the Assembly, in which a majority of the 99 nations represented can block all action. This majority, while not invariably adhering to the Russian line, is at least united in hostility to anything that savors of the old colonialism. Thus power has been transferred into the hands of those who lack strength, and a situation has been created which is dominated by uncertainty. Uncertainty and the unpredictable are dangerous elements in any international situation. It is impossible to conduct sound banking when there exists no stability of exchange.

## V

The former theory of the balance of power, the device of the Concert of Europe, has, since the First World War, been replaced by international tribunals, such as the League of Nations and the United Nations. It was not foreseen by those who drafted the Charter at San Francisco 15 years ago that the principle of one-state-one-vote might in the end prove irrational. Today the votes of the 99 sovereign states in the Assembly bear no relation to the amount of power they can exercise or the degree of responsibility they can assume. The strength of the United Nations is subject to so many variables that the exercise of its authority is unpredictable. Valuable as the tribunal ought to be in arranging for the pacific settlement of disputes, the incidence of its authority is too uncertain to give its decisions the inevitability of public law. The veto has paralyzed the Executive and the voting system may paralyze the Assembly. The major decisions in this world are taken by those who possess power and are prepared to exercise it. The substitution of consent, or votes, for force has given the United Nations a certain unreality which hampers its authority.

The principle of one-man-one-vote is conditional on the existence of the rule of law. But there is no international rule of law, only a few accepted conventions; thus it is fallacious to suppose that peace can be preserved by votes. The fact that the world is obliged to rely for peace on an organization that so obviously lacks realism, if not reality, is a major misfortune. I do not blame those who 15 years ago drafted the Charter. In many ways it is an honest and competent document. Yet the gap which has been created between reality and unreality constitutes a serious menace. Would it be better to admit that the future of the world depends upon the force that can be brought to bear by the U.S.S.R. and the United States? I fear that I am unable to recommend anything other than this stark reality.

The pessimism implicit in such a conclusion does not mean that

I believe international diplomacy has no part to play or that the nations of the world are entirely dependent upon what may be willed or decided in Moscow or in Washington. It means that the nations of the world, and especially of the Western world, should avoid separating practice from principle, as was done at the time of Suez and Cuba, and should avoid placing themselves in the wrong. There does exist such a thing as international morality. Its boundaries are not visibly defined nor its frontiers demarcated; yet we all know where it is. If other countries transgress these frontiers, we at least should respect them. *Aliis licet: tibi non licet.* That is to say, what is right for others is not right for us. That should be our motto; by that we shall in the end prevail.

# 70 / American Foreign Policy — Freedoms and Restraints

RAYMOND ARON

It is a truism that we rarely see ourselves as others see us. American views of United States diplomacy are prone to a dangerously misleading subjectivity. Thus, there is value in giving attention to the views of a perceptive foreign observer. In this selection, the author incisively analyzes American diplomacy, its strengths and weaknesses.

HOW DOES AMERICAN diplomacy look to a European observer who is well disposed to the United States? I do not feel really qualified to answer this question . . . because I know too many of the men responsible for American policy and have been in Washington too often to share some of the illusions and fears prevailing in Europe. If I were to give my own personal interpretation of "United States diplomacy," it would probably resemble that of some Americans rather than typify a European point of view. It may be more useful, therefore, to summarize the

Reprinted from *Daedalus,* Journal of the American Academy of Arts and Sciences, XCI, 4 (Fall, 1962), 717–32. By permission of the American Academy of Arts and Sciences and the author.

Raymond Aron, a leading French scholar in the field of international affairs, is professor in the Faculty of Letters, University of Paris. He is a member of the Institut d'Etudes Politiques and a contributor to *Le Figaro.* His many publications include *The Century of Total War* (1954) and *On War* (1958).

criticisms most frequently leveled at American diplomacy by various European schools of thought. A discussion of these criticisms may help enlighten American readers about the attitudes of their allies in the Old World.

Let us start with a proposition that is obvious but often overlooked: the United States has and must have a world-wide diplomacy, whereas European nations, even Great Britain and France, no longer have the resources required for action on a world scale. When France was at war in Indochina, she depended even more on the United States, because she was incapable of carrying on the war without transatlantic military and financial aid.

This difference between a world-wide perspective and a purely European one has been responsible for misunderstandings and tensions between the United States and its European allies. It could not be otherwise. Europeans would have thought it normal for the United States, as an ally, to take sides with them under all circumstances; but viewed from Washington, the Atlantic partners appear merely as links in a chain surrounding the Soviet Union. Of course there is a greater agreement on moral ideals between western Europe and the United States than there is between the United States and any Latin American or Asiatic nation, even if officially allied to the American Republic. Of all the treaties signed by the United States since 1945, the Atlantic Pact is the most important. It is the foundation of the entire American system of alliances. Nevertheless, it is one instrument of action among others, and no United States administration has thought of carrying out the formula, so often suggested by French leaders, to extend the sphere of the Atlantic Pact to the rest of the world. French ministers might demand, "Is it possible to be allies in the heart of Europe and not in the Near East?" "Certainly," American spokesmen (Democrats or Republicans) might have replied, had they chosen to be frank. At the time of the Suez crisis, the American stand against the British and French in support of President Nasser was a striking demonstration, not of American duplicity, but of the dualism, or better, the pluralism of the considerations the President of the United States must bear in mind. The ultimate goal is the same everywhere: to contain the power of Soviet Russia and prevent the growth of Communist regimes, but the means employed may be in Europe the Atlantic Pact, and in the Near East, concessions to Arab nationalism, however anticolonial and anti-European those means may be.

We may summarize this rapid preliminary analysis by stating that the object of American diplomacy throughout the entire world is to oppose the principal enemy, the U.S.S.R. (or the Russo-Chinese bloc).[1]

---

[1] The United States has not yet taken into account the split between Moscow and Peking.

The United States, therefore, refuses to subordinate its actions to the preferences and interests of its allies, even if they are partners in a regional pact. Specifically, the United States has always sympathized with movements of national liberation and with anticolonial ideologies, being always sufficiently discreet not to provoke the indignation of the particular colonial power involved and sufficiently frank not to abandon to the Soviets a monopoly of the words assumed to be popular in the Afro-Asian nations.

Inevitably and logically, Europeans who refuse to "liquidate the empire" or to "free oppressed peoples" have felt American policy to be a threat. Oddly enough, the men of the European Left, especially in France, ought to have agreed with American policy (despite their anti-Americanism) because it was anticolonial, but they have seldom recognized that they share this attitude, and they have almost never expressed it. United States' support of France in Indochina after 1950 also provided ammunition for those who denounced "American imperialism" and wished to ignore the anticolonial intentions of the United States.

American diplomacy, concerned with all five continents, must express the wishes, not of a prince and his advisers, but of the most talkative and on surface the most incoherent political system in the world. In the last months of 1950, while the Eighth Army was fighting a hard war against the North Koreans and the Chinese volunteers, scarcely a day passed without some general or Senator airing militant views which rocked the boat in political circles in Washington and made the British, whose diplomatic style still bears the stamp of aristocratic traditions, tremble. The sudden trip of Clement Attlee to Washington in November 1950 was caused by rumors (growing out of indiscretion) about the eventual use of atomic weapons in Korea. The polemic on Cuba between John F. Kennedy and Richard M. Nixon during the presidential campaign of 1960 is another example of the "democratic style" of American diplomacy, which is deplorable in foreign eyes. The television exchange between the two candidates about Quemoy and Matsu is another example of American diplomatic practice which is easier to denounce than to change.

President Kennedy has issued several directives with the object of reducing the number of American spokesmen on foreign policy as well as controlling their oratory and their imagination. Generals and admirals are to submit their speeches to official screening. A Senate committee is investigating this abridgement of free expression, and it wonders whether it is constitutional thus to muzzle free citizens of the United States. I hope the American reader will not accuse me of meddling in domestic affairs if I indicate my approval of this "preventive censoring." In spite of everything, American diplomacy will continue to

be noisy, controversial, and hotly contested, with a single man who must make great decisions at any moment but tens of hundreds of men who believe themselves qualified to declare policy, denounce it, influence it, correct it, or comment on it.

So much for criticisms aimed at obvious contradictions in the diplomacy of a nation which has only one enemy and many allies, the diplomacy of the most verbose democracy in history. These weaknesses result from the nature of both the United States and of the world as it actually is.

If we except Communists and radical reformers, having already excepted the defenders of Empire, the majority of Europeans all but unanimously agree with the goals of American diplomacy: to contain the expansion of Communism without risking general war, or, if one prefers, to contain Communism by reducing the risks of a general war to a minimum. What are the principal criticisms of the means adopted to carry out these goals, of the method of action in general? For purposes of analysis, one might say there are two types of criticisms: those of the so-called realists, and those of the so-called idealists.

The objections of the realist school obviously vary with the different phases of American policy. They think that during the war American diplomacy was led astray by a failure to understand the nature of the Soviet regime. President Roosevelt was anxious to win the war as fast and as cheaply as possible. He postponed the problem of the political organization of the world until after the victory. He did not see that the conduct of operations and the strategy adopted at the time predetermined the peace settlement. Thus the United States allowed the Soviet Union to "liberate" and "Sovietize" Eastern Europe even while the United States kept a monopoly of atomic weapons. If I may paraphrase Sir Winston Churchill, never has a state had such a superior force and taken so little advantage of it. In 1945, however, the great concern of the United States was "to bring the boys home." A diplomat, nostalgic for the old days, asks wistfully, "How can one trust the fate of the West to a republic which sacrifices half of Europe to appease popular and political clamor?"

From 1945 to 1950, the realists say, the United States allowed the Communist parties to carry out revolutions managed from above to their logical conclusion unchecked. It was capable neither of supporting Chiang Kai-shek nor of abandoning him to his destiny. The Americans hastened to demobilize their army and their naval and air fleets but not to produce the atomic weapons on which American superiority rested. Not until the Korean War did President Truman make the decision to rearm seriously and turn a deaf ear to "economists" who thought inflation a greater threat than the Soviet Union and who foresaw the end of "free enterprise" if the day should come when the budget for national

defense broke the ceiling of $15 billion. The ceiling of $50 billion was broken for the year 1962–1963, and free enterprise survives.

In the period 1948 to 1962, the European realists would reproach American diplomacy for having been "timid," for having abandoned the initiative to the Soviets, and for never having tried to win a real victory. In 1948, when the Russians, using the pretext of technical difficulties, gradually established the blockade of Berlin, American diplomacy sought and found a way out in the air lift, but it did not risk sending an armed convoy to break the blockade. In Korea, the United States leaders ceased military operations and consented to armistice negotiations as soon as Moscow expressed a desire to negotiate—in the spring of 1951. For a war between the United States and North Korea (aided by Chinese volunteers) to end in a stalemate and not in American victory was in the eyes of the world the equivalent of a defeat for the nation supposed to be the strongest on earth. Similarly, in the second Berlin crisis since 1958, American diplomacy has constantly made moves toward negotiation "under threat of force," whereas (according to General de Gaulle) all that would have been needed was to "stand firm" until Moscow had stopped threatening and a calm atmosphere appropriate to peaceful talks had been restored. We shall return later to the dialogue between the Europeans and the new administration of President Kennedy. Suffice it to say that, to the realist school of European critics, American diplomacy—in the years when United States territory was safe from attack and when the Strategic Air Command was capable of striking at Soviet territory—erred by ineptitude or by an excess of caution, so that it was not able to win in Korea, and it did not choose to aid the Hungarian rebels.[2]

At present (1962), the realists attack particularly the conduct of American diplomacy toward the uncommitted nations and the United Nations. In this respect General de Gaulle is a good spokesman for the realist school. The European realist does not at all dispute the idea that the United States should keep in touch with the Afro-Asian nations as much as possible and influence them away from the Soviet bloc. What he questions is the conception of competing for the allegiance of the uncommitted nations formulated by the American diplomat, and the methods he uses to win out over his rival.

Is it wise to give representatives of the new nations an exaggerated idea of their own importance? Is it right to let them believe that their words or commitments will seriously affect the relationships of world power? Is it advisable to flatter them and suggest that we need them,

---

[2] Is it necessary to add that, if American diplomacy had done or attempted to do what the realist school reproaches it for not doing, many Europeans, probably a majority, would have accused the United States of warmongering?

when they in fact need us much more? Furthermore, American opinion (including diplomatic opinion) tends to picture the uncommitted nations as choosing sides according to their sentiments and according to the morality and generosity they see in the great powers, while in fact they are or will be affected much more by their passions or their guesses about the outcome of the struggle. To the European realist, nothing seems more ridiculous than the attention paid by the State Department or the White House to what they call "world opinion."

There is no such thing as world opinion on the political level. The representatives of the uncommitted nations meeting in Belgrade did not condemn the Soviet resumption of nuclear tests, but they would have denounced the United States indignantly if it had taken the same initiative. Why this double standard, to use an American expression? There are several reasons, and different critics would choose a different combination: the uncommitted nations are more afraid of the U.S.S.R. than of the United States, they know the Soviets are less sensitive to moral condemnation, they are naturally more anti-capitalist than anti-Communist. They know that positive neutralism—that is, noncommitment expressed in language closer to the language of the Soviets than to that of the West, in general pays off. Positive neutralism, shrewdly practiced, often leads to competitive bidding among the great powers for the good will of the neutrals, even to competitive financial generosity. The lesson is simple: the uncommitted nations are not the arbiters of justice and injustice; popular opinion and the opinion of politicians is no more impartial in the neutral world than in the West or in the Soviet bloc. Where is that world opinion to which Adlai Stevenson is so sensitive, outside his imagination? The realists would say, "Let the United States do what its own defense and that of the free world requires and stop being frightened by a phantom."

The American attitude toward the United Nations falls under the same criticism. What basis is there for attributing to the votes of the General Assembly, at present consisting of the delegates of one hundred and four states, a superior value to decisions taken by the states or by a bloc of states? The members of the United Nations behave in New York as they do elsewhere. They are selfish, seeking their own advantage, power, or prestige. What results from their debates is not the "general will" dreamed of by Jean-Jacques Rousseau, it is not always even a fair compromise, but rather an equivocal text on which a majority was able to agree because in its last precise formulation the text was unacceptable only to a minority.

It is true that a considerable number of American diplomats have no illusions about the United Nations. President Kennedy referred to the world organization as "a hope and an instrument." Setting aside the hope, the instrument remains. Mr. Khrushchev attacked the instrument

because it made it possible for the Anglo-French Suez operation to be liquidated without too much damage, because it maintained a degree of peace on the frontiers between Israel and her neighbors, and because in the Congo it aided the formation of a government which wished to be moderate and neutral.

This reasoning would not convince the realists, for whom General de Gaulle is a leading spokesman. They would say that the Congo problem should have been handled by the coordinate action of the powers directly concerned. In the opinion of the French President, United Nations intervention adds the confusion of the protector to the chaos of the protected. The United States will not allow itself to intervene openly and frankly, but it subjects itself to the opinion of the majority in the Security Council or the General Assembly. This means that the international community is dependent on contingents from Ethiopia or Ghana to establish order, even to bring Tshombe into line.

Even if the United Nations finally succeeds, even if Kasavubu and Adoula eventually establish a power acceptable to the West, to the neutral nations, and to the Congolese alike, General de Gaulle would not think in retrospect that he had been wrong and the White House right. As an instrument of diplomatic action, the international organization would still seem to him to be burdened with all the defects of parliamentary politics, at the mercy of demagoguery and disorder. Rational diplomacy is diplomacy that is quietly but firmly conducted by the great powers, disregarding the outcries of newspapers, the invective of the Kremlin, and the factitious indignation of the new masters of new nations. If it were argued that Western intervention in the Congo would have provoked intervention by the Soviet bloc, General de Gaulle would reply that the Kremlin has neither the means nor the wish to commit itself seriously in central Africa.

In short, in the opinion of European realists, American diplomacy was not able to foresee postwar problems during the hostilities, nor was it able to exploit its own superior resources in the early postwar period. American diplomacy maintained a defensive position, sometimes clumsy and always timid, when it could have taken the initiative. It was satisfied merely not to lose in Berlin and in Korea, and never did it either take the risks or face the cost of a winning policy. Today, with the uncommitted nations the subject of rivalry between the two blocs, American diplomacy confuses support of the United Nations (at best a tactical measure, useful in some circumstances) with development of strategy, and, by fearing a world opinion which exists only in the minds of some diplomats, it subjects United States action to a ridiculous concern with prestige, to the anticolonial or anti-Western prejudices of the transient leaders of states which owe their existence (more ficti-

tious than real) to the distintegration of European empires and to the rival ideologies of the two great powers.

The interpretation of United States diplomacy by the idealist school, although perhaps not contradictory to the foregoing, is quite different. It has four main themes, in my opinion. (1) *The anti-Communist obsession* has degenerated into excessive fear of the danger created by the men and ideas of the Kremlin. There are several expressions of this obsession and various arguments against it. In New Delhi one of the most influential newspapermen, speaking of American diplomacy, told me, "By crying 'wolf' when there is none, the United States may end by speaking to deaf ears when the wolf appears." In Europe, a dozen years ago, the French equivalent of the Indian journalist would probably have said, "American diplomacy acts as if there were imminent danger of military aggression from the East, whereas the Communist danger, if there is one, is more political than military, more a long-range threat than an immediate one." This school would add that the effectiveness of all the measures taken by American diplomacy, including the justifiable ones, is blunted because anti-Communism rather than a positive policy seems to be both their cause and their goal.

(2) Communism being not only the primary but virtually the absolute enemy, *any government, even a reactionary one, seems worthy of American support if it is or seems to be the only alternative to power in the hands of men oriented toward Moscow.* The best informed critics of the idealist school would recognize that in certain cases American diplomacy did not have much choice, that a despot or a military oligarchy was the only possible alternative for the exercise of power excluding Communists or radical reformers. Critics would maintain, however, that sometimes American diplomacy unduly restricts its own choices by equating radical reformers with Communists, and at other times it adapts itself too easily to a despotism which is neither necessary nor inevitable until it becomes intolerable and is overthrown by a popular revolt. When the leaders of such a revolt reproach Washington for leniency toward despotism and thus appear to be anti-American, they are treated as enemies by American diplomats. In this way the United States risks being considered an ally of reaction and an enemy of progress. The result is that a movement like the Cuban revolution slides into Moscow's camp.

(3) Cuba illustrates another error committed by American diplomacy over the years: that of putting too much confidence in alliances or military pacts. Up to 1945 American diplomacy remained faithful to the tradition of avoiding alliances or commitments which would limit American freedom of action. This tradition is composed of two distinct elements: the desire to avoid international conflicts (isolationism), and concern not to be bound by agreements made in advance. It asserted

itself again after World War I and was responsible for the Senate's rejection of the Treaty of Versailles and of membership in the League of Nations. Since 1945 the United States, glorifying what it had condemned, has indefatigably accumulated treaties: the North Atlantic Pact, the South-East Asia Pact, the Reciprocal Defense Pacts with South Korea, Japan, the Philippines, Australia, and New Zealand. In South America, under the pretext of defending the hemisphere against military aggression (one wonders from where) the United States has supplied arms to all governments of whatever stamp. Fidel Castro's guerrillas fought against tanks furnished to Batista by the Pentagon. Further afield, critics wonder whether a pact with or the supply of arms to Pakistan helped to stabilize the situation, or whether on the contrary they did not provoke a kind of local arms race between the two successor states to British India.

(4) Finally, the idealists consider American diplomacy to have been exceptionally rigid, especially in John Foster Dulles' time. In Asia, more than ten years after the assumption of power by Mao Tse-tung, American diplomacy stubbornly continues to recognize the survivors of the Nationalist Chinese regime in Formosa as the legitimate government of China, even though they are incapable of setting foot in it. Perhaps the reader will object that American policy should not be accused of being at the same time too lenient toward the neutrals and too rigid toward the Soviet Union and Communist China, but this is in fact the image of American foreign policy abroad: it stands firm in Quemoy and Matsu, it forbids Japan and the Philippines to renew diplomatic relations with Communist China, and on the other hand it supports Nasser against the British and French after the nationalization of the Suez canal. To be sure, John Foster Dulles refused to finance the high dam at Aswan, and even based his refusal on arguments which could not but hurt the Egyptian president, but apart from this decision, expressed in an unnecessarily aggressive style, American diplomacy, because of its anti-Communist obsession, is always ready to make concessions to the neutral uncommitted nations in the hope of preventing them from making a commitment against the West.

At this point the idealists end up by joining the realists. What the former explain by the anti-Communist obsession, the latter explain by weakness or confusion, but they both hold it against American diplomacy that the United States seems less concerned to remain faithful to its friends than to please the uncommitted or somewhat hostile nations. The realists see in this a sign of mistaken idealism, a respect for "world opinion," which is invented to meet United States needs; the idealists denounce it as a result of the anti-Communist obsession. In the last analysis, the allies of the United States (the European allies, for example) are least likely to slide into Communism, and the neutrals, even

if they are unfriendly, are most likely to commit themselves to the other side. If American diplomats seem at times to pay more attention to the neutrals than to the allies, it is not because they prefer the former, but because they are more afraid that the neutrals may decide to take the fatal plunge of adhesion to the Communist bloc. In this sense, the hierarchy of importance established by American diplomacy seems to be an inversion rather than an expression of the hierarchy of friendship. The uncommitted nations have the advantage of being the most removed from American affections, with the sole exception of the Communists. Fidel Castro could have gained much if he had stayed on the threshold instead of entering the temple.

Let us summarize the two types of criticism and try first to discern the valuable elements they have in common, and then to see how other elements cancel out by contradicting one another, so to speak. In the realist criticism, there are two themes which are generally accepted by enlightened opinion, even in the United States: the conduct of the war by Franklin D. Roosevelt and his administration was dictated by strictly military considerations and showed an absolute indifference to the problems of the peace. Everything that happened seemed to indicate that the American President did not understand the long-range implications of the various ways in which the war could be won. Similarly, there is no doubt that in 1945, after the capitulation of Japan, the United States demobilized too fast and did not know how to use the striking superiority it had at the time to prevent the sovietization of eastern Europe and impose a just settlement.

What can be argued is the extent to which these errors were *necessary*. Could Roosevelt have followed Sir Winston Churchill's suggestion of a major operation in the Balkans in order not to let eastern Europe be "liberated" by the Red army alone? Could he have placed less confidence in Stalin, or at least left his successor instructions to reverse the policy imposed by the war against Germany as soon as possible? Could Truman not have resisted the demand to "bring the boys home" and thus have saved eastern Europe from sovietization by using threats, if not force? It would be futile to pretend to give categorical answers to these questions. What is indisputable is that between 1941 and 1945 American diplomacy had only one enemy, Hitler's Germany, that from 1945 to 1948 it deprived itself of the military means it actually had, which a great power cannot do without, following a war which had put the territorial settlement of the entire planet at stake.

Concerning the period 1948 to 1958, both the realists and the idealists are right; American diplomacy acted with moderation but sometimes spoke in extremes. Obsessed with anti-Communism, the United States took a minimum of risks and maintained a consistently defensive policy. It avoided the dangers of action even when it could have brought

victory, not merely avoiding defeat. Not even in such cases would the United States risk the cost. Could not American vision have been broader? Could not the United States' objective have been to defeat the "Chinese volunteers" and not merely to repulse the North Koreans? Was a local military victory possible without a serious risk of spreading the war? I am tempted, with hindsight, to give affirmative answers to these questions, but I am not sure that this was my conviction at the time, and I am sure that more dynamic action would have been denounced as aggression and warmongering by a majority of Europeans. In other words, the realists are not wrong in suggesting that the United States could have taken greater advantage of its superiority, and the idealists are not wrong in stressing the rigidity of American diplomacy and its obsession with anti-Communism. Both would be wrong to forget, however, that the foreign actions of the United States in Europe and in Asia were essentially in line with the ideas of moderate Europeans.[3] Action was defensive because the Western democracies had no desire for conquest or reconquest, and, in a test of force between democracies and totalitarian regimes, it is always the latter who take the offensive. The action was finally cautious and in no way warlike, not because the United States is a "paper tiger," but because its only goal was to contain communist expansion.[4]

We come then to the last theme on which the idealists and realists meet, although they do not use the same words or formulate the same reproaches: the American attitude toward the uncommitted world. In fact, it is useful to distinguish between different times and various regions of the world. In Africa and in Asia the United States was dealing with the colonies of its European allies. It wanted to show its sympathy for movements of national liberation without breaking the Atlantic Pact. Even though the Europeans more than once cursed the powerful transatlantic ally, the United States can congratulate itself on having virtually accomplished the task it set itself. Decolonization is almost complete, and relations between the United States and its partners in the North Atlantic Pact are no worse than they were ten years ago. It may be that Portugal will prefer to leave the Atlantic alliance tomorrow rather than resign itself to decolonization, but even a break with Portugal (which is rather improbable) would be a failure of only secondary importance in a policy which has been on the whole successful.

Although American policy toward national liberation movements and European nations has been criticized by some as too favorable to the former and by others as too careful of the latter's feelings, the

---

[3] Errors of execution must also be excepted, like the possible misunderstanding of American intentions that was probably at the bottom of the Korean campaign.

[4] We pass over the main American defeat, the victory of the Communist party in China, because at the time Europeans were primarily absorbed in their own problems.

most serious crises have arisen in regions where it was not really a question of decolonization properly so-called, for example, on the occasion of the nationalization of the Suez canal by the Egyptian government. It is the general attitude of the United States toward the uncommitted nations which is criticized, an attitude dominated by anti-Communism and expressed in military pacts, in support of reactionary governments and in rabble-rousing rivalry with the Soviet Union, resulting eventually in concessions to the most determined of the neutral leaders.

The American leader may answer that the various expressions of the American attitude toward the uncommitted nations can be more or less justified by the circumstances. I willingly agree. It is easy to denounce the inadequacies of Diem's government in South Viet Nam, but it remains to be proved that any other would be better. Similarly, military pacts, even with countries not exposed to direct aggression, can be a means of reinforcing a weak government and of showing interest in the political fate of a new state. Only a detailed analysis would enable us to measure precisely the advantages and disadvantages of the measure taken in each case.

Having made these reservations, I am nonetheless inclined to support the fundamental objection: United States policy, because of its anti-Communist obsession, ends by giving the states it protects the feeling that the normal order is reversed. The protector state accepts conditions imposed by the protected states, as if in escaping Communism these states were doing a service to the United States rather than to themselves. American diplomacy would have everything to gain in dissipating the impression it has itself created that, wherever Communism is or seems to be a threat, the United States is ready to intervene with pacts, with dollars, even with soldiers. The fate of the United States does not depend on the domestic government of "Ruritania." The day when the State Department makes it clear that it is tired of "blackmail by threat of communism" and that it is determined not to yield to it any longer, a great step will have been taken.

Next, American policy should try to control its tendency to oscillate from one extreme to the other: yesterday hostile to neutrality, today resigned or even favorable to neutralism; yesterday accumulating military pacts, today concerned only with economic aid and alliance for progress; yesterday supporting any *de facto* government as long as it is anti-Communist, today trying to impose social reform and making such reform the condition of economic aid.

Finally and most importantly, American policy, even if it continues to act through the United Nations in some circumstances, should not be taken in by its own propaganda. Effective or not as an instrument, the United Nations is neither an impartial arbiter nor the expression

573

of a "universal conscience," nonexistent at present. Concessions to the neutrals in order to obtain a majority in the Security Council or the General Assembly run the danger of being ultimately too expensive. In serious matters like armament and disarmament, there is no need to pay much attention to the opinions or prejudices expressed on all occasions by the governments of states which do not share the responsibility. Even in matters of secondary importance, it would be wrong for the United States to show too much concern with the judgments of the uncommitted nations. On the world scene, it is not a good thing for the strong to perpetuate the farce of submission to the weak. The U.S.S.R. never plays such a game, and it is none the worse off. The competition between the Soviet Union and the United States is neither a tournament of morality nor a rivalry in generosity.

In conclusion, it may be useful to note briefly European reactions to the Kennedy administration. Let us skip the first months of the administration, dominated and darkened by the Cuban fiasco. Now, a year and a half after the inauguration, what are the distinctive characteristics of Kennedy's methods, that is, of a policy whose goals and principal means cannot be modified by a change of President?

In relation to the uncommitted world, I note three characteristic actions. The Alliance for Progress in Latin America shows an effort to make economic aid conditional on social reform. The action in South Viet Nam and Laos shows American willingness to make a virtual military commitment, if need be, to contain Communist subversion. Finally, the recourse to the United Nations in the Congo operation, the military support given by the United States to the United Nations forces opposing the secession of Katanga, can be interpreted in idealist terms (the United Nations is the guarantor of peace or the hope of mankind) but also in realist terms (in certain cases the United Nations is a useful instrument for preventing a direct clash between the two blocs). These three actions in Latin America, Southeast Asia, and the Congo suffice to show that the Kennedy administration is not dogmatic but is ready to use the language of social reform, the language of guns, or the language of international law, depending on the particular situation. This eclecticism or flexibility, once recognized for what it is, should be approved by moderate opinion in Europe. Up to the present time, critics have paid most attention to the third case, United States support of a *military* operation on the part of the United Nations.

As regards the Soviet Union, the originality of the Kennedy policy lies chiefly in the serious attention given to the ideas of academic specialists, especially in regard to arms, disarmament, or arms control. These ideas have been cautiously received in Europe, partly because they are not understood, but also because they are purely technical and overlook the political aspects of the problem.

The new administration is even more opposed than the Eisenhower administration to the spreading dissemination of atomic weapons, but its leaders did not consider in advance the probable reaction of the British, French, and Germans to a system in which Americans would retain exclusive control of nuclear weapons, while the Europeans devoted their resources to conventional weapons. Meanwhile, since the Russians have resumed testing, and since negotiations about stopping tests have definitely failed, the Kennedy administration is forced to "rethink" its policy. It is not enough to show that "rationally" a world with only two thermonuclear powers is more stable than a world with three or four deterrent forces; it is also necessary to convince both the allies and the neutrals that the possession of the decisive weapons should be reserved to the United States and the Soviet Union. I have never thought that the experts of the Massachusetts Institute of Technology or the Rand Corporation would succeed in convincing General de Gaulle, Mao Tse-tung, or even Mr. Strauss.

Imperfectly understood, the Pentagon's ideas have disturbed Europeans, who see in them the germ of a partial withdrawal. If Americans demanded of Europeans an increased effort in conventional arms, it would mean that they are no longer prepared to give Europeans protection by the threat of thermonuclear reprisals. The result is to draw a radical distinction between the Old World and American territory, the former not protected, the second protected by a deterrent force exclusively under the orders of the President of the United States.

At the present hour, President Kennedy's advisers are discovering that an *explicit* agreement between the Big Two to close the Atomic Club is not possible. They are learning that technically correct ideas may be politically inapplicable. In short, they are leaving the ivory towers and dealing with politics, measuring the distance between Cambridge and the White House, between the models of the game theory and the reasoning processes of statesmen. General de Gaulle never played poker at Princeton, and he probably has never opened the book of J. von Neumann and Morgenstern, but he knows the force of a "no" in a game where the rules forbid laying the cards on the table. Or, if you like, he knows the value of a refusal in a test of will which does not permit the open use of force. I am sure the day will soon come when these American leaders, their minds trained in rational disciplines, will make the inevitable concessions to others' motives, even if these appear irrational in their own eyes. On that day, the policy of the Kennedy administration will be grand.

# 71 / Diplomacy as an Instrument — A Secretary of State's View

DEAN RUSK

**It would be instructive to place oneself hypothetically in the shoes of an American Secretary of State in order to try to understand the problems of American foreign policy in the contemporary world, particularly the question of the limits and potentialities of actions by the United States. Perhaps even more instructive is the testimony of a Secretary of State as he discusses with a Senate committee the dimensions of American diplomacy. The following is such a statement.**

I SHOULD LIKE to note certain factors which suggest to me that our objective should be that of steady improvement in organization procedures, but that we would be deluding ourselves if we expected from such efforts miraculous differences in our relations with the rest of the world.

In foreign affairs we are dealing with a world which we can influence, but not control, and it is a world of rapid change. We do business now with more than 112 governments. During the present calendar year, there will have been elections or changes in government in more than 50 of them, including 10 of the 15 NATO countries.

If we are to get an accurate impression of that outside world, we should look at not less than 110 maps, each centered on one of the nations we deal with, reminding us that we are the center of the world only to ourselves, and that each nation looks outward from where it is.

I am not suggesting that we are not an important country. In fact, we ourselves should act on the basis that what we do is of the greatest importance, because that is the way of fulfilling our responsibility. Certainly in times of crisis our role is magnified, but in the ordinary flow of events our impact upon other countries is much less than we and others sometimes suppose.

Reprinted from Hearing, U. S. Senate Government Operations Subcommittee on National Security Staffing and Operations, 88th Cong., 1st sess., Part 6, December 11, 1963, pp. 386–92.

Dean Rusk has been Secretary of State in both the Kennedy and Johnson administrations. He was president of the Rockefeller Foundation and before that was an Assistant Secretary of State.

For example, the Alliance for Progress represents about 2 percent of the GNP of Latin America. The 2 percent can influence, but cannot determine what happens with the 98 percent. We cannot buy countries or their policies with 2 percent of their GNP or less than 1 percent of our own, nor would we wish to do so. In any event, minor changes in organization within our own Government will not resolve quarrels between neighbors in distant parts of the world, nor blunt the objectives of international communism, nor make the rest of the world more responsive to our wishes.

The elementary problem of organization, at least to one who has experienced and seen many reorganizations in Government, is to find men of the highest competence to deal with problems which tax human capacity to its limits. The real organization, contrasted with that erected by law and pictured in organization charts, is determined by the flow of confidence from top to bottom and the performance which earns that confidence from bottom to top.

I emphasize the quality of people, and there could be some debate on this, I am sure, because organization seldom stands in the way of good people and seldom converts mediocrity into excellent performance.

Further, I would support the view . . . that the organization of the U.S. Government for the conduct of its foreign relations cannot be effectively studied or significantly improved by an examination of the executive branch alone. The Congress is deeply involved in the conduct of our foreign relations. It plays a decisive role in all actions requiring men or money. It has a great deal to do with the ability of the Government to recruit the best talent and to move at the speed required by the rapidly changing international environment.

It had not been my purpose . . . to go into this aspect of the role of Congress as it applies to the subject before us, but I might mention two points which illustrate what I have just said.

We have had some discussion in recent weeks on amendments to the foreign aid bill, amendments which would have a decisive bearing upon our relations with a number of countries on a bilateral basis. The Executive has urged that the bill be as clean as possible. Now, one of the reasons for this is not just the traditional constitutional tension between the Executive and the Congress on such matters, but one of the reasons for this is that the legislative cycle is annual, at least annual, and events are moving much more rapidly than that annual cycle can deal with on a flexible and, I think, intelligent basis.

Along with that, when the legislature plays a card, that card is played and gone. We are thereby deprived of that card in our international negotiations and our international dealings. That lever is gone, and it is used.

Therefore, I hope that at some stage there can be discussion among

577

the appropriate committees of Congress as to the role which Congress itself plays in the conduct of our foreign relations, and not just in setting policies but in the conduct of our foreign relations, to see how that fits into the requirements of a fast-moving world situation.

Now, at the other end of the spectrum, a matter that is not nearly so important although sometimes more painful, there are eight or nine committees or subcommittees of the Congress interested in the administration of the Department of State. Those committees frequently disagree with each other on such matters as personnel. To one committee an individual becomes a person of the highest qualification and competence. To another committee, that person ought to be fired from the service.

From my point of view as Secretary of State, I cannot see any other answer but that committees of the Congress should be very careful about getting into those matters which are, by statute, a responsibility of the Secretary of State. Otherwise, these tensions among the committees of the Congress make administration difficult and sometimes almost impossible.

Let me come back now to what seemed to me to be the starting point of our problem. I mentioned doing business with more than 112 countries. I mentioned that in more than 50 of those there would have been elections and changes of government during this calendar year. Now, I suppose there would be 10 or 12 of those changes of government which were unscheduled. I don't say necessarily unpredicted or surprises, but at least unscheduled. That creates a turbulence in our scene which, if anything, is going to increase somewhat, because we will have at least 125 or 130 independent countries before this process ends.

The little island of Zanzibar becomes an independent state this month. How many islands of the Pacific will want to be independent states? The prospect here is to me unsettling, at least.

But this multiplication of states has greatly changed the conduct of business and foreign policy in the Department of State over the last 30 to 40 years. I am told that the Department of State receives every working day throughout the year about 1,300 incoming cables. I will see 20 to 30 of those on a usual day. We send out 1,000 cables a day, on every working day, and I will see perhaps 6 of those; the White House may see 1 or 2. So when the committee says that delegation is inevitable, this is entirely right. Junior officers in the Department today deal with and have to deal with matters which before World War II would have come to the Secretary of State. The desk officer is the key post in the Department in our bilateral relations with other countries.

I feel myself that we should find ways and means, and I have taken certain steps to do this in some test cases, of upgrading the standing and the experience of the desk officer. He is the man who has the op-

portunity to brood 24 hours a day about the problems of a particular country. It is he who in Government makes a decision when he puts on his hat at the end of the day and closes the door without having done a particular thing that might have been done that day. It is he who is in the best position to alert the Assistant Secretary or the Secretary that a problem is festering, that it needs attention, that there may be action to be taken to prevent a problem or there may be opportunities where by early attention we can sustain and promote American interests.

I think the State Department ought to move steadily toward—and this was implied also in one of your reports—the concept at least in its policy sections of all chiefs and no Indians, or at least far more chiefs and far fewer Indians. This would expedite and it would get greater attention and greater competence at points which are critically important in the conduct of our affairs, and would, I think, make it easier to get a broad understanding of policy and policy objectives through the machinery that actually is responsible for the conduct of our relations.

Then I would emphasize the role of the Assistant Secretaries, the next critical point. The Assistant Secretary at any given time may have 50 or 75 or 100 matters which should be of concern to him which ought to be on his worry list. Again, those higher up are somewhat at the mercy of the judgment of the Assistant Secretary, and his sensing of the art of policy in deciding what matters ought to be dealt with, and when.

I think we could all agree that there is a time for action and a time for letting a situation mature, but which is suitable in a given situation? When is a matter ripe for action? One can look at a worry list, as I have had occasion to do in the past, which is a year old. We used to use these lists when I was Assistant Secretary. If you look at a list that is a year old, it is really quite revealing to see what has happened to that list in the course of a year—which matters improved and which matters got worse, and which matters remained the same—and to find out whether there is any relation between your action or inaction and the course of events, and whether matters improved or worsened. At the end of a year, you can look back and decide that it might have been better to have left a particular item alone and it might have been better to have done something more about some other item. In this respect, the Assistant Secretary is in the crucial post in terms of the art of management of policy in our relations with the rest of the world.

Now, some, or most of our problems, in this tumultuous and, given modern weapons systems, increasingly dangerous world—most of our problems are not so much in the formulation of policy in its broadest sense, in its formulation of objectives. We are a certain kind of Nation and we are a certain kind of people. We have some well established

concepts of policy to which we are committed and, indeed, if Government strays too far away from those broadest concepts of policy, the American people have a very effective way of bringing it back into the mainstream of our national policy.

No one, for example, up or down the line thinks that the United States will make an agreement with the intention of breaking it. No one will suppose that we will not try to conduct ourselves to the maximum extent possible in accordance with the norms of international law. No one supposes that we take frivolously the commitments in the preamble and in articles I and II of the United Nations Charter. The general principles of policy are pretty well established and rooted deeply in the nature of our society. But these principles do conflict with each other in a given situation. They compete with each other, and in a tumultuous and highly controversial situation in some part of the world, the problem is how the principles bear upon that particular situation, which principles get priority.

It is the application of policy to particular situations that take almost all of our time. That means that we cannot always be verbally consistent in dealing with one situation as compared with another, because the situations themselves are contradictory. Therefore, if we support American interests in all of these situations, there will be times when our policy appears to be verbally inconsistent.

Now, in this process, it seems to me that there are two or three key points that need attention in addition to those indicated by the committee. The one is the matter of getting accurate and relevant information. The ghost that haunts the policy officer or haunts the man who makes the final decision is the question as to whether, in fact, he has in his mind all of the important elements that ought to bear upon his decision or whether there is a missing piece that he is not aware of that could have a decisive effect if it became known.

I think we can be proud of the extraordinary improvement in our intelligence- and information-gathering activities in the last 20 years. The need for it has been multiplied many times by the fragmentation of the world political structure, and the breadth, character, and depth of the information we need mounts steadily. When I was assigned to G-2 in 1941, well over a year after the war had started in Europe, I was asked to take charge of a new section that had been organized to cover everything from Afghanistan right through southern Asia, southeast Asia, Australia, and the Pacific. Because we had no intelligence organization that had been giving attention to that area up to that time, the materials available to me when I reported for duty consisted of a tourist handbook on India and Ceylon, a 1924 military attaché's report from London on the Indian Army, and a drawer full of clippings from the New York Times that had been gathered since World War I. That

was literally the resources of G-2 on that vast part of the world a year after the war in Europe had started.

We have greatly improved our ability to gather relevant information. However, our problem is how to get it to the people at the top. When a crisis occurs, it is then almost too late to educate those who have to make the decision. The great problem we have is to prepare the minds of those who are going to make decisions for the decisions that have not yet appeared. How does the educational process go on? There are many ways of doing it.

There are systematic daily publications of all classifications from the intelligence community which feed to the top. I spend a good deal of my own time reading these and find them invaluable. I have been greatly helped in the past year and a half by a series of one- or two-page intelligence notes on the greatest variety of questions. I may get 12, 15, or 20 of these in the course of a day—just little snippets of comment and information about what is going on here and there, coming out of the machinery that has available to it the widest range of information. Many of them look ahead to possibilities, because a part of this matter of information is to alert the leadership to what can happen and what the possibilities are in terms of alternative courses of action that might protect American interests in that contingency if it occurs in that way.

So I think that we need continually to work on the question of how to get information to those responsible for making the decisions in time to be of use to them. I emphasize the time factor. You can't go back and take a course in the problems of a particular area when you have to move within hours, or make a decision by not moving; so this is of some importance.

Then I think that we have a problem of how to get information to the Congress, since it does play a crucial role in our foreign affairs. I don't think we have fully found the answer to that question. Part of the problem is congressional time, because Senators and Congressmen have not only an interest in or responsibility for having judgments on these very complex matters of foreign relations, they also have a host of domestic problems before them, apart from the political processes by which they remain Senators and Congressmen.

So our problem is to find and expand the time made available by Senators and Congressmen to give us a chance to talk with them and get more information. We are more ready to talk to individuals or groups of Congressmen, than perhaps the Congress realizes. But we realize the limited time available to us. Through Mr. Dutton and others, and personal contacts by myself, I have indicated I would be glad to come down as often as I can get a hearing, in the most informal fashion, to talk over some of these problems for the information of the Congress.

We believe it critically important that Congress be in a position to understand the full flow, the full complexity and the full backdrop of particular problems, since its participation affects how we organize ourselves for national security and national security matters.

I would like to underscore what the committee has said about the responsibility of the top leadership for administration. I believe this is important, and I give administration a good deal of my own time because administration should not become a thing in itself, but should know that its purpose is to administer something called foreign policy, and that the end object of administration remains foreign policy. It is not just a machine of its own.

Secondly, administration involves choices in using short resources for potentially unlimited demands—for additional services and additional personnel. The normal trend, not necessarily a happy trend of large organizations, is to grow. Allocation of short resources among different needs and demands itself presents major policy questions in establishing the priorities, and I think only those who are responsible at the top ought to establish those priorities.

Last year, for example, I took a series of Saturdays throughout the fall conducting my own hearings on our budget. I had the responsible officers come in and talk about personnel and personnel assignments and budget, not only to prepare them but to prepare me for the presentations to the Bureau of the Budget and also in preparation for the hearings of the four committees of the Congress. I think the administration itself has a very important responsibility of leadership.

On the role of the Ambassador I might make this comment: I don't believe it is true that the role of an Ambassador has been diminished by the increase in the speed and expansion of communications. If you look back to the period when communications were slow or poor, the role of the Ambassador was not in my judgment nearly so important as his role today. One reason is connected with communications and the other is not.

The speed of communications greatly increases the pace of events. Therefore, the judgment of the man on the spot is just as important today as it was in clipper-ship days, because events are moving that much faster. There is almost never a week that passes when we don't have instances of a judgment that had to be made immediately on the spot by an Ambassador to deal with a situation before he could get this town to comment or give him instructions. I think that we ought to continue to set our sights on Ambassadors who have that capability even though there may be times when he is not called upon to use that capability in the most dramatic sense.

The other factor is that what the United States does in the world is so much more important now than it was 40 or 50 years ago, and

this, too, greatly enlarges the responsibility and role of the Ambassador.

The principal reason why Ambassadors have to refer back so many things to Washington is that if he were left alone to decide what should be done to strengthen to the maximum our bilateral relations with the country in which he is posted, we would have accumulated requirements upon the United States for men or money far exceeding the resources available to us. Further, there is a vast complex of relevant legislation on which the Ambassador himself can't be an expert, and he may not know whether we, in fact, are able to do what he would like to see us do.

Then there is a third element—sound foreign policy. This runs directly into important domestic policies and domestic interests. I say this not in a pejorative sense at all, because these domestic interests are real. But an Ambassador has to have judgment from Washington on such a matter as straightening out our problem with Mexico on the salinity of the Colorado River. He can't move on matters involving oil imports or textiles or similar problems without Washington making the decision in the light of all of the factors, domestic and foreign, that might be involved.

On the question of personnel abroad, we are making a very intensive study at the present time on the staffing of our embassies, beginning with some of the larger ones, and particularly regarding the staffing from other agencies of Government. I am concerned that there are at least 44 agencies of Government represented in our Embassy in London. I would hope the committee would give us a little time to sort that one out before it looks too closely at that situation, because I am reminded of a remark that General Marshall made to me when he was Secretary of State. He recalled that in 1923 the Army sent a special task force to Europe to locate a good many officers who were left behind on various missions at the end of World War I, and couldn't be located. They were drawing their pay, but for 5 years they had disappeared from sight, and so the Army sent a mission that was called the "live graves registration team" to locate these individuals.

Well, there is a little of that that has to be looked into at every stage, and we are trying to do something about it.

### SENATE SUBCOMMITTEE ON NATIONAL SECURITY STAFFING AND OPERATIONS

If the diplomat's traditional functions in recent times have changed radically, so has the size and scope of the job of the modern American ambassador abroad. He not only has to represent his country, negotiate, and report, but he also faces the enormous task of coordination and executive management of numerous disparate American agencies which may have representatives in his domain. This fact earns him the label "the harassed ambassador." The dimensions of this problem are sketched in this excerpt from a report of the U. S. Senate Government Operations Subcommittee on National Security Staffing and Operations (the Jackson Committee). The report follows testimony before the committee by numerous diplomatic officials.

I am sorry to know nothing more of the subject than that letter after letter has been written to you thereon, and that the office is in possession of nothing more than acknowledgements of your receipt of some of them so long ago as Aug. 1786, and still to add that your letter of Jan. 24, 1791, is the only one received of later date than May 6, 1789. You certainly will not wonder if the receipt of but one letter in two years & an half inspires a considerable degree of impatience.

Secretary of State Thomas Jefferson, Letter to William Carmichael, American Chargé in Spain, Nov. 6, 1791

SECRETARY JEFFERSON'S "impatience" with Mr. Carmichael is not likely to be echoed in 1964. Today the daily volume of telegraphic traffic alone between the State Department and the embassies is more than 400,000 words.

The jet plane and electronic communications on the one hand, and America's world involvements, on the other, have combined to complicate enormously and in part transform the role of American Ambassador.

The traditional functions—negotiation, representation, and reporting—have changed because issues can be referred rapidly to Wash-

Reprinted from U. S. Senate Government Operations Subcommittee on National Security Staffing and Operations, *Administration of National Security*, 88th Cong., 2d sess., Committee print (June 15, 1964), pp. 1–3.

ington, or handled by officers coming from Washington, or decided in Washington in talks with visiting heads of state, prime ministers, foreign ministers, or other high officials. If all roads once led to Rome, all airways now lead to Washington.

With respect to negotiation, the role of the modern Ambassador is much reduced—often he is but one part of a negotiating team in a complex diplomatic operation. If an issue is of some importance, the matter will probably be handled directly between the Department of State and the Foreign Office, with the Ambassador playing an intermediary or supporting role. When the Ambassador conducts negotiations, he will receive detailed instructions. To be sure, the modern Ambassador is not a mere onlooker—his advice will be sought. Particularly men in remote posts, off diplomacy's beaten tracks, or assigned to countries not at the top level of Washington concern, have some scope in practicing the art of negotiation. Even so the cables run hot and heavy, and it is a far cry from the day when an Ambassador had to operate alone for long periods, guided by his own wisdom and wit, with very general instructions.

With respect to representation, it used to be that an Ambassador represented his sovereign at the court of the other sovereign. Now things are different. An Ambassador still has the tedious round of official parties and entertainment. He must still participate in the pomp and ceremony of official life. But he must also hold the hands of newsmen, open doors for businessmen, and attend to visiting Congressmen. Besides, today's Ambassador is expected to get away from the capital and to acquire first-hand knowledge of the country's political, social and economic life. What the people are saying is often more important than the gossip of high society, and his business suits and even more informal attire may wear out sooner than his white tie and tails.

Posts, of course, vary greatly. In an emerging African nation, the host government may turn to the American Ambassador for advice on economics, or administration, or military affairs, or even internal political matters which would seldom, if ever, be sought by older and more established governments. In some areas, work with regional and international organizations is an added dimension for American diplomacy.

With respect to reporting, 50 years ago it may have been sufficient to cover the affairs of the court and the capital. No more. Now an Ambassador is called upon to view the society as a whole, to analyze the forces working for change, and to relate the problems of his country to wider problems and policies. Hence his reports must penetrate more deeply while the horizon of relevance has widened—and at the same time the number of reporters other than the Ambassador has grown with the number of agencies making up the American establishment.

Thus each of the elements of an Ambassador's traditional respon-

585

sibility has altered. Meanwhile, a new executive role has been laid upon our Ambassadors. Since World War II the American Executive Branch has reproduced itself abroad in something approaching its full panoply of separate agencies—with all that implies in terms of overlapping jurisdictions, incompatible assignments, mutual jealousies, surplus staff, and the ruminations of innumerable committees. Not only State, but AID, USIS, the service attachés (Army, Navy, and Air Force), military assistance advisory groups (MAAGS), CIA, Treasury, Agriculture, science attachés, and the Peace Corps may be found at our major posts. There may also be an area military commander.

In Britain, for example, with which we have old ties and many common interests, at least 44 American agencies are represented in the Embassy. In the Soviet Union, where the "court" is still a dominating fact of life, the American mission more nearly resembles the classic embassy with limited tasks. In Korea our involvement is recent but very deep and the American establishment includes sizable American forces and military bases as well as a host of civilian agencies.

Except for the Communist bloc and a few small posts where our responsibilities are limited, the number of agencies and operating programs demands on-the-spot coordination and central supervision, lest inter-agency pulling and hauling dissipate American influence.

To meet this need Washington has turned to the Ambassador, whose authority is reinforced by his Presidential appointment and diplomatic precedence. Gradually, if unevenly, since World War II, the Truman, Eisenhower, and especially the Kennedy Administrations have tried to build the Ambassador's coordinating role into our tradition and get it accepted in the day-to-day operations of government agencies.

But Washington giveth and Washington taketh away. In theory, the Ambassador is now more than *primus inter pares*. He is the active leader and director of American policies and programs. But practice often falls short, not least because Washington frequently undercuts the leadership and direction it asks him to provide.

In principle, our modern Chiefs of Mission are, like the President they serve, chief executives of large complex establishments, and as their other roles have changed—sometimes diminishing—this new executive role has come to the fore.

The result may be called the Ambassador's dilemma.

*One:* He is expected to perform his traditional diplomatic functions in a most untraditional setting, with less independence and less policy authority than Ambassadors once exercised—and with far more people under foot;

*Two:* He is expected to contribute to the policy process from the perspective of a single-country mission, while those at home who have to make the policies treat almost nothing as a single-country problem;

*Three:* He is expected to serve as leader and coordinator of his "country team" while lacking power or even much influence over the budgets, the personnel systems, the reporting requirements, and the operating policies of many of the field staffs theoretically subordinate to him.

His dilemma places a great burden on an Ambassador and ways must be found to improve and increase the support Washington gives him.

# 73 / *Impressions of a Recent Ambassadorial Experience*

GEORGE F. KENNAN

For a closer look at the operational problems of American diplomacy, one may with benefit turn to an eloquent ambassador serving in an important foreign capital. One such is the author of this selection, whose testimony below came at the culmination of two and a half years as United States ambassador to Yugoslavia, 1961–63. In the memorandum which follows, Mr. Kennan discusses the ambassador's relationship with other United States personnel assigned to the country in which the ambassador is chief of mission, the ambassador's relationship with Washington, with Congress, and the general restrictions under which he himself had to work.

## 1. The Position of the Ambassador with Relation to the Country Team

I assume that the members of the subcommittee will be interested, in the first instance, to have my impressions about relations between the

Reprinted from *Administration of National Security,* Hearing, U. S. Senate Government Operations Subcommittee on National Security Staffing and Operations, 88th Cong., 1st sess., Part 5 (December 11, 1963), pp. 358–63.

George F. Kennan has had a dual career as diplomat and distinguished historian. He is a permanent professor at the Institute for Advanced Studies, Princeton, New Jersey, and has written numerous works, including *American Diplomacy, 1900–1950* (1951), *Russia and the West under Lenin and Stalin* (1962), and *On Dealing with the Communist World* (1964).

Ambassador and other members of the country team, on the basis of this recent experience as Ambassador in Belgrade. I must say at once that I encountered no difficulty whatsoever in exerting what seemed to me to be adequate authority over the entire American establishment in Yugoslavia. It may be that I was favored in being surrounded with a group of exceptionally able and loyal assistants, whose abilities I myself admired, whose judgment I valued, and whose attitude toward myself was at all times eagerly and enthusiastically cooperative. But aside from this fortunate circumstance, I had the impression that the authority of an Ambassador over official American personnel stationed in his country is just about whatever he wants to make it. So long as they are in his territory, they have to respect his authority, if he insists they do so. This applies even to those who represent other agencies.

If he requires them to do things they consider contrary to their general instructions from Washington, or intrinsically unwise to an intolerable degree, their recourse is in Washington. They can take appeal, in effect, from the Ambassador's judgment; and if they are upheld, appropriate instructions will eventually be issued from Washington to both him and them, and the matter will be settled. But so long as they are there, in his bailiwick, and so long as Washington has not specifically overruled the Ambassador, they have to respect his authority. Anything else would be insubordination; and in a case of flagrant and persistent insubordination, he could require them to leave the country. We, fortunately, had no such situations in Belgrade, and nothing even resembling one.

## 2. Relations with the Department of State and Other Agencies in Washington

A much more serious limitation on my own effectiveness in shaping policy toward the country in which I was stationed was presented by inability to get recommendations accepted in Washington. I rarely had difficulty in this respect when it was a case of policy matters on which the Department of State had discretion to act, although, of course, there were such cases, too. The trouble usually occurred where the Department of State, or at least its central organs, did not have primary responsibility for the decision. The difficulties were greatest, it seemed to me, when the matters in question were ones considered to lie within the primary competence of AID, of the Pentagon, of the budgetary or fiscal authorities, or of those authorities (I am ashamed to say that I do not know exactly who they are) which backstop the Department of State in, and in some respects control, such matters as the issuance of passports, visas, reentry permits, etc.

With these latter, in particular, I felt the lack of any effective liaison.

They included, I suppose, people in the Immigration Service, and in the FBI. I was never sure that they understood, or shared, or respected, the policy determinations of the Department of State with relation to Yugoslavia. I had the impression, perhaps erroneous, that many of these were going on the assumption that Yugoslavia was a member of the Soviet bloc, a thesis contrary to our own observations and to the established analysis of the Department. This hampered our operations and had, in a number of instances, what I considered to be adverse effects on our operations in the field.

In budgetary and fiscal matters, again, the Ambassador was sadly powerless. In general, he simply took what he got. The Department of State might receive his recommendations sympathetically; but the Department itself was too lacking in flexibility and authority to put them into effect with any firmness or promptness. Such recommendations had a habit of trailing off into the mysteries of the Budget Bureau, or the Treasury, or congressional appropriations committees, to a point where all track of them was lost, where months and years went by, and the Ambassador eventually either was transferred or forgot he had made them. At an early stage in my ambassadorship, I made recommendations for new fencing around the residence in Belgrade, owned by our Government, also for a swimming pool for staff recreational purposes, and for an extension of the Embassy residence. The changes were obviously desirable. We had literally tens of millions of dollars piled up in local currency, which might have been drawn on for most of the costs of these improvements, and much of which, if not used in this way, will probably never be used at all by us. Nevertheless, nothing actually occurred during my time there as Ambassador. Things are now about to occur, I understand; but the delays were long and discouraging. I should think that if a man enjoys such confidence on the part of his Government that he can be entrusted with the responsibilities of an important diplomatic mission, it ought also to be possible to entrust him with a limited control over funds, not major funds, just governmental pocket money, so that he could at least make minor dispositions affecting Government property at his post, without waiting years for approval.

With the respect to matters falling under the competence of AID, I found our governmental procedures slow and inflexible to an alarming degree. In general, I felt that the time for aid to Yugoslavia had passed. The aid programs were, in fact, generally dismantled during the period of my service there; and this was in accordance with my own recommendations. But there were times when a minor area of discretion on the part of the Ambassador would have yielded dividends from the standpoint of national interest, and when the absence of it was frustrating and embarrassing. This, again, was primarily a matter of congressional policy —particularly of the existence of sweeping and rigid restrictions on aid,

or anything that smacked of aid, toward Yugoslavia. As an example, we were seriously handicapped by these legislative restrictions when it came to trying to render assistance in the case of the Skoplje earthquake. This was surely unnecessary. If the legislative stipulation had only allowed us a relatively small sum, to be used at the discretion of the Ambassador or the Secretary of State in instances when there appeared to be special need, we would have been spared this sort of embarrassment.

### 3. Relations with Congress

I mention with some hesitation these instances of the limitations placed by legislative action on the ability of the Ambassador to play his part effectively. I have no choice but to do so; for these were the main impediments I experienced to the full deployment of my usefulness at my post. I do not need to remind you of the restrictions placed last year, not only on the extension of anything under the heading of aid, but even on the extension of normal trading facilities to Yugoslavia. These restrictions were adopted in the face of the most solemn and formal sort of warnings and objections on my part, conveyed to congressional leaders on many occasions and in many ways. It seems to me that a problem is arising here to which we shall, all of us, have to give attention sooner or later.

If I had known, for example, when I was offered the position of Ambassador in Yugoslavia, how little value the Congress would assign to my own judgment, in the light of an experience of nearly 30 years in the affairs of the Eastern European area, I would not have accepted the appointment; for without the support of Congress it was impossible to carry out an effective policy there. I do not know how this sort of a situation can be avoided; but I think Members of Congress might wish to bear in mind that there is usually a price to be paid, not just in terms of the peace of mind of the person most affected, but in terms of the national interest itself, when an Ambassador's recommendations are wholly disregarded on the legislative side of the Government; for it is not just his usefulness in the given question, but his usefulness as a whole, which is thereby affected.

### 4. Lack of Access to Information in Files at Home

I found myself particularly handicapped, as Ambassador, by lack of information as to what was going on at home in matters affecting our work in Belgrade, or of information about Yugoslavia to which other departments or agencies of the Government were privy. For example, it was important to us, from the standpoint of determining policy toward Yugoslavia, to know definitely whether the Yugoslavs were or were not

conducting any sort of activity in this country to which we could object. It was my impression they were not; and if anything they were doing here lent itself to any such interpretation, this is something I think I could have discussed to good effect with the Yugoslav authorities in Belgrade. But in the absence of any sort of liaison with the internal security organs of our own country, we simply had to bat in the dark in all such matters. The same was true with regard to the rather complicated affairs of the Serbian church authorities in North America— affairs in which the patriarchate in Belgrade was intimately involved and which it fell to me to discuss officially, on more than one occasion, with the Serbian patriarch in person. Again, although our naval authorities obviously had good information on the question of the use, or non-use, of Yugoslav vessels in trade with Cuba, and although this, too, was a matter which I was obliged to discuss officially from time to time with the Yugoslav authorities, I was never adequately informed even of what our Government knew about this subject. On all such matters, and others as well, the Yugoslavs with whom we had to deal were better informed, as a rule, than we were.

I understand the reasons that impel our intelligence-gathering authorities to be cautious about divulging to anyone information they have in their files. But the Department of State and the Foreign Service cannot do their work properly if they are denied information, already in the Government's files, which is pertinent to their determinations of policy. I am reluctant to believe that means could not be found, compatible with governmental security, to keep the Foreign Service at least as well supplied with such information as the governments with which it has to deal.

### 5. Overstaffing

Members of this subcommittee may recall that I was one of those who at one time expressed himself as being of the opinion that Department of State and Foreign Service were both greatly overstaffed. I cannot speak, today, for the Department of State. But I should like to say that so far as the official establishment in Yugoslavia was concerned, I found myself in most respects corrected. It is true that this establishment was a great deal larger than the Foreign Service establishments in which I had served before the war. It included, for one thing, a large USIS component—something which we did not know at all in earlier days. The administrative section, too, was larger than anything we knew in earlier days. There were also some minor instances of what seemed to me to be excessive paternalism. But when I looked around and asked myself where I could cut, beyond those major cuts which attended the dismantling of the aid mission, it was not easy to find the places. I could

have objected to the size of the informational establishment, had it not been for the fact that these people were doing an extraordinarily perceptive and effective job, and making, as it seemed to me, the fullest possible use of their time and facilities. Either one wanted these things to be done, or one did not. To me, they seemed obviously constructive and desirable; and they could hardly have been better accomplished than they were. These activities were conducted by talented, devoted people who gave all they had to the job. Who was I to complain?

It was difficult for me to judge the necessity for the relatively large military staffs. I suspected they were larger than they needed to be; but what was at issue here might have been a matter of two or three people. A cut of this order would not have helped us much.

As for the administrative overhead, I am pleased to report that the centralized administrative section, so unfamiliar to those of us who were brought up in the old Foreign Service, actually proved to be a timesaver to myself. It too, was well conducted; and it was quite effective, as it was intended to be, in freeing my own time for substantive questions. In all instances, the redeeming feature was excellence of personnel and able executive leadership of the respective sections. Perhaps the answer to quantity is quality; certainly, the former without the latter is fatal.

### 6. Quality of Staff

I think I may have been particularly fortunate, in Belgrade, in the quality of personnel assigned to work with me. In the case of the regular Foreign Service officers, I cannot say whether this happy result was achieved as a result of the arrangements for selection and promotion with the Service, or in spite of them. I still have misgivings about a Service so large and so impersonal in its administration. I suspect that this feature—the feeling of being a lost cog in a great machine where no one really knew you and your fate would be decided largely by what came out of a business machine—rested heavily, at times, on the morale of the men themselves. But in general, the Foreign Service work breeds its own morale, outwardly undemonstrative, often not externally visible, but inwardly far tougher and more devoted than is generally realized. I can only say that my officers were, without exception, fine men, only too anxious to give loyalty where loyalty was given in return, anxious to learn, to grow in their work, and to serve effectively. If men of this caliber do not become effective diplomats, the Government had best look to its own procedures for handling, training, developing, and encouraging its personnel. As of today, it seems to me that the country has a Foreign Service second to no other, and better than it has a right to expect, given the lack of appreciation and respect exhibited by the public at large for its tasks and its achievements.

## 7. Inspection Arrangements

Shortly before my departure, the Belgrade Embassy was inspected. I would like to say that I have never seen an inspection better conducted; that is, more thoroughly, more rigorously, yet with greater tact or with greater benefit to the staff and to the functioning of the mission. The Inspection Service of the Department of State has come a long way from the days of the 1920's and 1930's; and the results are beginning to make themselves visible. All that it needs is what the Department and Foreign Service, in general, most desperately need; namely, a demonstration of Executive and congressional confidence and above all a reasonable measure of administrative stability—the privilege of doing one thing long enough to let it work.

## 8. Career versus Noncareer

On the law of averages, professional training in the Foreign Service should constitute the best preparation for service as chief of mission, and the majority of our mission chiefs should normally be drawn from this source. There will always be room, however, for people who have come up other ladders, particularly when they enjoy a special intimacy with President or Secretary of State and are well qualified in other respects. In the course of a long career, I have seen a number of talented people come into these positions from other walks of life. In Belgrade, one did not have to go far to find such an instance: we had, next door in Bulgaria, Mrs. Eugenie Anderson, for whose performance there many of us felt much admiration. Any system so rigid as to forfeit the services of such people would be self-defeating. On the other hand, I am profoundly convinced that the day has passed when the United States can afford to place in high diplomatic positions people who represent anything other than the best available talent for the work in question, whatever their origin, their professional background, or their services to a political party.

## 9. Tours of Duty

I feel that, in general, the ambassadorial tour of duty should be 3 to 4 years, at a minimum. The same is true of foreign service personnel who have special training in, and knowledge of, a particular area. I felt that our performance in Belgrade was definitely weakened by too rapid a turnover in qualified personnel.

## 10. General Organization of Government from Standpoint of Foreign Affairs

It remains my view, as it has been for many years, that the President requires something in the nature of a prime minister for the conduct, on his behalf, of the external affairs of the Nation, political, economic,

and military. To my mind, this can only be the Secretary of State; and I would like to see him given the requisite authority. Such a change implies, however, a readiness to establish and to maintain, not just in time of war but in time of peace as well, what the German historian Meinicke described as the "priority of foreign policy"—meaning the principle that the external problems of the country should be given precedence over the internal ones, and that foreign policy should not be permitted to become a function of domestic-political convenience. To me, it seems urgently necessary that this change, which is one of the state of mind rather than of administrative reform, come over us all at an early date, for our situation now, in what is nominally a state of peace, is far more parlous than it ever was, prior to 1945, in time of war. But obviously, such an effort to centralize and strengthen the conduct of foreign policy will never be effective unless it has the support of Congress and, to a limited and reasonable extent, of the two great political parties.

# 74 / Dimensions of the New Diplomacy

## CARNEGIE COMMITTEE ON FOREIGN AFFAIRS PERSONNEL

**What are the dimensions of the "new diplomacy"? What changes in modern world politics particularly affect diplomacy as an instrument of American foreign policy? Especially important is the problem of attuning government personnel policies to the requirements of today's and tomorrow's world. The complexity of world-wide demands on American government personnel and the kinds of training required to fulfill these demands are among the important questions discussed in this selection from the Report of the Committee on Foreign Affairs Personnel, sponsored by the Carnegie Endowment for International Peace. Its chairman was Christian A. Herter, former Secretary of State. Staff director was Frederick C. Mosher, professor of political science, University of California, Berkeley.**

Reprinted from *Personnel for the New Diplomacy*, Report of the Committee on Foreign Affairs Personnel, Christian A. Herter, chairman. Published by and under the auspices of the Carnegie Endowment for International Peace, Washington, D. C., December, 1962, pp. 1–8.

THE PRACTICE OF DIPLOMACY between states is among the most ancient and honored institutions of civilized societies. Its maturation among the nations of Europe in the nineteenth century was a significant achievement. It provided, and still provides, the principal mechanism whereby sovereign states can communicate with one another and settle their differences short of war. The European system was the model for the diplomacy of the United States and for the other nations of the world, and European diplomatic services influenced the evolution of the United States service.

However effective this diplomatic model was in years gone by, it is clear that the old system, though still useful and even essential in its central elements, is inadequate by itself for the United States of today. The reasons for this are many, and most of them derive from changes in societies and relationships among peoples that could hardly have been foreseen even a quarter of a century ago. A second and accompanying category of changes stems from the revolutionized role of the United States in world affairs. Behind both these types of change are the enormous and still accelerating technological and scientific developments of recent decades.

## The World Setting

The characteristics of the revolution in international affairs in the past quarter-century are generally well known, but their significance in terms of the staffing of the United States' foreign affairs agencies is not as fully appreciated. It is necessary, therefore, to recall some of these factors in order to point out their impact on our foreign affairs personnel systems.

The most obvious, pervasive, and crucial element in the world situation today is the conflict between the free countries, struggling to build a world of free, independent, peaceful, and progressive peoples, and the Communist world. While the United States and other nations in the past opposed and periodically warred against absolutism in one form or another, never before, short of all-out hostilities, have international energies been so mobilized and so committed to a struggle of this kind. This struggle motivates many international activities, and it colors virtually everything that is done in world affairs. Furthermore, with the quickening pace of incidents at various points in the world and the danger of their rapid escalation to world crises, the critical nature of decisions in foreign affairs has become truly awesome. In no other field of social or political action are the stakes comparable.

A second obvious change has been the shrinkage of the world in terms of the relations among states and between any given state and its emissaries abroad. There is today an immediacy in foreign affairs and a

demand for speed of decision and action unknown in the past. International communication can be virtually instantaneous, international travel extremely rapid. Direct conversation between heads of states has become a frequent part of diplomatic machinery.[1] American citizens are made particularly aware of this immediacy by the presence of the United Nations at their very doorstep on the east side of Manhattan Island. The machinery of this organization makes possible frequent contacts not only among friendly nations but also between them and others that are non-aligned and even with most of those that are hostile.

An accompanying factor is the interlocking of states and of conflicting or parallel interests all around the world. Disturbances in Laos or Berlin or Cuba may touch off diplomatic problems thousands of miles away. Keeping up with developments and correlating them with policies and programs in a consistent manner have become problems of the greatest complexity.

A fourth element of change in diplomacy has arisen from the need to deal with *peoples* of nations as well as with their governments. Traditional diplomacy was designed almost exclusively to govern relationships between representatives of heads of states. Today, much foreign activity involves the representation of whole peoples before whole peoples of other societies. This relationship between peoples is most conspicuous in connection with information programs, cultural programs, educational exchanges, trade fairs, and like enterprises. It is equally important in most international development undertakings in which foreign representatives deal not only with government ministries but also with a great variety of institutions, organizations, and individuals in the local society. Even in the more traditional activities of foreign services, a great deal more attention must be paid than formerly to the many forces, factions, and interests on the local scene in addition to the government in power. And in the view of local populations, official representatives, no matter what their function and no matter what agency has sent them, are seen and judged as prototypes, for better or worse, of the nation they represent.

A further dimension of change in the diplomatic area arises from the sudden and dramatic emergence of new states, particularly in Africa and Asia. There are, at this writing, 110 members of the United Nations, and its membership continues to grow. Twenty-five years ago we exchanged ambassadors with only 17 nations, and ministers with 43. Today, there are more than 100 ambassadorial posts.

A most significant source of change in diplomacy today derives from the demands for rapid social, economic, and political progress

---

[1] In the first year and three-quarters of the Kennedy Administration, for example, more than fifty chiefs of state or heads of government visited Washington.

in so many of these nations, as well as in the older nations of Latin America. No longer can the purpose of diplomacy be confined to a narrow or insular view of national interest. Our diplomacy, as well as that of many other industrialized nations, is now committed to assisting developing countries to achieve their aspirations for growth.

Traditional diplomacy, with its conventions and accepted practices, assumed that relations between states would normally be carried out on a bilateral basis. Today, account must also be taken of a complex of international and regional machinery, most of it created since World War II. In addition to the United Nations itself, there are many permanent international organizations operating in such specialized fields as agriculture, health, banking, investment, communications, and labor. Beyond these are a variety of regional organizations such as the North Atlantic Treaty Organization, the Southeast Asia Treaty Organization, the Organization of American States, the Intergovernmental Committee for European Migration, and others; and there are countless other multilateral arrangements of one or another type—temporary, *ad hoc,* periodic. Indeed, part of the challenge of diplomacy today lies in the invention of new forms and structures of international relations to meet emerging problems.

### The Role and Activities of the United States

The new dimensions cited above have had a particular impact on the United States because of the transformation of this country's role in the affairs of the world. The posture of the United States changed dramatically in the direction of active participation in foreign affairs at the time of the Spanish-American War. The movement toward a more activist policy in foreign affairs has been sporadic rather than consistent but was greatly accelerated as a consequence of both the world wars of this century. By the 1950's there could be no doubt that we had acquired, however gladly or however reluctantly, leading responsibilities among the nations of the free world. Our interest in every part of the world is today extensive, and our commitment to the pursuit of growth and progress among the free nations is well-nigh total.

In pursuit of our international goals, we have developed an arsenal of instruments more varied than ever before. They include: all the tools of traditional diplomacy; international law; intelligence; political action; technical assistance and various types of foreign economic aid; military aid programs; information and psychological programs; monetary policies; trade development programs; educational exchange; cultural programs; and, more recently, measures to counter insurgency movements. Most of these fall outside the older definition of diplomacy, but all of them must be considered actual or potential elements of United

States programs. Together they constitute what is here called the "new diplomacy."

With the expansion of our commitment and of our instruments for effectuating foreign policy goals has come an intermingling of foreign affairs considerations with other national objectives and interests. The most dramatic example of this is the connection between foreign affairs policy and military policy, a combination now widely known as national security policy. Not too long ago, our diplomatic and military establishments planned and operated with comparatively little relation or attention one to the other. Diplomacy was presumably predominant until we overpassed the brink of war; then the military agencies took over. Today, many of the most important foreign policy problems are also military problems. Under the President, the foreign affairs and defense agencies must work in continuous concert and with mutual understanding, both in peace and in war.

The fusion of foreign policy considerations with domestic problems is illustrated across the whole range of national interests. Every major department and agency of the national government has an immediate concern in some phase of our foreign policy. Indeed, the distinction between what is foreign and what is domestic is often more confusing than useful. Our relationships with other nations are tied inextricably to our internal growth, our prosperity, our scientific and technological development, and our domestic politics.

With increasing United States commitment abroad, the problems of coordinating, correlating, and administering the overseas programs have become enormous. For example, some 28 Federal agencies employ about 32,000 United States citizens in civilian capacities in some 127 foreign countries, colonies, and dependencies. About 58 per cent of these employees work for the Department of Defense; another 37 per cent are employed by the State Department, the Agency for International Development, and the United States Information Agency; and the remaining 5 per cent are scattered among 20 other Federal departments and agencies. These figures exclude some 95,000 foreign nationals who are also employed by United States agencies abroad.

The complexity can be illustrated in other ways. The United States Government must provide representation in the governing bodies of a growing number of international and regional organizations. It must provide for the participation of United States officials and private citizens in an ever increasing number of international conferences—474 between July 1, 1961, and June 30, 1962, alone, or an average of almost two new ones starting every workday in the year. Almost 2,800 United States delegates participated.

There is one further aspect of United States diplomacy which represents a substantial departure from the traditional diplomacy of the past.

It arises from the remarkable growth of interest in foreign policy among millions of United States citizens and from their legitimate concern about the costs, particularly of defense and foreign aid. Diplomacy today involves more than representation of the United States' interests abroad; it requires, in effect, a continuous representation of foreign policy questions to the people. The increased interest and concern of our people in the conduct of foreign affairs is reflected in the role played by the Congress in the formulation and execution of foreign policy. Under our constitutional form of government, the powers vested in the Congress take on special significance in meeting the demands of the new diplomacy. While the Executive Branch under the President must exercise leadership in the formulation of policies and programs, the Congress not only provides the requisite authorization and appropriations in their support, but may and often does assume the initiative. In short, diplomacy cannot operate in a vacuum at home and our Congressional leaders and responsible officials in the Executive Branch must give attention to the temper of the people at large and to the many groups and organizations that reflect the diversity of our society, including private businesses, labor organizations, the educational world, and a host of other public and private groups.

### The New Diplomats

The basic and rapid changes in the nature of the world and in the role of the United States have clearly called into being a new and an enlarged concept of foreign affairs, and this in turn entails a different conception of the role and the kinds of personnel engaged in it. In this report, the Committee offers a number of recommendations directed to equipping our foreign affairs personnel better to handle the problems of the new diplomacy. Principal among the objectives are the following three:

First, it is apparent that our foreign policy goals cannot be pursued in a posture of passivity—of observing and reporting. To be sure, there is as great a stake as ever in accurate, perceptive, up-to-date information about developments in other countries, and the Committee would certainly not condone any slighting of the reportorial functions. But all of the foreign affairs agencies are heavily involved in operations, in *doing* things overseas. Their responsibilities include not only watching things happen and reporting them, but also helping to make them happen or at least influencing their happening. We have an overriding need to utilize the instruments available to us in ways that will help give a positive and constructive orientation to the forces of change. Our personnel systems must be adapted to recruiting and developing officers oriented to, and capable of, this kind of performance.

Equally clearly, the responsibilities of this country in world affairs cannot be adequately met by "generalists" with a superficial knowledge of all relevant specialties. Quality is required, as it always has been, but today the need is for quality in many different areas and many different professions. Our personnel systems must be adapted to recruiting and developing and utilizing a growing diversity in talents and skills.

Finally, our representatives overseas are not merely representatives of the individual agencies that sent them there or of their particular specialties or professions. They are first and foremost representatives of the United States. It is therefore essential that there be an underlying level of understanding and agreement among foreign affairs officials as to the goals of our nation and our democratic system. These officials should also understand and agree on the content and use of the various possible instruments in achieving those goals. The very diversity of skills and knowledges mentioned above makes more necessary, and also more difficult, a common appreciation of national purpose. Such an appreciation must be built on a foundation of knowledge of the circumstances in which we operate, the tools we may employ, and the relations of those tools one to the other. There is always a danger, in large and complex enterprises, of compartmentation, divisiveness, jealousy, and parochialism. In the chapters that follow, the Committee proposes measures to achieve a greater degree of unity amid the diversity of talents, perspectives, and efforts required in foreign affairs. This is merely another way of stating the national motto, which has both described and served the United States so very well for so very long. The personnel systems in foreign affairs should be so conceived as to contribute both to the diversity and to the unity.

### Political Leadership and Careers

In the field of foreign affairs, the President, the Secretary of State, and other high officials carry a fearful burden of responsibility for prompt and courageous decisions which are the more difficult for being essentially irreversible. Political leadership alone, however, cannot cope unaided with the complexities of foreign affairs. It must be undergirded by professional career services whose members, drawn from all segments of society, are well grounded in their understanding of, and capacity to use, the instruments of the new diplomacy.

The use of career public servants in filling top executive posts raises an important issue of public policy which the Committee believes merits special comment. The Committee takes it as self-evident that the President must and will have freedom to choose from the entire national pool of qualified men and women in selecting key appointive officials in foreign affairs. Career officers should constitute a prime

resource within the national pool. They should receive no less consideration than others as potential choices for the highest executive posts; they should neither enjoy an automatic priority nor suffer from an adverse presumption. Rather they should be deemed available and encouraged to aspire to such posts with the knowledge that they will be appraised in competition with others drawn from any part of the nation's human resources. They can ask or expect no more. If the quality, training, and experience of career officers are steadily upgraded as recommended in this report, increasing numbers of them are bound to be selected for high executive posts at home as well as abroad.

This concept is consistent with, and does no violence to, the principle of Presidential control. Political direction must, of course, emanate from the President, but political direction need not conflict with the need for depth of experience in, and professional knowledge of, foreign affairs, whether acquired within or outside the career services. Whoever is appointed to positions of top executive responsibility must enjoy the confidence of the responsible political head—the President, the Secretary of State, or heads of other foreign affairs agencies, as the case may be. Those so appointed must also be prepared to accept the political hazards implicit in these positions.

. . . . .

The Committee is impressed, as all Americans should be, by the long strides our foreign affairs establishment has already taken in adjusting to, and even in pioneering, the new diplomacy. Our capacity to respond to changed situations improves year by year. Only in part is the new diplomacy a goal to be achieved; in many respects, it exists now. It is to the remaining tasks and possible improvements that this report is addressed.

# 75 / *Diplomacy in the United Nations*

THOMAS HOVET, JR.

**A major and probably increasingly important sector for applying the diplomatic instrument is the United Nations. What is**

Reprinted from *Journal of International Affairs*, XVII, 1 (1963), 29–41. Published by the School of International Affairs, Columbia University. Reprinted by permission.

Thomas Hovet, Jr., is professor of international relations, Graduate School of Arts and Sciences, New York University. His publications include *Bloc Politics in the United Nations* (1960) and *Africa in the United Nations* (1964).

the setting for United Nations diplomacy? What role does the U.N. organization play as an arena for applying national diplomacies? What are the identifiable features of U.N. diplomacy?

DIPLOMACY in the United Nations has been characterized in many ways. Traditionally it has been called multilateral diplomacy, public diplomacy, conference diplomacy, or parliamentary diplomacy. On occasion it has been termed bloc diplomacy, diplomacy by groups, and even diplomacy by majorities. When the diplomatic processes in the United Nations have been more comparable to the classical methods of diplomacy, the methods there have been referred to as private or quiet diplomacy. When the features of public and quiet diplomatic methods were combined, the diplomatic process in the United Nations has been characterized as preventive diplomacy or the diplomacy of reconciliation.

The key to any understanding of United Nations diplomacy is a recognition of the role the organization plays as an instrument of diplomacy. As a diplomatic instrument the United Nations is, in some senses, a permanent international conference. Representatives of 110 nations are in almost continual attendance at the headquarters in Manhattan of the Organization, and their very presence provides a ready atmosphere for constant diplomatic negotiations. As a center for harmonizing the actions of states the United Nations provides a formal framework for diplomatic operations. In the thirteenth Annual Report of the Secretary-General, the late Dag Hammarskjold wrote that "...as an instrument for reconciliation and for worldwide co-operation the United Nations represents a necessary addition to the traditional methods of diplomacy as exercised on a bilateral or regional basis." Within the framework of its formal organization and agreed procedures the United Nations provides a diplomatic instrument that can be used at a moment's notice. While the preliminary negotiations for an *ad hoc* multilateral international conference may require months or even years to agree upon the procedures for the conference, the United Nations provides a framework already established to which states can bring their problems without delay. Because most states have established permanent missions at the United Nations headquarters, a state that does not want to avail itself of the formal procedures of the United Nations can have easy contact with the diplomats of other states and carry on negotiations in the traditions of the more classical forms of diplomacy. To the newer and smaller states which may not be able to afford diplomatic representation in a wide variety of countries, this center of diplomatic activity at the United Nations may provide their primary area of contact with other

states. Thus the United Nations is not only a diplomatic instrument itself, but it is also a center of diplomatic activity constantly available to states in their negotiations with other states.

Surveying the evolution of the diplomatic method in the United Nations, it appears that the process has evolved from one which stressed public or conference diplomacy to one which stresses private or quiet diplomacy. The use of "evolution" may be an oversimplification because diplomacy in the United Nations has not really been of one type or the other. The development of the diplomatic method in the United Nations has seen an increasing recognition of the possibilities of supplementing conference diplomacy with quiet diplomacy. Secretary-General Hammarskjold constantly argued for a greater awareness of the variety of diplomatic techniques that could be realized within the setting of the United Nations. In his tenth Annual Report, the Secretary-General explained that

Within the framework of the Charter there are many possibilities, as yet largely unexplored, for variation of practices. The United Nations is at a very early stage in that development. . . . It is my hope that solid progress can be made in the coming years in developing new forms of contact, new methods of deliberation and new techniques of reconciliation. . . .

The problem of diplomacy in the United Nations has been a question of evolving an adjustment between the processes of conference and quiet diplomacy. Diplomatic methods are in a constant state of evolution. A process applied in one situation may or may not be used in other situations. The problem for the diplomat in the United Nations is to recognize the strengths and weaknesses of particular diplomatic techniques, and to adjust to new diplomatic methods that may or may not require the particular type of skills generally associated with diplomacy in its classical sense. Diplomatic techniques in the United Nations can be called successful if they provide an atmosphere which allows negotiations to continue, and unsuccessful if the method or combination of methods inhibits the process of negotiation.

### Public Diplomacy

The emphasis on conference or public diplomacy in the United Nations is not only related to the adjustment of the diplomatic method to the growth of representative government, the impact of scientific developments, especially in the area of communications, and the experiences of the League of Nations; it also reflects concepts inherent in the minds of the drafters of the United Nations Charter. Basic to this type of diplomacy is a belief in the importance of public discussion and in the importance of world public opinion. By focusing the spotlight of public

opinion on a situation, it is felt that this public exposure can freeze a situation and prevent a chain of events that might lead to conflict. At the same time there is a feeling that public discussion of an issue provides an opportunity for states not directly involved in the situation to make their influence felt in resolving the issue. The focus of publicity on the actions of a particular state threatening the peace may place that state not in an offensive but rather in a defensive position in which it must justify and explain its actions. In many instances the use of this type of public diplomacy in the United Nations has had a bearing on the adjustment of a problem. The public discussions in the Security Council and the General Assembly in 1960 undoubtedly had an influence in minimizing the actions of the United States and the Soviet Union in the Congo. The Security Council considerations of the situation in Iran in 1946 had an influence on the withdrawal of Soviet troops from that country. The actions in 1956 of Great Britain and France in the Suez were curtailed by exposure to the spotlight of public discussion in the United Nations. The public consideration in the General Assembly in 1953 and 1954 of the Burmese complaint over the presence of Chinese Nationalist troops within its borders was a determining factor in the withdrawal of those forces. The public discussion in the Security Council in 1962 was a factor in the easing of tensions between the United States and the Soviet Union over the presence of Soviet missiles in Cuba. The states administering Trust Territories and Non-Self-Governing Territories have continually been forced to justify their policies publicly in the Trusteeship Council and the General Assembly, and there can be little doubt that their policies in these territories have been modified as a result. The continual discussions in conference of economic and social questions have served to isolate fundamental problems and to make all states aware of the variety of attitudes on these crucial issues.

While it is apparent that conference or public diplomacy in the United Nations has been a factor in preventing many particular situations from getting out of hand, it is just as clear that adjustment of a situation often cannot be resolved by public discussion. Public diplomacy may expose the issue, but its resolution is generally the result of quiet diplomacy. Too often, policy positions taken in the public eye of conference diplomacy prevent states from adjusting their attitudes on an issue. Public diplomacy places stress not on negotiation but on "success" or "failure." Having once taken a strong public policy position a state cannot easily adjust its position without having it interpreted as a concession; a public shift of policy is often interpreted as a diplomatic defeat. With its emphasis on formal voting and other procedures, public diplomacy in the United Nations often results in competition between states. The spotlight of publicity places undue pressure on a state not on its ability to adjust to a situation, but on its ability to preserve its position.

Delegates are tempted to play to the public arena instead of concentrating on negotiations that will resolve the problem; they may ridicule the representatives of other states because it is pleasing to their fellow countrymen, but it does not help the process of negotiation. They are constantly motivated to prove to the public in their own countries that they are defending national policy. In a sense they are placed in a position of acting as if they were representatives in a parliament, their constituents being the people in their own country. But they are not parliamentary representatives, because the United Nations is not a parliament.

The fact that resolutions are adopted in the United Nations by majority vote means that the diplomats are often tempted to negotiate for votes, not to negotiate for the adjustment of problems. The public spotlight emphasizes votes, not the resolution of international problems. The public spotlight de-emphasizes the fact that resolutions are not laws, but merely recommendations. The public spotlight inclines the representatives of states to take stands on issues which may not be of vital interest to their countries. In the resumed Thirteenth Session, for example, the Indian ambassador took a public stand on a question of the nature of elections in the Trust Territory of the Camerouns under French Administration. By his public stand he found himself in a position of being at odds with the representatives from all the African states. His motive may have been to seek what he thought was a proper action, but the result of taking this position in public meant that he openly antagonized a number of states on an issue that was of vital concern to them but of little concern to his country. Had his suggestions been made in private the ensuing animosity would have been negligible, because he could have reversed his position without any loss of prestige for India. Having taken the position in public, he could not reverse himself. Thus on an issue of no major importance to India he found himself creating not only conflict between India and the African states, but an atmosphere of animosity that would transfer to other issues at other times.

The ability to win votes and to pass resolutions, however, may not resolve issues. Between 1946 and 1962, fifty-six resolutions have been passed by the General Assembly, for example, on the question of South West Africa, more resolutions than have been passed on any other issue before the United Nations. Yet none of these resolutions has had any major impact upon the policies of South Africa towards the territory of South West Africa. Even if South Africa might want to adjust its policies towards South West Africa, it would be difficult to do so because it would appear to the South African public as if the Government were not defending its national interest. Any adjustment of its policy in the face of these resolutions would be interpreted as a defeat for the South African Government. Thus, in the face of these resolutions, the South African

Government has become more adamant. Rather than reducing the conflict between South Africa and the other states, the tension has increased.

### Quiet Diplomacy

While public diplomacy has an important role, especially in certain types of situations, it is apparent that the success of diplomacy in the United Nations depends upon the use of public diplomatic methods in conjunction with more quiet forms of diplomacy. If there has been the development of a distinctive diplomatic method in the United Nations, it has been the development of a wide variety of techniques that provide an opportunity to intermingle and balance public and private procedures of diplomacy.

This blending of public and quiet diplomacy gives a uniqueness to the diplomatic method of the United Nations that has been influenced by at least three factors: the growth of the role of the Secretary-General, the establishment of permanent missions, and the development of caucusing groups and blocs. Each of these three elements is, in a sense, an outgrowth of the nature of public diplomacy in the United Nations, but the significance of these elements has really been felt in the environment they have created for the development of quiet diplomacy.

As the United Nations developed and the agenda of each organ expanded, the Headquarters became the location for a continual round of meetings. The General Assembly hardly finishes its sessions before the Trusteeship Council and the Economic and Social Council together with their commissions and committees, are in session. Moreover, the Security Council is organized so as to be able to meet at any moment. Even if a state is not a member of one or another of these organs, its ability to keep abreast of the issues demands that it have some sort of permanent representation at United Nations Headquarters. By 1962 almost all of the members of the United Nations had permanent missions located at the seat of the Organization. It is natural that the existence of these permanent missions provides a basis for continual contact between nations. States are thus provided with another area of diplomatic contact in addition to the normal exchange of ambassadors. In some respects, contact between states at the United Nations has the advantage of being more informal than contact between ambassadors at a national capital. The existence of these permanent missions, therefore, provides a convenient framework for quiet diplomacy.

With the impact of the Cold War frustrating the anticipated development of the Security Council, the role of the General Assembly has increased and so, too, has the role of the Secretary-General. While the concept of the role of the Secretary-General has evolved in many ways in the seventeen years of the United Nations, the most significant aspect of

this development has been the tendency of delegates to thrust heavy responsibilities upon the Secretary-General. While the General Assembly in 1956 agreed upon the creation of a United Nations Emergency Force in the Middle East, it gave the Secretary-General the responsibility of attending to the details involved in establishing such a force. His success in carrying out these tasks, and many similar ones, has influenced the General Assembly and the other organs to entrust even more responsibilities to him. In part, the willingness to give these responsibilities to the Secretary-General have been an expression of confidence in him as a person. During the tenure of Dag Hammarskjold, the tendency to "let Dag do it" was a tribute to his ability to facilitate, through the devices of quiet diplomacy, a resolution of issues that could not be brought to fruition by public diplomacy. Gradually the Office of the Secretary-General has developed as a third factor in diplomatic negotiations.

The Secretary-General serves as a catalyst in facilitating quiet diplomacy. An issue may be brought to public attention, as was the Cuban situation in the fall of 1962, but once the issue has been exposed, the negotiations between the United States and the Soviet Union were not only conducted quietly between their permanent missions, but also through the good offices of the Secretary-General which served as a medium for the exchange of views and as a source of suggestions of means for negotiation and reconciliation. Having the maintenance of peace as his only interest in an issue, the Secretary-General can use his initiative in facilitating negotiations. His success in encouraging negotiations depends upon the degree to which states have confidence in his role as a catalyst in the negotiations; consequently, his role is limited if states feel that he is concerned with a particular solution of a problem. In order to maintain this role as a catalytic force the Secretary-General has resorted to a number of techniques, one of the most important being the creation of informal advisory committees. The United Nations Emergency Force Advisory Committee and the Advisory Committee on the Congo were created by the Secretary-General to provide a diplomatic sounding board in which he could weigh with the delegations concerned the moves he intended to take in implementing resolutions of the General Assembly and the Security Council. The efforts of the Secretary-General have not been the efforts of secret diplomacy. His concern has been with the preliminary phase of behind-the-scenes negotiations in preparation for reaching open covenants with public diplomacy. From the very beginnings of the United Nations, the Office of the Secretary-General has served as a go-between for states in preliminary negotiations. Traditionally, the Office of the Secretary-General has not entered negotiations unless it has been requested by one of the parties to an issue. However, the Secretary-General has not always waited for states to call upon his assistance in facilitating negotiations, but at times has taken the initiative; an example

was the Beck-Friis mission to Cambodia and Thailand. Nevertheless, the extent to which the Secretary-General may of his own initiative enter into this quiet phase of United Nations negotiations depends heavily upon his personal rapport with the delegations. Therefore, the role of the Secretary-General is two-fold: it may be a role in the preliminary stages before the public discussion of an issue; or it may enter in the phases that follow a public discussion. Both roles are concerned with making it possible for negotiations to proceed.

The third element that has facilitated the development of quiet diplomacy in conjunction with public diplomacy at the United Nations has been the gradual evolution of caucusing groups and blocs within the membership of the Organization. While groups of states with similar interests were initially drawn together primarily to agree upon candidates for election to the non-permanent seats on the Security Council and the other organs, these groups have gradually emerged as an informal diplomatic apparatus.

By January 1963 there were eleven caucusing groups and one caucusing bloc apparent within the membership of the United Nations . . . . A *bloc* may be defined as a group of states which meets regularly in caucus, the members of which are bound by their votes in the United Nations by the caucus decision; the Soviet Bloc is the only bloc. A *caucusing group* is a term applied to any group of states which has some degree of formal organization, holds fairly regular meetings, and is concerned with substantive issues and procedural matters; the eleven caucusing groups are the Afro-Asian Group, the African Group, the Brazzaville Group, the Casablanca Group, the Arab Group, the Western European Group, the European Community Group, the Benelux Group, the Scandinavian Group, the Latin American Group, and the Commonwealth Group. Most of the members of the United Nations belong to at least one of these groups, and some members belong to several. The United States, China, Israel, and South Africa do not belong regularly to any caucusing group. This group development has been criticized for encouraging vote-bargaining on resolutions. Such criticism oversimplifies the role that these groups play in the diplomacy of the United Nations.

Caucusing groups are concerned with attempts to mobilize strength to influence formal decisions of the various organs of the United Nations. But they also perform a significant role in preliminary stages of negotiation before the public debates, votes, and resolutions. The very informal Commonwealth Group, for example, is not concerned with agreeing on common policies, its members belong to a number of other groups, and the meetings of the Commonwealth Group therefore provide informal means of expressing various points of view. These caucusing groups constitute a channel of communications between countries with

similar interests. They can, within their meetings, work for an accommodation of viewpoints to prevent clashes within the arena of the public debates that would lead to a hardening of relations. In the Sixteenth Session of the General Assembly, for example, Nigeria and Guinea were in disagreement in the plenary debate over a procedural point on the consideration of items on the agenda. Before the discussion became too involved, Ghana proposed that the Assembly adjourn to allow the African Group time to see if it could work out the difficulty. At the next session of the Assembly the Delegate of Madagascar, as chairman of the African Group, announced that the issue had been resolved and he proposed a compromise procedure which had the support of both Guinea and Nigeria.

Concerned as they are with achieving support for formal proposals, the group-majority recognizes that unless concessions are made to gain that support, it may only create friction and bitterness. Negotiations between groups, then, often tend to blunt an otherwise sharply worded resolution. Where public consideration tends to separate issues, negotiation within and between groups can relate concessions on one issue to concessions on other issues. New delegations and delegates can test their skills with other states in an informal caucus atmosphere of frank exchange that is not possible within a more formal public discussion. A state can thus test a proposal without fear that it is publicly taking a viewpoint that cannot be adjusted.

One of the fundamental difficulties in dealing with any international issue is the problem of determining precisely what is actually at dispute. The groups in their discussions provide a place in which delegations can share information informally, and thus assist in determining what is the point at issue. Questions can be asked without embarrassment in this group process, and delegations can become better informed on the problems that will be considered at a later time in the public debates.

In addition to the permanent missions, the role of the Secretary-General, the function of the group process, and the very nature of the composition of the General Assembly also provide a bridge between public and quiet diplomacy that is unique. The fact that in session after session more and more foreign ministers, prime ministers, and chiefs of state attend General Assembly meetings means that there is an opportunity for contact between states that is unparalleled. While foreign ministers participate in the public debates, especially in the initial stages of the Assembly, they also use the opportunity to meet informally with their counterparts from other countries. Even their participation in the General Assembly is significant. The foreign ministers usually participate in the so-called general debate at the beginning of each General Assembly session. The general debate provides these foreign policy leaders with an opportunity to assess the current nature of international problems from a

new perspective. It also provides all members with an awareness of the general philosophical approach of each state to significant problems. The Charter provides for the Security Council to serve on occasion as a meeting ground of heads of state. While this development has been encouraged by the Secretary-General, it has not come into operation.

As the United Nations evolves, these various developments create a bridge between techniques of public and quiet diplomacy. It is not easy, however, to develop the proper balance between the areas in which quiet diplomacy is most useful and those areas in which public diplomacy is most useful. One problem lies in the nature of the diplomatic skills that are required. It is an unusual delegate who is skilled in the techniques of both public and quiet diplomacy. A diplomat used to more traditional forms of diplomacy may be shocked at his first experience in the General Assembly where the procedure is more similar to that of a parliament or a state legislature. Skills may be needed in coping with the rules of procedure. In this situation the member of a delegation who may have come up through the ranks of a political party will find himself more at home. He is familiar with parliamentary give and take. Such an individual, however, may become so concerned with manipulating the procedure that he will lose sight of the fact that the United Nations is not a parliament, that success is measured not in passing resolutions but in providing means through which negotiations can continue. There is a temptation to insult other delegates, a temptation to consider resolutions passed as victories, and a temptation to demonstrate proficiency in the use of procedural rules. Such temptations, if not curbed, can create more disharmony than advance the cause of peace.

The delegate accustomed to more traditional forms of diplomacy may be inclined to overlook elements in United Nations diplomatic method that are necessary for the achievement of his tasks. For example, he may confine his contacts with delegations to the ambassadorial level. But within the United Nations, the interplay is as much between delegations as between leaders of delegations. Within each delegation individuals are assigned particular tasks, and to some extent they develop areas of speciality upon which their delegation leaders place considerable reliance. Depending upon the category of issue that is being considered, there are, sometimes, informal leaders within a delegation whose influence is substantial in determining the policy attitudes of a delegation. Successful negotiation may depend, therefore, upon discerning the identity of these leaders. The delegation that confines its contacts to the ambassadorial level may, as a result, find its negotiations fruitless. Successful negotiation between delegations should involve contact at every level so as to provide useful intelligence on the latitude of instructions given to delegations, and therefore the areas within which an accommodation of viewpoints can be negotiated.

Most of the major powers have a problem in this process of the interplay of public and private diplomacy precisely because they are major powers, with wide interests in virtually all issues before the United Nations. Their latitude for give and take may be limited because of this universality of interests. Conversely, smaller states must be constantly aware that, though they may build voting majorities, no resolutions in the United Nations can be realistic unless concessions are made to the power relationships among the larger states.

The United Nations has only begun to explore the variety of techniques of diplomacy that are at its disposal to facilitate negotiations between states. While all of its attempts have not been successful, it has nonetheless achieved success in a variety of cases. One of its most notable developments has been in the area of what Mr. Hammarskjold called preventive diplomacy—that which combines both elements of public and quiet diplomacy. In the Introduction to the fifteenth Annual Report, the late Secretary-General explained that

. . . preventive diplomacy . . . is of special significance in cases where the original conflict may be said either to be the result of, or to imply risks for, the creation of a power vacuum between the main blocs. Preventive action in such cases must, in the first place, aim at filling the vacuum so that it will not provoke action from any of the major parties, the initiative for which might be taken for preventive purposes but might in turn lead to a counter action from the other sides. The ways in which a vacuum can be filled by the United Nations so as to forestall such initiatives differ from case to case, but they have this in common: temporarily, and pending the filling of the vacuum by normal means, the United Nations enters the picture on the basis of its non-commitment to any power bloc, so as to provide to the extent possible a guarantee in relation to all parties against initiatives from others. . . .

This type of preventive diplomacy has been exercised by the United Nations in different circumstances and with different techniques. In Greece, the Special Committee on the Balkans focused attention upon foreign sources of subversion. The United Nations Observation Group in Lebanon checked reports of foreign intervention. In Laos, a Security Council subcommittee verified whether a crisis existed. In the Congo, the United Nations prevented intervention by outside powers by providing assistance in the maintenance of law and order when the established government there collapsed. These cases illustrate the fact that although the diplomatic method evolving in the United Nations has the ability to achieve concrete results, its full potential has not been reached. Progress is nevertheless being made, for the ability to produce conditions in which negotiations can proceed is a mark of good diplomacy.

At the same time that a distinctive diplomatic method is gradually evolving, the expansion in United Nations membership is creating

problems for diplomacy. The procedures and the structure of the General Assembly are being strained by the size of its membership. There are more issues on the agenda, more delegates desiring to speak, more draft resolutions submitted, more amendments introduced, more votes requested, more meetings to attend, and more delegates to be consulted. As the sessions become longer, it is more difficult for foreign ministers and heads of states to participate, except for brief periods. Delegations, especially small ones, are severely taxed in providing representatives to attend the increased number of meetings. States cannot afford to allow key individuals in their foreign offices to spend one-third or one-half of their time at the United Nations. They must either rotate personnel attending sessions there or else send less qualified officials. On the other hand, to be effective, public diplomacy needs persons experienced in its procedures and qualified to deal with the issues being considered.

Up to the present the evolution of diplomatic method in the United Nations has been concerned with an expansion of opportunities for quiet diplomacy. In the future the adjustment of procedures of public diplomacy to the enlarged membership will probably be the more serious problem faced by the world body. The ability of the United Nations to balance techniques of public and quiet diplomacy will depend upon the successful development of workable procedures integrating the two diplomatic methods.

# For Further Reading

BLOOMFIELD, LINCOLN. *The United Nations and U. S. Foreign Policy* (Boston: Little, Brown, 1960).

CLEVELAND, HARLAN, GERARD J. MANGONE, and JOHN C. ADAMS. *The Overseas Americans* (New York: McGraw-Hill, 1960).

CRAIG, GORDON, and FELIX GILBERT. *The Diplomats 1919–1939* (Princeton: Princeton University Press, 1953).

KERTESZ, STEPHEN D., ed. *American Diplomacy in a New Era* (Notre Dame, Ind.: University of Notre Dame Press, 1961).

MC CAMY, JAMES L. *Conduct of the New Diplomacy* (New York: Harper and Row, 1964).

MORGENTHAU, HANS J. "The Disparagement of Diplomacy," *Dilemmas of Politics* (Chicago: University of Chicago Press, 1958), ch. 15, pp. 270–80.

NICOLSON, HAROLD. *Diplomacy*, 2d ed. (New York: Oxford University Press, 1950).

PEARSON, LESTER B. *Diplomacy in the Nuclear Age* (Cambridge, Mass.: Harvard University Press, 1959).

PRICE, DON K., ed. *The Secretary of State* (Englewood Cliffs, N. J.: Prentice-Hall, 1960).

ROSSOW, ROBERT. "The Professionalization of the New Diplomacy," *World Politics*, XIV, 4 (July, 1962), 561–75.

SEABURY, PAUL. *Power, Freedom and Diplomacy* (New York: Random House, 1963).

THAYER, CHARLES W. *Diplomat* (New York: Harper, 1959).

THOMPSON, KENNETH W. *American Diplomacy and Emergent Patterns* (New York: New York University Press, 1962).

WILCOX, FRANCIS O., and H. FIELD HAVILAND, JR. eds. *The United States and the United Nations* (Baltimore, Md.: The Johns Hopkins Press, 1961).

# VIII PEACE, COEXISTENCE, OR WAR?

# 76 / The Prevention of World War III

## KENNETH E. BOULDING

A categorical imperative of any great nation's foreign policy in the nuclear age is the prevention of general war. The following article is concerned with preventing World War III. How can this be done? The author argues that international relations may be viewed as a system. This is to suggest that international "actors" behave in relatively stable and predictable patterns. Potentially, this allows for prediction and control of the patterns of change in the system. The author argues that the present "system" is headed towards disaster. He sets forth a series of five steps that, if followed, might avoid thermonuclear disaster.

WHEN we talk about preventing something we imply two things. We imply, first, that there is a dynamic system which is now proceeding that, if allowed to proceed unchanged, will result in an event which is regarded as undesirable and which, therefore, we want to prevent. We imply also that it is possible to change the dynamic system in question and replace it by another dynamic system in which the unwanted event does not occur. Thus, suppose we find ourselves driving towards a railroad crossing and suddenly we see the red lights flashing and a train approaching. Our dynamic system at the moment consists simply of velocity and direction. We are proceeding, say at 50 miles per hour, towards the crossing. The distant early warning system of our eyes informs us the crossing is dangerous. The knowledge which we have of our existing dynamic system informs us that if it continues we will arrive at the crossing at the precise moment when the train is there. The

Reprinted from the *Virginia Quarterly Review*, XXXVIII (Winter, 1962), 11–21. By permission.

Kenneth E. Boulding is professor of economics, University of Michigan. He is the author of *Conflict and Defense: A General Theory* (1962) and other important works.

combination of a distant information system coupled with the simple dynamics of automobiles enables us, however, to prevent the disaster. We do this by putting on the brakes long before we get to the crossing. This in effect changes the dynamic system under which we have been operating. It introduces a new variable into it, indeed a new dimension, deceleration. Because of this, we are able to prevent the disaster, as we are able to avoid simultaneous occupancy of the crossing by ourselves and the train.

We must be careful, of course, in applying the analogy of a simple psycho-mechanical system like a man driving a car to the enormous complexities and uncertainties of the international system. However, the international system is still a system, even though it has important random elements in it. Because it is not entirely random, it has elements of predictability. One of the greatest difficulties lies precisely in the stochastic nature of the system. We are driving a car, as it were, that may or may not respond to brakes according to whether dice held by the driver indicate "respond" or "fail." The situation is made all the more difficult by the fact that we face here a stochastic system with a very small universe, that is, a very small number of cases. Stochastic systems with a large number of cases can be treated by the theory of probability. We have a pretty fair idea, for instance, how many people are going to die in automobile accidents next year, although we do not know exactly who they are.

The problem of reducing the total number of automobile accidents is a very different kind of problem from the one that faces the driver of the preceding paragraph. Nevertheless, even with our present knowledge it would not be difficult to design an automobile and a road system which would kill, let us say, 20,000 people a year instead of 40,000. What we would be doing here would be to reduce the probability of disaster on the part of a single individual. It is by no means impossible to think of the international system in a rather similar way, and to talk about the things we can do to reduce the probability of disaster. What we mean by this is that if we had a very large number of planets roughly identical with our own we could postulate changes in the system which would reduce the number of cases in which disaster occurred. This would be the analogue of treating road deaths as a public health problem and seeking to reduce their probability. As far as we know, however, we do not have a large number of planets like ours and for our purposes at least there is only one. Hence, reducing the probability of disaster does us very little good if the disaster actually occurs. The problem of stochastic systems with a small number of cases has received insufficient attention in the theoretical literature. It is precisely this kind of system, however, with which we have to deal in international affairs.

I believe the present international system to be one which has a

significant probability built into it of irretrievable disaster for the human race. The longer the number of years we contemplate such a system operating, the larger this probability becomes. I do not know whether in any one year it is one per cent, ten per cent, or even fifty per cent. I feel pretty sure, however, that it is of this order of magnitude, not, shall we say, of the order of magnitude of .01 per cent. The problem of system change, therefore, is urgent and desperate, and we are all in terrible danger. This is largely because of a quantitative change in the parameters of the international system under which we now live. This is still essentially the system of unilateral national defense in spite of the development of the United Nations and certain international organizations. Unilateral national defense is workable only if each nation can be stronger than its potential enemies in its home territory. This is possible under two circumstances. The first is that the nations must be far enough away from each other, and the extent to which their power declines as they operate further away from their own home bases must be sufficiently great. Then each nation can be stronger than the other *at home* with on-the-spot forces because of the fact that in a nation's home territory the enemy operates at a certain disadvantage. There is a second condition, however, which is that each nation must be able to dominate an area around its home base equal in depth to the range of the deadly missile. Because of quantitative changes in these conditions even in the last few years the system of unilateral national defense has become infeasible on a world scale. No nation is now far enough away from potential enemies to be sure that it can dominate even its own territory. Furthermore, the range of the deadly missile is rapidly reaching 12,500 miles, which means that the second condition cannot possibly be fulfilled. The condition which unilateral national defense attempts to establish, therefore, which I call *unconditional viability,* is now no longer possible.

The urgent and desperate nature of the present situation is created by the universality of the disaster with which we are threatened. The system of unilateral national defense has never given permanent security. The rise and fall of nations and empires is a testament to this fact. Indeed, looking with a large historical eye, one may say that unconditional viability has never existed except perhaps for brief periods and the best that unilateral national defense could do for any society was to postpone disaster. The situation of the individual society, that is, is rather analogous to that of the individual, whose life, on this earth at any rate, must also end in irretrievable disaster, that is, in death. Where we have a large number of individuals, however, death for the individual is not death for the race. In fact death for the individual is necessary if the race is to survive. Where the number of individuals becomes smaller and smaller, however, there comes to be a critical point where death for the individual is also death for the race and the irretrievable disaster which the

individual suffers is likewise irretrievable disaster for the species. The unilaterally defended national state now seems to me to have got to this state in its development. It is no longer appropriate as a form of organization for the kind of technical society in which we live. Its death throes, however, may destroy the whole human race. The age of civilization out of which we are passing was characterized by a large number of nation-states or independent political organizations practicing unilateral national defense. Because of the large number of these organizations there were always some being born and always some ready to rise into the places of those which suffered disaster. With the number of effectively independent nation-states now reduced to two or perhaps at most three, the possibilities of irretrievable disaster become much greater.

The problem which we face, therefore, is how to effect a system change in the international order, or perhaps we should say the world political order, sufficient to lower the probability of disaster to a tolerable level. The critical problem here might be described as that of "system perception." To revert again to the analogy of the car and the railroad crossing, if the driver of the car does not see that he is approaching the crossing, if the warning lights are not working, and if he cannot see the train approaching, he will naturally not take any steps to avert the disaster. The world problem here is perhaps psychological rather than mechanical. There is a fairly widespread sense abroad of impending doom. The doom, however, is so large that we do not really believe it and we go about our daily actions as if it did not exist. This is the mechanism, as Jerome Frank has pointed out, known to the psychologists as "denial." Up to a point this is actually healthy. We all know that we are going to die sometime and we may die tomorrow; but we act pretty much as if we are going to live forever. We do not spend much time in taking tearful farewells and in writing our last wills and testaments. We plan ahead for months and even for years, in spite of the fact that these plans may never come to fruition. This perfectly legitimate response to uncertainty becomes pathological when it prevents us from taking steps which would postpone disaster or make it less likely. The man who is afraid that he has a cancer but who will not go to a doctor because he might find out that he has one is a good example. Where the prospect of disaster, therefore, is so vague or so uncertain that it merely results in pathological denial, it is necessary to bring the actor to a more realistic appraisal of the system within which he is acting.

If the problem of "denial" is to be overcome, it is necessary to do more than merely scare people with horrendous pictures of the possible future. Indeed, the more horrendous the picture which is drawn, the more it is likely to result in denial and pathological inactivity. The future which faced our driver at the railroad crossing was also horrendous, but instead

of denying this and continuing on his way he presumably applied the brakes, that is, initiated a system change. The problem in the international system is that we seem to have no brakes. That is, it is hard for people to visualize the nature of the system change which is necessary for survival. This, then, is one of the major tasks today of the political scientist, the philosopher, the journalist, and the prophet: to give the people an image of changes in the international system which seems small enough to be feasible yet large enough to be successful. It is not useful to picture Utopias which seem utterly unattainable—this perhaps is the main difficulty with the World Federationists—even though the function of Utopias in providing a constant driving force in social dynamics should not be underestimated. The present situation, however, calls not for Utopia, but for political solutions. Indeed, one of our great difficulties today is that we have too many Utopias. We need to think, therefore, in terms of a world social contract: that is, a minimum bargain between the contending parties which will give the world a sufficient system change to relieve it from the intolerable burden which it now bears. This social contract does not even have to be explicit or contractual. It can begin by being tacit; indeed, one can argue that a world social contract already exists in a tacit embryo form. We can visualize perhaps the following five stages of development.

1. The stage of tacit contract. In systems which have an inherent instability, such as duopoly in the relations of firms, or a bipolar system of mutual deterrence in the relations of states, it is often possible to maintain a quasi-stable position for a long time through tacit contract: that is, through mutually consistent unilateral behavior on the part of each party. A quasi-stable position is like that of an egg on golf-tee—it is stable for small disturbances but not for large. For considerable periods of time, however, the disturbances may be small enough so that Humpty-Dumpty does not fall. Comes a slightly larger disturbance, however, and all the King's horses and men cannot put him together again. The international system under the Eisenhower administration exhibited this kind of quasi-stability. An important element in that stability was a tacit agreement between the United States and the Soviet Union to do nothing effective about civil defense. We agreed, in effect, that our civilian populations should be mutually exchanged as hostages, for we each had the power to destroy large numbers—at least half—of each other's civilians. This meant that the chance of deliberate nuclear war was very small, though the chance of accidental war was appreciable; indeed, the missiles almost went off on at least two occasions. A natural accident, such as a large meteor, or an electronic breakdown, or a social accident, such as a mad pilot, or a political accident, such as an unwise commitment to an irresponsible third party, could under these circumstances easily set off a mutual exchange of nuclear weapons, so that the system could not be regarded as more than a temporary expedient.

Another example of tacit contract was the mutual suspension of nuclear tests, recently broken by the Soviet Union. Here the fear, perhaps, of world opinion, and the fear also of the technical consequences of an uncontrolled race for technical development of weapons, created a temporary tacit agreement. We have had similar tacit agreements in regard to spheres of influence and intervention in third-party quarrels. The United States did not interfere in Hungary, nor the Soviet Union in Egypt during the Suez crisis. The Russians allowed themselves to be thrown out of the Congo, and are not threatening to be more than a nuisance in Cuba. The conflicts in Korea and Viet Nam were temporarily settled by latitudinal partitions. The Arab-Israeli conflict does not become an arena of the cold war. All these represent systems of mutuality of conduct which might be classified as tacit agreement.

2. The fate of the tacit agreement on nuclear testing, and what looks like the impending fate of the tacit agreement on civil defense, is a testimony to the inherent instability of the tacit agreement in the long run. It is something like the gentleman's agreement in economic competition, which suffers from the defect that not all people are gentlemen. The danger is that in the absence of organization between contending parties their only means of communication is by a "threat system." A threat system, which is characteristic of unilateral national defense, is based on the proposition, "If you do something bad to me I will do something bad to you," by contrast with an exchange system, which is based on "If you do something good to me I will do something good to you." Both systems tend to lead to consummation, but whereas the consummation of exchange is an increase of goods, the consummation of threats is an increase of "bads." War is mainly the result of the depreciation in the credibility of threats in the absence of their consummation; and hence a threat system has a basic instability built into it, which tacit contract may postpone but cannot ultimately avoid. The great problem, therefore, is how to get rid of threat systems. This, I suspect, happens historically mainly by their being overlaid with other systems of relationship—trade, communication, organization—until they fall so much to the bottom of the pile that they are no longer significant.

The essential instability of threat systems and the weakness of tacit agreements, therefore, make it highly desirable to pass into the second stage of formalized agreement, and the building of what might be called "peace-defending" organizational structures. The first of these obviously is an arms control organization designed at first perhaps only to limit the present arms race but capable of the ultimate hope of policing genuine disarmament. We could begin, perhaps, with an organization for the prevention of accidental war. This will be a joint organization of the major armed forces of the world. Once this has been accomplished, a major system change is under way. It is the organizational disunity of

the armed forces of the world which constitutes the real threat to humanity. If they were united they might threaten us with a great many disagreeable consequences but they would not threaten us with extinction. An arms control organization, therefore, would be the beginning of a very powerful social change. It would constitute the formal recognition of the fact that unilateral national defense is no longer possible. Once this initial break is made, system change may be expected to take place quite rapidly. It may be that we shall have to look forward to a substantial separation of the armed forces organization from the states which they are supposed to defend, and which they can no longer defend. Just as we solved the problem of religious wars by the separation of church and state, so we may be able to solve the problem of nuclear war by the separation of the armed forces from the state. The plain fact is that today the threat which the armed forces of the world present to their own civilian populations is much greater than any conflict among the nations. Arms control will be the beginning of the recognition of this social fact.

3. Arms control must move fairly rapidly into disarmament; otherwise it will be unstable. The organization of the world armed forces will be a loose and unstable one at first, and it will always threaten to break up. It may be, of course, that the major pressure towards disarmament will come from the economic side. Once the threat of war is removed by arms control and by organizational unity of the world armed forces, the economic burden of maintaining these monstrous establishments will seem intolerable, especially in view of the fact that it is the arms burden (equal to the total income of the poorest half of the human race!) which perhaps prevents the world from really tackling the problem of economic development and which condemns hundreds of millions of people and their descendants to live in misery. One looks forward, therefore, to the third stage of rapid and total disarmament, under the arms control organization. There are many difficult problems involved in this which have not been worked out and on which research desperately needs to be done. One research program is on the way at the moment on the broad problems of the economics of disarmament, conducted by Professor Emile Benoit of Columbia University. The United Nations is about to inaugurate a similar study. However, the organizational and social-psychological problems involved are very great and quite unprecedented. Growth is always much easier than decline and the problems of adjustment involved in a rapid decline in the world's armed forces still have to be faced. These problems, however, are difficult rather than insoluble.

4. Even universal total disarmament, however, is not enough, for this too is likely to be unstable even though disarmament itself will reduce many of the sources of conflict, especially those which arise out of strategic considerations. It will not eliminate all conflicts by any means.

In a world as divided as this, ideologically and economically, we may expect serious conflicts continually to arise. These conflicts will constantly present the temptation to the losing side to resort to violence and to redevelop organized armed forces. If disarmament is to be stable, therefore, there must be a system of conflict control. Conflict control is one of the essential functions of government. It is not, however, the only function. In thinking of world government, this is probably where we ought to begin. In the early stages it is more important to establish conflict control than to establish justice or to solve all social problems. Conflict control as a function of government has been inadequately studied and identified. This is perhaps because the study of conflict systems themselves is still in its infancy. However, this is a rapidly developing body of social science and one hopes that it may be possible in the not-too-distant future to develop a substantial body of knowledge on the identification and control of conflict systems. The problem, of course, is the identification of conflict processes in early stages before they become pathological. There are very difficult problems here in the definition of the pathology of conflict, as this, of course, goes very deep into our value systems. Conflict which is regarded as pathological by one person may not be so regarded by another. If, however, we regard violence as generally a sign of pathological conflict, we may be able to identify the processes of social dynamics which lead towards it, and we may therefore be able to interpose counterweights which will correct these processes. We may revert once more to the analogy of the car at the crossing. We need to develop both perception of dangers ahead and also organizations which can act as brakes. These processes have been fairly well worked out in industrial relations, where a whole profession of mediators and conciliators and personnel experts has come to being. There is no reason why these principles should not be applied in other fields of social life and especially to the conflict of states.

5. The last stage, of course, is true world government, capable not only of controlling conflict but of expressing and developing the common concerns and aims of mankind. At the moment this seems to be a long way off. Fortunately, the prevention of war does not depend, I think, on the establishment of full world government. If the stages of development which I have outlined can be pursued rapidly enough, war may be postponed for longer and longer periods until the postponement becomes indefinite by the establishment of a true world government. We must therefore find half-way houses and quarter-way houses which are moderately habitable. We must not allow Utopian longings to deprive us of political bargains. The actual negotiation of the world social contract is going to be a long and arduous business. We need to put many more resources into this than we are now doing. Nevertheless, there is something here which can be done. There is a road which leads some-

where. If we are to break out of the apathy, irrationality, and despair which beset us, we must gain a vision of that road of escape and make at least one step along it. This is the great significance of the growing movement for peace research. Just as we no longer accept depressions as "acts of God," wholly unpredictable and uncontrollable, so we need no longer accept mass violence as unpredictable and uncontrollable. The fact that we cannot yet predict or control it should stir us to a great intellectual effort in this direction, for this way lies hope. The only unforgivable sin in the present crisis of mankind is despair.

# 77 / From *Commencement Address at the American University, Washington, D. C., June 10, 1963*

## JOHN F. KENNEDY

In October, 1962, President Kennedy and Premier Khrushchev, in a confrontation over Soviet missiles in Cuba, found themselves staring down the gun barrel into nuclear war. For each it was patently an edifying experience. In the Soviet Union it ultimately produced foreign policies apparently less hostile to the United States. In the United States it produced a new search for an acceptable "strategy for peace." In one of the most important speeches of his 1,036 days as President, John F. Kennedy, on June 10, 1963, set forth his conception of a peace plan. We must wait for future historians to measure the ultimate impact of this significant statement.

. . . I HAVE . . . chosen this time and place to discuss a topic on which ignorance too often abounds and the truth is too rarely perceived—and that is the most important topic on earth: peace.

What kind of peace do I mean and what kind of peace do we seek? Not a Pax Americana enforced on the world by American weapons of war. Not the peace of the grave or the security of the slave. I am talking about the genuine peace—the kind of peace that makes life on earth worth living—and the kind that enables men and nations to grow and to hope and build a better life for their children—not merely peace for

Americans but peace for all men and women—not merely peace in our time but peace in all time.

I speak of peace because of the new face of war. Total war makes no sense in an age where great powers can maintain large and relatively invulnerable nuclear forces and refuse to surrender without resort to those forces. It makes no sense in an age when a single nuclear weapon contains almost ten times the explosive force delivered by all the Allied air forces in the second world war. It makes no sense in an age when the deadly poisons produced by a nuclear exchange would be carried by wind and water and soil and seed to the far corners of the globe and to generations yet unborn.

Today the expenditure of billions of dollars every year on weapons acquired for the purpose of making sure we never need them is essential to the keeping of peace. But surely the acquisition of such idle stock-piles—which can only destroy and can never create—is not the only, much less the most efficient, means of assuring peace.

I speak of peace, therefore, as the necessary rational end of rational men. I realize the pursuit of peace is not as dramatic as the pursuit of war—and frequently the words of the pursuer fall on deaf ears. But we have no more urgent task.

Some say that it is useless to speak of peace or world law or world disarmament—and that it will be useless until the leaders of the Soviet Union adopt a more enlightened attitude. I hope they do. I believe we can help them do it.

But I also believe that we must re-examine our own attitudes—as individuals and as a nation—for our attitude is as essential as theirs. And every graduate of this school, every thoughtful citizen who despairs of war and wishes to bring peace, should begin by looking inward—by examining his own attitude towards the course of the cold war and toward freedom and peace here at home.

First: Examine our attitude towards peace itself. Too many think it is unreal. But that is a dangerous defeatist belief. It leads to the conclusion that war is inevitable—that mankind is doomed—that we are gripped by forces we cannot control.

We need not accept that view. Our problems are manmade. There-fore, they can be solved by man. And man can be as big as he wants. No problem of human destiny is beyond human beings. Man's reason and spirit have often solved the seemingly unsolvable—and we believe they can do it again.

I am not referring to the absolute, infinite concepts of universal peace and good will of which some fantasies and fanatics dream. I do not deny the value of hopes and dreams but we merely invite dis-couragement and incredulity by making that our only and immediate goal.

## Concrete Actions Needed

Let us focus instead on a more practical, more attainable peace—based not on a sudden revolution in human nature but on a gradual evolution in human institutions—on a series of concrete actions and effective agreement which are in the interests of all concerned.

There is no single, simple key to this peace—no grand or magic formula to be adopted by one or two powers. Genuine peace must be the product of many nations, the sum of many acts. It must be dynamic, not static, changing to meet the challenge of each new generation. For peace is a process—a way of solving problems.

With such a peace, there will still be quarrels and conflicting interests, as there are within families and nations. World peace, like community peace, does not require that each man love his neighbor—it requires only that they live together with mutual tolerance, submitting their disputes to a just and peaceful settlement. And history teaches us that enmities between nations, as between individuals, do not last forever. However fixed our likes and dislikes may seem, the tide of time and events will often bring surprising changes in the relations between nations and neighbors.

So let us persevere. Peace need not be impracticable—and war need not be inevitable. By defining our goal more clearly—by making it seem more manageable and less remote—we can help all people to see it, to draw hope from it, and to move irresistibly towards it.

And second: let us re-examine our attitude towards the Soviet Union. It is discouraging to think that their leaders may actually believe what their propagandists write.

It is discouraging to read a recent authoritative Soviet text on military strategy and find, on page after page, wholly baseless and incredible claims—such as the allegation that

American imperialist circles are preparing to unleash different types of war . . . that there is a very real threat of a preventive war being unleashed by American imperialists against the Soviet Union . . . (and that) the political aims,

and I quote,

of the American imperialists are to enslave economically and politically the European and other capitalist countries . . . (and) to achieve world domination . . . by means of aggressive war.

Truly, as it was written long ago: "The wicked flee when no man pursueth." Yet it is sad to read these Soviet statements—to realize the extent of the gulf between us. But it is also a warning—a warning to the American people not to fall into the same trap as the Soviets, not to see only a distorted and desperate view of the other side, not to see conflict

as inevitable, accommodation as impossible and communication as nothing more than an exchange of threats.

No government or social system is so evil that its people must be considered as lacking in virtue. As Americans, we find Communism profoundly repugnant as a negation of personal freedom and dignity. But we can still hail the Russian people for their many achievements—in science and space, in economic and industrial growth, in culture, in acts of courage.

Among the many traits the peoples of our two countries have in common, none is stronger than our mutual abhorrence of war. Almost unique among the major world powers, we have never been at war with each other. And no nation in the history of battle ever suffered more than the Soviet Union in the second world war. At least 20,000,000 lost their lives. Countless millions of homes and families were burned or sacked. A third of the nation's territory, including two-thirds of its industrial base, was turned into a wasteland—a loss equivalent to the destruction of this country east of Chicago.

Today, should total war ever break out again—no matter how—our two countries will be the primary targets. It is an ironic but accurate fact that the two strongest powers are the two in the most danger of devastation. All we have built, all we have worked for, would be destroyed in the first 24 hours. And even in the cold war—which brings burdens and dangers to so many countries, including this nation's closest allies—our two countries bear the heaviest burdens. For we are both devoting massive sums of money to weapons that could be better devoted to combat ignorance, poverty and disease.

We are both caught up in a vicious and dangerous cycle with suspicion on one side breeding suspicion on the other, and new weapons begetting counter-weapons.

In short, both the United States and its allies, and the Soviet Union and its allies, have a mutually deep interest in a just and genuine peace and in halting the arms race. Agreements to this end are in the interests of the Soviet Union as well as ours—and even the most hostile nations can be relied upon to accept and keep those treaty obligations and only those treaty obligations, which are in their own interest.

So, let us not be blind to our differences—but let us also direct attention to our common interests and the means by which those differences can be resolved. And if we cannot end now our differences, at least we can help make the world safe for diversity. For, in the final analysis, our most basic common link is that we all inhabit this small planet. We all breathe the same air. We all cherish our children's future. And we are all mortal.

Third: Let us re-examine our attitude towards the cold war, remem-

bering we are not engaged in a debate, seeking to pile up debating points.

We are not here distributing blame or pointing the finger of judgment. We must deal with the world as it is, and not as it might have been had the history of the last eighteen years been different.

We must, therefore, persevere in the search for peace in the hope that constructive changes within the Communist bloc might bring within reach solutions which now seem beyond us. We must conduct our affairs in such a way that it becomes in the Communists' interest to agree on a genuine peace. And above all, while defending our own vital interests, nuclear powers must avert those confrontations which bring an adversary to a choice of either humiliating retreat or a nuclear war. To adopt that kind of course in the nuclear age would be evidence only of the bankruptcy of our policy—or of a collective death-wish for the world.

To secure these ends, America's weapons are non-provocative, carefully controlled, designed to deter and capable of selective use. Our military forces are committed to peace and disciplined in self-restraint. Our diplomats are instructed to avoid unnecessary and purely rhetorical hostility.

For we can seek a relaxation of tensions without relaxing our guard. And, for our part, we do not need to use threats to prove that we are resolute. We do not need to jam foreign broadcasts out of fear our faith will be eroded. We are unwilling to impose our system on any unwilling people—but we are willing and able to engage in peaceful competition with any people on earth.

Meanwhile, we seek to strengthen the United Nations, to help solve its financial problems, to make it a more effective instrument for peace, to develop it into a genuine world security system—a system capable of resolving disputes on the basis of law, of insuring the security of the large and the small, and of creating conditions under which arms can finally be abolished.

At the same time we seek to keep peace inside the non-Communist world, where many nations, all of them our friends, are divided over issues which weaken Western unity, which invite Communist intervention or which threaten to erupt into war.

Our efforts in West New Guinea, in the Congo, in the Middle East and the Indian subcontinent have been persistent and patient despite criticism from both sides. We have also tried to set an example for others— by seeking to adjust small but significant differences with our own closest neighbors in Mexico and Canada.

Speaking of other nations, I wish to make one point clear. We are bound to many nations by alliances. These alliances exist because our concern and theirs substantially overlap. Our commitment to defend Western Europe and West Berlin, for example, stands undiminished

because of the identity of our vital interests. The United States will make no deal with the Soviet Union at the expense of other nations and other peoples, not merely because they are our partners, but also because their interests and ours converge.

Our interests converge, however, not only in defending the frontiers of freedom, but in pursuing the paths of peace.

It is our hope—and the purpose of allied policies—to convince the Soviet Union that she, too, should let each nation choose its own future, so long as that choice does not interfere with the choices of others. The Communist drive to impose their political and economic system on others is the primary cause of world tension today. For there can be no doubt that, if all nations could refrain from interfering in the self-determination of others, the peace would be much more assured.

This will require a new effort to achieve world law—a new context for world discussions. It will require increased understanding between the Soviets and ourselves. And increased understanding will require increased contact and communication.

One step in this direction is the proposed arrangement for a direct line between Moscow and Washington, to avoid on each side the dangerous delays, misunderstanding, and misreadings of the other's actions which might occur in a time of crisis.

We have also been talking in Geneva about other first-step measures of arms control, designed to limit the intensity of the arms race and reduce the risks of accidental war.

Our primary long-range interest in Geneva, however, is general and complete disarmament—designed to take place by stages, permitting parallel political developments to build the new institutions of peace which would take the place of arms. The pursuit of disarmament has been an effort of this Government since the 1920's. It has been urgently sought by the past three Administrations. And however dim the prospects are today, we intend to continue this effort—to continue it in order that all countries, including our own, can better grasp what the problems and the possibilities of disarmament are.

The only major area of these negotiations where the end is in sight—yet where a fresh start is badly needed—is in a treaty to outlaw nuclear tests. The conclusion of such a treaty—so near and yet so far—would check the spiraling arms race in one of its most dangerous areas. It would place the nuclear powers in a position to deal more effectively with one of the greatest hazards which man faces in 1963—the further spread of nuclear weapons. It would increase our security—it would decrease the prospects of war.

Surely this goal is sufficiently important to require our steady pursuit, yielding neither to the temptation to give up the whole effort nor the temptation to give up our insistence on vital and responsible safeguards.

I am taking this opportunity, therefore, to announce two important decisions in this regard:

First: Chairman Khrushchev, Prime Minister Macmillan and I have agreed that high-level discussions will shortly begin in Moscow towards early agreement on a comprehensive test ban treaty. Our hopes must be tempered with the caution of history—but with our hopes go the hopes of all mankind.

Second: To make clear our good faith and solemn convictions on the matter, I now declare that the United States does not propose to conduct nuclear tests in the atmosphere so long as other states do not do so. We will not be the first to resume. Such a declaration is no substitute for a formal binding treaty—but I hope it will help us achieve one. Nor would such a treaty be a substitute for disarmament—but I hope it will help us achieve it.

Finally, my fellow Americans, let us examine our attitude towards peace and freedom here at home. The quality and spirit of our own society must justify and support our efforts abroad. We must show it in the dedication of our own lives—as many of you who are graduating today will have an opportunity to do, by serving without pay in the Peace Corps abroad or in the proposed National Service Corps here at home.

### Peace and Freedom Related

But wherever we are, we must all, in our daily lives, live up to the age-old faith that peace and freedom walk together. In too many of our cities today, the peace is not secure because freedom is incomplete.

It is the responsibility of the executive branch at all levels of government—local, state and national—to provide and protect that freedom for all of our citizens by all means within our authority. It is the responsibility of the legislative branch at all levels, wherever the authority is not now adequate, to make it adequate. And it is the responsibility of all citizens in all sections of this country to respect the rights of others and respect the law of the land.

All this is not unrelated to world peace. "When a man's ways please the Lord," the Scriptures tell us, "he maketh even his enemies to be at peace with him." And is not peace, in the last analysis, basically a matter of human rights—the right to breathe air as nature provided it—the right of future generations to a healthy existence?

While we proceed to safeguard our national interests, let us also safeguard human interests. And the elimination of war and arms is clearly in the interest of both.

No treaty, however much it may be to the advantage of all, however tightly it may be worded, can provide absolute security against the risks of deception and evasion. But it can—if it is sufficiently in the interests

of its signers—offer far more security and far fewer risks than an unabated, uncontrolled, unpredictable arms race.

The United States, as the world knows, will never start a war. We do not want a war. We do not now expect a war. This generation of Americans has already had enough—more than enough—of war and hate and oppression. We shall be prepared if others want it. We shall be alert to try to stop it. But we shall also do our part to build a world of peace where the weak are safe and the strong are just.

We are not helpless before that task or hopeless of its success. Confident and unafraid, we labor on—not toward a strategy of annihilation but toward a strategy of peace. Thank you.

# 78 / *Coexistence or Victory —*
# *A Partisan Debate*

### BARRY GOLDWATER AND
### J. WILLIAM FULBRIGHT

The debate on "coexistence" versus "victory" in the cold war takes place on several levels, none the least of which is on the partisan political level. The following dual selection represents the foreign policy debate over basic objectives as it occurs at the level of partisan debate. This one occurred in August, 1963.

### Senator Goldwater

. . . We are being told that things are not as they seem, not as they actually are, but only as the NEW FRONTIER says they are. We are asked in every area of Government policy to base our judgment, not on achievement but on Presidential rhetoric. We are supposed to overlook the unsolved problems, the looming threats, the lack of decision and abject failures and devote our time instead to marveling at sweet-sounding verbal assessments emanating from the White House.

Reprinted from the *Congressional Record* (daily ed., August 2, 1963), pp. 13172–174. Senator Goldwater's remarks were originally made at the Human Events Conference, July 12, 1963.

Barry Goldwater spoke as the junior Senator from Arizona and as a Republican Presidential aspirant. William Fulbright spoke as the junior Senator from Arkansas and as a liberal foreign-policy Democrat.

This is particularly true in the field of foreign affairs. We are to "ask not" why it was necessary for the President of the United States to travel over Europe promising that the United States would honor its commitment to defend Western Europe in the event of a Communist attack. Our task is to take our cue from cheering thousands in Europe and join the chorus. We are not supposed to ask why other American Presidents never had to give such resounding personal assurances. We are not supposed to see that personal assurances were all the President had to give because the record of his administration does nothing—let me repeat, does nothing—to reassure the people of Western Europe that we would react strongly and affirmatively to a Communist attack. How can we expect Western Europe to take us at the President's word when they have only to look at Cuba to realize that we haven't reacted strongly enough to meet a Communist threat on our own doorstep?

I suggest that those Europeans who had read the President's speech at American University must have wondered at his promises that the United States would not hesitate to defend Europe from Communist attack. In that speech, you may remember, the President credited the Soviet Union with having a deep interest in "a just and genuine peace." He urged the American people to re-examine their attitude toward the Soviet Union and pointed out that our two nations had never waged war against each other. He drew attention to Soviet losses in World War II—as though this had some special bearing—and urged an effort to "make the world safe for diversity."

Now that last—make the world safe for diversity—is a nicely turned phrase. It has a statesmanlike ring to it. It is the kind of rhetorical expression we have learned to expect from the President. But what does it mean? I would suggest that you think long and hard on that phrase—make the world safe for diversity. For diversity, as practiced by the Soviet Union, means many things. It means slavery and oppression and tyranny and bigotry. It means Godlessness, a lack of honor, the degrading of human dignity, a national policy of falsehood. It means pogroms and purges and concentration camps. It means mass murder and aggression. Why, in the name of everything that is honorable, should the United States strive to make the world safe for that kind of diversity?

I suggest that the President's plea is just another way of saying that the New Frontier is determined to coexist with international communism wherever it thrives—even in the Western Hemisphere. This is merely an extension of the liberal fallacy which can never seem to realize that there can be a serious threat to the security of the United States and the freedom of the world coming from the left of the political spectrum. Apologists for the Communist way and Communist objectives continue to abound in the liberal circles of America despite the years of experience we have had with Soviet duplicity. I suggest that there is something

wrong—something radically wrong—with the liberal orientation for the cold war. And I am beginning to despair of its ever being able to overcome what amounts to a deep-seated prejudice in favor of far leftists' objectives.

. . . . . .

Today's conservative, I am proud to say, is standing where history once placed the true liberal. He is standing for freedom in its true meaning both at home and abroad. He is standing for individual rights, for justice and order, and honor in a world which the modern-day liberal says is changing so fast that we must erase even the virtues and traditions which have withstood the test of many thousands of years.

I believe today's liberal is so frightened of the future that he is incapable of acting in the present. Why else are we confronted today with a virtual paralysis of policy? Why else does Cuba remain a festering, Soviet powerbase on our very doorstep? Why else are we trying to pretend that international communism is mellowing and not out to enslave the entire world? Why else are we pushing, ever more frantically, for an accommodation with the Soviet Union on disarmament and a nuclear test ban?

I say that the cause for our indecision and inaction is a deep-rooted fear on the part of the liberal establishment which forecloses the possibility of any action at all that may contain a slight element of risk. And I don't have to tell you that such craven fear is completely out of character with the American spirit. I have no doubts about the American people. They know that to stand for principle, to oppose oppression, to fight tyranny involves a certain risk. This is nothing new. Think of the risk our revolutionary forefathers ran at Lexington and Concord. I doubt if we will ever see the day when you and I live in a risk-free world, where our every action is guaranteed absolutely safe before we take it. The good things in this life do not come easily and without risk. They require boldness and courage and determination on the part of those who seek. So it is with the United States of America. To lead the free world, we must measure up to the demands of leadership—yes, even to the taking of risks in the name of freedom and justice.

### Senator Fulbright

I read the Senator's speech with interest and enjoyment. It is indeed a remarkable speech. At no point does it burden the reader with the complexities of current foreign and domestic problems.

The Senator has a rare gift of clarity. So lucid is his discourse that he makes us wonder what all the fuss has been over nuclear weapons and international tensions and unemployment and all the other stubborn problems that perplex the American people. In the Senator's penetrating analysis, all these problems can be made to evaporate if we will only

declare a "bold" and "courageous" policy abroad and return to "fundamentals" at home. It is regrettable that, for whatever excellent reasons, the Senator did not see fit to elaborate on his noble sentiments or to spell out how and where and by what means he proposes to take "bold" action abroad or to explain to us which precise "fundamentals" he would have us return to in our domestic life.

Undoubtedly, the Senator from Arizona intends to do these things in some future pronouncement. . . . .

•  .    .    .    .    •

The Senator from Arizona is opposed to coexistence; so are the Chinese Communists. The Senator is opposed to the nuclear test ban treaty; so are the Chinese Communists. The Senator thinks it is cowardly to try to avoid nuclear war; so do the Chinese Communists.

I am confident that no fairminded American will misinterpret the interesting parallel between the Senator's views on these matters and those of the Chinese Communists. The Senator, without doubt, is a loyal and patriotic American.

I was particularly interested in . . . his views on coexistence. . . . "To coexist," according to Webster, is "to exist together or at the same time." The Senator, as we all know, is unalterably opposed to such an arrangement between the Communist countries and the free world. It would seem to follow that the Senator considers it essential for one side or the other—presumably the Communist side—to stop existing at once.

The problem, of course—which the Senator has not yet seen fit to comment on—is precisely how the Communists can be persuaded or coerced to terminate their existence. It seems reasonable to suppose that they will not do so voluntarily, so the problem is really one of compulsion. It is precisely at this interesting point that the Senator leaves us in suspense.

He is absolutely clear, however, in his conviction that "coexistence" is craven, cowardly and un-American. It is, in fact, a Communist idea, based on Khrushchev's apparent confidence that if the two sides engage in peaceful competition for the allegiance of mankind, his side will win. For an American to favor coexistence, he would have to believe that democracy is far stronger than communism, that a free society can create a far better life for the individual than a totalitarian society, that freedom has a magnetism and promise for mankind that communism can never hope to match.

Of this heresy no one can accuse the junior Senator from Arizona. He has stated unequivocally that he favors "boldness and courage and determination" over craven "coexistence." These words, of course, are a bit vague and the Senator has not yet seen fit to translate them into specific proposals for a "bold" and "courageous" foreign policy.

But perhaps we can speculate. Both the United States and the Soviet Union possess hydrogen bombs and intercontinental missiles with which to destroy each other's societies. Neither has the means of preventing the other from doing so. Under these circumstances the only alternative to "coexistence" is mutual destruction. This, perhaps, is the key to the foreign policy favored by the Senator from Arizona—a "bold," "courageous," and "determined" policy of "coannihilation."

This, of course, is speculation because the Senator has not yet chosen to reveal his foreign policy proposals. It may be some time before he does so. In the meantime, there is nothing for us to do but restrain our eagerness and contemplate the delay with equanimity.

# 79 / House Joint Resolution No. 444 ("The Victory Resolution")

## DONALD C. BRUCE

How should the basic foreign policy objective of the United States be stated? Victory over Communism? Coexistence with Communism? Containment of Communism? A positive statement of the "victory" advocates is contained in the following proposal, submitted by Representative Donald C. Bruce, Republican of Indiana, to the 87th Congress, 1st Session, June 12, 1961, and commonly known as "The Victory Resolution." This proposal and others like it have been introduced in Congress over a number of years, but as of the end of the 88th Congress (1964) no action has been taken by Congress as a whole.

"DECLARATION of will of the American people and purpose of their Government to achieve complete victory over the forces of the World Communist Movement":

Whereas numerous findings, resolutions, and condemnations in United States law, Presidential proclamations, and treaties which bind the United States, proclaim that the World Communist Movement pursues invariably the same object, world conquest, and evinces a clearcut design to reduce all peoples under its absolute despotism; and

Reprinted from *Congressional Record*, 87th Cong., 1st sess. (June 12, 1961).

Whereas the supranational World Communist Movement does not represent the Russian and other peoples under its totalitarian control, but rather, in violation of their legitimate national aspirations, commands their lands and resources as an industrial-military base for its global campaign; and

Whereas the World Communist Movement operates on every level of human activity, using all conceivable pressures—ideological, psychological, economic, military, paramilitary, etc.—to bring about a widening influence and ultimately absolute control over every human thought, aspiration and action in the nations it subverts and conquers; and

Whereas the United States of America has taken numerous steps including the use of armed forces to withstand the global aggression of the World Communist Movement in certain areas in various foreign countries and within our borders; and

Whereas these steps which constituted a determination to resist certain individual thrusts of that aggression, in their totality have not met the full challenge of the global state of hostility that has been declared in dogma and prosecuted in deed by the World Communist Movement; and

Whereas the nature of the threat demands the engagement of the full will of the American people against the hostile universal dedication of the enemy, and the application of a complete global policy to meet and defeat on every front the widespread coordinated forces of the World Communist Movement; therefore be it

*Resolved by the Senate and House of Representatives of the United States in Congress assembled,* That a state of hostility exists, and, finding no longer tolerable the abuses and usurpations of the global aggression unjustly thrust upon men by the World Communist Movement, in order to bring peace and security to this Nation and the family of nations and to realize the hopes expressed in law for the freedom of Communist-enslaved peoples, it hereby is and henceforth shall be, the indomitable national will of the people of the United States of America and the unswerving purpose of their Government to achieve complete victory over the forces of the World Communist Movement in all its names, its parties and sections, and to this great end we urge similar action by all independent nations and humbly beseech the strength and guidance of Almighty God; and be it further

*Resolved,* That the President shall prepare for the approval of the Congress, a program to achieve this total victory.

# 80 / Ten Misconceptions of Anti-Communism

JOHN LUKACS

In making an end-means analysis of future United States foreign policy, it is crucially important what assumptions one
makes about the ends and means of the adversary. Nothing
is more dangerous to the national interest than to conceive a
foreign policy upon false assumptions. American foreign policy since 1946 has been fundamentally anti-Communist. It is
useful to consider the conceptions—or misconceptions—upon
which this foreign policy has been based. The following selection is a provocative analysis of "misconceptions"—as of
1959—of anti-Communism.

MOST THINKING PERSONS in the Western world will recall how,
during World War II, certain overly optimistic conceptions about Russia
and Communism grew up in the United States. These mistaken conceptions contributed to, though they did not alone cause, the expansion of
Soviet Russian power in the confused period during the last phase of that
war and even for some time afterwards. The writer of this article, a refugee from a Sovietized Hungary, was therefore not alone in having welcomed a corrective article which he read about ten years ago in an
American magazine. Though the name of the magazine and the author
of the article now escape him, the title of the piece, "Ten Misconceptions
About Communism," does not. Its author took an energetic whack at
whatever confused or illusionary conceptions about Communism may
still have lingered in American minds. He explained clearly and with
trenchant examples how it was not true that the Communist system
helped the working man, how the character of Communism had not
changed for the better, how Communists were not radical idealists, how
the Chinese Communists were not "agrarian reformers," how Communists
did not believe in certain elementary freedoms. And so on.

Reprinted, by permission, from United States Naval Institute, *Proceedings,*
LXXXV, 5 (May, 1959). Copyright © 1959 by the United States Naval Institute.
The opinions or assertations in this article are the private ones of the writer and are not
to be construed as official or reflecting the views of the United States Naval Institute
or the United States Government.

John Lukacs, a graduate of the University of Budapest, left Hungary in 1946
and is now an American citizen. He is professor of history at Chestnut Hill and La Salle
Colleges in Philadelphia. His published works include *The Great Powers and Eastern
Europe* (1954) and *A History of the Cold War* (1961).

Such misconceptions about Communism do not linger on in American minds today, certainly not in the minds of the readers of the *Proceedings*. I believe, however, that during the past ten years another set of misconceptions about Communism may have grown up from a different direction. The most important of them, we may as well term the "ten misconceptions of anti-Communism," since they consist of misconceptions held by honest anti-Communists and they include certain mistaken notions about Soviet Russia.

### First Misconception

*That the idea of revolutionary Communism represents the greatest danger to Western Civilization.*

The greatest danger to the West is represented not by the idea of Communism but by the extraordinary power of a potentially aggressive Russia, by the growing power of a hostile China, and by the fact that Russian armies are stationed in the very middle of Europe. Notwithstanding the relatively considerable percentage of Communist voters in two or three European nations, it may be said that the attraction of the Communist idea has failed throughout the Western world. There, in contrast to the record of other ideological or revolutionary forces, there has not been a single instance of a spontaneous Communist revolution resulting in the more or less permanent establishment of a Communist regime in the 112 years that have now elapsed since the publication of Marx's *Communist Manifesto*. And the Hungarian Revolution in 1956 demonstrated the utter failure of Communist indoctrination.

### Second Misconception

*That the infiltration of the Communist idea represents the greatest danger to the United States.*

The most complete refutation of Marxian theories lies implicit in the recent history of the United States. Despite the economic orientation of American education and culture, even during the catastrophic economic crisis of 1929–33, the Communist Party was unable to gather more than 103,000 votes in the Presidential election of 1932. Out of a voting population of nearly forty million people of whom twelve million were unemployed at the time, Communist candidates polled barely 0.25 per cent of the actual, and less than 0.1 per cent of the potential, votes. This does not mean, of course, that Communists in America did not, at times, exercise a pernicious influence far in excess of their numbers. They represent a potential danger, however, not when they act as revolutionary agitators but when some of them are potential Russian agents. It is not the

successes of the Communist idea but only the occasional successes of Russian espionage in this country that require Americans to be on guard against the infiltration of Communists.

### Third Misconception

*That the main purpose of Soviet Russia is to extend the rule of international Communism all over the world.*

The main purpose of the rulers of Soviet Russia is to establish and maintain the maximum amount of power and security for their country. Their concept of maximum security now includes the maintenance of a ring of satellite governments (at the cost of suppressive terror, if necessary) in nations bordering the Soviet Union proper, the imposing of limits on the power of a resurgent Germany, and the furthering of anti-American forces on the edges of the great Eurasian continent. Serious historians of Soviet Russia find little evidence to support the theory that the spreading of international Communism has been the *primary* purpose of Russian governments. Evidence to the contrary was especially obvious during the long rule of Stalin, who eliminated from the Soviet hierarchy the outstanding world revolutionary, Trotsky. Stalin cynically referred to the European Communist refugees assembled in Moscow as "beggars." He made treaties with Hitler's Germany and Mussolini's Italy with no consideration at all for the Communists of those countries who were languishing in concentration camps. He suggested to Churchill that he had a very low opinion indeed of certain European Communists. During and after the last war, he employed Communist parties and movements as a means for the promotion of Great Russian strategic and imperial interests. His policy in the East European captive nations and to some extent even within the Soviet Union was to prefer agents of the Russian national cause over convinced international-minded Communists with long-standing records. It is indeed a paradox that these very nationalistic, terroristic, and un-Marxian policies made Stalin's conquests relatively successful. It is true that the rulers of the Soviet Union still believe, or at least profess to believe, in the "inevitable" victory of the Communist idea throughout the world. Yet this hardly determines their main political actions any more than the idea of Islam determines the policies of Nasser's Egypt. Somewhat like the secondary elements of Pan-Slavism a century ago, Communism is a secondary lever but not a primary motive of Russian action. A consistent adherence to the cause of world Communism would on occasion impede rather than further the national interests of Soviet Russia, prohibiting the Russians, for instance, from concluding advantageous agreements with anti-Communist states or from interfering with the independence of non-Russian Communist states, like Poland or Yugoslavia, for example.

## Fourth Misconception

*That the international Communist conspiracy made it possible for Russia to enslave a whole chain of satellite countries in Europe.*

The cause of the deplorable division of Europe is not Communism but World War II in which the nations of Europe tore themselves apart and from which Russia naturally profited—just as World War I was the inevitable prerequisite for the success of Lenin in Petrograd in 1917. Though a more determined American policy between 1944 and 1947 may have prevented some (surely not all) of the now captive nations from falling wholly within the Russian sphere, the fundamental fact remains that, whatever the mistakes of the Allied statesmen, it was the world war launched by Hitler that resulted in the Eastern European empire of Stalin. Within Eastern Europe, then, perhaps with the single exception of Yugoslavia, it was not Communist subversion and not Communist revolutions but the military occupation or the pressure of the Soviet Russian Army that imposed the Communist system on these unfortunate nations.

## Fifth Misconception

*That, through Communism, Soviet Russia has already achieved hitherto unparalleled successes in Asia.*

It is true that the Communist idea has more attraction for Asians and for colored races in general than for white nations with their Western and Christian and European traditions. It is noteworthy even in the Middle East, where Russia has now pursued an active policy after the departure of Britain and France, Communist or Russian successes have not been spectacular. It is true that China has gone Communist. Even there we may ask whether the World War II victory of Russia and her subsequent occupation of Manchuria was not an inevitable prerequisite of the eventual Communist victory in the Chinese civil war. None of these conditions should, however, obscure the fact that during the past ten years Russia has been retreating throughout the Far East where she now occupies only the position of a marginal power. Not only the Soviet regime but Tsarist Russia before the Bolshevik Revolution often enjoyed a preëminent influence in Manchuria, possessed naval bases in China, controlled the strategically important Chinese Eastern Railroad, exercised primary control over North Korea and the frontier province of Sinkiang, and enjoyed monopoly control over Outer Mongolia. None of these conditions exists today, since it is Chinese predominance which asserts itself in most of these territories. Indeed, it may be said that not for long decades have Russia's holdings in the Far East been as limited as they are today. And perhaps never in modern

history has Russia had to face the serious prospects of growing Chinese pressure against her thinly inhabited eastern frontierlands.

### Sixth Misconception

*That Communism appeals especially to people suffering from economic distress.*

This is perhaps the most persistent of all misconceptions. It has already caused some damage to American policies and certainly to American pocketbooks. There seems to be very little correlation between economic conditions and the appeal of the Communist idea throughout the world. Detailed electoral statistics in certain European countries indicate that the poorest districts often vote strongly anti-Communist, while relatively prosperous industrial and farming precincts may furnish Communist majorities. The best example, again, is available from the United States where the relatively greatest extent of Communist infiltration had taken place within some of the highest-paid unions, while the poorest class of workers and the poorer sections of the country showed consistently strong anti-Communist attitudes, not to speak of the circumstances that many Communists and fellow-travellers in this country were recruited not from the lower but from the upper classes of the population.

### Seventh Misconception

*That, after more than forty years, a completely Communist and wholly atheistic society within Russia has been constructed.*

Though in contradiction to the theories of Marx (who prophesied the victory of Communism in the most completely industrialized nations of the West and who excluded Russia from his calculations) it was in Russia, and perhaps in Russia alone, that a Communist government succeeded in establishing itself permanently, the evolution of Russian society shows a considerable number of tendencies away from Communism. Indeed, it may be said that the two outstanding achievements in recent Russian history, the endurance of the Russian armed forces during the last war and some of the recent successes of Russian science, have come about because their activities during crucial phases were not strongly circumscribed by Communist dogma (though they were, of course, subordinated to the regimentation prevailing in every military and totalitarian state). There are strong evidences for the emergence of a managerial and professional class within the Soviet Union, for an increasing desire for private possessions which the government no longer wishes to restrict drastically, for a general and passive indifference especially among younger people (which, however, must not be mistaken for actual hostility) to Communist doctrines, for a gradual

resurgence of the attraction of the specifically Russian Orthodox Church (whose connections abroad the Soviet regime, like the Tsars, has frequently exploited for its own imperialist purposes ever since Stalin). In this respect we must observe that, whatever the official and, by now, less and less frequent Soviet claim for militant atheism, the persecution of the Christian churches within the captive nations of the Russian empire, unlike the mass murders of believing Christians during the Ottoman and Mongol occupations of Eastern Europe, is aimed less at the eradication of religious practice than at the complete subordination of the Churches to the State—which is, again, not a Communist but rather the age-old Byzantine ideal and practice. In sum, though the Communist leaders of Russia would probably not admit this even to themselves, the Soviet system within Russia does not represent such a total break with the Russian past as their people are told and as we are accustomed to think. The nationalist bonds of the Russian past are now intertwined with the Soviet strings of the present. Since this union seems to strengthen rather than weaken the power of the Soviet Russian state, this in itself is no source of comfort to the West.

### Eighth Misconception

*That every anti-Russian cause deserves American support.*

Though the principal opponent of the United States and of the Western world is the Soviet Russian Imperial State, it is no more in the interest of the United States or of Europe to aim at the total collapse of Russian power than it was in our interest to have aimed for the permanent collapse of Germany after the last war. It is in our interest to promote the independence of the captive Eastern European nations; it is not in our interest to promote the partition of the Soviet Union proper. Any large-scale weakening of the Russian State itself, apart from her imperial holdings, would not only decisively affect the tremendous political balance of the Eurasian continent but would virtually assure the embittered hostility of the Russian people against the West and the United States under no matter what violent and brutal leadership.

### Ninth Misconception

*That every anti-Communist cause deserves American support.*

The logic of this contention would mean that the principal figure of the twentieth century worthy of American support would have been Hitler.

### Tenth Misconception

*That anti-Communism must be the basic principle governing American thought and American action.*

Rejection of the doctrines and repugnance to the practices of Communism should, by now, be a natural and reasonable reaction for every decent person in the Western world. But the rejection of the wrong and the repugnance to the abnormal are natural reactions, like breathing: thus they cannot represent a principle. Moreover, while "isms" are ideas and systems of ideas, the principles of Western Christendom are such eternal values as decency, loyalty, honesty, courage, justice, charity. The illegitimate elevation of ideas to the level of absolute principles results in intellectual confusion and eventually in totalitarianism. Anti-Communism cannot become a basic yardstick of American behavior. The extent of the American's loyalty cannot be measured by the self-professed degree of fervency in a political belief. It is not by accident that the disloyalty and the personal dishonesty of Communist agents so often go hand in hand. Conversely, the loyalty of the patriotic American remains inseparable from the evidences of his personal decency and honesty and from his personal recognition of the duties of justice, courage, and charity. It does not depend on his profession of a transitory political idea—especially when we consider that one day we may face a Russia which is no longer Communist, but the imperial power of which may menace us no less than it does today.

Let us now tie together the above discussed ten misconceptions in one paragraph:

*The idea of revolutionary Communism represents the greatest danger to Western civilization; the infiltration of the Communist idea represents the greatest danger to the United States. The main purpose of Soviet Russia is to extend the rule of international Communism all over the world; the international Communist conspiracy made it possible for Russia to enslave a whole chain of satellite countries in Europe. Through Communism, Soviet Russia has already achieved hitherto unparalleled successes in Asia, (since) it appeals especially to people suffering from economic distress. By now a wholly atheistic Communist society within Russia has been constructed. (Therefore) every anti-Russian cause deserves American support; every anti-Communist cause deserves American support. Anti-Communism must be the basic principle governing American thought and American action.*

I have now tried to explain how every one of these propositions is considerably mistaken. Yet reread the above paragraph; could it not serve for a text taken from a speech made by an honest and patriotic American in our days? Of course it could—because in our times we suffer not so much from an inflation of money as from an inflation of words, not so much from the automatic weakening of monetary values as from the automatic weakening of verbal values through their rhetorical inflation, imprecision, and repetition.

At this point a word must be said about the author of this article.

The complexities and the sentiments engendered about arguments concerning Communism make it necessary that the personal position of those who advance them should be made clear, for it is always from a personal position that the motives and the purposes of an otherwise "objective" proposition or article inevitably issue. It is natural for a person of Russian origin to try to establish evidence that, despite the prevalence of the Soviet system, the Russian people are basically anti-Communist. It is natural for a Communist sympathizer to argue otherwise. I feel, therefore, that in concluding this article I should make it clear that this writer has suffered the loss of his native country and of his family through Communism imposed by Russian armed forces; that he escaped from Hungary with the active help of an American naval officer of high rank; that he is a Catholic by religion and has been a professor of history in American Catholic colleges for the past twelve years; that his anti-Communist activities and writings have been frequent; that they have been quoted approvingly by anti-Communist American scholars and authorities long before the present phase of the "cold war"; and that he has been generally considered a conservative thinker and writer.

I put all this down not to defend myself from eventual criticism but to point out how the views advanced in this article may be consistently held by conservative and anti-Communist men throughout the Western world. Indeed, their consideration may not only be consistent but necessary components of our attitude toward the Russian challenge. Continued and widespread misconceptions about anti-Communism may, on the other hand, weaken or compromise our view of our great opponent, thus playing into the hands of the most vicious and unscrupulous elements latent among the leadership groups of the present Russian State. In the end, they may even contribute to perhaps the greatest peril that the white race and Western Civilization may face: the rise of a Red Mongol Empire of over a billion men, pushing across the great plains of Eurasia to the common peril of Russians, Europeans, and Americans alike.

# 81 / Where Are We Heading?

WALT W. ROSTOW

## IV

HOW . . . SHALL WE describe the period through which we are now [November 1963] passing?

So far as the *détente* is concerned Khrushchev has explicitly set narrow limits. He has said that he will not contemplate a German settlement which does not recognize the legitimacy of the Ulbricht government; he has said he will contemplate German unity only under communism; he has said that he will not accept effective international inspection of the Soviet Union, thus narrowly limiting the range of arms control measures; he has said there shall be no ideological coexistence, and Soviet actions on the world scene indicate that this means that he will continue to use Communist parties abroad to exploit every weakness and division in the Free world for Soviet and Communist advantage.

In the atmospheric test ban and in the hot line agreement he has indicated some awareness that he shares with the United States an interest in checking the spread of nuclear weapons and in avoiding a war by accident or miscalculation. Moreover, he has shown interest in expanding trade with the world outside the Communist bloc.

This is, then, at the moment a very narrow terrain of common understanding and common action. In fact, the most fundamental thing to be said about this period of pause is that the ambitious post-Sputnik offensive has been brought—for a time at least—to a halt; and that both at home and abroad the Kremlin faces extremely serious problems as well as the need to devise a fresh strategy.

What implications does this have for the policy of the United States and the West? What should be our objectives in this period of pause which has been earned substantially by the strength, resoluteness, and the unity of the Free World?

First, let me put the answer negatively. The greatest danger we face is that we and our allies take the occasion of this pause to let down our strength or dilute our will to grapple with the many dangerous situations we still confront on the world scene. As the men in the Kremlin look about them, their best hope must be that the United States and the West may prove incapable of staying the course; that, out of a

Reprinted from U. S. Department of State Press Release No. 594 (November 19, 1963), pp. 5–11; excerpt from an address by Mr. Rostow at the University of California at Los Angeles, Calif., November 20, 1963.

A brief biographical sketch of Mr. Rostow accompanies selection 9.

false sense, the cold war is coming to an end; that, out of boredom or domestic preoccupations or a desire to get on with purely national objectives on the world scene, we will open up new opportunities for the Communists to advance.

Thus, the five basic questions which we as a nation and a community of free men have had to answer in the course of Stalin's and Khrushchev's offensives since 1946, we must be prepared to answer again and again. That is, the United States commitment to the security of the Western world must remain firm; Western Europe must continue to demonstrate its economic, social, and political viability; the whole of the West must be prepared to deal effectively with any Communist thrust across the frontiers of the cold war; we must continue the still incomplete demonstration in the underdeveloped areas that, with our help, these peoples and governments can maintain their independence and move on to build and shape modern societies in conformity with their own traditions, cultures, and ambitions; and, above all, the West must continue so to equip itself and so to behave as to make nuclear blackmail a counter-productive diplomatic or military technique.

Having tested us hard, since 1946, in many dimensions, there may be some reluctance in Moscow to return to methods which were not successful; but communism is not a self-containing phenomenon. We can be sure that any perceived weakness within the Free World will be exploited, if Moscow judges that it commands the capacity to exploit it without excessive cost and risk. We must minimize the number of openings available to the Communists and we must make sure that the cost and risk of their attempted exploitation remain prohibitively high.

## V

If this view is correct, certain things follow.

First, there must be no let down in our military capacity to bring force effectively to bear. This is not merely a matter of military budgets, but the question of maintaining overseas our own forces and those of our allies required to make the use of force unattractive to the Communists on the spot—whether it be nuclear weapons or slogging infantrymen.

Second, as Khrushchev made clear on the occasion of the forty-sixth anniversary of the Communist revolution on November 7, and as the Communists in Peiping, Hanoi, and Havana make clear every day, the struggle to advance communism by subversion and guerrilla warfare has by no means been abandoned. Although our own capacity to deal with this kind of attack from within has increased and the ability and will of the governments and peoples in the developing nations to defend their independence have been widely demonstrated, the Communists

have not wholly lost hope in what they call wars of national liberation. This is ultimately the issue at stake in South Viet-Nam where a war against South Vietnamese independence is being conducted day by day, directed from North Viet-Nam, with the backing of both Moscow and Peiping.

It is altogether likely that, frustrated in Europe, we shall see a renewed and heightened effort by the Communists in Asia, the Middle East, Africa, and Latin America over coming months and years, despite some Communist setbacks in recent years.

Third, it follows directly from this fact that we must maintain our own foreign aid program and continue to urge our allies in Western Europe and Japan to expand theirs. I can think of nothing more likely to encourage Communists all over the world than a let down in the American foreign aid effort. Our foreign aid program is a critically important instrument for helping maintain the independence of the developing nations. In the short run, the military aid increases their capacity for defense; in the longer run, the build-up of their economies, accompanied by measures that insure social progress, is an essential foundation for the maintenance of their independence.

The struggle to help the developing nations through the historic transition from traditional or colonial ways of life to the attainment of stable, modern societies is a long, difficult struggle. The Communists perceive in this revolutionary transition openings to intrude, upset, and take over these societies. They have never been more alert or eager to move in than they are right now. They remain the scavengers of the process of modernization—as they have been since Lenin formed the first modern Communist party in Russia, itself then in the midst of modernization.

Foreign aid, in all its various dimensions, is one of the few effective instruments we have to help see these countries through. I have worked on foreign aid problems inside and outside of government for more than a decade. The justification for foreign aid in the United States interest has never been sounder than it is today. The objective case for a reduction in foreign aid has never been weaker.

I can understand why members of the Congress might, in one part of their minds, find foreign aid a burden. It is easier not to vote money for expenditure abroad than to vote it—even though foreign aid money, in the end, is spent almost wholly in the United States. I can understand why they should look about for a way to shift or reduce the burden— even though that burden has been declining in terms of our national income and is only a small proportion of what we spend on national defense. I can understand the political difficulty with a program which has no organized constituency behind it in the United States.

But history will neither understand nor forgive us if, at a critical

645

moment in a great and mortal struggle, we denied ourselves one of the few proven weapons available in the battle for the independence of nations and human freedom.

The impulse in the Congress radically to cut foreign aid is as serious and dangerous to the national interest as was the impulse in 1945 and 1946 to bring our troops home and to dismantle our armed forces. We disarmed unilaterally and convinced Stalin that even a devastated and war-torn Russia could realistically seek to achieve a decisive shift in the global balance of power and, in time, world domination. To reduce foreign aid at this time is a form of unilateral disarmament.

In one sense the matter is even more serious. Thus far in the cold war the main body of Communist and United States military power has not engaged. Our military strength and that of our allies have proved an effective deterrent, excepting the attack in South Korea and various Communist adventures in guerrilla warfare. But the non-military struggle for the independence of the developing nations is an active war, going forward every day. Foreign aid is by no means our only instrument in the struggle; and dollars alone cannot win it. But every dollar available for foreign aid is useful and will be brought to bear. For every dollar withdrawn from foreign aid, this nation will pay a disproportionate price in the form of a reduced ability to deal with a world caught up in revolutionary changes which Communists seek to capture.

In laying out our missile programs we properly ensure that Communist targets are covered and deterrence will be effective by a safe margin. There are no such safe margins now built into our programs of military or economic aid. A reduction in foreign aid will simply reduce effective United States power and influence on the world scene.

As Secretary Rusk said the other day—this is no time to quit. This is a time patiently and stubbornly to stay the course—and to do so with an underlying confidence that, in aligning ourselves actively with the cause of national independence and human freedom, we are aligned with the forces of history that will prevail. But there is nothing inevitable about history unless it is backed by determined men. And right now there is no substitute in the Free World for the resources and commitment to this cause of the American people.

We must persist patiently and stubbornly not merely with our part in the struggle to maintain the independence of the developing nations, but also in building in the northern half of the world an effective partnership among the more advanced nations—notably in Western Europe, although Japan, Canada, Australia, New Zealand, and other nations have an expanded role to play in this partnership.

Having fully recovered from the war and enjoyed a remarkable decade of development, the nations of Western Europe are reassessing

what their role should be on the world scene. They feel—and they feel properly—that they should take a greater hand in the life-and-death issues, both of defense and of construction, on which their fate, as well as our own, depends. What is at stake—as they move from dependence towards a role of increased responsibility—is how Europe should be organized and what their future relations to the United States and to each other shall be.

It is natural that this transition should involve debate and differences of opinion. It is the biggest piece of international architecture ever undertaken at a time of peace. But the underlying fact is that, as these debates go forward—capturing the headlines—the ability and the will of the more advanced nations of the Free World to work together is improving in one field after another—in aligning concepts of military strategy; in the coordination of foreign aid; in monetary matters; in trade; and in the field of political consultation. There will certainly be difficulties and differences of view. But, if we are patient and capable of staying the course—in this field of policy as elsewhere—there is every reason to believe that what will emerge is an effective expression of a profound underlying common interest: in the end we of the Atlantic community are the principal guardians of the great heritage of Western civilization; and in a world of modern weapons and communications, in the face of the phenomenon of communism, in the face of the great revolutionary forces sweeping Asia, the Middle East, Africa, and Latin America, we can only ensure a world in which that heritage can survive and prosper if we work together.

## VI

I have tried to describe the sequence of the cold war in terms of two great offensives: Stalin's of 1946–51 and Khrushchev's of 1957–62. There is, of course, another side to this sequence. In the immediate postwar days, in the mid-1950's, and at present, there have been serious and sustained efforts to see whether negotiation could move us towards a more peaceful and stable world. As I said in a recent article in *Foreign Affairs,** we are engaged in what might be called the third round of such negotiation.

The key issues are precisely those to which Khrushchev has referred in setting the limits to the present *détente:* the problems of self-determination and security in Central Europe; the problems of inspection and arms control; and the commitment of the Communists to seek to advance their cause by techniques of subversion and guerrilla warfare, not only in the developing areas but elsewhere as well.

---

* "The Third Round," *Foreign Affairs*, XXXXII, 1 (October 1963), 1–10.

On the basis of statements and policies emerging from Moscow, there is no reason at the moment to believe that we are on the eve of great final settlements of these fundamental issues. If we are to move towards a more peaceful world, it will be, as nearly as we can perceive, by an historical process and not by some clear-cut event. We see no signs that peace will suddenly break out and the cold war come to an end.

What, then, are our prospects in such an historical process? What right have we to hope that, if we can stay the course, history will move towards a peaceful resolution of the dangerous issues whch have wracked the planet for a generation and are still outstanding?

The first thing to be said is that communism has moved forward when the U.S. and the West appeared weak or vulnerable; and we have seen relatively stable periods when Communist offensives were frustrated. It was undoubtedly American unilateral demobilization in 1945–46, as well as the economic, social, and political state of Western Europe, which inflamed Stalin's hopes.

It was the apparent weakness and vulnerability of Asia which inflamed Stalin's and Mao's hopes in the latter part of the 1940's.

It was the believed vulnerability of the West to nuclear blackmail and the apparent vulnerability of the developing nations to Communist intrusion which formed the foundation for Khrushchev's post-Sputnik offensives.

The first lesson of our experience is, therefore, that the prospects for peace are directly related to the strength and unity of the West and the effectiveness of our policies in every quarter of the globe.

But there is something more to be said. The forces at work within the Communist bloc all push in a similar direction. Nationalism is on the rise in Communist China, Eastern Europe, and, indeed, in the Soviet Union itself. One of the oldest claims of communism—namely, that it is a doctrine and movement which transcended the ancient claims of nationalism—has never looked less persuasive. On the contrary, despite debate and difficulty, the non-Communist world is making real progress in finding ways in which dignified and proud national states can concert for larger common purposes: within Europe, in the Atlantic community, in the expanding relations of Japan, both with the Atlantic community, within Asia, and in other parts of the world; within Latin America and in our hemispheric relations with Latin America; and within Africa. Dangerous clashes of nationalism exist in many parts of the Free World and absorb a high proportion of the energies of diplomacy in the search for pacific settlement. But building on the most fundamental of the commitments of free men—namely, to search and find collective solutions in an environment of diffuse authority—we are making real progress.

Second, the claim of Communists that they have found a more efficient, if more ruthless, method for developing an underdeveloped area, can no longer be sustained. And there is an inescapable reason for this failure; namely, that the techniques of Communist control are incompatible with the efficiency of agriculture in an underdeveloped area where three-fourths of the people are normally engaged in rural life. This is what Communist China has massively demonstrated to the world in the past five years. And its demonstration has been reenforced by the failures in North Viet-Nam and in Castro's Cuba. There are ample problems on our agenda in proving the compatibility of economic progress and human liberty in Asia, the Middle East, Africa, and Latin America. But there is no reason for any of us to believe that communism offers a realistic and effective alternative.

Similarly, in more advanced societies the more we observe of the evolution of the Soviet Union and Eastern Europe, the more clear it is that communism, as a technique for organizing a modern society, has nothing to offer men—either in growth, stability, or social equity— that intelligent, democratic societies cannot do better. We in the more advanced democracies have an ample agenda. But we can approach that agenda in confidence that events and hard facts—not theoretical debate—are demonstrating that communism is a technically inferior as well as inhumane alternative.

In Eastern Europe there is also a solid basis for hope. After almost a generation's monopoly in propaganda and education, the young are not turning to communism for inspiration or guidance. In the social sciences they look to the lively evolution of thought in the West; in culture they reach back to their national traditions which are closely linked to those of the nations in Western Europe.

In Eastern Germany we see an imposed regime of virtual occupation which, every day, appears before the world as an historical anachronism.

None of these historical facts or trends will, in itself, bring us movement towards peace unless we of the West stay the course, maintain our strength, struggle for increased unity, and build an increasingly effective community of free nations.

But if we in the West demonstrate a capacity to persist doggedly along the lines of current policy and commitment—lines which have been built up in three postwar administrations and by a generation's effort throughout the West—we have every reason to believe not only that we shall not be buried, but that the principles for which we stand shall triumph.

# 82 / *What the U.N. Can Do — If It Will*

ARTHUR LARSON

The peace-keeping task in the world has changed sharply
since the United Nations was created in 1945. Can the United
Nations function as an effective peace-keeping agency in the
nuclear age? What are some of the precedents?

THE INITIATION by the United Nations of two more peace-keeping operations—in Cyprus and on the South Vietnam–Cambodia border
—supplies a good occasion for reminding ourselves of the changed character of the peace-keeping task since World War II.

We have all heard people say: "What good is the U.N. if it cannot
stop a major power from launching a nuclear attack?" Or, "If the land
armies of the Soviet Union started crunching across Central Europe,
what could those fifteen judges in the World Court do to stop them?"

The answer is: that is not the way wars start now.

Since 1945 there has been a marked downturn in the prospect of
direct armed conflict between major powers—and a marked upsurge
in direct armed conflict between smaller countries.

The reason for the former is the nuclear deadlock. The reason for
the latter is the breakup of the colonial empires. Whatever else may be
said of colonialism, it necessarily minimized the opportunities for military
clashes among its component parts. Now, with dozens of new nation-
states free to arm themselves, with ancient hatreds—communal, religious,
tribal—unrestrained by a strong colonial power, and with the major
powers as willing as in the past to fish in such troubled waters, the main
everyday peace-keeping job has changed.

The significance of this fact is that the United Nations, even with
its present limitations, has the techniques and the power to deal with
such conflicts—always assuming that its members want it to do so.
We can therefore spend less time worrying about the U.N.'s obvious
inability to coerce a nuclear power bent on direct military aggression,
and more time exploiting techniques for controlling the local conflicts
that are a prime threat to peace, because almost all of them have the
capacity for exploding into major wars.

Reprinted from *Saturday Review*, June 27, 1964, p. 20. By permission.

Arthur Larson is director of the World Rule of Law Center, Duke University. He
has served in various government posts, including the directorship of the U. S. Information Agency. He is the author of several works on international law and organization and numerous essays.

The U.N.'s peace-keeping techniques have been devised—indeed, one might almost say improvised—to meet a variety of demands during the past eighteen years. Enough experience has now been gained to make it useful to sort these techniques into categories, so that when situations like Cyprus and South Vietnam come along, the existence of precedents will facilitate prompt adoption of suitable devices. A check-list of these techniques, in descending order of forcefulness, would include:

*Regular fighting force:* Under direct U.N. command, authorized by Security Council, to control internal disorder containing threat to international peace: U.N. force in the Congo (ONUC). Under U.N. aegis but national command, authorized by Security Council, to resist aggression: Korean action.

*Armed buffer force and border patrol:* Under direct U.N. command, authorized by General Assembly, to separate hostile forces of Israel and Egypt: United Nations Emergency Force (UNEF).

*Control of subversive border crossings:* Authorized by General Assembly, to observe and report on compliance with resolutions calling for end of aid to Communist guerrillas in Greek Civil War: the U.N. Special Committee on the Balkans (UNSCOB). Authorized by Security Council, to check on illegal infiltrations into Lebanon to foment revolt: the U.N. Observer Group in Lebanon (UNOGIL). Authorized by Security Council, and financed by the parties, to eliminate foreign involvement in Yemeni civil war: United Nations Yemen Observation Mission (UNYOM).

*Truce supervision:* Authorization by Security Council, to observe compliance with cease-fire between India and Pakistan in Kashmir: United Nations Commission for India and Pakistan (UNCIP). Authorized by Security Council, to report on observance of General Armistice Agreements between Israel and Egypt, Lebanon, Jordan, and Syria: U.N. Truce Supervision Organization (UNTSO).

*Territorial administration:* Established by Secretary-General, authorized by General Assembly, and financed by the parties, to administer territory of West Irian (West New Guinea) during transfer from Netherlands to Indonesia, supported by an armed U.N. police force: U.N. Temporary Executive Authority (UNTEA).

One value of this kind of checklist is that it demonstrates that, even without looking beyond tried techniques, the U.N. can today piece together the components necessary to cope with a wide variety of contingencies. Is the problem one of subversive crossing of borders, as in South Vietnam? We have the precedent of the Lebanon action—and it is gratifying that the beginnings of a control action appear to have been undertaken in respect to South Vietnam's border with Cambodia. Is the problem one of maintaining a cease-fire, as in Cyprus? There are

651

the lessons of Kashmir and the Middle East. Is the problem lack of money, as in every current action? There is the device of having individual parties or contributing countries pay the bill, as in Korea, Yemen, West Irian, and Cyprus. Is the problem inability to get Security Council action? There are the precedents of UNEF, the Greek action, and the West Irian action for General Assembly action.

If there is a problem, then, of effective use by members of U.N. facilities to control this type of conflict, the problem is not "can't—it is "won't." It is to be hoped that this "won't" will steadily recede as all nations, particularly the major powers, fully comprehend the mutuality of their interest in the systematic control of any apparently minor or local armed conflict that could escalate into general war.

# 83 / From *Peace on Earth* (Pacem in Terris)

POPE JOHN XXIII

One of the most eloquent and potentially influential statements on world peace to be issued during the era of the cold war was by Pope John XXIII. In an encyclical, or circular letter, issued on April 10, 1963, from the Vatican, and addressed not only to faithful Catholics but to "all men of goodwill," the Pope warned of the danger of nuclear war, stressed the concept of international community, and urged the strengthening of international organization for peace, among other things.

*PART III: Relations between States*

SUBJECTS OF RIGHTS AND DUTIES

*Disarmament.* . . . It is with deep sorrow that we note the enormous stocks of armaments that have been and still are being made in more economically developed countries, with a vast outlay of intellectual and economic resources. And so it happens that, while the people of these countries are loaded with heavy burdens, other countries as a

From Parts III and IV of the text of the encyclical *Pacem in Terris,* from the translation supplied by the Vatican Press Office, June 10, 1963, as published in *The New York Times,* June 11, 1963, pp. 17–19. Footnotes have been omitted.

result are deprived of the collaboration they need in order to make economic and social progress.

The production of arms is allegedly justified on the grounds that in present-day conditions peace cannot be preserved without an equal balance of armaments. And so, if one country increases its armaments, others feel the need to do the same; and if one country is equipped with nuclear weapons, other countries must produce their own, equally destructive.

Consequently, people live in constant fear lest the storm that every moment threatens should break upon them with dreadful violence. And with good reason, for the arms of war are ready at hand. Even though it is difficult to believe that anyone would deliberately take the responsibility for the appalling destruction and sorrow that war would bring in its train, it cannot be denied that the conflagration may be set off by some uncontrollable and unexpected chance. And one must bear in mind that, even though the monstrous power of modern weapons acts as a deterrent, it is to be feared that the mere continuance of nuclear tests, undertaken with war in mind, will have fatal consequences for life on the earth.

Justice, then, right reason and humanity urgently demand that the arms race should cease. That the stockpiles which exist in various countries should be reduced equally and simultaneously by the parties concerned. That nuclear weapons should be banned. And that a general agreement should eventually be reached about progressive disarmament and an effective method of control. In the words of Pius XII, our predecessor of happy memory: "The calamity of a world war, with the economic and social ruin and the moral excesses and dissolution that accompany it, must not be permitted to envelop the human race for a third time."

All must realize that there is no hope of putting an end to the building up of armaments, nor of reducing the present stocks, nor, still less, of abolishing them altogether, unless the process is complete and thorough and unless it proceeds from inner convictions: unless, that is, everyone sincerely cooperates to banish the fear and anxious expectation of war with which men are oppressed. If this is to come about, the fundamental principle on which our present peace depends must be replaced by another, which declares that the true and solid peace of nations consists not in equality of arms, but in mutual trust alone. We believe that this can be brought to pass, and we consider that it is something which reason requires, that it is eminently desirable in itself and that it will prove to be the source of many benefits.

In the first place, it is an objective demanded by reason. There can be, or at least there should be, no doubt that relations between states, as between individuals, should be regulated not by the force of arms,

but by the light of reason, by the rule, that is, of truth, of justice and of active and sincere cooperation.

Secondly, we say that it is an objective earnestly to be desired in itself. Is there anyone who does not ardently yearn to see war banished, to see peace preserved and daily more firmly established?

And finally, it is an objective which will be a fruitful source of many benefits, for its advantages will be felt everywhere, by individuals, by families, by nations, by the whole human family. The warning of Pius XII still rings in our ears: "Nothing is lost by peace. Everything may be lost by war."

Since this is so, we, the vicar on earth of Jesus Christ, Saviour of the world and author of peace, and as interpreter of the very profound longing of the entire human family, following the impulse of our heart, seized by anxiety for the good of all, we feel it our duty to beseech men, especially those who have the responsibility of public affairs, to spare no labor in order to insure that the world events follow a reasonable and human course.

In the highest and most authoritative assemblies, let men give serious thought to the problem of a peaceful adjustment of relations between political communities on a world level: an adjustment founded on mutual trust, on sincerity in negotiations, on faithful fulfillment of obligations assumed. Let them study the problem until they find that point of agreement from which it will be possible to commence to go forward towards accords that will be sincere, lasting and fruitful.

We, for our part, will not cease to pray God to bless these labors so that they may lead to fruitful results.

*In Liberty.* It has also to be borne in mind that relations between states should be based on freedom, that is to say, that no country may unjustly oppress others or unduly meddle in their affairs. On the contrary, all should help to develop in others a sense of responsibility, a spirit of enterprise and an earnest desire to be the first to promote their own advancement in every field.

*The Evolution of Economically Underdeveloped Countries.* Because all men are joined together by reason of their common origin, their redemption by Christ and their supernatural destiny, and are called to form one single family, we appealed in the encyclical *Mater et Magistra* to economically developed nations to come to the aid of those which were in the process of development.

We are greatly consoled to see how widely that appeal has been favorably received. And we are confident that even more so in the future it will contribute to the end that the poorer countries, in as short a time as possible, will arrive at that degree of economic development which will enable every citizen to live in conditions in keeping with his human dignity.

But it is never sufficiently repeated that the cooperation, to which reference has been made, should be effected with the greatest respect for the liberty of the countries being developed, for these must realize that they are primarly responsible, and that they are the principal artisans in the promotion of their own economic development and social progress.

Our predecessor Pius XII already proclaimed that in the field of a new order founded on moral principles, there is no room for violation of freedom, integrity and security of other nations, no matter what may be their territorial extension or their capacity for defense. It is inevitable that the powerful states, by reason of their greater potential and their power, should pave the way in the establishment of economic groups comprising not only themselves but also smaller and weaker states as well. It is nevertheless indispensable that in the interests of the common good they as all others, should respect the rights of those smaller states to political freedom, to economic development and to the adequate protection, in the case of conflicts between nations, of that neutrality which is theirs according to the natural, as well as international, law. In this way, and in this way only, will they be able to obtain a fitting share of the common good, and assure the material and spiritual welfare of their people.

It is vitally important, therefore, that the wealthier states, in providing varied forms of assistance to the poorer, should respect the moral values and ethnic characteristics peculiar to each, and also that they should avoid any intention of political domination. If this is done, a precious contribution will be made towards the formation of a world community, a community in which each member, whilst conscious of its own individual right and duties, will work in a relationship of equality towards the attainment of the universal common good.

*Signs of the Times.* Men are becoming more and more convinced that disputes which arise between states should not be resolved by recourse to arms, but rather by negotiation.

It is true that on historical grounds this conviction is based chiefly on the terrible destructive force of modern arms. And it is nourished by the horror aroused in the mind by the very thought of the cruel destruction and the immense suffering which the use of those armaments would bring to the human family. And for this reason it is hardly possible to imagine that in the atomic era war could be used as an instrument of justice.

Nevertheless, unfortunately, the law of fear still reigns among peoples, and it forces them to spend fabulous sums for armaments; not for aggression, they affirm—and there is no reason for not believing them—but to dissuade others from aggression.

There is reason to hope, however, that by meeting and negotiating,

men may come to discover better the bonds that unite them together, deriving from the human nature which they have in common. And that they may also come to discover that one of the most profound requirements of their common nature is this: that between them and their respective peoples it is not fear which should reign but love, a love which tends to express itself in a collaboration that is loyal, manifold in form and productive of many benefits.

## PART IV: Relationship of Men and of Political Communities with the World Community

*Interdependence between Political Communities.* Recent progress of science and technology has profoundly affected human beings and influenced men to work together and live as one family. There has been a great increase in the circulation of ideas, of persons and of goods from one country to another, so that relations have become closer between individuals, families and intermediate associations belonging to different political communities, and between the public authorities of those communities. At the same time the interdependence of national economies has grown deeper, one becoming progressively more closely related to the other, so that they become, as it were, integral parts of the one world economy. Likewise the social progress, order, security and peace of each country are necessarily connected with the social progress, order, security and peace of all other countries.

At the present day no political community is able to pursue its own interests and develop itself in isolation . . . .

*Insufficiency of Modern States to Ensure the Universal Common Good.* The unity of the human family has always existed, because its members were human beings all equal by virtue of their natural dignity. Hence there will always exist the objective need to promote, in sufficient measure, the universal common good, that is, the common good of the entire human family.

In times past, one would be justified in feeling that the public authorities of the different political communities might be in a position to provide for the universal common good, either through normal diplomatic channels or through top-level meetings, by making use of juridical instruments such as conventions and treaties, for example: juridical instruments suggested by the natural law and regulated by the law of nations and international law.

As a result of the far-reaching changes which have taken place in the relations between the human family, the universal common good gives rise to problems which are complex, very grave and extremely urgent, especially as regards security and world peace.

On the other hand, the public authorities of the individual polit-

ical communities—placed as they are on a footing of equality one with the other—no matter how much they multiply their meetings or sharpen their wits in efforts to draw up new juridical instruments, they are no longer capable of facing the task of finding an adequate solution to the problems mentioned above. And this is not due to a lack of good will or of a spirit of enterprise, but because of a structural defect which hinders them.

It can be said, therefore, that at this historical moment the present system of organization and the way its principle of authority operates on a world basis no longer correspond to the objective requirements of the universal common good.

*Connection between the Common Good and Political Authority.* There exists an intrinsic connection between the common good on the one hand and the structure and function of public authority on the other. The moral order, which needs public authority in order to promote the common good in human society, requires also that the authority be effective in attaining that end. This demands that the organs through which the authority is formed, becomes operative and pursues its ends must be composed and act in such a manner as to be capable of bringing to realization the new meaning which the common good is taking on in the historical evolution of the human family.

Today the universal common good poses problems of worldwide dimensions, which cannot be adequately tackled or solved except by the efforts of public authorities endowed with a wideness of powers, structure and means of the same proportions: that is, of public authorities which are in a position to operate in an effective manner on a worldwide basis. The moral order itself, therefore, demands that such a form of public authority be established.

*Public Authority Instituted by Common Consent and Not Imposed by Force.* A public authority, having worldwide power and endowed with the proper means for the efficacious pursuit of its objective, which is the universal common good in concrete form, must be set up by common accord and not imposed by force. The reason is that such an authority must be in a position to operate effectively yet, at the same time, its action must be inspired by sincere and real impartiality: in other words, it must be an action aimed at satisfying the objective requirements of the universal common good. The difficulty is that there would be reason to fear that a supernational or worldwide public authority, imposed by force by the more powerful political communities, might be or might become an instrument of one-sided interests and even should this not happen, it would be difficult for it to avoid all suspicion of partiality in its actions, and this would take from the efficaciousness of its activity.

Even though there may be pronounced differences between polit-

ical communities as regards the degree of their economic development and their military power, they are all very sensitive as regards their juridical equality and their moral dignity. For that reason, they are right in not easily yielding in obedience to an authority imposed by force, or to an authority in whose creation they had no part, or to which they themselves did not decide to submit by conscious and free choice.

*The Universal Common Good and Personal Rights.* Like the common good of individual political communities, so too the universal common good cannot be determined except by having regard to the human person. Therefore, the public authority of the world community, too, must have as its fundamental objective the recognition, respect, safeguarding and promotion of the rights of the human person. This can be done by direct action when required, or by creating on a world scale an environment in which the public authorities of the individual political communities can more easily carry out their specific functions.

*The Principle of Subsidiarity.* Just as within each political community the relations between individuals are governed by the principle of subsidiarity, so too the relations between the public authority of each political community and the public authority of the world community must be regulated by the light of the same principle. This means that the public authority of the world community must tackle and solve problems of an economic, social, political and cultural character which are posed by the universal common good. For, because of the vastness, complexity and urgency of those problems, the public authorities of the individual states are not in a position to tackle them with any hope of a positive solution.

The public authority of the world community is not intended to limit the sphere of action of the public authority of the individual political community, much less to take its place. On the contrary, its purpose is to create, on a world basis, an environment in which the public authorities of each political community, its citizens and intermediate associations, can carry out their tasks, fulfill their duties and exercise their rights with greater security.

*Modern Developments.* As is known, the United Nations Organization (U.N.O.) was established on June 26, 1945, and to it there were subsequently added intergovernmental agencies with extensive international tasks in the economic, social, cultural, educational and health fields. The United Nations Organization had as its essential purpose the maintenance and consolidation of peace between peoples, fostering between them friendly relations, based on the principles of equality, mutual respect, and varied forms of cooperation in every sector of human society.

An act of the highest importance performed by the United Nations Organization was the Universal Declaration of Human Rights, approved

in the General Assembly of December 10, 1948. In the preamble of that declaration, the recognition and respect of those rights and respective liberties is proclaimed as an ideal to be pursued by all peoples and all countries.

Some objections and reservations were raised regarding certain points in the declaration. There is no doubt, however, that the document represents an important step on the path towards the juridical-political organization of the world community. For in it, in most solemn form, the dignity of a person is acknowledged to all human beings. And as a consequence there is proclaimed as a fundamental right, the right of free movement in the search for truth and in the attainment of moral good and justice, and also the right to a dignified life, while other rights connected with those mentioned are likewise proclaimed.

It is our earnest wish that the United Nations Organization—in its structure and in its means—may become ever more equal to the magnitude and nobility of its tasks, and that the day may come when every human being will find therein an effective safeguard for the rights which derive directly from his dignity as a person, and which are therefore universal, inviolable and inalienable rights. This is all the more to be hoped for since all human beings, as they take an ever more active part in the public life of their own political communities, are showing an increasing interest in the affairs of all peoples, and are becoming more consciously aware that they are living members of a world community.

# 84 / Can We Survive Technology?

## JOHN VON NEUMANN

United States foreign policy objectives and commitments are to some extent the inevitable consequence of modern technology. Whether our foreign policies can maintain pace with an accelerating technology is a significant question. The even more crucial question, whether we can survive technology, is brilliantly discussed in this selection.

Reprinted from *Fortune*, June, 1955, pp. 106ff. Copyright © 1955 by Time, Inc. and reprinted by special permission.

John von Neumann was professor of mathematics, Institute for Advanced Study, Princeton, New Jersey. Possessing one of the most gifted minds of this century, he was a member of the United States Atomic Energy Commission at the time of his death.

... IN THE FIRST HALF of this century the accelerating industrial revolution encountered an absolute limitation—not on technological progress as such but on an essential safety factor. This safety factor, which had permitted the industrial revolution to roll on from the mid-eighteenth to the early twentieth century, was essentially a matter of geographical and political *Lebensraum*: an ever broader geographical scope for technological activities, combined with an ever broader political integration of the world. Within this expanding framework it was possible to accommodate the major tensions created by technological progress.

Now this safety mechanism is being sharply inhibited; literally and figuratively, we are running out of room. At long last, we begin to feel the effects of the finite, actual size of the earth in a critical way.

Thus the crisis does not arise from accidental events or human errors. It is inherent in technology's relation to geography on the one hand and to political organization on the other. The crisis was developing visibly in the 1940's, and some phases can be traced back to 1914. In the years between now and 1980 the crisis will probably develop far beyond all earlier patterns. When or how it will end—or to what state of affairs it will yield—nobody can say.

In all its stages the industrial revolution consisted of making available more and cheaper energy, more and easier controls of human actions and reactions, and more and faster communications. Each development increased the effectiveness of the other two. All three factors increased the speed of performing large-scale operations—industrial, mercantile, political, and migratory. But throughout the development, increased speed did not so much shorten time requirements of processes as extend the areas of the earth affected by them. The reason is clear. Since most *time* scales are fixed by human reaction times, habits, and other physiological and psychological factors, the effect of the increased speed of technological processes was to enlarge the *size* of units— political, organizational, economic, and cultural—affected by technological operations. That is, instead of performing the same operations as before in less time, now larger-scale operations were performed in the same time. This important evolution has a natural limit, that of the earth's actual size. The limit is now being reached, or at least closely approached.

Indications of this appeared early and with dramatic force in the military sphere. By 1940 even the larger countries of continental Western Europe were inadequate as military units. Only Russia could sustain a major military reverse without collapsing. Since 1945, improved aeronautics and communications alone might have sufficed to make any geographical unit, including Russia, inadequate in a future war. The advent of nuclear weapons merely climaxes the development. Now the effectiveness of offensive weapons is such as to stultify all plausible

defensive time scales. As early as World War I, it was observed that the admiral commanding the battle field could "lose the British Empire in one afternoon." Yet navies of that epoch were relatively stable entities, tolerably safe against technological surprises. Today there is every reason to fear that even minor inventions and feints in the field of nuclear weapons can be decisive in less time than would be required to devise specific countermeasures. Soon existing nations will be as unstable in war as a nation the size of Manhattan Island would have been in a contest fought with the weapons of 1900.

Such military instability has already found its political expression. Two superpowers, the U.S. and U.S.S.R., represent such enormous destructive potentials as to afford little chance of a purely passive equilibrium. Other countries, including possible "neutrals," are militarily defenseless in the ordinary sense. At best they will acquire destructive capabilities of their own. . . . Consequently, the "concert of powers"— or its equivalent international organization—rests on a basis much more fragile than ever before. The situation is further embroiled by the newly achieved political effectiveness of non-European nationalisms.

These factors would "normally"—that is, in any recent century— have led to war. Will they lead to war before 1980? Or soon thereafter? It would be presumptuous to try to answer such a question firmly. In any case, the present and the near future are both dangerous. While the immediate problem is to cope with the actual danger, it is also essential to envisage how the problem is going to evolve in the 1955–80 period, even assuming that all will go reasonably well for the moment. This does not mean belittling immediate problems of weaponry, of U.S.–U.S.S.R. tensions, of the evolution and revolutions of Asia. These first things must come first. But we must be ready for the follow-up, lest possible immediate successes prove futile. We must think beyond the present forms of problems to those of later decades.

Technological evolution is still accelerating. Technologies are always constructive and beneficial, directly or indirectly. Yet their consequences tend to increase instability—a point that will get closer attention after we have had a look at certain aspects of continuing technological evolution.

First of all, there is a rapidly expanding supply of energy. It is generally agreed that even conventional, chemical fuel—coal or oil—will be available in increased quantity in the next two decades. Increasing demand tends to keep fuel prices high, yet improvements in methods of generation seem to bring the price of power down. There is little doubt that the most significant event affecting energy is the advent of nuclear power. Its only available controlled source today is the nuclear-fission reactor. Reactor techniques appear to be approaching a condition in which they will be competitive with conventional (chemical) power

sources within the U.S.; however, because of generally higher fuel prices abroad, they could already be more than competitive in many important foreign areas. Yet reactor technology is but a decade and a half old, during most of which period effort has been directed primarily not toward power but toward plutonium production. Given a decade of really large-scale industrial effort, the economic characteristics of reactors will undoubtedly surpass those of the present by far.

Moreover, it is not a law of nature that all controlled release of nuclear energy should be tied to fission reactions as it has been thus far. It is true that nuclear energy appears to be the primary source of practically all energy now visible in nature. Furthermore, it is not surprising that the first break into the intranuclear domain occurred at the unstable "high end" of the system of nuclei (that is, by fission). Yet fission is not nature's normal way of releasing nuclear energy. In the long run, systematic industrial exploitation of nuclear energy may shift reliance onto other and still more abundant modes. Again, reactors have been bound thus far to the traditional heat-steam-generator-electricity cycle, just as automobiles were at first constructed to look like buggies. It is likely that we shall gradually develop procedures more naturally and effectively adjusted to the new source of energy, abandoning the conventional kinks and detours inherited from chemical-fuel processes. Consequently, a few decades hence energy may be free— just like the unmetered air—with coal and oil used mainly as raw materials for organic chemical synthesis, to which, as experience has shown, their properties are best suited.

It is worth emphasizing that the main trend will be systematic exploration of nuclear reactions—that is, the transmutation of elements, or alchemy rather than chemistry. The main point in developing the industrial use of nuclear processes is to make them suitable for large-scale exploitation on the relatively small site that is the earth or, rather, any plausible terrestrial industrial establishment. Nature has, of course, been operating nuclear processes all along, well and massively, but her "natural" sites for this industry are entire stars. There is reason to believe that the minimum space requirements for her way of operating are the minimum sizes of stars. Forced by the limitations of our real estate, we must in this respect do much better than nature. That this may not be impossible has been demonstrated in the somewhat extreme and unnatural instance of fission, that remarkable break-through of the past decade.

What massive transmutation of elements will do to technology in general is hard to imagine, but the effects will be radical indeed. This can already be sensed in related fields. The general revolution clearly under way in the military sphere, and its already realized special aspect, the terrible possibilities of mass destruction, should not be viewed as

typical of what the nuclear revolution stands for. Yet they may well be typical of how deeply that revolution will transform whatever it touches. And the revolution will probably touch most things technological.

Also likely to evolve fast—and quite apart from nuclear evolution— is automation. Interesting analyses of recent developments in this field, and of near-future potentialities, have appeared in the last few years. Automatic control, of course, is as old as the industrial revolution, for the decisive new feature of Watt's steam engine was its automatic valve control, including speed control by a "governor." In our century, how- ever, small electric amplifying and switching devices put automation on an entirely new footing. This development began with the electrome- chanical (telephone) relay, continued and unfolded with the vacuum tube, and appears to accelerate with various solid-state devices (semi- conductor crystals, ferromagnetic cores, etc.). The last decade or two has also witnessed an increasing ability to control and "discipline" large numbers of such devices within one machine. Even in an airplane the number of vacuum tubes now approaches or exceeds a thousand. Other machines, containing up to 10,000 vacuum tubes, up to five times more crystals, and possibly more than 100,000 cores, now operate faultlessly over long periods, performing many millions of regulated, preplanned actions per second, with an expectation of only a few errors per day or week.

Many such machines have been built to perform complicated scien- tific and engineering calculations and large-scale accounting and logis- tical surveys. There is no doubt that they will be used for elaborate industrial process control, logistical, economic, and other planning, and many other purposes heretofore lying entirely outside the compass of quantitative and automatic control and preplanning. Thanks to sim- plified forms of automatic or semi-automatic control, the efficiency of important branches of industry has increased considerably during recent decades. It is therefore to be expected that the considerably elaborated newer forms, now becoming increasingly available, will effect much more along these lines.

Fundamentally, improvements in control are really improvements in communicating information within an organization or mechanism. The sum total of progress in this sphere is explosive. Improvements in com- munication in its direct, physical sense—transportation—while less dra- matic, have been considerable and steady. If nuclear developments make energy unrestrictedly available, transportation developments are likely to accelerate even more. But even "normal" progress in sea, land, and air media is extremely important. Just such "normal" progress molded the world's economic development, producing the present global ideas in politics and economics.

Let us now consider a thoroughly "abnormal" industry and its poten-

tialities—that is, an industry as yet without a place in any list of major activities: the control of weather or, to use a more ambitious but justified term, climate. One phase of this activity that has received a good deal of public attention is "rain making." . . .

But weather control and climate control are really much broader than rain making. All major weather phenomena, as well as climate as such, are ultimately controlled by the solar energy that falls on the earth. To modify the amount of solar energy, is, of course, beyond human power. But what really matters is not the amount that hits the earth, but the fraction retained by the earth, since that reflected back into space is no more useful than if it had never arrived. Now, the amount absorbed by the solid earth, the sea, or the atmosphere seems to be subject to delicate influences. True, none of these has so far been substantially controlled by human will, but there are strong indications of control possibilities.

The carbon dioxide released into the atmosphere by industry's burning of coal and oil—more than half of it during the last generation—may have changed the atmosphere's composition sufficiently to account for a general warming of the world by about one degree Fahrenheit. The volcano Krakatao erupted in 1883 and released an amount of energy by no means exorbitant. Had the dust of the eruption stayed in the stratosphere for fifteen years, reflecting sunlight away from the earth, it might have sufficed to lower the world's temperature by six degrees (in fact, it stayed for about three years, and five such eruptions would probably have achieved the result mentioned). This would have been a substantial cooling; the last Ice Age, when half of North America and all of northern and western Europe were under an ice cap like that of Greenland or Antarctica, was only fifteen degrees colder than the present age. On the other hand, another fifteen degrees of warming would probably melt the ice of Greenland and Antarctica and produce worldwide tropical to semi-tropical climate.

Furthermore, it is known that the persistence of large ice fields is due to the fact that ice both reflects sunlight energy and radiates away terrestrial energy at an even higher rate than ordinary soil. Microscopic layers of colored matter spread on an icy surface, or in the atmosphere above one, could inhibit the reflection-radiation process, melt the ice, and change the local climate. Measures that would effect such changes are technically possible, and the amount of investment required would be only of the order of magnitude that sufficed to develop rail systems and other major industries. The main difficulty lies in predicting in detail the effects of any such drastic intervention. But our knowledge of the dynamics and the controlling processes in the atmosphere is rapidly approaching a level that would permit such prediction. Probably intervention in atmospheric and climatic matters will come in a few decades, and will unfold on a scale difficult to imagine at present.

What could be done, of course, is no index to what should be done; to make a new ice age in order to annoy others, or a new tropical, "interglacial" age in order to please everybody, is not necessarily a rational program. In fact, to evaluate the ultimate consequences of either a general cooling or a general heating would be a complex matter. Changes would affect the level of the seas, and hence the habitability of the continental coastal shelves; the evaporation of the seas, and hence general precipitation and glaciation levels; and so on. What would be harmful and what beneficial—and to which regions of the earth—is not immediately obvious. But there is little doubt that one *could* carry out analyses needed to predict results, intervene on any desired scale, and ultimately achieve rather fantastic effects. The climate of specific regions and levels of precipitation might be altered. For example, temporary disturbances—including invasions of cold (polar) air that constitute the typical winter of the middle latitudes, and tropical storms (hurricanes)—might be corrected or at least depressed.

There is no need to detail what such things would mean to agriculture or, indeed, to all phases of human, animal, and plant ecology. What power over our environment, over all nature, is implied!

Such actions would be more directly and truly worldwide than recent or, presumably, future wars, or than the economy at any time. Extensive human intervention would deeply affect the atmosphere's general circulation, which depends on the earth's rotation and intensive solar heating of the tropics. Measures in the arctic may control the weather in temperate regions, or measures in one temperate region critically affect one another, one-quarter around the globe. All this will merge each nation's affairs with those of every other, more thoroughly than the threat of a nuclear or any other war may already have done.

Such developments as free energy, greater automation, improved communications, partial or total climate control have common traits deserving special mention. First, though all are intrinsically useful, they can lend themselves to destruction. Even the most formidable tools of nuclear destruction are only extreme members of a genus that includes useful methods of energy release or element transmutation. The most constructive schemes for climate control would have to be based on insights and techniques that would also lend themselves to forms of climatic warfare as yet unimagined. Technology—like science—is neutral all through, providing only means of control applicable to any purpose, indifferent to all.

Second, there is in most of these developments a trend toward affecting the earth as a whole, or to be more exact, toward producing effects that can be projected from any one to any other point on the earth. There is an intrinsic conflict with geography—and institutions based thereon—as understood today. Of course, any technology interacts with geography, and each imposes its own geographical rules and modalities.

The technology that is now developing and that will dominate the next decades seems to be in total conflict with traditional and, in the main, momentarily still valid, geographical and political units and concepts. This is the maturing crisis of technology.

What kind of action does this situation call for? *Whatever* one feels inclined to do, one decisive trait must be considered: the very techniques that create the dangers and the instabilities are in themselves useful, or closely related to the useful. In fact, the more useful they could be, the more unstabilizing their effects can also be. It is not a particular perverse destructiveness of one particular invention that creates danger. Technological power, technological efficiency as such, is an ambivalent achievement. Its danger is intrinsic.

In looking for a solution, it is well to exclude one pseudosolution at the start. The crisis will not be resolved by inhibiting this or that apparently particularly obnoxious form of technology. For one thing, the parts of technology, as well as of the underlying sciences, are so intertwined that in the long run nothing less than a total elimination of all technological progress would suffice for inhibition. Also, on a more pedestrian and immediate basis, useful and harmful techniques lie everywhere so close together that it is never possible to separate the lions from the lambs. This is known to all who have so laboriously tried to separate secret, "classified" science or technology (military) from the "open" kind; success is never more—nor intended to be more—than transient, lasting perhaps half a decade. Similarly, a separation into useful and harmful subjects in any technological sphere would probably diffuse into nothing in a decade.

Moreover, in this case successful separation would have to be enduring (unlike the case of military "classification," in which even a few years' gain may be important). Also, the proximity of useful techniques to harmful ones, and the possibility of putting the harmful ones to military use, puts a competitive premium on infringement. Hence the banning of particular technologies would have to be enforced on a worldwide basis. But the only authority that could do this effectively would have to be of such scope and perfection as to signal the *resolution* of international problems rather than the discovery of a *means* to resolve them. . . .

What safeguard remains? Apparently only day-to-day—or perhaps year-to-year—opportunistic measures, a long sequence of small, correct decisions. And this is not surprising. After all, the crisis is due to the rapidity of progress, to the probable further acceleration thereof, and to the reaching of certain critical relationships. Specifically, the effects that we are now beginning to produce are of the same order of magnitude as that of "the great globe itself." Indeed, they affect the earth as an entity. Hence further acceleration can no longer be absorbed as

in the past by an extension of the area of operations. Under present conditions it is unreasonable to expect a novel cure-all.

For progress there is no cure. Any attempt to find automatically safe channels for the present explosive variety of progress must lead to frustration. The only safety possible is relative, and it lies in an intelligent exercise of day-to-day judgment.

The problems created by the combination of the presently possible forms of nuclear warfare and the rather unusually unstable international situation are formidable and not to be solved easily. Those of the next decades are likely to be similarly vexing, "only more so." The U.S.–U.S.S.R. tension is bad, but when other nations begin to make felt their full offensive potential weight, things will not become simpler.

Present awful possibilities of nuclear warfare may give way to others even more awful. After global climate control becomes possible, perhaps all our present involvements will seem simple. We should not deceive ourselves: once such possibilities become actual, they will be exploited. It will, therefore, be necessary to develop suitable new political forms and procedures. All experience shows that even smaller technological changes than those now in the cards profoundly transform political and social relationships. Experience also shows that these transformations are not *a priori* predictable and that most contemporary "first guesses" concerning them are wrong. For all these reasons, one should take neither present difficulties nor presently proposed reforms too seriously.

The one solid fact is that the difficulties are due to an evolution that, while useful and constructive, is also dangerous. Can we produce the required adjustments with the necessary speed? The most hopeful answer is that the human species has been subjected to similar tests before and seems to have a congenital ability to come through, after varying amounts of trouble. To ask in advance for a complete recipe would be unreasonable. We can specify only the human qualities required: patience, flexibility, intelligence.

# For Further Reading

BOWIE, ROBERT R. *Shaping the Future: Foreign Policy in An Age of Transition* (New York: Columbia University Press, 1964).

BRZEZINSKI, ZBIGNIEW, and SAMUEL P. HUNTINGTON. *Political Power: U.S.A./ U.S.S.R.* (New York: Viking, 1964).

CHAMBERLAIN, WILLIAM HENRY. *Appeasement: Road to War* (New York: Rolton House, 1962).

CLAUDE, INIS L., JR. *Swords Into Ploughshares*, 2d ed. (New York: Random House, 1959).

COUSINS, NORMAN. *In Place of Folly* (New York: Harper, 1961).

FROMM, ERIC. *May Man Prevail* (Garden City, N.Y.: Doubleday, 1961).

GOLDWATER, BARRY. *Why Not Victory?* (New York: McGraw-Hill, 1962).

KENNAN, GEORGE F. *On Dealing with the Communist World* (New York: Harper and Row, 1964).

KENNEDY, JOHN F. *The Burden and the Glory*, ed. Allan Nevins (New York: Harper and Row, 1964).

LAIRD, MELVIN, ed. *The Conservative Papers* (Garden City, N.Y.: Doubleday Anchor, 1964).

LARSON, ARTHUR, ed. *A Warless World* (New York: McGraw-Hill, 1963).

MILLIS, WALTER, and JAMES REAL. *The Abolition of War* (New York: Macmillan, 1963).

OSGOOD, CHARLES E. *An Alternative to War and Surrender* (Urbana, Ill.: University of Illinois Press, 1962).

President's Commission on National Goals. *Goals for Americans* (Englewood Cliffs, N. J.: Prentice-Hall, 1960).

RANSOM, HARRY HOWE. *Can American Democracy Survive Cold War?* (Garden City, N.Y.: Doubleday, 1963; Anchor ed., 1964).

ROCK, VINCENT P. *The Strategy of Interdependence* (New York; Scribner's, 1964).

ROOSEVELT, JAMES, ed. *The Liberal Papers* (Garden City, N.Y.: Doubleday Anchor, 1962).

RUSSELL, BERTRAND. *Has Man a Future?* (New York: Simon and Schuster, 1962).

WOLFERS, ARNOLD. *Discord and Collaboration* (Baltimore, Md.: The Johns Hopkins Press, 1962).

WRIGHT, QUINCY, ed. *Preventing World War III: Some Proposals* (New York: Simon and Schuster, 1962).

# Index

accidental nuclear war, 207, 208-209,
618-19, 653
Acheson, Dean, 4, 147, 372
Act for International Development, 483
Adams, Charles Francis, 91n, 94n
Adams, Charles Francis, Jr., 99
Adams, John, 89n, 91
Adams, John Quincy, 80-81, 94n
Adenauer, Konrad, 119, 297
Africa, 58, 281, 291, 377, 531, 572
Communist offensive in, 123-24, 125,
382, 383, 495, 513, 645, 649
nineteenth century, U.S. in, 96-97
and political stability, 468-78, 504-
505
effect of racial disorders on, 305-307
in United Nations, 596, 605, 608, 609
*see also under specific countries*
Agency for International Development
(AID), 368, 375, 376, 383, 598
ambassador's relations with, 588-90
aggression
indirect, the term, 250, 252
piecemeal, 204-206
Soviet range of, 232-35
*see also* deterrence
agriculture
and economic disparity, 330
land reform programs for, 8, 364,
431-32, 473
in socialist systems, 362-63, 364,
649
and surplus distribution, 59, 376,
434-35
Agriculture, Department of, 376
Aguinaldo, Emilio, 498
aid programs (*see* economic development
aid; foreign aid)
airpower
and the manned bomber, 215, 217,
223
in nuclear strategy, 144, 146-47, 150,
164-65, 169, 183, 208
status of, 227-30
Alaska, 80
Albania, 461, 462

Algeria, 195, 491
Allen, George V., 278
Alliance for Progress, 125, 281, 377-78,
384, 386-88, 511, 574, 577
alliances
commitment to, 118, 154, 285, 626-27
and Communist bloc countries, 69,
125-26, 233-35, 356, 637
and nuclear strategy, 146-47, 152-54,
156-62, 168-77, 184-87, 192-93
and U.S. diplomacy, 74, 91, 94,
116-20, 563-64, 569-70
in Washington's Farewell Address,
78-79
for world security, 55-57, 647
*see also* North Atlantic Treaty
Organization
Allied Control Commissions, 145
Alsop, Joseph, 218
Altschul, Frank, 53n
ambassadors
number of posts, 596
role of, 546-49, 555-59, 582-94
selection of, 547-48, 593
*see also* diplomacy
American Revolution, 88-92
Amory, John Forth, 285-95
Anand, R. P., 531n
Anderson, Eugenie, 593
Anderson, Robert, 370
Angola, 462
anticolonialism
as guerrilla war technique, 450, 451
in U.S. policy, 564, 572
anti-Communism
in governments, and U.S. support,
365, 418-19, 421, 423, 569, 573
misconceptions of, 635-42
as propaganda technique, 277, 288
as U.S. principle, 640-41
appeasement, 5, 116-17, 118
Arab-Israeli conflict, 619, 651
Arbenz Guzman, Jacobo, 484, 515, 524
Areval, Juan, 484
arms control, 161, 174, 197, 574, 643
negotiations for, 61-63, 185-87, 190-
93, 627

*An American*

*An American Foreign Policy Reader*